Bebop BYTES Back

An Unconventional Guide to Computers

Clive 'Max' Maxfield
Alvin Brown

Foreword by Lee Felsenstein

Doone
Publications
• ◂ • ◂ • ◂ ◂ • ◂

Charlies Babbage
(1792 - 1871)

M axfield
&
ontrose
Interactive

The authors and publisher have used their best efforts in preparing this book, the CD-ROM accompanying
this book, and the programs and data contained therein. However, the authors and publisher make no
warranties of any kind, expressed or implied, with regard to the documentation or programs or data contained in this book or CD-ROM, and specifically disclaim, without limitation, any implied warranties of
merchantability and fitness for a particular purpose with respect to the CD-ROM, the programs and/or data
contained therein, or the techniques described in the book. In no event shall the authors or publisher be
responsible or liable for any loss of profit or any other commercial damages, including but not limited to
special, incidental, consequential, or any other damages in connection with or arising out of furnishing,
performance, or use of this book or the contents of the CD-ROM.

Maxfield
&
Montrose
Interactive

P.O. Box 857,
Madison,
AL 35758,USA
Email: bebopbb@aol.com

**Doone
Publications**

• ◂ • • ◂ • ◂ • ◂ • ◂

7950 Hwy 72W, #G106,
Madison, AL 35758, USA
Tel/Fax: USA 205-837-0580
or 1-800-311-3753
Email: asmith@doone.com

To my mother and father, Margaret and Reginald Maxfield,
for their unfailing confidence and support, even when the teachers
at my high school said that I was a complete and utter
idiot who would never make anything out of myself.

Clive "Max" Maxfield

Clive "Max" Maxfield

To my mother and father, Pat and John Brown, for the
encouragement they gave me to make the most of the talents
that were bestowed upon me. I hope that my children, Barnaby
and Holly, realize by this effort that *nothing* is impossible!

Alvin Brown

Alvin Brown

Foreword

This book is not for everyone.

It's for people who want to make a dinosaur dance... to exactly the tune that suits them at the moment. Who want to take the most complex, precision-built machines available and make them do something bizarre, inexplicable, or totally unexpected.

It's for people who keep looking for what's underneath the surface, who never stop wondering "how does this work?" And when they find what's underneath, they want to know how that works.

It's for young people, or more exactly, people who haven't grown old. People who don't believe that they've already done everything remarkable they're ever going to do. It's for people with a future.

If you're the right person for this book, you need to know a few facts:

1. The more time you spend with this book and its accompanying CD-ROM, the more you'll get out of it. Skimming through it won't take you where you want to go. Paying serious attention, on the other hand, will teach you more about computers than you can imagine. (You might also see a few beautiful sunrises.)

2. The labs work on two levels: on and under the surface. When you're performing the labs you'll need to look for patterns that build up from individual events.

3. When you're done, you won't look any different. You won't get a trophy or a certificate to hang on your wall. You'll have some knowledge, and some skill, and you'll be ready to find more knowledge and develop more skill. Much of this will be recognizable only to someone who has the same knowledge and skill.

This book will admit you to the company of people who have deep knowledge of computer technology. It is only a beginning (there is no end), and there are many possible directions for you to go.

And this book makes it fun. Written by a couple of wise-cracking English computer engineers with overactive imaginations, it is rich in jokes, trivial information, and overblown vocabulary (with a lexicon). Maxfield and Brown have masterfully made the task of learning computer technology engaging.

Good luck, enjoy your voyage of discovery, and I expect to see some of you in the near future.

Lee Felsenstein
Moderator, Homebrew Computer Club
Designer, Osborne-1 and Sol-20 computers, Pennywhistle -103 modem
Co-founder, Community Memory Project

About the Authors

Clive "Max" Maxfield and Alvin Montrose Brown are both eminent in the field of electronics, although Alvin was already eminent when Max's eminence was merely imminent.

Max is 6'1" tall, outrageously handsome, English and proud of it. In addition to being a hero, trend setter, and leader of fashion, he is widely regarded as an expert in all aspects of electronics (at least by his mother). After receiving his B.Sc. in Control Engineering in 1980 from Sheffield Polytechnic (now Sheffield Hallam University), England, Max began his career as a designer of central processing units for mainframe computers. To cut a long story short, he now finds himself Member of the Technical Staff (MTS) at Intergraph Computer Systems, Huntsville, Alabama, USA, where he gets to play with their high-performance 3D graphics workstations. To occupy his spare time (Ha!), Max is a contributing editor to *Electronic Design News (EDN)* magazine and a member of the advisory board to the *Computer History Association of California (CHAC)*. In addition to numerous technical articles and papers appearing in magazines and at conferences around the world, Max is also the author of the outstandingly successful prequel to this tome, *Bebop to the Boolean Boogie (An Unconventional Guide to Electronics)*. On the off-chance that you're still not impressed, Max was once referred to as an *"industry notable"* and a *"semiconductor design expert"* by someone famous who wasn't prompted, coerced, or remunerated in any way!

Alvin is a well-traveled English gentleman, being born in Assam India where his father managed several tea plantations. After enjoying a lifestyle that most of us can only dream of, Alvin returned to England at the age of 9 to suffer the rigors of the English educational system. Upon leaving college, Alvin spent 10 years acquiring an extensive knowledge of electronics computer-aided design whilst working for a UK-based defense contractor. During this time Alvin devoted himself to developing thick and thin film hybrid microelectronics circuits and writing computer aided design software, and he subsequently held a number of managerial positions in software development and consultative services groups. Alvin moved to the United States in 1989, where he lives with his wife Susan and their two children, Barnaby and Holly. Alvin is currently a Product Manager for Intergraph Computer Systems, Huntsville, Alabama, USA, where he is responsible for the technical marketing of high performance 3D graphics workstations specializing in Virtual Simulation (VIZSIM) and Distributed Interactive Simulation (DIS). Alvin has also presented papers at international conferences and has published a number of technical articles.

Bebop Bytes Back is Max and Alvin's first attempt at a collaborative venture. Surprisingly, they are still talking to each other.

Acknowledgments

When one has spent more than two years on a project such as *Bebop BYTES Back*, slaving every evening and weekend over a hot computer keyboard, it's easy to fall into the trap of believing that you've done the whole thing single-handedly. But when the authors brushed the cobwebs off their shoulders and reemerged from their studies into the grim light of day, it quickly became apparent that many people had contributed to this work.

In the case of the book itself, our thanks go to Preston Jett and John Huggins for their sage advice on every subject under the sun, and to Andy "Crazy" Glew, microprocessor architect at Intel Corporation, for his insights into arcane computer lore. Thanks also go to Julie Feazel and Barbara Castlen for reviewing the early versions of the text; to Kip Crosby, President of the *Computer History Society of California (CHAC)* (http://www.chac.org/index.html), for his consultations on the history of computers, his sterling work as "first reader," and for his enthusiastic support throughout the course of this project; and to Stephanie Maxfield for leaping into the breach at the last minute to help with proof reading and the index. We would also like to offer our appreciation to Doug Brewster for providing the photographs in Chapter 1, to graphics artist extraordinaire Bob Sallee for furnishing the "Dinosaur and Walnut" image in Chapter 1 and the outstanding caricatures of famous people in Chapter 15, and to Victor Johnson for his help in digitally processing all of the images. Thanks also to Chuck and Rita Paglicco for the "*Best Clam Chowder in the World*" recipe that appears in Appendix J, and to Alvin's wife and Max's mother for their contributions to the Lexicon in Appendix K.

Turning our attention to the *Beboputer Computer Simulator*, we offer grateful thanks to Ed Smith for designing and implementing the core of the *Beboputer's* assembler utility, and to digital effects and graphics czars David Biedny and Nathan Moody (*IDIG*, http://www.microweb.com/idig) for designing the toolbar icons. When David first glimpsed at the prototype interface, he forced a rictus smile to his face and said between clenched teeth: "*It's really very nice and I don't want you to take this the wrong way, but can I ask if you're totally committed to this particular color scheme......?*" A few days later, a superb set of hand-crafted, color-coordinated icons were winging their way to us across the Internet. Thanks also go to David and Nathan for the superb graphics they created for the *Beboputer's* Web pages, and to Terri Gates for organizing and formatting the content of these pages. We would also like to thank Alvin's son, Barnaby, for entering the contents of the *Beboputer's* Character ROM, and to Kip Crosby and Chris Lott (professional bit-manipulator at Phase IV Systems Inc., Huntsville, AL) for the tremendous efforts they expended beta-testing the *Beboputer*.

With regards to the *Beboputer's* multimedia extravaganza, we demanded the best that money could buy on a zero-dollar budget. First and foremost our thanks to those who stride the corridors of power in the Digital Media division of Intergraph Computer Systems, Huntsville, AL, for granting us permission to use their extensive television studio facilities in the dead of night. Thanks also to television and video expert Liz Cernadas, who acted as our producer and camera operator; audio specialist Lucas Wilson, who created the sound effects and original music and acted as our sound engineer; and multimedia expert Bryan Wiersma, who spent countless evenings editing and compositing the video and pulling everything together. For those who are interested in this sort of thing, the video editing and compositing were performed on an Intergraph StudioZ CGI/Video Authoring Workstation featuring four 200 MHz Pentium® Pro processors and serial-digital video capture and playback (if this was a games machine running a flight simulator, you'd be splattered all over the landscape before your hand touched the joystick!).

Last but certainly not least, our grateful thanks to the "cast of thousands" who provided us with the myriad video clips and animations featured in the multimedia: IBM for their archive videos of 1950s and 1960s computers in lab 1 (and also the photos of early computational devices and other memorabilia that appear in Chapter 15 of the book); Thiokol Corporation, Huntsville, AL, for allowing us to video the switch panel in lab 1; Vince Mazur for the video of his Altair computer in lab 1; Bryan Wiersma for the *"Theater"* animation in lab 1, United Printed Circuits, Huntsville, AL for allowing us to video their paper tape punch in lab 2; Patrick Breithaupt for his Morse Code skills in lab 2; David Duberman (*Motion Blur Media*, duberman@dnai.com) for the *"Laser"* animation in lab 3 (David is the author of *"3D Modeling Construction Kit,"* Waite Group Press); Martin Foster (*Animatrix*, mfoster@earthlink.net), for the *"Captain Carnage"* animation in lab 4 (Captain Carnage is based on an original 2D character designed by Jeff Cook); Martin Foster again for the live action/animation *"Leopard"* composite in lab 7 (film footage courtesy of Ashok Amritraj from his film *"Jungle Boy"*); Tim Forcade (*Forcade and Associates*, 72007.2742@compuserve.com) for the *"Alien"* animation in lab 5 (Tim is the author of a number of books, his most recent being the *"3D Studio® IPAS Plug-in Reference,"* New Riders); Linda Case for demonstrating her touch-typing skills in lab 5; Dan Stiles for the "Flat Cow" animation in Lab 9; and Bill Farnsworth, bon vivant and raconteur, who created the *"Flying Logo"* animation for lab 6 and the *"Talking Cow"* animation for lab 9...... Phew! Also please note that the *"Band"* animation in lab 8 was created by Corel Corporation, and all of the videos and animations mentioned above (along with the original music by Lucas Wilson) are copyrighted by their respective owners and may not be used without express permission in writing from said owners.

As usual, we take full credit for everything that came out right, and any errors that may have slithered in can only be attributed to cosmic rays and spurious events of unknown origin.

Contents

We commence our voyage into the unknown by briefly summarizing the way in which computers became available to society at large, and then presenting the concept of the *Beboputer* virtual computer. Along the way we also discover why this chapter is numbered '0'.

Here we learn what a computer is and what it does. We also introduce the concepts of transistors and integrated circuits, investigate the various pieces that go to form a typical home computer, and discover how Grandma passes her evenings in a virtual reality system.

Now we're ready to commence our plunge into the bowels of a computer system, where we are formally introduced to its central processing unit (CPU), memory devices (RAM and ROM), and the input/output ports with which the CPU communicates with the outside world. Along the way we are introduced to a herd of rampaging aunts and discover the binary and hexadecimal number systems used to represent data inside computers.

The first computers didn't have typewriter-style keyboards to enter data and they weren't equipped with television-type monitors to display results. Instead, users programmed these machines using banks of switches, while the computer responded using panels of flashing lights. In this lab we use a virtual switch panel to enter a simple program and discover just how tedious operating a computer used to be.

Modern computers contain "hard disks," which they use to store ferocious quantities of data, but these devices were not available to the designers of early computers. As an alternative, data was stored on a variety of perforated paper products, including paper tapes and punched cards. In this lab we use a virtual paper tape device to store and retrieve a program entered using our switch panel.

Labs 1 and 2 employed a simple output device consisting of eight light-emitting diodes (LEDs). In this lab we experiment with alternative arrangements of LEDs in the form of 7-segment displays that can be used to present decimal and hexadecimal numbers.

Chapter 6: Primitive Logic Gates 6-1

Computers are formed from simple logical functions called "primitive gates." In this chapter we introduce these primitive gates and consider how they can be connected together to form more complex functions.

Chapter 7: Binary Arithmetic 7-1

The number system with which we are most familiar is decimal – a base-10 system that uses ten digits. The decimal system is not well-suited for computers, which instead prefer the base-2 system known as binary. In this chapter we discover the difference between unsigned and signed binary representations, along with techniques for performing binary additions and subtractions.

Chapter 8: Rampaging Around a CPU 8-1

The "brain" of a computer is its central processing unit (CPU). In this chapter we examine the *Beboputer's* CPU, including its arithmetic/logic unit, accumulator, status register, instruction register, and control unit. We also investigate the CPU's addressing logic, which includes the program counter, stack pointer, index register, and interrupt vector. Along the way we introduce the *Beboputer's* instruction set and addressing modes.

Chapter 9: The Hex Keypad (Lab 4) 9-1

In labs 1 through 3 we discovered how time-consuming and tedious entering programs using a switch panel can be. In this lab we replace our switch panel with a hexadecimal keypad, then use this device to enter a program that inputs binary numbers and displays their decimal equivalents using the 7-segment displays from lab 3. Next we modify our program to actually speak the numbers using a virtual sound card device.

Chapter 10: The QWERTY Keyboard (Lab 5) 10-1

One of the ways in which we feed information to a modern computer is by means of a typewriter-style keyboard. In this lab we discover why early typewriters looked like sewing machines, then chart their evolution into computer keyboards. Next we plug a virtual keyboard into one of the *Beboputer's* input ports; then we use our hex keypad to enter a program that monitors the keyboard and, when a key is pressed, displays the corresponding code on our 7-segment output devices.

In this lab we trace the development of the television from its humble beginning in the late-1800s, and observe its evolution into modern computer displays. Next we create a program that monitors our QWERTY keyboard and, when a key is pressed, displays the corresponding character on a virtual computer screen called a memory-mapped display.

Thus far we've entered all of our programs as numbers in a form referred to as machine code. In this lab we design our own assembly language, which allows us to specify programs at a higher level of abstraction and makes our lives much easier. We then create programs in our new language, automatically convert them into machine code using a program called an assembler, and debug them using a CPU register display and other tools.

In this lab we use an editing tool to create a file containing character patterns for use with the memory-mapped display introduced in Chapter 11. Next we use a special tool to program a virtual Character ROM, then we "plug" this device into our *Beboputer* and use it to display our new characters.

Now we're ready to take all that we've learned in the previous labs and put it to good use. In this lab we plug the shell of a calculator into the *Beboputer's* input and output ports. Your mission, should you decide to accept it, is to write a program to make our shell perform the duties of a simple four-function calculator.

In this, the final Chapter, we investigate the evolution of computers, commencing 350 million years ago when the first terapods clawed their way our of the Earth's oceans, and cumulating with the advent of today's personal computers. Along the way we discover the hidden dangers of tally sticks and meet some surprising characters whose contributions to computing have been largely forgotten in the mists of time.

Chapter 0

What is a *Beboputer*?

In this chapter we will discover:

Why the prospect of computers weighing only
1.5 tons used to be exciting

How computers became available to society
at large

What we mean by the term "*Beboputer*"

How each *Beboputer* lab has a multimedia
introduction

In what way the *Beboputer* is "Internet-ready"

Why this chapter is numbered '0'

Contents of Chapter 0

The relentless march of science

"Computers of the future may weigh no more than 1.5 tons!" trumpeted an article forecasting the relentless march of science in a 1949 edition of Popular Mechanics magazine. To many of their readers this prediction seemed wildly optimistic, considering that a typical computer of that era might occupy 1,000 square feet of floor-space, weigh-in at approximately 30 tons, and require enough power to light a small town!

In those days of yore, computers were a mystery to the vast majority of people – very few understood what a computer was and even fewer had actually seen one "in the flesh." By comparison, these days a tremendous number of people have access to home computers and this number is increasing all the time. We're also used to working with computers in a highly interactive fashion, and we've grown to expect, nay demand, systems equipped with an abundance of features, such as large quantities of memory, high-resolution graphics monitors, CD-ROM drives, fax modems, sound cards, and so forth.

Many youngsters seem to assume that things have been this way since ancient times, but nothing could be further from the truth. During the 1950s and 1960s computers were physically huge (you'd be hard pushed to fit one in a barn), extremely expensive (they typically cost millions of dollars), and you could count the people who even considered computers for the home on the fingers of one foot, but the times they were a'changin'. Following the development of the transistor in 1947 and the integrated circuit in 1958, the first microprocessor (or, in loose terms, computer-on-a-chip) made its debut in 1971, and the world of computing began to undergo a dramatic transformation.

The mid-1970s saw the arrival of the first home computers. By today's standards these were incredibly simple affairs – they had a very small amount of usable memory (only enough to store between 256 and 1,024 characters of information), they didn't have any way to remember programs when they were turned off, and they didn't have a keyboard or a computer screen. In fact, the only way to program these early home computers was by means of a bank of switches called a switch panel (Figure 0.1), and the only way to see what they were doing was by means of flashing lights. Also, these little rascals usually arrived as a kit of parts in a zip-lock bag and it was up to their proud owners to assemble them.

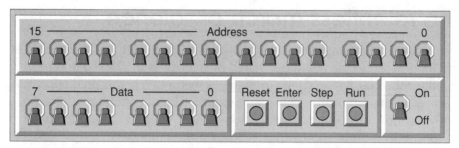

Figure 0.1: Switch panel (home computer circa early-1975)

At that time, it was popularly believed that anyone who could understand computers was a hero or heroine with a size-16 turbo-charged brain, and people who worked with computers enjoyed a certain amount of prestige. However, much to everyone's surprise, a tremendous demand arose for these do-it-yourself kits, and it began to dawn on the industry that perhaps, just maybe, but don't quote me, the general public *were* interested in owning their own computers and *were even* capable of learning how to use them (although this latter point was considered heresy in some circles)!

It didn't take too long for owners of the early systems to discover just how tedious it was to enter programs using a switch panel, so there was a collective sign of relief at the introduction of the hex keypad (Figure 0.2).[1] Hex keypads were so named because they allowed users to enter their programs in the hexadecimal (base-16) numbering system, which was far more efficacious than the binary (base-2) system the operators had previously been obliged to employ when using a switch panel.

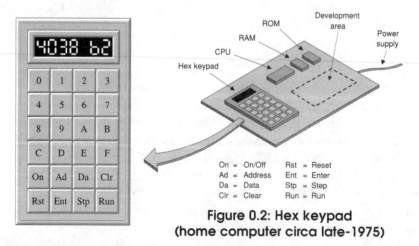

On = On/Off	Rst = Reset
Ad = Address	Ent = Enter
Da = Data	Stp = Step
Clr = Clear	Run = Run

**Figure 0.2: Hex keypad
(home computer circa late-1975)**

[1]Many of the early systems actually employed octal (base-8) keypads, but we aren't going to discuss octal in this book for reasons that will become apparent in the fullness of time.

In addition to the hex keypad, these rudimentary single-board systems typically featured a simple microprocessor; a small amount of *read-only memory (ROM)*, which contained a "hard-wired" program to monitor the keypad; a minuscule quantity of *random access memory (RAM)*, which held the user's programs; and a development area for the user to add their own bits and pieces of hardware.

Developments in home computing continued to be fast and furious, and by 1977 (only twenty years ago as we pen these words) a few lucky souls could boast home systems sporting typewriter-style keyboards and antediluvian monitors that could display a few lines of chunky-looking text (Figure 0.3).

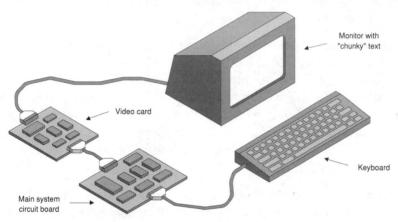

Figure 0.3: Keyboard and monitor (home computer circa 1977)

While these systems may not seem outrageously impressive today, they were considered to be revolutionary at the time. Of course, few people in those days had any conception of how quickly computers would evolve and how powerful they would become, to the extent that even a run-of-the-mill home system of today would have caused a hardened expert of yesteryear to squeal in delight.

However, although the majority of us now have access to home computers and use them for a tremendous range of tasks, only a very small proportion of users have more than a rudimentary comprehension as to how they actually function. This is unfortunate, because computers can be a tremendous amount of fun, and the fun increases the more one understands what's going on "under the hood."

So, just what is a *Beboputer?*

Ah, now there's a question. The prequel to this book, *Bebop to the Boolean Boogie (An Unconventional Guide to Electronics)*, was received with tumultuous acclaim from critics and readers alike. So many of our fans were *"Beboping"* along that, with tears in our eyes, we were moved to continue our epic saga with this new tome on computers. In conjunction with the little squiggly black notations that festoon the pages of this book, what we've *"been and gone and done"* is to design a very simple microprocessor which understands a limited set of instructions. Next, we designed a simple computer system based on our microprocessor and we christened this system a *Beboputer*™.

Now comes the capriciously cunning part of our tale. Instead of constructing the *Beboputer* in hardware (out of physical devices), we implemented it as a virtual machine in software (as a program). We have also furnished you with a wealth of virtual devices that can be plugged into your *Beboputer*, including a medley of useful tools, a variety of sumptuous output displays, and a smorgasbord of other treats such as a virtual sound card.[2] The *Beboputer* and its associated grab-bag of goodies are provided for your delectation and delight on the CD-ROM accompanying this book.

During the course of the book, you will perform a series of interactive labs that will allow you to experience the evolution of computers and to learn what they do and how they actually do it. For example, in Lab 1 you will enter a simple program using an old-fashioned switch panel; in Lab 2 you will learn how to save a program onto a virtual paper tape; in Lab 4 you will be introduced to a hex keypad; and by the time you reach Lab 5 you will be using your hex keypad to write a program to load values from a virtual keyboard and display the corresponding characters on a dual 7-segment display (Figure 0.4).

Along the way, you will plunge into the metaphorical bowels of the *Beboputer's* central processing unit (CPU), which is considered to be the "brain" of a computer. You will also explore the instruction set that we designed for the *Beboputer* (including the tradeoffs that we made) and learn how to write programs in both machine code and assembly language.

---

[2]Note that, to persuade your *Beboputer* to speak as described in Chapter 9, your main computer system must boast a real sound card.

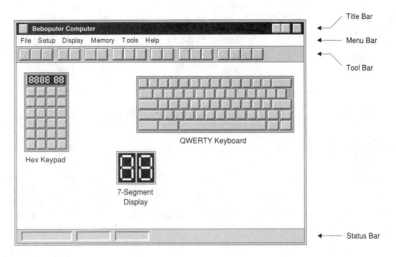

Figure 0.4: The *Beboputer* project window for Lab 5

We're Multimedia-equipped and Internet-ready

In addition to a veritable cornucopia of tools and utilities that will aid you on your quest, each lab comes equipped with a multimedia introduction featuring a fabulous fun-fest of information and trivia, including archive videos of early computers and other memorabilia.

Incidentally, the *Beboputer* is one of the first of a new breed of programs that are classed as "Internet-ready," because it features immediate access to special pages on the *World Wide Web* (or Web for short), from which you can download programs written by other users (and submit your own programs if you so desire), access "hints and tips," communicate directly with the authors, locate information on any *Beboputer* enhancements and additional utilities as they become available, and much, much more.[3]

Why is this chapter numbered '0'?

Computer programmers typically start counting, indexing, and referencing things from zero, so to keep in the spirit of things we decided to follow the same convention. The reasons for counting from zero and related conventions will become apparent as you progress through this book. Along the way, you'll also learn all of the necessary buzz-words to be able to

---

[3]Your system must be equipped with a modem and have access to the Web.

gabble gregariously and hold your own in any conversation. Yes, you too will be able to wantonly wield words like: *hardware, software, firmware, vaporware, opcode, operand, bit, tayste, nybble, byte, playte,* and ...... the list goes on.

All things considered, there's a lot of it about

OK, there's good news and there's bad news ...... which do you want first? Ah, you'd like to start off with the good news would you? Well, the good news is that computers aren't nearly as complex as you fear – all that is required is to learn the basic concepts and to then build on these one piece at a time.

The bad news is that, although the individual pieces are relatively simple there are a lot of them about. For example, although Chapter 1 will be easy on your nerves, Chapter 2 is jam-packed with enough concepts to make your brains want to leak out of your ears. Whatever you do, **don't despair!** While it would be advantageous to digest the entire contents of Chapter 2 before proceeding further, you don't have to guzzle it down in one big chunk. If you should find that your brain is beginning to overheat, proceed immediately to Chapter 3 (Lab 1) where the real fun begins – you can always pop back to visit Chapter 2 at a later date.

Above all else, never forget that computers provide endless things to discover and enjoy. The authors have been in this business for more years than we care to remember, and there's always something new to discover and more fun to be had. On this note ...... Aaaaaaaaa ...... we'd like to say that we hope that you have as much pleasure learning about and playing with the *Beboputer* as we had creating it.

Max and Alvin (November 1994 – January 1997)

Except where such interpretation is inconsistent with the context ....

Except where such interpretation is inconsistent with the context, the singular shall be deemed to include the plural, the masculine shall be deemed to include the feminine, and the spelling and punctuation shall be deemed to be correct.

Chapter 1

What is a Computer?

In this chapter we will discover:

The sock color of choice for the discerning
Viking warrior

What computers are and what they do

The difference between analog and digital
computers

That computers can be constructed using
electronic, mechanical, and even
pneumatic components

Transistors and integrated circuits

How Grandma passes the evenings
ensconced in her virtual reality system

Contents of Chapter 1

Fearsome warriors or slaves to fashion?

Many of us are used to thinking of the Vikings as fearsome warriors (this isn't your mother's computer book), who descended from the northlands and rampaged and pillaged across Europe. These fearless warriors are popularly believed to have laughed at danger and scoffed at the elements, so the recent archaeological discovery that many Vikings wore red woolly socks is, to many of us, somewhat disconcerting. However, we digress ......

What is a computer?

In the 1800s, mathematical tables such as logarithmic and trigonometric functions were generated by teams of mathematicians working day and night on primitive mechanical calculators. Due to the fact that these people performed *computations* they were referred to as *computers*. But over the course of time, the term *computer* became associated with machines that could perform the computations automatically.

In its broadest sense, a computer is a device that can accept information from the outside world, process that information, make decisions based on the results of it's processing, and then return the information to the outside world in its new form (Figure 1.1).

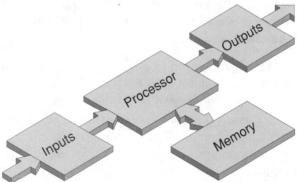

Figure 1.1: Block diagram of generic computer system

The "brain" of the computer is the *processor*, which performs mathematical and logical operations on the information presented to its inputs, makes any decisions that need making, and determines what information to output. The processor makes use of *memory* which contains instructions that are used to guide the processor through the operations it performs, and this memory can also be used to store intermediate results.

Although we typically think of computers in the context of electronics, they can be implemented in a variety of ways, including mechanical, hydraulic, and pneumatic systems. This book focuses on electronic implementations, because these account for the overwhelming majority of today's computing systems.

Information can be viewed in different ways which are referred to as *analog* and *digital*. Analog information represents a continuously varying quantity, such as a light controlled by a dimmer switch, while digital information represents a quantity that can be considered as being in one of a number of discrete states, such as a light switch which is either **ON** or **OFF**. It is possible to construct computers that operate in either an analog or a digital fashion using any of the engineering disciplines referred to above; for example, a mechanical analog computer called the *differential analyzer* was constructed at MIT in 1930. In fact, the majority of early electronic computers were analog, because simple functions such as integrators, summers, multipliers, dividers, and function generators (which produce mathematical functions like sine-waves) can be constructed as analog circuits requiring relatively few components. Sophisticated problems can be modeled by connecting these simple functions together, and analog computers still find application for such tasks as real-time simulation. However, the accuracy of an analog computer depends on the accuracy of each function, which, in turn, depends on the tolerances of the individual components. Thus, the overall accuracy of the system tends to deteriorate as more and more functions are connected together.

Digital computers can also be used to process analog information, the only requirement being that this information must first be converted into a digital form. Similarly, the outputs generated by a digital computer can be translated into analog equivalents where necessary. Digital computers were initially not as popular as their analog counterparts, because they required large quantities of components to perform relatively simple operations and digital implementations were not well understood. However, the invention of the integrated circuit (as discussed in the next section) made it possible to miniaturize electronic components to an extraordinary degree and to mass-produce complex digital functions. Eventually digital computers became smaller, cheaper, more accurate, and much more flexible than their analog predecessors. This book focuses on digital computers as these account for more than 99% of systems in use today.

Transistors and integrated circuits

Digital computers essentially consist of a lot of switches connected together in such a way that they can perform logical and arithmetic operations. For example, assuming that you live in a house with two floors, consider the light switches at the top and bottom of the stairs. If both of the switches are UP or both are DOWN the light is ON, but if only one of the switches is UP and the other is DOWN then the light is OFF. Thus, we might consider these switches to be making a simple logical decision, In fact, this particular example provides a classic illustration of a fundamental logical function known as an XNOR (exclusive-NOR). However, mechanical switches can only be operated a few times a second, while their electronic equivalents can be operated millions of times a second.

The first true electronic computers used vacuum tubes which acted as switches. These systems were monsters; for example, ENIAC, which was constructed between 1943 and 1946 at the University of Pennsylvania, was 10 feet tall, occupied 1,000 square feet of floor space, weighed in at approximately 30 tons, and used more than 18,000 vacuum tubes which required enough power to light a small town. It was therefore obvious to everyone that this approach was less than likely to result in pocket calculators or computers for home use.

Around the mid-1940s, scientists and engineers began to investigate a little known group of substances called *semiconductors*.[1] These materials were of interest because they could be persuaded to act as both conductors and insulators. It was considered that devices formed from semiconductors had potential as amplifiers and switches, and could therefore be used to replace the prevailing technology of vacuum tubes. On December 23rd 1947, physicists in America created a semiconductor switch which they dubbed a *transistor* (derived from *transfer resistor*). These components were of a type known as point-contact devices, but they were soon superseded by more sophisticated versions, including *bipolar junction transistors (BJTs)* and *field-effect transistors (FETs)* (Figure 1.2).

We can think of both mechanical switches and transistors as being devices with three terminals. In the case of the mechanical switch, there are only two physical terminals to which wires are connected, while the third "virtual" terminal is the control which is provided by a human operator or some other agency. If the switch is CLOSED electricity can flow between its terminals, but if the switch is OPEN the flow of electricity is cut off.

[1]These materials actually began to receive attention as early as the 1920s (see also Chapter 15).

By comparison, in the case of the transistor, all of the terminals are physical. The presence or absence of an electrical signal at the control terminal causes the transistor to be **ON** or **OFF** (corresponding to the mechanical switch being **CLOSED** or **OPEN**), thereby facilitating or blocking the flow of electricity between the other two terminals.

Thus, the mechanical switch and the transistor are conceptually very similar. However, the transistor can be smaller than a grain of sand and, more significantly, the signal controlling the transistor can be generated by other transistors. This latter point is very important, because it means that transistors can be switched **ON** and **OFF** millions of times a second.

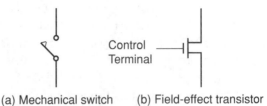

(a) Mechanical switch   (b) Field-effect transistor

Figure 1.2: Mechanical switch and field-effect transistor symbols

Although the piece of semiconductor used to form a transistor is very small, an individually packaged transistor is somewhat larger. An individually packaged device, which is referred to as a *discrete component*, consists of the semiconductor material and its connections to external leads, all encapsulated in a protective package. The package protects the semiconductor from moisture and other impurities and helps to conduct heat away from the transistor when it's operating. The package also facilitates the handling of these devices (it's not easy to work with something the size of a grain of sand), and stops you waving a sad farewell to a year's salary if you should happen to sneeze while holding a handful of the little tinkers (Figure 1.3).

Figure 1.3: Dime, discrete transistor, and transistor-based circuit board

Early electronic circuits were constructed using discrete components, which were mounted on a non-conducting board with holes drilled through it. These components were then connected using individual pieces of insulated copper wire. The thankless tasks of drilling the holes, mounting the components, and wiring the components together were all performed by hand, which was boring, time-consuming, prone to errors, and expensive.

By the 1950s, a new interconnection technology had gained commercial acceptance: *printed circuit boards (PCBs)*. In the case of the simpler boards, an insulating base layer has conducting tracks printed onto one or both sides. Over the years, the processes of printing tracks, drilling holes, and attaching components to the board began to be performed by automatic, computer-controlled machines.

Unfortunately, although discrete transistors are much smaller than the vacuum tubes they replaced, even a simple computer requires an awful lot of them. Computers based on individually packaged transistors required a substantial number of large, heavy circuit boards, and the closest these systems came to being portable was if one had a large flat-bed truck, an electric generator, and a wind-tunnel sized cooling fan.

Actually, although there was a general desire to make electronic systems smaller, faster, and cheaper, there was little thought that one of the results would be personal computers for the masses. In fact the requirement for miniaturization was primarily driven by the demands of the American space program. For some time people had been thinking that it would be a good idea to be able to fabricate entire circuits on a single piece of semiconductor. The first public discussion of this idea is generally credited to the British radar expert G.W.A. Dummer in a paper he presented in 1952. However, it was not until the summer of 1958 that Jack Kilby, working for Texas Instruments, succeeded in creating the first such device, which we now refer to as an *integrated circuit* (Figure 1.4).

Figure 1.4: Dime, unpackaged integrated circuit, and packaged integrated circuit

An integrated circuit has transistors and the connections between them formed on the surface layer of a sliver, or chip, of a single piece of semiconductor. Although a variety of semiconductor materials are available, the most commonly used is silicon and integrated circuits are popularly known as *silicon chips*. As silicon is the main constituent of sand and one of the most common elements on earth,[2] we aren't in any danger of running out of it in the foreseeable future.

Modern integrated circuit manufacturing techniques allow the construction of transistors whose dimensions are measured in fractions of a millionth of a meter, and a single device can contain millions of transistors. In the same way that computers constructed using individually packaged transistors were thousands of times smaller and faster than their vacuum-tube ancestors, computers created using integrated circuits are thousands of times smaller and faster than their discrete-transistor cousins. Thus, if we were to compare a vacuum-tube computer to a hulking dinosaur with a brain the size of a walnut, then we could compare a modern computer to a jet-propelled walnut with a brain the size of a dinosaur (Figure 1.5).

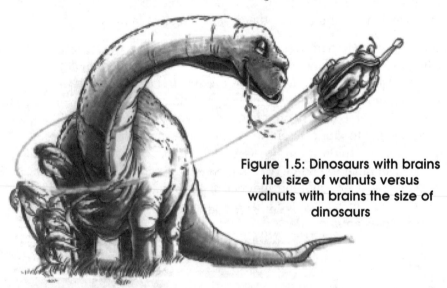

Figure 1.5: Dinosaurs with brains the size of walnuts versus walnuts with brains the size of dinosaurs

Ultimately, the development of the integrated circuit paved the way for the proliferation of personal computers. Today, systems small enough to fit in the palm of your hand can be created with far more processing power than monsters weighing tens of tons only a decade or two ago.

---

[2] Silicon accounts for approximately 28% of the earth's crust.

A typical home computer system

If we were to take a stroll through the mists of time, sometime after the Jurassic period when dinosaurs ruled the earth (say around the middle of the 1970s), we would find relatively few people with access to any form of computer system. But time flies when you're having fun, and an increasingly large proportion of us now have access to a computer in our own homes. Although details vary, a typical home system may resemble the one shown in Figure 1.6.

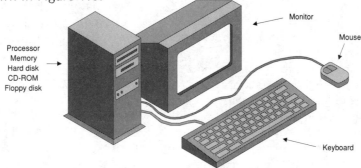

Figure 1.6: Typical home computer system circa 1997

The major constituents of such a system are the *processor, monitor, keyboard,* and *mouse*. The keyboard and mouse are used to enter data into the computer, while the monitor is used to display results (the display area of the monitor is often referred to as the *screen*). In addition to containing the "brain" of the computer, the processor cabinet also accommodates the following components:

- A quantity of fast semiconductor memory in the form of integrated circuits.

- Long-term, bulk-storage memory in the form of magnetic media known as a *hard disk*.

- Removable storage in the form of floppy disk and CD-ROM drives.

- Standard interfaces to support external devices such as printers and modems (these external devices are known as peripherals).

So here we are in our new utopia. Young children happily explore the universe using computer-based interactive encyclopedias; teenagers rush home to write their school reports using word processors; and sweet little old ladies (who, not too many years ago, covered their electric sockets: *"To stop the electricity leaking out my dear!"*) spend a quiet evening at home immersed in their virtual reality systems, rampaging through alien worlds and decimating hordes of loathsome creatures with their laser cannons.

But there are clouds a'brewin' on the horizon and flies the size of fruit-bats in the ointment (we never metaphor we didn't like). Paradoxically, although a tremendous number of people use computers on a daily basis, only a very small proportion of them have the faintest clue as to how their computers actually work inside. As that great British prime minister Sir Winston Spencer Churchill might have said: "*Never in the field of human endeavor was so much obscure to so many and known to so few.*"[3]

Although integrated circuits are very small and very fast, they may not be suitable for use in certain hostile environments. For example, electronic components located close to the core of a nuclear power plant have a life expectancy approaching that of an ice cube in the Sahara desert. One alternative is to use pneumatic devices, in which logical functions are implemented using the flow of air through small pipes and valves. A number of simple logical functions may be constructed in a package reminiscent of a large integrated circuit, except that the inputs and outputs to the package are actually small, hollow tubes. These packages are mounted on a rack and connected together using flexible pipes. Sadly, although it is theoretically possible to construct a fully functional computer using these techniques, it would be an immense undertaking and not worth the effort. However, an electronic computer housed in the safety of a control room can be used to direct small blocks of decision-making pneumatic logic residing in the hostile environment.

And so, finally, it becomes clear why we have labored so long and so hard in a cruel, uncaring world to bring you this masterpiece. No longer are the ancient mysteries of the computer to be available only to the members of the inner sanctum — those furtive creatures of dubious morals who perform eldritch rituals and bind themselves with arcane oaths. Someone has to rend the veils asunder and we're just the men for the task. Now, read on ......

---

[3]What he actually said in a tribute to the Royal Air Force at the House of Commons (August 20th, 1940) was: "Never in the field of human conflict was so much owed by so many to so few."

Quick quiz #1

1) What color socks did some Vikings wear?

2) When did the term computer originate?

3) What is a general definition of a computer?

4) What technologies can be used to implement computers?

5) What is the difference between analog and digital information?

6) Which devices acted as switches in the first true electronic computers?

7) What is a semiconductor and what is the most commonly used semiconductor?

8) When was the first point-contact transistor constructed?

9) In what way can a transistor be considered to act like a switch?

10) What is an integrated circuit?

> For those who are interested and want to know more about transistors, integrated circuits, and the best time of day to eat smoked fish; these topics are presented in greater detail in this book's companion volume: *Bebop to the Boolean Boogie (An Unconventional Guide to Electronics)*, ISBN 1-878707-22-1.

Chapter 2

Roaming Around
a Computer

In this chapter we will discover:

The central processing unit (CPU), and why it's considered
to be the "brain" of the computer

The control, data, and address busses

The binary, quinary, and hexadecimal numbering systems

How to convert from hexadecimal to binary (and back
again) while retaining a sense of humor

How binary numbers can be used to represent different
types of data

How the computer stores information in its RAM and ROM
memory devices

How the computer communicates with the outside world
using its input and output ports

Contents of Chapter 2

There's nothing to fear but fear itself

So here we are, seconds away from plunging into the bowels of a computer system, our knees aquiver and butterflies in our stomachs. Indeed, some of the more faint-hearted amongst us may feel the same dread as occurs when we find ourselves with one foot dangling over the edge of a bottomless pit and the other balanced on a bar of wet soap. But fear not my braves, because there's nothing to fear but fear itself. As my dear old dad used to tell me when I was but knee-high to a grasshopper: *"A coward dies a thousand deaths – a brave man only once."* So let's bite the bullet and take a quick peek through our splayed fingers at Figure 2.1.

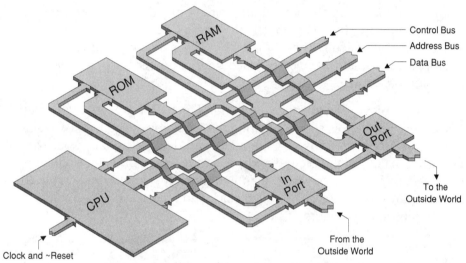

Figure 2.1: The bowels of a computer

DON'T PANIC! Just take a deep breath and hold it .... mentally count down from 999,999 to 0 .... and breath out again.[1] You see, you've stopped worrying already! Look on the bright side – it's got to be a whole lot easier for you to understand this figure than it was for us to draw it! In fact, as we shall come to see, this really isn't very complicated at all – it just seems that way because it's unfamiliar. All that is required for enlightenment to dawn is to dismantle the system into its constituent parts, examine them individually in a little more detail, give them a quick polish, and then glue them back together again.

But first, a word of warning before we proceed. There is a lot of information in this chapter and you may feel somewhat overwhelmed at first. Don't

---

[1]Bearing in mind that litigation is viewed as a national sport in America, we should perhaps point out that this is a joke (so don't try it at home unless you're a professional).

worry, because you don't have to digest everything at once. At a minimum, skim through the following topics to get a general idea of what's going on and then slip into Chapter 3 where the real fun begins – you can always return to review any subjects that you're unsure of after you've really started to enjoy yourself.

The central processing unit (CPU)

The *central processing unit (CPU)* is where all of the number crunching and decision making is performed. In the more heroic industrial-sized computers, the CPU may be formed from a large number of integrated circuits and may even require multiple circuit boards. By comparison, in the majority of today's home computers the entire CPU is implemented as a single integrated circuit. These single-chip CPUs are known as *microprocessors*, and computers based on microprocessors are called *microcomputers*.

In the system-level illustration presented in Figure 2.1, a large arrow marked "clock and ~reset" was shown entering the CPU from stage left. This large arrow was used for purposes of simplicity and, let's be brutally honest, because it balanced the picture and was aesthetically pleasing (something engineers pay more attention to than you might imagine).[2] In fact this arrow represents two distinct signals called **clock** and **~reset**, which are more clearly illustrated in Figure 2.2.

The *clock generator* block is similar to the drum master on a slave galley – pounding out a measured beat to keep all of the rowers in step. However, in our case the beat is actually an electronic signal which switches back and forth between two

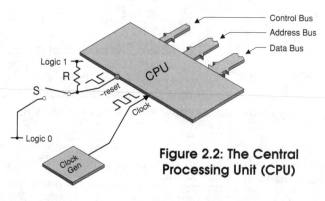

Figure 2.2: The Central Processing Unit (CPU)

voltage levels millions of times a second. This signal drives the CPU's clock input and is used to synchronize its internal actions.[3]

---

[2]It is not uncommon for an engineer to select one component in preference to another based purely on its color or aesthetically pleasing shape!

[3]Some computers employ more complex clocking schemes involving multiple clock signals.

Now turn your attention to the CPU's ~reset input. When power is first applied to the CPU causing it to "wake up," it feels somewhat disorientated to say the least. To gain some idea of the CPU's predicament, imagine being awakened by a bucket of freezing cold water hurled in your face, only to find a high-school marching band parading around your bedroom (I hate it when that happens). To cut a long story short, the poor little rascal hasn't got a clue where it is or what it is supposed to do. This is where the ~reset signal comes into play, because, much like someone sneaking up and bursting a paper bag just behind your head, it causes the CPU to pause for a moment of quiet reflection and to look at things from a new perspective.

> The reason the ~reset signal has a tilde character ("~") (pronounced "till-da") as part of its name is to indicate that this signal's active state is a *logic 0*. Similarly, the small circle (called a *bobble* or *bubble*) on the side of the CPU symbol is also used to indicate that this signal's active state is a *logic 0*. The reasons for using *logic 0* as the active state are many, varied, long, and tortuous, so you may be grateful that we won't go into them here. However, throughout the course of our discussions you will see that many control signals share this characteristic.

Before we proceed, we first need to recall our discussions in Chapter 1, in which it was noted that digital computers are constructed from transistor switches. These switches can be in one of two states, **OFF** or **ON**, which physically correspond to two different voltage levels. However, we generally have only minimal interest in the actual voltages used and, for reasons that will become apparent, the terms **OFF** and **ON** are not particularly useful or relevant in this context. So rather than thinking in terms of voltage levels or in terms of **OFF** and **ON**, we generally use more abstract logical terms called *logic 0* and *logic 1*.

Now, consider the circuit connected to the ~reset input in Figure 2.2. The switch **S** is usually open, which means that the ~reset input is connected to a *logic 1* value through the resistor **R**. When the switch is closed it connects the ~reset input directly to a *logic 0*, which causes the CPU to be initialized into a well-known state. The switch is of a type that springs open when released, thereby returning ~reset to a *logic 1* value and permitting the CPU to start to do its cunning stuff.

Sometimes even the best computer becomes hopelessly lost and confused, usually due to programming errors caused by its human operators. In this case the system may be reinitialized by means of the ~reset signal as discussed previously. Also, an additional circuit (not shown here) is used to automatically apply a *logic 0* pulse to the ~**reset** signal when power is first applied to the system; this is referred to as a *power-on reset*.

Protruding from the right-hand side of the CPU symbol are three busses: the *control bus*, *address bus*, and *data bus*. The operation of these busses is discussed in more detail below. Suffice it to say that the CPU uses the address bus to "point" to other components of the system; it uses the control bus to indicate whether it wishes to "talk" or to "listen"; and it uses the data bus to convey any information between itself and the other components. In fact the CPU is similar to a traffic policeman standing at the center of a crossroads, pointing to cars (or data in this case) and deciding who goes where and when.

Due to the fact that the CPU performs the bulk of the decision making, it is often referred to as the "brain" of the computer. However, on any scale of intelligence a CPU actually scores a lot lower than an amoeba and only slightly higher than a pickled onion. In fact the CPU doesn't really have any intelligence at all (unlike pickled onions which have evolved to be remarkably adept at scurrying away from between one's fingers).

Now this may seem to be at odds with the power you perceive computers to have, because they can appear capable of performing extremely sophisticated tasks. However, even the most complex problem can be broken down into a sequence of simple steps. In fact the CPU only ever performs relatively uncomplicated operations, such as adding two numbers together or comparing them to see which one is bigger. The CPU just does what it's told to do without any real understanding of what it's doing or why it's doing it (much like a man about to depart on a shopping expedition with his wife); it doesn't have a clue what it's about to do until it receives its next instruction (much like a man *on* a shopping expedition with his wife); and it can barely remember what it did just a moment ago (much like a man recently returned *from* a shopping expedition with his wife).

Having said this, although the CPU can only perform very simple operations it can execute millions of these operations every second, which makes it appear to be excruciatingly clever. But the real intelligence is in the intellectual content of these sequences of operations, known as *programs*, which are created by humans.

The data bus

The term *bus* is used to refer to a group of signals which carry similar information and perform a common function. As was previously noted, a computer system employs three busses called the *control bus*, *address bus*, and *data bus*. Purely for the sake of being contrary we will examine these in reverse order. In the case of our computer, we are going to assume that the data bus is composed of eight wires (Figure 2.3).

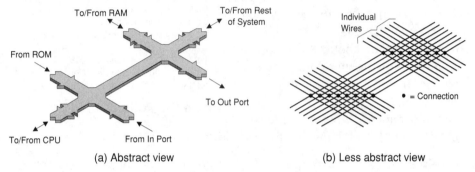

(a) Abstract view   (b) Less abstract view

Figure 2.3: The data bus

The more abstract view of the data bus shows arrows indicating the directions in which signals can travel between the various components attached to the bus. The less abstract view omits these arrows to emphasize the fact that the bus is physically composed of simple wires. In reality, the only thing that determines which way signals are traveling on the bus at any particular time is the CPU. By means of its control and address busses, the CPU can dictate which component is currently permitted to "talk" (drive signals onto the data bus) and which component is allowed to "listen" (receive those signals from the data bus). Due to the fact that signals can travel in either direction on the data bus, this bus is said to be *bidirectional*.

Remembering that we are considering conventional digital systems,[4] each wire may be used to represent one of two values: *logic 0* or *logic 1*. The actual values being driven onto the wires may change from one moment to the next, but, at any particular moment in time, a group of n wires can carry 2^n different combinations of these values (where 2^n means *"two to the power of n"* or *"two multiplied by itself n times"*). For example, two wires can be used to represent $2^2 = (2 \times 2) = 4$ different patterns of 0s and 1s (00, 01, 10, and 11). Similarly, the eight wires in our data bus can carry

---

[4]Some evaluations have been performed on tertiary logic; that is, logic gates based on three distinct voltage levels. Tertiary logic opens up all manner of mind-boggling possibilities which, you can thank your lucky stars, we aren't going to consider here.

$2^8 = (2 \times 2 \times 2 \times 2 \times 2 \times 2 \times 2 \times 2) = 256$ different patterns of 0s and 1s (Figure 2.4).

Before we discuss the types of information that can be represented using these patterns, it is worth pausing to consider a few important snippets of information contained within this figure. We must give the wires forming the data bus names so that we can refer to them in such a way that everybody knows what we're talking about. As an alternative to giving them meaningless individual names such as **big-boy**, **cuthbert**, and **fang**, it is preferable to give them a meaningful common name such as **data**, and to then distinguish the individual wires in some way.

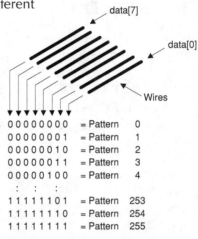

data[7]

data[0]

Wires

0 0 0 0 0 0 0 0	= Pattern 0
0 0 0 0 0 0 0 1	= Pattern 1
0 0 0 0 0 0 1 0	= Pattern 2
0 0 0 0 0 0 1 1	= Pattern 3
0 0 0 0 0 1 0 0	= Pattern 4
: : :	
1 1 1 1 1 1 0 1	= Pattern 253
1 1 1 1 1 1 1 0	= Pattern 254
1 1 1 1 1 1 1 1	= Pattern 255

Figure 2.4: Patterns of 0s and 1s

One solution would be to call the wires something like **data0**, **data1**, **data2**, and so on, but this can be painfully longwinded. A more advantageous solution is to append the common name with an index along the lines of **data[0]**, **data[1]**, **data[2]**, and so forth. Now, your first reaction may be that this solution is even more longwinded than the first, but the solution based on indexes has the advantage that it permits groups of wires to be specified as a range.

For example, **data[2:5]** can be used to represent the range of wires from **data[2]** to **data[5]**; that is, **data[2]**, **data[3]**, **data[4]**, and **data[5]**. Thus, the expression **data[2:5]** = 1010 is a compact way of indicating that the wires **data[2]** and **data[4]** are currently being used to represent *logic 1* values, while **data[3]** and **data[5]** are currently being used to represent *logic 0s*.

The previous example was based on an ascending range, but descending ranges such as **data[5:2]** may also be used. Thus, the expression **data[5:2]** = 0101 (in which the descending range is complemented by reversing the order of the values being assigned to the wires) is identical in intent to the original expression **data[2:5]** = 1010. In fact, for reasons that will become apparent, the data and address busses are usually considered in terms of a descending range. For example, it is far more common to see an expression in the form of **data[7:0]** = 01010011, than to see the equivalent expression **data[0:7]** = 11001010.

Another somewhat related point is that, given the way in which computers work, people who work with computers typically start counting at zero. This is why the wires forming our data bus are named data[0] through data[7], as opposed to using data[1] through data[8] which may appear to be more intuitive. Similarly, the 256 patterns illustrated in Figure 2.4 are actually numbered from 0 to 255. The reasoning behind these conventions will be made clear as we delve deeper into the nether regions of our discussions.

An overview of number systems

One type of information that we would use our patterns of 0s and 1s to represent would be numerical values, but first we need to establish what we mean by "numerical." The number system with which we are most familiar is the decimal system, whose name is derived from the Latin decem, meaning "ten."

The decimal system is based on ten digits: 0, 1, 2, 3, 4, 5, 6, 7, 8, and 9. Thus, it is said to be *base-10* or *radix-10*, where the term radix comes from the Latin word meaning "root." However, decimal is certainly not the only possible number system, and people have experimented with many alternative systems over the years, including *quinary (base-5)* systems (counting using the fingers of only one hand); *duo-decimal (base-12)* systems (counting using the finger joints of one hand by pointing at them with the thumb of that hand); *vigesimal (base-20)* systems (counting using both fingers and toes); and even *sexagesimal (base-60)* systems, which were used by the Sumerians and the Babylonians thousands of years ago. This all serves to illustrate the fact that number systems with bases other than ten are not only feasible, but positively abound throughout history.

The decimal system that we know and love so well is a *place-value* system, in which the value of a particular digit depends both on the digit itself and on its position within the number. Every column in a place-value system has a "weight" associated with it, and each digit is correlated with its column's weight to determine the final value of the number (Figure 2.5).

Once again, 10^n means *"ten to the power of n"* or *"ten multiplied by itself n times"*, so $10^3 = (10 \times 10 \times 10) = 1000$. Any base to the power of one is equal to itself, so $10^1 = 10$. Strictly speaking a power of zero is not part of the series, but by convention any base to the power of zero equals 1, so $10^0 = 1$.

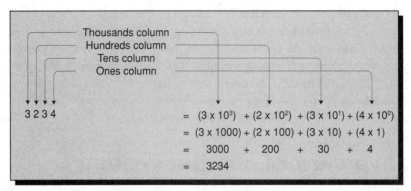

Figure 2.5: Combining digits with column weights in decimal

To prepare us for the ordeals to come, it is important to have a firm grasp of how different number systems work. Before we plunge with reckless abandon into the systems used by computers, it is well worth our time to take a glance at something a little closer to home, such as the quinary (base-5) system, which uses five digits: 0, 1, 2, 3 and 4. This system is particularly interesting in that a quinary finger-counting scheme is still in use today by some merchants in the Indian state of Maharashtra near Bombay.

As with any place-value system, each column in a quinary number has a weight associated with it, where the weights are derived from the base. Each digit is correlated with its column's weight to determine the final value of the number (Figure 2.6).

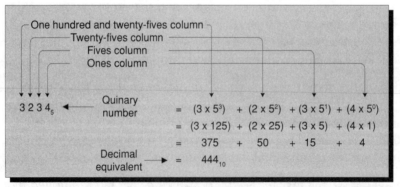

Figure 2.6: Combining digits with column weights in quinary

When we use systems with bases other than ten, subscripts are used to indicate the relevant base; e.g. $3234_5 = 444_{10}$ ($3234_{QUINARY} = 444_{DECIMAL}$). By convention, any value without a subscript is assumed to be in decimal.

Counting in quinary commences at 0 and progresses up to 4_5, at which point all of the available digits have been used. Thus, the next count causes the first column to be reset to 0 and the second column to be incremented resulting in 10_5 (which equals 5 in decimal) (Figure 2.7).

Quinary	Decimal
0_5	0_{10}
1_5	1_{10}
2_5	2_{10}
3_5	3_{10}
4_5	4_{10}
10_5	5_{10}
11_5	6_{10}
12_5	7_{10}
13_5	8_{10}
14_5	9_{10}
20_5	10_{10}
21_5	11_{10}
$\vdots$	$\vdots$
43_5	23_{10}
44_5	24_{10}
100_5	25_{10}
$\vdots$	$\vdots$

Figure 2.7: Counting in quinary

Similarly, when the count reaches 14_5 (which equals 9 in decimal), the next count causes the first column to be reset to zero and the second column to be incremented resulting in 20_5 (which equals 10 in decimal).

Life becomes more interesting when the count reaches 44_5 (which equals 24 in decimal). The next count causes the first column to be reset to zero and the second column to be incremented. But as the second column already contains a 4, this causes *it* to be reset to 0 and the third column to be incremented resulting in 100_5 (which equals 25 in decimal).

Now you may be wondering why we have wandered off the beaten path into this number-systems maze. At a first glance it might appear to be jolly advantageous to use the decimal numbering system all of the time – after all, that's the one that we slaved over for years learning at school. However, although base-10 systems are anatomically convenient they have few other advantages to recommend them. In fact, almost any other base (with the possible exception of 9) would be as good as, or better than, base-10. Even worse, as fate would have it, none of the number systems discussed above are particularly efficacious when it comes to computers. And thus we find ourselves with our backs against the wall, compelled against our wills to master new ways of looking at numbers in the form of the *binary* and *hexadecimal* systems.

The binary number system

As we previously discussed, each wire on the data bus can be used to carry one of two values: *logic 0* and *logic 1*. If we decide that we wish to treat these values as numerical digits, an obvious move is to consider the *binary (base-2)* number system, which uses only two digits: 0 and 1 (Figure 2.8).

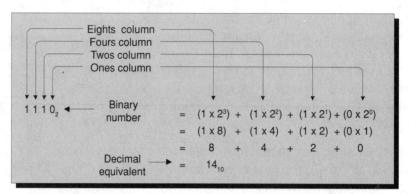

$$1110_2 = (1 \times 2^3) + (1 \times 2^2) + (1 \times 2^1) + (0 \times 2^0)$$
$$= (1 \times 8) + (1 \times 4) + (1 \times 2) + (0 \times 1)$$
$$= 8 + 4 + 2 + 0$$
$$= 14_{10}$$

Figure 2.8: Combining digits with column weights in binary

As is usual in a place-value system, each column in a binary number has a weight associated with it, where the weights are derived from the base, and each digit is correlated with its column's weight to determine the final value of the number. Once again, subscripts are used to indicate the relevant base; for example, $1110_2 = 14_{10}$ ($1110_{BINARY} = 14_{DECIMAL}$).

The phrase *binary digit* is usually abbreviated to *bit*, so our data bus, which is composed of eight wires, would be said to have a width of eight bits or to be eight bits wide. Groupings of eight bits are common in computers and are given the special name of *byte*.

It now becomes apparent that one of the options available to us is to use the 256 patterns of 0s and 1s that can be carried by our 8-bit data bus to represent positive binary numbers in the range 0 to 255 (Figure 2.9).

In the same way that a group of eight bits are given the special name of *byte*, a group of four bits, which is also common, may be referred to as a *nybble* (or sometimes a *nibble*). The idea that "two nybbles make a byte" is in the way of being a computer engineer's idea of a joke. Thus we find that people who work with computers do have a sense of humor, it's just not a particularly sophisticated one.

Continuing this theme, there have been sporadic attempts to construct terms for groups of other sizes; for example, tayste or crumb for a 2-bit group, playte or chawmp for a 16-bit group, dynner or gawble for a 32-bit group, and tayble for a 64-bit group. However using anything other than the standard terms byte and nybble is extremely rare.

It also becomes obvious that unlike numbers written with pencil and paper, in which both decimal and binary values can be of any size (limited only by the dimensions of your paper and your endurance), the numbers manipulated within a computer have to be mapped onto a physical system of logic gates and wires. Thus, the maximum value of an individual numerical quantity represented by the data bus is dictated by the width of the bus; that is, the number of bits available to describe that quantity. To extricate ourselves from this predicament it's possible to play cunning tricks that allow us to use our 8-bit data bus to represent both positive and negative numbers of any desired size, but these tricks won't be revealed until a little later in the game.

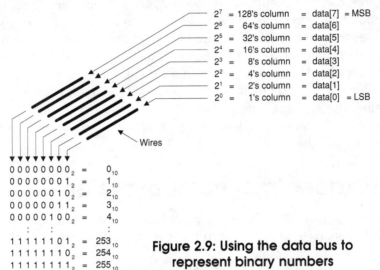

$$2^7 = 128\text{'s column} = \text{data}[7] = \text{MSB}$$
$$2^6 = 64\text{'s column} = \text{data}[6]$$
$$2^5 = 32\text{'s column} = \text{data}[5]$$
$$2^4 = 16\text{'s column} = \text{data}[4]$$
$$2^3 = 8\text{'s column} = \text{data}[3]$$
$$2^2 = 4\text{'s column} = \text{data}[2]$$
$$2^1 = 2\text{'s column} = \text{data}[1]$$
$$2^0 = 1\text{'s column} = \text{data}[0] = \text{LSB}$$

Wires

$$00000000_2 = 0_{10}$$
$$00000001_2 = 1_{10}$$
$$00000010_2 = 2_{10}$$
$$00000011_2 = 3_{10}$$
$$00000100_2 = 4_{10}$$
$$\vdots \qquad \vdots \qquad \vdots$$
$$11111101_2 = 253_{10}$$
$$11111110_2 = 254_{10}$$
$$11111111_2 = 255_{10}$$

Figure 2.9: Using the data bus to represent binary numbers

Representing binary numbers is a common practice in digital computing, which unveils the reasoning behind some of the conventions introduced in our discussions on the data bus. The rationale for numbering the patterns starting with zero matches the binary sequence which starts with all 0s, which in turn represents 0_{10}. Similarly, a wire representing the binary value 2^n has the index n; that is, the wire representing 2^0 is **data[0]**, the wire representing 2^1 is **data[1]**, and so forth.

Due to the fact that **data[0]** represents the least-significant binary value, it is referred to as being the *least-significant bit (LSB)*. Similarly, **data[7]** is referred to as being the *most-significant bit (MSB)*, because it represents the most-significant binary value. In fact the MSB depends on the width of the bus; if we were working with a system with a 16-bit data bus called **data[15:0]**, then **data[0]** would still be the LSB, but the MSB would now be **data[15]**.

In any numbering system it is usual to write the most-significant digit on the left and the least-significant digit on the right. For example, when you see a decimal number such as 825, you immediately assume that the '8' on the left is the most-significant digit (representing eight hundred) while the '5' on the right is the least-significant (representing five). This explains why we previously observed that: *"It is far more common to see an expression in the form data[7:0] = 01010011 than to see the equivalent expression data[0:7] = 11001010,"* because the former style reflects the way in which we usually visualize binary numbers as being assigned to the bus.

Counting in binary commences at 0 and progresses rather quickly up to 1_2, at which point all of the available digits have been used. Thus, the next count causes the first column to be reset to 0 and the second column to be incremented resulting in 10_2 (which equals 2 in decimal). Similarly, when the count reaches 11_2 (which equals 3 in decimal), the next count causes the first column to be reset to zero and the second column to be incremented. But as the second column already contains a 1, this causes it to be reset to 0 and the third column to be incremented resulting in 100_2 (which equals 4 in decimal).

The hexadecimal number system

Although the concept of the binary number system is relatively easy to understand, humans tend to find such numbers rather difficult to work with. For example, the binary value 11010111_2 is quite long and relatively awkward to conceptualize, while its decimal equivalent of 215 is comparatively easy. One solution to this problem devolves from the fact that any number system having a base that is a power of two (2, 4, 8, 16, 32, and so on) can be easily mapped into its binary equivalent, and vice versa. For this reason, people who work with computers typically make use of either the *octal (base-8)* or *hexadecimal (base-16)* systems.

As a base-16 system, hexadecimal requires sixteen individual symbols to represent all of its digits. This poses something of a problem, because we only have ten Hindu-Arabic[5] symbols (0 through 9) available to us in decimal. One solution would be to create some new symbols, but many would regard this as less than optimal, not the least that we'd all have to learn them and it would require existing typewriters and computer keyboards to be modified. As an alternative, the first six letters of the alphabet are brought into play (Figure 2.10).

The rules for counting in hexadecimal are the same as for any other place-value system; when all the digits in a column are exhausted, the next count sets that column to zero and increments the column to the left (Figure 2.11).

---

[5]The symbols we use to represent decimal numbers arrived in Europe around the thirteenth century from the Arabs, who in turn borrowed them from the Hindus.

Hexadecimal	0	1	2	3	4	5	6	7	8	9	A	B	C	D	E	F
Decimal	0	1	2	3	4	5	6	7	8	9	10	11	12	13	14	15

Figure 2.10: The sixteen hexadecimal digits

Binary and hexadecimal numbers are often prefixed by leading zeros to pad them to some desired width, thereby providing an indication of the physical number of bits used to represent these values within the computer. Thus, the binary values in Figure 2.11 are padded to make them 8-bits wide, because this is the width we've chosen for our data bus. Similarly, any single-digit hexadecimal values are padded with a leading zero, where each hexadecimal digit is equivalent to four binary digits.

Decimal	Binary	Hexadecimal
0	0000 0000	00
1	0000 0001	01
2	0000 0010	02
3	0000 0011	03
4	0000 0100	04
5	0000 0101	05
6	0000 0110	06
7	0000 0111	07
8	0000 1000	08
9	0000 1001	09
10	0000 1010	0A
11	0000 1011	0B
12	0000 1100	0C
13	0000 1101	0D
14	0000 1110	0E
15	0000 1111	0F
16	0001 0000	10
17	0001 0001	11
18	0001 0010	12
⋮	⋮	⋮
etc.	etc.	etc.

Figure 2.11: Counting in hexadecimal

The binary values shown in Figure 2.11 have spaces dividing them into two 4-bit sections. This representation is not outrageously common, but is used here to emphasize the fact that each hexadecimal digit is equivalent to four binary digits. For example, $0_{16} = 0000_2$, $9_{16} = 1001_2$, $C_{16} = 1100_2$, and $F_{16} = 1111_2$. This means that it is very easy to convert hexadecimal numbers into their binary equivalents, and vice versa (Figure 2.12).

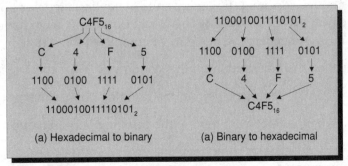

(a) Hexadecimal to binary   (a) Binary to hexadecimal

Figure 2.12: Mapping hexadecimal to binary and vice versa

Just to make life a little more interesting, these examples involve the conversion of a 16-bit number from hexadecimal to binary and back again. In the case of the hexadecimal to binary conversion, each hexadecimal digit is mapped into its corresponding 4-bit binary equivalent, and these 4-bit groups are then stuck back together to form the full 16-bit value. By comparison, in the case of the binary to hexadecimal conversion, the 16-bit binary value is split up into groups of four bits, each of these groups is mapped to its corresponding hexadecimal digit, and these digits are then glued together to give the result.

In the original digital computers, bus widths were often multiples of three bits (such as 9-bits, 12-bits, 18-bits, 24-bits, and so on). As an octal digit can be directly mapped onto three bits, these bus values were easily represented in octal, which provides one of the reasons behind the original popularity of the octal system.

More recently, computers have tended to standardize on bus widths that are multiples of eight bits (such as 8-bits, 16-bits, 32-bits, and so on). Although octal can be used to represent the values on these busses, hexadecimal is more commonly used because each hexadecimal digit can be directly mapped onto four bits. This is one of the main reasons for the decline in popularity of the octal system and the corresponding ascendancy of hexadecimal.

Performing simple arithmetic operations in binary or hexadecimal is fairly straightforward once you've got the hang of it, but it can be a bit of a stumbling block for beginners. Rather than confuse the issue by delving into this topic now, we've relegated it to Chapter 7 and Appendix G.

The *Beboputer's* calculator utility

Amongst the *Beboputer's* treasure chest of tools you will find a calculator utility to aid you in translating numbers back and forth between binary, decimal, and hexadecimal. If you haven't already installed your *Beboputer* from the CD ROM accompanying this book, do so now by following the instructions in Appendix A. Once you've completed the installation:

a) Click on the **Start** button on the Windows® 95 taskbar[6,7]

b) Click on the **Programs** item in the resulting pop-up menu

c) Click on the **Beboputer** item in the resulting pop-up menu

[6]All of the instructions in this book are based on the Microsoft Windows® 95 operating system (the only system for which the *Beboputer* is certified).
[7]Microsoft and Windows are registered trademarks of Microsoft Corporation.

d) Click on the **Calculator** item in the resulting pop-up menu. This will invoke your *Beboputer's* calculator utility as shown in Figure 2.13.

Figure 2.13: The calculator utility

The calculator powers-up using the decimal numbering system by default. This is indicated by the fact that the **Dec** button is highlighted. Use your mouse to enter the decimal number 61642, then click on the **Hex** button to see F0CA, which is your number's 4-digit hexadecimal equivalent. Now click on the **Bin** button to receive 1111000011001010, which is your original number's 16-bit binary equivalent. The calculator also powers-up assuming that you wish to use two bytes (sixteen bits) to display your hexadecimal or binary values (remember that each hexadecimal character corresponds to four bits). This is indicated by the fact that the **2Byte** button is highlighted. Click on the **1Byte** button and note that the display changes to 11001010; these eight bits are the least-significant bits of your number. (Note that the **1Byte** and **2Byte** buttons have no effect when displaying decimal numbers).

The calculator's remaining buttons work in the standard way of such utilities, although you may not be familiar with the **AND, OR, XOR, NOT, ROL, ROR, SHL,** and **SHR** buttons. These buttons represent logical and bit-manipulation operations, and they correspond to some of the *Beboputer's* instructions which will be introduced in later chapters.[8]

---

[8]The **ROL** and **ROR** calculator buttons work slightly differently to the *Beboputer's* **ROLC** and **RORC** instructions, which are discussed in detail in Chapter 8 (you can find out more about the calculator in the online help provided with the *Beboputer*).

Play around with the calculator for a while to familiarize yourself with its operation, then dismiss it by clicking on the Exit button in its title bar. Note that when you invoke the main *Beboputer* as discussed in the next chapter,

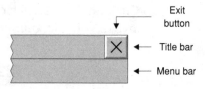

you'll find an icon for the calculator in the project window's toolbar and you can access the calculator at any time by clicking on this icon.

Different types of data

Imagine that it's Christmas and you've just eaten enough food to sustain Conan the Barbarian on a week's forced march. All you want to do is to let your belt out three notches and moan and groan for a few hours, but instead you find yourself obliged to join in one of those endlessly involved party games organized by a rampaging herd of aunts.

Our imaginary game is based on pieces of paper on which numbers are written. Before the game starts, the game master (the biggest, most ferocious aunt you ever saw) has instructed one of your uncles on the meaning of certain numbers. The trick is that these numbers mean different things at different times. When your uncle is presented with his first number it will represent an instruction as follows: if he receives a 65 he has to hop up and down on one leg, if he sees a 66 he has to make annoying sounds with his armpit, and if he is presented with a 67 he has to expound his views on the current political situation at great length.[9]

Your uncle is further informed that his second number will represent a letter of the alphabet: the number 65 will represent the letter 'A', 66 will represent 'B', 67 will represent 'C', and so on. Thus, when he receives his second number, he has to determine which letter that number represents and shout it out. Your long-suffering uncle is also instructed that his third number will be exactly what it appears to be (a number), so when he receives his third slip of paper he simply has to inform everyone as to the number he finds there. Last but not least, your uncle learns that the whole sequence will start again, with his fourth number representing a new instruction. Obviously this game is not going to oust Trivial Pursuit™ as a party favorite, but bear with us, because there's reason behind our madness.

Assume that the game master deals your uncle a sequence of paper slips which commence with the following numbers: 65, 67, 66, and 67. Your

---

[9]Unfortunately we all have uncles who do this sort of thing without prompting, but dealing with issues like these is outside the scope of this book.

uncle will first hop up and down on one leg, then shout out the letter 'C', then declaim "sixty-six", then inform everyone what he thinks about politicians, and so it goes ...... pandemonium reins and a good time is had by all. Note that the number 67 appears twice, but it means something different each time based on its position in the sequence.

One interesting point is that your uncle must be present at the beginning of the game when the first slip of paper is passed. Imagine the confusion if he slipped out to the rest room for a few moments (as you do), and only returned in time to receive the third slip. If he mistakenly assumed that *this* was an instruction, then instead of declaiming *"sixty-six"* he would immediately commence to make annoying sounds with his armpit. Similarly, every succeeding slip of paper would be treated incorrectly. Oh, the confusion that would ensue, the shame that would have to be endured, and how the neighbors would talk.

But as usual we digress. Aside from the fact that our party game bears a strong resemblance to the way in which computers work, the point behind all of this rigmarole is that symbols such as numbers are under our control and they only represent what we want them to represent. Also, numbers may represent different things at different times; the trick of course is to know what they are supposed to represent at any particular time. And so we return to the patterns of 0s and 1s carried by our 8-bit data bus, which can be used to represent a variety of different things depending on the occasion (Figure 2.14)

Before we examine Figure 2.14 in detail, we've been throwing the term data around rather freely, so this might be an appropriate time to try to define exactly what we mean. The dictionary defines data as: *"Things that are certainly known, or which can be taken to be known, from which inferences can be drawn."* As luck would have it, this definition is as close to useless for our purposes as it could be, so we'll have to take a stab at one ourselves. As far as we're concerned "data" may be loosely defined as any information which is accepted, processed, or generated by the computer. By this definition, any instructions used to direct the computer may also be regarded as being a form of data. While this is true, it is common practice to refer to *instructions* and *data* as being distinct entities. This is just one of those cases where you have to fumble your way along very carefully; it's difficult to describe, but by the time you finish this book you'll know as much as anyone else.

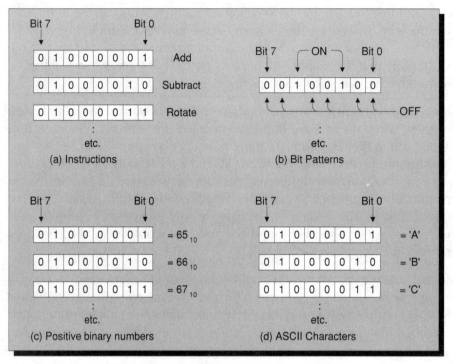

Figure 2.14: Different types of data

The first thing the CPU does after it's been reset is to request an instruction, which duly appears on the data bus (this process is discussed in more detail a little later on). Figure 2.14a illustrates some possible instructions.[10] In addition to directing the computer as to what to do, an instruction also tells the CPU whether the next byte of information to appear on the data bus will be another instruction, or whether it will be an additional piece of data associated with this first instruction (once again, we will examine this process in more detail a little later on).

The data associated with an instruction can come in many forms. As we have already discussed, the patterns of 0s and 1s on the data bus may be used to represent positive binary numbers as illustrated in Figure 2.14c. Similar patterns may also be used to represent negative binary numbers, but that topic has been largely relegated to Chapter 7.

Alternatively, the patterns of 0s and 1s may be a simple bit pattern as shown in Figure 2.14b. For example, the CPU may direct this pattern to one of the output ports where it could be used to drive something in the outside world,

---

[10]Note that the particular patterns of 0s and 1s shown here were selected only for the purpose of illustrating certain points in these examples.

such as a set of light bulbs in your house. In this case each bit in the pattern might be used to control an individual light – a *logic 1* on that bit might turn a particular light **ON**, while a *logic 0* could turn that light **OFF**. Of course, we need to keep in mind the fact that the values *logic 0* and *logic 1* have little relevance in the outside world. Thus, we might decide that a *logic 0* should turn the light **ON** and a *logic 1* should turn it **OFF**. The actual actions caused by the logical values depend on whatever is present on the other side of the output port (the use of output ports will also be covered in more detail later on).

Last but not least (and remembering that only a few possibilities have been discussed here), we might use different patterns of 0s and 1s to represent characters such as 'A', 'B', 'C', and so on (Figure 2.14d). However, unlike the mapping of positive binary numbers which is pretty intuitive, the mapping of characters is somewhat less obvious. The problem is that everybody has to agree that we're all talking about the same thing. For example, your program may direct the CPU to send the binary pattern 01000001_2 to an output port that's connected to a printer. In this case, assuming that you are assuming that this pattern represents a letter 'A', it would be sort of useful if the printer assumed the same thing.

Now, your first reaction might be why don't we make 00000000_2 correspond to an 'A' and proceed from there, but someone else might suggest that we start with a lowercase 'a'. Yet another person might wish to commence with the characters that represent decimal digits ('0', '1', '2', '3', and so on), and then there are such things as punctuation characters and special characters like '!', '@', '#', and '$'.

What we need is a standard, but there is an engineering joke that goes: *"Standards are great, everyone should have one"* – the problem being that almost everyone does! However, there is one code that is very widely

Another code that deserves some mention is the *Extended Binary Coded Decimal Interchange Code (EBCDIC)* from IBM, primarily because of the pain and suffering it has caused the authors over the years.

The beauty of ASCII is that all of the alpha characters are numbered sequentially; that is, 65 = 'A', 66 = 'B', 67 = 'C', and so on until the end of the alphabet. Similarly, 97 = 'a', 98 = 'b', 99 = 'c', and so forth. This means that you can perform programming tricks like saying ('A' + 23), and having a reasonable expectation of ending up with the letter 'X'. To cut a long story short, if you were thinking of doing this with EBCDIC ...... don't. Fortunately, the chances of your running into EBCDIC are relatively slight (and they're close to zero in this book).

used, the *American Standard Code for Information Interchange (ASCII).* Using ASCII (pronounced "*ass-key*"), the letter 'A' is represented by the number 65 in decimal, which is 41_{16} in hexadecimal and 01000001_2 in binary (hence the reason for the examples selected above). We will return to consider the use of ASCII again in Chapters 4, 10, and 11. Also, the full ASCII code is presented for your delectation and delight in Appendix E.

The address bus

Imagine a series of thousands upon thousands of boxes standing side-by-side and stretching away into the dim and distant beyond. Each box is numbered sequentially commencing with zero (Figure 2.15).

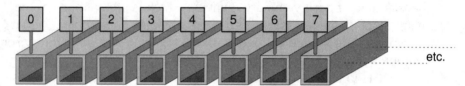

Figure 2.15: A series of boxes[11]

Remembering the party games we discussed above, imagine that some of the boxes contain slips of paper with numbers written on them, while others remain empty waiting for us to put something in them. Further suppose that some of the boxes are open to the elements, while others have transparent pieces of bullet-proof glass sealing their ends.

In the case of an open box, we could write a number on a slip of paper and insert it into that box. In the case of a box that already contains a slip of paper, we might simply read the number on the slip but leave the slip where it is; we might copy the slip and place the copy in another box; or we might erase the number on the slip and write a new number in its place. Finally, in the case of a box that is sealed with a glass cover, we can read the number on the slip inside the box, but we can't alter it in any way.

Strange as it may seem, this is the way that the CPU views its world – as a series of boxes containing numbers (which may represent different things as discussed above). However, we manly computer men don't think "boxes" is a grandiose enough term, so instead we call them *memory locations,* which sounds much more impressive when you're trying to baffle and bewilder your friends. Now the CPU needs a way to indicate which memory location it is currently interested in, and for this it uses its *address bus* (Figure 2.16).

---

[11]Oh, the hours we spent inventing catchy titles for our figures.

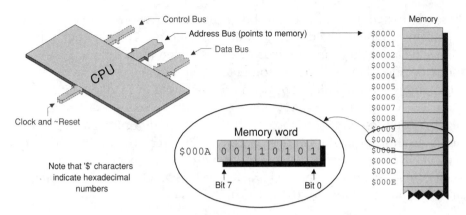

Figure 2.16: The address bus

Each location in the memory is referred to as a *word*, and each word has the same width as the data bus. Thus, as the data bus in our *Beboputer* is 8-bits wide, each word in the memory must also be 8-bits wide. Each bit in a memory word can be used to store a *logic 0* or a *logic 1*, and all of the bits forming a word are typically written to or read from simultaneously.

There are several possible origins for the term address. Remembering the series of boxes in Figure 2.15, the numbers used to reference them may be likened to house addresses that are used to locate mail boxes. Alternatively, this term may be derived from the concept that the CPU addresses itself to the memory, along the lines of: *"Excuuussseee me, but were you addressing that remark to me Sir?"* But we don't have the time to wander off down the highways and byways of word origins here (you can check out the lexicon at the back of the book should you find yourself with time on your hands). Wherever the term came from, the CPU uses its address bus to point to memory locations, each of which has a unique identification number, or address.

The totality of memory locations that can be addressed by the computer are referred to as its *address space*. In the case of our *Beboputer*, we're going to assume that the address bus is sixteen bits (two bytes) wide. This means that our address bus can carry 2^{16} unique combinations of 0s and 1s, which can therefore be used to point to 65,536 different memory locations numbered from 0 to 65,535. However, for a variety of reasons it is not very convenient to refer to the addresses of memory locations using a decimal notation, so rather than referring to a location such as 48,259 using its decimal value (or worse, its binary equivalent of 1011110010000011_2), it is common practice to refer to addresses using a hexadecimal notation such as $BC83_{16}$.

By some strange quirk of fate, this brings us to the reason why we used '$' characters to indicate hexadecimal values in Figure 2.16. Although it is relatively easy for humans to recognize subscripted numbers such as $BC83_{16}$ and to decide what they mean, computers aren't tremendously good at this sort of thing. For example, consider a program used to read text into a computer. Unless it was particularly clever, such a program could easily become confused and "see" the subscripts as being normal numbers. To circumvent this problem a variety of conventions may be used to indicate numbers in bases other than decimal. In our case, we decided to prefix hexadecimal numbers with '$' characters (e.g. $BC83) and binary numbers with '%' characters (e.g. %1011110010000011).

The control bus

And so we come to the last bus used by a computer system: the *control bus*, which, as its name might suggest, wields ultimate authority over the coming and going of data throughout the system. Paradoxically, in some respects the control bus is the simplest bus of all — in our system it only consists of two wires named ~read and ~write (Figure 2.17).

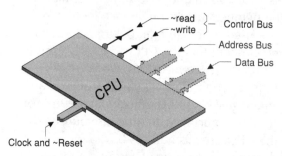

Figure 2.17: The control bus

In fact, in many systems these two signals are combined on a single wire, in which case a *logic 1* is used to indicate a read operation and a *logic 0* is used to indicate a write (or vice versa). In our case we chose to keep them separate for the sake of clarity.

To be perfectly honest, the **clock** and ~reset inputs are also considered to form part of the control bus, but these signals are often treated separately as is illustrated in our diagrams. Additionally, the control bus may also include some other signals which are used to interrupt the CPU's normal operation, but this topic has been set aside for detailed discussion in Appendix D.

Both the ~read and ~write signals are active when they carry *logic 0* values. This is indicated by the tilde characters ('~') in their names, and also by the small circles (called *bobbles* or *bubbles*) on the side of the CPU. The CPU uses its ~read signal to indicate when it wishes to receive (read) some data from whichever memory location it is currently pointing to with its address bus. The location selected by the address bus passes the required data to the CPU by means of the data bus. Similarly, the CPU uses its ~write signal to indicate when it wishes to send (write) some data to whichever memory location it is currently pointing to with its address bus. The CPU passes the data to the targeted location by driving it out onto the data bus. One way to illustrate the processes of reading and writing is by means of a timing diagram (Figure 2.18).

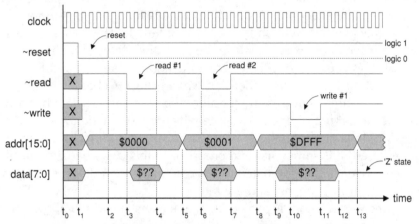

Figure 2.18: Timing diagram for reading and writing data

As with many other things associated with computers, timing diagrams can appear to be pretty complex to the uninitiated, but they are really not as frightening as they first appear. The vertical y-axis shows the signals that we're interested in, while the horizontal x-axis represents time progressing from left to right. As we move through time, individual signals such as ~reset are shown to switch between lower and higher levels. A lower level is assumed to represent a *logic 0* and a higher level is assumed to represent a *logic 1*. In the case of the address and data busses, which represent multiple signals, the hexadecimal values representing the group are shown in shaded boxes.

In the case of our timing diagram, everything starts when the computer is first switched on at a time we have chosen to call t_0. The actions of all of the signals are related to the clock, which is oscillating furiously between *logic 0* and *logic 1*. Although there seems to be a lot of it, this diagram actually only represents four major sequences known as *machine cycles*, each of which is divided into a series of actions. From left to right, these sequences involve resetting the computer, performing a read cycle, performing a second read cycle, and performing a write cycle. A breakdown of these sequences into their individual actions follows.

Resetting the Computer: When power is first applied to the system at time t_0 everything is in disarray. The CPU feels as though it has been hit over the head with a mallet and it doesn't know whether it's coming or going. This is indicated by the X values shown on the ~read and ~write signals and on the address and data busses, where X's are used to indicate unknown values.

In a real system a special *power-on reset* circuit would be used to ensure that the ~reset signal was active from the word go, but we've ignored this to better illustrate the effect of this signal. In our example the ~reset input is placed in its active state (which is a *logic 0*) at time t_1. This causes the CPU to place its ~read and ~write signals in their inactive states (which are *logic 1s*). It also causes the CPU to direct the address bus to point to memory location $0000 (remember that we're using '$' characters to indicate hexadecimal values), and for all of the wires on the data bus to be driven to a special *high-impedance* state which is usually denoted by Z characters.[12] In fact, although the expression *"driven to high impedance"* is commonly used, it is somewhat inappropriate in this case, because all of the devices connected to the data bus have actually been disconnected from the bus by electronic means, and are therefore not driving anything. Finally, at time t_2, the ~reset signal is placed in its inactive state which allows the CPU to start to do its funky stuff.

Read Cycle #1: Following a reset, the first thing that the CPU does is to read an instruction from the memory location at address $0000. To do this the CPU places the ~read signal in its active state (which is a *logic 0*) at time t_3. When the memory location at address $0000 "sees" the active ~read signal, it responds by placing a copy of its contents onto the data bus. We've shown these contents as being $?? to indicate that we don't really care what they are at this stage in our discussions; suffice it to say that they represent an instruction for the CPU to act upon. Once the CPU has acquired the instruction and stored a copy internally, it places the ~read signal in its inactive state (which is a *logic 1*) at time t_4. When the memory location at address $0000 realizes that the ~read signal has gone inactive, it disconnects itself from the data bus and returns to driving Z values onto the bus.

Read Cycle #2: Depending on the instruction it received during the previous read cycle, the CPU may now perform either a read cycle or a write cycle – in our case we're assuming another read cycle. Additionally, the previous instruction may have informed the CPU that the next read cycle will return data associated with that instruction, or it may have informed the

---

[12]The concept of high impedance is discussed in more detail in Chapter 6.

CPU to expect a completely new instruction. In our case we're assuming that the CPU expects a new instruction which will, by default, be in the next memory location.

At time t_5 the CPU increments the address bus to point to memory location $0001. At time t_6 the CPU places the ~read signal in its active state. When the memory location at address $0001 "sees" that the ~read signal is active, it places a copy of its contents onto the data bus. Once again we've shown these contents as being $?? to indicate that we don't really care what they are at this stage in our discussions. At time t_7 the CPU places the ~read signal in its inactive state. When the memory realizes that the ~read signal has gone inactive, it disconnects itself from the data bus and returns to driving **Z** values onto the bus.

Write Cycle #1: For the purposes of this discussion, we will assume that the instruction from the second read cycle told the CPU to write some data to memory location $DFFF. Thus, at time t_8 the CPU changes the address bus to point to memory location $DFFF. At time t_9 the CPU places the information it wishes to write onto the data bus (as usual we've used $?? to indicate that we don't really care what this value is at the moment). At time t_{10} the CPU places the ~write signal in its active state. When the memory location at address $DFFF "sees" that the ~write signal is active, it takes a copy of the value on the data bus and squirrels it away. After waiting a few moments to give the memory time to store the data, the CPU places the ~write signal in its inactive state at time t_{11}. At time t_{12} the CPU stops driving its data onto the data bus and returns to driving **Z** values onto the bus. Finally, at time t_{13} the CPU places a new value onto the address bus and is ready to commence a new cycle.

If the preceding discussion made perfect sense to you, then you can award yourself ten points and a prize coconut. But don't worry if it seemed confusing on this first pass, because you really don't need to know a computer system at this level of detail to be able to use it.[13] As we proceed you'll find yourself returning to this timing diagram of your own accord, and each time you return it will make more and more sense. Trust us on this — have we ever lied to you before?

---

[13]This is fortunate, as otherwise computers would not be nearly so popular as they are.

The memory (RAM and ROM)

We were going to start this section with a cunningly capricious quip about memory devices …… but it seems to have slipped our minds! Alright, alright, we know that this isn't outrageously amusing, but you have do the best with the material you have available (and these are the jokes that the Muppet Show refused).

As we will see, computers can use a variety of methods for storing binary data for later use. However, the technique of interest to us at the moment involves special integrated circuits of which there are two main categories: *read-only memory (ROM)* and *read-write memory (RWM)*. For a number of reasons, mainly historical, RWMs are more commonly known as *random-access memories (RAMs)*.

The data contained by ROMs is hard-coded into them during their construction.[14] ROMs are referred to as being *non-volatile*, because their data remains intact when power is removed from the system. The CPU can read (extract) data from ROM devices, but cannot write (insert) new data into them. By comparison, data can be read out of RAM devices and new data can be written back into them. The act of reading data out of a RAM does not affect the master copy of the data stored in the device. When power is first applied to a system, RAM devices initialize containing random *logic 0* or *logic 1* values. Thus, any meaningful data stored inside a RAM must be written into it by the CPU after the system has been powered-up. Also, RAMs are said to be *volatile*, because any data they contain is lost when power is removed from the system.

The smallest unit of memory is a *cell*, which can be used to store a single bit of data; that is, a *logic 0* or *logic 1*. A number of cells physically grouped together are classed as a word, and all of the cells in a word are typically written to or read from at the same time. The core of a memory device is made up of a number of words arranged as an array (Figure 2.19).

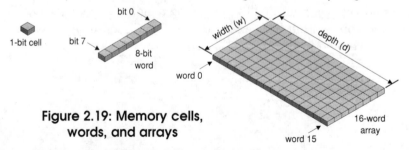

**Figure 2.19: Memory cells,
words, and arrays**

---

[14]See also the discussion on PROMs, EPROMs, and EEPROMs in Chapter 13.

Remember that this is simply a pictorial representation that provides us with a way in which to view the world. In reality, each cell in the array is composed of a number of transistors, and all of the cells (and the connections between them) are fabricated on a single integrated circuit.

The width **w** of the memory is the number of bits used to form a word, where the bits are usually numbered from 0 to (**w** - 1); thus, an 8-bit wide word has bits numbered from 0 to 7. Similarly, the depth **d** of a memory is the number of words used to form the array, where the words are usually numbered from 0 to (**d** - 1); thus, the 16-word array illustrated in Figure 2.19 would have its words numbered from 0 to 15.

In addition to the memory array itself, some decoding and control logic is also needed to make the device function as required, but we will gloss over this for the nonce. Although their internal construction is quite different, packaged ROM and RAM devices are very similar in external appearance (Figure 2.20).

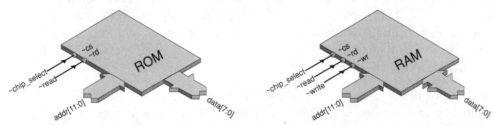

Figure 2.20: ROM and RAM

Both ROMs and RAMs have a ~cs input, which is used to inform them when their services are required (where "cs" is a common abbreviation for "chip select"). Similarly, both devices have a ~rd input, which informs them when the CPU wishes to perform a read operation. However, only the RAM has a ~wr input, which is used to inform it when the CPU wishes to perform a write operation. The ROM does not have this input because, as was previously noted, you can't write new data into a *read-only* memory. As the tilde characters in their names and the bobbles on the diagrams would suggest, the active states for the ~cs, ~rd, and ~wr inputs are *logic 0s*, which is usually the case for control signals.

For the CPU to reference a particular word in one of these memory devices, it must specify that word's address by placing appropriate values onto the device's address bus (this address is subsequently decoded inside the device to select the appropriate word). Remembering that our CPU's address bus has 16-bits called **addr[15:0]**, you may have wondered why the individual devices are shown as only having 12-bit address inputs called **addr[11:0]**. The reason is fairly simple – it's possible to obtain memory devices with a bewildering variety of widths and depths, and it's certainly possible to get a device with 65,536 words (each 8-bits wide) which would require a 16-bit address. But this would mean that we could only use a single memory device in our system – either a ROM or a RAM. Obviously this is not acceptable, because a general-purpose computer requires both types of memory, so we have to use smaller chunks of memory and connect them together in such a way that we can achieve our heart's desire.

Memory sizes

Without diverting too far from the path we're trying to tread, we now need to consider an interesting quirk associated with ROMs and RAMs. Memory devices are constrained to have a depth of 2^n words, where 'n' is the number of bits used to form their address. For example, a device with a 10-bit address could internally decode that address to select one of 1,024 words (2^{10} = 1,024). Now the suffix K (Kilo) is generally taken to represent one thousand; but, as we have seen, the closest power of two to one thousand is 2^{10}, which equals 1,024. Therefore a 1 K-word memory actually refers to a device containing 1,024 words.

For reasons of our own, we made the decision to use devices with 12-bit addresses as illustrated in the previous figure . These 12-bit address can be internally decoded to select one of 4,096 words (2^{12} = 4,096). Remembering that our words are 8-bits wide, and that 8-bits is usually referred to as a byte, this means that we are using 4 K-byte ROMs and RAMs in our system. Even to the untrained eye (or ear), it is obviously easier to say *"We're using four kilo-byte memory devices,"* than it would be to say *"We're using memory devices with four-thousand and ninety-six words."*

Memory address decoding

OK, we're really racing along now. So what we've got is a bucket of 4 K-byte ROM and RAM devices, and we want to connect them together in such a way that, to the CPU, they appear to be a single 64 K-byte memory (where 64 K-bytes equals the 65,536 byte-sized words that can be addressed by our CPU's 16-bit address bus). As we will see, all of the memory devices we use are going to be connected to the CPU's data bus. Similarly, all of the devices are going to be connected to bits **addr[11:0]** of the CPU's address bus. So what we need to do is to use the remaining four address bus bits, **addr[15:12]**, to select between the individual memory devices. Based on the fact that four bits can be used to represent sixteen different combinations of 0s and 1s, what we're going to do is to use a special device known as a 4:16 decoder (Figure 2.21).

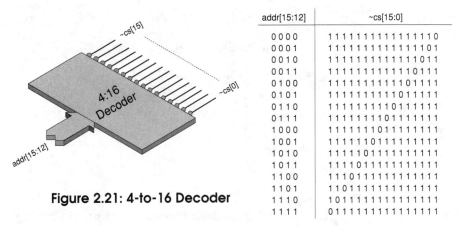

addr[15:12]	~cs[15:0]
0 0 0 0	1 1 1 1 1 1 1 1 1 1 1 1 1 1 1 0
0 0 0 1	1 1 1 1 1 1 1 1 1 1 1 1 1 1 0 1
0 0 1 0	1 1 1 1 1 1 1 1 1 1 1 1 1 0 1 1
0 0 1 1	1 1 1 1 1 1 1 1 1 1 1 0 1 1 1
0 1 0 0	1 1 1 1 1 1 1 1 1 1 0 1 1 1 1
0 1 0 1	1 1 1 1 1 1 1 1 1 0 1 1 1 1 1
0 1 1 0	1 1 1 1 1 1 1 1 0 1 1 1 1 1 1
0 1 1 1	1 1 1 1 1 1 1 0 1 1 1 1 1 1 1
1 0 0 0	1 1 1 1 1 1 0 1 1 1 1 1 1 1 1
1 0 0 1	1 1 1 1 1 0 1 1 1 1 1 1 1 1 1
1 0 1 0	1 1 1 1 0 1 1 1 1 1 1 1 1 1 1
1 0 1 1	1 1 1 0 1 1 1 1 1 1 1 1 1 1 1
1 1 0 0	1 1 0 1 1 1 1 1 1 1 1 1 1 1 1
1 1 0 1	1 0 1 1 1 1 1 1 1 1 1 1 1 1 1
1 1 1 0	1 0 1 1 1 1 1 1 1 1 1 1 1 1 1
1 1 1 1	0 1 1 1 1 1 1 1 1 1 1 1 1 1 1

Figure 2.21: 4-to-16 Decoder

This diagram and its associated truth table make the operation of the decoder clear for all to see. The device has four inputs connected to **addr[15:12]**, and sixteen outputs connected to a set of wires called ~cs[15:0]. As you should know by now, the tilde characters in their names and the bobbles on the diagram indicate that the active states of the outputs are *logic 0s*. Each pattern of 0s and 1s on the inputs causes an individual output to be driven to its active state, and each of these outputs is used to select a particular memory device. The only thing that remains to be done is to connect the decoder to sixteen of our 4 K-byte memory devices in such a way that the CPU is fooled into thinking that it is looking at a single 64 K-byte chunk of memory (4 K-bytes x 16 = 64 K-bytes) (Figure 2.22).

In this configuration the four most-significant bits of the address bus, **addr[15:12]**, are fed into our 4:16 decoder. Each of the outputs from the decoder can be used to select a 4 K-byte ROM or RAM device.[15] The remaining address bits, **addr[11:0]**, which are connected to all of the memory devices, are used to point to a particular word within whichever device is selected by the decoder. Due to lack of space, this diagram only shows three ROM devices – the remaining ROMs and RAMs would be connected in a similar fashion. Note that the ~read signal from the CPU is connected to all of the ROMs and RAMs, but the ~write signal would only be connected to the RAMs.

---

[15] As you will soon discover, we're actually only going to use the ~cs[14:0] outputs to select memory devices, because we're saving ~cs[15] to select the input and output ports.

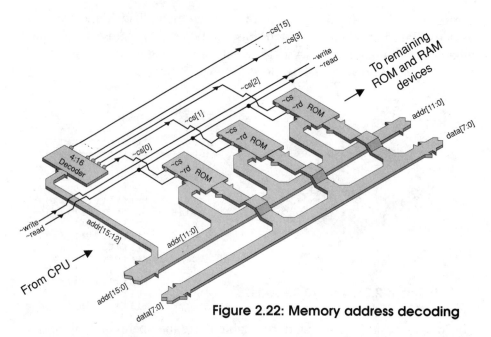

Figure 2.22: Memory address decoding

The main point to note is that the CPU doesn't know anything about the tricks we're playing here. As far as *it's* concerned the address bus appears to be pointing to 64 K-bytes of contiguous memory, which means that the CPU is as happy as a clam.

The memory map

A common method for describing the way in which the computer's memory is organized is by means of a diagram called a *memory map* (Figure 2.23).

As we have previously discussed (and as we will see if we ever get to finish this rapscallion of a chapter), a large part of what we're going to do is based on a simple virtual computer that we've called the *Beboputer*. On the CD-ROM that accompanies this book is software that will allow your hunky home computer to pretend to be our *Beboputer*.

Now your real computer probably contains a very sophisticated CPU along with millions of bytes of memory. However, in the not-so-distant past, the best computer that the average person could hope to own would probably have contained a CPU that was little more sophisticated than the *Beboputer*, and it would most likely have had far less memory than we're going to give you to play with (because memory used to be considerably more expensive than it is today).

From the memory map we see that the *Beboputer* has 16 K-bytes of ROM (in four 4 K-byte chunks) starting at address $0000. Following the ROM there are 44 K-bytes of RAM (in eleven 4 K-byte chunks) starting at address $4000.

Note that the last 4 K-byte chunk of the map doesn't actually contain any memory. What? How can this be? Well if you rewind your brain to the beginning of this chapter (Figure 2.1), you will recall our mentioning the *input ports* and *output ports* that the CPU uses to communicate with the outside world. There are a variety of ways in which the system can be configured to allow the CPU to "talk" to its input/output (I/O) ports, but one of the most common is known as *memory-mapped I/O*, in which we fool the CPU into believing that these ports are actually standard memory locations. Theoretically we could use all of

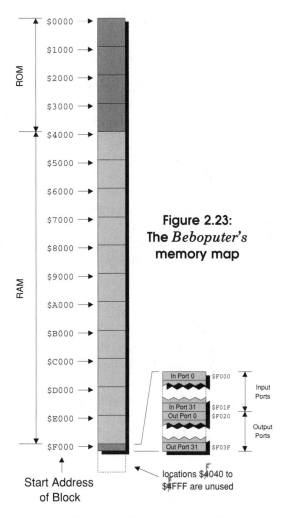

Figure 2.23: The *Beboputer*'s memory map

the top 4,096 locations in the memory map as input and output ports, but this would be somewhat excessive to say the least. In the case of the *Beboputer*, we decided to employ thirty-two input ports located at addresses $F000 through $F01F and thirty-two output ports at addresses $F020 through $F03F. These ports are discussed in more detail in the next (and final – hurrah) section of this chapter.

The input and output ports

And so we wend our weary way towards the checkered flag that marks the close of this chapter, with only the one last hurdle of input and output ports to slow us down. But turn that frown upside down into a smile, because this final topic isn't so much of a hurdle as a leisurely stroll that will lead us onwards and upwards into Chapter 3 – a chapter which promises to be absolutely jam-packed with oodles of scrumptious fun.

Imagine that you lock yourself in a room, disconnect your telephone, radio, television, and music center, draw the drapes (or curtains if you're in England), turn off the lights, sit in a chair, and don't move a muscle. While you're hanging around you could think the most amazingly interesting thoughts that anyone ever "thunked," but what's the point if you can't communicate your ideas to someone else?[16] Similarly, it would be possible to create a computer that performed cunningly complicated calculations and was isolated from the outside world. But if there's no way to see the results or tell the little rascal to do something else, then once again, what's the point?[17] Thus, for a computer to be of any use it has to be able to communicate with the outside world, and for this purpose it employs input and output ports.

Input ports

As their name suggests, the computer uses its input ports to allow the CPU to receive information from the outside world. As we noted above, there are a variety of ways in which systems can be configured, but one of the most common, known as *memory-mapped I/O*, is to fool the CPU into believing that the ports are actually standard memory locations. First consider an input port (Figure 2.24).

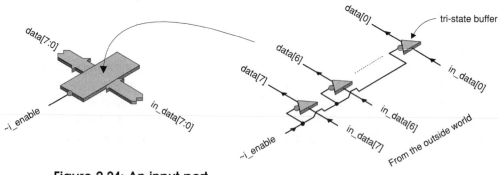

Figure 2.24: An input port

---

[16]Of course the French philosopher Jean Paul Sartre might have a few words to say on this subject – he usually did. If you really want to learn how to suffer, you could do worse than reading his book, "Being and Nothingness."

[17]Yes, Jean Paul, we know, we know.

Note that this input port is 8-bits wide, which is the same width as our data bus. The inputs to the port, in_data[7:0], would be driven by something in the outside world; for example, switches connected in such a way that they can represent either *logic 0* or *logic 1* values. The outputs from the port, data[7:0], are connected to the CPU's data bus.

Inside the port are logic gates known as *tri-state buffers*, one for each of the data signals.[18] These buffers act in such a way that when their control inputs are in their active state (which is a *logic 0*) they pass whatever is on their data inputs through to their data outputs. However, when their control inputs are in their inactive state, the buffers effectively disconnect themselves from the data bus and start to drive high-impedance **Z** values (similar buffers are used inside memory devices to disconnect them from the data bus when they are not selected).

When the CPU wishes to read the values being presented to the port's inputs, it must somehow cause a *logic 0* to be applied to that port's ~i_enable signal. In the case of the *Beboputer*, we have decided that there are going to be thirty-two such input ports located at addresses $F000 to $F01F. In order for the CPU to individually address these ports, it must be able to generate a unique ~i_enable signal for each port.

There are numerous ways of generating such signals and, to be honest, we really aren't all that bothered with this here. However, in order to tickle your curiosity we'll give you a few clues. First of all we can use the most significant output from the 4:16 decoder, ~cs[15], to indicate that we wish to address a location greater than or equal to $F000. We can then combine this signal with some additional logic that decodes the least significant address bus bits to give us thirty-two signals corresponding to addresses $F000 to $F01F. Finally, we could combine each of these signals with the CPU's ~read signal to give us thirty-two unique control signals, one for each input port.

Output ports

In the case of an output port, the inputs to the port, data[7:0], are connected to the CPU's data bus, while the port's outputs, out_data[7:0], would be used to drive something in the outside world; for example, lights connected in such a way that a *logic 0* value would turn them **OFF** and a *logic 1* value would turn them **ON** (or vice versa) (Figure 2.25).

---

[18]Tri-state buffers are discussed in more detail in Chapter 6.

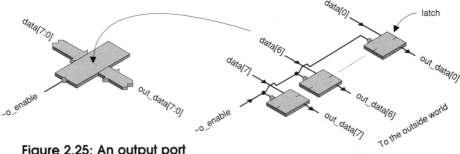

Figure 2.25: An output port

Inside the port are logic functions known as *latches*,[19,20] one for each of the data signals. These latches act in such a way that, when their control inputs are in their active state (which is a *logic 0*), they pass whatever is on their data inputs through to their data outputs. However, when their control inputs are in their inactive state the latches remember the last values they were driving and continue to drive them to the outside world (similar functions may be used inside RAM devices to store data).

When the CPU wishes to send a value to the port's outputs, it must somehow cause a *logic 0* to be applied to that port's ~o_enable signal. In the case of our *Beboputer*, we have decided that there are going to be thirty-two such output ports located at addresses $F020 to $F03F. In order for the CPU to individually address these ports, it must be able to generate a unique ~o_enable signal for each port.

Once again there are numerous ways of generating such signals. For example, we can use the most significant output from the 4:16 decoder, ~cs[15], to indicate that we wish to address a location greater than or equal to $F000. We can then combine this signal with some additional logic that decodes the least significant address bus bits to give us thirty-two signals corresponding to addresses $F020 to $F03F. Finally, we could combine each of these signals with the CPU's ~write signal to give us thirty-two unique control signals, one for each output port.

Input/output (bidirectional) ports

For reasons of clarity we decided that our input ports should have different addresses to our output ports. However, a moments reflection tells us that as the function of an input port is complementary to the function of an output

---

[19]Actually there are a variety of different types of output ports – we decided to concentrate on those containing latches because they're relatively common and easy to understand.
[20]Latches are discussed in more detail in Chapter 6.

port, it should be possible to have both an input port and an output port having the same address. In this case, the CPU would first set up the appropriate address and then, depending on whether it made its ~**read** or ~**write** signals active, it would either access the input port or the output port, respectively. These dual ports, which may be referred to as input/output (I/O) ports or bidirectional ports, are very common.

That's it! We've made it! We just roamed around the inside of a computer system (figuratively speaking) and lived to tell the tale. You really deserve to give yourself a pat on the back, because the above isn't simple by any stretch of the imagination. But battling through this hard part early on as we have done will greatly smooth the stuff to come. The worst is behind us, and all we have to look forward to now is pure unmitigated, unadulterated, unadorned fun ...... Chapter 3, here we coommmeeee ......

Quick quiz #2

1) How many deaths does a coward die?

2) Which number system is used inside digital computers?

3) Which part of the computer makes decisions and performs logical and arithmetic operations?

4) What are the *data, control*, and *address* busses used for?

5) Name four different types of information that might be conveyed by the data bus.

6) What are the **clock**, ~**reset**, ~**read**, and ~**write** signals used for?

7) What are ROMs and RAMs used for and what are the major differences between them?

8) What does "1 K-byte" actually mean?

9) What is a memory map used for?

10) What do input and output ports do and how do they do it?

For those who are interested and want to know more about number systems, logic gates, memory devices, and musical socks; these topics are presented in greater detail in this book's companion volume: *Bebop to the Boolean Boogie (An Unconventional Guide to Electronics)*, ISBN 1-878707-22-1.

Chapter 3

The Switch Panel

In this chapter we will discover:

How a 1960s computer would compare to
your home computer

Why early computers used magnetic
beads to store information

How early computer operators used switch
panels to control computers

What flowcharts are and how to use them

How to invoke your *Beboputer*

How to enter and run a program using
a switch panel

How to speed up or slow down your
Beboputer's system clock

The *Memory Walker* display and how
to use it

What to do if your mother calls you
down to dinner

Contents of Chapter 3

Peering through the mists of time

If we were to give our crystal ball a stern rubbing and peer back through the mists of time, say to the early 1960s, very few people knew what a computer was and even fewer had actually seen one "in the flesh." In those days computers used to cost tens of millions of dollars and they were bigger than big. In fact, by present day standards they were outrageously, gynormously, humongously huge. The cooling systems alone could weigh several tons, and you'd be hard pushed to squeeze even a medium-sized computer into a large barn!

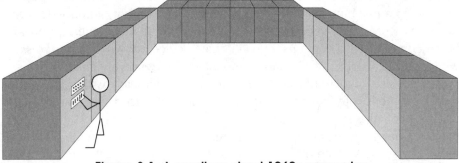

Figure 3.1: A medium-sized 1960s computer

These hulking brutes, which were referred to as *mainframe computers*,[1] required temperature-controlled, air-conditioned environments, and they were so expensive that you needed a security clearance to gain access to them. To pay their way they had to run twenty-four hours a day, so any company who owned one was obliged to rent computer time out to other firms in the wee hours of the night. They were so unreliable that, when you bought one, it typically came with one or more engineers who were on call day and night to keep it running. Anyone who knew which buttons to press (or, more importantly, which buttons *not* to press) was automatically classed as a computer expert, and such a person was held in high esteem by their colleagues and in outright awe by the general populace. Ah, the good old days!

But those were the times when individually packaged transistors were still considered to be the state-of-the-art, and the first rudimentary integrated circuits were only just beginning to appear on the scene. So although they were big and ugly, in almost every respect these monsters were far less

---

[1]Early computers were constructed in a number of cabinets, each of which required a strong internal frame to support the weight of the components. Thus, the term "mainframe" derives from the fact that the main cabinet (or main frame) housed the central processing unit and the main memory.

powerful than a typical home computer system is today, with none of the bells and whistles that we have come to take for granted. You will see what we mean as we proceed with our first laboratory, in which we use the *Beboputer* to emulate some of the characteristics of its great-grandfathers.

A 1960s computer versus your home computer

Before we start to use our *Beboputer* to craft some simple programs, perhaps it would be a good idea to quickly compare your home computer of today to a machine from the days of yore. First of all, in addition to the ROM and RAM integrated circuits that we introduced in Chapter 2, your home computer also contains a bulk-storage device known as a *hard disk*, which can be used to store a large amount of data relatively cheaply. This device consists of a circular disk a few inches in diameter, which is covered with a magnetic material and which is spun at high speed. The hard disk unit also contains special read/write heads (similar in concept to the record/playback heads in your music cassette recorder). These read/write heads can move across the surface of the disk, record data onto the disk, and recover that data later. Your computer can use its hard disk to store several hundreds of millions of bytes (megabytes) of information.

Because magnetic media retains its data when power is removed from the system, it is said to be *non-volatile* (similar to ROM devices). One of the major disadvantages of currently available bulk storage units is their relatively slow speed,[2] which means that the CPU can process data at a much higher rate than the bulk storage device can supply or store it. Semiconductor memories such as RAM devices are a great deal faster

As we discussed in Chapter 2, memory devices are constrained to have a depth of 2^n words, where 'n' is the number of bits used to form their address. Now, the suffix M (mega) is generally taken to represent one million, but the closest power of two to one million is 2^{20}, which equals 1,048,576. Therefore, 1 M-byte (one megabyte) actually refers to a device containing 1,048,576 bytes.

than bulk storage, but in addition to being volatile they are also significantly more expensive.

Moving along ...... when you turn your home computer's power switch to its ON position, the *power-on reset* circuit (as discussed in Chapter 2)

---

[2]Note the use of the qualifier "*relatively.*" Modern bulk storage is actually amazingly fast, but not as fast as the rest of the system.

causes the CPU to be reset and to read an instruction from a specific memory address; in the case of the *Beboputer* this address is $0000. The components forming the system are connected together in such a way that this hard-wired address points to a location in a ROM device. The ROM contains a sequence of instructions known as the *basic input/output system (BIOS)*, which is used by the CPU to initialize both itself and other parts of the system. This initialization is known as *boot-strapping*, which is derived from the phrase *"pulling himself up by his boot-straps."* At an appropriate point in the initialization process, instructions in the ROM cause the CPU to copy a set of master programs known collectively as the *operating system* from the hard disk into the RAM. The ROM instructions then direct the CPU to transfer its attention to the operating system instructions in the RAM. The operating system brings up a user-interface onto your screen, and the computer is finally ready for you to enter the game.

> In 1968, the designers of the Hewlett-Packard Model 9100 desktop "calculator" created the first (and almost certainly the last) electromagnetic circuit board ROM. They laid out "drive tracks" on the circuit board with "kinks" to the left or the right, where these kinks were used to represent *logic 0s* or *logic 1s*. Another set of tracks called "sense tracks" were then laid over the top of the drive tracks, and each sense track was connected to the input of an amplifier. Thus, when signals were applied to the drive tracks, electro-magnetic coupling caused pulses to be seen on the sense lines, where the polarity of these pulses ("up" or "down") corresponded to the direction of the kinks in the drive tracks.

Now let's return to a 1960's computer and compare it to the above. First of all these early computers didn't contain anything comparable to our semiconductor ROM devices. Instead, when power was first applied or the computer was reset, the CPU read its first commands from some pseudo memory locations that contained hard-wired (often hand-wired) instructions. These instructions, of which there were very few, were used to implement a very simple program that observed a bank of switches called a *switch panel* to see what the operator was doing with them. Because this program monitored the switch panel it was referred to as the *monitor* routine.[3] You may care to note that the operator in Figure 3.1 is using just such a switch panel.

---

[3]To avoid any misunderstanding, we should note that even the most rudimentary of monitor programs in the form described in this chapter were not available on the first computers (whose switch panels were hard-wired directly into the "guts" of the system), but the concept of a monitor program serves as a basis for our discussions here. A more detailed look at the role of monitor programs is presented in Chapter 12.

Similarly, a 1960s computer didn't contain any semiconductor RAM devices (the first such device, which was manufactured by Fairchild, wasn't introduced until 1970 and only contained 256 <u>bits</u>). Instead, they used something called *magnetic core memory* (also known as *core store* or simply *core*), which consisted of ferromagnetic beads threaded with wires (Figure 3.2).

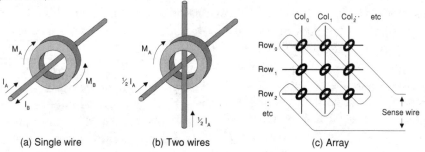

(a) Single wire   (b) Two wires   (c) Array

Figure 3.2: Magnetic core store

First consider the case where such a bead has a single wire threaded through it (Figure 3.2a). If a small current is passed through the wire then nothing happens. But if a current of sufficient magnitude, which we will call I_A, is passed through the wire, it causes the bead to be magnetized in the direction M_A. Similarly, if a current of equal magnitude called I_B is passed through the wire in the opposite direction, the bead will be magnetized in the direction M_B. A bead magnetized in direction M_A can be used to represent a *logic 0*, while a bead magnetized in direction M_B can be used to represent a *logic 1* (or vice versa).

The point is that a magnetized bead will remain magnetized after the current is removed, and will therefore "remember" the logic value it is being used to represent.[4] As it happens this single-wire scheme is not particularly useful to us, because if we were to string a number of beads on the wire, then every time we applied a current to the wire they would all be magnetized in the same direction.

To solve this problem, consider the case in which a bead has two wires threaded through it (Figure 3.2b). If a current of $\frac{1}{2}I_A$ is passed through each wire, the total effect is identical to that of a single wire carrying I_A, and the bead is again magnetized in the direction M_A (similarly, if each wire were used to carry a current of $\frac{1}{2}I_B$, the bead would be magnetized in direction M_B). This dual-wire scheme is of use, because it allows us to construct an

---

[4]In this respect a core store is similar to a ROM, because it is non-volatile and any stored data is retained after power has been removed from the system.

array of such beads (Figure 3.2c), each of which can be individually magnetized by applying signals to its associated *row* and *column* wires.

The ability to individually magnetize each bead in direction M_A or M_B is only part of the story, because it is also necessary to be able to "read" a bead to determine the direction in which it was magnetized; that is, to see whether it is currently storing a *logic 0* or a *logic 1*. This is where the *sense wire* comes into play (Figure 3.2c).

Assume that a bead magnetized in direction M_A represents a *logic 0*, while a bead magnetized in direction M_B represents a *logic 1*. Now assume that we want to detect which logic value is currently being represented by the bead in the middle of our array. One technique is to apply signals of $\frac{1}{2}I_A$ to the wires **Row$_1$** and **Col$_1$** which, irrespective of the bead's current state, will cause it to be magnetized in direction M_A. However, there is a cunning trick here, because if the bead was already magnetized in direction M_A then nothing will happen, but if the bead was initially magnetized in direction M_B, then causing it to reverse its state results in a pulse of current appearing on the *sense wire*.

Thus, by detecting the absence or presence of a pulse on the *sense wire*, we can determine whether the bead was originally storing a *logic 0* or a *logic 1*, respectively. The only problem with this technique is that if the bead was initially storing a *logic 1*, then we've just overwritten it with a *logic 0* (that is, if the bead was originally magnetized in direction M_B, then it's now magnetized in direction M_A). This is referred to as a *destructive read*, which means that each read operation in a core store is normally followed by a write cycle to restore the original data.[5]

> The concept of using magnetic toroids for digital memory originated in 1950 and is credited to Jay Forrester at MIT. Although his invention was originally based on Permalloy tape-wound cores, the idea was quickly extended to use ferrite beads which were smaller, faster, and easier to mass produce.

The invention of the core store meant that, for the first time, a reasonably useful form of memory was available to computer designers. Although the idea of core stores seems rather strange today ...... they worked. If you think that these are bad, you ought to have seen what designers were obliged to use before! Previous attempts to create computer memory had involved such esoteric technologies as mercury delay lines, which were

---

[5]Semiconductor RAMs typically do not have a destructive read cycle; that is, the act of reading data out of a RAM does not affect the master copy of the data stored in the device.

sequential in nature (see also Chapter 15). To differentiate core stores from these sequential techniques, the term *random access memory (RAM)* was coined to emphasize the fact that data could be written to and read from any part of the core's array. This is why we use the term RAM to this day, as opposed to the possibly more meaningful appellation "*read-write memory (RWM)*" which was mentioned in Chapter 2.

In addition to being a lot slower than today's semiconductor memory devices, core stores were physically much larger and they could only hold a relatively small amount of data. The first core stores were effectively "knitted" together by teams of ladies with the appropriate skills, although automated techniques soon took over. The outer diameter of the original beads was around 2 mm (which is actually quite small), and they eventually shrank to around 0.2 mm (which is really, really small), but it still took a whole bunch of them to make a memory that could hold a reasonable amount of data.

A typical array from a core store might occupy a circuit board 50 cm x 50 cm (note that the size and configurations of core stores varied enormously). The array itself, which might be approximately 15 cm x 15 cm, would sit in the middle of the board like a spider in the center of its web, while the rest of the circuit board would be occupied by a gaggle of other electronic components required to drive signals into the array and sense any responses from the array. Additionally, if you consider the portion of an array shown in Figure 3.3c, you will observe that the entire array is served by a single *sense wire*, which means that the array could only be connected to a single bit of the data bus. Thus, each bit of the data bus would require its own array, so an 8-bit bus would require eight such circuit boards.

Your home computer probably contains at least 4M-bytes of RAM (that's 4,194,304 bytes), and it possibly contains a whole lot more. By comparison, users of our medium-sized 1960s computer would be lucky if they had access to as much as 8K-bytes of core store (that's only 8,192 bytes!). Furthermore, unlike your RAM, which occupies a few cubic centimeters and weighs only a few grams, core store required one or more cabinets, each of which was the size of a large washing machine, and each of which required a fork-lift truck to move it around!

We know, we know – we've wandered off into the weeds again, but you have to admit that it's quite interesting. As a final point in our comparison, we noted that your home computer has a bulk storage device called a hard disk, which can be used to store hundreds of millions of bytes of information for later use. This technology simply wasn't available to the designers of the early computers. Instead, they used a variety of more mundane techniques, most of which involved punching holes in paper tapes or semi-rigid paper cards. We'll return to consider these storage techniques in Chapter 4.

We're almost ready to rock and roll, but..

We can sense your anticipation and the adrenaline rush that's beginning to flood throughout your nervous system, but there are two more points we must briefly introduce before hurling ourselves into the fray. The first is the concept of a flowchart, which is a graphical means of describing a sequence of operations. For example, consider the case where a school bully has expressed his fervent belief that you rank lower on the evolutionary scale than pond slime. When delivering your response, you may well decide to follow the sequence of actions illustrated by the flowchart in Figure 3.3.

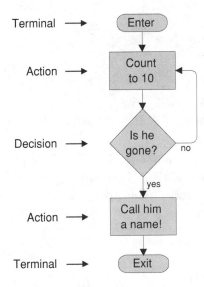

Figure 3.3: Flowcharts

Flowcharts get their name from the fact that they chart the flow, or passing of control, from one operation to the next. By default, the flow is assumed to be from top-to-bottom and from left-to-right, but this may be modified by the use of the arrows on the flowlines linking the symbols.

Flowcharts can employ a wide variety of symbols, but we will generally employ a limited subset. The two main types of symbols are the *action symbol* (rectangle), which indicates some form of activity or processing; and the *decision symbol* (diamond), which indicates some form of evaluation or test. The *terminal symbols* simply indicate the entry point to, and exit point from, the flowchart.

The first action in our example is to count to ten, which is always a good course to follow in these situations. The next stage in the process is to decide whether the bully has left the vicinity; if he isn't out of hearing range then we count to ten again. It is only when we are sure he has departed the scene that we decide to bravely speak our minds (using a controlled acting technique that the uninitiated may confuse with a whisper).

Flowcharts are extremely useful for documenting the operation of computer programs, and they provide an excellent means of communicating the intent of a program. However, we will also discover that although flowcharts are strong on "*what*" and "*how*," they are a little weaker on "*when*" and "*why*."

The last thing you need to be aware of before experiencing the utmost in delectation and delight is that, amongst other things, the CPU in our *Beboputer* contains an 8-bit register called the *accumulator*. As its name might suggest, the accumulator is where the CPU gathers, or accumulates, intermediate results (Figure 3.4).

The mysterious internal workings of the CPU (including the accumulator) are more fully discussed in Chapter 8. Suffice it to say that the CPU can be instructed to *load* a byte of data from any location in the memory into its accumulator. (The loading process actually involves taking a copy of the data in the memory; the contents of the memory at that location remain undisturbed.) The CPU can also be instructed to perform a variety of arithmetic and logical operations on the data in the accumulator. Last but not least, the CPU can be instructed to *store* whatever data is currently contained by the accumulator into any location in the memory. This operation overwrites any existing contents in that memory location, but leaves the contents of the accumulator undisturbed.

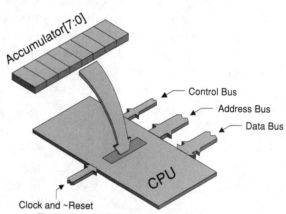

Figure 3.4: The accumulator

Winding up the *Beboputer*

So we're finally ready to rock-and-roll. If you haven't already installed the *Beboputer* from the CD that came with this book, then consult Appendix A and do so with extreme haste. The rest of us will hang around twiddling our thumbs and waiting for you to catch up ......

Tick-tock, tick-tock, tick-tock ...... Are you finally ready now? Why do you always have to leave everything until the last minute. No, don't bother to apologize, we've wasted enough time already. (Good Grief, I'm turning into my Mother!)

Make sure that the *Beboputer* CD is in the appropriate drive in your computer, then open up the *Beboputer* by clicking on the Start button in the task bar, followed by the Programs item, the Beboputer item, and the Beboputer Computer item. Once the *Beboputer's* project window has opened, click the File item on its menu bar, click the Open Project entry in the resulting pull-down menu, then select the Lab 1 project from the ensuing dialog. This will invoke the first lab which, depending on the size of your screen and the resolution you are using, will hopefully bear a passing resemblance to Figure 3.5.

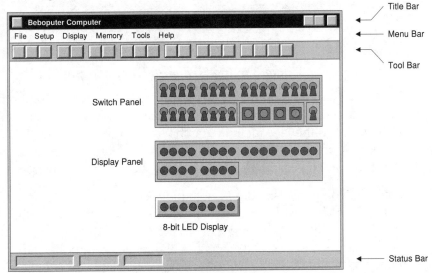

Figure 3.5: The *Beboputer* project window for Lab 1

In the case of this first lab, the working area of the project window contains just three items: a switch panel, a display panel, and an 8-bit LED display[6] (just to give you a clue, the switch panel is the one with all of the switches). In ye olden tymes, the switch panel was one of the main methods for the operator to instruct the computer as to which operations it was to perform. Correspondingly, the display panel was one of the main techniques for the operator to see what the computer had actually decided to do (as we have all learnt to our cost, what you want and what you get aren't necessarily the same thing).

Running along the upper half of the switch panel are sixteen switches, which correspond to the signals forming the *Beboputer's* 16-bit address bus.

---

[6]LED is the abbreviation for *light-emitting diode*. These devices are discussed in more detail in Chapter 5.

Similarly, the lower left-hand side of the switch panel contains eight switches, which correspond to the *Beboputer's* 8-bit data bus. In the bottom right-hand corner is the main ON/OFF switch, which is used to power-up the *Beboputer* (we'll look at the other buttons in due course).

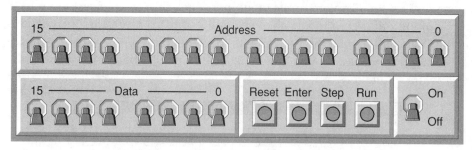

Figure 3.6: The *Beboputer's* switch panel

Before we proceed, you may care to note the multimedia icon on the toolbar. By clicking on this icon you'll be presented with a short multimedia introduction to the lab, including archive video of 1950s and 1960s computers, magnetic core store, and a number of other goodies (unless you're good at lip-reading a sound card is strongly recommended).[7]

Similarly, you may also care to note the Web icon on the toolbar. Clicking on this icon will invoke your default Web browser and cause it to display a page of information delivered with your *Beboputer*. This page contains hyperlinks (the colored text), which will connect you to the *Beboputer's* home pages on the World Wide Web (WWW). You can use these pages to download programs written by other users (and submit your own programs if you so desire), access "hints and tips", communicate directly with us (the authors), locate information on any *Beboputer* enhancements and additional utilities as they become available, and much, much more.[8]

Now, close your eyes and imagine that ...... Hmmm, that won't work will it? If you close your eyes then you won't be able to follow along with us. Let's try that one again. Pretend that you've closed your eyes, and imagine that you're walking slowly and purposefully down a long corridor towards a set of double doors, on either side of which is a big, mean security guard. To your rear you hear rustlings and mutterings as the president of the company, numerous vice presidents, managers, bean-counters,[9] and gophers jostle for position to be as close to you as possible. But no one

---

[7]Each lab has its own multimedia introduction.
[8]Your system must be equipped with a modem and have access to the Web.
[9]A "bean-counter" is the somewhat disparaging (and totally undeserved) term used by engineers to refer to accountants.

dares to jostle *you*, because, after all, you are the only person who knows how to make their new computer work.

As you approach the end of the corridor the security guards blanch at your steely gaze and, nervously throwing the doors asunder, they salute you as you stride into the computer room to take possession of your domain (you don't even need to swagger – everyone is already just about as impressed as they can be).

Calmly and surely you advance toward the main switch panel – the crowd hold their breaths. You reach out your hand ...... and brush an imaginary piece of lint off your lapel – the crowd sighs. You reach out again ...... pause ...... flex your fingers ...... and depress the main power switch on the switch panel – the crowd gasps. For the briefest moment ...... nothing happens ...... and then ...... and then ...... the cooling fans begin their plaintively ascending whine as they wind up to speed, the lights on the display panel commence to flash in seemingly random but strangely mesmerizing patterns, and the gyroscopic trumble grunges begin their syncopated oscillations against the perambulating notchet tattles.[10]

Can you hear it? Can you feel it? Can you taste it? Is your heart pounding? Are your little toes curled in anticipation? Are you ready? ...... Then **Now** is the time for you to re-enact these actions of yesteryear in glorious Technicolor in the comfort of your living room. Move your mouse cursor over the **ON/OFF** switch on the switch panel and click it with your mouse button. The switch toggles, the display lights flash, and, if your home computer is equipped with a sound board, you'll hear the cooling fans begin to roar into action (if you didn't shell out the extra lucre for a sound board ...... we bet you're sorry now).

So here you are with your *Beboputer* virtual computer running at full nerve-tingling, gut-wrenching, super-duper-mega-thruster power – it's actually quite awe-inspiring isn't it? What? ...... What do you mean *"Is that it?"* ...... Well what did you expect? ...... Oh, we see, you thought that something really impressive was going to happen didn't you. Well we're sorry to be the bearers of bad tidings, but what you see is pretty much the way it used to be. In those antediluvian days there weren't any computer terminals with high-resolution color graphics displays or computer-synthesized voices saying *"I'm sorry Dave, but I really don't think that's a good idea."* In fact,

---

[10]Sorry, we started to get a bit carried away there. Before anyone in the know starts moaning and groaning, the last part about the *"gyroscopic trumble grunges"* and the *"notchet tattles"* is meaningless drivel that we just made up on the spur of the moment (unless you happen to be running one of the old Wurtsle-Grinder Mark 4's of course).

there really wasn't much of anything that acted in the way you're used to seeing computers behave today. But fear not my braves, because you'll find that there's more to this simple user interface than meets the eye.

What should you do if your mother calls you down to dinner?

Before creating your first program, it might be wise to consider what you're going to do if you have to stop in the middle for any reason. For example, if your mother has been slaving for hours over a hot microwave, she's probably not going to be deliriously happy if you let your dinner get cold while you rush to complete this chapter. So, if you have to leave the lab for any reason, there are a couple of things you should know:

a) If you power-down the *Beboputer* using the ON/OFF switch on the main switch panel, then you can wave a fond farewell to any programs that you've entered into the *Beboputer's* memory, because you're not going to see them again.

b) Similarly, when you exit the lab you'll automatically lose any programs that you've created (exiting the lab is discussed in more detail at the end of this chapter).

As it happens, the programs in this chapter are very simple, so it probably wouldn't cause you untold grief if you had to reenter them later. However, there are ways to save the contents of the *Beboputer's* memory that we'll be introducing in future labs (if you're desperate, you can check out the use of the Save RAM entry under the Memory pull-down menu as described in the *Beboputer's* online help).

Using the switch panel to enter a program

The first thing we're going to do is to use the switch panel to enter a rudimentary program that will flash the lights on the 8-bit LED display. As we previously discussed, an easy way to illustrate the program's intent is by means of a flowchart (Figure 3.7).

From the flowchart we see that the first action the program is to perform is to load the accumulator (abbreviated to ACC) with an initial value. In the case of this particular program, we decided to load the hexadecimal value $03 (or 0000 0011 in binary).

The program's next action is to store the contents of the accumulator into a memory location. Remember that this operation overwrites any existing contents in the memory location, but leaves the contents of the accumulator undisturbed. Additionally, in this case we're going to trick the CPU, because although it thinks it's writing to memory, the address we're using actually points to an output port. This output port is the one that's connected to the 8-bit LED display.

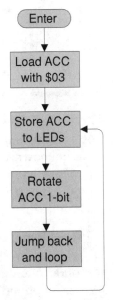

Figure 3.7: "Rotate" flowchart

The third action in the program is to rotate the contents of the accumulator one bit to the left. That is, the original contents of bit 0 in the accumulator are copied into bit 1; the original contents of bit 1 are copied into bit 2; and so on up to the original contents of bit 6, which are copied into bit 7. Additionally, the original contents of bit 7 are copied into a temporary location called the *carry flag*, and the original contents of the carry flag are copied into bit 0 of the accumulator. Don't worry if you aren't too sure about any of this, because all will become clear when we actually run the program. (Note that the relationship between the rotate operation and the carry flag is discussed in more detail in Chapter 8.)

The program's fourth and final action (at least, the final action as far as the flowchart is concerned) is to jump back to the point at which it stores the contents of the accumulator into the memory location. Thus, our program does not make any decisions, it just performs a series of actions. Note that this program will never end, but will keep on looping around rotating the accumulator and displaying its contents until we do something to halt it or the universe ends (whichever comes first).

So, armed with our trusty flowchart, your next step is to load the program into the *Beboputer's* memory. If you cast your mind back to Chapter 2 (Figure 2.23), you'll remember that the *Beboputer* has 16K-bytes of ROM (spanning addresses $0000 through $3FFF) and 44K-bytes of RAM (spanning addresses $4000 through $EFFF). We obviously can't load our program into the ROM area because that's *read-only*, so we have to use the RAM. We could load the program anywhere in the RAM, but for aesthetic purposes we'll start at the first available location at address $4000.

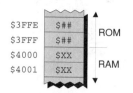

$3FFE	$##
$3FFF	$##
$4000	$XX
$4001	$XX

ROM

RAM

Figure 3.8: X and #

Remembering that we've only just turned the *Beboputer* on, all of the RAM locations will have powered up containing random, unknown *logic 0* and *logic 1* values. If we were able to peer inside the *Beboputer's* memory and focus on the boundary between the ROM and the RAM, we would see something like Figure 3.8. For the purposes of this illustration, we're using 'X' characters in the RAM area to indicate unknown values. By comparison, the '#' characters in the ROM area indicate that these values (which were programmed into the ROM when it was constructed) are fixed, stable *logic 0s* and *logic 1s*; it's just that we have little interest in them at the moment.

Now use your mouse to control the address switches on the switch panel and play around with them for a while. A switch in the UP position corresponds to a *logic 1* (its center shows green), while a switch in the DOWN position indicates a *logic 0* (its center shows red). There's no particular reason for linking UP or green to *logic 1* (or DOWN or red to *logic 0*) – this just happens to be the way we decided to do things. Note that as you manipulate these address switches the lights in the corresponding positions on the display panel are updated to match the switch positions. Once you've had your fill of listening to the satisfying "clunk" the switches make as they toggle from one position to another, make them match the positions shown in Figure 3.9.

As we see, all of the switches should be DOWN (*logic 0*), with the exception of addr[14] which should be UP (*logic 1*). Remembering that each group of four switches corresponds to one

Figure 3.9: Address $4000

hexadecimal digit, the binary pattern represented by the switches (0100 0000 0000 0000) is equivalent to an address of $4000 in hexadecimal. If you're at all confused by this, now would be a good time to zip back to Chapter 2 to re-read the discussions on Figures 2.10, 2.11, and 2.12 (especially 2.12). You really do need to be 100% confident about this before we proceed, because we'll be seeing a lot of this sort of thing in the future.

Next use your mouse to control the data switches on the switch panel. As before, the lights in the corresponding positions on the display panel are updated to match the switch positions. Once again you can play around with these for a while, then make the data switches match the positions shown in Figure 3.10. The binary pattern represented by the data switches

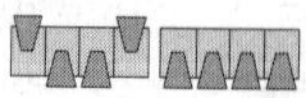

Figure 3.10: Data $90

(1001 0000) is equivalent to $90 in hexadecimal — we will learn the significance of this particular value in a moment.

When we first applied power to the *Beboputer*, its virtual power-on reset circuit automatically caused our system to enter its *reset mode* (as is indicated by the status bar at the bottom of the project window). While the *Beboputer* is in its reset mode, the address and data lights on the display panel track the status of their related switches on the switch panel. But now we're at the exciting part. Flex your fingers, then use your mouse to click on the Enter button on the switch panel. Although nothing much seems to have happened, appearances can be deceptive, because you've just taken a great leap forward. The best way to illustrate what you have just done is to once again consider what we'd see if we were able to peer inside the *Beboputer's* memory (Figure 3.11).

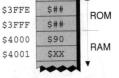

"Well smite my grunions with a spreckle rake!" When you clicked on the Enter button you caused the values on the data switches ($90) to be copied into the memory location pointed to by the address switches ($4000). As it happens, the contents of address $4000 are going to be the first byte in the first instruction in our program ($90 directs the CPU to load the contents of the next memory location into its accumulator). Of course we've still got a long way to go, but we have successfully converted the first half of the first action in the flowchart in Figure 3.7 into something that the *Beboputer* can understand.

Figure 3.11: Load instruction

Our program actually requires us to load nine bytes of data into the RAM. We've already loaded the first byte, so we only have eight more bytes to go. To speed things up a little, simply execute the following instructions. Once we've loaded the entire program we'll return to discuss what each of these bytes mean.

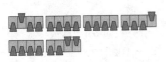 Set address and data switches as shown, then click the Enter button to load $03 into address $4001.

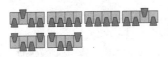 Set address and data switches as shown, then click the Enter button to load $99 into address $4002.

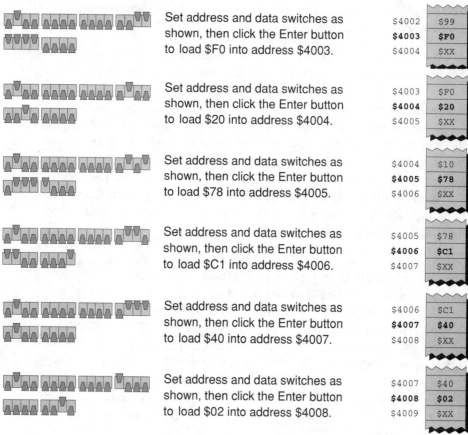

Set address and data switches as shown, then click the Enter button to load $F0 into address $4003.	$4002	$99
	$4003	**$F0**
	$4004	$XX
Set address and data switches as shown, then click the Enter button to load $20 into address $4004.	$4003	$F0
	$4004	**$20**
	$4005	$XX
Set address and data switches as shown, then click the Enter button to load $78 into address $4005.	$4004	$10
	$4005	**$78**
	$4006	$XX
Set address and data switches as shown, then click the Enter button to load $C1 into address $4006.	$4005	$78
	$4006	**$C1**
	$4007	$XX
Set address and data switches as shown, then click the Enter button to load $40 into address $4007.	$4006	$C1
	$4007	**$40**
	$4008	$XX
Set address and data switches as shown, then click the Enter button to load $02 into address $4008.	$4007	$40
	$4008	**$02**
	$4009	$XX

And that's the lot, you've entered the entire program. Unfortunately, there's no way (or none that we've told you about yet) for you to peer inside the *Beboputer's* memory to make sure that you didn't make any mistakes. However, if you think that you did made an error at a particular location, you can always reset the address and data switches to their correct positions for that location and click on the Enter button again.

We're almost ready to run the program, but before we do, it would be appropriate to compare our original flowchart with its actual realization that we just loaded into the RAM (Figure 3.12)

As we can see, the program consists of four instructions, which correspond to the four action blocks in the flowchart: a *load*, a *store*, a *rotate*, and a *jump*. Each instruction requires a different number of bytes: the type of *load* we used requires two bytes, the *store* and *jump* take three bytes each, while the *rotate* only occupies a single byte.

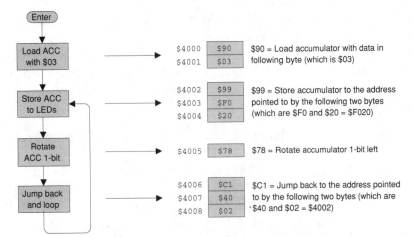

Figure 3.12: Rotate accumulator program

The first byte of each instruction is called the *opcode*, which is an abbreviation of "operation code." The opcode instructs the CPU as to the type of operation it is to perform. For those instructions which occupy multiple bytes, any bytes following the opcode are referred to as the *operand*.

In the case of the load instruction, the $90 opcode instructs the CPU to copy the contents of the following byte into its accumulator. As the following byte (at address $4001) is in fact $03, this is the data that will be loaded into the accumulator.

Similarly, in the case of the store instruction, the $99 opcode instructs the CPU to copy the contents of its accumulator into the memory location specified by the address contained in the following two bytes. When we designed our *Beboputer*, we made the decision that addresses would be stored in memory with the most-significant byte first. Thus, the contents of the two bytes stored at addresses $4003 and $4004 ($F0 and $20 respectively) are understood by the CPU to represent the address $F020. If you were to return the memory map shown in Chapter 2 (Figure 2.23), you would see that this is the address of output port 0. As we're omnipotent (at least as far as the *Beboputer* is concerned), we happen to know that the 8-bit LED display on your screen is plugged into this output port.

> Many commercial microprocessors expect addresses to be stored in memory with the least-significant byte first. The reason for this is primarily based on something called addressing modes, which we haven't looked at yet. However, it's generally more intuitive for beginners if addresses are stored in memory with the most-significant byte first, so that's the way we decided to do it.

In the case of the rotate instruction, the $78 opcode instructs the CPU to rotate the contents of its accumulator one bit to the left. Once again, the effects of this instruction will become apparent when we come to actually run the program. The rotate instruction contains everything that needs to be said as far as the CPU is concerned, so this instruction does not have any operand bytes.

Finally, in the case of the jump instruction, the $C1 opcode at address $4006 instructs the CPU to jump back to the memory location specified by the address contained in the following two bytes. The contents of the two bytes stored at addresses $4007 and $4008 ($40 and $02 respectively) are understood by the CPU to represent the address $4002. If you look at the flowchart in Figure 3.12, you'll see that this is the address of the first byte in the store instruction. When we decide to run a program, the CPU will commence at whichever initial address we give it ($4000 in the case of this example). The CPU will automatically continue to proceed through ascending addresses until something occurs to change the flow of the program. In this program the jump instruction at address $4006 causes just such a change to occur.

One point that you may have been wondering about is the opcodes themselves. Why is it that the codes $90, $99, $78, and $C1 represent *load*, *store*, *rotate*, and *jump* instructions respectively. Did this just happen? Are these international standards? Do these codes work with every computer? Well as fate would have it, the answers to these questions are No, No, and ...... wait for it ...... No. Each type of computer understands its own set of opcodes which are hard-wired into the core of the CPU by its designers. The opcodes $90, $99, $78, and $C1 just happen to be the ones that we (in our omnipotence) decided the *Beboputer* should use. We will return to consider opcodes in more detail in Chapter 8.

Using the switch panel to run a program

In order to run our program, we first need to set the address switches on the switch panel to the program's start address of $4000 (Figure 3.13). When it comes to executing our program we have two options: to *Step* through it or to *Run* it. Now remember that we're currently in the *Beboputer's* *reset*

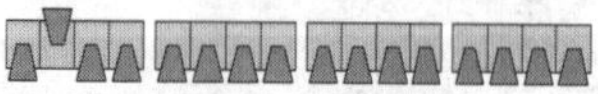

Figure 3.13: Start address $4000

mode (as is indicated by the status bar at the bottom of the project window). In this mode, both the Step and Run buttons on the switch panel will cause the program to be executed from the start address as specified by the address switches.

Initially we will use the *step mode*, so click the **Step** button with your mouse, which causes the lights on the display panel to flicker between values and then settle down again. As we see, the address lights on the display panel have ceased to correspond to the address switches on the switch panel. Instead, these lights now show $4002 (or 0100 0000 0000 0010 in binary). Similarly, the data lights now reflect the contents of the memory at this address (these contents are $99, or 1001 1001 in binary). The action of the **Step** button was to take one step through the program; that is, to execute both of the bytes associated with the first instruction (the *load*). Thus, the address lights are now pointing to the first byte of the second instruction (the *store*).

Also note that the status bar at the bottom of the project window now indicates that we are in the *step mode*. In this mode, both the **Step** and **Run** buttons will ignore the address switches on the switch panel, and will instead cause the program to be executed from the current address as indicated by the address lights on the display panel.

For the moment we will remain in the *step mode*, so once again click the **Step** button, which causes several things to happen. As soon as they've settled down, the address lights show $4005 (or 0100 0000 0000 0101 in binary). Similarly, the data lights now reflect the memory contents at this new address ($78 or 0111 1000 in binary). The action of the **Step** button was once again to take a single step through the program; that is, to execute all three of the bytes associated with the second instruction (the *store*). Thus, the address lights are now pointing to the only byte in the third instruction (the *rotate*).

Perhaps of more interest, the two rightmost LEDs on the 8-bit LED display just turned green. The reason for this is easily understood; the first instruction in the program loaded the accumulator with $03 (or 0000 0011 in binary), while the second instruction stored the contents of the accumulator to the LED display. The red and green lights on the LED display correspond to the 0s and 1s in the accumulator, respectively.

Now click the **Step** button again to execute the rotate instruction. As we'd expect, the address and data lights update to reflect the fact that they are now pointing to the first byte of the last instruction (the *jump*). Additionally, although we can't see them, the contents of the accumulator have been rotated left by one bit. That is, the accumulator's contents have been modified from $03 (or 0000 0011 in binary) to $06 (or 0000 0110 in binary).

To actually display the new contents of the accumulator, first click the **Step** button to execute the jump instruction. Remembering that the jump instruction directed the CPU to jump back to address $4002, it should come as little surprise to find that the address and data lights update to reflect the fact that they are now pointing to the first byte of the store instruction again. Clicking the **Step** button one more time executes the store instruction, which causes the accumulator's *new* contents to be copied to the 8-bit LED display.

You may continue to click the **Step** button to your heart's content. Once your clicking frenzy has run its course, click on the **Run** button to unleash the full power of the *Beboputer*. Apart from anything else, note that the status bar at the bottom of the project window now indicates that we are in the *run mode*.

Modifying the *Beboputer's* system clock

Depending on the power of your home computer, the lights on the 8-bit LED display are either crawling along at a snail's pace or flashing before your eyes in a furious blur (as we're well-acquainted with *Murphy's Law* ("What can go wrong will go wrong!") we've discounted the third possibility that the display is changing at just the right speed).

Fortunately we are prepared for just such an eventuality. Use your mouse to click the **Setup** item on the project window's menu bar, then click the **System Clock** entry in the resulting pull-down menu. This will invoke the appropriate dialog window as shown in Figure 3.14. It should not be a major revelation to find that clicking on the arrows marked **Slow** and **Fast** and then clicking on the **Apply** button will cause the system clock to slow down or speed up, respectively. Note that we aren't actually affecting the speed of your real computer, only the speed of our *Beboputer*. Also note that the effects of changing the *Beboputer's* system clock will only persist for the current session; that is, the next time you use the *Beboputer*, its clock will automatically be returned to its default setting (which is to go as fast as possible).

Figure 3.14: Modifying the system clock

We would like you to modify the system clock so that the patterns on the 8-bit LED display change approximately once per second; that is, somewhere around the same rate that you'd count *"Thousand one, thousand two, thousand three, ..."* This will ensure that you can see whatever it is that we're describing at the time. However, please note that we can't work miracles (our rule is no more than three a day), so we can't squeeze more speed out of your main computer than it's inherently capable of. When you've altered the system clock to your satisfaction, dismiss the dialog window by clicking on its Cancel button.

We now have a fairly graphic idea of the actions that the *Beboputer* is performing, and the speed with which the address and data lights on the display panel are changing compared to the speed of the 8-bit LED display also tells a story. Remember that our program is nine bytes long. The first two bytes (the *load* instruction) are only employed to load an initial value into the accumulator at the beginning of the program. The CPU then loops around the remaining seven bytes and, once every cycle, it updates the 8-bit LED display. This explains why the lights on the main display panel are so much more active than those on the 8-bit LED display; the main display is updated for each of the three instructions forming the loop, while the 8-bit LED display is only updated once.

There are only two ways to exit from the *run mode*; one is to click on the Step button on the switch panel, which will return us to the *step mode*. Do this now. You will observe that it's impossible to predict the point at which you will break into the program – the *Beboputer* will simply halt at the beginning of whichever instruction it was about to perform when you clicked the mouse.

Once in the *step mode*, you may continue to click on the Step button as before. By some strange quirk of fate, there are also only two ways to exit from the *step mode*; one is to click on the Run button on the switch panel, which will return us to the *run mode*. Do this now. You will observe that the lights on the displays resume their frenzied activity.

Using the switch panel to modify a program

Suddenly, on the spur of the moment, out of the blue, like a shot in the dark, we've decided that we don't like our existing program. Instead of rotating the contents of the accumulator, which, after all, anyone can do, we'd like to do something a little bit more meaty. Perhaps we'll start by loading the accumulator with zero, and then loop around incrementing its contents by one. Obviously, the first thing we'll need is a trusty flowchart (Figure 3.15).

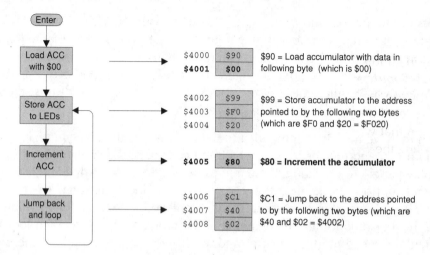

Figure 3.15: Increment accumulator program

From the flowchart we see that the first action is to load the accumulator with an initial value of $00. As before, the second action is to store the contents of the accumulator to the 8-bit LED display. The third action is to increment the contents of the accumulator by one; that is, to add the number 1 to whatever the accumulator already contains. The fourth and final action is to jump back to the store instruction.

Fate is obviously smiling down on us, because it appears that we only have to modify the contents of two bytes to coerce our original program into this new manly-man's version (how lucky can you get?). The first byte to be modified is the initial value that's loaded into the accumulator, where this value was stored at address $4001 – we need to change this byte from $03 to $00. The second byte to be modified is at address $4005; we need to change this byte from $78 (the original opcode that rotated the accumulator) to $80 (a new opcode that increments the accumulator).

However, we're still in the *run mode*, and we can't change anything if we're in either the *run mode* or the *step mode*. Try clicking on the address switches if you like. You'll find that although they'll toggle, they don't have any other effect. The problem is that the *Beboputer's* monitor program isn't paying any attention to us – the only thing on its mind is to continue executing our first program like a gerbil running endlessly around a wheel.

Somehow we have to get the *Beboputer's* attention, and the way to do this is to click your mouse on the **Reset** button on the switch panel. (Please, please, PLEASE .... whatever you do .... **Do Not** press the physical reset button on your real computer). Clicking on *our* **Reset** button has the same effect on the *Beboputer* that a handful of ice cubes dropped down the back of your shirt would have on you — it causes it to sit up and pay attention! In fact, in an identical manner to the *power-on reset*, the Reset button causes the *Beboputer* to return to address $0000, which is the location of the first instruction in our monitor program. (We'll discuss the monitor program in more detail a little later). Note that the 8-bit LED display retains the last pattern that was written to it — for reasons of our own we decided that resetting the *Beboputer* should not affect the output ports.

As usual, the status bar at the bottom of the project window indicates that we're now back in the *reset mode*. Also, as we'll see, pulling a reset did not affect the contents of the RAM, so our original program is still there. All you have to do to modify the program is perform the following actions:

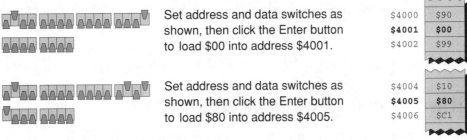

$4000	$90
$4001	**$00**
$4002	$99

Set address and data switches as shown, then click the Enter button to load $00 into address $4001.

$4004	$10
$4005	**$80**
$4006	$C1

Set address and data switches as shown, then click the Enter button to load $80 into address $4005.

Once again, in order to run our program we first need to set the address switches on the switch panel to the program's start address of $4000 (Figure 3.16). As before, to execute our program we have two options: to *Step* through the program or to *Run* the program; and due to the fact that we're currently in the *reset mode*, both the Step and Run buttons on the switch panel will cause the program to be executed from the start address as specified by the address switches.

Figure 3.16: Start address

But before we run this program, let's make sure that we're all tap-dancing to the same set of bongos and we're one-hundred percent sure as to what it's going to do. We already know that the program will load the accumulator with an initial value of $00, and then loop around adding one to the contents of the accumulator on each pass through the loop. Thus, we may reasonably expect that the lights on the 8-bit LED display will follow the sequence shown in Figure 3.17.

Obviously this is a standard binary count, which is pretty much what we'd anticipate from our flowchart. However, one interesting question would be: *"When all of the lights on the 8-bit LED display are green (corresponding to the accumulator containing 1111 1111 in binary), then what do you expect*

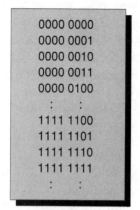

```
0000 0000
0000 0001
0000 0010
0000 0011
0000 0100
  :    :
1111 1100
1111 1101
1111 1110
1111 1111
  :    :
```

Figure 3.17:
Expected output

the next action will be?" If you're not sure about the answer to this question, stick around because we'll find out shortly.

Click on the **Step** button enough times to travel around the loop once or twice to make sure that you're entirely comfortable with the way in which the program is working. Then, when you're ready, click on the **Run** button and let the *Beboputer* rip.

It shouldn't take too long before you discover the answer to the question we posed above. Our accumulator contains eight bits, which can only represent 256 different patterns: $00 through $FF in hexadecimal. Thus, when the accumulator contains $FF (or 1111 1111 in binary), the next increment instruction causes it to overflow and return to $00 (or 0000 0000 in binary).

The memory walker display

By now it's probably beginning to dawn on you that working with one of the early computers was not as effortless as one might have hoped. Remember that when you modified our original program, you were aided by the fact that we'd written everything down for you. Imagine what life would be like if your program was thousands of bytes long – during the process of creating the program you would have had to write down each byte on a piece of paper along with a description of its purpose.

Additionally, the only way to check the contents of any particular memory location in the early days was by means of the display panel. In fact, the original computers often had substantially larger display panels than we've shown here. These panels could display the contents of dozens of locations at the same time, which is why the producers of old science fiction films tended to make their computers resemble Christmas trees; this wasn't a *"pigment of their fig-newtons"* – it was actually quite realistic for the time!

But there's no need for us to continue to beat our heads against the wall, because *we* have far better ways of doing things. First, return to the *reset mode* by clicking the **Reset** button on the switch panel. Next we'll bid a fond

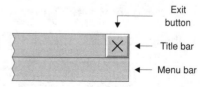

Exit
button

Title bar

Menu bar

farewell to the display panel. You can do this by clicking the exit button in its title bar.

What we're going to do now is to use a utility that we've dubbed the *Memory Walker Display*. One way to invoke this utility would be to click the Display item on the project window's menu bar, then click the Memory Walker entry in the resulting pull-down menu. However, on the basis that you'll probably be using this utility extensively, we've provided a short cut in the form of a Memory Walker icon on the project window's tool bar. Single-clicking on this icon will also invoke the memory walker display.

	BP	Step	Address	Data	
▶			$4000	$90	▲
			$4001	$00	
			$4002	$99	
			$4003	$F0	
			$4004	$20	
			$4005	$80	
			$4006	$C1	
			$4007	$40	
			$4008	$02	
			$4009	$XX	
			$400A	$XX	▼

Figure 3.18: Memory-walker display

Use either of these methods to bring up the memory walker (Figure 3.18). As you'll see, the two right-hand columns display addresses and data, respectively (we'll ignore the two left-hand columns for the moment). By default, the display commences at the first location in the RAM (at address $4000). As our program consists of only nine bytes occupying addresses $4000 to $4008, addresses $4009 and above display 'X' characters to indicate that these locations still contain unknown, random values.

To the right of the display there is a scroll bar. You can click on the arrows at the top and bottom of the scroll bar to move up and down through the memory. Alternatively, you can use your mouse to drag the thumb (the small box in the middle of the scroll bar), which allows you to traverse the display much faster.

If the memory walker is too large or too small for your preference, you can re-size it by dragging the bottom of the display with your mouse. Similarly, if the display appeared at an inconvenient position in your project workspace, you can relocate it by dragging its title bar with your mouse. Note that dragging the display out of the project workspace will cause scroll bars appear on the main project window. This is because the project window supports a virtual workspace, which can represent a much larger area than can be displayed on your screen. We would urge caution here, because it's easy to lose things in a virtual workspace if you forget where you left them (but you'll probably discover that for yourselves).

In addition to the scroll bar, there are a variety of other techniques that allow you to quickly navigate around the memory. At the top of the memory walker display is a toolbar. Clicking on the O/P Port icon will cause the display to scroll to the area in memory occupied by the output ports, such as the one driving our 8-bit LED display at address $F020. Similarly, clicking on the related I/P Port icon will cause the display to jump to the memory locations dedicated to our input ports, which commence at address $F000.

Next click on the ROM icon, which automatically scrolls the display to the start of the ROM at address $0000. Note that there is some data representing the monitor program in the ROM (we'll return to consider this shortly).

Now click on the Goto icon. This brings up a dialog window which allows you to enter an address in hexadecimal. When you've entered your target address, either click on the OK button or press the <Enter> key on your keyboard.

Finally (for the moment), click on the RAM icon to return us to the start of our program at address $4000. Now if you've been keeping pace with us and not wandered off into the boondocks to do your own thing, the address switches on the switch panel should still be set up to point to location $4000. (You might want to check that they still appear as shown in Figure 3.16; if not then please change them now).

Click the Step button on the switch panel, which causes the *Beboputer* to execute the instruction at address $4000 and pause at the beginning of the next instruction at address $4002. Note the chevron characters at address $4002 (in the second column from the left in the memory walker). Whenever the *Beboputer* is in its *step mode*, these chevrons appear in the memory walker and point to the first byte of the instruction that is waiting to be executed. Perform a few more steps, and observe both the chevrons and the 8-bit LED display.

Next click on the Run button in the switch panel, thereby unleashing the full spine-tingling power of the *Beboputer*. Note that the memory walker display "grays out," because continually updating this type of display while the *Beboputer* is in its *run mode* would bring your computer to its knees and slow everything down to an unacceptable level. (Any data values shown in the memory walker are not guaranteed to be valid whilst the display is grayed out.)

Now, while your mother isn't looking, click the **Reset** button on the switch panel. As you would expect, this forces the *Beboputer* back into its *reset mode* and the contents of memory walker are updated and returned to us. However, the most important point is that the memory walker gives us a visual confirmation that pulling the reset did not affect the contents of the *Beboputer's* memory.

But wait, there's more. Boldly click the **ON/OFF** switch on the switch panel. As soon as the power is cut the display lights on the switch panel flicker out and the memory walker goes gray; thereby indicating that it has nothing meaningful to say. Wait a few seconds to savor the moment, then click the **ON/OFF** switch again to bring the *Beboputer* back online. Good grief! Look at the memory walker! All of the memory locations show 'X' characters! What have you done? Where has our program gone? Is this the end of all life in the universe as we know it? Well, it's not quite as bad as that, but our program has certainly exited the stage and moved on to another plane of existence.

The problem is that our *Beboputer's* memory is based on (virtual) semiconductor RAMs, which lose their contents when power is removed from the system, and which initialize with unknown, random *logic 0s* and *logic 1s* when power is reapplied. How could we have forgotten that? Well, there's no use crying over spilt milk. Obviously we need some way to store our programs, but we'll leave that problem for Chapter 4.

Introducing the monitor program

It's almost time to close this chapter, but we're not quite finished yet. Click the memory walker display's **ROM** icon. As we see the monitor program is still present, because ROMs are non-volatile, so our ROM retained its contents when power was removed from the system. Use the down arrow on the scroll bar to scroll a little way down the display. You'll see that our monitor program is quite short; in fact, it only occupies 29 bytes in addresses $0000 to $001C. There are two very good reasons for this; first, a monitor program for a switch panel interface isn't very complicated; and second, what you see isn't really a monitor program at all!

Let's take these points in order. In a real machine of the 1960s vintage, the switch and display panels would be connected into input and output ports (unless they were hard-wired into the "guts" of the computer – see also Chapter 12). For example, the switch panel would require four input ports: two to handle the address switches, one to handle the data switches, and one to handle the Enter, Step, and Run buttons (each of these buttons would only require one bit of the port, while the Reset button would be hard-wired into the CPU's reset input). Similarly, the display panel would require three output ports: two for the address lights and one for the data lights (this is discussed in more detail in Chapter 9).

Thus, in a real machine the monitor program would simply loop around, reading the various switch ports, writing to the various display ports, loading data into a memory location (when instructed to do so by an Enter command), and passing control to another program (when instructed to do so by a Step or Run command). So in reality, a monitor program for one of these old machines wouldn't need to contain very many instructions at all. In a similar manner to their real counterparts, *our* switch and display panels are plugged into four of our input ports and three of our output ports, respectively. However, as we just noted, what you see here isn't really a monitor program – it could be, but it isn't. In fact the bytes you see in the ROM are there for just one purpose, which is to give you something to look at.[11] For technical reasons that are beyond our power to explain here, it proved to be advantageous for us to usurp the monitor program's function and to control the *Beboputer* from afar.

Hardware, software, firmware, wetware, and vaporware

We've mentioned the terms *hardware* and *software* before (and we'll doubtless be mentioning them again), so this is probably an appropriate time to define them formally. Hardware refers to all of the physical components of a computer system, including the circuit boards, integrated circuits, cables, cabinets, monitors, and even the nuts and bolts. By comparison, *software* refers to the programs (sequences of instructions) which are executed by the computer, while the term *firmware* is used to refer to any programs like our monitor routine that are stored in non-volatile memory devices such as ROMs.

---

[11]This isn't to say that the data in these bytes doesn't mean anything at all because it does, but it's up to you to work out what it is!

In addition to "hardware," "software," and "firmware," a number of other "–wares" have thrust their way onto the stage. The term *wetware* is often used to refer to any software that is still relatively new and untested (unfortunately, commercially released programs can sometimes fall into this category),[12] while *vaporware* refers to any hardware or software that exist only in the minds of the people who are trying to sell it to you. Other "–wares" that you may stumble across are *shareware* (for which you pay a nominal charge, based largely on an honor system) and *freeware* which, as its name would suggest, is software that is placed in the public domain at no charge.[13]

Exiting the lab and saving your environment

To exit the lab, you can simply click the **File** item on the project window's menu bar, then click the **Exit** entry in the resulting pull-down menu. However, this means that the next time you enter this lab it will be returned to its original pristine condition. If you've rearranged the various tools and displays to new positions on your screen, and assuming that you intend to return to this lab in the future, you may wish to save the project window just the way it is.

You can save your current environment by clicking the **File** item on the project window's menu bar, then clicking the **Save Project As** entry in the resulting pull-down menu. The ensuing dialog functions in a standard manner, thereby allowing you to save the lab under a new name. If you subsequently wish to return to your named project in the future, you can use the **File** → **Open** command to select your named project.

> **Note** that saving one of our pre-defined projects to a new name will automatically disable that particular lab's multimedia button, because we can no longer guarantee that our multimedia content will match your new configuration.

---

[12]"Wetware" is also sometimes used to refer to people's brains (or the thoughts and ideas therein).
[13]Some freeware is actually tremendously useful and well-written, but a lot is worth exactly what you pay for it. Hey, what do you want for nothing – your money back?

Quick quiz #3

1) What did computer memory have to do with ladies knitting?

2) What was magnetic core store and how did it work?

3) What were switch and display panels used for in early computers?

4) What does a RAM contain when power is first applied to a computer system?

5) What is a hard disk?

6) What are flowcharts and what are they used for?

7) What is a program?

8) What do you understand by the terms "opcode" and "operand" at this stage in our discussions?

9) What were the main tasks performed by a monitor routine?

10) Where would you expect to find an accumulator and what does it do?

Chapter 4

Paper Tapes and Punched Cards

In this chapter we will discover:

Who invented the accordion

When paper tapes were first used as a
medium for the preparation, storage, and
transmission of data

How to use the output ports dialog to
invoke new output devices

How to save a program from the
Beboputer's RAM onto a (virtual)
paper tape

How to load a program from a paper tape
into the *Beboputer*'s RAM

The differences between main (core) store
and bulk storage technologies

When, and by whom, punched cards were
first used in a data processing role

Contents of Chapter 4

Perforated paper products save the day

As was amply illustrated in the previous chapter, it was somewhat inconvenient to have a computer which forgot everything it knew if its operator turned it off before stepping out for a bite of lunch. Similarly, imagine a programmer's frustration if, after spending countless hours entering a program containing hundreds or thousands of bytes, the janitor carelessly disconnected the computer in order to vacuum the office. A few choice words would be (and often were) the order of the day, let me tell you!

There were also a variety of other considerations. For example, since the early computers had very little memory anyway, it was necessary to have some mechanism to store large amounts of data outside of the main memory. A program could then access and process small portions of the data on an as-needed basis. Also, if the operator had a number of different programs, but there wasn't enough memory to contain them all at the same time, then it was necessary to have some technique for storing the inactive programs. There was also the question of long-term archiving; that is, being able to store programs and data for use sometime in the future.

Yet another concern was being able to transport programs and data between computers located at different sites. For example, a programmer who created an interesting routine in Boston may well have wanted to share the fruits of his or her labors with colleagues in San Francisco. Although some flavors of early memories, such as magnetic core stores, were non-volatile, it was still somewhat less than practical to slip something the size of a large washing machine into an envelope and drop it into the mail.

For all of these reasons, it was obvious to everyone that it would be advantageous to have some kind of reliable, cheap, and efficient media for storing large amounts of computer data (and preferably something that weighed-in at substantially less than a ton). To satisfy these requirements, two techniques became very widely used: paper tapes and punched cards, both of which involved perforating paper-based products (try saying that ten times quickly).

The origin of paper tapes

By using paper tapes, like so many other aspects of computing, engineers took advantage of technology that already existed at the time. In 1837, the British physicist and inventor Sir Charles Wheatstone and the British electrical engineer Sir William Fothergill Cooke invented the first British electric telegraph.[1,2] This instrument made use of five wires, each of which drove a pointer at the receiver, where these pointers were used to indicate different letters. In the same year, the American inventor Samuel Finley Breese Morse developed the first American telegraph, which was based on simple patterns of "dots" and "dashes" called *Morse Code* being transmitted over a single wire. Morse's system was eventually adopted as the standard technique, because it was easier to construct and more reliable than Wheatstone's (Table 4.1).

A	•—	N	—•	0	—————
B	—•••	O	———	1	•————
C	—•—•	P	•——•	2	••———
D	—••	Q	——•—	3	•••——
E	•	R	•—•	4	••••—
F	••—•	S	•••	5	•••••
G	——•	T	—	6	—••••
H	••••	U	••—	7	——•••
I	••	V	•••—	8	———••
J	•———	W	•——	9	————•
K	—•—	X	—••—	,	——••—— comma
L	•—••	Y	—•——	.	—•—•—• period
M	——	Z	——••	?	••——••

Table 4.1: Subset of International Morse Code

The duration of a "dash" is three times the duration of a "dot." Note that this is only a subset of the code (although it's quite a large subset), but it's enough to give the general idea. Also note that this table shows *International Morse Code*, which is a slightly different flavor to *American Morse Code.*

Morse Code has a number of interesting features and, knowing us, you'll be lucky to escape this book without our mentioning at least a few of them. One little nugget of trivia we can't resist pertains to the code for the letter 'V'. In his early years, Morse was more attracted to the arts than he was to science. The rumor on the street is that Morse attended a performance of Beethoven's Fifth Symphony on one of his trips to England. Idle speculation further has it that this performance so impressed him that the *"dot dot dot dash"* code he

---

[1]Sir Charles was a busy man. Amongst other things, he also invented the *accordion* in 1829 and three-dimensional photographs in the form of his *stereoscope* in 1838.
[2]Apropos of nothing at all, 1837 was also the year that another "Charles", Charles Dickens, first published a story under his given name (prior to this he'd been using the pen-name "Boz").

used for the letter 'V' (which is also the Roman numeral for "five") was intended to emulate the symphony's opening sequence, which goes: "*Da Da Da Daaa*".[3,4]

The telegraph quickly proliferated thanks to the relative simplicity of Morse's system. However, a problem soon arose in that operators could only transmit around ten words a minute, which meant that they couldn't keep up with the public's seemingly insatiable desire to send messages to each other. This was a classic example of a *communications bottleneck*. Thus, in 1857, only twenty years after the invention of the telegraph, Sir Charles Wheatstone introduced the first application of paper tapes as a medium for the preparation, storage, and transmission of data (Figure 4.1).

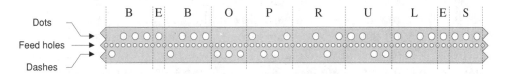

Figure 4.1: Wheatstone's perforated paper tape

Sir Charles' paper tape used two rows of holes to represent Morse's dots and dashes. Outgoing messages could be prepared off-line on paper tapes and transmitted later. By 1858, a Morse paper tape transmitter could operate at 100 words a minute. Unsuspectingly, Sir Charles had also provided the American public with a way to honor their heroes and generally have a jolly good time, because used paper tapes were to eventually become a key feature of so-called *ticker-tape parades*.

In a similar manner to Sir Charles' telegraph tape, the designers of the early computers realized that they could record their data on paper tapes by punching rows of holes across the width of the tape. The pattern of the holes in each *data row* represented a single data value or character. The individual hole positions forming the data rows were referred to as *channels* or *tracks*, and the number of different characters that could be represented by each row depended on the number of channels forming the rows. The original computer tapes had five channels, so each data row could represent one of thirty-two different characters. However, as users began to demand more complex character sets, including the ability to use both uppercase characters ('A', 'B', 'C', ...) and their lowercase equivalents ('a', 'b', 'c', ...), the number of channels rapidly increased, first to six and later to eight (Figure 4.2).

---

[3]You really had to be there!
[4]Not that we actually give these rumors much credence you understand.

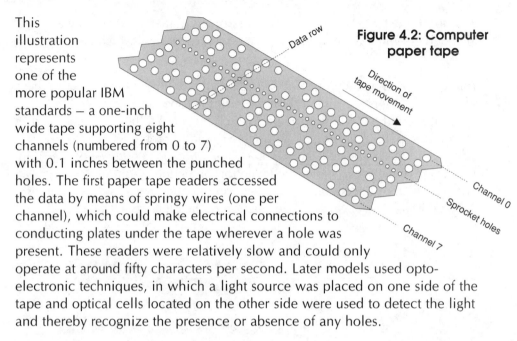

Figure 4.2: Computer paper tape

This illustration represents one of the more popular IBM standards — a one-inch wide tape supporting eight channels (numbered from 0 to 7) with 0.1 inches between the punched holes. The first paper tape readers accessed the data by means of springy wires (one per channel), which could make electrical connections to conducting plates under the tape wherever a hole was present. These readers were relatively slow and could only operate at around fifty characters per second. Later models used opto-electronic techniques, in which a light source was placed on one side of the tape and optical cells located on the other side were used to detect the light and thereby recognize the presence or absence of any holes.

In the original slower-speed readers, the small sprocket holes running along the length of the tape between channels 2 and 3 were engaged by a toothed wheel to advance the tape. The higher-speed opto-electronic models used rubber rollers to drive the tape, but the sprocket holes remained, because light passing through them could be detected and used to generate synchronization pulses. On the off-chance that you were wondering, the reason the sprocket holes were located off-center between channels 2 and 3 (as opposed to being centered between channels 3 and 4) was to enable the operator to know which side of the tape was which. Of course, it was still necessary to be able to differentiate between the two ends of the tape, so the operators used scissors to shape the front-end into a triangular point, thereby indicating that this was the end to be stuck into the tape reader.

Winding up the *Beboputer*

In case you hadn't guessed by now, the purpose of this lab is to save a program onto a virtual paper tape and to subsequently reload it back into the *Beboputer*. But first we need a program to be saved. Other than the fact that we are going to use this program in a future laboratory, we really don't care what it actually does; it's the act of saving and recovering it that we're interested in here. As we are *"Masters of the mystic arts,"* we could have used some capriciously cunning tricks to automatically create this program for you ...... but we didn't. Instead, we decided that it's necessary for you to suffer now in order that you will fully appreciate the wonders that are to come, and, more importantly, so that you will truly understand the trials and tribulations faced by the early computer pioneers. However, although we're firm we're also fair, so you may take heart in the knowledge that this is the very last program you will be forced to enter using the switch panel.

Make sure that the *Beboputer* CD is in the appropriate drive in your computer, then invoke the *Beboputer* as described in the previous Chapter. Once the *Beboputer's* project window has opened, click the File item on its menu bar, click the Open Project entry in the resulting pull-down menu, then select the Lab 2 project from the ensuing dialog. This will invoke the second lab (Figure 4.3).

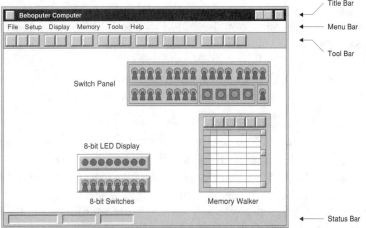

Figure 4.3: The *Beboputer* project window for Lab 2

The main switch panel, the memory walker, and the 8-bit LED device are all familiar to us from the previous lab. In fact the only new tool is a simple 8-bit switch device that we've plugged into one of our input ports. Note that the display panel (not shown here) also arrives on the screen, because it's intimately related to the switch panel. But the fact that we have the memory walker means that we no longer need the display panel, so dismiss this device by clicking the exit button in its title bar.

The program we are going to write will perform an endless loop, reading the state of the switches on the 8-bit input device and writing this state to the 8-bit LED display. The flowchart for this program, along with its associated opcodes and data bytes, is shown in Figure 4.4.

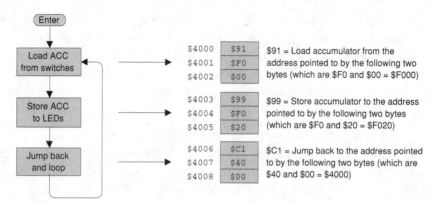

Figure 4.4: Load and store program

From the flowchart we see that the first action is to load the accumulator with whatever value is represented by the 8-bit switch input device. This is a slightly different load instruction to the one we used in our previous laboratory; in this flavor of a load, the $91 opcode at address $4000 instructs the CPU to load the accumulator with the contents of the memory location which is pointed to by the following two bytes.

As was discussed in Chapter 3, we (as designers of the *Beboputer*) decided that addresses would be stored in memory with the most-significant byte first. Thus, the contents of the two bytes stored at addresses $4001 and $4002 ($F0 and $00, respectively) are understood by the CPU to represent the address $F000. However, once again we're going to trick the CPU, because although it thinks it's reading from memory, the address we're using actually points to an input port into which we've connected the 8-bit switch device.

The other two instructions are identical to our previous program (with the exception of the address associated with the *jump* instruction). The $99 opcode at address $4003 instructs the CPU to copy the contents of its accumulator into the memory location specified by the address contained in the following two bytes (which actually contain the address of the output port that drives the 8-bit LED display). Finally, the $C1 opcode at address $4006 instructs the CPU to jump back to the memory location specified by the address contained in the following two bytes. In the case of this program, we've decided that the jump instruction should cause the CPU to return to address $4000, which is both the beginning of the program and the beginning of the loop.

By some strange quirk of fate, this program requires us to load only nine bytes of data, just like the programs we played with earlier, and the sooner we start the sooner we'll finish. First, click the **ON/OFF** switch on the main switch panel with your mouse to power-up the *Beboputer*, then perform the following actions to load the program. (Note that every time you click the main switch panel's **Enter** button, the memory walker updates to show that data):

Set address and data switches as shown, then click the Enter button to load $91 into address $4000.	$3FFF **$4000** $4001	$## **$91** $XX
Set address and data switches as shown, then click the Enter button to load $F0 into address $4001.	$4000 **$4001** $4002	$91 **$F0** $XX
Set address and data switches as shown, then click the Enter button to load $00 into address $4002.	$4001 **$4002** $4003	$F0 **$00** $XX
Set address and data switches as shown, then click the Enter button to load $99 into address $4003.	$4002 **$4003** $4004	$00 **$99** $XX
Set address and data switches as shown, then click the Enter button to load $F0 into address $4004.	$4003 **$4004** $4005	$99 **$F0** $XX
Set address and data switches as shown, then click the Enter button to load $20 into address $4005.	$4004 **$4005** $4006	$F0 **$20** $XX
Set address and data switches as shown, then click the Enter button to load $C1 into address $4006.	$4005 **$4006** $4007	$10 **$C1** $XX
Set address and data switches as shown, then click the Enter button to load $40 into address $4007.	$4006 **$4007** $4008	$C1 **$40** $XX
Set address and data switches as shown, then click the Enter button to load $00 into address $4008.	$4007 **$4008** $4009	$40 **$00** $XX

Don't forget that you can always correct any errors by overwriting a location's contents with new data. Once you've entered the program and

Figure 4.5: Start address

you're happy that all is as it should be, return the address switches to the program's start address of $4000 (Figure 4.5), then click the Run button to let the *Beboputer* rip.

Now, although not a lot seems to be happening, the *Beboputer* is actually working furiously, reading the values of the switches on the 8-bit input device and writing what it finds there to the 8-bit LED display. (The ways in which the switches and the LED display work are discussed in more detail in Chapter 5.) Use your mouse to click one of the 8-bit switches and note that the corresponding LED *appears* to respond almost immediately.

Play around for a while toggling the switches and watching the LEDs respond. When you're ready to proceed further, click the main switch panel's Step button to place the *Beboputer* in its *step mode*. As we know, it's impossible to predict the point at which you will break into the program – the *Beboputer* will simply halt at the beginning of whichever instruction it was about to perform when you dropped into the *step mode*. So once you've entered this mode, keep on clicking the Step button until the chevrons in the memory walker fall on address $4006. Now perform the following sequence of actions:

a) Make a note of the current state of the lights on the 8-bit LED display; that is, which ones are red and which ones are green.

b) Click one of the 8-bit switches to change its state and record which one you changed. Note that nothing happens to the 8-Bit LEDs.

c) Click the Step button to execute the *jump* instruction, which results in the chevrons pointing to address $4000 in the memory walker. Note that nothing happens to the 8-Bit LEDs.

d) Click another of the 8-bit switches to change its state. Make sure that this isn't the same switch that you changed last time and record which one you changed this time. Note that nothing happens to the 8-Bit LEDs.

e) Click the Step button to execute the *load* instruction, which results in the chevrons in the memory walker pointing to address $4003. Note that nothing happens to the 8-Bit LEDs.

f) Click another of the 8-bit switches to change its state. Make sure that this isn't the same as either of the switches that you changed above and record which one you changed this time. Note that nothing happens to the 8-Bit LEDs.

g) Click the **Step** button one last time to execute the *store* instruction, which results in the chevrons in the memory walker pointing to address $4006. Note that two of the LEDs did change this time.

The main point of the above exercise is to illustrate the fact that the CPU doesn't inherently know exactly when something changes in the outside world.[5] Thus, when you altered the first switch at point (b) the CPU didn't actually pay any attention. Similarly, when you stepped through the instruction at point (c), the CPU didn't look at the switches, it just executed the *jump* instruction. Once again, when you modified the second switch at point (d), the CPU didn't actually notice that you'd done anything. It was only when you executed the *load* instruction at point (e) that the CPU copied the state of the switches into its accumulator. Thus, when you changed the third switch in point (f), the CPU didn't pay any attention, because it had already loaded the switches' values on the previous instruction. So when you finally executed the *store* instruction at point (g), the only LEDs to be updated were those corresponding to the first two switches that you had altered.

Without touching the 8-bit switches, click the **Step** button three more times and observe that the third LED *does* change. If the reason for this is not immediately obvious, then spend a few moments going through the sequence in your mind until you're satisfied that you understand what's going on. Last but not least, the reason why we didn't notice any of this when we were happily toggling the switches in the *run mode* was that the *Beboputer* was racing around the loop, reading the switches and updating the LEDs faster that you could say: *"Buy the authors a three course meal and put it on my tab!"*

Saving our program on paper tape

As we know to our cost, the fact that our program is stored in RAM means that we will lose it when we power-down the *Beboputer*. So what we are going to do is to store our program onto a virtual paper tape. But first, click the main switch panel's **Reset** button to return us to the *reset mode*. Next click the **Setup** item on the project window's menu bar, then click the **Output Ports** entry in the resulting pull-down menu. Alternatively, you can

---

[5]See also the discussions on interrupts in Appendix D.

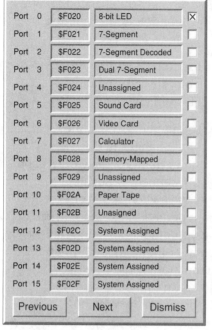

Port 0	$F020	8-bit LED	☒
Port 1	$F021	7-Segment	☐
Port 2	$F022	7-Segment Decoded	☐
Port 3	$F023	Dual 7-Segment	☐
Port 4	$F024	Unassigned	☐
Port 5	$F025	Sound Card	☐
Port 6	$F026	Video Card	☐
Port 7	$F027	Calculator	☐
Port 8	$F028	Memory-Mapped	☐
Port 9	$F029	Unassigned	☐
Port 10	$F02A	Paper Tape	☐
Port 11	$F02B	Unassigned	☐
Port 12	$F02C	System Assigned	☐
Port 13	$F02D	System Assigned	☐
Port 14	$F02E	System Assigned	☐
Port 15	$F02F	System Assigned	☐

Previous	Next	Dismiss

Figure 4.6: Outport ports dialog form

simply click the **Output Ports** icon in the project window's toolbar. Either of these methods will invoke a dialog window similar to the one shown in Figure 4.6.

This dialog reveals that there are a number of output devices available to us. Note that the button associated with Port 0 already has an 'X' in it, thereby indicating that this device is turned on (or "plugged in" if you will); this corresponds to the 8-bit LED display that we've been using thus far.

Now click the button associated with Port 10, which corresponds to a paper tape reader/writer. As soon as you click this button, the appropriate device appears in the main project window (Figure 4.7). We'll be using the reader/writer in a moment, but first we should note that our **Output Ports** window can also be used to turn off (or unplug) output devices. To check this out, click the **Port 10** button again and observe that the reader/writer immediately disappears from the main project window.

But we can't play around all day because we've got serious work to do, so click the **Port 10** button one last time to return the paper tape reader/writer to the project window, then click the dialog window's **Dismiss** button to discard this form.

Tape in →

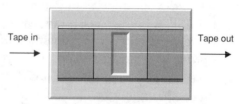

← Tape out

Figure 4.7: Paper tape reader/writer

As usual, if the reader/writer device appears at an inconvenient location on your screen, you can move it by dragging its title bar with your mouse. If you find yourself with too many

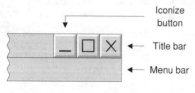

Iconize button

Title bar

Menu bar

devices on your screen for comfort, you can iconize our main displays by clicking the appropriate button in the top right-hand corner of their title bars. Once a device has been iconized, you can move its icon by dragging it around with the mouse. When you wish to restore an iconized device, simply click its restore button to return it to its previous size and location. You may wish to try iconizing and restoring the memory walker before we continue.

Now pay attention, because this next bit is a little tricky. The picture in the reader/writer window represents a top-down view of the mechanism that will actually punch holes in the tape. However, the reader/writer doesn't actually initiate any actions itself, because the *Beboputer* is in charge. To fully understand the process, click the ROM icon in the memory walker's tool bar, which automatically scrolls the memory walker to the start of the ROM at address $0000 where our main monitor program resides. Now use the scroll bar (or the Goto icon) to wander through the memory to address $0030. As you will see, there's a subroutine hanging out in addresses $0030 through $0042. (At this stage of our discussions, we may consider a subroutine to be a program segment that's called from a higher level – in this case you're going to summon it manually).[6] As it happens, this is the subroutine that will write our program to the paper tape.

In the real world you would first have to load a blank paper tape into the mechanism before running the subroutine. Also, at some stage you would have to write a name, or label, onto the paper tape to remind you what it contained in the future. Every tape has to have a label – imagine how silly you'd feel if, after neglecting to label your tapes, someone suddenly appeared crying: *"Quick, don't ask any questions, just give me the program that deactivates the rocket's automatic self-destruct sequence!"*

Things work a little differently in our virtual world, but not dramatically so. First set the address switches on the main switch panel to point to the subroutine's start address of $0030 (Figure 4.8), then click the switch panel's Run button. This opens up a dialog window prompting you to give the tape a name. The name of your tape can contain from one to eight alphabetic, numeric, and underscore characters, but spaces aren't allowed and you can't have an underscore as the first character. Baring these restrictions in mind,

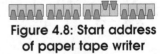

Figure 4.8: Start address of paper tape writer subroutine

you can name your tape pretty much anything you wish, but we suggest that you call it "mytape1" so we can refer to it as such later in these notes.

Type in a name for your tape, then either press the <Enter> key on your keyboard or click the window's Save button. This causes the main monitor program to enter the *run mode* and to hand control over to the paper tape

---

[6]The concept of subroutines is introduced in greater detail in Chapters 8 and 12.

writer subroutine. At this point you'll observe a blank tape being loaded into the hole puncher mechanism, then the subroutine will copy the contents of the *Beboputer's* RAM, one byte at a time, to the output port that drives the paper tape writer. Every time the writer receives a byte from the *Beboputer's* output port it punches the corresponding holes into the paper tape (our particular monitor program will only copy the 512 bytes occupying addresses $4000 to $41FF onto the tape).

Once the subroutine has copied all of the bytes comprising our program to the paper tape writer, it returns control to the main monitor program and retires gracefully from the scene. Actually, to be absolutely honest, much of the above is complete subterfuge, because in the same way that our *Beboputer* doesn't really have a main monitor program (see Chapter 3), it also doesn't really have a paper tape writer subroutine. Once again we're playing the puppet master by controlling the *Beboputer* from afar. However, if we did have a real monitor program and a paper tape writer subroutine, then this is the general way in which everything would hang together.

One further point that we might be moved to mention is that real paper tapes used to stream out of the writer at prodigious rates, and they usually ended up in a humongous tangle on the floor. Even in high-tech institutions, a strategically placed waste bucket usually served to gather the tape and prevent passers-by from trampling all over it. A brand-new tape would be approximately 1,000 feet in length, but the operator would tear off the tape a few inches after the last holes had been punched. Also, an extremely useful gadget to own was a hand-operated winder, which greatly speeded up the process of coiling your punched tape onto a reel.

Reloading our program from paper tape

Before we reload our program from the paper tape, we first need to remove the copy of the program that's already resident in the *Beboputer's* memory (otherwise we wouldn't be able to tell whether the paper tape reader was working or not). Click the **RAM** icon in the memory walker to return us to the start of the RAM so we can see the program. As we've already discovered, one way to lose a program is to power-down the machine, but there's a less drastic alternative that will prove useful in future laboratories.

Click the **Memory** item on the project window's menu bar, then click the **Purge RAM** entry in the resulting pull-down menu. This invokes a dialog window that allows you to purge the RAM of its contents. The resulting dialog allows you to select a range of addresses to be purged, so you could enter $4000 as the start address, $4008 as the end address, and then click the Apply button. Alternatively, as we don't have anything else in the RAM anyway, you can simply click the Purge All button followed by the Apply button. As you might expect, the memory walker updates with 'X' characters to show that the locations containing our program have been returned to random, unknown values.

Now click the ROM icon in the memory walker's tool bar to return us to the main monitor program, then use the scroll bar (or the Goto icon) to wander down to address $0050. As you'll see, there's a second subroutine hanging out in addresses $0050 through $0066, and it's this subroutine that will read our program from the paper tape.

Figure 4.9: Start address of paper tape reader subroutine

In order to run this second subroutine we need to set the address switches on the main switch panel to point to the subroutine's start address of $0050 (Figure 4.9). But before executing this subroutine, click the RAM icon in the memory walker's tool bar so that we can see our program as it appears in the memory.

Now click the switch panel's Run button, which opens a dialog window prompting you to select the name of the tape you wish to load. In addition to mytape1 (or whatever name you chose to give your tape in the previous section), you will also see the names of one or more other tapes. These additional tapes contain programs that we've already created for use in future laboratories. For the moment, click mytape1 and then click the dialog's Open button, which causes the main monitor program to enter the *run mode* and to hand control over to the paper tape reader subroutine. In turn, this subroutine reads the data, one byte at a time, from an input port that's connected to the paper tape reader. Every time the subroutine reads a byte from the input port, it copies that byte into the next free location in the RAM.

Once the subroutine has copied all of the bytes from the paper tape into the RAM, it returns control to the main monitor program and exits stage left. You can check that the program still works by returning the address switches to the program's start address of $4000 (check Figure 4.5 if you're unsure of the switch positions), then clicking on the Run button and playing with the 8-bit switches. Once you've finished, power-down the *Beboputer* by clicking the ON/OFF switch on the main switch panel. To exit this laboratory, click the File item on the project window's menu bar, then click the Exit entry in the resulting pull-down menu.

Teleprinters and batch modes

These days we're used to working with computers in what we call an *interactive mode*; that is, one issues a command via the keyboard or the mouse and the computer responds almost instantly. Additionally, during the course of the program your computer may request further information from you, and both of you can interact together in real time.

This level of interaction was almost undreamed of in the past. Although controlling a computer by means of its switch panel was interactive in its own way, it's not what we would regard as being interactive today. Furthermore, there was only one switch panel, but it could take many hours to create a program byte by painful byte. Thus, if the switch panel had been the only way to enter programs, it would have been a pitiful sight to see professional programmers manhandling each other in a desperate attempt to claw their way to the panel.

In reality, the computer's time was far too valuable to have it sitting around twiddling its metaphorical thumbs while operators entered programs via the switch panel. Due to their extremely high price-tags, the only way for early computers to be cost effective was for them to be performing calculations and processing data twenty-four hours a day. Thus, although it had other system-management functions, the switch panel was mainly employed to enter simple boot-strap routines when power was first applied to the system. These routines were then used to load more complex programs from external devices such as paper tape readers.[7]

The end result was that, to support the most efficient use of computing resources, programs had to be created off-line. This makes a lot of sense when you realize that it might take the computer only a few seconds to run a program that had required many hours to enter. One technique for creating a program off-line was by means of a *teleprinter*,[8] which looked something like a typewriter on a stand with a large roll of paper feeding through it. In fact, a teleprinter was essentially an electromechanical typewriter with a communications capability. In addition to the roll of paper (which was used by the operator to check what he or she had actually typed), the teleprinter could also contain other devices such as a paper tape reader/writer.

---

[7]This process is discussed in far greater detail in Chapter 12.
[8]Teleprinters were often referred to as *teletype machines* or *teletypes*. However, this was a brand name (much as "Hoover" is for vacuum cleaners) for a series of teleprinters manufactured by International Telephone and Telegraph (ITT).

Due to the fact that teleprinters were relatively inexpensive (compared to the millions of dollars invested in the computer), a typical installation usually included a large number of them, thereby allowing many people to create programs at the same time. Groups of programs were subsequently presented to the computer operators in a batch, and the computer was said to be running in a *batch mode*.[9] As computers evolved and became more powerful, teleprinters began to be connected directly to them. This allowed the operators and the computer to communicate directly with each other, which was one of the first steps along the path toward the interactive way in which we use computers today.

By some strange quirk of fate, the use of teleprinters for program preparation brings us to an interesting diversion that will help to explain the origins of certain terms used in future chapters. But first let's note that in order to handle textual documents, a complete and adequate set of characters should include the following:

> The terms *uppercase* and *lowercase* were handed down to us by the printing industry, from the compositors' practice of storing the *type* for capital letters and small letters in two separate cases. When working at the type-setting table, the compositors invariably kept the capital letters and small letters in the upper and lower cases, respectively; hence, *uppercase* and *lowercase*. Prior to this, scholars referred to capital letters as *majuscules* and small letters as *minuscules*, while everyone else simply called them capital letters and small letters.

    a) 26 uppercase alphabetic characters ('A' through 'Z')

    b) 26 lowercase alphabetic characters ('a' through 'z')

    c) 10 numeric digits ('0' through '9')

    d) Approximately 25 special characters for punctuation and other special symbols, such as '&', '%', '@', '#', and so forth.

To be *machine-readable* (that is, to be understandable by an electronic device), each of these characters has to be assigned a unique binary code. Additionally, as these character codes have to be recognized by diverse devices such as computers, printers, and teleprinters (to name but a few), it would obviously be useful if everybody could agree on a common standard.

Of course, in the spirit of free enterprise, everyone and his dog came up with their own standard! However, to cut a long story short, one standard that came to be very widely used is the *American Standard Code for Information Interchange (ASCII)*. We will be considering this standard in

---

[9]The phrase *batch mode* is now commonly used to refer to a program that's running as a background task, using whatever resources are available when interactive users aren't hogging all of the computer's capacity

more detail in Chapters 10 and 11, but for the moment we need only note that the ASCII codes corresponding to the characters we use to represent hexadecimal digits are as shown in Table 4.2:

Hex Digit	ASCII Code	Hex Digit	ASCII Code
0	00110000	A	01000001
1	00110001	B	01000010
2	00110010	C	01000011
3	00110011	D	01000100
4	00110100	E	01000101
5	00110101	F	01000110
6	00110110		
7	00110111		
8	00111000		
9	00111001		

Table 4.2: ASCII codes for hexadecimal characters

In fact ASCII only covers 128 different characters, which means that it only requires a 7-bit field to encode them. However, because 8-bit bytes are common in computers, ASCII codes are commonly embedded in 8-bit fields, where the most-significant bit is either set to *logic 0* or used for other purposes that we're not concerned with here. The point is that when the programmer pressed a key on his or her teleprinter, this key generated an 8-bit ASCII code, and it was this code that was subsequently punched into the paper tape.

Now this next bit can appear somewhat convoluted at first, so let's take it step by step. Consider the program that we created earlier in this laboratory (Figure 4.4). Although we used a hexadecimal notation to refer to the bytes forming this program, the actual values that we entered on the switch panel (and which were subsequently used by the *Beboputer*) were *logic 0s* and *logic 1s*; that is, like all modern computers, our *Beboputer* really sees the world in binary. Consider the first byte of our program, which we documented as hexadecimal $91. In order to arrive at this value, we split the 8-bit byte into two 4-bit nybbles, and then converted each of these nybbles into its hexadecimal equivalent (Figure 4.10).

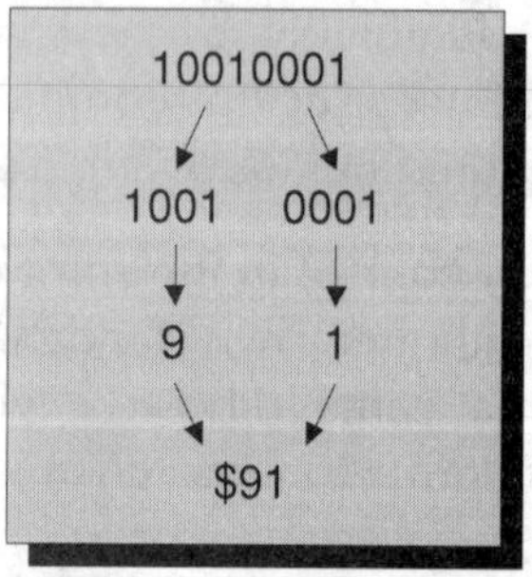

The reason we prefer to use hexadecimal is that humans find these numbers far easier to remember, read, and recognize than their binary equivalents.

Figure 4.10: Arriving at $91 in hexadecimal

Also, if the data is being entered on a teleprinter, then keying-in two hexadecimal characters as opposed to eight binary 0s and 1s immediately reduces the chances of error by 75%. In fact, if we take account of the reduction in boredom and fatigue when using hexadecimal numbers, and combine this with the ease of recognizing any miss-typed sequences (compared to recognizing them in binary), then the operator's error rate is reduced by far more than 75%.

Returning to the problem at hand, the result of a teleprinter operator keying in the characters "91" would have been two 8-bit ASCII characters punched into the paper tape. But these ASCII characters are useless to the computer, which wants to see a single 8-bit byte. To illustrate this graphically, we'll compare the paper tape generated by a teleprinter to the tape that was created when we saved our program (Figure 4.11).

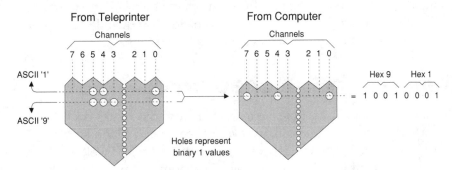

Figure 4.11: Teleprinter paper tape versus computer tape

As we see, if we'd been using a teleprinter, the resulting paper tape would have two data rows of punched holes (each representing an ASCII character) for every byte in our original program. Note that this is not a major problem and it even conveys certain advantages; for example, a tape generated on a teleprinter can also be directly read by a teleprinter, which can immediately reprint the ASCII characters in a form suitable for humans to read.

But the tape generated by the teleprinter still cannot be used directly by the computer. One way to overcome this problem might be to create a simple translator program to be run on the computer. This program would read an ASCII tape from a teleprinter, convert each pair of ASCII characters into their one-byte binary equivalents, and write out a new tape in binary (Figure 4.12).

Of course, the first generation of this program would have to be entered using the main switch panel. However, any future versions (containing more "bells-and-whistles") could be prepared on a teleprinter and then translated into binary using the original program.

These two tapes, ASCII and binary, are referred to as the *source* and *object* tapes, respectively. The origin of the term "source" (meaning "root" or "beginning") appears reasonably obvious, as in *"The source of the river Nile."* Similarly, the term "object" probably stems from "objective,"

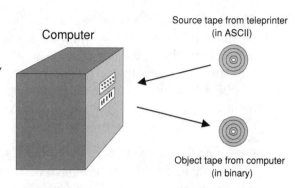

Figure 4.12: Translating a teleprinter tape

"mission," "target," or "goal," as in *"This is the object of the exercise."* To the best of the authors' knowledge, both of these terms first came into common usage in the context of this form of tape translation. However, as we will see in future chapters, these terms have subsequently come to be associated with other things such as programs and files.

The origin of punched cards

The practice of punching holes in cards to record data dates back to the early 1800s, when a French silk weaver called Joseph Marie Jacquard invented a way of automatically controlling the warp and weft threads on a silk loom by recording patterns as holes in a string of thin wooden boards or cards. In the years to come, variations on Jacquard's punched cards were to find a variety of uses, including representing music to be played by automated pianos and programs to be executed by computers.

The first practical use of punched cards for data processing is credited to the American inventor Herman Hollerith. During the 1880s, Hollerith decided to use Jacquard's punched cards to represent the data gathered for the American census, and to read and collate this data using an automatic machine. The resulting tabulating machines were successfully used to gather and process the data from the 1890 census, and Hollerith's company grew from strength to strength. In addition to solving the census problem, Hollerith's machines proved themselves to be extremely useful for a wide variety of statistical applications, and some of the techniques they used were to become significant in the development of the digital computer. In February 1924, Hollerith's company changed its name to International Business Machines, or IBM.

Many references state that Hollerith originally made his punched cards the same size as the dollar bills of that era, because he realized that it would be convenient and economical to buy existing office furniture, such as desks and cabinets, that already contained receptacles to accommodate stacks of bills. Other sources consider this to be a popular fiction. Whatever the case, we do know that these cards were eventually standardized at $7^3/_8$ inches by $3^1/_4$ inches, and Hollerith's many patents permitted his company to hold an effective monopoly on punched cards for many years.[10]

Although other companies came up with innovative ways to bypass Hollerith's patents, they failed to capitalize on their advances, thereby giving IBM a chance to regain the high ground. For example, Hollerith's early cards were punched with round holes, because his prototype machine employed cards with holes created using a tram conductor's ticket punch. Hollerith continued to use round holes in his production machines, which effectively limited the amount of data that could be stored on each card. By the early 1900s, Hollerith's cards supported 45 columns, where each column could be used to represent a single character or data value. This set the standard until 1924-1925, when the Remington Rand Corporation evolved a technique for doubling the amount of information that could be stored on each card. But they failed to exploit this advantage to its fullest extent, and, in 1929-1931, IBM responded by using rectangular holes, which allowed them to pack 80 columns of data onto each card. Although other formats appeared sporadically (including some from IBM), the 80 column card overwhelmingly dominated the punched card market from around the 1950s onward (Figure 4.13).

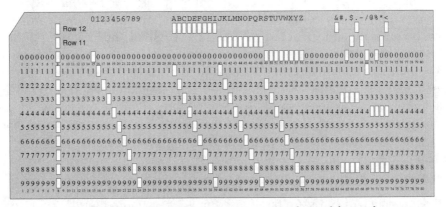

Figure 4.13: IBM 80-column punched card format

---

[10]Hollerith, who was no one's fool, had quickly realized that the real money was not to be made in the tabulating machines themselves, but rather in the tens or hundreds of thousands of cards that were used to store data.

Figure 4.13 shows one of the early 80 column IBM cards (not to scale). Each card contains 12 rows of 80 columns, and each column is typically used to represent a single piece of data such as a character. The top row is called the "12" or "Y" row; the second row from the top is called the "11" or "X" row; and the remaining rows are called the "0" to "9" rows (indicated by the numbers printed on the cards). This figure (which took a long time to draw let me tell you) illustrates one of the early, simpler coding schemes, in which each character could be represented using no more than three holes. (Note that we haven't shown all of the different characters that could be represented.) Over the course of time, more sophisticated coding schemes were employed to allow these cards to represent different character sets such as ASCII and EBCDIC; the rows and columns stayed the same, but different combinations of holes were used.

One advantage of punched cards over paper tapes was that the textual equivalent of the patterns of holes could be printed along the top of the card (one character above each column). Another advantage was that it was easy to replace any cards containing errors. However, the major disadvantage of working off-line (with both punched cards and paper tapes) was that the turn-around time to actually locate and correct any errors was horrendous.

Generally speaking, if you make a programming error on one of today's interactive systems, the system quickly informs you of your mistake and you can fix it almost immediately. By comparison, in the days of the batch mode, you might slave for hours at a teleprinter with a card puncher attachment, march miles through wind and rain to the computer building carrying a one-foot high stack of cards, only to hear: *"We're a bit busy at the moment, can you come back next Monday?"* So you left your cards with the operator and spent the weekend in delightful anticipation, but on returning the following week to collect your results, you'd probably receive a few inches of computer printout carrying the words: *"Syntax error on card 2: missing comma."* Arrgggh – if the computer knew enough to tell that there was a missing comma, why didn't the callous swine know enough to stick one in for you? The result was that debugging even a trivial program could take weeks and weeks. In fact, by the time you eventually got a program to work, you were often hard-pushed to recall what had prompted you to write it in the first place!

Although punched cards are rarely used now, we endure their legacies to this day. For example, the first computer monitors were constructed so as to display 80 characters across the screen. This number was chosen on the basis that you certainly wouldn't want to display fewer characters than were on an IBM punched card, and there didn't appear to be any obvious advantage to being able to display *more* characters than were on a card.

Similarly, long after interactive terminals became commonly available, the formatting of certain computer languages continued to follow the rules laid down in the era of punched cards. To this day, many assembly languages (see Chapter 12) have unnecessarily restrictive rules along the lines of *"Labels can only occupy columns 1 through 8."* Even the first high-level languages such as *FORTRAN* (an abbreviation of *Formula Translation*) had comparable rules.

As a final example, consider the case of the program called *SPICE (Simulation Program with Integrated Circuit Emphasis)*, which is used by engineers for evaluating analog circuits. The first generation of this program appeared commercially around the beginning of the 1970s and its descendants are used to this day. The point is that it is still common practice to refer to the data used by this program as a *"SPICE deck,"* which is a hangover from those times when such data was stored using punched cards ("deck of cards" – get it?).[11]

Alternative storage technologies

Although there are a baffling and bewildering variety of storage technologies, for the purposes of this closing discussion we will focus on two principal categories: *main store* (or *core store*) and *bulk storage*. (In the context of present-day usage, the term "core store" no longer implies magnetic core memory, but this is almost certainly where the term is derived from.) The main store is where the computer keeps any programs and data that are currently active, while bulk storage is used to hold dormant programs and data. We may generalize the main store as being relatively fast, large, expensive, and (typically) volatile, while bulk storage is relatively slow, small, cheap, and (always) non-volatile.[12] Bulk storage should also ideally be portable.

In the case of main store, the early computers used an assortment of Heath Robinson technologies,[13] including rotating drums containing capacitors,

---

[11]Later versions of SPICE came equipped with a simple user interface called *"Nutmeg."* This name had no relevance other than the fact that nutmeg is a spice (Oh, how we laughed).
[12]Referring to bulk storage devices as being "small" and "cheap" has to be taken in the context of the amount of data they hold. This means that if you compare main store with bulk storage in terms of cubic-inches-per-megabyte and dollars-per-megabyte, then bulk storage is smaller and cheaper.
[13]Where Heath Robinson is the British counterpart to the Americans' Rube Goldberg.

rotating drums covered with a magnetic coating, electrostatic storage, and mercury delay lines (see also Chapter 15). The first type of main store that wouldn't cause today's users to throw up their hands in absolute disbelief was magnetic core store, which was invented in the 1950s (see also Chapter 3). Unlike most forms of main store, magnetic core store was non-volatile, but it had little potential as a bulk storage technology, because of its large physical size and the fact that you didn't get very much of it for your money (for a long time, 8K-bytes of magnetic core store was considered to be pretty huge).

The picture began to change dramatically at the beginning of the 1970s with the advent of the first semiconductor memories. Although early devices could only hold a few hundred bits, their capacity expanded rapidly and prodigiously, culminating in modern devices that can hold mega-bytes of data. Due to the restricted amount of memory available with the original computers, the early programmers learnt to be extremely frugal with their memory usage. In fact, many microprocessor text books dating from around 1976 confidently stated that the majority of applications would need no more than 1K-byte, and that no application should require more than 4 K-bytes! Six years later, in 1981, the founder of Microsoft, Bill Gates, stated that: *"640 K-bytes should be enough for anyone."*[14] Only fifteen years later, in 1996, home computers typically came equipped with a minimum of 8M-bytes, many had 16 M-bytes, and the lucky few splashed out the cash for 24 M-bytes, 32 M-bytes, or more.

In the context of bulk storage, paper tape and punched cards began to be augmented, then replaced, by magnetic media, including magnetic tapes, magnetic drums, and magnetic disks (generally speaking only tapes and disks remain with us today). Between magnetic tapes and disks, the tapes were initially much cheaper and could store more data,[15] but they had the problem of only being able to store and access data sequentially, which meant that you had to start at the beginning of the tape and work your way through it until you reached the information you were looking for. By comparison, early magnetic disk drives were relatively expensive and prone to error, but they had the advantage of being able to store and access data in a random manner, which meant that you could quickly locate the data you were looking for.

---

[14]Where 640 K-bytes was the maximum amount of memory that could be supported by the first IBM personal computers (PCs). Actually, it's hard to hold Bill's comment against him, because most people agreed with him at the time.

[15]Even though the first tape drives were relatively simple, a single tape could store the same amount of data as 400,000 IBM punched cards!

Some of the early magnetic disks were heroic in their proportions; for example, one system built by the Librascope Corporation in the late-1960s used disks that were four feet in diameter (these devices weren't tremendously reliable, but their disks performed sterling duty as coffee tables)! However, magnetic media underwent phenomenal development over the years. In the early 1980s, a common form of hard disk called a "removable disk" came equipped with a drive the size of a top-loading washing machine (Figure 4.14). The disk-pack itself comprised a number of platters mounted on a central axis, looked like a large wedding cake, weighed in at around 20 pounds, and the one used by the authors could only store about 15 M-bytes of data. By comparison, in the early 1990s, a floppy disk 3.5" in diameter and 1/8" thick could hold a respectable 1.5 M-bytes.[16] By 1995, desktop home computers commonly contained hard disks (including the drives) that weighed about 0.5 pounds and could store between 500 and 1,000 M-bytes of data. Similarly, notebook computers in 1995 commonly contained hard disks that were around 0.5 inches thick and weighed a couple of ounces, yet could store 200 M-bytes or more.

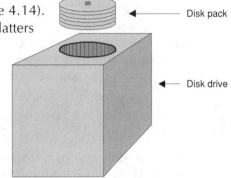

Disk pack

Disk drive

Figure 4.14: Removable hard disk

And the world continues to move on. The transportable bulk storage medium of choice for the majority of computer users in the 1990s is the CD-ROM, which is based on the same technology as the compact discs that were originally invented to store music. (For reasons unknown, the "disk" in *magnetic disk* and *floppy disk* is spelt with a 'k', while the "disc" in *compact disc* is spelt with a 'c'.) By 1995, CD-ROMs could contain around 600 M-bytes of data, and it is confidently expected that in the fairly immediate future they will be able to contain a giga-byte or more (where *giga* stands for one thousand million). Additionally, although existing CD-ROMs are read-only (hence the "ROM" postfix), it is anticipated that they will support both reading and writing of data in the very near future.

As to the longer term, only a brave man would dare to predict where we'll all end up. A host of alternative technologies are undergoing experimental evaluation, including optical and protein memories which hold the promise

---

[16]In 1976, a company called iCOM started to advertise an eight-inch floppy drive called the "*frugal floppy*," which sold for $1,200.

of being able to store tera-bytes of data in a few cubic centimeters (where *tera* stands for one million million).

Perforated paper products never die, they simply....

Finally, a word of caution. Although we have predominantly been referring to 1960s computers as our baseline, do not be misled into believing that paper tapes and punched cards have completely exited the stage. The halcyon days for paper tapes and punched cards were certainly the 1960s and 1970s. In those days it was easy to spot anyone who had anything to do with computers, because their offices, briefcases, jacket pockets, and hands were usually overflowing with reels of paper tape and decks of punched cards (*"Holy paper products, Batman"*).

However, although paper tapes and punched cards may seem delightfully antiquated, many institutions, including universities, continued to use these forms of data storage well into the 1980s, and both techniques are still to be found in the odd technological backwater to this day. Indeed, paper tapes continue to find a role to play in certain hostile environments. For example, in some manufacturing and heavy engineering facilities, computer-controlled machine tools may be located close to strong magnetic fields and electromagnetic noise. Many of today's storage technologies (such as floppy disks) tend to be corrupted in these conditions, but, much like the Energizer Bunny™ in the television commercials, paper tape products (especially modern varieties formed from materials such as Mylar) keep on going, and going, and going, and ......

Quick quiz #4

1) Who invented the accordion (and why)?

2) What were the main reasons for the widespread use of paper tapes and punched cards in the 1960s and 1970s?

3) Can you spot any interesting features associated with the subset of Morse Code shown in Table 4.1?

4) When was paper tape first used for the preparation, storage, and transmission of data?

5) What were the major features of an IBM 1-inch paper tape?

6) What was the difference between a paper tape generated by a teleprinter and one created by a computer?

7) In what context were the terms "source" and "object" originally used in regard to paper tapes?

8) When and by whom were punched cards first used in a data-processing role?

9) What were the main advantages of punched cards over paper tapes?

10) What are the primary differences between main store and bulk storage?

Chapter 5

Seven-Segment Displays

In this chapter we will discover:

The difference between normal diodes and
light-emitting diodes (LEDs)

How to use LEDs to construct our simple 8-bit
output display

How to rearrange our LEDs to form an
undecoded 7-segment display

How to augment an undecoded 7-segment
display to form its decoded counterpart

How we can attach two decoded 7-segment
displays to a single 8-bit output port

How to create a program that can display
values from $00 to $FF on our two
7-segment displays

Contents of Chapter 5

Diodes can be rather cunning when you get to know them

In the preceding chapters we used an output device that we dubbed an 8-bit LED display. This display consisted of a panel of eight lights, one for each of the bits coming from its associated output port (Figure 5.1).

Corresponds to output bit 7

Corresponds to output bit 0

Figure 5.1: A simple 8-bit LED display output device

We also noted that a red light indicates that its corresponding output port bit is driving a *logic 0*, while a green light indicates a *logic 1*. Now we could simply assume that this display is constructed using standard incandescent light bulbs, and we could completely ignore the way in which the output port drives the display. However, as we will be using a number of derivations of this type of display in future laboratories, it won't cause you irreparable harm to learn what LEDs are, how they work, and how we're using them (in our virtual world of course).

First of all the term LED is the abbreviation for *light-emitting diode*, which (it may not surprise you to learn) is similar to a normal *diode* except that it emits light. *"But what is a normal diode?"* you cry plaintively (and rather pathetically, we might add). Well, if you'll settle down for a moment and make yourselves comfortable we'll tell you, but first we need a stirring subtitle to make us strong.

Diodes and light-emitting diodes (LEDs)

Ah, there's nothing like a warm subtitle on a cold night. Now, where were we? Oh yes, we were talking about diodes, which can be cunning little rascals when you get to know them. A diode is an electronic component with two terminals that only conducts electricity in one direction. If you don't think this is terribly impressive, then try to do it yourself.[1] The first diodes were created using vacuum tubes (see also Chapter 15), but these were eventually superseded by semiconductor equivalents.

---

[1]Once again, this is a joke. For goodness sake don't go sticking your fingers (or any other parts of your anatomy) into a power outlet, because if you do you'll receive a nasty shock (Ho ho ho, shock, get it? ...... Oh well, be that way).

A semiconductor diode may be considered to be two-thirds of a transistor (or not, depending on your point of view).[2] When a diode is connected across two voltage sources such that its *anode* terminal is at a more positive (+ve) potential than its *cathode* terminal (Figure 5.2b), then the diode will conduct and current will flow. But, if the diode's anode is at a more negative (-ve) potential than its cathode (Figure 5.2c), then the diode will prevent current from flowing.

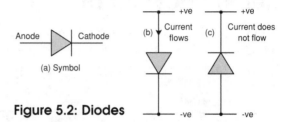

(a) Symbol

Figure 5.2: Diodes

Generally speaking we can consider electricity as consisting of vast herds of electrons migrating from one place to another, while electronics is the art of controlling these herds: starting them, stopping them, telling them where they can roam, and instructing them what to do when they eventually get where they're going. The point is that electrons are negative, and they actually flow from a more negative source to a more positive target, but Figure 5.2b showed the current as flowing from +ve to -ve, a conundrum indeed!

The reason for this inconsistency is that electricity was discovered long before it was fully understood. Ancient artifacts in the form of clay pots lined with copper and with carbon rods inserted in their necks are said to have been discovered at archeological sites in Egypt. If so, then these pots could conceivably have acted as batteries,[3] yet it wasn't until the early part of the 20th Century that George Thomson actually proved the existence of electrons at the University of Aberdeen in Scotland. The men and women who established the original theories about electricity had to make decisions about things that they didn't fully understand (so what else is new?), and the direction in which current actually flows is one such example. For a variety of reasons (including a number of theological and philosophical arguments), it was originally believed that current flowed from positive to negative. By the time the grim, unwashed truth was discovered it was too late to change all of the text books! As you may imagine, this inconsistency can, and does, cause endless problems for the unwary.[4]

---

[2] Ha! Let the pedantic university professors argue with that sentence (he said bitterly).
[3] Some people believe that the ancient Egyptians used these batteries to electroplate things, while others say that the whole idea of them having batteries is a load of rubbish.
[4] Not the least that different branches of engineering may indicate current as flowing in either the classical or the actual sense. Also different countries have adopted one direction or the other as their standard.

However, once again we have digressed. Scientists discovered that by introducing extremely thin layers of esoteric materials into diodes during their construction, they could be made to emit light when they were conducting (Figure 5.3). Depending on the materials used, it is possible to create LEDs that emit red, green, yellow, orange, and, most recently, blue light. The red ones are the cheapest and the easiest to make, which is why all of the original calculators and digital watches used them, while the blue ones are comparatively rare and expensive. Unlike incandescent bulbs,

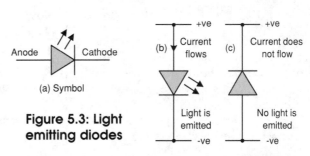

Figure 5.3: Light emitting diodes

which are power-hungry and tend to have relatively limited life-spans, LEDs are very energy-efficient and exceptionally durable. In fact the authors once saw an advertisement stating that a particular product's LEDs would last for 80,000 years.[5] However, claims like this should be taken with a pinch of salt, not the least that the average life-span of any article in an environment that contains small children (which includes the entire planet Earth) is typically measured in hours if you're lucky.

For the sake of simplicity, Figure 5.3 shows the LEDs as being connected directly across the power lines. A more usual arrangement would include a resistor in series with each diode in order to limit the amount of current that can pass through them. However, if you've got more money than sense, it is possible to obtain LEDs that contain their own current regulating circuits, and we're nominally using this type here. But should you actually decide to play with real LEDs at any stage, then we would suggest that you refer to any basic electronics "cookbook," which will describe how to calculate the value of the current-limiting resistor.

8-Bit LED displays

As we previously noted in Chapter 2, rather than thinking in terms of voltage levels or labels such as OFF and ON, we generally use the more abstract concepts of *logic 0* and *logic 1* when dealing with the logic gates inside a computer. However, when we interface a computer to the outside world, it once again becomes necessary to view signals as real voltage

---

[5]You could presumably ask for your money back if they failed after only 75,000 years!

On February 9, 1907 a letter from Mr. H.J. Round of New York, NY, was published in *Electrical World* magazine as follows:

A Note on Carborundum

To the Editors of Electrical World:

Sirs: –During an investigation of the unsymmetrical passage of current through a contact of carborundum and other substances a curious phenomenon was noted. On applying a potential of 10 volts between two points on a crystal of carborundum, the crystal gave out a yellowish light.

Mr. Round went on to note that some crystals gave out green, orange, or blue light. This is quite possibly the first documented reference to the effect upon which LEDs are based.

values. On this basis, and because these are reasonably common, we will assume that our *logic 0* and *logic 1* values actually equate to 0 volts and +5 volts, respectively.

Now sit up, straighten your back, chest out, stomach in, breath deeply, and pay attention, because although this next bit is really quite simple, by Murphy's Law it also manages to be tortuously tricky at the same time. Our computer "talks" to the outside world via its output ports.[6] Consider some of the ways in which a single bit of one of these ports might be connected to one or more LEDs (Figure 5.4).

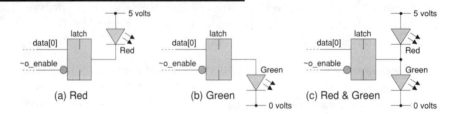

(a) Red   (b) Green   (c) Red & Green

Figure 5.4: Connecting LEDs to an outport port

In all three cases we're considering the same bit of the port; that is, the output from the latch that's connected to the **data[0]** signal on the computer's data bus. In the first example (Figure 5.4a), we've connected a red LED between the output from the latch and +5 volts. The way in which we've connected this LED means that when the latch is driving a *logic 0* (0 volts), the diode's anode will be at +5 volts, its cathode will be at 0 volts, and the diode will be turned on and glow red. However, when the latch is driving a *logic 1* (+5 volts), both of the diode's terminals will be at the same potential, so nothing will happen and the diode will be turned off. Note that if this diode had been flipped over such that it's anode were connected to the latch's output and its cathode were connected to +5 volts, then it would never turn on (remember that diodes only conduct in one direction).

---

[6]Output ports were introduced in Chapter 2

Similarly, in the second example (Figure 5.4b), we've connected a green LED between the output from the latch and 0 volts. The way in which we've connected *this* LED means that when the latch is driving a *logic 1*, the diode's anode will be at +5 volts, its cathode will be at 0 volts, and the diode will be turned on and glow green. However, when the latch is driving a *logic 0*, both of the diode's terminals will be at the same potential, so nothing will happen and the diode will be turned off.

Finally, in the third example (Figure 5.4c), we've attached both red and green diodes to the latch's output. In this case a *logic 0* in the latch will turn the red diode ON and the green diode OFF, while a *logic 1* in

There's no particular reason why we used red and green LEDs where we did; we could have swapped them over or even exchanged them for different colors (so long as we continued to observe the same polarity). It's simply that when we designed our output displays, we took a vote and decided that *logic 0s* and *logic 1s* would be represented by red and green, respectively. For those who are into this sort of thing, we should note that if the integrated circuit used for the output port were constructed using a technology called *transistor-transistor logic (TTL)*, then only the red LEDs in Figure 5.3 would work. This is because TTL can't output a *logic 1* that's strong enough to drive a LED (the green LEDs in this case). However, we're assuming that our output port is constructed using another very common integrated circuit technology called *complementary metal-oxide semiconductor (CMOS)*, which *is* capable of driving both the red and green LEDs as shown.

the latch will turn the green diode ON and the red diode OFF. Returning to our 8-bit display, we're assuming that each of the output port's eight bits have both red and green LEDs attached to them. As the red LEDs have their anode terminals connected together, they are said to be in a *common anode* configuration. Similarly, the green LEDs have their cathode terminals connected together, so they are said to be in a *common cathode* configuration (Figure 5.5).

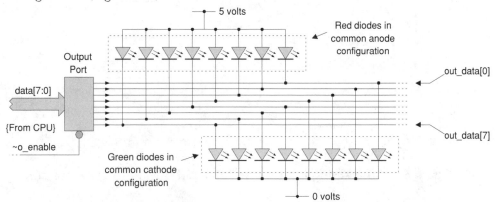

Figure 5.5: Common anode and common cathode configurations

For the purposes of our 8-bit display, we're assuming that each bit on the actual display panel consists of its associated green and red LEDs mounted together under a shared transparent plastic "window."

8-Bit switch devices

In the previous laboratory we also introduced an 8-bit switch input device (Figure 5.6). As we're going to be using the same input device in this laboratory, it will be advantageous if we understand a little more about the way in which it works.

Figure 5.6: A simple 8-bit switch input device

Once again, because we're using these switches to interface the computer to the outside world, it's necessary to view any signals as real voltage values. To be consistent with our earlier discussions, we will continue to assume that our abstract *logic 0* and *logic 1* values equate to 0 volts and +5 volts, respectively. Fortunately this device is quite simple; each switch has one terminal connected directly to a *logic 1*, while its other terminal is connected to a resistor, which is, in turn, connected to a *logic 0*. Each bit on the input port is connected to a point between a switch and its associated resistor (Figure 5.7).

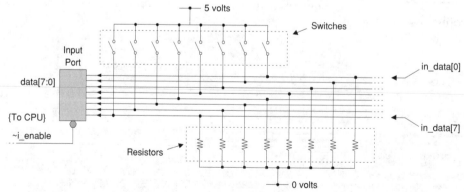

Figure 5.7: Connecting the 8-bit switch input device to the input port

When a switch is OPEN, its corresponding resistor pulls the wire connected to the input port down to *logic 0* (0 volts), but when the switch is CLOSED, it overrides the resistor and connects that bit of the input port directly to *logic 1* (+5 volts). (Had we wished to, we could have easily have reversed the positions of the switches and resistors, in which case a CLOSED switch would have equated to a *logic 0* and an OPEN switch to a *logic 1*.)

Note that this circuit diagram does not give any indication as to how the physical positions of the switches correspond to OPEN or CLOSED. In the case of our input device, we decided that a switch in the DOWN position would be OPEN (*logic 0*) and a switch in the UP position would be CLOSED (*logic 1*). Also note that this relationship was based on a purely arbitrary value judgment with no merit whatsoever, which is that light switches in America tend to follow the convention: UP = CLOSED = light is ON, while DOWN = OPEN = light is OFF.[7]

However, be warned that while the terms UP and DOWN do have some meaning for us (in the case of this particular input device), the terms ON and OFF are much trickier customers. The only thing we are really in a position to say is that, if things are indeed connected together and are physically oriented as we described them to be in the discussions above, then a switch that is DOWN is OPEN and represents a *logic 0*, while a switch that is UP is CLOSED and represents a *logic 1*. The point is that it's up to us (and the computer programs we write) to decide whether a *logic 0* means OFF and a *logic 1* means ON, or vice versa. In fact we can change our minds "on the fly" as often as we like, although we tend to try to avoid doing this sort of thing in order to hold onto what little sanity we have left!

Winding up the *Beboputer*

Armed with our new understanding of the 8-bit LED display and the 8-bit switch panel, let's plunge into the laboratory that will eventually lead us to 7-segment displays, which are, after all, what this chapter is supposed to be about. Make sure that the *Beboputer* CD is in the appropriate drive in your computer and summon the *Beboputer*. Once the *Beboputer*'s project window has opened, click the File item on its menu bar, click the Open Project entry in the resulting pull-down menu, then select the Lab 3 project from the ensuing dialog. This will invoke the third lab (Figure 5.8).

---

[7]Light switches tend to work the opposite way around in Great Britain, and you take your chances in the rest of the world.

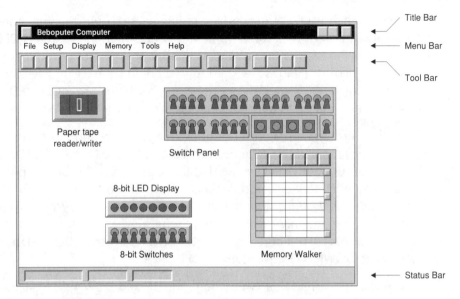

Figure 5.8: The _Beboputer_ project window for Lab 3

Once again, the main display panel (not shown here) also arrives on the screen, because it's intimately related to the switch panel; but we don't need the display panel for this lab, so dismiss it by clicking the exit button on its title bar. To kick-off the laboratory we're going to load the program that you saved on your virtual paper tape in the previous chapter. First click the ON/OFF switch on the main switch panel to power-up the _Beboputer_.

Figure 5.9: Start address of paper tape reader subroutine

Next set the address switches on the main switch panel to point to start address of our paper tape reader subroutine at $0050 (Figure 5.9).

Now click the switch panel's Run button. This opens up the usual dialog window prompting you to enter the name of the paper tape you wish to load. Click on mytape1, or whatever name you gave your program in the previous chapter (if you skipped the previous chapter or simply didn't bother to save your program, then click on the lab3_p1 entry, which is a paper tape that we previously created for you). Finally, click the dialog's Open button, which causes the main monitor program to enter the _run mode_ and to hand control over to the paper tape reader subroutine.

In turn, this subroutine reads the data, one byte at a time, from an input port that's connected to the paper tape reader. Every time the subroutine reads a byte from the input port, it copies that byte into the next free location in the RAM. As usual, once the subroutine has copied all of the bytes from the paper tape into the RAM, it returns control to the main monitor program and exits stage left.

As you may recall, our program performs an endless loop, reading the state of the switches on the 8-bit input device and writing this value to the 8-bit LED display. The flowchart for this program, along with its associated opcodes and data bytes, is shown once more in Figure 5.10.

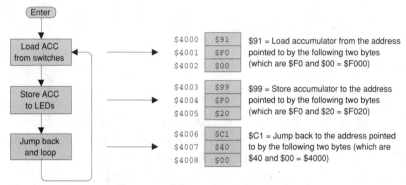

Figure 5.10: Load and store program

From the flowchart we see that the $91 opcode at address $4000 instructs the CPU to load the accumulator with whatever value is represented by the 8-bit switch input device. The $99 opcode at address $4003 instructs the CPU to copy the contents of the accumulator to the 8-bit display. Finally, the $C1 opcode at address $4006 instructs the CPU to jump back to the start of the loop, from whence it will proceed to do the whole thing all over again.

To remind yourself as to how this program actually performs, set the address switches on the main switch panel to point to our program's start address of $4000 (Figure 5.11) and click on the Run button. Play around for a while toggling the switches on the 8-bit switch panel and watching the 8-bit display respond. When you're ready to proceed further, click on the main switch panel's Reset button to return the *Beboputer* to its *reset mode*.

Figure 5.11: Start address

Undecoded 7-segment displays

Although the 8-bit displays that we've been using thus far can be very useful, we would sometimes prefer to see information displayed in a more human-readable form. In fact, by discarding our red LEDs and manipulating our existing green LEDs in a very rudimentary way, we can come up with a very useful device called an undecoded 7-segment display (Figure 5.12).

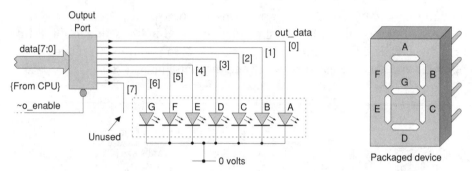

Figure 5.12: Undecoded 7-segment display

The LEDs forming this device are encapsulated in a common package (similar to an integrated circuit package) that can be attached to a display panel or a circuit board. The LEDs are arranged as segments and only seven are required, which is why we call this a 7-segment display.[8] In this example the package would only require eight pins, one for each of the LEDs and a common pin connected to *logic 0* (0 volts). The package's actual pin numbers are irrelevant to us, so long as we connect the pin associated with LED 'A' to out_data[0], the pin associated with LED 'B' to out_data[1], and so forth.

By some outrageous stroke of good fortune, we happen to have just such a display available for the *Beboputer*. To access this display, click the Setup item on the project window's menu bar and then click the Output Ports entry in the resulting pull-down menu. This will invoke the same dialog window that we used in the previous chapter. Note that the buttons associated with Port 0 and Port 10 are already turned on; these correspond to the 8-bit display and the paper tape reader. Don't disturb either of these buttons, because we'll be using both of these devices later. Instead, click the button associated with Port 1 to open our undecoded 7-segment display, then click on the Dismiss button to dismiss the Output Ports dialog window.

Use your mouse to drag the 7-segment display by its title bar and place it just above the 8-bit display. Next we need to modify our program such that, instead of it writing to the 8-bit display, it now writes to our new 7-segment display. This is quite simple, because all we need to do is to modify the address used by the store instruction (Figure 5.13).

---

[8]Had we wished, the unused bit from the output port could have been employed to drive an additional LED on the display, which could have been used to represent a decimal point.

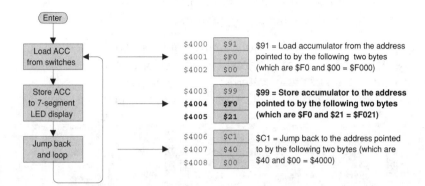

Figure 5.13: Modified load and store program

Actually, the original data stored at addresses $4004 and $4005 was $F0 and $20, respectively. Combined, these gave $F020, which is the address of output port 0 (the one connected to the 8-bit display). As it happens, the address of output port 1 (the one connected to the undecoded 7-segment display) is $F021, so all we really need to do is to modify the data stored at address $4005 from $20 to $21.

One way to modify this data would be to use the switch panel as described in Chapter 3, but we don't want to make you suffer unduly, so we've provided you with a short cut. Simply double-click on the data entry ($20) associated with address $4005 in the memory walker. This entry highlights to indicate that it's ready for editing, so use the keyboard to enter the new data of $21. Yes, it's true, you can use the memory walker to enter or modify programs!

Beware! As soon as you begin to modify the data in the memory walker, a pencil icon appears in the extreme left column associated with address $4005. This icon indicates that you're in the edit mode, but that your new data has not yet been accepted. Due to the way in which the memory walker functions, you have to click your mouse on another row in the display to cause it to accept your new data (or press the <Enter> key on your real computer's keyboard), at which point the pencil icon will disappear.

Now ensure that the address switches on the main switch panel still represent address $4000, click on the switch panel's Run button to set the *Beboputer* going, and play with the switches on the 8-bit panel to build up patterns on the undecoded 7-segment display. Note that only the right-hand seven switches have any effect, because this display only has seven segments, which means that the output port bit corresponding to the most-significant switch isn't connected to anything.

As the display contains seven individually-controllable segments, you can compose 2^7 = 128 different patterns! However, for our purposes we're only interested in sixteen of these patterns; the ones that we can use to represent the hexadecimal digits 0 through 9 and A through F (Figure 5.14).

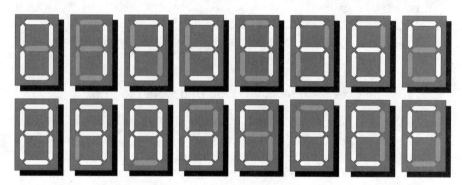

Figure 5.14: Generating hex digits with the undecoded 7-segment display

Use the switches to create at least a couple of these hexadecimal digits, then, when you've had as much fun as you can handle in one sitting, click on the main switch panel's **Reset** button to once again return the *Beboputer* to its *reset mode*.

Note that the hexadecimal digits 'b' and 'd' have to be displayed as lowercase characters in this type of display, because an upper case 'B' would be identical to the number '8', while an uppercase 'D' would be indistinguishable from the number '0'. It's also really easy to confuse the letter 'b' with the number '6' (as you will no doubt learn to your cost in the not-so-distant future). More sophisticated displays are available that allow you to adequately represent all of the letters of the alphabet, but they require more segments (and therefore more output port bits to control them) and are more expensive. Also, we don't usually need to display all of the letters of the alphabet on pocket calculators and related devices, so such products commonly employ basic 7-segment displays similar to those described here.

While you were playing with the 8-bit switches and observing the 7-segment display's response, you should have noticed that our original 8-bit display retained the last pattern the *Beboputer* wrote to it before you modified the program. This is because our new program only updates the 7-segment display, but it would be advantageous for us to be able to compare the two displays, so we need to upgrade our program such that it will output data to both of them. To persuade our program to write to both displays we need to add a second *store* instruction (Figure 5.15).

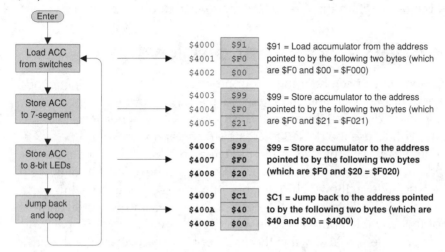

Figure 5.15: Modified program that writes to two displays

As we see, this is very similar to our previous program, with the addition of the three extra bytes required to implement the store instruction for our 8-bit display. However, although we only wish to add three bytes, one problem that immediately becomes apparent is that these new bytes occupy addresses $4006 through $4008, which were originally occupied by the jump instruction. This means that we've actually got to enter six bytes, the three new bytes for the second store instruction, followed by the three original bytes for the jump instruction, where this latter trio have to be relocated to addresses $4009 through $400B. In later chapters we'll consider some alternative techniques for creating programs that will alleviate this problem, but we'll just have to "bite the bullet" for now and do it by hand.

Use your new-found ability to directly edit data values using the memory walker to modify the values associated with addresses $4006 through $400B such that they match those shown in Figure 5.15. Remember that after you've entered the final value, you still have to click your mouse on another row in the display, thereby forcing it to accept the last piece of data and make the pencil icon disappear.

Once you've modified the program, ensure that the address switches on the main switch panel still represent address $4000, click the switch panel's Run button, and then play around with the 8-bit switch panel again.

As you'll see, the program now writes to both of the displays, which makes it a little easier to visualize what's happening behind the scenes. When you're ready to move on to the next exercise, click the main switch panel's **Reset** button to return the *Beboputer* to its *reset mode*.

Decoded 7-segment displays

The reason we've been referring to our new output device as an <u>undecoded</u> 7-segment display is that each LED in the packaged device required a separate bit to drive it. However, this isn't tremendously efficient unless we actually wish to use the device to create strange and wonderful (non-numerical) patterns. In addition to tying up a lot of the output port's bits, whenever we required a program to display a hexadecimal digit we'd have to specify exactly which segments (output bits) should be set to *logic 0s* and *logic 1s* to create the desired pattern. Even if we used some form of lookup table approach, this would still be something of a pain. A better alternative is to use a slightly more sophisticated version of the device called a <u>decoded</u> 7-segment display (Figure 5.16).

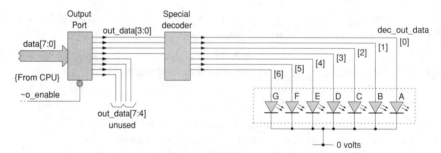

Figure 5.16: Decoded 7-segment LED display

As usual this really isn't as complicated as it might first appear. From our discussions in Chapter 2 we know that any four bits (such as the four least-significant bits from the output port, out_data[3:0]), can assume 2^4 = 16 different patterns of *logic 0s* and *logic 1s*. We can use these patterns to drive a special decoder device, which, in turn, drives the 7-segment display. When any of the sixteen binary patterns are presented to the decoder's inputs, it generates the appropriate signals on its **dec_out_data[6:0]** outputs, and these signals are used to drive the seven segment display in such a way as to present the appropriate hexadecimal digit (Figure 5.17).

out_data[3:0]	Hex	dec_out_data[6:0]
0 0 0 0	0	0 1 1 1 1 1 1
0 0 0 1	1	0 0 0 0 1 1 0
0 0 1 0	2	1 0 1 1 0 1 1
0 0 1 1	3	1 0 0 1 1 1 1
0 1 0 0	4	1 1 0 0 1 1 0
0 1 0 1	5	1 1 0 1 1 0 1
0 1 1 0	6	1 1 1 1 1 0 1
0 1 1 1	7	0 1 0 0 1 1 1
1 0 0 0	8	1 1 1 1 1 1 1
1 0 0 1	9	1 1 0 0 1 1 1
1 0 1 0	A	1 1 1 0 1 1 1
1 0 1 1	B	1 1 1 1 1 0 0
1 1 0 0	C	0 1 1 1 0 0 1
1 1 0 1	D	1 0 1 1 1 1 0
1 1 1 0	E	1 1 1 1 0 0 1
1 1 1 1	F	1 1 1 0 0 0 1

Figure 5.17: Decoder truth table

Note that we've been assuming that the LEDs in our 7-segment displays are connected in a *common cathode* configuration, but *common anode* configurations are also available. If we did happen to be using a common anode device, then we could still obtain the required results by simply inverting all of the *logic 0s* and *logic 1s* on the decoder's outputs.

Using the truth table in Figure 5.17, it would be quite a simple task to extract the Boolean equations for the decoder, and then to implement it using a couple of handfuls of primitive logic gates (which are introduced in the next chapter).[9] In fact it's possible to obtain a decoder such as this in the form of a special integrated circuit. Alternatively, the decoder logic could be bundled up inside the 7-segment display's package. In this latter case the display would be referred to as a decoded 7-segment display.

As usual, we just happen to have a decoded 7-segment display for you to play with. To access this display, click the **Setup** item on the project window's menu bar followed by the **Output Ports** entry in the resulting pull-down menu. This will invoke the same dialog window that you used earlier. Next click the button associated with **Port 1** to close the undecoded 7-segment display we've just been playing with, then click the button associated with **Port 2** to open our new decoded 7-segment display, and finally click the **Dismiss** button to close the **Output Ports** dialog window.

Once again, use your mouse to drag the decoded 7-segment display by its title bar and place it just above the 8-bit display. Of course, we now need to modify our program such that it writes to the appropriate output port for our new display, but this really is a "no-brainer." If you glance back to Figure 5.15, you'll see that it's only necessary to modify the data at address $4005 from its current contents of $21 to its new contents of $22, and we can quickly do this using the memory walker. Double-click the $21 data

---

[9]Extracting Boolean equations from truth tables is discussed in this book's companion volume, *Bebop to the Boolean Boogie (An Unconventional Guide to Electronics)*.

entry associated with address $4005 in the memory walker, enter the new value of $22, and click another row in the memory walker to make it accept the new data.

Ensure that the address switches on the main switch panel still represent address $4000, click on the switch panel's Run button, then play around with the 8-bit switch input device for a while. Use the truth table in Figure 5.17 to confirm that the right-hand four switches (and the associated bits on the 8-bit display) correspond to the hexadecimal digits appearing on the decoded 7-segment display. Note that although the left-hand four switches do modify their associated bits on the 8-bit display, they don't affect the 7-segment display (for reasons that are pretty obvious if you refer back to Figure 5.16). When you're ready to proceed to the next part of this laboratory, click the main switch panel's Reset button to return the *Beboputer* to its *reset mode*.

Dual decoded 7-segment displays

We're almost done, but there's just one more experiment we need to perform before we move onwards and upwards to new wonders and delights. As we have already discovered, using a decoded 7-segment display makes our lives a lot easier, because our 4-bit binary codes are automatically converted into the appropriate hexadecimal patterns. Also, we've only used four bits of our output port, so we've still got another four bits available to us, which means that the next obvious step would be to plug a brace of decoded 7-segment displays into the port (Figure 5.18).

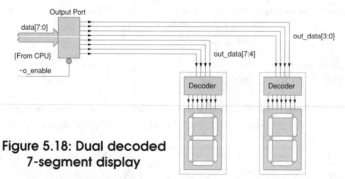

Figure 5.18: Dual decoded 7-segment display

By now it should not come as an outrageous surprise to find that we have a dual decoded 7-segment display cunningly hiding up our sleeves. You know what to do ...... click the Setup item on the project window's menu bar followed by the Output Ports entry in the resulting pull-down menu. Next click the button associated with Port 2 to close the 7-segment display we've just been playing with, then click the button associated with Port 3 to open our new dual decoded 7-segment display, then click the Dismiss button to close the Output Ports dialog window.

As per usual, use your mouse to drag the dual decoded 7-segment display by its title bar and position it just above the 8-bit display. Also, we now need to modify our program so that it writes to the appropriate output port for our new display. Once again, it's only necessary to modify the data at address $4005 from its current contents of $22 to its new contents of $23. Double-click on the $22 data entry associated with address $4005 in the memory walker, enter the new value of $23, and click another row in the display to make it accept the new data.

Ensure that the address switches on the main switch panel still represent address $4000, click the switch panel's Run button to instruct the *Beboputer* to execute our program, and play around with the 8-bit switch input device for a while. When you're ready to proceed to the last part of this laboratory, click the main switch panel's Reset button to return the *Beboputer* to its *reset mode*.

We really are just about done ...... honest. If you cast your mind back to Chapter 3, you'll remember that we used a program that looped around incrementing the accumulator and displaying the result. For your delectation and delight, we've created a modified version of that program to drive the dual decoded 7-segment display.

Set the address switches on the main switch panel to point to the start address of our paper tape reader subroutine at $0050 (Figure 5.19). Now click the switch panel's Run button, which opens the usual dialog window prompting you to enter the name of the tape you wish to load. Select the lab3_p6 entry, which is the name of a paper tape we've already created for you, then click the dialog's Open button to load the new program into the *Beboputer*'s memory. As you'll see, this program only comprises five instructions (Figure 5.20).

Figure 5.19: Start address of paper tape reader subroutine

At this stage in the game our new program should require relatively little explanation. The first instruction at address $4000 loads the accumulator with zero; the second and third instructions at $4002 and $4005 store the contents of the accumulator to the dual 7-segment and 8-bit displays, respectively; the fourth instruction at $4008 increments the contents of the accumulator; and the fifth instruction at $4009 causes the program to jump back to the first store instruction in the loop.

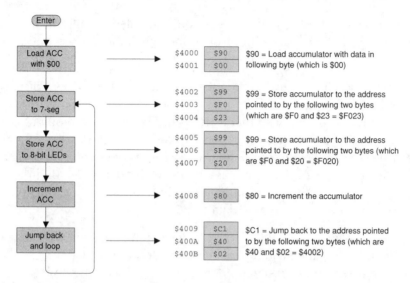

Figure 5.20: New increment accumulator program

Modify the address switches on the main switch panel such that they represent address $4000, click the switch panel's Run button, and watch the two displays counting up (each in their own way) from $00 to $FF. Remember that when the count reaches $FF, the next increment instruction will cause the accumulator to overflow and to roll around to $00 again. Also remember that if the display is counting too fast, you can modify the speed of the *Beboputer's* system clock as discussed in the previous chapter.

And finally, you may wish to bid a fond farewell to the main switch panel and the paper tape reader, because we're soon to discover more sophisticated ways of doing things. So, with tears rolling down your cheeks, power-down the *Beboputer* by clicking the ON/OFF switch on the main switch panel, then exit this laboratory by clicking the File item on the project window's menu bar followed by the Exit entry in the resulting pull-down menu.

Quick quiz #5

1) What is the average life span of any electronic product in an environment containing small children?

2) What are diodes and what do they do?

3) What is the main difference between standard diodes and LEDs?

4) What are the main differences between incandescent light bulbs and LEDs?

5) Why did early digital calculators and watches use red LEDs as opposed to other colors?

6) In the case of our simple 8-bit displays, why did we use red and green LEDs to represent *logic 0* and *logic 1* values respectively?

7) Are 7-segment displays always preferable to simple 8-bit displays?

8) What do the terms "common anode" and "common cathode" mean in the context of diodes?

9) The single decoded 7-segment display we used in this lab was said to be based on a common cathode configuration; hence the truth table shown in Figure 5.17. Create the corresponding truth table for a single decoded 7-segment display based on a common anode configuration.

10) What are the relative advantages and disadvantages of undecoded and decoded 7-segment displays?

Chapter 6

Primitive Logic Gates

In this chapter we will discover:

NOT gates

AND, OR, and XNOR gates

NAND, NOR, and XNOR gates

Tri-state gates and bi-directional buffers

How to use primitive gates to build other functions

The difference between combinational and sequential functions

Contents of Chapter 6

Are the hairs on the back of your neck starting to quiver?

Previously we noted that digital computers are essentially comprised of a large number of transistor-based switches, which are connected together in such a way that they can perform logical and arithmetic functions. The problem is that a computer can contain a huge number of these switches, and comprehending the inner workings of a computer would be almost impossible if we were to continue to think of it in these terms. The solution is to view things at higher levels of abstraction, the first such level being a group of logical elements called *primitive logic gates*. Fairly soon we're going to plunge into the bowels of the computer's central processing unit (CPU), and having even a rudimentary understanding of what logic gates are and what they do will definitely help us on our way.

Several different families of transistors are available to designers and, although the actual implementations vary, each can be used to construct primitive logic gates. One transistor family is known as *metal-oxide semiconductor field-effect transistors (MOS FETs)*. This is a bit of a mouthful to say the least, so we'll try to avoid saying it again. The main point as far as we're concerned is that there are two basic flavors of these devices called PMOS and NMOS transistors. There are a number of ways in which these transistors can be used to create primitive logic gates, but one very common technique, referred to as *complementary metal-oxide semiconductor (CMOS)*, employs both PMOS and NMOS transistors connected together in a complementary manner.

If the hairs on the back of your neck are starting to quiver and you're beginning to break out into a cold sweat, then settle down and try to relax, because this is going to be a lot simpler than you fear. So make yourself comfortable, and we'll begin ......

NOT gates

As we've already mentioned, when dealing with logic gates inside a computer, rather than thinking in terms of voltage levels or in such terms as OFF and ON, we generally prefer the more abstract concepts of *logic 0* and *logic 1*. However, when we move to consider an actual implementation, it once again becomes necessary to view signals as real voltage values. On this basis, and because these are reasonably common, we will assume that our *logic 0* and *logic 1* values actually equate to 0 volts and +5 volts, respectively. Bearing this in mind, consider one of the simplest logic gates, which is called a NOT (Figure 6.1).

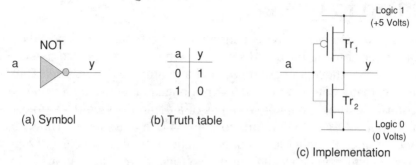

(a) Symbol   (b) Truth table   (c) Implementation

Figure 6.1: CMOS implementation of a NOT gate

In the case of the symbol (Figure 6.1a), the small circle on the output (referred to as a *bobble* or *bubble*) indicates that this is an inverting function. Associated with the symbol is a truth table (Figure 6.1b), which provides a convenient way to represent the function of this gate, which is that a *logic 0* presented to its input will cause the output to return a *logic 1*, and vice versa. Finally, it is only when we consider the actual implementation of the gate (Figure 6.1c) that we need to take any voltage levels into account.

The bobble on the control input of transistor Tr_1 indicates that this is a PMOS transistor. In the context of our implementation this transistor has an *active-low* control, which means that applying a *logic 0* to the control input turns the transistor **ON**, while a *logic 1* turns it **OFF**. By comparison, the lack of a bobble on the control input of transistor Tr_2 indicates that this is an NMOS transistor. In the context of our implementation this transistor has an *active-high* control, which means that applying a *logic 1* to the control input turns the transistor **ON**, while a *logic 0* turns it **OFF**.

Thus, when a *logic 0* is applied to input a, transistor Tr_1 is turned **ON** and transistor Tr_2 is turned **OFF**, which means that output y is connected to *logic 1* via Tr_1. Similarly, when a *logic 1* is applied to input a, transistor Tr_1 is turned **OFF** and transistor Tr_2 is turned **ON**, resulting in output y being connected to *logic 0* via Tr_2. It may help to visualize the operation of the NOT gate in terms of switches rather than transistors (Figure 6.2).

And it's as simple as that. The point is that instead of thinking in terms of transistors (or switches), it's a lot easier to think in terms of NOT gates and their bigger cousins, such as AND, OR, and XOR.

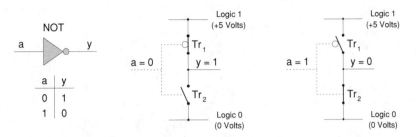

Figure 6.2: NOT gates's operation represented in terms of switches

AND, OR, and XOR gates

Although the NOT is the simplest of the primitive gates, the AND, OR, and XOR aren't tremendously more complicated (Figure 6.3).

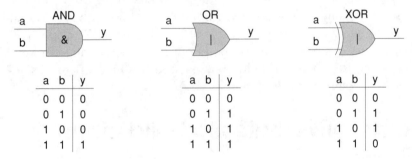

a	b	y
0	0	0
0	1	0
1	0	0
1	1	1

a	b	y
0	0	0
0	1	1
1	0	1
1	1	1

a	b	y
0	0	0
0	1	1
1	0	1
1	1	0

Figure 6.3: AND, OR and XOR gates

In the case of the AND, the output is only TRUE (*logic 1*) if both of the inputs are TRUE, otherwise the output is FALSE (*logic 0*); that is, the output y is TRUE if a AND b are TRUE. Similarly, in the case of the OR, the output y is TRUE if a OR b are TRUE. In fact the OR should more properly be referred to as an *inclusive-OR*, because its TRUE output cases <u>include</u> the case where both of the inputs are TRUE. Contrast this with the *exclusive-OR*, or XOR, in which the TRUE output cases <u>exclude</u> the case where both of the inputs are TRUE.

NAND, NOR, and XNOR gates

Now consider the effect or attaching a NOT gate to the output of an AND. Due to the fact that this combination occurs frequently in designs it is given its own symbol, along with the name NAND (NOT-AND); similarly for a NOR (NOT-OR) and an XNOR (exclusive-NOR) (Figure 6.4).

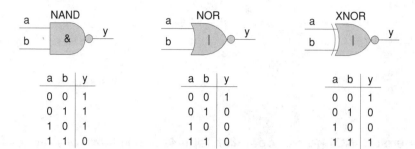

Figure 6.4: NAND, NOR, and XNOR gates

As usual, the bobbles on the symbols' outputs indicate inverting functions; one way to visualize this is that the symbol for the NOT gate has been forced back into the preceding symbol until only its bobble remains. Not surprisingly, the output from the NAND (as illustrated in its truth table) is the inverse, or negation, of the output from an AND. Similarly, the outputs from the NOR and XNOR are the inverse of the OR and XOR, respectively. Note that, for reasons beyond the scope of our discussions, the term XNOR (exclusive-NOR) is typically used in preference to NXOR (NOT-exclusive-OR); however, both terms are acceptable.

Using primitive gates to build other functions

It may surprise you to learn that, with few exceptions (such as the tri-state gates we'll discuss a little later on), the seven gates NOT, AND, OR, XOR, NAND, NOR, and XNOR are pretty much all you need to construct any digital system, up to and including a computer. In fact you could struggle along if all you had was a large bag of NANDs (or NORs), because you can finagle all of the other gates out of them using a few cunning tricks; for example, you can make a NAND perform the duties of a NOT by simply connecting both of its inputs together.

Now it is not the purpose of this book to teach the principles of digital electronics. However, the following notes illustrate a few of the more common functions that can be constructed using these primitive gates. This won't take long, but it will aid your understanding of some of the concepts we've already covered, and it will also help to clarify certain topics that will be hurling our way in future chapters.

Decoders

One function of interest is a decoder, which uses a binary value, or address, to select between a number of outputs, and then asserts the selected output by driving it to its active logic value. For example, consider a 2:4 (two-to-four) decoder (Figure 6.5).

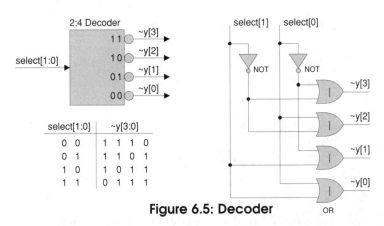

select[1:0]	~y[3:0]			
0 0	1	1	1	0
0 1	1	1	0	1
1 0	1	0	1	1
1 1	0	1	1	1

Figure 6.5: Decoder

The 00, 01, 10, and 11 annotations on the decoder symbol represent the various patterns of 0s and 1s that can be presented to the **select[1:0]** inputs, and are used to associate each input pattern with a particular output.

The truth table shows that when an output is selected it is asserted to a *logic 0* value (unselected outputs therefore assume *logic 1* values). Due to the fact that its outputs are asserted to *logic 0s*, this type of function is said to have *active-low* outputs (similar functions can be created with *active-high* outputs). The active-low nature of the outputs is also indicated by the bobbles on the symbol and the tilde characters in the names of the output signals.

For the purposes of these discussions we are not overly concerned with the method by which we extracted the Boolean (logic) equations from the truth table to obtain the actual logic gates used to implement this function,[1] but rather with the fact that only a few primitive gates are required to do the job. It would also be quite easy to create larger versions of this function, such as 3:8 (three-to-eight) or 4:16 (four-to-sixteen) decoders. In fact, you may recall that we used just such a 4:16 decoder to implement our memory address decoding in Chapter 2, while the special decoders used to drive our decoded 7-segment displays in Chapter 5 could be constructed using similar techniques.

---

[1]This is just one of a number of possible implementations.

Multiplexers

Another function of interest is a multiplexer, which uses a binary value, or address, to select between a number of inputs, and then conveys the data from the selected input to the output. For example, consider a 2:1 (two-to-one) multiplexer (Figure 6.6).

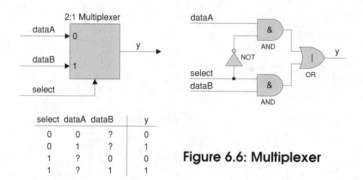

select	dataA	dataB	y
0	0	?	0
0	1	?	1
1	?	0	0
1	?	1	1

Figure 6.6: Multiplexer

The 0 and 1 annotations on the multiplexer symbol represent the values that can be presented to the **select** input, and are used to indicate which data input will be selected.

The ? characters in the truth table are used to indicate *don't care* values. When the **select** input is presented with a *logic 0*, the output from the multiplexer depends only on the value on **dataA**, and we don't care about the value on **dataB**. Similarly, when the **select** input is presented with a *logic 1*, the output from the multiplexer depends only on the value on **dataB**, and we don't care about the value on **dataA**.

As for the decoder, we are not particularly concerned with the way in which we extracted the Boolean equations from the truth table to obtain the actual logic gates used to implement the multiplexer,[2] but rather with the fact that only a few gates are necessary to perform the task. It would also be quite easy to create larger versions of this function, such as 4:1 (four-to-one) or 8:1 (eight-to-one) multiplexers. Although we haven't explicitly discussed any cases where we've used multiplexers thus far, you can bet your little cotton socks that we'll be tripping all over the little rascals in the not-so-distant future.

---

[2]This is just one of a number of possible implementations.

Latches and flip-flops

Digital logic functions may be categorized as being either *combinational* (otherwise called *combinatorial*) or *sequential*. In the case of a combinational function, the logic values at that function's outputs are directly related to the current <u>combination</u> of values on its inputs (decoders and multiplexers fall into this category). By comparison, the logic values on a sequential function's outputs depend not only on its current input values, but also on previous input values; that is, the output values depend on a <u>sequence</u> of input values.

The bottom line is that sequential functions can act as memory elements. Although there are many flavors of these functions, we shall concentrate our attentions on only two: D-type latches and D-type flip-flops (Figure 6.7).

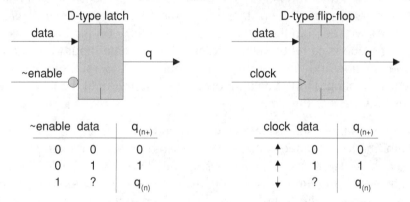

Figure 6.7: Latches and flip-flops

By convention the output from a latch or a flip-flop is named q (although the authors don't have the faintest clue why). The $q_{(n+)}$ labels in the truth tables indicate that these columns refer to future values on the outputs (the n+ subscripts represent some future time, or *now-plus*). Similarly, the $q_{(n)}$ output assignments indicate the current value on the outputs (the n subscripts represent the current time, or *now*). Thus, the last line in each of the truth tables indicates that, for these combinations of inputs, the future values on the outputs will be the same as their current values.

In the case of the D-type latch, the ~enable input is *level-sensitive*, which means that its effect on the function depends only on its current logic value or level, and is not directly related to that input transitioning from one logic value to another. Also, in this particular example, the ~enable input is *active-low*, as is indicated by the bobble on the symbol and the tilde character prefixing the signal's name. As usual the truth table offers a more complete description of the function's operation. When the ~enable input is in its active state (*logic 0*), any value on the data input will be propagated through the function to its output. Note that any changes on the data input will ripple through to the output so long as the ~enable input remains in its active state. Also, when the ~enable input returns to its inactive state (*logic 1*), the function will "remember" the last value on the data input, and will continue to present this value at its output. Alternative versions of the latch with *active-high* enable inputs can also be easily constructed.

In the case of the D-type flip-flop, the clock input is *edge-sensitive*, which means that it only affects the function when it transitions from one logic value to another. The fact that this input is edge-sensitive is indicated by the chevron (v-shape) on the symbol. In this particular example, the lack of a bobble on the symbol indicates that this clock input is sensitive to a *rising edge* (also referred to as a *positive edge*); that is, a transition from *logic 0* to *logic 1*. As we see from the truth table, a rising edge on the clock causes whatever value is currently being presented to the data input to be loaded into the function and to be propagated through to its output. Note that any subsequent changes to the data input will be ignored until the next active edge is presented to the clock.

In many ways these sequential functions aren't much more complex than the combinational functions that we considered earlier. For example, it is possible to construct a simple latch using only two NAND (or NOR) gates, while the latch and flip-flop shown here could be constructed using five and six gates, respectively.[3] On the other hand, due to the fact that sequential functions depend on outputs (or internal equivalents) being fed-back as internal inputs, these functions can require a little lateral thinking to tie them down. Fortunately we're not particularly interested with the actual implementation of these functions here; we just need a basic understanding as to what they can do. One example of the use of D-type flip-flops is provided by the CPU's *accumulator*, which we introduced in Chapters 3, 4, and 5, and these functions will be further explored in Chapter 8, when we start to plunge deeper into the nether regions of the CPU.

Tri-state gates

And finally (for the moment), we come to a special class of functions known as *tri-state gates*, whose outputs can adopt three values: *logic 0*, *logic 1*, and *logic Z* (hence the "tri-state" appellation). In fact all of the primitive

---

[3] It is also possible to "hand-craft" latches and flip-flops that require very few transistors.

gates discussed thus far can be constructed so as to support tri-statable outputs, but at this time we're only interested in a simple function called a *tri-state buffer* (Figure 6.8).

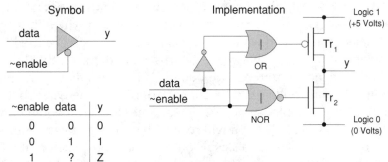

Figure 6.8: Tri-state buffer

This particular example has an active-low ~enable input, as is indicated by the bobble on the symbol and the tilde character in the signal's name (similar functions with active-high enable inputs are also easy to create).

When the ~enable input is in its active state (*logic 0*), any value on the data input will be propagated through the buffer to appear at its output. Note that any changes on the data signal will ripple through to the output so long as the ~enable input remains in its active state. However, when the ~enable input returns to its inactive state (*logic 1*), the output from the buffer will assume a *logic Z* value, irrespective of the value on the data input (which is why we use a ? character indicating *don't care* in the truth table for this case).

In fact a *logic Z* isn't a real value at all. Unlike *logic 0s* and *logic 1s*, which are ultimately related to real, physical voltage levels, a *logic Z* represents a condition known as *high-impedance*, in which the gate is effectively disconnected from its own output. When the ~enable input is presented with a *logic 1* (its inactive state), it causes the output of the OR gate to be forced to a *logic 1* and the output from the NOR gate to be forced to a *logic 0*, thereby turning both the Tr_1 and Tr_2 transistors OFF, respectively. With both of these transistors turned OFF, the output y is disconnected from the *logic 1* and *logic 0* voltage levels, and is therefore in the high impedance (*logic Z*) state.

By comparison, when the ~enable input is presented with a *logic 0* (its active state), the outputs of the OR and NOR gates are determined by the value on the data input. The circuit is arranged such that only one of the Tr_1 and Tr_2 transistors can be ON at any particular time. If the data input is presented with a *logic 0*, transistor Tr_2 is turned ON, thereby connecting the output y to *logic 0*. Similarly, if the data input is presented with a *logic 1*, transistor Tr_1 is turned ON, thereby connecting the output y to a *logic 1*.

As usual, don't worry if this all appears somewhat confusing at first. In reality we are not particularly concerned with the way in which these gates are constructed, but only in what they do and what they can be used for. The important point here is that when the tri-state buffer is disabled it is effectively disconnected from its own output. This means that the outputs from multiple tri-state buffers can be connected to the same wire, so long as only one of them is enabled at any particular time. In fact, if you return to our discussions in Chapter 2, you will realize that tri-state gates are used to buffer any device that can drive signals onto the *data bus*, such as the CPU, RAMs, ROMs, and input ports. The control signals generated by the CPU dictate which particular device is enabled (can "talk") at any particular time, while the rest of the devices are automatically disabled (forced to "listen").

Only one question remains. It is easy to see how tri-state buffers can be used by devices such as ROMs or input ports to allow them to drive signals onto the *data bus* or to isolate them from the bus. But what about devices such as RAMs or the CPU itself, which, in addition to being able to drive signals onto the *data bus*, also have to be capable of reading signals from the bus? The answer is to use two tri-state gates connected in a back-to-back configuration, thereby creating a *bidirectional buffer.* (Figure 6.9).

By disabling the output buffer and enabling the input buffer, the device can accept a signal from the *data bus* (this signal would then be used to drive other logic gates inside the device).

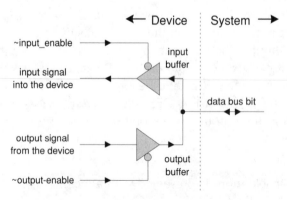

Figure 6.9: Bidirectional buffer

Similarly, by enabling the output buffer and disabling the input buffer, the device can drive a signal onto the *data bus* (this signal would then be acquired by whichever device the CPU decides should be in its listening mode).

If both the input and output buffers are disabled, then the device is effectively disconnected from the *data bus*; that is, it is neither "talking" or "listening." Finally we should observe that the bidirectional buffer illustrated in Figure 6.9 only applies to a single bit on the *data bus*. Remembering that our hypothetical system's *data bus* is eight bits wide, each device connected to the bus would require eight of these buffers. Note however that all eight of the ~input-enable signals (inside the device) would be connected together, and would be driven by a single control signal from the outside world (similarly for the ~output-enable signals).

Quick quiz #6

1) Why is it preferable to view digital logic in terms of primitive gates as opposed to transistors?

2) What does a NOT gate do and how does it do it?

3) What does a bobble on the output of the symbol for a primitive gate indicate?

4) What is the difference between an AND gate and a NAND gate?

5) Describe the similarities and differences between decoders and multiplexers.

6) Create the symbol and truth table for a 3:8 decoder with active-high outputs.

7) Describe the difference between combinational and sequential functions.

8) Create the symbols and truth tables for a D-type latch with an active-high enable and a D-type flip-flop with a negative-edge clock.

9) What is a tri-state buffer used for and what does a *logic Z* state represent?

10) Create symbols and truth tables for tri-statable OR and NOR gates.

For those who are interested and want to know more about logic gates, extracting and using Boolean equations, and seafood gumbo; these topics are presented in greater detail in this book's companion volume: *Bebop to the Boolean Boogie (An Unconventional Guide to Electronics)*. ISBN 1-878707-22-1

Chapter 7

Binary Arithmetic

In this chapter we will discover:

The difference between signed and
unsigned binary numbers

How to perform binary additions

How to use primitive logic gates to
construct an adder function

Nine's, ten's, one's, and two's
complement numbers

How to perform binary subtractions using
complement techniques

The ancient process called
"Casting out the nines"

Contents of Chapter 7

Cease your whimpering and whining

As fate would have it, we've arrived at the point in our discussions where we must consider the way in which a computer visualizes and manipulates numbers. Now settle down, wipe your nose, and cease your whimpering and whining, because there's simply no other way to proceed; if we don't tackle this subject and show it who's in charge here and now, then it will sneak up behind us while we're not looking and give us an unpleasant surprise. On the brighter side, we are only going to consider addition and subtraction in this chapter — we'll return to look at multiplication and division some way down the road.[1]

Unsigned binary numbers

Since digital computers are constructed from logic gates which can represent only two states, they are obliged to employ the binary number system, which provides only two digits: 0 and 1. Also, unlike calculations on paper in which both decimal and binary numbers can be of any size, numerical quantities within a computer have to be mapped onto a physical system of logic gates and wires. Thus the maximum value of an individual numerical quantity inside a computer is dictated by the width of the computer's *data bus*; that is, by the number of bits available to describe that value.

One way to represent such data is as *unsigned binary numbers*, which, as their name might suggest, can only be used to represent positive values. Consider the range of such numbers that can be represented using an 8-bit data bus (Figure 7.1).

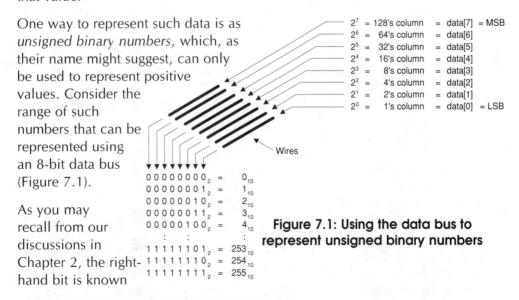

$$2^7 = 128\text{'s column} = \text{data[7]} = \text{MSB}$$
$$2^6 = 64\text{'s column} = \text{data[6]}$$
$$2^5 = 32\text{'s column} = \text{data[5]}$$
$$2^4 = 16\text{'s column} = \text{data[4]}$$
$$2^3 = 8\text{'s column} = \text{data[3]}$$
$$2^2 = 4\text{'s column} = \text{data[2]}$$
$$2^1 = 2\text{'s column} = \text{data[1]}$$
$$2^0 = 1\text{'s column} = \text{data[0]} = \text{LSB}$$

Wires

$$00000000_2 = 0_{10}$$
$$00000001_2 = 1_{10}$$
$$00000010_2 = 2_{10}$$
$$00000011_2 = 3_{10}$$
$$00000100_2 = 4_{10}$$
$$\vdots \qquad \vdots$$
$$11111101_2 = 253_{10}$$
$$11111110_2 = 254_{10}$$
$$11111111_2 = 255_{10}$$

Figure 7.1: Using the data bus to represent unsigned binary numbers

As you may recall from our discussions in Chapter 2, the right-hand bit is known

---

[1]Multiplication and division are discussed in Appendix G.

as the *least-significant bit (LSB)*, because it represents the least significant value. Similarly, the left-hand bit is known as the *most-significant bit (MSB)*, because it represents the most significant value. Also, as every bit can be individually assigned a value of 0 or 1, a group of eight bits can be assigned $2^8 = 256$ unique combinations of 0s and 1s, which means that an 8-bit unsigned binary number can be used to represent values in the range 0_{10} through $+255_{10}$.

Binary addition

Binary numbers may be added together using a process identical to that used for decimal addition. However, even though such additions are basically simple, they can prove confusing to a rookie, so we'll take things one step at a time. First of all, consider a series of simple one-digit additions using the decimal system with which we're all comfortable (Figure 7.2).

$$\begin{array}{rr} & 0 \\ + & 0 \\ \hline = & 0 \end{array} \qquad \begin{array}{rr} & 0 \\ + & 6 \\ \hline = & 6 \end{array} \qquad \begin{array}{rr} & 8 \\ + & 0 \\ \hline = & 8 \end{array} \qquad \begin{array}{rr} & 8 \\ + & 6 \\ \hline = & 14 \end{array}$$

Figure 7.2: Simple 1-digit decimal additions

As we would expect, there's nothing too surprising here. The only special case that has to be taken into account is when the result of an addition overflows the maximum value that can be stored in a decimal digit, which happens in the last example of 8 + 6.

In fact we're so familiar with the decimal system that you probably didn't even blink when you glanced at this case, but it's key to what is to come. One way to view this last example is to say it aloud in the way of students at school, which is: "*Eight plus six equals four, with one carried forward into the next column.*" Now hold this thought as we consider some one-digit additions in binary (Figure 7.3).

$$\begin{array}{rr} & 0 \\ + & 0 \\ \hline = & 0 \end{array} \qquad \begin{array}{rr} & 0 \\ + & 1 \\ \hline = & 1 \end{array} \qquad \begin{array}{rr} & 1 \\ + & 0 \\ \hline = & 1 \end{array} \qquad \begin{array}{rr} & 1 \\ + & 1 \\ \hline = & 10 \end{array}$$

Figure 7.3: Simple 1-digit binary additions

Note that since we explicitly stated that these *are* binary numbers, it is permissible to omit the customary '2' subscripts. The "odd man out" in this figure is the last example, which may have caused you to pause for thought, but which really isn't too different from its decimal equivalent. The point to remember is that a binary digit can only represent two values (0 and 1), which means that any result greater than 1 causes a carry into the next column. Thus, $1 + 1 = 10_2$ (where 10_2 in binary equals 2 in decimal); or, to put this another way: *"One plus one in binary equals zero, with one carried forward into the next column."*

Now consider what happens when we extend this concept to multi-digit binary numbers. Using the same technique that we'd employ for a decimal addition, the two least-significant bits are added together to give a sum and, possibly, a carry-out to the next stage. This process is repeated for the remaining bits progressing towards the most-significant. For each of these remaining bits there may be a carry-in from the previous stage and a carry-out to the next stage. To fully illustrate this process, consider the step-by-step addition of two 4-bit binary numbers (Figure 7.4).

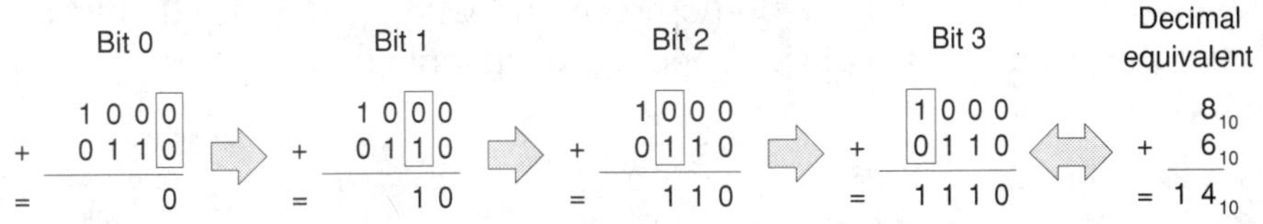

Figure 7.4: Simple 4-digit binary addition

Since we explicitly stated that there were *binary* additions, it behooves us to use subscripts in the case of the decimal equivalent. Just in case you're wondering, the reason why we're looking at 4-digit binary additions (as opposed to using 8 digits which is the width of our data bus) is simply that they're easier to illustrate and discuss. Also, as a point of interest, several early microprocessors and a lot of microcontrollers were based on 4-bit data busses (and some still are).

If you're having any difficulty relating binary values to their decimal equivalents, then you may wish to flick back to Chapter 2 (Figure 2.11) for a moment. In fact our first example wasn't too taxing, because each stage never involved more than a single '1' (bit 0 is $0 + 0 = 0$, bit 1 is $0 + 1 = 1$, bit 2 is $0 + 1 = 1$, and bit 3 is $1 + 0 = 1$). So if you're starting to feel a bit friskier about all of this, cast your twinkling orbs over a second example that's just a little more thought-provoking (Figure 7.5).

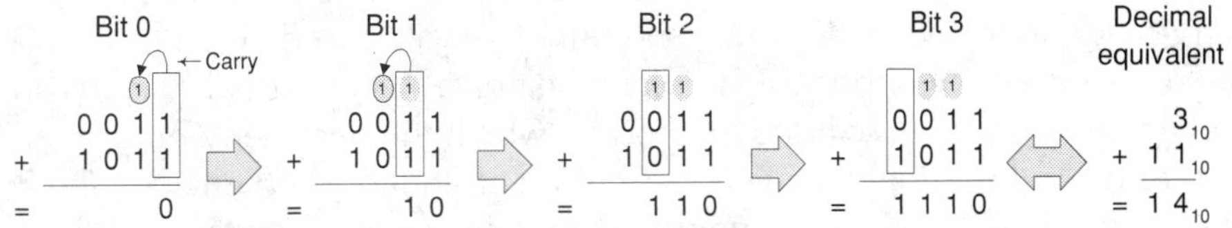

Figure 7.5: Another simple 4-digit binary addition

This example is of interest because certain bit positions require us to add multiple 1s together. In the case of bit 0 we add two 1s; that is, $1 + 1 = 10_2$ (where 10_2 in binary equals 2 in decimal); or, as we previously noted: *"One plus one in binary equals zero, with one carried forward into the next column."* But it's when we move to consider the bit 1 column that our eyes begin to glaze over, because here we have to add three 1s – the two original 1s from the numbers and the carry-in from the addition of bit 0. Thus, the addition for bit 1 is $1 + 1 + 1 = 11_2$ (where 11_2 in binary equals 3 in decimal); or, to put this another way: *"One plus one plus one in binary equals one, with one carried forward into the next column."* Life gets easier again when we move to bit 2, because even though we have a carry-in from the previous column, there aren't actually any 1s in the main numbers, so $1 + 0 + 0 = 1$. Finally, in the case of bit 3, we don't have a carry from the previous stage and we're back on home ground with $0 + 0 + 1 = 1$. Just to hammer the point home, consider one more example in this series (Figure 7.6).

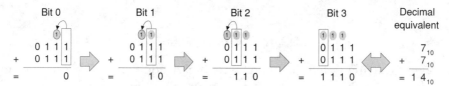

Figure 7.6: Yet another simple 4-digit binary addition

In this case we're really caught between a rock and a hard place, because the addition of each of the first three bit positions results in a carry to the next column (bit 0 is $0 + 1 + 1 = 10_2$, bit 1 is $1 + 1 + 1 = 11_2$, bit 2 is $1 + 1 + 1 = 11_2$, and bit 3 is $1 + 0 + 0 = 1$).

Now let's change direction slightly to consider how we might implement an addition function with our primitive logic gates. Our first task is to determine how to handle simple 1-digit additions. A designer might proceed to do this by (a) drawing a symbol, (b) writing out the truth table associated with the symbol, and (c) extracting the logical equations from the truth table and implementing them as primitive gates (Figure 7.7).

The signals cin and cout are common abbreviations for "carry-in" and "carry-out," respectively. As usual, the primitive gates used here illustrate only one of a variety of possible implementations. Also as usual, we are not overly concerned here with the method by which the designer would extract the Boolean (logic) equations from the truth table and decide which gates to use. In fact the only thing that we are interested in here is the way in which we can use primitive logic gates to perform arithmetic operations.

Let's extend this concept to perform 4-digit binary additions; for example, assume that we wish to add two 4-bit binary numbers called a[3:0] and b[3:0] (Figure 7.8).

One way to achieve this is to connect four of our 1-digit adders together in series. Note that we've connected the first digit's carry-in input to a *logic 0*, which means that this input doesn't have any effect on the result. Also note that we've rotated the symbols for the individual 1-digit adders and oriented them such that they match our earlier 4-digit addition examples. Glance back to the additions that we performed in Figures 7.4, 7.5, and 7.6, and imagine presenting the two numbers to

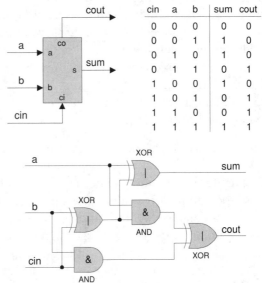

cin	a	b	sum	cout
0	0	0	0	0
0	0	1	1	0
0	1	0	1	0
0	1	1	0	1
1	0	0	1	0
1	0	1	0	1
1	1	0	0	1
1	1	1	1	1

Figure 7.7: Simple 1-digit binary adder

be added together to the a[3:0] and b[3:0] inputs of our adder function; the 4-bit result would eventually appear at the s[3:0] outputs. (For the moment we'll simply assume that the result on the carry-out output is discarded – we'll consider what we actually do with this signal in a little while.)

Also, don't forget that the only reason we're playing with 4-digit numbers here is because they're easier to describe and understand. In the case of our *Beboputer*, which has an 8-bit data bus, we would have to extend our adder to handle 8-digit numbers. Assuming the style of adder illustrated in Figure 7.8, this could be easily achieved by appending four more 1-digit adders onto the end of the chain.

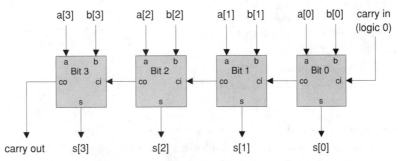

Figure 7.8: Simple 4-digit binary addition

This form of adder is known as a *ripple adder*, because the result ripples down through the chain. Consider what happens when we present two binary numbers to the a[3:0] and b[3:0] inputs. The bit 0 adder immediately starts to add a[0] and b[0], the bit 1 adder immediately starts to add a[1] and b[1], the bit 2 adder immediately starts to add a[2] and b[2], and the bit 3 adder immediately starts to add a[3] and b[3]. The problem is that the bit 1 adder cannot generate the correct result until the bit 0 adder has finished its calculation and generated its carry-out signal. Similarly, the bit 2 adder has to wait for the bit 1 adder to finish *its* calculation and generate *its* carry-out signal, and so on down the line.

Thus, the s[1], s[2], and s[3] outputs may toggle backwards and forwards between *logic 0* and *logic 1* for a while as the intermediate carry signals propagate through the chain. The end result is that, even though adders of this type can perform calculations in a few millionths of a second, they remain relatively slow in computer terms and their delay increases as more stages are added. (We could redesign our adder using additional logic gates such that it generated the result for all four bits simultaneously, but this is beyond the scope of this book.) Now bearing in mind what we've just learned, let's consider one final 4-digit binary addition (Figure 7.9).

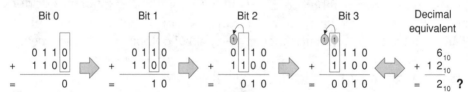

Figure 7.9: One final 4-digit binary addition

Arrggghh! How can this be? How can the result of adding six and twelve equal two? The problem is that, although the result should actually be eighteen, four bits can only carry $2^4 = 16$ different patterns of 0s and 1s, so our 4-bit result can only represent unsigned binary numbers in the range 0_{10} through 15_{10}. This is illustrated in Figure 7.9 by the fact that there's nowhere to stick the carry-out from the bit 3 addition.

However, remembering that our logic-gate implementation of an adder had a carry-out output, then we might be able to get things back on track if we could somehow make use of this signal (Figure 7.10).

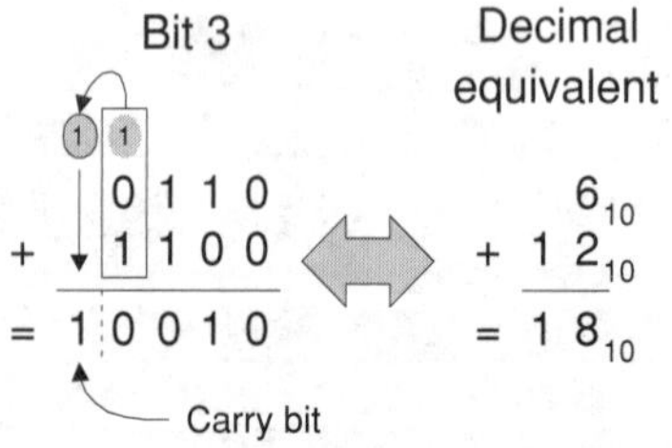

We previously observed that, although the maximum value of an individual numerical quantity is dictated by the width of the

Bit 3   Decimal
equivalent

$$
\begin{array}{r}
0\ 1\ 1\ 0 \\
+\ 1\ 1\ 0\ 0 \\
\hline
=\ 1\ 0\ 0\ 1\ 0
\end{array}
\qquad
\begin{array}{r}
6_{10} \\
+\ 1\ 2_{10} \\
\hline
=\ 1\ 8_{10}
\end{array}
$$

Carry bit

Figure 7.10: The carry bit

binary field used to represent it, it's possible to play cunning tricks which allow us to represent numbers of any size. Well, this is where we'll begin to reveal some of these tricks. The first thing to note is that there's simply no way to make a 4-bit quantity hold more than sixteen different binary patterns, so the obvious solution is to use more bits. But we can't simply keep on increasing the width of our computer's data bus, because no matter how wide we make it there will always be some bright spark who wants to use bigger numbers than the bus can hold. Just for the purposes of these discussions, let's assume that we're working with a computer that only has a 4-bit data bus (in which case each memory location would also only be 4 bits wide). Further assume that the adder inside the CPU is also only 4 bits wide (just like the adder that we constructed earlier), but that we actually wish to play with 8-bit numbers, which would allow us to represent values in the range 0_{10} through $+255_{10}$. As a particular example, consider the case whereby we wish to add the two 8-bit numbers 00110110_2 and 00011100_2 to give 01010010_2 (which equates to $54_{10} + 28_{10} = 82_{10}$ in decimal). The way in which we can achieve this using our 4-bit adder is illustrated in Figure 7.11.

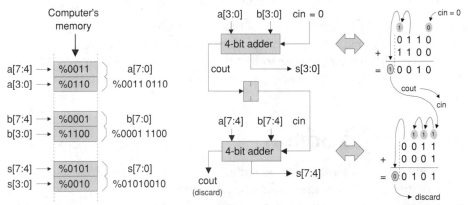

Figure 7.11: Performing an 8-bit addition using 4-bit quantities

Somewhere in the computer's memory we would use two 4-bit words to store the first 8-bit number, which we will refer to as a[7:0]. We would also require a second pair of 4-bit words to store the second 8-bit number, which we can call b[7:0]. Last but not least, we would need to reserve a final pair of 4-bit words to store the 8-bit result, which we will refer to as s[7:0]. (Note that the '%' characters in this figure are used to indicate binary values.)

At this stage we don't need to know exactly how the computer performs its operations, but we are interested in the general sequence as follows.

The CPU reads the least significant 4 bits from the numbers in memory, a[3:0] and b[3:0], and adds them together. For the purposes of this first addition, the CPU ensures that the **carry-in** into the adder is forced to a *logic 0*. The result from this addition is written back into the memory as s[3:0], while the value on the **carry-out** signal is stored inside the CPU in a 1-bit register (either a latch or a flip-flop), which is known as the *carry flag*.

The CPU next reads the most significant 4 bits from the numbers in memory, a[7:4] and b[7:4], and adds *these* together using the same adder function (that is, the same physical logic gates) as for the first addition. However, in this case the CPU ensures that the **carry-in** into the adder is driven by the *carry flag* register, which currently contains the carry-out from the first addition. The result from this addition is written back into the memory as s[7:4]. Note that the value on the **carry-out** signal from this second addition would also be stored in the *carry flag* register, thereby overwriting its existing contents. Thus, if we have the ability to store the carry-out from each 4-bit addition and to use that value as a carry-in to a subsequent addition, then we can effectively represent numbers of any size by partitioning them into 4-bit quantities.

Of course our *Beboputer* is actually based on an 8-bit data bus, which means that handling 8-bit binary numbers is not a problem. However, should we wish the *Beboputer* to handle any larger values, such as 16- or 32-bit numbers, then we can do so using similar techniques to those described here.

Binary subtraction

Unsigned binary numbers may be subtracted from each other using a process identical to that used for decimal subtraction. However, for reasons of efficiency, computers rarely perform subtractions in this way, but instead these operations are typically performed by means of *complement techniques*.

There are two forms of complement associated with every number system, the *radix complement* and the *diminished radix complement*, where the term "radix" refers to the base of the number system. Under the decimal (base-10) system, the radix complement is also known as the *ten's complement* and the diminished radix complement is known as the *nine's complement*. First consider a decimal subtraction performed using the nine's complement technique – a process known in ancient times as "*Casting out the nines*" (Figure 7.12).

The standard way of performing this operation would be to subtract the subtrahend (283) from the minuend (647), which, as in this example, may require the use of one or more borrow operations. To perform the equivalent operation using a

Figure 7.12: Nine's complement decimal subtraction

nine's complement technique, each of the digits of the subtrahend is first subtracted from a 9. The resulting nine's complement value is added to the minuend, then an *end-around-carry* operation is performed. The advantage of the nine's complement technique is that it is never necessary to perform a borrow operation.

Now consider the same subtraction performed using the ten's complement technique (Figure 7.13). The advantage of the ten's complement approach is that it is not necessary to perform an end-around-carry, because any carry-out resulting from the addition of the most-significant digits is simply dropped from the final result. The disadvantage is that, during the process of creating the ten's complement, it is necessary to perform a borrow operation for every non-zero digit in the subtrahend. This

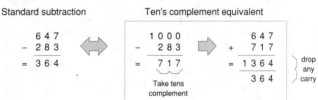

Figure 7.13: Ten's complement decimal subtraction

problem can be overcome by first taking the nine's complement of the subtrahend, adding one to the result, and then performing the remaining operations as for the ten's complement.

Similar techniques may be employed with binary (base-2) numbers, where the radix complement is known as the *two's complement* and the diminished radix complement is known as the *one's complement*. First consider a binary subtraction performed using the one's complement technique (Figure 7.14).

Once again, the standard way of performing the operation would be to subtract the subtrahend (00011110_2) from the minuend (00111001_2), which may require the use of one or more borrow operations. (Don't beat your head against a wall trying to understand the standard binary subtraction, because we won't ever be doing one — simply take our word as to the result.) In order to perform the equivalent operation using the one's complement technique, each of the digits of the subtrahend is first subtracted from a 1. The resulting one's complement value is added to the minuend, then an end-around-carry operation is performed.

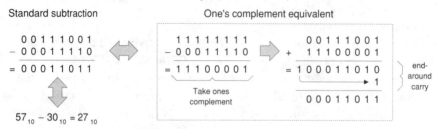

Figure 7.14: One's complement binary subtraction

The advantage of the one's complement technique is that it is never necessary to perform a borrow operation. In fact <u>it isn't even necessary to perform a subtraction operation</u>, because the one's complement of a binary number can be generated simply by inverting all of its bits; that is, by exchanging all of the 0s with 1s, and vice versa. This means that even if we stopped here, you already know how to perform a simple binary subtraction using only inversion and addition, without any actual subtraction being involved! Now consider the same binary subtraction performed using the two's complement technique (Figure 7.15).

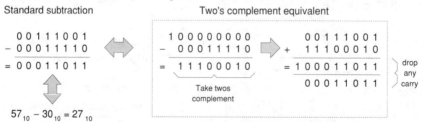

Figure 7.15: Two's complement binary subtraction

The advantage of the two's complement approach is that it is not necessary to perform an end-around-carry, because any carry-out resulting from the addition of the two most-significant bits is simply dropped from the final result. The disadvantage is that, during the process of creating the two's complement, it is necessary to perform a borrow operation for every non-zero digit in the subtrahend. This problem can be overcome by first taking the one's complement of the subtrahend, adding one to the result, and then performing the remaining operations as for the two's complement.

As fate would have it, there is also a short-cut approach available to generate the two's complement of a binary number. Commencing with the least significant bit of the value to be complemented, each bit up to and including the first 1 is copied directly, then the remaining bits are inverted (Figure 7.16).

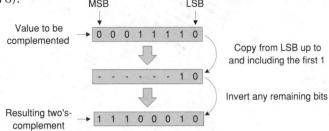

Figure 7.16: Shortcut for generating a two's complement

Unfortunately, all of the previous examples will return incorrect results if a larger value is subtracted from a smaller value; that is, for these techniques to work, the final result must be greater than or equal to zero. The reason for this is pretty obvious, because subtracting a larger number from a smaller number results in a negative value; but we've been using unsigned binary numbers, which, by definition, can only be used to represent positive values. It is obviously impractical to only ever perform calculations that will have positive results, so we are obliged to come up with some way of representing negative quantities. One solution is to use *signed binary numbers* as discussed below.

Signed binary numbers

In the case of standard decimal arithmetic, negative numbers are typically represented in *sign-magnitude* form, which means that we prefix the value with a minus sign; for example, a value of minus twenty-seven would be indicated as -27. However, computers rarely employ the sign-magnitude form, but instead use the signed binary format, in which the most significant bit is also called the *sign bit*. Signed binary numbers can be used to represent both positive and negative values, and they do this in a rather ingenious way (Figure 7.17).

The cunning ruse underlying the signed binary format is that the sign bit is used to signify a negative <u>quantity</u> (not just a sign). Thus, in the case of a signed 8-bit number, a 1 in the sign bit represents -2^7 (= -128), while the remaining bits are used to represent positive values in the range 0_{10} through $+127_{10}$. So when the value represented by the sign bit is combined with the values represented by the remaining bits, an 8-bit signed binary number can be used to represent values in the range -128_{10} through $+127_{10}$.

To illustrate the differences between the sign-magnitude and signed binary formats, consider a positive sign-magnitude decimal number and its negative equivalent; for example, +27 and -27. As we see, the

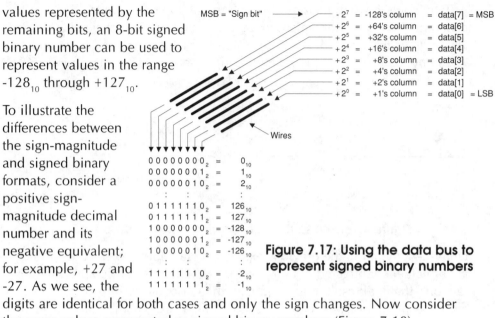

MSB = "Sign bit"

-2^7 = -128's column	= data[7]	= MSB
$+2^6$ = +64's column	= data[6]	
$+2^5$ = +32's column	= data[5]	
$+2^4$ = +16's column	= data[4]	
$+2^3$ = +8's column	= data[3]	
$+2^2$ = +4's column	= data[2]	
$+2^1$ = +2's column	= data[1]	
$+2^0$ = +1's column	= data[0]	= LSB

Wires

$$00000000_2 = 0_{10}$$
$$00000001_2 = 1_{10}$$
$$00000010_2 = 2_{10}$$
$$\vdots \qquad \vdots$$
$$01111110_2 = 126_{10}$$
$$01111111_2 = 127_{10}$$
$$10000000_2 = -128_{10}$$
$$10000001_2 = -127_{10}$$
$$10000010_2 = -126_{10}$$
$$\vdots \qquad \vdots$$
$$11111110_2 = -2_{10}$$
$$11111111_2 = -1_{10}$$

Figure 7.17: Using the data bus to represent signed binary numbers

digits are identical for both cases and only the sign changes. Now consider the same values represented as signed binary numbers (Figure 7.18).

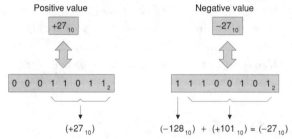

Positive value

$+27_{10}$

Negative value

-27_{10}

$0\ 0\ 0\ 1\ 1\ 0\ 1\ 1_2$ $1\ 1\ 1\ 0\ 0\ 1\ 0\ 1_2$

$(+27_{10})$ $(-128_{10}) + (+101_{10}) = (-27_{10})$

Figure 7.18: Comparison of positive and negative signed values

In this case the bit patterns of the two binary numbers are very different. This is because the sign bit represents an actual quantity (-128_{10}) rather than a simple plus or minus; thus, the signed equivalent of -27_{10} is formed by combining -128_{10} with $+101_{10}$.

At a first glance the signed binary concept may appear to be an outrageously complex solution to a fairly simple problem. In addition to representing an asymmetrical range of negative and positive numbers (-128_{10} through $+127_{10}$ in the case of an 8-bit value), the way in which these values are formed is, to put it mildly, alien to the way we're used to thinking of numbers. Why then, you may ask, don't we simply use the most-significant bit to represent the sign of the number (for example, 0 = positive and 1 = negative) and leave it at that?

Well as you may expect, there's reason behind our madness. First, if we did use the most significant bit to represent only the sign of the number, then such numbers would accommodate both +0 and -0 values. Although this may not seem like a particularly significant point, computers are essentially dumb and it would introduce complications in recognizing whether or not a given value was less than zero or equal to zero. But there's a lot more to signed binary numbers than this. Now pay attention, because this is the clever part; closer investigation of the two binary values in Figure 17.18 reveals that each bit-pattern is the two's complement of the other! To put this another way; taking the two's complement of a positive signed binary value returns its negative equivalent, and vice versa (the only problem with this scheme being that, due to the asymmetrical range, the largest negative number can't be negated; for example, in the case of an 8-bit signed binary number, you can't negate -128_{10} to get $+128_{10}$, because the maximum positive value that's supported is $+127_{10}$).

The end result of all this is that using signed binary numbers (which may be referred to as *two's-complement numbers*) greatly reduces the complexity of operations within a computer. To illustrate why this should be so, consider one of the simpler operations: addition. Compare the following additions of positive and negative decimal values in sign-magnitude form with their signed binary counterparts (Figure 7.19).

First examine the standard decimal calculations – the one at the top is easy to understand, because it's a straightforward addition of two positive values. However, even though you are familiar with decimal addition, you probably found the other three a little harder, because you had to decide exactly what to do with the negative values. By comparison, the signed binary calculations on the right are all simple additions, irrespective of whether the individual values are positive or negative.

Decimal sign-magnitude		Signed binary
5 7		0 0 1 1 1 0 0 1
+ 3 0	⟺	+ 0 0 0 1 1 1 1 0
= 8 7		= 0 1 0 1 0 1 1 1
5 7		0 0 1 1 1 0 0 1
+ -3 0	⟺	+ 1 1 1 0 0 0 1 0
= 2 7		= 0 0 0 1 1 0 1 1
-5 7		1 1 0 0 0 1 1 1
+ 3 0	⟺	+ 0 0 0 1 1 1 1 0
= -2 7		= 1 1 1 0 0 1 0 1
-5 7		1 1 0 0 0 1 1 1
+ -3 0	⟺	+ 1 1 1 0 0 0 1 0
= -8 7		= 1 0 1 0 1 0 0 1

Figure 7.19: Comparison of sign-magnitude versus signed binary additions

Similarly, if a computer was forced to use a binary version of the sign-magnitude form to perform additions, then instead of performing its calculations effortlessly and quickly, it would have to perform a painful sequence of operations. First it would have to compare the signs of the two numbers. If the signs were the same, the computer could simply add the two values (excluding the sign bits themselves), because the result would always have the same sign as the original numbers. However, if the signs were different, the computer would have to subtract the smaller value from the larger value, and then ensure that the correct sign was appended to the result.

As well as being time consuming, performing all of these operations would require a substantial amount of logic gates. Thus, the advantages of signed binary format for addition operations are apparent: signed binary numbers can always be directly added together to provide the correct result in a single operation, irrespective of whether they represent positive or negative values. That is, the operations a + b, a + (-b), (-a) + b, and (-a) + (-b) are all performed in exactly the same way, by simply adding the two values together. This results in computers that are simpler to design, use fewer logic gates, and execute operations faster.

Now consider the case of subtraction. We all know that 10 - 3 = 7 in decimal arithmetic, and that the same result can be obtained by negating the right-hand value and inverting the operation; that is, 10 + (-3) = 7. This technique is also true for signed binary arithmetic, although the negation of the right hand value is performed by taking its two's complement rather than by changing its sign. For example, consider a generic signed binary subtraction represented by a - b.[2] Generating the two's complement of b results in -b, thereby allowing the operation to be performed as an addition: a + (-b). This means that computers do not require two different blocks of logic (one to add numbers and another to subtract them); instead, they only require some logic to generate the two's complement of a number and an adder, which tends to make life a lot easier for all concerned. In the next chapter we will plunge into the bowels of a CPU, at which time we'll begin to see how the fruits of our labors can be implemented in hardware.

---

[2]For the sake of simplicity, only the case of a - b is discussed here. However, the operations a - b, a - (-b), (-a) - b, and (-a) - (-b) are all performed in exactly the same way, by simply taking the two's complement of b and adding the result to a, irrespective of whether a or b represent positive or negative values.

Be afraid, be very afraid

If all of the above seems too good to be true, you're right — it is! One of the biggest problems when using computers is mapping the numbers that we use (which are potentially infinite) into the way a computer thinks about them (which is as finite chunks).

Generally speaking these issues aren't outrageously complicated, but they do require a certain amount of lateral thought and mental gymnastics. So, instead of washing our clothes in public at this moment in time, we'll postpone any in-depth discussions for the nonce and return to consider this topic in more detail in Appendix G.

Quick quiz #7

1) Why do digital computers use the binary number system?

2) Why are numbers in a computer different from numbers written on a piece of paper?

3) What is the difference between unsigned and signed binary numbers?

4) What range of numbers can be represented by a 4-bit field if it (a) represents an unsigned quantity and (b) represents a signed quantity?

5) What is the two's complement of 00110101_2?

6) What is the carry flag used for in binary additions?

7) Use two's complement techniques to generate the result of $00110101_2 - 01001010_2$.

8) Show how a 6-bit data bus could be used to represent signed and unsigned binary values (yes, we really mean six bits).

9) What range of numbers could be represented by a 6-bit bus if we were using a signed-magnitude format, as opposed to standard signed binary numbers?

10) What are the advantages and disadvantages of standard signed binary numbers, as compared to using a signed-magnitude format?

Chapter 8

Rampaging around a CPU

In this chapter we will discover:

The accumulator and its related instructions

The grim truth about the origin of opcodes

The status register: what it is and what it does

The ALU: what it is and how it works

The instruction register and the instruction decoder

The addressing logic, including the program counter, index register, stack pointer, and interrupt vector

What subroutines are and what they do

What addressing modes are and how they're used

Contents of Chapter 8

Rampaging around a CPU

Everything we've discussed thus-far has merely been limbering-up exercises to prepare our mental muscles for the ordeals to come. Our real journey starts here and now as we quiver at the brink, poised to hurl ourselves into the bowels of the computer's *central processing unit (CPU)* where we'll rampage around to our heart's content. Our path will carry us on a rollicking roller-coaster ride (thrill-seekers only need apply), commencing at a slow crawl to lull us into a false sense of security, followed by a screaming plunge into the nether regions where we'll disappear for a while ...... until we rocket out of the other side, clutching our stomachs and gasping for more.

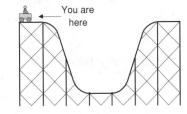

The accumulator (ACC)

Considering how far we've come together, it's surprising how woefully ignorant we remain as to what's actually inside the CPU. In fact the only thing we currently know is that the CPU's contents include a register called the *accumulator* (or **ACC** for short), which is used to gather, or accumulate, intermediate results. The accumulator is generally the same width as the computer's data bus, so the *Beboputer's* accumulator will be 8 bits wide (Figure 8.1).

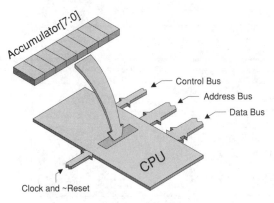

Figure 8.1: The accumulator (ACC)

The obvious next question would be: *"Now that we've got an accumulator, what can we actually do with it?"* Well we're glad you asked, because that's just what we're about to discuss. We'll commence our jaunt by considering some of the things we want the CPU to do with its accumulator, and then proceed to delve inside to see how it actually goes about doing them.

One of the first things we need to be able to do is to load data into the accumulator; that is, to read a byte of data from the system's memory (either ROM or RAM) and place a copy of that data into the accumulator. This process overwrites any data that was already in the accumulator, but does not affect the data in the memory location that's being copied. Similarly, we also need to be able to store the contents of the accumulator; that is, to write a copy of the accumulator into a byte in the system's memory (just the RAM in this case, because the ROM is "read-only"). The process of storing the accumulator overwrites any data that was already in the target memory location, but does not affect the contents of the accumulator.

In addition to loading and storing, we also need the ability to perform a variety of arithmetic, logical, and other miscellaneous operations on the data contained within the accumulator. A selection of accumulator operations we might wish to perform are summarized in Table 8.1.

Type	Mnemonic	Description
Loads and Stores	LDA	Load a byte from memory into the accumulator
	STA	Store the accumulator to a byte in memory
Arithmetic	ADD	Add a byte from memory into the accumulator
	SUB	Subtract a byte in memory from the accumulator
Logical	AND	AND a byte from memory into the accumulator
	OR	OR a byte from memory into the accumulator
	XOR	XOR a byte from memory into the accumulator
Miscellaneous	INCA	Increment the accumulator (add 1 to it)
	DECA	Decrement the accumulator (subtract 1 from it)
	ROLC	Rotate accumulator 1 bit left via the carry flag [1]
	RORC	Rotate accumulator 1 bit right via carry flag [1]
	SHL	Shift accumulator 1 bit left
	SHR	Shift accumulator 1 bit right

Table 8.1: Basic accumulator operations

---

[1]See also the discussions on the carry flag later in this chapter.

When engineers sit down to design a new CPU, one of their main tasks is to decide which instructions it will be capable of performing, where these instructions are referred to collectively as the *instruction set*. Selecting the instructions that will comprise the instruction set is non-trivial, because there are a variety of competing factors to be taken into account. In the case of the *Beboputer*, we desired an instruction set with the following attributes:

a) To be as small and compact as possible, thereby making it easy to understand, learn, and use.

b) To be comprehensive enough to adequately illustrate computer concepts and create meaningful and understandable programs.

These criteria are obviously somewhat contradictory, so we will endeavor to describe the various tradeoffs that we considered during the course of the project. At this point it is probably worth noting that the *Beboputer* is, to all intents and purposes, a real computer that the authors designed from the ground up, and also that the *Beboputer* is conceptually very similar to several early microprocessors dating from the mid- to late-1970s. The only really unusual aspect of the *Beboputer* is that we implemented it in software (as a program) rather than in hardware (as silicon chips).

Another aspect of the design process is assigning *mnemonics* to the various instructions, where a mnemonic is an abbreviated name suggestive of the operation to be performed; for example, **LDA** meaning *"load the accumulator"* and **STA** meaning *"store the accumulator."* Mnemonics serve as an aid to memory, and allow us to document programs and communicate their intent in an extremely efficient way. Once again there are tradeoffs, such as the fact that we want our mnemonics to be as short as possible, but we don't want them to be cryptic or obscure.

Unfortunately, each type of computer has its own unique instruction set and associated mnemonics. If all of this strikes you as being a minefield of potential confusion, then you're really beginning to get into the swing of things, because ...... it is! As we progress through the remainder of the book, we'll highlight some of the reasons why computers are designed this way, some of the problems that arise *because* computers are designed this way, and some of the ways in which we get *around* the problems that arise because computers are designed this way (phew!).

The ADD and SUB arithmetic instructions

The ADD instruction causes a byte stored in the memory (RAM or ROM) to be added to the current contents in the accumulator. The result from this operation is stored in the accumulator, thereby overwriting its original contents (the contents of the memory remain undisturbed). Similarly, the SUB instruction causes a byte from the memory to be subtracted from the current contents in the accumulator. To illustrate these instructions, assume that the accumulator originally contains 00111001_2 (57 in decimal), to which we either wish to add or subtract the contents of a location in memory that contains 00011110_2 (30 in decimal) (Figure 8.2).

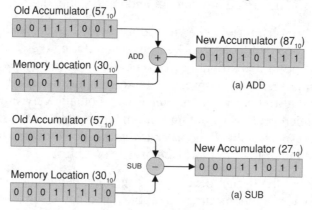

Figure 8.2: The ADD and SUB instructions

In fact, remembering our discussions on binary arithmetic in Chapter 7, if push came to shove we could probably make do without the SUB instruction. As you may recall, if we represent a generic subtraction as a - b, then we can achieve the same effect by negating the right-hand value and inverting the operation; that is, a - b is identical to a + (-b). Thus, we could generate the two's complement of the value in memory (using techniques that will be introduced later) and then add the result to the accumulator. However, this technique is non-intuitive, cumbersome, and time-consuming. Also, if there's anything we tend to do a lot of in computer programs it's adding and subtracting numbers, so it's more than worth our while to include both ADD and SUB in our instruction set.

The INCA and DECA (increment and decrement) instructions

As we've just discussed ADD and SUB, this is probably an appropriate time to quickly mention the INCA and DECA instructions. As its mnemonic suggests (or is supposed to suggest), the INCA instruction increments (adds 1 to) the contents of the accumulator. Similarly, the DECA instruction decrements (subtracts 1 from) the contents of the accumulator. To illustrate these instructions, once again assume that the accumulator originally contains 00111001_2 (57 in decimal), and consider what would happen if we were to increment or decrement this value (Figure 8.3).

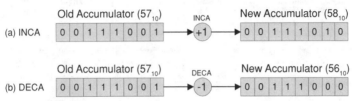

Figure 8.3: The INCA and DECA instructions

The reason we used INCA and DECA for mnemonics (as opposed to simply using INC and DEC, respectively) is that we are probably going to want to be able to perform similar operations on other registers inside the CPU, so appending an 'A' to the end of these mnemonics distinguishes the fact that they relate to the accumulator.

Of course, one might question why we need these instructions at all. After all, instead of INCA we could use an ADD with an argument of +1; similarly, instead of DECA we could use a SUB with an argument of +1 (or an ADD with an argument of -1 if we really wanted to grasp at straws). One answer is that the ADD and SUB instructions require a minimum of two bytes in the memory, while INCA and DECA only require one byte (this aspect of our instructions is discussed in more detail a little later); thus, having INCA and DECA will make our programs smaller and faster. Additionally, as we tend to do a lot of incrementing and decrementing in programs, having these instructions goes a long way to making said programs easier to read by better communicating their intent. Trust us on this one – you'll thank us for these instructions later.

The AND, OR, and XOR logical instructions

In addition to arithmetic operations such as ADD and SUB, we often desire to perform logical operations on the contents of the accumulator. The AND, OR, and XOR instructions cause a byte stored in the memory to be logically AND-ed, OR-ed, or XOR-ed to the current contents in the accumulator, respectively. The results from these operations are stored in the accumulator, thereby overwriting its original contents (as usual, the contents of the memory remain undisturbed). To illustrate these instructions, assume that the accumulator originally contains 00001111_2, and that we wish to AND, OR, or XOR this value with a memory location containing 01010101_2 (Figure 8.4).

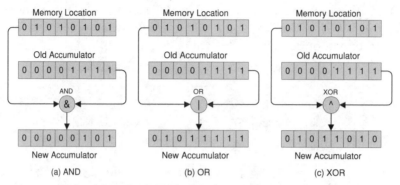

Figure 8.4: The AND, OR, and XOR instructions

The main point to note about these logical operations is that they function in a bit-wise fashion; that is, on a bit-by-bit basis. For example, in the case of the AND, mem[0] is AND-ed with old-acc[0] to give new-acc[0], mem[1] is AND-ed with old-acc[1] to give new-acc[1], and so forth. The truth tables for these bit-wise operations are identical to those for the primitive gates of the same names (as presented in Chapter 6).

The NOT logical instruction (and why we don't have one)

The AND, OR, and XOR are the only logical instructions supported by the *Beboputer*. Now you might be wondering about other logical operators, such as a NOT to invert all of the bits in the accumulator. There's no doubt that having a NOT instruction would actually be quite useful, but in the spirit of keeping the *Beboputer's* instruction set as small as possible, we decided that we could learn to get by without one (Figure 8.5).

As this illustration demonstrates, it's possible to achieve the same effect as a NOT by simply XOR-ing the accumulator with all 1s. For example, 00110101_2 XOR-ed with 11111111_2 results in 11001010_2, which is identical to inverting all of the bits in the original number. (In the future we will refer to this technique as a *pseudo-NOT*.)

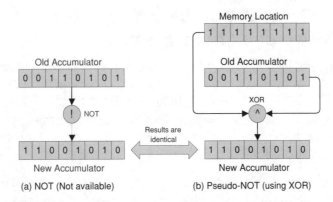

Figure 8.5: The NOT instruction (which we don't have)

The NAND, NOR, and XNOR logical instructions (and why we don't have them)

In the same way that we don't have a **NOT** instruction, we also don't have **NAND**, **NOR**, or **XNOR** instructions. However, once again this isn't as dire as it may seem. If you cast your mind back to our discussions in Chapter 6, you will recall that a **NAND** gate can be realized by inverting the output of an **AND** gate with a **NOT**. Baring this in mind, we can achieve the same effect as a **NAND** instruction by using an **AND** followed by a **NOT** (Figure 8.6).

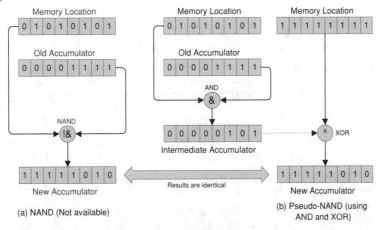

Figure 8.6: The NAND instruction (which we don't have)

Of course, as we don't actually have a **NOT** instruction, we are obliged to use a pseudo-NOT based on the "*XOR with all 1s*" technique discussed above. Similarly, equivalent results to the **NOR** and **XNOR** instructions can be achieved by appending pseudo-NOTs to **OR**s and **XOR**s, respectively.

The SET 'n' and CLR 'n' bit manipulation instructions (and why we don't have them)

Some computers include SET 'n' and CLR 'n' instructions in their repertoire, where 'n' is an integer in the range 0 to 7 (for an 8-bit accumulator). If they are available, SET n and CLR n facilitate the setting of individual bits in the accumulator to a *logic 1* or clearing them to a *logic 0*, respectively. However, once again we decided that we could muddle along without these instructions.

Now, it may seem as though all we're doing is chanting an endless litany about the instructions that we *don't* have. But the instructions themselves are not particularly important, so long as we can perform any tasks demanded by our programs. In the case of a SET n, we can achieve exactly the same functionality using an OR; it's just a little slower to execute and somewhat less convenient to program (Figure 8.7).

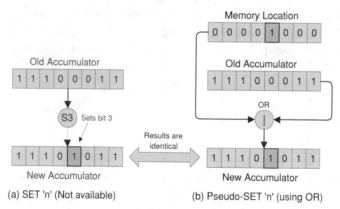

(a) SET 'n' (Not available)   (b) Pseudo-SET 'n' (using OR)

Figure 8.7: The SET 'n' instruction (which we don't have)

For example, if the accumulator originally contained 11100011_2, then a SET 3 instruction (if we had one) would cause bit 3 in the accumulator to be set to 1, resulting in 11101011_2. **(Remember that we number the bits in the accumulator commencing with zero and counting from the left.)** But we can achieve the same effect by OR-ing the accumulator with a 1 in that bit position; for example, 11100011_2 OR-ed with 00001000_2 equals 11101011_2 (note that if the targeted accumulator bit was already a 1, then this OR would have no effect).

Similarly, in the case of a CLR n, we can realize the same functionality with an AND (once again, it's just a little slower and somewhat less convenient). For example, if the accumulator originally contained 11100011_2, then a

CLR 6 instruction (if we had one) would cause bit 6 in the accumulator to be cleared to a 0, resulting in 10100011_2. But we can achieve the same effect by AND-ing the accumulator with a 0 in that bit position; for example, 11100011_2 AND-ed with 10111111_2 results in 10100011_2 (Figure 8.8).

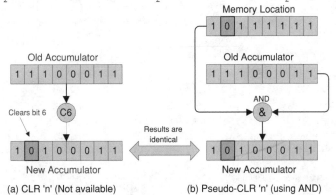

(a) CLR 'n' (Not available)   (b) Pseudo-CLR 'n' (using AND)

Figure 8.8: The CLR 'n' instruction (which we don't have)

Note that if the targeted accumulator bit was already a 0, then this AND would have no effect. The end result is that, as we can easily achieve the same effect as SET 'n' and CLR 'n' instructions using ORs and ANDs, respectively, we decided that there was no pressing need to equip the *Beboputer* with these instructions.

The COMP (two's complement) instruction (and why we don't have one)

Another instruction that might occasionally come in handy would be a COMP, which could be used to generate the two's complement of the value in the accumulator (two's complements were introduced in the previous chapter). For example, assuming that the accumulator originally contains 00111001_2 (+57 in decimal) and that we're viewing this as being a signed binary value, then a COMP instruction (if we had one) would result in the accumulator containing 11000111_2 (-57 in decimal), and vice versa (Figure 8.9).

However, once again, we decided that we could survive without having a dedicated COMP instruction. If you remember our discussions in Chapter 7, you will recall that one way to generate the two's complement of a number is to invert all of its bits and then add one to the result. Thus, we can achieve the same effect as a COMP by performing a pseudo-NOT on the contents of the accumulator (XOR-ing it with all 1s) followed by an INCA (or an ADD with an argument of +1).

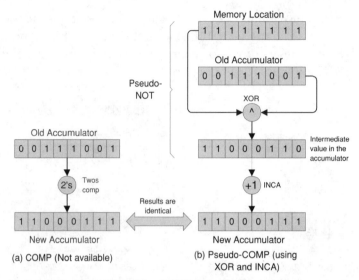

Figure 8.9: The COMP instruction (which we don't have)

Now all of this jiggery-pokery may seem painfully confusing at first, but, perhaps surprisingly, it can turn out to be quite a lot of fun. For anything that you want to do with a computer, there are invariably a variety of ways to achieve the same end-result, but out of all of the options there may be one solution that's slightly more advantageous than the others, and finding this solution can impart a certain amount of satisfaction. In fact, in the not-so-distant past, electronics magazines used to pick a popular computer of the day and sponsor competitions in which readers would strive to describe the most elegant solution to a relatively simple problem. In this case "elegant" translated to a solution that required the fewest instructions (or bytes in memory), executed the fastest, or preferably both.

The ROLC and RORC (rotate through carry) instructions

Just for the heck of it, why don't we change direction and look at some of the instructions that the *Beboputer does* support? A brace of instructions we've provided to manipulate data inside the accumulator are the rotates, where the mnemonics ROLC and RORC stand for "*rotate left through the carry flag*" and "*rotate right through the carry flag*," respectively. Some instruction sets allow you to specify by how many bits the accumulator will be rotated, but the *Beboputer* only supports single-bit rotates (Figure 8.10).

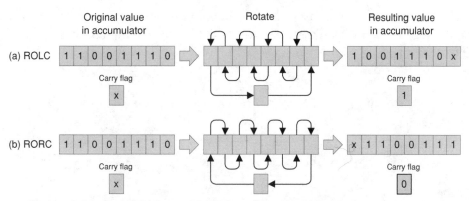

Figure 8.10: The ROLC and RORC (rotate through Carry) instructions

The rotate instructions are relatively simple to understand, with the possible exception of the *carry flag*, which we haven't formally introduced yet. For the nonce, let's simply assume that the carry flag is a 1-bit register that can contain either a *logic 0* or a *logic 1* (which is indicated as an 'x' in this figure). In the case of a ROLC, the original contents of bit[0] of the accumulator move into bit[1], the original contents of bit[1] move into bit[2], and so on down the line until we arrive at bit[7], which moves into the carry flag, which, in turn, rolls back into bit[0]. Similarly, in the case of a RORC, the original contents of bit[7] move into bit[6], the original contents of bit[6] move into bit[5], and so forth until we arrive at bit[0], which moves into the carry flag, which, in turn, rolls back into bit[7]. (We'll return to these instructions and the carry flag when we come to consider the *status register* later in this chapter.)

The SHL and SHR (shift) instructions

The final group of instructions we've provided to manipulate data inside the accumulator are the shifts, where the mnemonics SHL and SHR stand for "*shift left*" and "*shift right*," respectively. As with the rotates, some instruction sets allow you to specify by how many bits the accumulator will be shifted, but the *Beboputer* only supports single-bit shifts.

Unfortunately, the shift instructions require a little more thought than the rotates. When we turn our attention to shifts in general we discover two main flavors, which are referred to as *arithmetic* and *logical shifts*. Some computers support both types, in which case they would typically have four shift instructions named something like ASHL ("*arithmetic shift left*"), LSHL ("*logical shift left*"), ASHR ("*arithmetic shift right*") and LSHR ("*logical shift right*"). However, on the basis that the *Beboputer* only supports arithmetic shifts, we decided to call our mnemonics SHL and SHR for simplicity (Figure 8.11).

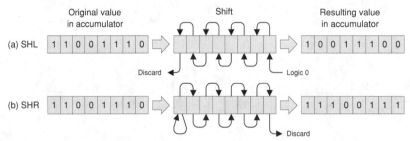

Figure 8.11: The SHL and SHR (shift) instructions

At this point you may be wondering whether the lack of logical shift instructions will be detrimental to your ability to write useful programs and your general standing in the community. As it happens you don't need to be overly concerned, not the least that arithmetic and logical shift lefts are actually identical, because they both shift a *logic 0* into bit[0] and they both discard the original bit[7].[2] In fact the main reason we differentiate between arithmetic and logical shift lefts is for aesthetic considerations (to counter-balance the shift rights). By comparison, shift rights are slightly more interesting (or not, depending on your point of view). In the case of an *arithmetic* shift right (the type supported by the *Beboputer*), the most significant bit of the accumulator (bit[7] in our case) is copied back into itself – we'll discuss the rationale behind this in a moment. In the case of a *logical* shift right (which *isn't* supported by the *Beboputer*), a *logic 0* would be shifted into bit[7]. Both flavors of shift right end up discarding bit[0].[3]

It now becomes obvious why we don't need to worry too much about the lack of a logical shift right instruction, because we can achieve exactly the same effect by performing our arithmetic shift right followed by AND-ing the result with 01111111_2, where this AND-ing operation has the effect of clearing bit[7] to a *logic 0* (return to our earlier discussions on the CLR n instruction if you're at all unsure of what we're talking about).

Beyond the fact that they're generally useful, one interesting facet of shift left instructions is that they can be used to multiply the value in the accumulator by two. For example, if the original contents of the accumulator were 00011011_2 (27 in decimal), then performing a SHL would

---

[2]To be perfectly honest, saying that we "discard bit[7]" is a bit of an overstatement, but we'll return to investigate this point when we come to consider the carry flag later in this chapter.
[3]Once again, saying that we "discard bit[0]" is not strictly true as we shall come to see.

result in the accumulator's containing 00110110_2 (54 in decimal) (Figure 8.12a).

This also works with negative (two's complement) numbers; for example, if the accumulator originally contained 11100010_2 (-30 in decimal), then performing a **SHL** would result in 11000100_2 (-60 in decimal) (Figure 8.12b).

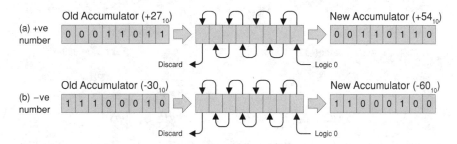

Figure 8.12: Using SHL to multiply by two

Beware! There's more to this than meets the eye and you can run into trouble if you're not one hundred percent sure of what you're doing. For example, if we were to perform a **SHL** on the value 10110110_2, then the result would be 01101100_2. This is of course perfectly acceptable if we're visualizing the accumulator as containing a simple pattern of 1s and 0s, because the result is exactly what we'd expect. However, if we're visualizing the accumulator as containing two's complement numbers, then a **SHL** on 10110110_2 (-74 in decimal) would result in 01101100_2 (+108 in decimal), which would obviously be incorrect.

The problem is that, if we *are* visualizing the contents of the accumulator as being a two's complement number, then what we're trying to do in this particular example is to multiply -74 by 2 (which we would expect to return a result somewhere in the vicinity of -148). Unfortunately, as we previously discussed, our 8-bit accumulator can only represent two's complement numbers in the range -128_{10} through $+127_{10}$. A slightly more visual manifestation of this problem is that our shift caused the 1 in the sign bit (**bit[7]**) to drop off the end, thereby presenting us with a positive result. In fact this is all tied up with the same issues that we briefly mentioned at the close of the previous chapter, which are the problems of mapping the numbers that we wish to use (which are potentially infinite) into the way a computer thinks about them (as finite chunks). However, we will discover a way around this problem when we come to consider the *status register* and the *carry flag* a little later on.

In the same way that shift lefts can be used to multiply the value in the accumulator by two, shift right instructions can be used to divide by two. For example, if the original contents of the accumulator were 01010100_2 (84 in decimal), then performing a SHR would result in the accumulator containing 00101010_2 (or 42 in decimal) (Figure 8.13a).

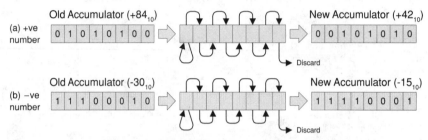

Figure 8.13: Using SHR to divide by two

Once again, this technique also works with negative (two's complement) numbers; for example, if the accumulator originally contained 11100010_2 (−30 in decimal), then performing a SHR would result in 11110001_2 (-15 in decimal). In fact this is the reason why there is such a beast as an arithmetic shift in the first place, because for this to work with negative numbers it's necessary to shift in a copy of the sign bit (bit[7] in our case), which is why our SHR instruction copies bit[7] back into itself.

Fortunately there are no problems with shift right instructions exceeding the range of numbers that can be represented by the accumulator, because dividing by two can only make the number smaller. However, remembering that bit[0] is discarded in the case of a shift right, we should note that any remainder will be lost when using this technique to divide odd numbers. For example, performing an SHR on 01010101_2 (or 85 in decimal) will result in 00101010_2 (or 42 in decimal), because the 1 in bit[0] of the original accumulator value is discarded when the shift takes place. In fact there's a little more to these instructions than we're showing here (including a way to counteract the problem of losing the remainder), but we'll return to them again when we come to consider the *status register* later in this chapter.

Introducing the implied, immediate, and absolute addressing modes

Throughout these discussions we've been wont to wield words along the lines of: "*The xxx instruction causes a byte of data stored in the memory to be yyy-ed to the current contents in the accumulator.*" This is all well and good, but it glosses over the fact that an instruction can't just direct the CPU to "*Use any old data that you happen to find lying around,*" but instead it must explicitly define where the data is to be found.

It is common practice to refer to an instruction's *addressing modes*, which refers to the way in which the CPU determines or resolves the addresses of any data to be used in the execution of its instructions. At this stage in the proceedings, we shall consider only three types of addressing modes: *implied*, *immediate*, and *absolute*.

Before examining these modes in detail, we should remind ourselves that the user instructs the CPU where to start executing a program, and the CPU responds by pointing its address bus at that location. Thereafter the CPU will automatically increment its address bus and stroll through the memory sequentially until directed to do otherwise (we'll examine the mechanism behind this later in this chapter). We should also recall that the first byte of an instruction is called the *opcode*, which is an abbreviation of "operation code." The opcode instructs the CPU as to the type of operation it is to perform, such as ADD, SUB, AND, OR, and so forth. For those instructions which occupy multiple bytes, any bytes following the opcode are referred to as the *operand*. When a program is written or viewed in terms of "bits and bytes" (opcodes and operands), that program is said to be in *machine language* or *machine code*, because this is the form that's directly understood and executed by the machine (computer).

The implied addressing mode

Certain instructions only require one byte, because they have an opcode but no operand. Instructions of this type don't require an operand, because the location of their data is *implied* by the instruction itself, hence they are said to use the *implied addressing mode*. Examples of this type of instruction are INCA, DECA, ROLC, RORC, SHL, and SHR, all of which operate on the data stored inside the accumulator, and which therefore don't require any operand (data) bytes to be associated with them.

Assume that during the process of executing a program the CPU arrives at address 'n' in the memory. Further assume that the CPU is expecting a new instruction, which means that the first thing it will do is to read the opcode from the memory location pointed to by its address bus (Figure 8.14). (Note that the question marks in this figure simply indicate that we aren't particularly interested in the contents of these locations at this time.)

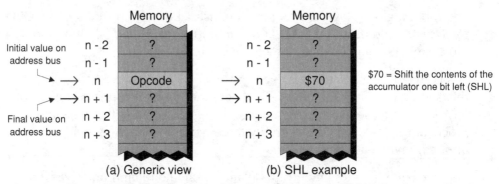

Figure 8.14: One-byte instructions (implied addressing)

In the case of the *Beboputer's* instruction set, the $70 opcode instructs the CPU to perform a **SHL** (*"shift left"*) on any data currently stored within its accumulator. Thus, when the CPU "sees" this opcode, it immediately realizes that it's dealing with a one-byte instruction; that is, the CPU inherently understands that this instruction is using the implied addressing mode. (Don't concern yourself with the reason why $70 means **SHL** at the moment – we'll come to consider this in a little while.)

Note that as soon as the CPU has read the opcode and performed the **SHL** instruction, it automatically increments its address bus to point to the next memory location ('n + 1' in this example).[4] Due to the fact that the CPU understands $70 is a one-byte instruction, it will automatically assume that the byte at location 'n + 1' is the first byte (the opcode) of a new instruction, so it will read that byte and continue to do its cunning stuff.

The immediate addressing mode

Unlike instructions that only manipulate the existing contents of the accumulator, an instruction such as an **LDA** requires data to load into the accumulator, while an instruction such as **ADD** requires data to add to the contents of the accumulator (similarly for **SUB**, **AND**, **OR**, and **XOR**). One way to provide this data is to locate it in the byte *immediately* following the opcode; thus, these two-byte instructions are said to use the *immediate addressing mode*.

Once again we'll assume that the CPU is executing a program, that it arrives at address 'n' in the memory, and that it is currently expecting a new

---

[4]To be perfectly honest, the CPU may well increment its address bus *at the same time* that its performing the SHL, but you'll find it easier to visualize these things as occurring sequentially.

instruction. So the first thing the CPU will do is read the opcode from the memory location pointed to by its address bus (Figure 8.15).

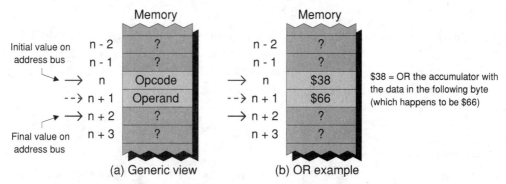

(a) Generic view   (b) OR example

Figure 8.15: Two-byte instruction (immediate addressing)

In the case of the *Beboputer's* instruction set, the $38 opcode instructs the CPU to **OR** the contents of the next memory location with the current contents of the accumulator (and to store the result in the accumulator). Thus, when the CPU "sees" the $38 opcode, it immediately realizes that it's dealing with a two-byte instruction; that is, the CPU inherently understands that this instruction is an **OR** that's using the immediate addressing mode. (Once again, don't concern yourself with the reason why $38 indicates an **OR** using the immediate addressing mode for the moment; just take our word for it.)

As soon as the CPU has read the opcode, it automatically increments its address bus to point to the next memory location ('n + 1' in this example). Because the CPU understands that $38 is a two-byte instruction, it will automatically read the operand byte at location 'n + 1' (which happens to be $66 in hexadecimal or %01100110 in binary for this example) and perform the **OR** operation using this data.

As usual, as soon as the CPU has read the operand and performed the **OR** instruction, it automatically increments its address bus to point to the next memory location ('n + 2' in this example). Due to the fact that the CPU understands $38 was a two-byte instruction, it will automatically assume that the byte at location 'n + 2' is the first byte (the opcode) of a new instruction, so it will read that byte and continue on its merry way.

The absolute addressing mode

As opposed to storing the data associated with instructions like **LDA** or **ADD** in the byte immediately following the opcode, one alternative is to use the *two* bytes following the opcode to represent an *absolute* address in memory where the data is to be found; thus, these three-byte instructions are said to use the *absolute addressing mode*.

Once again, assume that the CPU is executing a program, that it arrives at address 'n' in the memory, and that it is currently expecting a new instruction. So the first thing it will do is to read the opcode from the memory location pointed to by its address bus (Figure 8.16).

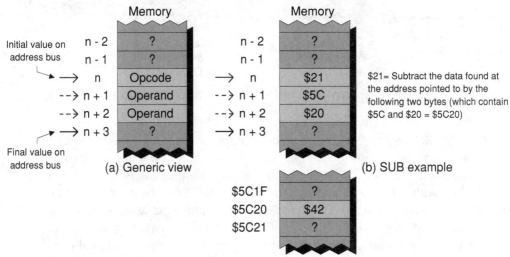

Figure 8.16: Three-byte instructions (absolute addressing)

In the case of the *Beboputer's* instruction set, the $21 opcode represents a SUB operation using the absolute addressing mode. That is, this opcode instructs the CPU to subtract some data from the current contents of the accumulator (and to store the result in the accumulator). Furthermore, this opcode instructs the CPU that the data to be subtracted will be found in a memory location whose address is specified by the following two bytes. So when the CPU reads the $21 opcode, it immediately realizes that it's dealing with a three-byte instruction. (As before, we don't need to concern ourselves with the reason why $21 indicates a SUB instruction using the immediate addressing mode at this time.)

As soon as the CPU has read the opcode, it automatically increments its address bus to point to the next memory location ('n + 1' in this example). Because the CPU understands that $21 represents a three-byte instruction, it will automatically read the operand byte at location 'n + 1' (which happens to be $5C in this example). The CPU knows that this byte forms the first part of an address, so it will store this data in the most-significant half of a 16-bit temporary location within itself. As soon as the CPU has performed this read, it automatically increments its address bus to point to the next memory location (which will be 'n + 2'). Remembering that the CPU understands it's dealing with a three-byte instruction, it will now read the operand byte at location 'n + 2' (which happens to be $20 in this example). Once again, the CPU knows that this byte forms the second part of an address, so it will store this data in the lest-significant half of the 16-bit temporary location within itself. As usual, the CPU will now automatically increment its address bus to point to the next memory location ('n + 3' in this example).

OK, let's pause for breath and briefly recap where we are. When the CPU "saw" our $21 opcode, it realized that it was dealing with a three-byte instruction (a SUB using the absolute addressing mode), so it proceeded to read the following two operand bytes and to

store them in a temporary location within itself, leaving the address bus pointing at location 'n + 3'. Now the CPU understands that the combination of the two operand bytes represents the address of the data that it is supposed to use (Figure 8.17). Furthermore, in the case of the *Beboputer*, the CPU assumes that the first and second operand bytes of an absolute instruction represent the most-significant and least-significant bytes of the target address, respectively.[5] Thus, in the case of this particular example, the CPU knows that the data it requires is contained in memory location $5C20.

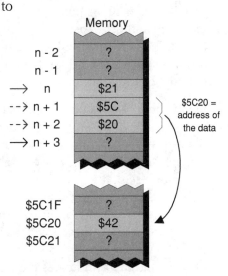

Figure 8.17: Absolute addressing

So in order to complete the instruction, the CPU now drives the $5C20 value stored inside its temporary location onto the address bus, thereby pointing to the memory location containing the data. The CPU then reads this data (which happens to be $42 in this example) and performs the relevant operation, which is to subtract the data from the accumulator. As soon as the CPU has finished performing the operation, it will return the address bus to point to its previous location ('n + 3' in this example). As you

---

[5]As we have previously mentioned, many commercial microprocessors would expect addresses to be stored in memory with the least-significant byte first, because this facilitates something called *relative addressing*, which is introduced in more detail in Chapter 12.

might expect by now, the CPU will automatically assume that the byte following a three-byte instruction is the first byte (the opcode) of a new instruction, so it will read that byte and start the process all over again.

The grim truth about the origin of opcodes

A key point to note at this juncture is that certain instructions can employ more than one addressing mode; for example, the LDA, ADD, SUB, AND, OR, and XOR instructions can all use either *immediate* or *absolute* addressing. So a good question to ask would be: *"How can we (humans) tell them apart?"* Well one technique would be to simply append the mnemonics with a suffix indicating the addressing mode; for example, LDA-imm and LDA-abs. (There are more convenient techniques, but you'll have to bide awhile until we meet these.) However, the CPU cannot accept any ambiguity, and stridently demands that each instruction has a unique opcode for every addressing mode (Table 8.2).

Don't Panic! This is not complicated! As we have remarked on a number of occasions, these things just appear to be on the complex side because they're new. Let's take things one step at a time. The column headers *imp*, *imm*, and *abs* represent the *implied*, *immediate*, and *absolute* addressing modes, respectively; while the sub-column header *op* stands for *opcode* and the # indicates the number of bytes required by that instruction. Thus, we can see that the LDA-imm instruction (with its immediate addressing) has an opcode of $90 and requires a two-byte instruction, while its LDA-abs counterpart (with its absolute addressing) has an opcode of $91 and requires a three-byte instruction. Now be fair, it's not as bad as you thought, is it?

	imp		imm		abs	
	op	#	op	#	op	#
LDA			$90	2	$91	3
STA					$99	3
ADD			$10	2	$11	3
SUB			$20	2	$21	3
AND			$30	2	$31	3
OR			$38	2	$39	3
XOR			$40	2	$41	3
INCA	$80	1				
DECA	$81	1				
ROLC	$78	1				
RORC	$79	1				
SHL	$70	1				
SHR	$71	1				

Table 8.2: Addressing modes and associated opcodes

The next point to consider is the origin of the opcode values themselves. For example, why does it happen that the *Beboputer* understands the opcodes $90, $70, and $99 to represent the **LDA-imm** (immediate), **SHL-imp** (implied), and **STA-abs** (absolute) instructions, respectively? Well as we already discussed, when engineers sit down to design a new computer, one of their main tasks is to agree on the instructions that will be included in its instruction set. What we didn't mention is that a significant part of the process is to assign individual opcodes to each of these instructions. Deciding on an instruction set and assigning opcodes to these instructions is something of a mystic art that depends on a smorgasbord of interrelated factors (such as the proposed internal structure of the CPU, which is referred to as its *architecture*). For the nonce, let's simply assume that one designer says: *"I'd like to use $91 as the opcode that tells the CPU to load the accumulator using the absolute addressing mode,"* and that his or her chums reply: *"That sounds good to us, now let's go out for lunch!"* Similarly, in the case of the *Beboputer*, we just happened to decide to use the $90 as the opcode for **LDA-imm**, $70 as the opcode for **SHL-imp**, and so forth. (Actually, there's a bit more to it than this, but nothing that we wish to become embroiled in here.)

The end result is that, in addition to having its own unique instruction set, each type of computer has its own unique opcodes. One obvious problem with this way of doing things is that programs written in the machine code for one computer won't run on a different type of computer (this problem is somewhat mitigated by the use of higher level languages, which are discussed in Chapter 12). So why do computer designers insist on doing things this way? One answer is that computers are constantly evolving and different design teams keep on coming up with ideas for better and faster ways of doing things. Another reason is that instruction sets are proprietary commercial property, which can be valuable in their own right. Last but not least, every design team accepts as an article of faith that the gods are smiling upon them, and that divine inspiration will provided them with the best of all possible schemes.

So let's put this all together, and consider a segment of a simple program that commences at memory location $4000 (Figure 8.18).

First the CPU recognizes the $90 opcode in location $4000 as an **LDA-imm** (meaning *"Load the accumulator using the immediate addressing mode"*), so it loads the data that it finds in location $4001 (which happens to be $03 in this example) into the accumulator.

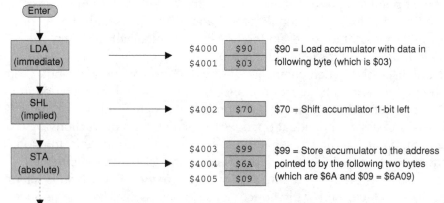

Figure 8.18: Putting it all together

The CPU next reads the $70 opcode from location $4002 and recognizes it as a SHL-imp (meaning "*Shift the accumulator one bit left using the implied addressing mode*"), so it simply shifts the contents of the accumulator one bit to the left. (Note that as the accumulator originally contained $03, shifting it one bit left leaves it containing $06.)

After performing the shift, the CPU moves on to read the $99 opcode at location $4003. The CPU recognizes this as a **STA-abs** (meaning "*Store the accumulator using the absolute addressing mode*"), so it loads the two bytes that it finds in locations $4004 and $4005 (which, in this example, happen to be $6A and $09, respectively) into the temporary location within itself.

The CPU then drives the value $6A09 contained within its temporary location out onto the address bus and stores the contents of the accumulator ($06) into that memory location. Finally, the CPU returns its address bus to point to the next instruction at location $4006, and continues to Bebop along with whatever it finds there.

The status register (SR)

Before commencing our headlong plunge into the bowels of the CPU, there's one more register that deserves mention: the *status register (SR)* (Figure 8.19). Each bit in the status register is called a *status bit*, but they are also commonly referred to as *status flags* or *condition codes*, because they serve to signal that certain conditions have occurred. As we shall see, each status bit is essentially independent of the other status bits. In fact the status bits are so autonomous that the main reason we consider them collectively (in the form of the status register) is to facilitate manipulating them as a group.

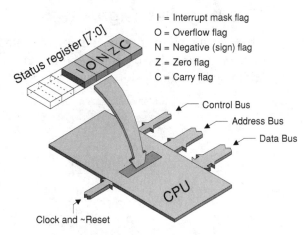

I = Interrupt mask flag
O = Overflow flag
N = Negative (sign) flag
Z = Zero flag
C = Carry flag

Since we may require to load the status register from, or store it to, the memory (albeit in a different manner to the way in which we handle the accumulator), it is usual to regard this register as being the same width as the data bus (which is 8 bits in our virtual system). However, in the case of the *Beboputer* we only actually employ five status flags: the

Figure 8.19: The status register (SR)

interrupt mask flag, overflow flag, negative flag, zero flag, and *carry flag.* These are the most generic status flags and are common to almost every microprocessor on the face of the planet. For no particular reason other than aesthetic considerations, we determined that our status flags would occupy the five least-significant bits of the status register. Thus, the three most significant bits of the register exist only in our imaginations, which means that their non-existent contents are, by definition, undefined.

Before we consider the *Beboputer's* status flags in more detail, we need to be aware of certain conventions as follows:

a) A status flag is said to be "set" if it contains a *logic 1*, which is used to indicate a **TRUE** condition. For example, if the zero flag is set (contains a *logic 1*), it indicates that the current value stored in the accumulator is zero (that is, all of the bits in the accumulator currently contain zeros).

b) A status flag is said to be "cleared" if it contains a *logic 0*, which is used to indicate a **FALSE** condition. For example, if the zero flag is cleared (contains a *logic 0*), it indicates that the current value stored in the accumulator is non-zero (that is, one or more of the bits in the accumulator contain a *logic 1*).

Note that although the zero flag is predominantly used to indicate whether or not the accumulator currently contains a zero value as we just discussed, this status flag is multifaceted and can be used to indicate other conditions depending on the actual operation being performed (see also the discussions on the zero flag and the **CMPA** instruction later in this chapter).

The negative (sign) flag

The negative flag contains a copy of the most significant bit *in* the accumulator following an operation *on* the accumulator (including arithmetic, logical, shift, rotate, and load operations) (Figure 8.20).

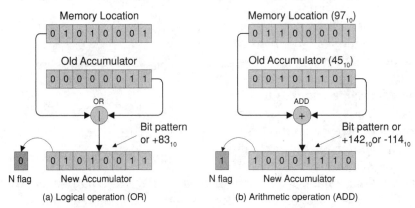

Figure 8.20: The negative status flag

This status flag is called the *negative flag* because, if the value in the accumulator is considered to be a signed (two's complement) binary number, then a *logic 1* in the most-significant bit indicates a negative number. Similarly, the reason this flag is sometimes referred to as the *sign flag* is that the most-significant bit of a signed binary number is referred to as the *sign bit*.

However, this leads us to an excruciatingly important point, which is that a value stored in the accumulator can represent whatever we want it to at any particular time. For example, in the case of the logical operation shown in Figure 8.20a, we can regard the resulting value in the accumulator as being either a simple bit pattern or a binary number representing $+83_{10}$. Similarly, in the case of the arithmetic operation illustrated in Figure 8.20b, even though this *is* an arithmetic operation, we can still view the final value stored in the accumulator as being a non-numerical bit pattern if we so desire. Alternatively, we might wish to consider this value as representing either the unsigned binary number $+142_{10}$ or the signed (two's complement) binary number -114_{10}.

The point is that the CPU doesn't have a clue as to how we're viewing the contents of the accumulator at any particular time. All the CPU can do is ensure that the negative status flag contains a copy of the most significant bit in the accumulator. Thus, if we (the programmers) decide to consider the value in the accumulator as representing a two's complement binary number, then we may also say that a *logic 1* in the negative flag indicates that this number is negative. But if we decide to regard the value in the accumulator as representing a simple bit pattern or an unsigned binary number, then all we can say is that the negative flag contains a copy of the most-significant bit in the accumulator and leave it at that.

The zero flag

The zero flag is predominantly used to indicate whether or not the accumulator contains a value of zero following an operation that affects the accumulator (including arithmetic, logical, shift, rotate, and load operations) (Figure 8.21).

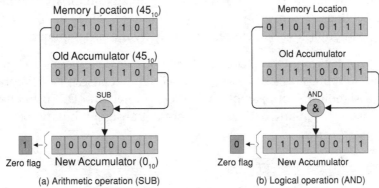

Figure 8.21: The zero status flag

Remember that a status flag which is "set" (contains a *logic 1*) indicates a **TRUE** condition, while a status flag that is "cleared" (contains a *logic 0*) indicates a **FALSE** condition. Thus, in the case of the arithmetic operation shown in Figure 8.21a, the zero flag is set to *logic 1* to say: "*It's* <u>true</u> *that the accumulator contains a zero value.*" Similarly, in the case of the logical operation illustrated in Figure 8.21b, the zero flag is set to *logic 0* to say: "*It's* <u>false</u> *(not true) that the accumulator contains a zero value.*" Unfortunately, this can be a bit confusing for beginners, who generally feel that a *logic 0* in the zero flag should indicate a zero value in the accumulator. However, as we progress you will begin to understand that the way in which the zero flag functions is logically consistent with the rest of the CPU's universe.

Also note that in addition to indicating a zero value in the accumulator, the zero flag is occasionally used for other purposes which will be noted in due course (see also the discussions on the **CMPA** instruction and the *index register* later in this chapter).

The carry flag

The carry flag is perhaps the most multifarious of all the status flags, in that it's used for a smorgasbord of different purposes, but it's most obvious task is to store any carry-out from arithmetic operations performed on unsigned binary numbers.

Additions and the carry flag

Once again, remember that the CPU doesn't have any way of telling what the values it is manipulating are supposed to represent. These values can symbolize simple bit patterns without any particular numerical significance, unsigned binary numbers, or signed (two's complement) binary numbers; but the CPU doesn't know, because whatever these values happen to stand for at any particular time is determined solely by the programmer.

However, the fact that the CPU cannot tell what its data values are currently being used to represent is somewhat immaterial, because it can simply make an assumption. For example, when performing an **ADD** instruction the CPU can assume that any data values represent unsigned binary numbers (Figure 8.22).

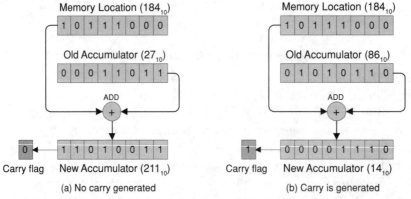

Figure 8.22: The carry status flag (carries from unsigned additions)

Remember that if the value in the accumulator is considered to represent an unsigned binary number, then our 8-bit accumulator can represent values in the range 0_{10} through $+255_{10}$. So if we add two numbers such as 184_{10} and 27_{10} together (Figure 8.22a), the result of 211_{10} can be accommodated in the accumulator and the carry flag is cleared to *logic 0*, thereby saying: *"It's false (not true) that this addition resulted in a carry out."*

By comparison, if we attempt to add two numbers such as 184_{10} and 86_{10} together (Figure 8.22b), the result of 270_{10} cannot be accommodated in the accumulator (whose 8-bit field would actually end up containing 14_{10}). In this case the carry flag is set to *logic 1*, thereby saying: *"It's true that this addition resulted in a carry out."* Of course the way in which the carry flag is subsequently employed is now in the hands of the programmer. For example, a *logic 1* in the carry flag can simply be used to indicate an error condition along the lines of: *"The accumulator wasn't big enough to hold the result generated by adding these two numbers."* The programmer could then use this information to issue an error message or to pursue another course of action. Alternatively, the carry flag can be used to allow the programmer to perform multi-byte additions (which are discussed in more detail in Appendix G). As a point of interest, if we consider the combination of the 1-bit carry flag and the 8-bit accumulator to form a 9-bit field, then the value 100001110_2 does indeed represent 270_{10}, which would be the correct result from the operation in Figure 8.22b (and which is the basis for multi-byte additions in the first place).

Subtractions and the carry flag

The carry flag is also used in the case of subtractions. As usual, the CPU doesn't actually know what the values it is manipulating are supposed to represent, but when presented with a SUB instruction it once again assumes that any data values represent unsigned binary numbers.

Just to add to the confusion, when we subtract one number from another we don't actually generate *carries*, but instead we generate *borrows* (think about how a subtraction is performed in decimal). Thus, although we continue to refer to this status bit as the "carry flag," it actually ends up containing the status pertaining to any requirements for a borrow in the case of a SUB instruction (Figure 8.23).

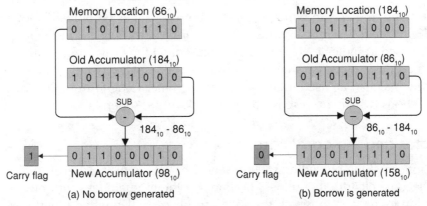

(a) No borrow generated   (b) Borrow is generated

Figure 8.23: The carry status flag (borrows from unsigned subtractions)

To further muddy the waters, borrows act in a manner opposite to carries. By this we mean that if the carry flag contains a *logic 1* following a SUB instruction, then this indicates a "no borrow" condition; but if the carry flag ends up containing a *logic 0*, then this indicates that a borrow *was* generated. Due to this inversion, the contents of the carry flag following a SUB instruction are sometimes referred to as representing a *borrow-out-not* or a *borrow-not* condition.

Now all of this may seem incredibly convoluted and involved, but you've got to have "*confidence in nonsense*" and hang in there. The reasons for borrows acting in an opposite manner to carries makes perfect sense once you understand the underlying number theory. Also, this will all become much clearer when we start to consider how the logic gates inside the CPU actually perform additions and subtractions.

For the nonce, we need only note that subtracting a smaller number like 86_{10} from a larger number like 184_{10} (Figure 8.23a) results in the accumulator containing the correct value of 98_{10} and the carry flag containing a *logic 1* (thereby indicating that no borrow was generated from this operation). By comparison, when we subtract a larger number like 184_{10} from a smaller number like 86_{10} (Figure 8.23b), the result of -98_{10} cannot be accommodated in the accumulator. The reason for this is obvious when we recall that the CPU sets or clears the carry (borrow) flag based on the assumption that its data values represent *unsigned* binary numbers. By definition, unsigned binary numbers can only be used to represent positive values, so we can't subtract a larger value from a smaller value and expect to receive the correct result. (This is why subtracting 184_{10} from 86_{10} actually results in the accumulator containing the incorrect value of $+158_{10}$ in this example.)

Once again, the way in which the carry (borrow) flag is employed following a SUB instruction is in the hands of the programmer; a *logic 0* in the flag can be used to indicate an error condition, which the programmer can detect and use to pursue a certain course of action. Alternatively, the carry (borrow) flag can be used to allow the programmer to perform multi-byte subtractions (which are discussed in more detail in Appendix G).

Rotates and the carry flag

Don't worry if the preceding section seemed a bit confusing, because all will become clear in the fullness of time. For the moment let's turn our attention to the way in which the CPU uses its carry flag when it performs rotate instructions (Figure 8.24).

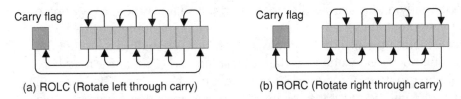

(a) ROLC (Rotate left through carry)   (b) RORC (Rotate right through carry)

Figure 8.24: The carry status flag's relationship to the rotate instructions

As you may recall, in the case of a **ROLC** (*"rotate left through the carry bit"*), the original contents of bit[0] of the accumulator move into bit[1], the original contents of bit[1] move into bit[2], and so on down the line until we arrive at bit[7], which moves into the carry flag, which, in turn, rolls around into bit[0]. Similarly, in the case of a **RORC** (*"rotate right through the carry bit"*), the original contents of bit[7] move right into bit[6], the original contents of bit[6] move right into bit[5], and so forth until we arrive at bit[0], which moves into the carry flag, which, in turn, rolls around into bit[7].

Although it may not be immediately obvious, performing our rotate instructions through the carry flag in this way becomes extremely useful should we wish to perform multi-byte rotates (classic examples of this occur in our multiplication subroutines as described in Appendix G).

Shifts and the carry flag

In our previous discussions on the shifts, we stated that bit[7] or bit[0] of the accumulator would be discarded in the case of a left or right shift, respectively. However, we weren't exactly telling the full story, because these bits are in fact copied into the carry flag (Figure 8.25).

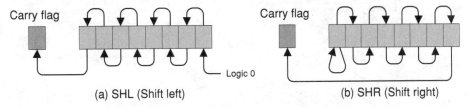

(a) SHL (Shift left)   (b) SHR (Shift right)

Figure 8.25: The carry status flag's relationship to the shift instructions

In fact the relationship between the shift instructions and the carry flag is somewhat similar to that of the rotates. Whichever bit conceptually "drops off the end" from a **SHL** (*"shift left"*) or **SHR** (*"shift right"*) is copied into the carry flag, which becomes extremely useful should we wish to perform multi-byte shifts.

Additionally, in our earlier discussions on the shift instructions we noted that there could be problems if we used a **SHL** to multiply a value by two, because our 8-bit accumulator may not be large enough to represent the resulting numerical value in certain cases. Similarly, we noted that there could be problems using a **SHR** to divide a number by two, because the remainder will be lost if the original value was an odd number. However, the fact that whichever bit "drops off the end" during a shift is stored in the carry flag provides us with the ability to detect and correct these problems.

The overflow flag

Previously we noted that the carry flag can be used to store the carries (or borrows) generated by arithmetic operations on unsigned binary numbers. We also noted that the CPU doesn't actually know whether the values it's manipulating are supposed to represent unsigned or signed binary numbers, but it assumes unsigned quantities for the purposes of updating the carry flag when it encounters **ADD** or **SUB** instructions.

The key point here is the qualification *"for the purposes of updating the carry flag."* The designers of the CPU are well aware that the programmer may be considering the data values as representing signed (two's complement) binary numbers. The problem is that the carry flag has little meaning if the data values *do* represent two's complement numbers,[6] so the CPU's designers also include the overflow status flag (Figure 8.26).

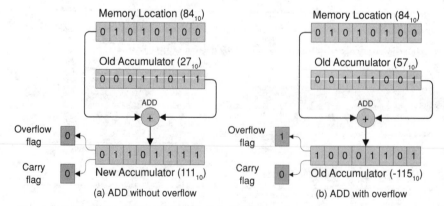

Figure 8.26: The carry status flag's (for signed arithmetic operations)

---

[6]Although we said that the carry flag has "little meaning" with regard to arithmetic operations on two's complement numbers, we didn't say it was "meaningless." In fact the carry flag does serve a useful purpose when we come to consider multi-byte operations on such numbers (see also Appendix G).

Remember that our 8-bit accumulator can be used to represent two's complement numbers in the range -128_{10} through $+127_{10}$. Thus, if we add two numbers such as 84_{10} and 27_{10} together (Figure 8.26a), the result of 111_{10} can be accommodated in the accumulator and the overflow flag is cleared to *logic 0*, thereby saying: *"It's <u>false</u> (not true) that this addition resulted in an overflow."* By comparison, if we attempt to add two numbers such as 84_{10} and 57_{10} together (Figure 8.26b), the result of 141_{10} cannot be accommodated in the accumulator (whose 8-bit field would actually end up containing -115_{10}). In this case the overflow is set to *logic 1*, thereby saying: *"It's <u>true</u> that this addition resulted in an overflow."*

An important point to note here is that the carry flag was cleared to logic zero in both of these examples. The reason for this is that if the values *were* considered to be unsigned binary values, then both of the operations actually generated the correct result. That is, the final value in the accumulator only represents -115_{10} if we consider that value to be a two's complement number, but if we consider it to be an unsigned binary number then the bit pattern *does* equate to 141_{10}.

Although this may appear to be somewhat confusing at first, the underlying mechanism is actually quite simple. Let's return to the fact that the CPU doesn't know whether the programmer is considering the data values to represent unsigned or two's complement numbers. To resolve this conundrum, we might visualize the CPU as saying:

a) *"First I'll regard these values as being unsigned binary numbers, so I'll perform an unsigned binary addition (or subtraction) and load the carry flag accordingly."*

b) *"Next I'll regard the values as being two's complement numbers, so I'll perform a two's complement addition (or subtraction) and load the overflow flag accordingly."*

Of course this isn't the way in which the CPU actually works, because it would be dreadfully inefficient to perform two operations every time we wanted to add (or subtract) a pair of numbers. In reality the CPU only performs a single addition (or subtraction), because the arithmetic processes for unsigned and signed numbers are absolutely identical, excepting the way in which the carry and overflow flags are set. The carry flag is simply treated as an additional (ninth) accumulator bit, so any carry out from bit[7] of the result is simply dumped into this flag. By comparison, the overflow flag is generated as an **XOR** of any carry into, and out of, bit[7] of the result.

However, we don't really need to understand exactly how the overflow flag is generated at this time (we will return to consider this later). For the moment we need only understand that the overflow flag is used to indicate when the result of an arithmetic operation using two's complement numbers produces a result that cannot be represented correctly. For example, if two positive numbers are added together such that the result would be greater than $+127_{10}$, or if two negative numbers are added together such that the result would be less than -128_{10}, then the overflow flag would be set (this latter case is sometimes referred to as an *underflow*). It's also worth pointing out that the overflow flag works in exactly the same way for both **ADD** and **SUB** instructions, and it could care less whether or not the data values represent positive or negative numbers. In every case the overflow flag will be set to *logic 1* if the result of the operation cannot be correctly represented as a two's complement number in the accumulator.

The interrupt mask flag

Last but certainly not least, the interrupt mask flag is used to enable or disable external devices from interrupting the CPU in its normal course of operation. However, for our purposes at this time, we need only be aware that this flag initially powers-up such that external interrupts are disabled and it's up to the programmer to enable them. (The subject of interrupts is presented in nerve-tingling detail in Appendix D).

The CMPA instruction

As we've now been formally introduced to the status flags, we can turn our attention to an instruction that we've ignored thus far – **CMPA** (*"compare accumulator"*) – which can be used to compare the value in the accumulator to a value in a specified memory location, and to store the result of that comparison in the zero and carry status flags (Figure 8.27).

If the value in the accumulator is *greater than* the value in the designated memory location (Figure 8.27a), then the carry flag is set to *logic 1* and the zero flag is cleared to *logic 0*; thus, the carry flag is used to indicate a greater-than condition. By comparison, if the value in the accumulator is *equal to* the value in the memory location (Figure 8.27b), then the carry flag is cleared to *logic 0* and the zero flag is set to *logic 1*; thus, the zero flag is used to indicate an equal-to condition. Finally, if the value in the accumulator is *less than* the value in the memory location, both carry and zero flags will be cleared to *logic 0*. The programmer can use the fact that both of the flags are *logic 0* to recognize the corresponding less-than condition.

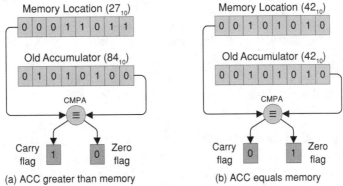

Figure 8.27: The CMPA instruction

Note that the **CMPA** instruction does not disturb the original contents of either the accumulator or the memory location. Also note that, in the case of the *Beboputer*, the **CMPA** instruction assumes that both of the numbers being compared represent *unsigned* binary values. (Some CPUs support both signed and unsigned compare instructions, but for those supporting only one flavor, the unsigned compare is the more common of the two.)

Summary of how the instructions affect the status flags

And so we've reached the point in our musings where we can relate the instructions introduced thus far to the status flags and see how well they fly (Table 8.3).

To refresh our memories, the column headers *imp*, *imm*, and *abs* represent the *implied*, *immediate*, and *absolute* addressing modes, respectively; while the sub-column header *op* stands for *opcode* and the # indicates the number of bytes required by that instruction. Thus, we can see that our new CMPA

	imp		imm		abs		flags				
	op	#	op	#	op	#	I	O	N	Z	C
LDA			$90	2	$91	3	-	-	N	Z	-
STA					$99	3	-	-	-	-	-
ADD			$10	2	$11	3	-	O	N	Z	C
SUB			$20	2	$21	3	-	O	N	Z	C
AND			$30	2	$31	3	-	-	N	Z	-
OR			$38	2	$39	3	-	-	N	Z	-
XOR			$40	2	$41	3	-	-	N	Z	-
CMPA			$60	2	$61	3	-	-	-	≥	≥
INCA	$80	1					-	-	N	Z	-
DECA	$81	1					-	-	N	Z	-
ROLC	$78	1					-	-	N	Z	↔
RORC	$79	1					-	-	N	Z	↔
SHL	$70	1					-	-	N	Z	↔
SHR	$71	1					-	-	N	Z	↔

Table 8.3: Instructions versus status flags

instruction has two addressing modes: the 2-byte **CMPA-imm** (immediate addressing) with an opcode of $60, and the 3-byte **CMPA-abs** (absolute addressing) with an opcode of $61.

Moving on to the status flags themselves, we see that everything is pretty much the way we'd expect it to be (note that the '-' symbol indicates "no change"). For example, the **LDA** ("*load accumulator*") instruction only affects the zero flag and the negative flag, while the **STA** ("*store accumulator*") instruction doesn't affect any flags at all.

The **ADD** and **SUB** arithmetic instructions are the most active, because they affect the overflow, negative, zero, and carry flags. By comparison, the logical operations **AND**, **OR**, and **XOR** only affect the negative and zero flags, while our new (semi-logical) **CMPA** instruction only affects the zero and carry flags (we're using the '≥' symbol to indicate that these flags are affected by our special magnitude comparison operation).

Not surprisingly, the **INCA** ("*increment accumulator*") and **DECA** ("*decrement accumulator*") instructions only affect the negative and zero flags. Last but not least, the shift and rotate instructions (**SHL**, **SHR**, **ROLC**, and **RORC**) affect the negative and zero flags in the standard way. These instructions also affect the carry flag, in that whichever bit conceptually "falls off the end" is copied into this flag (we're using the '↔' symbol to indicate that the carry flag is modified as part of a shift or rotate).

Finally, it's worth noting that none of the instructions we've discussed thus far have any effect on the interrupt mask flag, because this flag has to be explicitly set or cleared using its own special instructions. (Once again, the topic of interrupts is examined in gruesome detail in Appendix D.)

The Arithmetic-Logic Unit (ALU)

The heart (or perhaps the guts) of the CPU is the *arithmetic/logic unit (ALU)*, in which all of the number crunching and data manipulation takes place. As the *Beboputer's* data bus is 8 bits wide, its ALU works with 8-bit chunks of data (Figure 8.28).

The ALU accepts two 8-bit words A[7:0] and B[7:0] as input, "scrunches" them together using some arithmetic or logical operation, and outputs an 8-bit result which we've named F[7:0]. Whatever operation is performed on the data is dictated by a pattern of logic 0s and 1s called the ALU instruction. For example, one pattern may instruct the ALU to add A[7:0] and B[7:0] together, while another may request the ALU to logically **AND** each bit of A[7:0] with the corresponding bit in B[7:0].

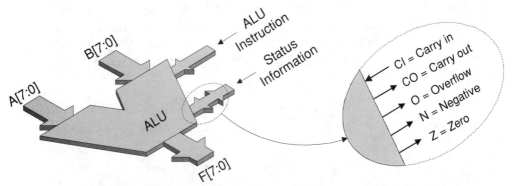

Figure 8.28: The ALU is where the "number crunching" takes place

Note that the ALU is completely asynchronous, which means that it is not directly controlled by the main system's clock. As soon as any changes are presented to the ALU's data, instruction, or carry-in inputs, these changes will immediately start to ripple through its logic gates and will eventually appear at the data and status outputs.

The "core" ALU

The number of instruction bits required to drive the ALU depends on the number of functions we require it to perform: two bits can be used to represent four different functions, three bits can represent eight functions, and so forth. This leads us to an interesting point, in that we can consider the ALU as having layers like an onion, and we might visualize the core of the *Beboputer's* ALU as performing only five simple functions (Table 8.4).

Function	Outputs F[7:0]	Flags Modified
Logical AND	A[7:0] & B[7:0]	N, Z
Logical OR	A[7:0] | B[7:0]	N, Z
Logical XOR	A[7:0] ^ B[7:0]	N, Z
Addition (ADD)	A[7:0] + B[7:0] + CI	CO, O, N, Z
Compare (CMP)	A[7:0] ≡ B[7:0]	CO, Z

Figure 8.4: The *Beboputer* ALU's five core functions

Note that the CMP function shown here will eventually be used to implement the CPU's CMPA ("*compare accumulator*") instruction that we introduced in our discussions on the status register. The instruction-bit patterns we might assign to these functions are not important for our purposes at this time; suffice it to say that the five functions shown here would only require three instruction bits. As we shall see, implementing a core ALU to perform these tasks is really not too complex. First consider how we could implement the AND function, which actually requires only eight 2-input AND gates (Figure 8.29).

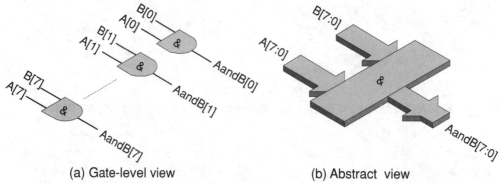

(a) Gate-level view   (b) Abstract view

Figure 8.29: Implementing the ALU's AND function using primitive gates

Similarly, the OR and XOR functions would only require eight 2-input OR gates and XOR gates, respectively. Things are a little more complex in the case of the ADD function, but not unduly so. Assuming we decide to use the technique described in Chapter 7, then our basic 8-bit adder will require a total of sixteen AND gates and twenty-four XOR gates, plus an additional XOR gate to generate the *overflow* output.[7] Similarly, the CMP (compare) is a little more complex than the primitive logical functions, but nothing that a few handfuls of cunningly connected gates can't handle. Thus, it wouldn't take us long to generate our five core functions as individual entities (Figure 8.30).

Note that the Oadd ("*overflow from the adder*") output from the ADD function would be directly connected to the main O ("*overflow*") output coming out of the core ALU. However, the ADD function's CIadd ("*carry-in to the adder*") input and COadd ("*carry-out from the adder*") output would *not* be connected to the core ALU's CI ("*carry in*") and CO ("*carry-out*") status flags, respectively, because we have other plans for these signals as we shall see.

---

[7]From our discussions earlier in this chapter, you will recall that the overflow output for an 8-bit adder can be generated by XOR-ing the carry-in and carry-out associated with bit[7] of the result.

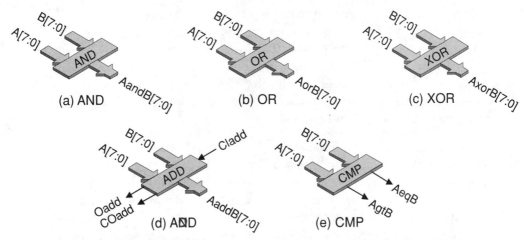

Figure 8.30: The *Beboputer*'s five core ALU functions in isolation

In the case of the CMP ("*compare*") function, the A[7:0] and B[7:0] inputs are considered to be unsigned binary numbers. On this basis, the AgtB output will be driven to *logic 1* if A[7:0] is *greater* than B[7:0], while the AeqB output will be driven to *logic 1* if A[7:0] is *equal* to B[7:0].

So at this stage in the proceedings we know how to implement the core ALU functions in isolation (although admittedly we've skimped on some of the nitty-gritty details). The next point to ponder is the means by which we can "glue" them all together to form the ALU itself. One approach would be to hurl a multiplexer into our cauldron of logic gates, stir things up a little, and see what develops (Figure 8.31).

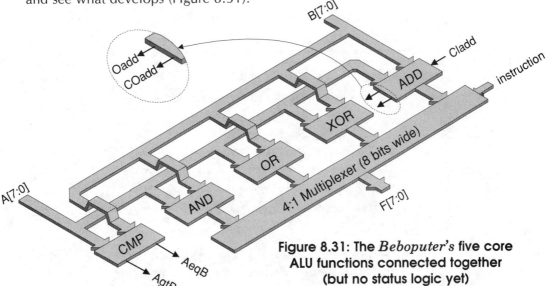

Figure 8.31: The *Beboputer*'s five core ALU functions connected together (but no status logic yet)

In this scenario we use two instruction bits (which can represent four patterns of 0s and 1s) to control a 4:1 multiplexer, where each of the input channels feeding the multiplexer is 8 bits wide. The A[7:0] and B[7:0] signals are presented to all of the functions, but only the outputs from the function of interest are selected by the multiplexer. The reason we only need a 4:1 multiplexer is that the fifth function, the CMP, only outputs status information, but doesn't generate any data as such.

The advantage of this multiplexer-based approach is that it's easy to understand, but, in fact, we would be unlikely to use it in a real-world implementation. This is because we're only interested in being able to perform a single function at any particular time, so we would examine the functions to find areas of commonality allowing us to share gates between them. To put this another way, instead of having multiple distinct functions feeding a multiplexer, we'd probably lose the multiplexer and "scrunch" all of the functions together into one "super function," thereby allowing us to reduce the ALU's total gate count and increase its speed. On the other hand, there's nothing intrinsically wrong with our multiplexer-based technique, so we'll stick with it for the purposes of these discussions.

So now we know how to implement the data-processing portion of our core ALU, but we've yet to decide how we're going to use the AgtB, AeqB, and COadd signals, and also how we're going to generate the CO, N, and Z status outputs (Figure 8.32).

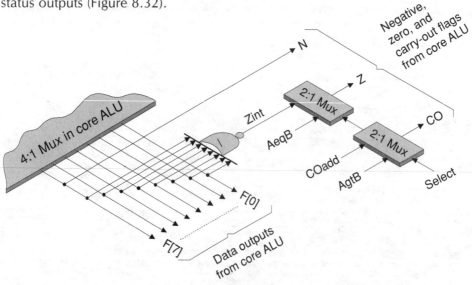

Figure 8.32: Generating the status outputs for the *Beboputer's* five core ALU functions

The N ("*negative*") status output is the easiest of all, because it's simply a copy of the most-significant bit of the data outputs (that is, F[7]). Things get a little more complicated when we come to the Z ("*zero*") output, because this signal depends on the type of operation the ALU is performing. In the case of the AND, OR, XOR, and ADD functions, the zero output is set to *logic 1* if the result from the operation is all 0s. We can create an internal signal called Zint to implement this by simply feeding all of the F[7:0] data outputs into an 8-bit NOR gate. However, in the case of the CMP function, we wish the Z output to be set to *logic 1* if the two data values A[7:0] and B[7:0] are equal (represented by the AeqB signal coming out of the CMP block).

The bottom line is that we've got a single output, Z, which we want to reflect the state of one of two signals, Zint and AeqB, depending on the function being performed. We can achieve this by feeding Zint and AeqB into a 2:1 multiplexer, whose select input is controlled by the third instruction bit driving the core ALU. Similarly, we usually want the CO status output to reflect the carry out from the ADD function on its COadd signal; but, if we're performing a CMP instruction, then we want the CO signal to be set to *logic 1* if the unsigned binary value on A[7:0] is greater than that on B[7:0]. Once again, we can achieve this by feeding both the COadd and AgtB signals into a 2:1 multiplexer controlled by our third instruction bit.

Extending the core ALU to perform subtractions and stuff

At this stage we've designed a core ALU that can perform five simple functions, but we know that our CPU requires more of us. For example, our core ALU has an ADD function that can add two 8-bit numbers together (along with the carry-in status input), but the CPU needs to be able to perform both additions and subtractions in the form of the ADD and SUB instructions that we defined at the beginning of this chapter. Furthermore, in order to perform multi-byte additions and subtractions, we're going to require two new instructions called ADDC and SUBC, in which the carry-in input to the adder block is fed by whatever value is currently stored in the carry flag. While we're pondering this poser, we might also decide to consider the INCA and DECA instructions, which will add 1 to, or subtract 1 from, the contents of the accumulator, respectively.

One thing we know (but you don't yet) is that, in the fullness of time, we're going to connect our 8-bit accumulator to the A[7:0] inputs feeding the ALU. Thus, we need to extend our core ALU in strange and wondrous ways such that we can control the value being fed into the B[7:0] inputs (Figure 8.33).

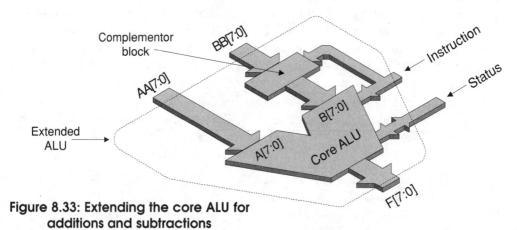

Figure 8.33: Extending the core ALU for additions and subtractions

Before delving into this new complementor block, it may be best to determine exactly what we want it to do. In the case of instructions such as AND, OR, XOR, ADD, and ADDC, we want the new block to pass whatever value is on the BB[7:0] inputs directly through to its outputs without any modification. In the case of SUB and SUBC instructions, our new block must negate the value on the BB[7:0] inputs before passing it on to the core ALU. Finally, in the case of instructions such as INCA and DECA, we want our new block to generate the appropriate value to be added to, or subtracted from, the accumulator (which, as we previously stated, is going to be connected to the AA[7:0] inputs) (Figure 8.34).

> Note that we are eventually going to require our extended ALU to perform sixteen different operations, which will therefore require four instruction bits. We can subsequently decode the various multiplexer controls and suchlike from these four bits inside the ALU.

Don't worry, this isn't as complicated as it looks ...... well maybe it is as complicated as it looks, but it's not quite as bad as you think it's going to be. In fact this new block contains only two functions: a 5:1 multiplexer and a negator, where the negator simply comprises eight NOT gates — one for each signal in the data path.[8] If the pattern on the instruction bits represents an operation such as AND, OR, XOR, ADD, or ADDC, then we'll decode them in such a way that they cause the 5:1 multiplexer to select the value on BB[7:0]. By comparison, a SUB or

---

[8]As opposed to constructing the negator block from NOT gates, we could decide to use eight 2-input XOR gates, each of which could have one of its inputs connected to a common control signal. In this case a *logic 0* on the control signal would pass the values on BB[7:0] through the XOR gates unmodified, while a *logic 1* would cause these values to be inverted. This would allow us to replace our 5:1 multiplexer with a 4:1 version that would require substantially fewer gates.

SUBC will cause the multiplexer to select the outputs from the negator block, whose value is the inverse of that found on BB[7:0]. In the case of a DECA, the multiplexer will select a hard-wired value of $FE (-2 in decimal), while an INCA will cause the multiplexer to select a hardwired value of $01 (+1 in decimal). The only other input to the multiplexer is a hard-wired value of $00 (0 in decimal), whose purpose will be revealed a little later.

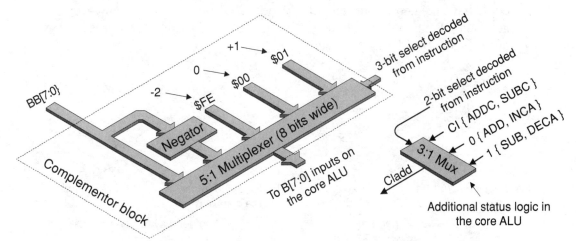

**Figure 8.34: Contents of the complementor block
(plus some additional status logic in the core ALU)**

One question that is probably on your lips is: *"Why does our complementor block only contain a negator (which generates the one's complement of the value on BB[7:0]) instead of a two's complementor?"* After all, we devoted a lot of effort in Chapter 7 to sing the praises of two's versus one's complement representations (*"In four-part harmony and stuff like that"*).[9] Similarly, if a DECA operation is intended to subtract 1 from the contents of the accumulator (which we're going to connect to the ALU's AA[7:0] inputs), then why does this operation actually cause the multiplexer to select the hard-wired value $FE, which equates to -2 in decimal. These questions are related, and the answers will make you begin to appreciate the wily ways of the CPU designer. But before we answer these points, let's first review what we know from Chapter 7:

    i)   We can perform a subtraction such as a - b by converting b into its negative equivalent and then performing an addition; that is, another way to represent a - b is to say a + (-b).

---

[9]From the song *Alice's Restaurant* by Arlo Guthrie

ii) We can convert **b** to - **b** by generating its two's complement.

iii) We already have an **ADD** function in the core ALU.

So one way to perform a simple **SUB** operation would be to cause the **Cladd** input to the **ADD** function in the core ALU to be forced to a *logic 0*, and to feed the **BB[7:0]** inputs through a two's complementor function (that we could have created in our new block had we wished to do so). However, generating the two's complement of a binary value requires us to invert all of the bits and add 1 to the result (Figure 8.35a).

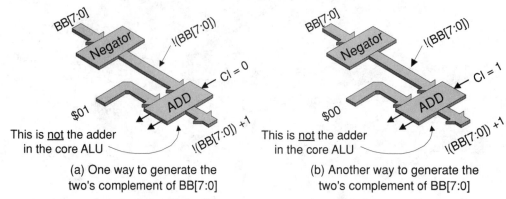

(a) One way to generate the two's complement of BB[7:0]

(b) Another way to generate the two's complement of BB[7:0]

Figure 8.35: Two techniques for generating the two's complement of BB(7:0)

Remember that we're not actually going to use a two's complementor; this portion of our discussions is simply intended to "set the scene." The process of inverting the bits using the negator is easy (we can simply feed each bit through a **NOT** gate), but adding 1 to the result would require us to build a second 8-bit adder, which would require an additional 41 logic gates.[10] Given a choice, we would prefer not to have two 8-bit adders in our ALU, but what can we do?

In fact the answer is floating around under our noses. Consider the methods for generating a two's complement shown in Figure 8.35. The first (Figure 8.35a) requires us to force this adder's CI input to a *logic 0*, and to connect its second set of data inputs to a hard-wired $01 value. Alternatively, we can achieve the same effect by connecting the second set of data inputs to a hard-wired $00 value and forcing the CI input to a *logic 1* (Figure 8.35b).

Hmmm, just a cotton-pickin' moment. Earlier in our discussions we noted that if we decided to use a two's complementor for a simple **SUB** operation,

---

[10]This assumes that we're using a simple *ripple adder* as described in Chapter 7. In a real CPU we'd typically employ a faster type of adder that, paradoxically, would require more gates.

then we would have to force the **Cladd** input to the adder in the core ALU to a *logic 0*. Let's play a little thought experiment and combine the two's complementor from Figure 8.35b with the main adder in the core ALU (note we've omitted the multiplexer in our complementor block to simplify the issue) (Figure 8.36).

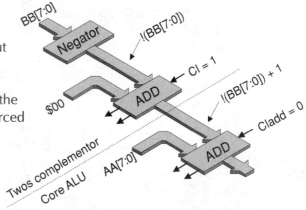

Does anything leap out at you from this figure? Well, the CI input to the adder in the two's complementor is being forced to *logic 1*, while the **Cladd** input to the adder in the core ALU is being forced to a *logic 0*. It doesn't take much thought to realize that we can achieve exactly the same effect by forcing the CI input to the adder in the two's complementor to a *logic 0*, and forcing the **Cladd** input to the adder in the core ALU to a *logic 1*.

Figure 8.36: If we were to use a two's complementor (which we aren't)

Now this is the clever bit. If the CI input to the adder in the two's complementor is forced to a *logic 0*, then this adder isn't actually doing anything at all. That is, we've ended up with a block that's adding one set of inputs (the outputs from the negator) to a value of $00 with a carry-in of zero. As any value plus zero equals itself, why do we need this adder? We don't! If we force the **Cladd** input to the adder in the core ALU to a *logic 1*, we can simply lose the adder from the twos complementor. Hence the fact that Figure 8.34 showed our new block as only containing a negator and a multiplexer. So now let's summarize where we're at so far:

a) To perform a **SUB** function (without a carry-in), we need to perform the operation a[7:0] - b[7:0]

b) We know that this is equivalent to a[7:0] + (-b[7:0])

c) We also know that we can generate (-b[7:0]) by taking the two's complement of b[7:0] using (!b[7:0] + 1), which gives us
a[7:0] + (!b[7:0] + 1)

d) But we don't want to use a two's complementor; we only want to use a negator (one's complementor). The one's complement of b[7:0] is !b[7:0], which would give us a[7:0] + (!b[7:0])

e) We know that the two's complement of a number equals its one's complement + 1, so we can also say that the one's complement of a number equals the two's complement -1. This means that a[7:0] + (!b[7:0]) is actually equivalent to a[7:0] + ((-b[7:0]) - 1)

f) So forcing the Cladd input to the adder in the core ALU to *logic 1* means that the operation we're actually performing is a[7:0] + ((-b[7:0]) - 1) + 1

If we cancel out the -1 and +1 in step (f), then we're left with an identical expression to that shown in step (b), which is what we wanted in the first place. It now becomes apparent why, in Figure 34, we added the 3:1 multiplexer to the core ALU (Figure 8:37). This allows us to force the Cladd signal to a *logic 1* for SUB and DECA operations. It also becomes apparent why we force the multiplexer in our complementor block to select $FE (-2 in decimal) for the DECA operation; in this case, the *logic 1* on the Cladd signal means that the operation

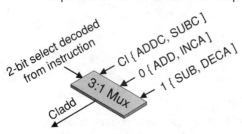

Figure 8.37: The multiplexer we added to the core ALU

actually performed by the extended ALU is A[7:0] -2 + 1, which equals A[7:0] -1, which is what we want our DECA operation to do (phew!).[11]

Extending the core ALU to perform shifts and rotates

Cheer up. After the previous section, this one is going to be a doddle. As we discussed at the beginning of this chapter, we want to be able to shift and rotate the contents of the accumulator using instructions that we called SHL (*"shift left"*), SHR (*"shift right"*), ROLC (*"rotate left through the carry bit"*), and RORC (*"rotate right through the carry bit"*). One way to achieve this is to further extend our core ALU by "gluing" another block onto it (Figure 8.38).

Note that although we've decided to attach this new block to the outputs of the core ALU, we could stick in a number of other places if we so desired. However, the fact that we have attached the shifter/rotator block to these outputs means that the logic we use to generate the Z (*"zero"*) and N (*"negative"*) status flags must be removed from the F[7:0] signals and

---

[11]There are a myriad ways to implement this sort of thing, this just happens to be the one we chose.

reattached to the extended ALU's FF[7:0] outputs (the logic for the Z and N status flags was illustrated in detail in Figure 8.32).

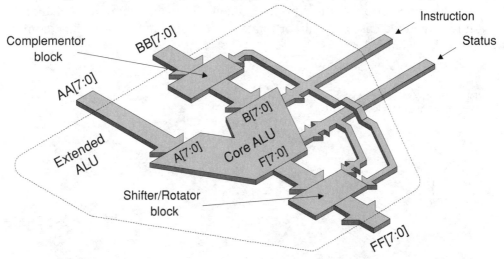

Figure 8.38: Extending the core ALU for shifts and rotates

Before leaping headfirst into this new block, there's one more point we should discuss. As you may recall, the multiplexer in our complementor block had one set of inputs connected to a hard-wired value of $00 (see figure 8.34), but we never got around to explaining why. Well remember that we're going to connect our accumulator to the extended ALU's AA[7:0] inputs. If we decide to perform a shift or rotate operation, then we want the values on the AA[7:0] inputs to be passed through the core ALU and fed directly into the shifter/rotator block without modification. But we know that the core ALU is always going to try to perform some sort of function on this data; after all, that's what it's there for! In fact there are a number of different ruses we could employ to solve this problem, but the technique we decided to use is as follows:

a) Assume that the extended ALU is presented with a SHL, SHR, ROLC, or RORC instruction.

b) This instruction is decoded in such a way that the multiplexer in the complementor block selects the hard-wired $00 value, while the core ALU is instructed to perform an ADD without carry (Cladd = *logic 0*).

c) Thus, the core ALU simply adds $00 to the value on the AA[7:0] inputs, **which has no effect whatsoever!** The unmodified AA[7:0] value is then handed on to the shifter/rotator block for it to perform the real operation (pretty cunning, huh?).

Now let's dive into the shifter/rotator block itself. In the case of instructions such as **AND**, **OR**, **ADD**, and **SUB**, we want our new block to simply pass whatever comes out of the core ALU straight through without modification. It is only in the case of a shift or rotate instruction that the new block comes into play (Figure 8.39).

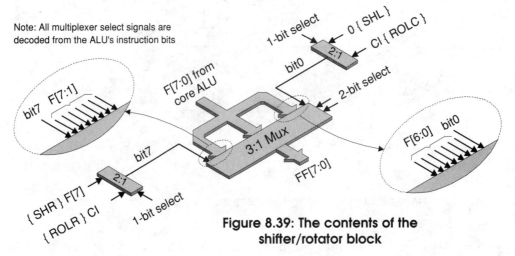

Figure 8.39: The contents of the shifter/rotator block

The mainstay of our shifter/rotator is a 3:1 multiplexer, in which each input channel is 8 bits wide. In the case of instructions like **AND**, **OR**, **ADD**, and **SUB**, we decode our instruction bits such that they cause this multiplexer to choose the F[7:0] outputs from the core ALU and pass them straight through to its FF[7:0] outputs. That is, the value on F[7] appears on FF[7], the value on F[6] appears on FF[6], and so on (this is represented by the multiplexer selecting the central set of inputs in Figure 8.39).

When we turn our attention to the **SHR** (*"shift right"*) or **RORC** (*"rotate right through the carry bit"*) instructions, a little thought reveals that we want both of them to shift whatever is coming out of the core ALU one bit to the right. That is, we want the value on F[7] to appear on FF[6], the value on F[6] to appear on FF[5], and so on (this is represented by the main multiplexer selecting the left-hand set of inputs in Figure 8.39). In fact the only difference between these instructions is the value that comes out of FF[7], which needs to be a copy of whatever was on F[7] for a **SHR**, or a copy of whatever is on the ALU's main CI (*"carry in"*) input for a **RORC**.[12]

To achieve all of this we use a simple 2:1 multiplexer to generate a signal called bit7; a **SHR** causes this multiplexer to select the input connected to

---

[12]You might wish to glance back to our earlier discussions on these instructions at this point.

F[7], while a RORC causes it to select the input being driven by CI. Now consider the magnified view of the left-hand inputs to the main multiplexer shown in Figure 8.39. As we see, the most-significant input is connected to the bit7 signal, while the remaining seven inputs are connected to F[7:1]. Thus, when the main multiplexer selects these inputs and passes them through to its outputs, the effect is to shift the bits coming out of the core ALU one bit to the right, and to insert whatever value is on the bit7 signal into the most-significant bit.

Similarly, we want both the SHL ("*shift left*") and ROLC ("*rotate left through the carry bit*") instructions to shift whatever is coming out of the core ALU one bit to the left. That is, we want the value on F[0] to appear on FF[1], the value on F[1] to appear on FF[2], and so on (this is represented by the main multiplexer selecting the right-hand set of inputs in Figure 8.39). In this case the only difference between these instructions is the value that comes out of FF[0], which needs to be a *logic 0* for a SHL, or a copy of whatever is on the ALU's main CI ("*carry in*") input for a ROLC.

Once again, we use a simple 2:1 multiplexer to generate a signal called bit0; a SHL causes this multiplexer to select the input connected to a *logic 0*, while a ROLC causes it to select the input being driven by CI. Now consider the magnified view of the right-hand inputs to the main multiplexer. As we see, the most-significant inputs are connected to the F[6:0] signals, while the least-significant input is connected to bit0. Thus, when the main multiplexer selects these inputs and passes them through to its outputs, the effect is to shift the bits coming out of the core ALU one bit to the left, and to insert whatever value is on the bit0 signal into the least-significant bit.

The only remaining task needed to complete our shifter/rotator is to modify the logic used to drive the CO ("*carry-out*") signal generated by the ALU. In our earlier discussions we used a 2:1 multiplexer to select between the COadd signal from the ADD function and the AgtB signal from the CMP function. To satisfy the requirements of our shifter/rotator, we now need to replace that 2:1 multiplexer with a 4:1 version (Figure 8.40).

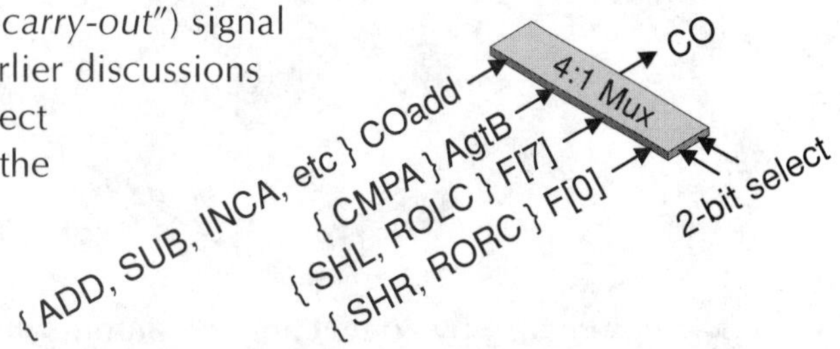

Figure 8.40: Modifying the carry-out logic to accomodate shift and rotate instructions

As usual, the select inputs controlling this multiplexer are decoded from the instruction bits driving the ALU. The ADD, OR, XOR, ADD, ADDC, SUB, SUBC, INCA, and DECA instructions all cause the multiplexer to select the COadd signal as before, while the CMPA instruction causes it to select the AgtB signal. In the case of the SHL or ROLC instructions, the multiplexer selects the input connected to the F[7] signal coming out of the core ALU, where F[7] is the bit that conceptually "drops off the end" when we shift everything to the left. Similarly, the SHR or RORC instructions cause the multiplexer to select the [F0] signal coming out of the core ALU, which is the bit that "drops off the end" when we shift everything to the right.

And that's your lot. The combination of the core ALU with the complementor and shifter/rotator blocks provides us with everything we need to satisfy all of the *Beboputer's* ALU-related instructions.

Connecting the accumulator and data bus to the ALU

Once we have a functional ALU we need to connect a number of doohickies to it in order to realize a fully-fledged CPU, where the first of these doodads is none other than our trusty old accumulator and a few of its closest friends (Figure 8.41).

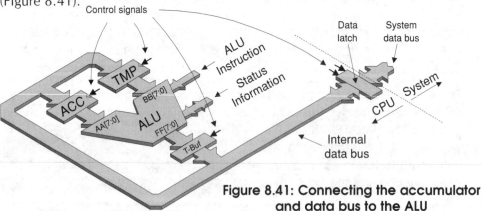

Figure 8.41: Connecting the accumulator and data bus to the ALU

We commence by connecting the outputs from our 8-bit accumulator (ACC) to the ALU's AA[7:0] inputs. Similarly, we connect an 8-bit temporary register (TMP) to the ALU's BB[7:0] inputs. The inputs to both the accumulator and the temporary register are driven by an internal 8-bit data bus, which is, in turn, linked to the "outside world" by means of an 8-bit bi-directional data latch.

Both the accumulator and the temporary register have control signals in the form of clocks. The fact that these signals are clocks is indicated by the chevrons ('v' shapes) on the symbols at the point where the signals enter them. Note that these clocks are not the same as the CPU's main clock input, although they are derived from it. Also note that these clocks can be activated individually, thereby allowing us to load one register or the other (or neither of them).

Now consider the bi-directional data latch linking the CPU's internal data bus to the main system's data bus. This latch also has control signals that dictate whether it will (a) read data into the CPU from the outside world; (b) write data from the CPU to the outside world; or (c) disconnect the internal data bus from the outside world.

Last but not least, we have an 8-bit tri-state buffer called **T-Buf**, which links the ALU's **FF[7:0]** outputs to the internal data bus. Depending on the state of the **T-Buf**'s control signal, it either propagates the outputs from the ALU onto the data bus or it isolates the ALU from the bus. All of the control signals for the registers, latches, and buffers are generated by some special logic that we haven't gotten around to worrying about yet.

To illustrate how this all hangs together, let's assume that we can control the ALU's instruction bits and drive values onto the control signals and data bus. Now assume that we want the ALU to add the values $2A (42 in decimal) and $14 (20 in decimal) together, and we then wish to retrieve the result $3E (62 in decimal). In order to achieve this, our first task will be to manually perform the same sequence of actions as would be caused by an **LDA** ("*load accumulator*") instruction (Figure 8.42).

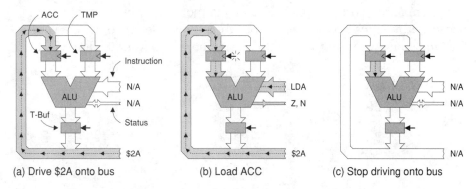

Figure 8.42: Manually performing the actions required to implement an LDA instruction

The first sub-action is to drive a value of $2A onto the internal data bus (Figure 8.42a). Note that we've only highlighted the path we're interested in at the moment; in reality this data would also be presented to the inputs of the temporary register (and to the outputs of the tri-state buffer, **T-Buf**). Next we force a binary pattern that's sort-of equivalent to an **LDA** instruction onto the instruction bits driving the ALU (we'll explain what we mean by "*sort-of*" in a moment), then we load the value on the data bus into the accumulator by triggering its clock input (Figure 8.42b). As soon as we've loaded the accumulator, this data appears at its outputs and slides into the ALU, thereby causing new values to appear on the **Z** and **N** status outputs (we'll consider what we do with this status information in the next section). Finally, we stop driving the $2A value onto the internal data bus, but the accumulator remembers this value and continues to drive it into the ALU (Figure 8.42c).

> Remember that the ALU itself is asynchronous and is therefore constantly doing something, so it will always take whatever is presented to its data inputs and generate something at its outputs. However, once again we've only highlighted the particular paths that are of interest to us at the moment.

The previous paragraph stated: "...... *force a binary pattern that's sort-of equivalent to an LDA instruction onto the instruction bits driving the ALU.*" The reason we said this is that the opcode for an **LDA** instruction will actually be processed by control logic we haven't considered yet, and it is this control logic that would generate the requisite patterns to be presented to the ALU's instruction bits.

After loading the accumulator, our next task is to manually perform the same sequence of actions as would be caused by an **ADD** ("*add data value to accumulator*") instruction. This is a little more complex than our **LDA**, because it requires two sequences of sub-actions, the first of which is to load the value we wish to add into our temporary register (Figure 8.43).

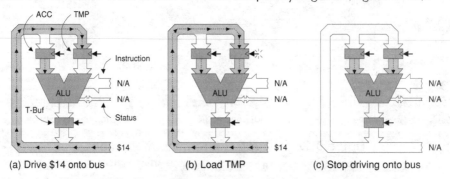

(a) Drive $14 onto bus   (b) Load TMP   (c) Stop driving onto bus

Figure 8.43: Manually performing the first sequence of actions required to implement an ADD instruction

This sequence is almost identical to the one we used to load the accumulator. However, instead of clocking the accumulator, we apply a clock signal to the temporary register (Figure 8.43b). So now we've caused the two values that we wish to add together to be presented to the ALU's inputs, which means that it's time to actually perform the ADD operation itself. But remember that the result from an operation such as an ADD is stored into the accumulator, so we need to do something rather cunning (Figure 8.44).

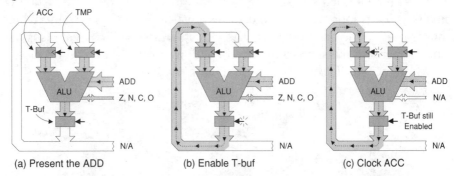

(a) Present the ADD   (b) Enable T-buf   (c) Clock ACC

Figure 8.44: Manually performing the second sequence of actions required to implement an ADD instruction

First we force a binary pattern that's sort-of equivalent to an ADD instruction onto the instruction bits driving the ALU. This causes the data outputs from the ALU to reflect the result of the addition, and it also causes new values to appear on the Z, N, C, and O status outputs (Figure 8.44a). Next we enable the tri-state buffer, T-Buf, which allows the result generated by the ALU to gain access to the internal data bus. This result roams throughout the entire data bus, but the path we're interested in is the one that wraps around to the accumulator's inputs (Figure 8.44b).

The cunning bit occurs when we clock the accumulator, which causes it to load the value being generated by the ALU (Figure 8.44c). Of course, as soon as we load the accumulator, its new contents are presented to the ALU's inputs. The ALU therefore modifies the results coming out of its outputs, and these results are presented to the internal data bus and eventually appear back at the accumulator's inputs. The reason this isn't a problem is that the registers forming the accumulator and the gates forming the ALU all have delays. This means that when we clock the result from the ALU into the accumulator, it takes a fraction of a second before the accumulator's outputs begin to respond.[13] Similarly, when the outputs from

---

[13]When we say *"fraction of a second,"* we are actually referring to a period measured in millionths (or even billionths) of a second.

the accumulator *do* respond, it takes some finite amount of time for the effect to ripple through the ALU and work its way back to the accumulator's inputs. Thus, by the time these unwanted signals present themselves to the accumulator, the result we're interested in is already safely stored away inside it. To complete the sequence, we would now disable our T-Buf tri-state buffers and remove the ADD from the ALU's instruction bits (these actions are not shown in Figure 8.44).

Once we've performed the ADD, the last task that we set ourselves when we commenced this journey into the unknown was to retrieve the result (which is now stored in the accumulator). The way in which we achieve this is to manually perform the same sequence of actions as would be caused by a STA ("*store accumulator*") instruction (Figure 8.45).

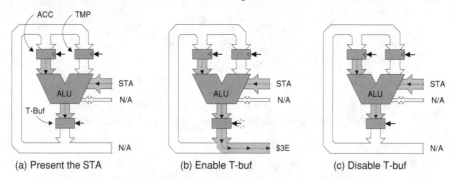

(a) Present the STA   (b) Enable T-buf   (c) Disable T-buf

Figure 8.45: Manually performing the actions required to implement an STA instruction

The first action in this sequence is to force a binary pattern that's sort-of equivalent to an STA instruction onto the instruction bits driving the ALU (Figure 8.45a). In fact all we really want the ALU to do is to pass the contents of the accumulator straight through to its outputs, but our ALU doesn't contain a "straight-through" path. To achieve this end, our accumulator-level version of an STA instruction actually coerces the ALU to add the contents of the accumulator to $00, which has no effect whatsoever (see also our earlier discussions on the complementor block).[14]

Next we enable the T-Buf tri-state buffers, which allow the value coming out of the ALU to gain access to the internal data bus. As usual this value roams throughout the entire bus, but the path we're interested in is the one that appears at the main outputs (Figure 8.45b). After passing the result to the

---

[14]There are a variety of other techniques we could use to pass the accumulator's contents through the ALU, including AND-ing them with $FF, OR-ing them with $00, or physically building a dedicated pathway to bypass the ALU completely. We just decided to do it using an ADD, so there.

outside world and storing it somewhere, we would disable the tri-state buffers, thereby disconnecting them from the internal data bus (Figure 8.45c). Finally, we would remove the STA from the ALU's inputs and get on with our lives.

Connecting the status register to the ALU and data bus

At certain stages during the acts of performing the LDA and the ADD instructions in the previous section, we showed the ALU generating values on its status outputs, but these outputs weren't connected to anything, thereby preventing us from making use of the status information. Thus, we need to connect these outputs to the status register (SR) (Figure 8.46).

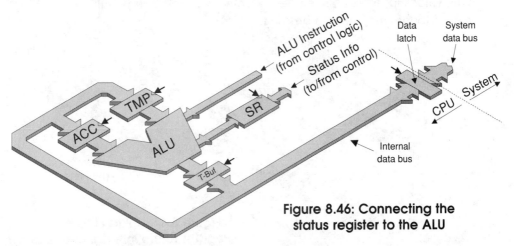

Figure 8.46: Connecting the status register to the ALU

In this simplified diagram, the status register is only shown as having a single clock. In reality, each of the five register bits forming our status register (I, O, N, Z, and C) would have individual clocks; alternatively they might share a common clock, but each would be equipped with an individual clock-enable. Once again, all of these control signals will be generated by some control logic we haven't looked at yet.

This leads us to a related consideration, in that the ALU is *always* outputting values on its O, N, Z, and C status outputs,[15] but in the previous section we only highlighted such outputs in Figures 42b, 44a, and 44b. Furthermore, Figure 42b only showed the N and Z outputs as being affected, while Figures 44a and 44b indicated that all four of the O, N, Z, and C outputs

---

[15]The interrupt mask (I) status bit is handled by a separate mechanism (see also Appendix D).

were affected. The fact is that, although the ALU is *always* outputting values on *all* of its status outputs, this doesn't mean that we're obliged to save them. Thus, depending on the particular operation that we're trying to perform, the control logic (that we promise to describe shortly) will only cause the appropriate status register bits to be loaded.

When we power-up or reset the *Beboputer*, all of the status bits are cleared to *logic 0s*; any subsequent values in the status bits depend on the results generated by whatever instruction has most recently been performed. For the vast majority of the time, only our elusive control logic typically pays much attention to the status register, because it uses the values in the status flags to make decisions, such as: "*If the carry flag is set (logic 1) I'll do one thing, but if it's cleared (logic 0) I'll do something else.*" Having said this, we do occasionally require the ability to directly read values from, and write values to, the status register.[16] Thus, we need to link our status register to the internal data bus (Figure 8.47).

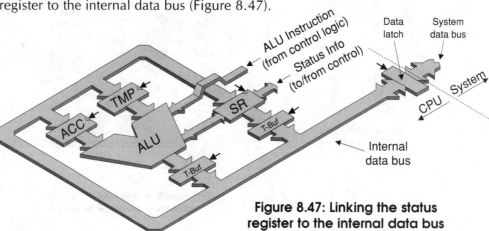

Figure 8.47: Linking the status register to the internal data bus

As usual this diagram is somewhat simplified. To better comprehend some of the more subtle details requires us to plunge a little deeper into the logic surrounding the status register (Figure 8.48). As we see, the inputs to our status register would actually be driven by a set of five 2:1 multiplexers, which are used to choose between the signals on the internal data bus and the outputs from the ALU. These multiplexers all share a common select control signal generated by our furtive control logic. Similarly, in Figure 8.47, we appeared to have two sets of outputs from the status register, where the first set was connected to our control logic and the second was used to drive the new tri-state buffer (T-Buf). However, the

---

[16]This ability is predominantly associated with subroutines and interrupts, as discussed in Chapter 12 and Appendix D, respectively.

status register really only has a single set of outputs that are used to drive both the control logic and the tri-state buffers (the tri-state buffers also share a common enable signal generated by our control logic).

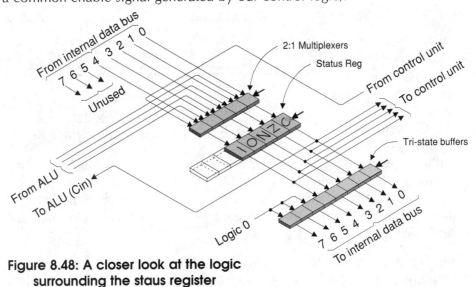

Figure 8.48: A closer look at the logic surrounding the staus register

Note that although some wires are shown as crossing over each other, the only points at which they are connected are those indicated by small black dots. Also remember that although we've only shown a single clock driving the status register, each bit forming the register would have an individual clock (or a common clock and an individual clock-enable).

Another point worth noting is that our internal data bus is 8 bits wide, but our status register only contains 5 bits. This isn't a problem in the case of writing a value to status register, because all we have to do is connect bits 0 to 4 of the internal data bus to the multiplexer inputs and forget about bits 5 through 7. However, things are a little trickier when we wish to read a value from the status register, because we only have 5 register bits available to drive our 8-bit bus. The solution to this problem is quite simple, because although the status register itself contains only 5 bits, we can make the tri-state buffer 8 bits wide and connect its three most-significant inputs to a logic value of our choice (we'll assume that they're connected to *logic 0*).

The circuit in Figure 8.48 also allows us to see how the carry flag can be driven by the ALU's carry-out (**Cout**) output and, at the same time, can be used to drive the ALU's carry-in (**Cin**) input. For example, in the case of one of our rotate instructions (**ROLC** and **RORC**), the bit that's shifted into the accumulator comes from the carry flag, while the bit that *"drops off the* end" of the accumulator is stored in the carry flag. Once again, this is possible due to the delays in the circuit, which mean that the original contents of the carry flag have already been utilized by the time the new contents overwrite them.

Finally, note once again that the interrupt mask flag is not connected to the ALU, but is instead driven directly by the control logic. The concept of interrupts is discussed in

	imp		imm		abs		flags				
	op	#	op	#	op	#	I	O	N	Z	C
SETIM	$08	1					1	-	-	-	-
CLRIM	$09	1					0	-	-	-	-

Table 8.5: Interrupt mask instruction

detail in Appendix D, so at this time we need only note that our CPU supports two special instructions called **SETIM** (*"set interrupt mask flag to logic 1"*) and **CLRIM** (*"clear interrupt mask flag to logic 0*). Both of these instructions use the implied addressing mode and therefore only occupy one byte (Table 8.5).

Some microprocessors support similar instructions for all of the status flags; for example, **SETC** and **CLRC** for the clear flag. If we had chosen to do this for the *Beboputer*, we would have been obliged to add eight more instructions to our instruction set, so we decided to live without them, because we're trying to keep our instruction set "mean and lean." On the other hand, if we *had* decided to support **SETC** and **CLRC**, then we could lose our **ADD** and **SUB** instructions, because we could combine **SETC** and **CLRC** with **ADDC** and **SUBC** to achieve the same results.

Adding the instruction register (IR) and control logic

And so, finally, we come to consider the control logic that's been lurking in the background for so long. In fact there are two pieces to the control logic: the *instruction register (IR)* and the *instruction decoder and executor* (we'll refer to the latter as the *instruction decoder* or the *control logic* for short) (Figure 8.49).

The instruction decoder is the real "brain" of the CPU, because it supplies all of the timing and control signals to the other members. This unit has two main inputs from the outside world: the system clock and the system reset. When the reset signal is activated (either explicitly or when power is applied to the system), the instruction decoder initializes the CPU by clearing the accumulator, status register, and instruction register (along with whatever else needs to be done).

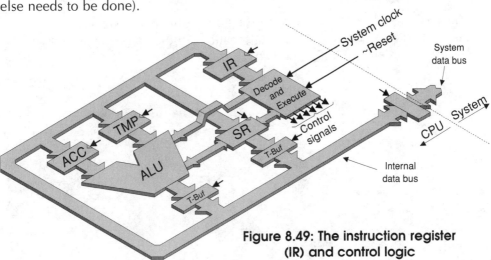

Figure 8.49: The instruction register (IR) and control logic

Following initialization, the instruction decoder causes the CPU to read an instruction from the main system's memory and stores it in the instruction register (the actual process behind this is discussed in the following sections). The decoder then generates whatever sequence of internal control signals are required to execute this particular instruction (you may wish to return to our previous discussions on Figures 42 through 45 for examples of these sequences). All of the decoder's actions are synchronized to the main system clock, and each instruction may require a number of clock cycles.

After a particular instruction has been executed, the instruction decoder causes the next instruction to be loaded from the main system's memory, and so it goes. Finally, before we proceed to the next section to discover just how all of this hangs together, remember that the instruction decoder can use the values stored in the status register to make decisions, along the lines of: *"If the zero flag is set I'll do one thing, otherwise I'll do something else."* We know that we've mentioned this before, but it's so key to  understanding the power of a computer that it's well-worth repeating, because it's this ability that allows the CPU to decide what it's going to do based on the results from a previous operation.

Adding the addressing logic

The last major block in the CPU is the addressing logic, which the instruction decoder uses to point to locations in the main system's memory and to the input and output ports (Figure 8.50).

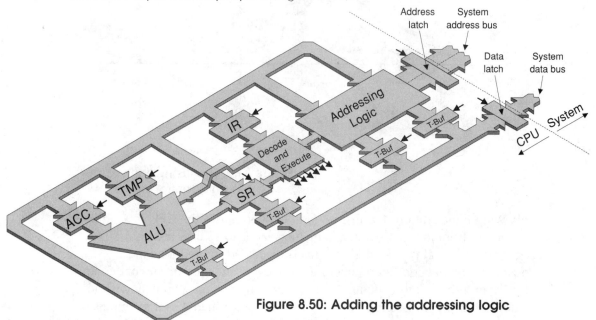

Figure 8.50: Adding the addressing logic

Remember that the *Beboputer* has a 16-bit address bus, which is why we show this bus as being twice the width of our 8-bit data bus. Inside the addressing logic block are a number of 16-bit registers, each of which may be loaded into the address latch and used to drive the address bus. Also, each of these 16-bit registers can be treated as two 8-bit registers (for the purposes of writing data into them and reading data out of them), which is why this figure shows two paths from the internal data bus into, and out of, the addressing logic block.

Not surprisingly, the complexity (or lack thereof) of its addressing logic dictates the sophistication (or lack thereof) of the addressing modes that can be supported by the CPU. As fate would have it, the educational nature of the *Beboputer* persuaded us that we should offer a reasonably varied potpourri of commonly used addressing modes, with the result that the addressing logic is quite ..... "hairy" (Figure 8.51).

A few moments ago we said that the addressing logic contains a number of 16-bit registers; however, for the sake of simplicity, Figure 8.51 only shows the main one which is referred to as the *program counter (PC)*. The program counter is actually formed from two 8-bit registers, which we've called PC-MS and PC-LS for the most- and least-significant bytes, respectively. The two halves of the program counter can be clocked independently or together (all of the control signals are driven by the instruction decoder that we introduced in the previous section). Thus, by means of the 2:1 multiplexers driving their inputs, we can individually load each half of the program counter with a value from the internal data bus. Similarly, the T-Buf tri-state buffers allow us to read the contents of PC-MS or PC-LS back onto the internal data bus.

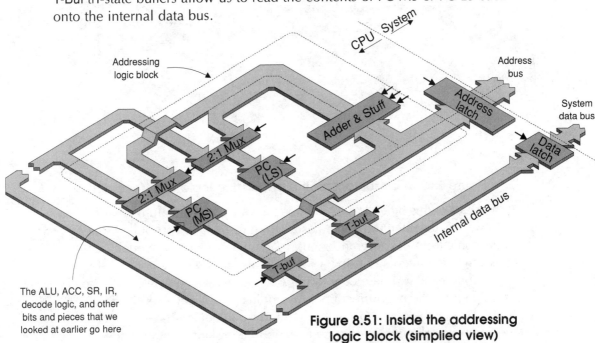

The ALU, ACC, SR, IR, decode logic, and other bits and pieces that we looked at earlier go here

Figure 8.51: Inside the addressing logic block (simplied view)

In order to point to a location in memory, the instruction decoder loads the outputs from both halves of the program counter into a 16-bit address latch, which, in turn, drives these signals onto the main system's address bus. Once the current value in the program counter is safely stored in the address latch, the instruction decoder may wish to modify its contents. For example, the instruction decoder might decide to increment the program counter to point to the next location in memory. In this case the decoder would use the 16-bit adder block to add $0001 to the current value in the program counter, and then store the result back into the program counter via the 2:1 multiplexers.

In the remaining sections of this chapter we'll investigate the ways in which the program counter (and other registers yet to be introduced) are used to access the memory, along with their relationships to various addressing modes. However, before we proceed, we need to take a slightly closer look at the contents of the addressing logic's adder block (Figure 8.52).

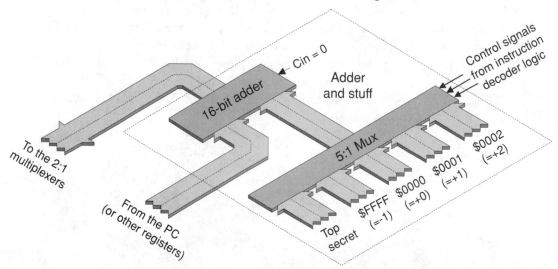

Figure 8.52: A closer look at the addressing logic's adder block

At the heart of this block is a 16-bit adder, which (not unnaturally) adds two 16-bit values together and generates a 16-bit result. One set of the adder's inputs come from the program counter (or another register), while the other set is generated internally using a 5:1 multiplexer under the control of the instruction decoder. In the case of the *Beboputer*, we can chose to modify the value from the program counter by adding it to $FFFF, $0000, $0001, or $0002, which equate to -1, +0, +1, and +2 in decimal, respectively (we'll consider the fifth, "top secret" option later). Note that adding -1 to the contents of the PC is exactly the same as subtracting +1 from it, thereby giving us the ability to decrement the contents of the PC should we so desire (the reason why we might want to add $0000 to anything will become clear in the fullness of time).

As a point of interest, the earliest microprocessors didn't have a dedicated adder block to serve the addressing logic, because the designers of that era were severely limited as to the number of transistors that could be squeezed onto a chip.[17] As an alternative, these primitive devices employed the

---

[17]The first microprocessor, Intel's 4004, only contained around 2,300 transistors (equivalent to approximately 500 primitive logic gates), which isn't all that many when you come to think about it. By comparison, modern microprocessors can easily contain millions of transistors.

adder in the ALU to increment the PC, which required splitting the contents of the PC into "chunks" and passing these chunks through the ALU. (If the *Beboputer* were based on this technique, it would use 8-bit "chunks"). Unfortunately, this technique drastically impacted the speed of the CPU, so as soon as it became possible to squeeze more transistors into integrated circuits, designers quickly beefed up their addressing logic by adding an adder (if you'll forgive the pun).

The program counter (PC)

Earlier we noted that our program counter is actually composed from two 8-bit registers; however, for the purposes of these discussions, we can simplify our view of the addressing logic by returning to consider the program counter as a single 16-bit register (so long as we remember that each half can be controlled independently) (Figure 8.53).

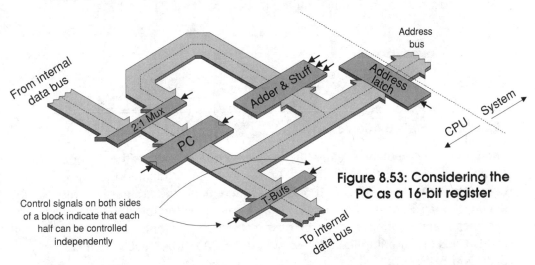

Figure 8.53: Considering the PC as a 16-bit register

Control signals on both sides of a block indicate that each half can be controlled independently

When the CPU is reset, the instruction decoder initializes the program counter to cause it to point to a specific memory location (address $0000 in the case of the *Beboputer*), and it is from this location that the CPU will retrieve its first instruction. To do this, the instruction decoder loads the outputs from the program counter into a 16-bit address latch, which, in turn, drives these signals onto the main system's address bus. Once the current value in the program counter has been safety squirreled away in the address latch, the instruction decoder increments the program counter such that it's ready to point to the next memory location, and for this we use our 16-bit adder block. In the real world we can save time by performing both tasks concurrently; that is, at the same time as we're loading the value coming out of the program counter into the address latch, we can also be incrementing it using the adder block and feeding it back into the program counter via the 2:1 multiplexers. As usual, the reason this works is because all of the logic blocks in the loop have internal delays (albeit small ones), which means that the original value in the program counter has been safely stored in the address latch by the time the new value comes out.

The implied addressing mode (imp)

As we previously discussed, the phrase "addressing mode" refers to the way in which the CPU determines or resolves the addresses of any data to be used in the execution of its instructions. The simplest form of addressing is the implied mode, which refers to instructions that only comprise an opcode without an operand; for example, INCA ("*increment accumulator*"). In this case, any data required by the instruction and the destination of any result from the instruction are implied by the instruction itself (Figure 8.54).

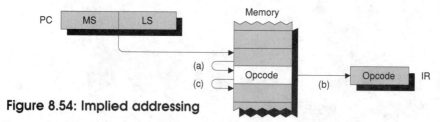

Figure 8.54: Implied addressing

The sequence commences when the program counter reaches the opcode for an implied instruction (Figure 8.54a), loads that opcode into the instruction register (IR) (Figure 8.54b), and increments the program counter (Figure 8.54c). Recognizing that this is an implied instruction, the CPU executes it and continues on to the next instruction. Examples of instructions that use implied addressing are: DECA, INCA, ROLC, RORC, SHL, and SHR.

The immediate addressing mode (imm)

Another simple form of addressing is the immediate mode, in which an instruction has one data operand byte immediately following the opcode; for example, ADD $03 ("*add $03 to the contents of the accumulator*") (Figure 8.55).

The sequence commences when the program counter reaches the opcode for an immediate instruction (a), loads that opcode into the instruction register (b), and increments the program counter (c). Recognizing that this is an immediate instruction, the CPU reads the data byte pointed to by the program counter, executes the instruction using this data, stores the result in the accumulator (d), and increments the program counter to look for the next instruction (e). Instructions that can use this form of addressing are: ADD, ADDC, AND, CMPA, LDA, OR, SUB, SUBC, and XOR.

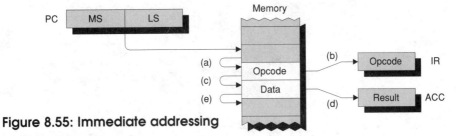

Figure 8.55: Immediate addressing

Temporary program counter A (TPCA)

If the only register in our addressing logic were the program counter, then the only forms of addressing we could support would be the implied and immediate modes as discussed above. Unfortunately, this would severely limit our ability to write useful programs, not the least that we would have to explicitly define every data value we wished to use in the body of the program itself. To illustrate the problem, consider the first instruction from one of our early programs in Chapter 4, in which we wish to load the accumulator with the value from the 8-bit switch device plugged into the input port at address $F000 (Figure 8.56).

Figure 8.56: A bit of a problem

This program commences when the instruction decoder copies the $91 opcode stored in memory location $4000 into the instruction register and increments the program counter to point to location $4001. The instruction decoder recognizes that the $91 opcode means *"load the accumulator with the value in the memory location whose address is stored in the following two bytes."* This technique is referred to as *absolute addressing*, because the two operand bytes specify an absolute address. However, if we load the most-significant byte of the target address ($F0) into our program counter, then we can't use the program counter to point to the least-significant byte of the target address ($00) stored at address $4002. Even worse, if we did manage to load the full $F000 value into the program counter, and managed to use this value to point to our input port, then how would we persuade the program counter to return to address $4003 after we'd copied the value from the input port into the accumulator? The solution is to augment our addressing logic with a register called TPCA (meaning "*temporary program counter A*")[18] (Figure 8.57).

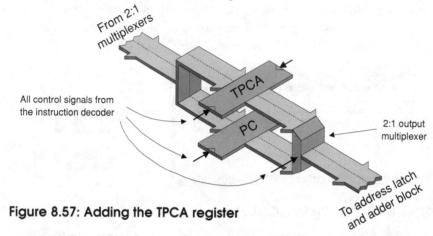

Figure 8.57: Adding the TPCA register

As we see, the signals from our original 2:1 multiplexers are used to drive both the program counter and the temporary program counter (both halves of which can be loaded individually or at the same time, just like the main program counter). Meanwhile, the outputs from the main program counter and temporary program counter are fed into a new 2:1 output multiplexer. As usual, this multiplexer is controlled by the instruction decoder, which can therefore choose to pass either the contents of the main program counter or the temporary program counter to the address latch and adder block (not to mention the tri-state buffers driving the internal data bus).

The absolute addressing mode (abs)

In the case of the absolute addressing mode, the opcode is accompanied by two address operand bytes, which are used to point to a byte of data (or to a byte in which to store data); for example, **ADD [$4B06]** ("*add the data stored in location $4B06 to the contents of the accumulator*) (Figure 8.58).[19]

The sequence commences when the program counter reaches the opcode for an absolute instruction (a), loads that opcode into the instruction register (b), and increments the program counter (c). Recognizing that this is an absolute instruction, the CPU reads the most-significant address byte from memory, stores it in the most-significant byte of the temporary program counter (d), and increments the main program counter (e). The CPU then

---

[18]The 'A' serves to inform us that there's a batting chance we'll have a TPCB ("*temporary program counter B*") before the sun goes down.
[19]The syntax "ADD [$4B06]" is more fully defined in Chapter 12.

reads the least-significant address byte from memory, stores it in the least-significant byte of the temporary program counter (f), and increments the main program counter once more (g).

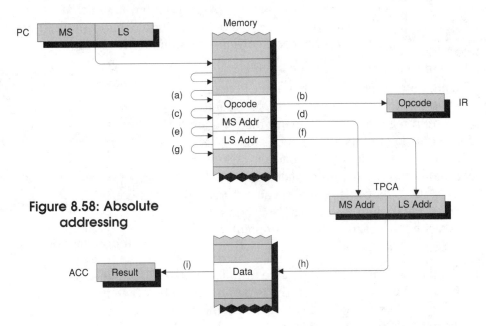

Figure 8.58: Absolute addressing

The main program counter is now "put on hold" while the CPU uses the temporary program counter to point to the target address containing the data (h). The CPU executes the original instruction using this data, stores the result into the accumulator (i), and then returns control to the main program counter to look for the next instruction. Examples of instructions that use absolute addressing are: ADD, ADDC, AND, CMPA, LDA, OR, STA, SUB, SUBC, and XOR. Note that in the case of a **STA** ("*store accumulator*"), the contents of the accumulator would be copied (stored) *into* the data byte in memory.

Unconditional jumps

The ability to use the temporary program counter to implement absolute addressing is obviously an important step forward, but there are more ramifications to this mode than the ability to access remote data. Without absolute addressing our programs would only ever be able to proceed in a linear manner, commencing at address $0000 (from a reset condition) and then casually strolling through succeeding locations, one after the other, until we eventually ran out of memory (Figure 8.59).

Memory

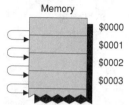

$0000
$0001
$0002
$0003

Figure 8.59: Strolling through the memory

In fact, to create any sort of meaningful program, the CPU must have the ability to change the flow of the program. The simplest example of this is a JMP ("*unconditional jump*") instruction, in which the CPU jumps directly to a new memory location. To illustrate this concept, consider a really simple program (Figure 8.60).

The program commences when the CPU copies the $90 opcode stored in location $4000 into the instruction register and increments the program counter to point to location $4001. Recognizing that the $90 opcode means "*load the accumulator using the immediate addressing mode*," the CPU copies the $00 value stored in location $4001 into the accumulator and increments the program counter to point to location $4002.

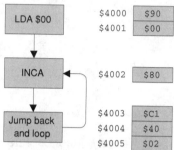

LDA $00	$4000	$90
	$4001	$00
INCA	$4002	$80
Jump back and loop	$4003	$C1
	$4004	$40
	$4005	$02

Figure 8.60: Unconditional jump

When the CPU reads the $80 value from location $4002, it recognizes this as being the opcode for an INCA ("*increment accumulator*") instruction, which it proceeds to do with alacrity, leaving the program counter pointing at location $4003.

Now this is the clever part. When the CPU reads the $C1 value at location $4003, it recognizes this as being an unconditional jump, so it uses the program counter to point to location $4004, and copies the $40 value it finds there into the most-significant byte of the temporary program counter. The CPU then uses the main program counter to point to location $4005, and copies the $02 value it finds there into the least-significant byte of the temporary program counter, which now therefore contains the full target address of $4002. Finally, the CPU copies the entire contents of the temporary program counter into the main program counter, and then continues to read the new opcode pointed to by the main program counter as if nothing had happened.[20]

Before we proceed further, the act of copying the temporary program counter into the main program counter deserves a few words, not the least that it explains the reason why we gave our adder block the ability to add $0000 to whatever value was passed into it (you may wish to refer back to

---

[20]If you're on your toes, you'll have realized that this program isn't particularly meaningful, because it never actually outputs anything, but it serves our purposes here, so "*what the hey?*"

Figure 8.52 at this juncture). First the control logic selects the outputs from the temporary program counter and feeds them into the adder block. At the same time, the control logic instructs the adder block to add $0000 to this value. This of course has no effect on the value coming out of the temporary program counter, which is just what we want. Finally, the control logic causes our original 2:1 multiplexers to select the value coming out of the adder block, then it clocks both halves of the main program counter, thereby loading it with the contents of the temporary program counter.

Finally, note that although Figure 8.60 only showed us jumping back in the memory, we can in fact jump in any direction. Also, programs can contain any number of jumps, so we might execute a few instructions then jump to a new location, execute a few more instructions and jump somewhere else, and so forth.

Conditional jumps

Unconditional jumps are very useful as you'll discover when you start to write your own programs, but we need something more. To be really effectual, the CPU must have the ability to change the flow of the program based on the result from an earlier operation. For example, after decrementing the accumulator, we might want the CPU to say: "*Hmmm, if the result from that operation wasn't zero then I should continue doing whatever it was that I was doing, but if the result was zero then I should start to do something else.*" (Figure 8.61).

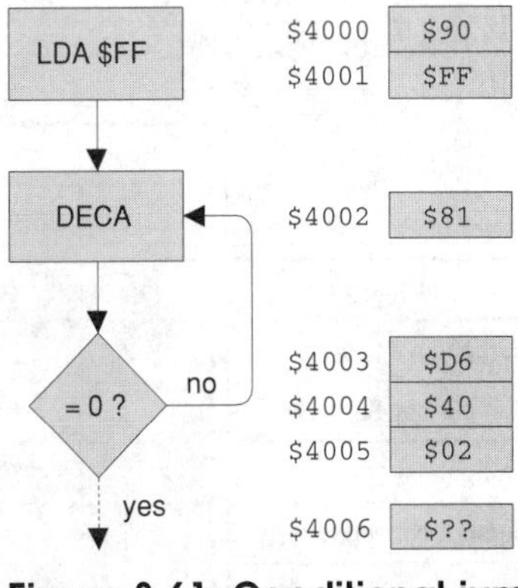

Once again, this simple (if meaningless) example serves to illustrate the point. First we load the accumulator with $FF, then we enter a loop that decrements the accumulator and tests its contents to see if they're zero. As long as the accumulator's contents are non-zero we jump back to location $4002, otherwise we continue on to the next instruction at location $4006.

The act of testing the accumulator and deciding what to do is performed by a conditional jump

Figure 8.61: Conditional jump

instruction. In this particular example, the $D6 stored in location $4003 is the opcode for a **JNZ** ("*jump if not zero*"), which bases its decision on the contents of the zero status flag. If the zero flag contains a *logic 0* (indicating a non-zero condition), then we perform the jump; otherwise, if the zero flag contains a *logic 1* (indicating that *all* of the bits in the accumulator are zero), then we fall through to the next instruction.

Now let's examine how the **JNZ** instruction works in a little more detail. When the main program counter arrives at location $4003, the CPU loads the $D6 opcode into the instruction register and increments the program counter to point to location $4004. Recognizing that this is a **JNZ**, the instruction decoder checks the value in the zero status flag. If the zero flag contains *logic 0* (indicating a non-zero condition) then the CPU proceeds as for a normal jump:

a) Copy the $40 value from location $4004 into the most-significant byte of the temporary program counter.

b) Increment the main program counter to point to location $4005.

c) Copy the $02 value from location $4005 into the least-significant byte of the temporary program counter.

d) Transfer the entire contents of temporary program counter ($4002) into the main program counter.

e) Read the new opcode pointed to by the main program counter as if nothing had happened.

Alternatively, if the zero flag contains a *logic 1* (indicating that *all* of the bits in the accumulator are zero), then the CPU simply uses the addressing logic's adder block to add $0002 to the current contents of the main program counter and stores the result back into the main program counter, thereby leaving it pointing at location $4006, from whence the CPU will read its next opcode.

As it happens, the *Beboputer* supports eight conditional jump instructions, allowing it to change the flow of a program based on the contents of the overflow, negative, zero, and carry flags (none of these jump instructions modify the contents of the flags themselves) (Table 8.6)

		imp		imm		abs		flags				
		op	#	op	#	op	#	I	O	N	Z	C
JMP	Unconditional jump					$C1	3	-	-	-	-	-
JO	Jump if overflow					$E9	3	-	-	-	-	-
JNO	Jump if not overflow					$EE	3	-	-	-	-	-
JN	Jump if negative					$D9	3	-	-	-	-	-
JNN	Jump if not negative					$DE	3	-	-	-	-	-
JZ	Jump if zero					$D1	3	-	-	-	-	-
JNZ	Jump if not zero					$D6	3	-	-	-	-	-
JC	Jump if carry					$E1	3	-	-	-	-	-
JNC	Jump if not carry					$E6	3	-	-	-	-	-

Table 8.6: Unconditional and conditional jump instructions

Note that these jump instructions may be considered to use the absolute addressing mode, on the basis that their opcodes have two operand bytes which are used to specify an absolute address.

Temporary program counter B (TPCB)

The implied, immediate, and absolute addressing modes, combined with the ability to perform conditional and unconditional jumps, allows us to create a fully functional computer capable of performing almost any task. In fact, if we wished, we could discard the immediate addressing mode and muddle along with only implied and absolute modes (we could take any data associated with our immediate instructions, stow it somewhere in the memory outside of the program's body, and then use absolute instructions to access it). The reasons we prefer to keep the immediate mode are twofold: these instructions execute faster than their absolute counterparts and they make our programs easier to understand (this latter point becomes somewhat less important when one employs higher-level programming languages as discussed in Chapter 12).

Also, although we could survive using only implied, immediate, and absolute instructions, we can make our lives easier (and more interesting) by adding some additional addressing modes. To do this we need to augment our addressing logic with more registers, the first of which might be called **TPCB** (*temporary program counter B*) (Figure 8.62).

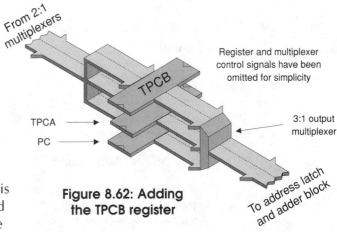

Figure 8.62: Adding the TPCB register

As for the other address registers, both halves of this new register can be loaded individually or at the same time. The signals from our original 2:1 multiplexers are now used to drive the main program counter and both of the temporary program counters; meanwhile, all three of these registers are connected to a 3:1 output multiplexer, which is used to drive the address latch and adder block (and the tri-state buffers feeding back into the internal data bus).

The indirect addressing mode (ind)

Adding a second temporary counter opens the doors to a host of possibilities, one of which is the ability to implement a new form of addressing known as the indirect mode. As for an absolute instruction, an indirect instruction has two address operand bytes following the opcode. However, these two bytes do not point to the target data themselves, but instead point to the first byte of another pair of address bytes, and it's *these* address bytes that point to the data (or to a byte in which to store data). Thus, indirect instructions are so-named because they employ a level of indirection. For example, consider an **LDA [[$4B06]]** (*"load the accumulator with the data stored in the location pointed to by the address whose first byte occupies location $4B06)* (Figure 8.63).[21]

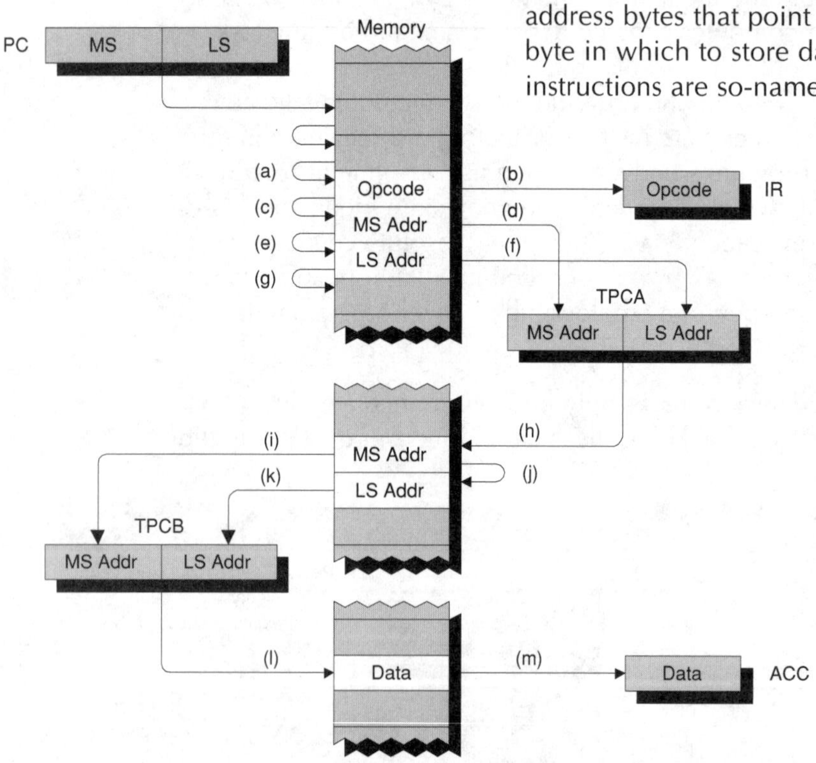

When the program counter reaches an indirect opcode (a), the CPU loads that opcode into the instruction register (b) and increments the program counter (c). Now the CPU reads the most-significant address byte from memory, stores it in the most-significant byte of temporary program counter A (d), and increments the main program counter (e). Next the CPU reads the least-significant address byte from memory, stores it in the least-significant byte of temporary program counter A (f), and increments the main program counter again (g).

Figure 8.63: Indirect addressing

The CPU now employs temporary program counter A to read the most-significant byte of the second address (h), stores it in the most-significant byte of temporary program counter B (i), and increments temporary program

---

[21]The syntax "**LDA [[$4B06]]**" is more fully defined in Chapter 12.

counter A (j). Next the CPU reads the least-significant byte of the second address and stores it in the least-significant byte of temporary program counter B (k). The CPU now uses temporary program counter B to point to the target data (l), and loads this data into the accumulator (m). Finally, the CPU returns control to the main program counter to look for the next instruction. Examples of instructions that can use indirect addressing are LDA, STA, and JMP (Table 8.7).

Note that there is no particular reason why instructions such as ADD, SUB, AND, OR, and XOR should not support indirect addressing (similarly for our conditional jump instructions). However, just because you can do

	imp		imm		abs		ind		flags				
	op	#	op	#	op	#	op	#	I	O	N	Z	C
JMP					$C1	3	$C3	3	-	-	-	-	-
LDA			$90	3	$91	3	$93	3	-	-	N	Z	-
STA					$99	3	$9B	3	-	-	-	-	-

Table 8.7: Some instructions that can use indirect addressing[22]

something doesn't mean that you have to, and CPU designers are certainly not obliged to support every possible addressing mode for every instruction. The point is that every time you add some functionality to a CPU, you also increase the complexity of the design, the number of transistors required to implement it, and the number of things that can go wrong (to name but a few). Thus, designers often balance their natural desire to create the "*all singing all dancing*" CPU against the fact that certain addressing modes are less likely to be used with some instructions than with others. For the pedantic amongst us, a few related points are as follows:

a) Even if a CPU has a limited instruction set and only supports a few addressing modes, it's almost always possible to create a program for any task (it just might take longer to run).

b) Even if a designer creates a really surrealistic instruction and associates a truly bizarre addressing mode with it, there's always going to be some maverick programmer who will find a use for it.

c) Irrespective of how *few* instructions and addressing modes a designer provides, there are always going to be critics jumping up and down saying that there are too many.

d) Irrespective of how *many* instructions and addressing modes a designer provides, there are always going to be connoisseurs proclaiming loudly and bitterly that there aren't enough.

---

[22]The JSR instruction can also use the indirect mode, but we haven't gotten around to that instruction yet.

In fact, with regard to the last point, some microprocessors seem to sport every possible instruction and addressing mode combination known to man (including some that you wouldn't recognize if they bit you on the leg). This is usually due to the fact that every time a new generation of a CPU is in the works, its designer's listen to every wacky idea that walks through the door, and they never seem to learn to say something like: *"If you can show me three people who will actually use this instruction in my lifetime, then maybe, just maybe I'll consider implementing it."*

The index register (X)

Another common register we might decide to add to our addressing logic is the index register (or X for short) (Figure 8.64).

As usual, both halves of the index register can be controlled independently, and the outputs from our original 2:1 multiplexers are now used to drive all four of our addressing registers. Also, all of these registers now drive a 4:1 output multiplexer. However, the index register is somewhat different to the registers that we've discussed thus far, in that we never actually load it's contents directly into the address latch, but instead we use it to modify the values coming out of the other registers.

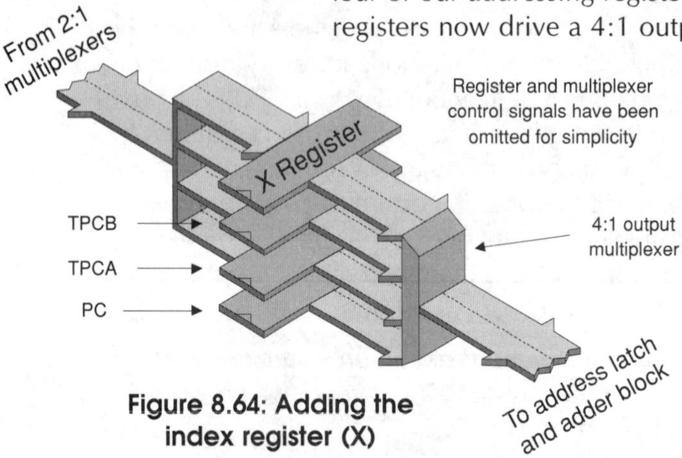

Figure 8.64: Adding the index register (X)

Register and multiplexer control signals have been omitted for simplicity

From 2:1 multiplexers

X Register

TPCB

TPCA

PC

4:1 output multiplexer

To address latch and adder block

The indexed addressing mode (abs-x)

Note that the previous figure is somewhat simplified, but before we delve into some of the more gory details, let's first ponder one of the ways in which we might employ our index register. Perhaps not surprisingly, the index register can be used to implement a new addressing mode known as indexed addressing. In fact, the indexed addressing mode is very similar to absolute addressing, except that we add the contents of the index register to the instruction's address operand bytes to generate the actual target address. For example, ADD [$4B06,X] (*"add the data stored in location ($4B06 + X) to the contents of the accumulator)* (Figure 8.65).[23]

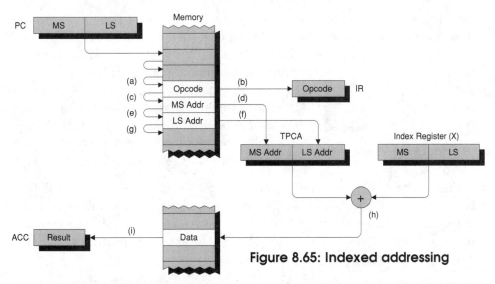

Figure 8.65: Indexed addressing

The sequence commences when the program counter reaches the opcode for an indexed instruction (a), loads that opcode into the instruction register (b), and increments the program counter (c). Recognizing that this is an indexed instruction, the CPU reads the most-significant address byte from memory, stores it in the most-significant byte of temporary program counter A (d), and increments the main program counter (e). The CPU then reads the least-significant address byte from memory, stores it in the least-significant byte of temporary program counter A (f), and increments the main program counter again (g).

The main program counter is now "put on hold" while the CPU adds the contents of the index register to the contents of temporary program counter A and uses the result to point to the target address containing the data (h). (The act of adding the index register to temporary program counter A does not affect the contents of the index register.) The CPU now executes the original instruction using this data and stores the result into the accumulator (i). Finally, the CPU returns control to the main program counter to look for the next instruction.

Examples of instructions that use indexed addressing are: ADD, ADDC, AND, CMPA, JMP, LDA, OR, STA, SUB, SUBC, and XOR. Note that, in the case of a STA ("*store accumulator*"), the contents of the accumulator would be copied (stored) *into* the data byte in memory. Also note that there's no particular reason why we shouldn't supply indexed versions of our conditional jump instructions; we just decided not to bother.

[23]The syntax "ADD [$4B06,X]" is more fully defined in Chapter 12.

Of course, we have to load a value into the index register before we can use it, so the *Beboputer* is equipped with a **BLDX** (*"big load index register"*) instruction. The reason we call this a *"big load"* is that we have to load two

Figure 8.66: BLDX (immediate)

bytes (16 bits) into the register. In fact there are two flavors of this instruction, thereby allowing us to load the index register using either immediate or absolute addressing. For example, consider the immediate mode (Figure 8.66).

In this example, the $A0 stored in location $4000 is the opcode for a **BLDX** using immediate addressing. As we see, this is similar to a standard immediate instruction, except that there are two data operand bytes instead of one. Similarly, in the case of the absolute form of this instruction, the two address operand bytes point to the first of a *pair* of data bytes.

In addition to the **BLDX** instructions, we also have **INCX** and **DECX** implied instructions to increment and decrement the index register, respectively. These instructions make the indexed addressing mode particularly useful for manipulating arrays or tables of values. Additionally, **INCX** and **DECX** affect the contents of the zero flag, which enables us to use the index register to control how many times we go around a loop. One consideration related to incrementing or decrementing the index register is that we might lose track of what it contains. Generally speaking this isn't a problem, but every now and again we might wish to peer inside this register to determine its current value. For this reason we also have a **BSTX** (*"big store index register"*) instruction, which is similar to an absolute-mode **STA** (*"store accumulator"*), except that it copies the contents of the index register into a *pair* of adjacent bytes somewhere in the *Beboputer's* memory.[24]

As we shall see in future labs, the index register can be exceptionally useful, often leaping to the fore when you least expect it. However, you will also find that you spend a lot of time using indexed versions of instructions such as **ADD** or **LDA** followed by an **INCX** or a **DECX** (alternatively, you may use an **INCX** or a **DECX** followed by an indexed instruction). For this reason, some CPUs support several additional opcodes that combine logical and arithmetic indexed instructions with the act of incrementing or decrementing the index register. In fact there are four flavors of these additional addressing modes:

---

[24]The BSTX instruction is also of use in preserving the contents of the index register should we call a subroutine that modifies this register (the concept of subroutines is introduced later in this chapter).

a) Pre-increment indexed   (Increment the index register then perform the instruction)

b) Pre-decrement indexed   (Decrement the index register then perform the instruction)

c) Indexed post-increment   (Perform the instruction then increment the index register)

d) Indexed post-decrement   (Perform the instruction then decrement the index register)

Important! This discussion on pre- and post-incremented/decremented indexed addressing modes is for interest only. The *Beboputer* doesn't support any of these additional modes, because they're really *"cream on the cake"* and we can survive quite happily without them.

	imp		imm		abs		abs-x		ind		flags				
	op	#	op	#	op	#	op	#	op	#	I	O	N	Z	C
BLDX			$A0	3	$A1	3					-	-	-	-	-
BSTX					$A9	3					-	-	-	-	-
INCX	$82	1									-	-	-	Z	-
DECX	$83	1									-	-	-	Z	-
ADD			$10	2	$11	3	$12	3			-	O	N	Z	C
ADDC			$18	2	$19	3	$1A	3			-	O	N	Z	C
SUB			$20	2	$21	3	$22	3			-	O	N	Z	C
SUBC			$28	2	$29	3	$2A	3			-	O	N	Z	C
AND			$30	2	$31	3	$32	3			-	-	N	Z	-
OR			$38	2	$39	3	$3A	3			-	-	N	Z	-
XOR			$40	2	$41	3	$42	3			-	-	N	Z	-
LDA			$90	2	$91	3	$92	3	$93	3	-	-	N	Z	-
STA					$99	3	$9A	3	$9B	3	-	-	-	-	-
JMP					$C1	3	$C2	3	$C3	3	-	-	-	-	-

Table 8.8: Summary of index register instructions[25]

---

[25]The **JSR** instruction can also use the indexed mode, but we haven't come to this instruction yet.

The gory details of connecting the index register

As we mentioned earlier, Figure 8.64 was something of a simplification, in that it didn't tell the whole story of how the index register is connected into the rest of the addressing logic. During our discussions on Figure 8.65, in which we described the act of performing an indexed instruction, we noted that it was necessary to add the contents of the index register to the contents of temporary program counter A. To do this we are going to require a 16-bit adder, but where are we going to find such a beast at this time of the night? Also, how can we add these two registers together, when our 4:1 output multiplexer can only select the contents of one register at any particular time? Just a moment, we already have a 16-bit adder in our addressing logic, so all we need to do is finagle things around a little (Figure 8.67).

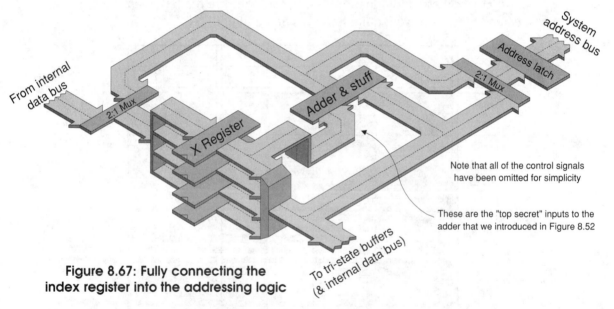

Note that all of the control signals have been omitted for simplicity

These are the "top secret" inputs to the adder that we introduced in Figure 8.52

Figure 8.67: Fully connecting the index register into the addressing logic

As we see, the index register is still connected to the 4:1 output multiplexer, which feeds it into the adder block in the usual way, thereby allowing us to increment or decrement its contents to perform our INCX and DECX instructions, respectively. However, we also take the outputs from the index register and feed them directly into a second set of inputs to the adder block. This second set of inputs form the *"Top Secret"* signals that we introduced in Figure 8.52. Thus, we can use the 4:1 output multiplexer to select the outputs from temporary program counter A (or one of the other registers) and feed them to the adder block, where we now have the ability to add them to the contents of the index register if we so desire.

Also, we've added a new 2:1 multiplexer to feed the address latch. This multiplexer can either select the signals from the 4:1 output multiplexer as before, or it can select the outputs from the adder block when we wish to load the sum of the index register and one of the other registers into the address latch.

The pre-indexed indirect (x-ind) and indirect post-indexed (ind-x) addressing modes

The most commonly used addressing modes are implied, immediate, absolute, indexed, and indirect as discussed above. However, the fact that we now have an index register allows us to add some additional modes that combine indexed and indirect addressing, the first of which is called *pre-indexed indirect*. This form of addressing is so-named, because the address in the opcode bytes is first added to the contents of the index register, and the result points to the first byte of the second address. For example, consider an **LDA [[$4B06,X]]** (*"load the accumulator with the data stored in the location pointed to by the address whose first byte occupies location ($4B06 + X)"*) (Figure 8.68).[26]

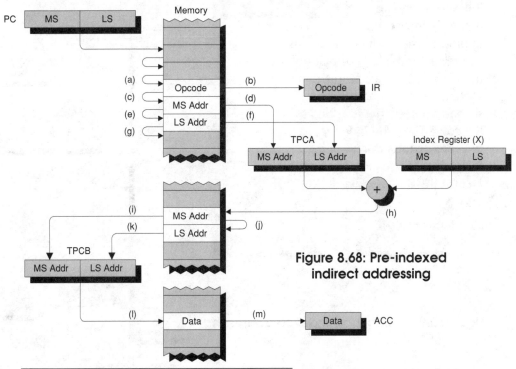

Figure 8.68: Pre-indexed indirect addressing

---

[26]The syntax "**LDA [[$4B06,X]]**" is more fully defined in Chapter 12.

When the program counter reaches a pre-indexed indirect opcode (a), the CPU loads that opcode into the instruction register (b), and increments the program counter (c). Next the CPU reads the most-significant address byte from memory, stores it in the most-significant byte of temporary program counter A (d), and increments the main program counter again (e). Now the CPU reads the least-significant address byte from memory, stores it in the least-significant byte of temporary program counter A (f), and increments the main program counter once more (g).

The CPU next adds the contents of the index register to the contents of temporary program counter A, uses the result to point to the most-significant byte of the second address (h), and stores this byte in the most-significant byte of temporary program counter B (i). The CPU then points to the least-significant byte of the second address (j), stores it in the least-significant byte of temporary program counter B (k), uses temporary program counter B to point to the target data (l), and loads this data into the accumulator (m). Finally, the CPU returns control to the main program counter to look for the next instruction.

Indirect post-indexed addressing is similar in concept to pre-indexed indirect addressing. However, in this case the address in the opcode bytes points to a second address, and it is this second address that is added to the contents of the index register to generate the address of the target data. For example, consider an LDA [[$4B06],X] (Figure 8.69).[27]

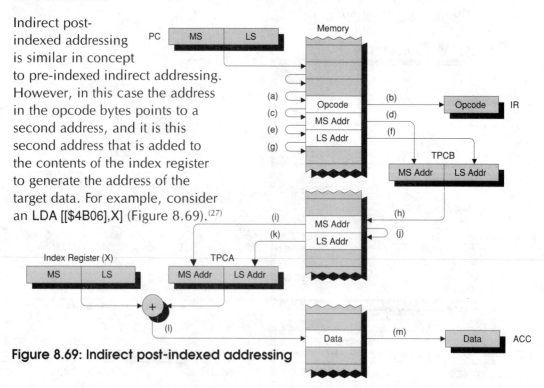

Figure 8.69: Indirect post-indexed addressing

---

[27]The syntax "LDA [[$4B06],X]" is more fully defined in Chapter 12.

When the program counter reaches an indirect post-indexed opcode (a), the CPU loads that opcode into the instruction register (b) and increments the program counter (c). Now the CPU reads the most-significant address byte from memory, stores it in the most-significant byte of temporary program counter A (d), and increments the main program counter again (e). The CPU next reads the least-significant address byte from memory, stores it in the least-significant byte of temporary program counter A (f), and increments the main program counter once more (g).

The CPU now uses the contents of temporary program counter A to point to the most-significant byte of the second address (h), and stores this byte in the most-significant byte of temporary program counter B (i). The CPU then increments temporary program counter A to point to the least-significant byte of the second address (j), and stores this byte in the least-significant byte of temporary program counter B (k). Now the CPU adds the contents of the index register to the contents of temporary program counter B, uses the result to point to the target data (l), and loads this data into the accumulator (m). Finally, the CPU returns control to the main program counter to look for the next instruction.

You may be pleased to learn that you probably won't find much use for the pre-indexed indirect and indirect post-indexed modes in the course of an average day, but they do tend to be applicable to the machine code that's generated from higher-level languages using automatic compilers (as discussed in Chapter 12)

	imp		imm		abs		abs-x		ind		x-ind		ind-x		flags				
	op	#	op	#	op	#	op	#	op	#	op	#	op	#	I	O	N	Z	C
LDA			$90	2	$91	3	$92	3	$93	3	$94	3	$95	3	-	-	N	Z	-
STA					$99	3	$9A	3	$9B	3	$9C	3	$9D	3	-	-	-	-	-
JMP					$C1	3	$C2	3	$C3	3	$C4	3	$C5	3	-	-	-	-	-

Table 8.9: Summary of x-ind and ind-x instructions[28]

You may recall that during our discussions on the indexed addressing mode, we noted the fact that some CPUs support a variety of derived modes called *pre-increment indexed*, *pre-decrement indexed*, *indexed post-increment*, and *indexed post-decrement*. Similarly, the designers of some CPUs use the same concept to create a whole slew of new modes derived from the pre-indexed indirect and the indirect post-indexed modes as follows:

---

[28]The JSR instruction can also use the x-ind and ind-x modes, but we haven't considered this instruction yet.

    a) Pre-increment pre-indexed indirect

    b) Pre-decrement pre-indexed indirect

    c) Pre-indexed post-increment indirect

    d) Pre-indexed post-decrement indirect

    e) Indirect pre-increment post-indexed

    f) Indirect pre-decrement post-indexed

    g) Indirect post-indexed post-increment

    h) Indirect post-indexed post-decrement

For example, in case (a) the CPU would first automatically increment the index register, and then use the new value in the index register as part of a standard pre-indexed indirect operation (you can work out the rest for yourself). As we previously stated, it doesn't matter how weird an instruction is or how convoluted its addressing mode, there will always be some programmer somewhere who will find a use for it. In fact, the modes above are actually quite reasonable when you come to think about it, which isn't to say that the *Beboputer* supports them. Once again, these modes would be "cream on the cake" as far as we're concerned, because we can achieve exactly the same effect using our existing modes and instructions, the main differences being that our programs will be a little larger and the *Beboputer* will take a little longer to run them.

The stack pointer (SP)

The penultimate register in the *Beboputer's* addressing logic treasure chest is the *stack pointer (SP)* (Figure 8.70)

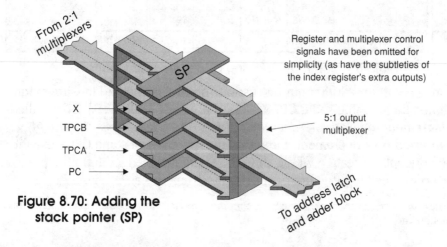

Register and multiplexer control signals have been omitted for simplicity (as have the subtleties of the index register's extra outputs)

5:1 output multiplexer

From 2:1 multiplexers

SP

X

TPCB

TPCA

PC

To address latch and adder block

Figure 8.70: Adding the stack pointer (SP)

The stack pointer comes in handy for a wide variety of tasks, but the way in which it works can be a little confusing to the uninitiated, so we'll start off with a simple example. Suppose we have a program that contains a loop, and every time it strolls around the loop it generates a value in the accumulator that we are going to need sometime in the future. This means that each time we pass through the loop, we have to copy whatever value is in the accumulator to some location in the *Beboputer's* memory, otherwise it will be overwritten the next time we cycle through the loop.

One approach would be to reserve a number of bytes in the memory and store the accumulator values there (employing instructions that use absolute, indexed, indirect, or similar addressing modes), but this means that we'd have to know the maximum (worse-case) number of values that we are ever going to want to play with. Apart from potentially tying up a lot of our available memory resources (which may not actually be required), there's a strong possibility that we would have to delve back into our program and modify it in the future if conditions ever change such that we need to store more values. Also, keeping track of the next free location in the area we've reserved is probably going to take a fair amount of messing around with additional instructions, which will slow our program down.

This is where the stack pointer leaps to the fore, because we have an immediate mode instruction called PUSHA ("*push the accumulator onto the stack*"), which causes the CPU to copy the contents of the accumulator to the memory location pointed to by the stack pointer, and to then automatically decrement the stack pointer to point to the next free location. For example, assume that the stack pointer's starting address is $4FFF (we'll discuss how this comes about in a little while), and further assume that our program has strolled around the loop three times, thereby executing three PUSHA instructions and placing three copies of the accumulator into the memory (Figure 8.71).

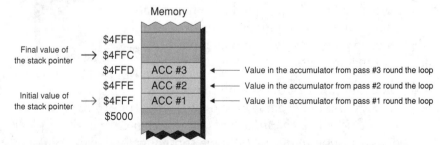

Figure 8.71: The state of the stack after three PUSHA instructions

The area occupied by this data is known as the *stack*, because we can visualize the bytes as being stacked one on top of the other. Note that the fact that the CPU automatically decrements the stack pointer means that it always ends up pointing to the first free location on the top of the stack.

To complement PUSHA, we also have a POPA (*"pop the accumulator off the top of the stack"*) instruction, which causes the CPU to increment the stack pointer to point to the last byte placed on the stack, and to then copy this byte into the accumulator. Once again, this results in the stack pointer pointing to the first free location on the top of the stack.

Using single-byte PUSHA and POPA implied mode instructions is much more efficient than using 3-byte absolute, indexed, or indirect mode versions. Additionally, this technique means that we don't have to define any specific number of bytes to be reserved, because the stack only uses the minimum amount of memory that it needs. Correspondingly, the stack can grow to be as big as necessary until it runs out of available memory.

One point that can cause confusion is the fact that the top of the stack occupies a lower address value than the bottom, because the stack "grows" in the opposite direction to the program. For example, assume that we initialize the stack pointer to address $4FFF, and then consider the portion of the memory map between the start of the RAM at addresses $4000 and the bottom of the stack at address $4FFF (Figure 8.72).

Note that we've tended to draw the memory map with address zero at the top and the most-significant address at the bottom. Some books do flip the map over and draw it the other way round, but the style we've used is the more common. One reason for this is that the addresses appear in the same order that we'd typically represent a binary count sequence, but a more important consideration is that this tends to reflect the way in which we document our programs.

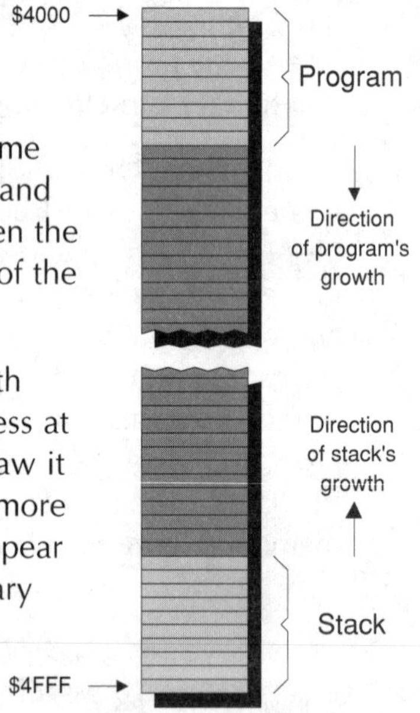

$4000 →

Program

Direction
of program's
growth

Direction
of stack's
growth

Stack

$4FFF →

Figure 8.72: Program vs stack

Of course, programs don't "grow" in the same sense that the stack does, but the effect is kind-of the same. For example, the programs we write for the *Beboputer* typically commence at address $4000, which is the first location in our RAM. If we subsequently decide to modify a program by adding more instructions, then our program will effectively "grow" down the memory map.

The reason the stack grows in the opposite direction to the program is to save programmers a lot of pain. If we commence the program at the lowest possible address and we initialize the stack to the highest possible address, then we can use all of our available memory to its maximum advantage until we push too much data onto the stack, at which point the top of the stack will collide with the end of the program and start to overwrite it. This condition, which is known as a *stack overflow*, is generally not considered to be a good thing to occur. Similarly, if we try to "pop" more data off the stack than we "pushed" onto it, then the result will be a *stack underflow* (for example, two PUSHAs followed by three POPAs will do the trick).

In addition to the PUSHA and POPA instructions, we also have their PUSHSR and POPSR counterparts, which push and pop the contents of the status register on and off the stack, respectively. Apart from anything else, this allows us to play some useful tricks, because the CPU only keeps track of where the stack pointer is currently pointing, but it doesn't retain knowledge as to the origin of any data on the stack. Thus, if we perform a PUSHSR followed by a POPA, we end up with a copy of the status register in the accumulator. Similarly, we can coerce the status register (and thus the status flags) to contain whatever values we wish, by first loading these values into the accumulator and then performing a PUSHA followed by a POPSR.

One point we should note is the stack pointer's initial address, which is shown as being $4FFF in the examples above. In the case of some computers, the stack pointer's initial address is hardwired into the CPU, such that it's automatically loaded into the stack pointer following a power-up or reset condition. However, other CPUs allow the stack pointer to be loaded under program control, and this is the tack we took with the *Beboputer*. Thus, the *Beboputer* is equipped with a BLDSP ("*big load stack pointer*") instruction, which allows us to load a 2-byte (16-bit) value into the stack pointer using either immediate or absolute addressing. This means that we can initialize the *Beboputer's* stack pointer to any location in the RAM portion of the memory, and we just happened to choose $4FFF for the sake of these examples.

The stack pointer usually takes care of itself, but every now and again we might wish to determine its current value. For this reason we also have a BSTSP ("*big store stack pointer*") instruction, which copies the contents of the stack pointer into a *pair* of adjacent bytes somewhere in the *Beboputer's* memory. (The BSTSP instruction is similar to the BSTX ("*big store index register*") we discussed earlier.)

Introducing subroutines

Assume that we wish to create a program to perform a certain task.
Generally speaking such a program will be composed of a sequence of sub-
tasks that are strung together to achieve the desired result. Further assume
that we already created one of these sub-tasks for use in an earlier program,
and that we'd like to re-use this set of instructions in our new program. One
way to do this would be by means of **JMP** (*"unconditional jump"*)
instructions (Figure 8.73a).

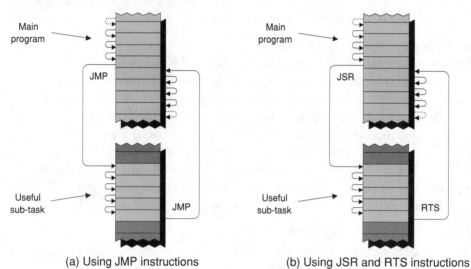

(a) Using JMP instructions   (b) Using JSR and RTS instructions

Figure 8.73: Introducing subroutines (using JSR and RTS instructions)

We could use the **JMP** in the main program to leap down to the instructions
comprising our sub-task, then use a second **JMP** at the end of the sub-task
to return to the main program. One problem with this scheme is that we
would need a way to remember the location in the main program to which
we wished to return, but there are techniques that make this a relatively
painless process as we'll discover in Chapter 12. In fact there's nothing
particularly wrong with the scheme in Figure 8.73a, *providing we only wish
to call the sub-task from a <u>single</u> location in the main program.* But what
happens if our sub-task is so useful that we'd like to call it again and again
from multiple locations in the main program? Actually calling the sub-task
multiple times isn't difficult; the problem arises when we wish to return to
the main program, because the **JMP** at the end of the sub-task can only be
used to return us to one of the calling locations.

The most common solution to this puzzle is to replace the **JMP** in the main
program with a **JSR** (*"jump to subroutine"*) instruction, while the **JMP** in the

sub-task would be replaced with a RTS ("*return from subroutine*") (Figure 8.73b). The cunning thing about a JSR instruction is that it causes the CPU to automatically place a copy of the 2-byte return address (as specified by the program counter) onto the top of the stack, and to decrement the stack pointer accordingly. Similarly, the RTS instruction causes the CPU to retrieve the 2-byte return address from the top of the stack (and to increment the stack pointer accordingly), copy this return address into the program counter, and then return control to the program counter.

	imp		imm		abs		abs-x		ind		x-ind		ind-x		flags				
	op	#	op	#	op	#	op	#	op	#	op	#	op	#	I	O	N	Z	C
BLDSP			$50	3	$51	3									-	-	-	-	-
BSTSP					$59	3									-	-	-	-	-
PUSHA	$B2	1													-	-	-	-	-
POPA	$B0	1													-	-	-	-	-
PUSHSR	$B3	1													-	-	-	-	-
POPSR	$B1	1													Φ	Φ	Φ	Φ	Φ
JSR					$C9	3	$CA	3	$CB	3	$CC	3	$CD	3	-	-	-	-	-
RTS	$CF	1													-	-	-	-	-

Table 8.10: Summary of stack instructions

Not surprisingly, the only stack instruction that modifies any of the status flags is the POPSR ("*pop the status register off the stack*") (we chose to use the Φ symbol in Table 8.10 to indicate that this was a somewhat special occurrence). Also, for reasons of our own, we decided that the JSR instruction should support the full range of addressing modes enjoyed by the JMP instruction. Finally, we should note that there's quite a lot more to the stack pointer and subroutines than we've discussed here, but we've decided to leave the really clever stuff for Chapter 12.

The interrupt vector (IV)

The final addressing register in the *Beboputer's* arsenal is the *interrupt vector (IV)*. This register is somewhat different to the others, in that once we've loaded it with a value it simply hangs around waiting for an interrupt to occur (Figure 8.74)

Interrupts, interrupt handling, and interrupt-related instructions are more fully discussed in Appendix D. Suffice it for the moment to say that when an interrupt occurs, the current contents of the program counter are copied onto the top of the stack (followed by a copy of the status register), then the contents of the interrupt vector are copied into the program counter.

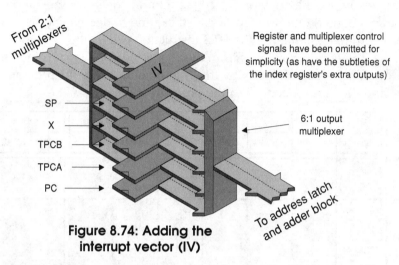

Register and multiplexer control signals have been omitted for simplicity (as have the subtleties of the index register's extra outputs)

6:1 output multiplexer

Figure 8.74: Adding the interrupt vector (IV)

Our fingers were crossed behind our backs

Earlier in this book we stated that Chapter 2 was the most difficult chapter in the book. Unfortunately, in that particular instance we weren't strictly adhering to the truth (which we obviously hold in high regard because we use it so sparingly). On the other hand we weren't exactly telling an untruth,

Never again!

because we had our fingers crossed behind our backs at the time, so whatever we said didn't really count (and our good characters therefore remain shiny-bright and without blemish). But now we can honestly say that this chapter was as bad as it gets and everything is going to be downhill from hereon in. Trust us, have we ever lied to you before?

Quick Quiz #8

1) If we were designing a computer that could only support two addressing modes, which ones would we choose?

2) Is there any particular reason why instructions such as **ADD** and **SUB** don't support the indirect, pre-indexed indirect, and indirect post-indexed addressing modes?

3) Why doesn't the *Beboputer* support **NOT**, **NAND**, **NOR**, and **XNOR** instructions?

4) In our discussions on the extended ALU, we forced the multiplexer in the negator block to select $FE (-2 in decimal) for a **DECA**; is there another way in which we could implement this instruction?

5) Which instructions would be most affected if the *Beboputer's* instruction set also included **SETC** (*"set carry flag to 1"*) and **CLRC** (*"clear carry flag to 0"*) instructions?

6) Describe two or more ways in which we might augment or enhance the *Beboputer's* **CMPA** (*"compare accumulator"*) instruction.

7) Why do we use certain status flags to represent multiple conditions (for example, the zero flag is also used to indicate equality in the case of the **CMPA** instruction)?

8) Describe a way in which we might enhance the *Beboputer's* **SHR** (*"shift accumulator right"*) instruction.

9) What are the advantages and disadvantages of the **ROLC** and **RORC** instructions rotating the accumulator through the carry flag?

10) How is it possible for us to use the value in the accumulator to drive the ALU, to perform an operation using the ALU, and to store the result back in the accumulator without messing everything up?

Chapter 9

The Hex Keypad

In this chapter we will discover:

What a hex keypad is and how one can be connected to a computer

What switch bounce is and how to cure it

What hierarchical flowcharts are and how to use them

How to use our hex keypad to enter and run a program that converts 8-bit binary numbers into their 3-digit decimal equivalents

How to make our program speak numbers aloud using the *Beboputer's* virtual sound card

Why our lives would have been easier if our forebears had decided to use the word *"onety"* instead of *"ten"*

Contents of Chapter 9

What can you do when a cornucopia of forces are afoot?

For a variety of reasons (which are discussed in more detail in Chapter 15), the advent of the microprocessor was not as assured as one might have expected. But, a cornucopia of forces were afoot,[1] some of which resulted in the introduction of the first microprocessor by Intel in 1971, and a brave new world of opportunities was born.

One of the more surprising developments, which was only envisaged by a few bold souls, was the emergence of the first home (hobbyist) microcomputers and development systems. The early versions of these systems were programmed using a bank of switches similar to a switch panel, and their results were presented on a set of lights not unlike a display panel, but later renditions adopted more streamlined interfaces based on octal or hexadecimal (hex) keypads (Figure 9.1).

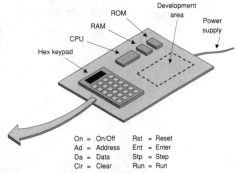

Figure 9.1: The Hex keypad

Amusingly enough, some of the early systems didn't support a *power-on reset* capability, and the reset button itself was often recessed behind a small hole to prevent it from being applied accidentally. Thus, an essential tool for many users was the *system toothpick* – a wooden toothpick which was used to trigger an initial reset following the first application of power to the system (and any subsequent resets as proved necessary).

These rudimentary trailblazers typically consisted of a single circuit board containing little more than a clock generator, the microprocessor, 1 K-byte of ROM (containing a primitive monitor program), between 256 bytes and 1 K-byte of RAM (to hold the user's programs), the keypad itself, and a small development area where the user could add some flashing lights or other devices to a limited number of input and output ports.

In this laboratory we will be using a hex keypad to enter and run a program on the *Beboputer*. The keypad acts as both an input and output device, thereby replacing the

---

[1]*"What's afoot? It's a dirty smelly thing on the end of your leg!"* – The Goon Show, circa1958.

switch and display panels. The four hexadecimal digits on the left of the display area indicate the current address, while the two digits on the right of the display show the memory's contents at that location.

The hex keypad versus switch and display panels

The monitor program (in the ROM) essentially performs the same task as it did for the switch and display panels, which is to loop around waiting for input from the user, process that input, display any relevant information, and, ultimately, transfer control to the user's programs. However, the monitor program does require some modification to reflect the physical differences between the hex keypad and the switch and display panels. Although you don't really need to know about this in any depth, it's worth taking a few moments to consider some of these physical differences and their implications, because this will greatly help your understanding of what's happening "behind the scenes."

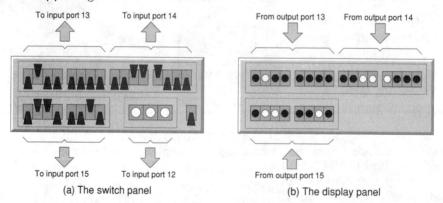

Figure 9.2: The ports used by the switch and display panels

In the case of the switch panel, we require four input ports to access all of the information from the switches. Two 8-bit ports are used to read the sixteen address switches, another 8-bit input port reads the eight data switches, and three bits of a final input port are required to read the Enter, Step, and Run buttons (the ON/OFF switch is connected to the power supply, while the Reset button is plugged directly into the CPU's reset input). When you had occasion to access the Input Ports dialog window in previous laboratories, you may have noticed that ports 12 through 15 were designated as being "System Assigned." In fact these are the ports that we use to handle the switch panel (Figure 9.2a).

The way this works is that the monitor program loops around reading the port connected to the **Enter**, **Step**, and **Run** buttons. When one of these buttons is activated, the monitor program reads the three ports connected to the address and data switches and uses this information to perform whatever task it's been instructed to do.

If we ignore the **ON/OFF** switch and the **Reset** button, the switch panel has twenty-seven switches and buttons. By comparison, the hex keypad has twenty-two buttons, but instead of assigning each button to an individual bit of an input port – which would again require the use of multiple ports – it is more efficacious to encode them and to only use a single port. Encoding the keypad's buttons makes our lives easier, because these buttons are used to represent both the address and the data, so it's more efficient for the monitor program to access a single port and then process the information internally.

Mapping the hex keypad's buttons

There are two aspects to bear in mind when we consider encoding the buttons on the hex keypad. First, we need to determine how we wish to map each button to a pattern of *logic 0s* and *logic 1s*; second, we have to decide on some physical mechanism to implement this encoding. From earlier discussions we know that an 8-bit field can represent 256 different patterns of *logic 0s* and *logic 1s*, and we could arbitrarily map each of the twenty-two buttons on the hex keypad to any of these patterns, the only requirement being that each pattern was unique. However, it's usually advantageous to partition any problem into smaller "chunks" and, in a case like this, to use meaningful assignments as far as possible (Figure 9.3).

As it happens, it's possible to derive some fairly intuitive assignments for our keypad. First we can use the four least-significant bits of the input port, in_data[3:0], to represent the hexadecimal digits '0' through 'F'. Next we can use in_data[5:4] to represent the **Address**, **Data**, and **Clear** buttons, while in_data[7:6] can be delegated to represent the **Enter**, **Step**, and **Run** buttons. Of course there are a multitude of other schemes that we could use, but this one has a certain

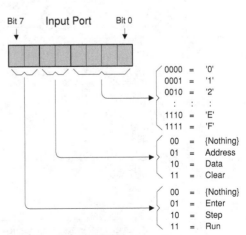

Figure 9.3: Mapping the keypad's buttons

aesthetically pleasing symmetry. One of the reasons that this particular arrangement works so well is that we inherently know that the user can only press a single button at a time. Actually, this latter point is only strictly true in the virtual world of the *Beboputer* – in the real world there's always the possibility of a button sticking, or a user with big fingers accidentally pressing two buttons at the same time. Also, as engineers are fond of saying: *"You can make it foolproof, but you can't make it proof against a total fool,"* and you can't ignore the possibility of a user deliberately pressing two buttons simultaneously, just because *"I wanted to see what would happen."*[2,3]

Encoding the hex keypad's buttons

Having settled on the patterns of *logic 0s* and *logic 1s* we intend to use to represent the keypad's buttons, we must now decide on a physical mechanism to implement this encoding. There are several techniques that could be employed, but one of the simplest to understand is based on a matrix of diodes (Figure 9.4).

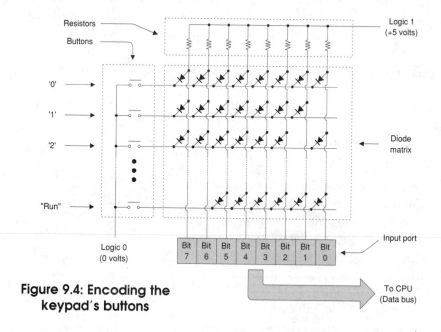

Figure 9.4: Encoding the keypad's buttons

---

[2]One should never underrate the ingenuity and creative genius of an inspired fool.
[3]Half of the safety features that engineers design into systems are there to ensure that some drongo hasn't turned the other half off.

As we see, each bit of the input port is connected to a "column" wire, which is, in turn, connected to a *logic 1* value via a resistor. Similarly, one side of each button on the keypad is connected to a *logic 0* value, while the other side is connected to a "row" wire. The important point to note is that the row and column wires aren't directly connected together; instead, selected row and column intersections are linked using diodes. It would certainly be possible to hand-build this type of diode matrix using individual components; alternatively, one could use a special programmable device called a PROM.[4]

If none of the buttons on the keypad are pressed, then the value $FF (or %11111111 in binary) would be presented to the input port. By comparison, when one of the buttons on the keypad *is* pressed, the row wire corresponding to that button is connected directly to a *logic 0* value. Wherever there is a diode at an intersection between this row wire and one of the column wires, that diode will conduct, thereby overriding the column wire's resistor and forcing the wire to assume a *logic 0* value. Thus, pressing a button on the keypad will cause a pattern of *logic 0s* and *logic 1s* to be presented to the input port, where the individual 0s and 1s correspond to the presence or absence of diodes, respectively.

The way in which this all works is that the monitor program starts off by happily looping around reading the input port and doing nothing as long as it sees a value of $FF. As soon as the monitor program sees any value other than $FF it knows that one of the buttons has been pressed, at which point it will use the ensuing pattern of *logic 0s* and *logic 1s* to determine which button is active and to perform any appropriate actions (Figure 9.5).

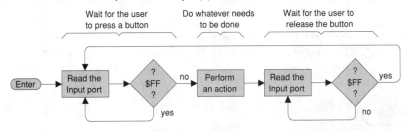

Figure 9.5: The monitor program reading the hex keypad's input port

Remembering that the CPU can execute millions of operations a second, we understand that the monitor program can perform an action and return to looking at the input port in an incredibly short time, long before the user is able to release the button. So the monitor program would be tempted to treat a single press of a button as though the user had actually pressed it

---

[4]PROMs are discussed in more detail in Chapter 13.

hundreds of times. One way to prevent this is in software, by writing the monitor program in such a way that, following an action, it enters a second loop waiting for the $FF value to return. The restoration of the $FF value indicates that the user has released the button, thereby permitting the monitor program to return to the start of the main loop where it waits for the user to press another button.

Another point to consider is a feature known as *switch bounce*. When you turn on a light switch in your house, it seems as though the switch simply closes and the light immediately appears. In reality the metal contact in the switch may bounce a number of times, much like the diving board at a swimming pool after a reckless youth has launched himself into a triple back-somersault with arms and legs flailing all over the place (at least, that's the way we do it). This isn't a problem in the case of a light switch, because it happens far too fast for you to ever notice the effect. However, the reaction time of the CPU is such that it can easily assume that the user is extraordinarily nimble-fingered, and thus misinterpret any switch bounce on the hex keypad's buttons for the user pressing the same button multiple times. Once again it is possible to use software to filter out these switch bounce effects, but it is more usual to add additional circuitry to de-bounce the switches in hardware.

Driving the hex keypad's 7-segment displays

Hopefully it did not escape your notice that the output mechanism used by the hex keypad is based on the 7-segment displays we introduced in Chapter 5. Also, as we previously noted, our original display panel required three output ports to drive it (Figure 9.2b). Similarly, we could, if we wished, employ the same output ports to drive three dual 7-segment displays on the hex keypad (Figure 9.6).

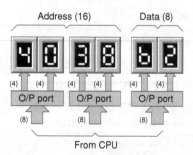

Figure 9.6: Driving the keypad's 7-segment displays (scheme A)

In this scheme the output from each 8-bit port is split into two 4-bit groups, and each 4-bit group is used to drive a decoded 7-segment display. In light of the alternatives that we'll be discussing shortly, you should remember that the output ports we've been considering thus far are assumed to latch the last data that was written into them by the CPU.

As an alternative to using three output ports to drive the displays, we might decide to perform the task using only a single port (Figure 9.7). In this case we could replace our latching output port with a simpler version containing only buffer gates. Next we could equip each 7-segment display with its own private 4-bit latch (in fact, it's possible to purchase these displays with built-in latches). Finally, we could use the four least-significant bits from the output port to drive all of the 7-segment displays (or at least, to drive the latches that drive the displays), and we could feed the four most-significant bits from the output port into a decoder, which could be used to generate enable signals for the latches. The decoder would be arranged such that only one set of 4-bit latches could be enabled at any particular time. (Note that the circuit shown here is only intended to illustrate a concept – in the real world we'd have to "tweak it" a little to make it work, because we've glossed over a few points for the sake of simplicity.)[5]

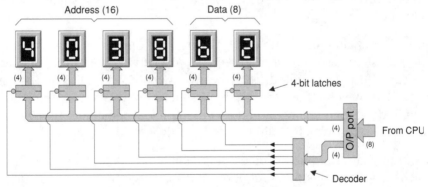

Figure 9.7: Driving the keypad's 7-segment displays (schemeB)

As yet another alternative, we could use the four least-significant bits from an output port to drive a chain of shift registers (Figure 9.8). In this case, the first time the monitor program writes a byte of data to the output port, this data would be loaded into the first set of 4-bit registers and the right-most digit (in this figure) would appear. The next time the monitor writes to the output port, the data in the second set of registers would be loaded with the data from the first set of registers, which would, in turn, be loaded with the new data from the port. Thus, each time the monitor program writes to the port, all of the digits will be shifted one place to the left. (Once again, we've omitted some nitty-gritty details from this figure for reasons of simplicity; for example, we haven't specified the origin of the load control which would be derived from the output port's enable signal.)

[5]*"Well, there's certainly something screwy going on around here"*– The Marx Brothers, *Room Service*, (1938)

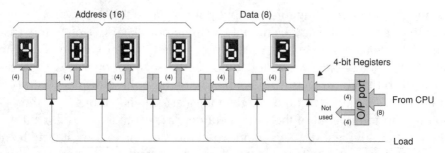

Figure 9.8: Driving the keypad's 7-segment displays (scheme C)

One of the problems with the shift register concept in scheme C is that modifying a single digit in the middle of the display would require the monitor program to re-write the entire six digits to the shift register chain (this problem could be mitigated to some extent by using a pair of output ports to drive two register chains: one for the address digits and one for the data digits).

In fact the main purpose behind this portion of our discussions is to illustrate the almost endless number of permutations that we could use. For example, instead of using two output ports to drive two register chains as was just suggested, we could use the four least-significant bits from a single output port to drive both chains, and use two of the four remaining bits as enable signals to select which chain should be activated.

Each alternative requires a different combination of hardware (registers, latches, decoders, and output ports) and software (the monitor program). In many respects scheme A (Figure 9.6) is the easiest to understand and implement. However, if the designer were limited as to the number of free output ports, then one of the other schemes may be preferred. Meanwhile, if a hobbyist were to construct this system as a home project, then the final implementation might well depend on whatever devices happened to be available in his or her treasure chest of spare parts.

Winding up the *Beboputer*

Well although the above may have been an interesting digression, it's time to move on to the body of this laboratory. Make sure that the *Beboputer* CD is in the appropriate drive in your computer and summon the *Beboputer*. Once the *Beboputer's* project window has opened, click the **File** item on its menu bar, click the **Open Project** entry in the resulting pull-down menu, then select the **Lab 4** project from the ensuing dialog. This will invoke our fourth lab (Figure 9.9).

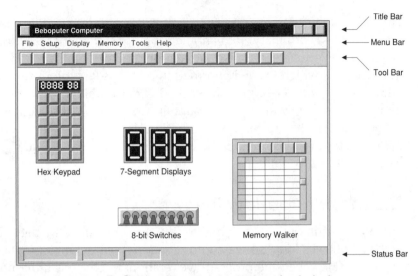

Figure 9.9: The *Beboputer* project window for Lab 4

Note our new hex keypad in the upper-left of the project window, and also note that this lab uses three 7-segment digits: the left-hand digit is supplied by our single decoded 7-segment display, while the two right-hand digits are represented by our dual decoded 7-segment display.[6]

Program to convert a binary number into its decimal equivalent

The first part of this laboratory involves creating a program to read the state of the switches on the 8-bit switch input device, to interpret the switch positions as being an 8-bit unsigned binary number, and to convert and display the decimal equivalent of this number using three 7-segment digits. The reason we need to use three digits is that an 8-bit field can represent 256 different patterns of *logic 0s* and *logic 1s*, so an unsigned binary number can be used to depict values in the range 0_{10} through 255_{10}. Thus, we require three digits to display the number in decimal (Figure 9.10).

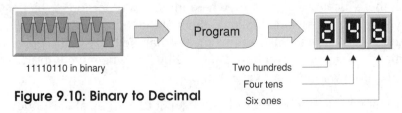

Figure 9.10: Binary to Decimal

---

[6]These displays were introduced in Chapter 5.

The heart of the task is to convert a value that's represented in one number system (base-2, or binary) into another number system (base-10, or decimal). Unfortunately, unlike the mapping between binary and hexadecimal, which we've performed in previous laboratories, mapping between binary and decimal presents a trickier problem. Before we continue, take a few moments to ponder how you might solve this assignment. However, don't worry that this is going to be more complicated than it is, because it's not (if you can follow this sentence, you shouldn't have any difficulty with our program).

The master (top-level) flowchart

The programs in our earlier laboratories were typically only between nine and twelve bytes long, so we could represent their actions using a single flowchart. However, the program we're about to create is a bit more "meaty," so it behooves us to partition the problem into manageable chunks. One particularly useful technique is to employ a hierarchical (multi-level) flowchart, which allows us to commence viewing the problem from a high level of abstraction, and to then work our way down to the nitty-gritty details (Figure 9.11).

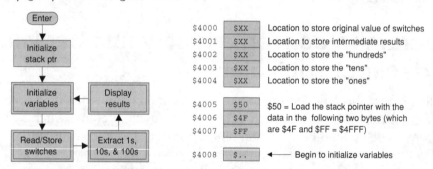

Figure 9.11: The master flowchart (and data storage locations)

Unlike our earlier programs, this one is going to require us to reserve some memory locations to store various values and intermediate results. We could establish these locations almost anywhere in the RAM portion of the memory map, but we decided to keep them at the top of the program in addresses $4000 through $4004. This means that the body of the program will actually commence at address $4005, which is where we'll instruct the CPU to run from when we arrive at that point.

As this program is (in the fullness of time) going to employ at least one subroutine, the first instruction at address $4005 initializes the stack pointer (the use of subroutines and the stack pointer was introduced in Chapter 8). Once again, we could initialize the stack pointer to point to almost anywhere in the RAM portion of the memory map, but we arbitrarily decided to point it at address $4FFF, which is the end of the first 4K block of RAM (remember that calling a subroutine decrements the stack pointer).

In the master flowchart, the "Initialize stack pointer" action box is drawn with a single border, thereby indicating that this box only represents a single, non-hierarchical task. By comparison, the other action boxes have double borders to indicate that they are hierarchical; that is, each of these boxes actually represents a number of tasks and decisions.

Finally, note that when we eventually finish whatever tasks are represented by the "Display Results" action box, the program will jump back to the first instruction in the "Initialize Variables" action box (which commences at address $4008). The reason we don't wish to jump back to the very first instruction in the program (at address $4005) is because we only need to initialize the stack pointer once.

Initializing the variables

Once it's loaded the stack pointer, our program's next task is to initialize the memory locations we're going to use to store our variables such that they contain known good values. In fact for reasons that will become apparent, we only actually need to initialize the locations at addresses $4002 through $4004 with values of zero (Figure 9.12).

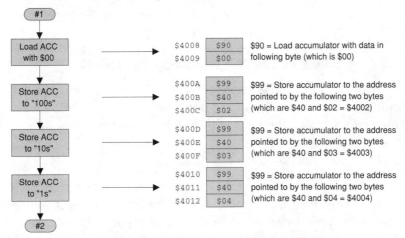

Figure 9.12: Intializing the Variables

This portion of the program is quite simple and doesn't contain anything that we haven't seen before. The first instruction loads the accumulator with a value of $00, while the following three instructions save this value to the memory locations at addresses $4002 through $4004. In fact, due to the way in which our program works, it's only strictly necessary to initialize the variables at addresses $4002 and $4003. However, as we aren't particularly concerned with creating the smallest program possible (at least in this instance), we decided to go ahead and initialize the variable at address $4004 as well.

Note that instead of containing the labels "Enter" and "Exit," the terminal symbols in this flowchart hold the labels "#1" and "#2", respectively. Using numerical labels such as these will help us understand how the various portions of the flowchart (and thus the program) are connected together.

Reading and storing the switches

Once we've initialized the variables, our next task is to read the state of the switches on our 8-bit input device and to save this value for later use (Figure 9.13).

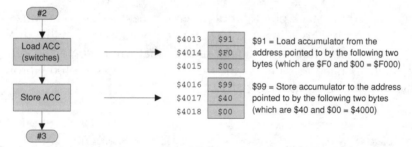

Figure 9.13: Loading and storing the switches

As you may recall, the address of the 8-bit switch's input port is $F000; thus, the first instruction loads the accumulator with whatever value is represented by switches. The second instruction then saves this value to the memory location at address $4000, which we reserved at the beginning of the program for just this purpose.

Once again, instead of containing the labels "Enter" and "Exit," the terminal symbols in the flowchart hold the labels "#2" and "#3", respectively. Note that the terminal symbol exiting the flowchart in Figure 9.12 and the terminal symbol entering the flowchart in Figure 9.13 both contain the label "#2", which indicates that these two points are connected together. Also note that, although this part of the program only contains two instructions, there are at least two good reasons why it is still appropriate to represent it as a discrete entity in our hierarchical flowchart: first, it's advantageous to keep the highest level of the flowchart (Figure 9.11) as uncluttered as possible for purposes of clarity; and second, it's good practice to partition a program into well-defined tasks to facilitate understanding and modifying the program in the future.

Extracting the "hundreds," "tens," and "ones"

Now the pace begins to pick up a little, because we have to determine how many "hundreds," "tens," and "ones" are represented by the 8-bit value we just stored in memory location $4000 (and which is still contained in the accumulator). Thus far our flowchart has only contained two levels of hierarchy; that is, the hierarchical blocks labeled "Initialize Variables" and "Read/Store Switches" in our top-level flowchart only contained low-level actions. However, extracting the "hundreds," "tens," and "ones" will be a little more complex, so this hierarchical block will itself contain a further level of hierarchy (Figure 9.14).

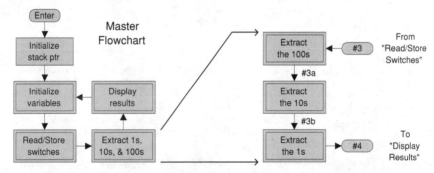

Figure 9.14: Extracting the "hundreds", "tens", and "ones"

The first task is to determine how many "hundreds" are represented by our 8-bit value. As is usual in computing, there are a number of different techniques we could use, but one of the easiest to understand is as follows:

a) Remember that the memory location at address $4002 (which is the location we're going to use to store the number of "hundreds") currently contains zero, because that's what we loaded it with in the "Initialize Variables" part of the program. Also remember that the accumulator currently contains the value we read from the switches.

b) Compare the contents of the accumulator to the number 99. If the result of this comparison shows that the contents of the accumulator are greater than 99, then the number obviously contains at least one "hundred." In this case increment the value in memory location $4002 (which contains the number of "hundreds") and subtract 100 from the value in the accumulator.

c) Repeat step (b) until the comparison shows that the value in the accumulator is not greater than the number 99.

This will result in the memory location at address $4002 containing the number of "hundreds" (0 = "no hundreds," 1 = "one hundred," 2 = "two hundreds," and so on), while the final value contained in the accumulator will equal the original value on the switches minus its "hundreds" component. And that's all there is to it (he said with a smile).[7] In fact this really isn't tremendously difficult to program, it's just that there are a few more steps involved when we consider the problem at the machine-code level (Figure 9.15).

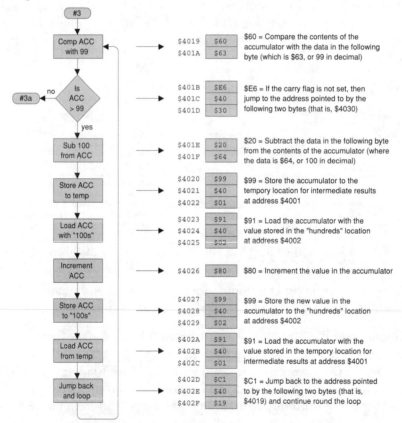

Figure 9.15: Extracting the "hundreds"

[7]*"From the moment that I picked up your book until I laid it down, I was convulsed with laughter. Some day I intend reading it." – Groucho Marx*

As usual ...... **Don't Panic!** Let's just take this step by step. The first instruction ($60 at address $4019) is a **CMPA**, which, in this case, compares the contents of the accumulator with the number 99 (or $63 in hexadecimal). As we discussed in the previous chapter, the **CMPA** instruction doesn't affect the contents of the accumulator, but it does set the carry flag to *logic 1* if the value in the accumulator is greater than the number it's being compared to (otherwise the carry flag is cleared to *logic 0*).

The next instruction ($E6 at address $401B) is a **JNC** (*"jump not carry"*), which will cause the program to jump to the location specified in the following two bytes if the carry flag contains a *logic 0*. In fact the target location at address $4030 will be the start of the program segment that extracts the "tens" (you may note that this is the first free location following the end of this segment to extract the "hundreds"). Thus, if the value in the accumulator is not greater than 99, the CPU will jump to the next part of the program at address $4030. However, if the value in the accumulator is greater than 99, the jump won't happen and the program will continue on to the next instruction at address $401E.

The remainder of this segment is reasonably self-explanatory. First we use a **SUB** instruction ($20 at address $401E) to subtract 100 (or $64 in hexadecimal) from the contents of the accumulator. Next we employ a **STA** instruction ($99 at address $4020) to store the accumulator to the temporary location we reserved for intermediate results (that is, the location at address $4001). Then we use a **LDA** instruction ($91 at address $4023) to load the accumulator with the contents of the location we reserved to use as a variable to store the number of "hundreds" (that is, the location at address $4002). This is followed by an **INCA** instruction ($80 at address 4026) to increment the contents of the accumulator. After incrementing the accumulator we use another **STA** instruction ($99 at address $4027) to return its contents to the "hundreds" variable, which therefore now reflects the fact that our program discovered another "hundred." Finally we use one more **LDA** instruction ($91 at address $402A) to reload the accumulator with our intermediate result, followed by an unconditional **JMP** instruction ($C1 at address $402D), which causes the program to loop back to the beginning of this segment to test for another "hundred."

So this really isn't too complicated; it's just that there seems to be rather a lot of it. The real problem is that it's tricky to work at the machine-code level where we're obliged to deal with opcodes and operands as numerical values. In fact there are easier techniques for representing programs as we'll discover in Chapter 12, but we aren't there yet. Also there's no gain without pain, and working with machine code (as we are here) will build a profound understanding that will serve you well in the future.

Moving on ...... the program segment to extract the "tens" will be almost identical to the segment that extracts the "hundreds," except that *its* CMPA instruction will be used to compare the contents of the accumulator with 9 instead of 99, the location used to store the "tens" value will be at address $4003, and the target addresses for the JNC and JMP instructions will have to be modified. (A listing of the entire program is shown a little later.) Finally, the program segment that extracts the "ones" will be extremely simple, because whatever is left in the accumulator after we've extracted the "hundreds" and the "tens" has to be the number of "ones." Thus, all this segment actually does is to store whatever value remains in the accumulator into the location we reserved to hold the "ones" value (that is, the location at address $4004).

Displaying the results

The last section of the program is comparatively simple. All we have to do is to load the accumulator with the values we stored in the "hundreds," "tens," and "ones" locations and copy these values to the output ports driving the 7-segment displays. However, there is just one small quirk, which devolves from the fact that one of our output devices is a dual 7-segment display (Figure 9.16).

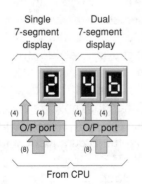

In the case of the left-hand digit, we're using our single 7-segment display to display the number of "hundreds." This means that all we have to do is to load the accumulator with the value we stored in the "hundreds" memory location, and then save it to the output port we're using to drive this display.

By comparison, in the case of the two right-hand digits, we're using our dual 7-segment display to display both the number of "tens" and the number of "ones." The problem here is that, as both of the digits on this display are driven by a single output port, and as our values for the "tens" and "ones" are stored in separate memory locations, we're going to have to perform a little jiggery-pokery.

Figure 9.16: A small quirk

Now this next bit might be a little difficult to wrap your brain around if you're a newbie, so let's take things one step at a time. The first thing to realize is that we know our "ones" location will only ever contain binary values in the range of 0000_2 through 1001_2 (which equates to 0 through 9 in decimal). If our original number contained any value greater than nine, then this would be reflected in the "tens" location (and possibly the "hundreds" location). To put this another way, ten "ones" really means one "ten" and no "ones," eleven "ones" really means one "ten" and one "one," twelve "ones" really means one "ten" and two "ones," and so on. Thus, we know that the number stored in our "ones" location will only ever occupy the four least-significant bits of this location.

Similarly, we know that our "tens" location will only ever contain binary values in the range of 0000_2 through 1001_2. These values equate to 0 through 9 in decimal, which we're taking to represent "no tens" through "nine tens"; that is, 0 = "no tens," 1 = "one ten," 2 = "two tens," and so on. We know there can't be more than nine "tens," because any greater value would be reflected in our "hundreds" location; so we know that the number stored in our "tens" location will only ever occupy the least-significant four bits of this location. Bearing all of this in mind, we are now poised to solve the problem ...... hmmm, perhaps it's time for another illustration (Figure 9.17).[8]

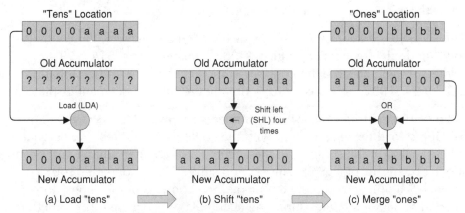

Figure 9.17: Merging the "tens" and "ones" values

Our first task is to load the accumulator with the value from the "tens" location (Figure 9.17a). Note that the 'a' characters shown in the four least-significant bits of the "tens" location are intended to indicate that these are the bits we're really interested in. Meanwhile, the question mark ('?')

---

[8]*"What is the use of a book,"* thought Alice, *"without pictures or conversations?"* — Alice's Adventures in Wonderland.

characters in the "Old Accumulator" indicate that we don't care what its contents were, because the load instruction will overwrite them.

The next step is to shift the contents of the accumulator four bits to the left (Figure 9.17b). However, as our shift left (SHL) instruction only shifts the accumulator one bit at a time, we'll have to use four of these instructions to achieve the desired result. When we finish the last of these shift left operations, the four least-significant bits of the accumulator will contain *logic 0s*, because one of the things a SHL does is to shift a zero into the accumulator's least-significant bit.

Last but not least, we OR the contents of the accumulator with the contents of the "ones" location (Figure 9.17c). The point to remember here is that logical instructions like OR operate on a bit-by-bit basis, so the original bit[0] in the accumulator is OR-ed with bit[0] of the "ones" location to generate the new bit[0] in the accumulator; the original bit[1] in the accumulator is OR-ed with bit[1] of the "ones" location to generate the new bit[1] in the accumulator; and so on.

The final result of these operations is that the accumulator's four most-significant bits end up containing the "tens" value, while its four least-significant bits contain the "ones" value. Thus, if we now save the contents of the accumulator to the output port driving our dual 7-segment display, we will achieve the effect we've been striving for (Figure 9.18).

The LDA ($91 at address $404A) loads the accumulator with the contents of the "hundreds" location at address $4002. Next we use a STA ($99 at address $404D) to store the contents of the accumulator to the output port at address $F022, which is the port driving the single 7-segment display.

Now comes the tricky bit, which commences with an LDA ($91 at address $4050) to load the accumulator with the contents of the "tens" location at address $4003. The contents of the accumulator are then shifted four bits to the left by means of four SHL instructions (the $70s at addresses $4053 through $4056). To complete the merge, the contents of the "ones" location at address $4004 are folded into the accumulator using the OR instruction ($39 at address $4057).

Following the merging of the "ten" and "ones" values into the accumulator, the STA ($99 at address $405A) is used to store the contents of the accumulator to the output port at address $F023, which is the port driving the dual 7-segment display. Finally, we use a JMP ($C1 at address $405D) to direct the CPU to jump back to the beginning of the main body of the program at address $4008. Thus, the program will continue to loop around, reading binary values from the switches and displaying their decimal equivalents on the 7-segment displays. (Once again, note that the reason the program returns to location $4008, as opposed to $4005, is because we only need to initialize the value of the stack pointer a single time. Also note that we haven't actually used the stack pointer in the code we've described thus far, but we will ...... Oh yes, we will).

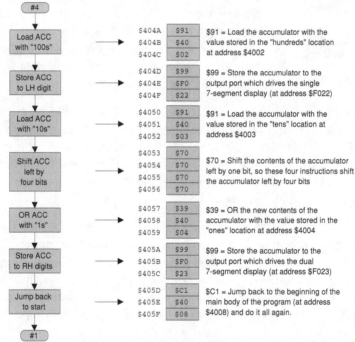

Figure 9.18: Displaying the results

Entering the program with the hex keypad

We've now arrived at the exciting bit where we enter our program, but first we need to power up the *Beboputer*, so click the **ON** button on the hex keypad. Note that the **Address (Ad)** button lights up to indicate that the address is the active field. Also note that all of the address and data digits initialize displaying hyphens, which indicates that they don't contain anything yet (Figure 9.19).

Figure 9.19: Blanks

If we ignore the memory locations we're using to store the various values and intermediate results, the first instruction in our program occurs at address $4005, so this is the address we need to enter. Using the keypad,

Figure 9.20: Address

click a '4', followed by a '0', another '0', and a '5', and watch the address build up in the address field (Figures 19.20a, 19.20b, 19.20c, and 19.20d, respectively).

Note that the individual characters initially arrive in the right-most address digit, but that they're shifted along to the left as successive characters are added. We used this technique because this is the way in which these devices often used to function and we saw no reason to break with tradition. Also note that the keypad's address and data fields display hexadecimal values.

Should you make a mistake, you can clear the address field by clicking the keypad's **Clear (Clr)** button, which will return the field's contents to hyphen characters. In fact the **Clear** button is *context-sensitive*, which means that its action depends on the context in which it's used. To put this another way, this button will clear either the address or the data field, depending on which field is active at the time.

Speaking of which, it's time to enter a value of $50 into the data field. First click the **Data (Da)** button on the keypad to make this field active. In this instance, the data field continues to show hyphens, because the memory location at address $4005 currently contains random, unknown values. In the real world you would be presented with whatever random value was contained by the location, but we decided to make the *Beboputer* more

Figure 9.21: Data

user-friendly. Note that, if we had previously entered a good value into this location, then this value would be displayed in the data field (we will return to this point a little later). Now click a '5', followed by a '0', and watch the data build up in the data field (Figures 19.21a and 19.21b, respectively).

To complete this operation, click the keypad's **Enter (Ent)** button. This causes the monitor program to load the data displayed in the data field ($50) into the memory location specified by the address field ($4005), and this

Figure 9.22: Enter

new data value will therefore be reflected in the memory walker display. Note that the *Beboputer* automatically increments the value in the address field (Figure 9.22). Once again the data field shows hyphens, because the memory location at address

$4006 currently contains random, unknown values. Also note that the Data (Da) button remains active, which allows you to alternate between entering data and clicking the Enter button with minimum inconvenience.

This leads us inexorably to the fact that we've still got a lot of program to enter and, as there's no time like the present, we'd better get on with it. (If you want to be a whining wallaby, the next section describes a short-cut method for loading this program. However, we strongly recommend that you enter at least a few of the instructions by hand, just to get the feel of using the keypad.) Remember that the address field currently contains $4006 and the data field is currently active, so start by entering the data associated with address $4006 from the following program listing (that is, click '4', followed by 'F', followed by the Enter button), and continue from there.

Address	Data	Instruction	Initialize the stack pointer
$4005	$50	BLDSP(imm)	Load the stack pointer with address $4FFF
$4006	$4F		
$4007	$FF		

Address	Data	Instruction	Initialize the variables
$4008	$90	LDA (imm)	Load the accumulator with $00
$4009	$00		
$400A	$99	STA (abs)	Store the accumulator to the "hundreds"
$400B	$40		location at address $4002
$400C	$02		
$400D	$99	STA (abs)	Store the accumulator to the "tens" location
$400E	$40		at address $4003
$400F	$03		
$4010	$99	STA (abs)	Store the accumulator to the "ones"
$4011	$40		location at address $4004
$4012	$04		

Address	Data	Instruction	Read and store the value on the switches
$4013	$91	LDA (abs)	Load the accumulator from the input port
$4014	$F0		connected to the 8-bit switch device at
$4015	$00		address $F000
$4016	$99	STA (abs)	Store the accumulator to the location we're
$4017	$40		going to use to preserve the original value
$4018	$00		on the switches (at address $4000)

Address	Data	Instruction	Extract the "Hundreds"
$4019	$60	CMPA (imm)	Compare the accumulator to $63 (99 in
$401A	$63		decimal)
$401B	$E6	JNC (abs)	If the carry flag isn't set to logic 1, which
$401C	$40		means that the value in the accumulator
$401D	$30		isn't bigger than $63, then jump forward to
			address $4030 (to extract the "tens")
$401E	$20	SUB (imm)	Subtract $64 from the contents of the
$401F	$64		accumulator (where $64 is 100 in decimal)
$4020	$99	STA (abs)	Store the accumulator to the temporary
$4021	$40		location which we use to save
$4022	$01		intermediate results at address $4001
$4023	$91	LDA (abs)	Load the accumulator with the contents of
$4024	$40		the "hundreds" location at address $4002
$4025	$02		
$4026	$80	INCA (imp)	Increment (add one to) the contents of
			the accumulator
$4027	$99	STA (abs)	Store the incremented contents of the
$4028	$40		accumulator to the "hundreds" location
$4029	$02		at address $4002
$402A	$91	LDA (abs)	Load the accumulator with the contents
$402B	$40		of the temporary location which we use
$402C	$01		to save intermediate results (at address
			$4001)
$402D	$C1	JMP (abs)	Jump back to the beginning of this
$402E	$40		segment of the program (at address $4019)
$402F	$19		and check to see if there are any more
			"hundreds"

Address	Data	Instruction	Extract the "Tens"
$4030	$60	CMPA (imm)	Compare the accumulator to $09 (which
$4031	$09		is 9 in decimal)
$4032	$E6	JNC (abs)	If the carry flag isn't set to logic 1, which
$4033	$40		means that the value in the accumulator
$4034	$47		isn't bigger than $09, then jump forward
			to address $4047 (to extract the "ones")
$4035	$20	SUB (imm)	Subtract $0A from the contents of the
$4036	$0A		accumulator (where $0A is 10 in decimal)
$4037	$99	STA (abs)	Store the accumulator to the temporary
$4038	$40		location which we use to save
$4039	$01		intermediate results (at address $4001)
$403A	$91	LDA (abs)	Load the accumulator with the contents
$403B	$40		of the "tens" location at address $4003

Address	Data	Instruction	
$403C	$03		
$403D	$80	INCA (imp)	Increment (add one to) the contents of the accumulator
$403E	$99	STA (abs)	Store the incremented contents of the
$403F	$40		accumulator to the "tens" location at
$4040	$03		address $4003
$4041	$91	LDA (abs)	Load the accumulator with the contents of
$4042	$40		the temporary location which we use to save
$4043	$01		intermediate results (at address $4001)
$4044	$C1	JMP (abs)	Jump back to the beginning of this segment
$4045	$40		of the program at address $4030 and check
$4046	$30		to see if there are any more "tens"

Address	**Data**	**Instruction**	**Extract the "Ones"**
$4047	$99	STA (abs)	Store whatever value remains in the
$4048	$40		accumulator (following the extraction of
$4049	$04		the "hundreds" and the "tens") to the
			"ones" location at address $4004

Address	**Data**	**Instruction**	**Display the results**
$404A	$91	LDA (abs)	Load the accumulator with the contents
$404B	$40		of the "hundreds" location at address $4002
$404C	$02		
$404D	$99	STA (abs)	Store the accumulator to the output port
$404E	$F0		connected to the single 7-segment
$404F	$22		display at address $F022
$4050	$91	LDA (abs)	Load the accumulator with the contents
$4051	$40		of the "tens" location at address $4003
$4052	$03		
$4053	$70	SHL (imp)	Shift the contents of the accumulator left one bit
$4054	$70	SHL (imp)	" " " " " "
$4055	$70	SHL (imp)	" " " " " "
$4056	$70	SHL (imp)	" " " " " "
$4057	$39	OR (abs)	OR the shifted contents of the accumulator
$4058	$40		with the contents of the "ones" location
$4059	$04		at address $4004
$405A	$99	STA (abs)	Store the accumulator to the output port
$405B	$F0		connected to the dual 7-segment display
$405C	$23		at address $F023
$405D	$C1	JMP (abs)	Jump back to the beginning of the main
$405E	$40		body of the program at address $4008
$405F	$08		and do the whole thing again, and again ...

Now although this may appear to be quite a long program, it actually required only thirty-six instructions and occupied only ninety-six bytes of memory (including the five bytes we reserved to store our temporary variables). However, you can readily understand why we would be reluctant to use this technique to enter a more substantial program, such as a full-featured word processor, which can easily occupy tens of millions of bytes. (Once again, we will start to examine more user-friendly ways of creating programs in Chapter 12.)

Before we continue, it's well worth pausing for a moment to reflect on how this program illustrates the generic way in which programs are created and computers work:

a) We commenced with a high-level problem we wished to solve.

b) We partitioned the problem into well-defined, manageable "chunks."

c) We derived a set of algorithms to solve the problem. For this example we represented our algorithms by means of flowcharts, but other techniques are also available. Note that the term *algorithm* is commonly used in computing, and is generally understood to refer to a sequence of formulas (which may be specified as a mixture of algebraic and logical steps) that can be used to solve a problem. To put this another way, an algorithm may be considered to be a step-by-step procedure for solving a complex problem.[9]

d) We translated our algorithms into machine-code instructions that the computer understands. In the case of this example we performed the translation by hand, but other techniques are available (see also Chapter 12).

Purely for the sake of interest, we've tallied the number of different instructions used in this program, which are:-

STA	Store accumulator	11	All absolute
LDA	Load accumulator	8	One immediate and seven absolute
SHL	Shift accumulator left	4	All implied (the only mode)
JMP	Jump unconditionally	3	All absolute

---

[9]Buzz words come and go with the seasons. Towards the end of the 1980s, the word on everyone's lips was *paradigm*, meaning "pattern" or "model," such as "*I'm working on a new design paradigm.*" Unfortunately, although it sounded clever when one person used it, it started to sound ridiculous when everyone was spouting forth (often pronouncing it incorrectly). By the early 1990s, "paradigm" had returned to relative obscurity (which means that we, the chosen few, can start using it again to sound intelligent).

JNC	Jump if not carry	2	Both absolute (the only mode)
CMPA	Compare accumulator	2	Both immediate
INCA	Increment accumulator	2	Both implied (the only mode)
SUB	Subtract from accumulator	2	Both immediate
OR	Logical OR with accumulator	1	Absolute
BLDSP	Load stack pointer	1	Big immediate (loads two bytes)

Is there anything we can conclude from this breakdown? This is a trick question, whose answer is obviously "*No.*" It isn't possible to determine anything useful on the basis of a single program, because a sample of one item is statistically meaningless. All we can say with any certainty is that this particular program uses ten different types of instructions, and that each instruction is used a certain number of times. However, it is interesting to note that there are more loads and stores than all of the other instructions combined. You might wish to perform a similar breakdown on future programs (both ours and your own) to see if you can spot any trends.

Short-cut technique for loading the program

We realize that it can be somewhat boring entering someone else's programs, and we know that you want to start writing your own as soon as possible, so we've already entered some of the programs described in this book and provided you with a shortcut technique for loading them.

Click the **Memory** item on the project window's menu bar, then click the **Load RAM** entry in the resulting pull-down menu. This will invoke the appropriate dialog window as shown in Figure 9.23.

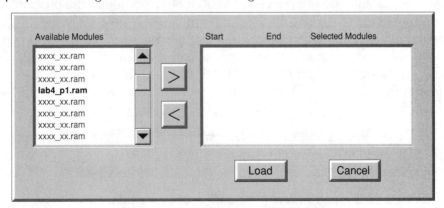

Figure 9.23: The Load RAM dialog

The scrolling list on the left-hand side of this dialog shows all of the programs that are available for you to load. (When you save your own programs using the corresponding Save RAM feature, they will also appear in this list.) The program we're interested in at the moment is called "lab4_p1," so locate this entry in the scrolling list. Now we wish to move this program into the list of programs to be loaded on the right-hand side of the dialog. There are two ways to do this as follows:

a) Single-click the "lab4_p1" entry in the scrolling list (the entry will be highlighted to indicate that it's been selected), then click the button with the right-pointing arrow located between the two lists.

b) Double-click the "lab4_p1" entry in the scrolling list, which automatically moves this entry into the right-hand list.

Whichever of these techniques you use, the right-hand list updates to reflect the addresses this program will occupy ($4005 through $405F). (Remember that locations $4000 through $4004 are used by the program to store data, but they aren't really a part of the body of the program.) In fact, this dialog will allow you to simultaneously load a selection of programs into different portions of the RAM, but we'll leave that feature for later consideration. For the moment, simply click the Load button, which will load the selected program(s) and automatically dismiss the dialog window.

Editing the program with the hex keypad

Suppose that you made a mistake entering the program, or that you've decided that you would like to make some changes, or that you'd simply like to take a peek into certain memory locations to see what's there. For example, assume that you'd like to check out that portion of the program where we loaded the value on the 8-bit switches and stored it in the *Beboputer's* memory (addresses $4013 through $4018). Of course we can always use our trusty memory walker to examine and modify the contents of the RAM, but this is a tool of convenience that we provided for the *Beboputer*. In the days of yore, the only tool that was available was the hex keypad itself.

So click the keypad's Address (Ad) button to make the address field active. Note that both the address and data fields display hyphens to indicate that nothing is selected. Now use the keypad to enter address $4013.

Try clicking the keypad's Enter (Ent) button. Nothing happens (except for an annoying beep), because the Enter button will only work if the data is the active field, so click the Data (Da) button to make this field active. Note that as soon as the data field becomes active, it displays the $91 value that we previously entered into this location. Now try clicking the Enter button again, and note that the address field increments to $4014, while the data field now displays the $F0 that we previously entered into *this* location.

Click the Enter button a few more times, and check that the data in the succeeding addresses is what we'd expect it to be. What you've just been doing is to write the existing data in these locations back into them. If you do wish to modify the data at a particular location, you first have to click the Clear (Clr) button to clear the data field, key-in some new data, and then click the Enter button to overwrite the existing data with your new data.

Running the program with the hex keypad

Ensure that the memory walker is set to the start of the RAM at location $4000. If you entered the program by hand, the first five memory locations, $4000 through $4004 (which the program uses to store data), will show unknown $XX values, because we haven't loaded anything into them yet. However, if you used the Memory → Load RAM command, then these locations will contain $00 values, which are automatically generated by the assembler tool we used to create this program for you (the assembler is introduced in Chapter 12). If you did load our existing program, then purely for the sake of the following discussions, use the memory walker to edit the data in locations $4000 through $4004 and replace the existing $00 values with $FF.

Click the keypad's Address (Ad) button to make the address field active, then enter the start address of the program, which is $4005. Next click the Step (Stp) button and note that the address field now displays $4008, because you've just stepped through the program's first instruction, which was to load the stack pointer with $4FFF. Now we're at the start of the "Initialize the Variables" segment of the program. Click the Step button to execute the LDA instruction, which loads the accumulator with $00. One more click on the Step button executes the STA instruction, which stores the accumulator to address $4002. Note that location $4002 in the memory walker updates to reflect the fact that this location now contains $00.

Keep clicking the Step button to walk through the program until the fun begins to fade, then click the Run button to let the *Beboputer* rip. (Note that you can switch between the *run mode* and the *step mode* at any time by clicking the appropriate button on the keypad.) As soon as the *Beboputer* enters the *run mode*, the hex keypad's address and data fields start to display '–' characters, the memory walker grays out, and the 7-segment displays light up to show three '0's, because this is the value that's currently represented by our 8-bit switches. Click the appropriate switches to build up an unsigned binary value of 11110110_2 (which equates to 246 in decimal) (Figure 9.24).

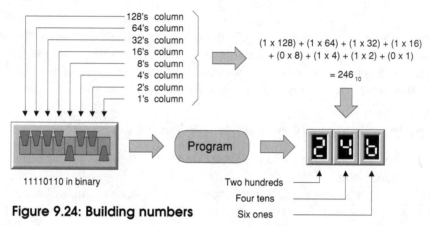

$$(1 \times 128) + (1 \times 64) + (1 \times 32) + (1 \times 16)$$
$$+ (0 \times 8) + (1 \times 4) + (1 \times 2) + (0 \times 1)$$
$$= 246_{10}$$

128's column
64's column
32's column
16's column
8's column
4's column
2's column
1's column

Program

11110110 in binary

Two hundreds
Four tens
Six ones

Figure 9.24: Building numbers

Remembering that each of the 8-bit switches corresponds to a different power of two, determine the switch positions required to build the decimal numbers 23, 86, 100, 128, 199, and 236, and test your solutions with our program. Finally, can you construct the decimal number 256 using our 8-bit switches? If not why not?[10]

At some point during the course of your experiments, dismiss the memory walker by clicking the **Exit** button in its title bar, and note how the speed of the *Beboputer's* response increases when you click on the 8-bit switches. Remember this for the future, because we are going to introduce additional tools to help us to understand what the *Beboputer* is doing, but every display you have open on the screen will have a significant impact on the *Beboputer's* speed.

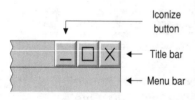

Iconize button

Title bar

Menu bar

When you've finished and are ready to proceed to the next part of this laboratory, click the keypad's **Reset (Rst)** button, which will halt the program and return the *Beboputer* to its *reset mode*.

[10]You can't use our 8-bit switches to represent 256 in decimal, because eight bits can only support 256 unique patterns of logic 0s and logic 1s, and we can therefore only represent unsigned numbers in the range 0_{10} through 255_{10}.

Augmented program that speaks the numbers

Now comes the really exciting part, in which we augment our program to generate the stuff that tickles your ears. That's right, we're going to instruct the *Beboputer* to actually speak your numbers out loud! Obviously this assumes that your real computer is equipped with a sound card. However, even if you haven't splashed out the cash for one of these little beauties, it's still worth your while to follow along with the rest of us, because we'll be introducing a few new ideas as we go.

Before we commence, we need to connect two new devices to the *Beboputer's* input and output ports. First click the Input Ports icon on the main project window's toolbar (not the one on the memory walker) to bring up the Input Ports dialog window. Click the Port 2 button to access the Big Red Button device (which we will refer to as "Big Red" henceforth), then click the Dismiss button to dismiss this form. Next click the Output Ports icon to invoke the Output Ports dialog window. Click the Port 5 button to access the *Beboputer's* Sound Card device, then click the Dismiss button to return the dialog window to whence it came. Finally, use your mouse to drag these devices by their banners and relocate them to wherever you think they look warm and fuzzy on your screen.

We will return to consider both "Big Red" and the sound card in more detail momentarily, but first let's discuss exactly what it is we intend to do. The way in which our original program functioned was to loop around reading the binary value on the 8-bit Switch input device, extract its "hundreds," "tens," and "ones" components, and display a decimal representation on our 7-segment displays (Figure 9.25a).

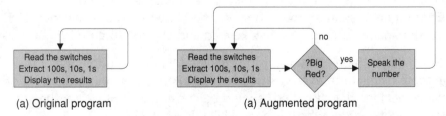

(a) Original program   (a) Augmented program

Figure 9.25: Original versus augmented programs

Now we wish to augment our program such that it speaks the numbers, which gives us a few things to consider. The first point is that you don't want the *Beboputer* to speak *every* time you change one of the 8-bit switches, because you might have to modify a number of switches to build up the number you require. The second point is that once you've set up a number, you might want to listen to it several times. This is where "Big Red" comes into play (Figure 9.25b). By default, our augmented program will continue to loop around reading the 8-bit switches and displaying the equivalent decimal number. However, after displaying this number, we are going to make the program check the state of "Big Red," which, if you've pressed it, will cause the number to be spoken.

The big red button

"Big Red" is simple in concept, because it's a single push-button switch that's connected to one bit of an input port, but there's a little more to it than that. First of all, there are an amazing number of different types of switches, including toggle switches, rocker switches, rotary switches, push-button switches, and even magnetic switches. (In fact switches are an interesting subject in their own right, with a baffling and bewildering set of terminology.) But we're only interested in two basic types, which we'll refer to as *toggle switches* and *momentary push-buttons* (Figure 9.26).

A toggle switch is similar to a light switch, in that it's either **ON** or **OFF**, and it stays that way until somebody causes it to alter its state. These are the sort of switches that are predominantly used in our original switch panel and our

(a) Toggle switch   (b) Momentary pushbutton

Figure 9.26: Toggle switch versus momentary pushbutton

8-bit switch device. Similarly, a standard push-button also remembers its last state, the only difference being that you push it in instead of flicking it up or down. By comparison, a momentary push-button only makes a connection while you're pressing it, while an internal spring (or similar mechanism) causes it to return to its **OPEN** position as soon as you release it. These are the sort of switches that are predominantly used on our hex keypad and also for "Big Red."

But wait, there's more, because we've decided that it would be useful to have some mechanism to tell us whether "Big Red" has been pushed or not. So we've decided that "Big Red" should be constructed with a transparent plastic window, under which is a red LED (Figure 9.27).

In this scenario (which is only one of many possibilities), one of the inputs to the latch is connected to the output from "Big Red." This input to the latch is usually connected to *logic 0* through the resistor, but, when "Big Red" is pressed, it connects the latch's input to *logic 1*.

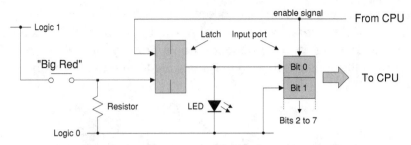

Figure 9.27: One possible scenario for "Big Red"

This particular latch is slightly different from those we've looked at before. For our purposes we will assume that when the input that's connected to "Big Red" is presented with a *logic 1*, the latch will begin to output a *logic 1*, which will cause the red LED to be turned on. (Remember that this LED is actually mounted inside "Big Red," and will therefore cause it to light up.) But, even when "Big Red" is released, the latch will "remember" what happened and will continue to drive its *logic 1* value.

Moving on ...... the output from the latch is connected to bit[0] of the input port, while all of the other bits are connected to *logic 0* values. Thus, when the CPU reads data from this input port, a value of 00000000_2 will indicate that nothing has happened, while a value of 00000001_2 will reflect the fact that "Big Red" has been pressed.

Finally, the enable signal that the CPU generates to read data from this input port can also be used to reset "Big Red's" latch, thereby returning it to driving a *logic 0* value until "Big Red" is pressed again. Note that the latch would be designed such that the enable signal will only reset it at the end of the CPU's read operation; that is, the latch will be reset by the enable signal returning to its inactive state (if the latch were reset at the beginning of the read operation, then the CPU would always see *logic 0s* and would never be able to tell whether "Big Red" had been pressed or not).

The *Beboputer's* sound card

Truth to tell, the *Beboputer* doesn't really have a sound card as such (let's face it, the *Beboputer's* existence is tenuous at best), so it uses the sound card in your real computer. The easiest way to envisage this is that you have two computers on your desk – your real computer and your *Beboputer* – and that both of them can communicate with the sound card (Figure 9.28).

Here's the way it works: Unlike the *Beboputer*, your real computer has a hard disk, on which we've stored some pre-recorded sound files. One of the

Beboputer's output ports (**Port 5** at address $F025) is connected to the sound card. When the *Beboputer* writes a byte of data to this port, the sound card uses that byte to access a corresponding sound file on your real computer's hard disk, and the sound card then plays this file through your real, physical loudspeaker.

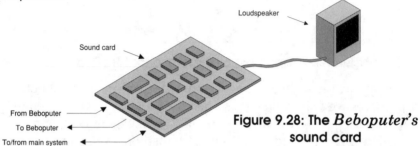

Figure 9.28: The *Beboputer's* sound card

As a byte can represent 256 different patterns of *logic 0s* and *logic 1s*, we can potentially use the *Beboputer* to play 256 different sound files, each of which could contain an interesting tone, a single word, a monologue, or Beethoven's 5th if we so desired. For the purposes of this laboratory, the sound files we're interested in are as follows:

Contents of byte from *Beboputer*	Contents of associated sound file
0_{10} (Binary 00000000, hex 00)	Says the word *"zero"*
1_{10} (Binary 00000001, hex 01)	Says the word *"one"*
2_{10} (Binary 00000010, hex 02)	Says the word *"two"*
3_{10} (Binary 00000011, hex 03)	Says the word *"three"*
4_{10} (Binary 00000100, hex 04)	Says the word *"four"*
5_{10} (Binary 00000101, hex 05)	Says the word *"five"*
6_{10} (Binary 00000110, hex 06)	Says the word *"six"*
7_{10} (Binary 00000111, hex 07)	Says the word *"seven"*
8_{10} (Binary 00001000, hex 08)	Says the word *"eight"*
9_{10} (Binary 00001001, hex 09)	Says the word *"nine"*
11_{10} (Binary 00001011, hex 0B)	Says the word *"eleven"*
12_{10} (Binary 00001100, hex 0C)	Says the word *"twelve"*
13_{10} (Binary 00001101, hex 0D)	Says the word *"thirteen"*
14_{10} (Binary 00001110, hex 0E)	Says the word *"fourteen"*
15_{10} (Binary 00001111, hex 0F)	Says the word *"fifteen"*
16_{10} (Binary 00010000, hex 10)	Says the word *"sixteen"*
17_{10} (Binary 00010001, hex 11)	Says the word *"seventeen"*
18_{10} (Binary 00010010, hex 12)	Says the word *"eighteen"*
19_{10} (Binary 00010011, hex 13)	Says the word *"nineteen"*

21_{10} (Binary 00010101, hex 15)	Says the word *"ten"*
22_{10} (Binary 00010110, hex 16)	Says the word *"twenty"*
23_{10} (Binary 00010111, hex 17)	Says the word *"thirty"*
24_{10} (Binary 00011000, hex 18)	Says the word *"forty"*
25_{10} (Binary 00011001, hex 19)	Says the word *"fifty"*
26_{10} (Binary 00011010, hex 1A)	Says the word *"sixty"*
27_{10} (Binary 00011011, hex 1B)	Says the word *"seventy"*
28_{10} (Binary 00011100, hex 1C)	Says the word *"eighty"*
29_{10} (Binary 00011101, hex 1D)	Says the word *"ninety"*
30_{10} (Binary 00011110, hex 1E)	Says the word *"hundred"*
31_{10} (Binary 00011111, hex 1F)	Says the word *"thousand"*
32_{10} (Binary 00100000, hex 20)	Says the word *"and"*
33_{10} (Binary 00100001, hex 21)	Says the word *"minus"*

It is important to note that the only relationship between the byte the *Beboputer* sends to the sound card and the sound file that's played is one that we (the masters of the *Beboputer's* universe) have set up behind the scenes. In fact you can modify our sound files or add your own if you wish (this is discussed in more detail in Appendix B).

One final point to consider is that the sound card works independently of the *Beboputer*. By this we mean that once the *Beboputer* has written a byte to the output port that's connected to the sound card, the card starts to play the corresponding sound file while the *Beboputer* continues on its merry way. The problem is that the *Beboputer* is running much faster than the sound card. For example, supposing we wish to use the sound card to say the phrase *"One hundred and sixty."* In this case we will instruct the *Beboputer* to send the following sequence of bytes to the sound card: $01, $30, $32, and $26. However, if we send these bytes one after the other without a pause, then the sound card won't have time to complete anything before it's told to do something else.

For example, when the sound card receives the $01 byte, it will locate the associated sound file and start to say *"One."* Unfortunately, the card will barely have started on the 'O' in *"One"* before it receives the $30 byte, so it will stop what it's doing, locate the new sound file, and start to say *"Hundred."* But once again, the card will only just have begun to say the 'H' in *"hundred"* when it receives the $32 byte which tells it to do something else, and so it goes.

In order to resolve this problem, we have also connected the sound card to one of the *Beboputer's* <u>input</u> ports (Port 5 at address $F005). Much like our Big Red Switch, the sound card only drives the least-significant bit of this port (the card drives a *logic 0* if it's free and a *logic 1* if it's busy). Thus, if the *Beboputer* reads this port when the sound card isn't doing anything, it will receive a value of $00 (or 00000000 in binary); but if the sound card is currently being used, then the *Beboputer* will receive a value of $01 (or 00000001 in binary). As we will see, we can use this feature to cause the *Beboputer* to wait for the sound card to complete whatever word it's currently working on before instructing it to begin speaking the next word.

What do we want our augmented program to do (in a general sort of way)?

Before we start to look at our augmented program in detail, it's worth pausing for a moment to consider exactly what it is that we want it to do. We know that we want our program to speak numbers in the form *"One hundred and forty,"* and we know that we've got to piece this sentence together out of the individual words *"One," "hundred," "and,"* and *"forty."* However, what's easy for us isn't necessarily easy for a computer (and vice versa). When we speak a number out loud, we unconsciously use several rules; for example, consider how you would say the following numbers:

Written Number	Spoken Number
0	*"Zero"*
6	*"Six"*
18	*"Eighteen"*
30	*"Thirty"*
57	*"Fifty seven"*
100	*"One hundred"*
106	*"One hundred and six"*
118	*"One hundred and eighteen"*
130	*"One hundred and thirty"*
157	*"One hundred and fifty seven"*

Just by looking at these examples, can you spot any obvious rules that we use when saying them aloud? Before you examine the way in which we attacked this problem, why not take the time to grab a pencil and a piece of paper and try to sketch out your own approach in the form of a flowchart? In fact, just because we really are quite nice when you get to know us, we'll give you a couple of hints. One of the tricky areas involves deciding when to say the word *"and,"* while another painful area involves the numbers *"eleven"* through *"nineteen."*

In this latter case, it's interesting to consider how much easier life would have been if our forefathers had decided to use the word *"onety"* instead of *"ten"* (where *"onety"* would have the same general meaning as *"twenty,"* *"thirty,"* *"forty,"* and so on). If this were the case, then instead of having *"eleven,"* *"twelve,"* *"thirteen,"* ...... up to *"nineteen"* as special cases which stick out like a sore thumb, we could have used *"onety-one,"* *"onety-two,"* *"onety-three,"* ...... and so forth up to *"onety-nine,"* respectively.

This might not strike you as being incredibly useful at the moment, because you've forgotten how difficult it was to learn the rules associated with speaking numbers when you were young. So as we said, have a stab at sketching out your own flowchart (no peeking now), and it shouldn't take too long for you to appreciate what we've been babbling on about.

The augmented program flowchart

So how did you do? You probably found that it wasn't as easy as you thought it was going to be, but that's only because thinking at this step-by-step level isn't the way we usually go about doing things. Don't worry, because it gets a lot easier with only a little practice. Of course you may have zipped through it, in which case may we offer you our heartiest congratulations!

Irrespective of whether you found it excruciatingly difficult or ridiculously easy, compare your solution to our approach below, but don't be overly concerned if your technique differs from ours, because there are an almost unlimited number of alternatives.

The first part of our solution concentrates on speaking the "hundreds" (if there are any), and deciding on whether or not to say the word *"and"* (Figure 9.29).

Note that the entry point, which is labeled *"#5"*, is assumed to be bolted on to the end of our original program, just

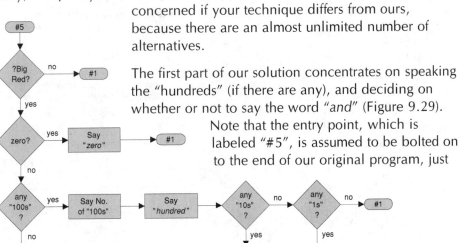

Figure 9.29: Speak-the-numbers (part 1)

after we've displayed the results, thereby overwriting the final unconditional jump back to the start of the main body of the program.

The first thing we do is to check our Big Red Switch. If "Big Red" has remained undisturbed, we immediately jump back to the start of the main body of the program (indicated by the "#1" label); but if "Big Red" has been pressed, then we know we've got to speak the number.

Remembering that we stored the original number at the beginning of the program, it's easy for us to test whether it was zero, in which case we simply say "*zero*" and return to the beginning of the main body of the program.

If our original number was non-zero, the next thing we do is to check to see if there are any "hundreds." If there aren't any, we can leave this part of the program and continue on our way (indicated by the "#6" label). If there are some "hundreds," then we need to say their number followed by the word "*hundred*." Now we check to see whether there are any "tens" or "ones." If there aren't any we've completed our mission, so we return to the beginning of the main body of the program. Alternatively, if there are some "tens" or "ones," we say the word "*and*" and proceed to the next part of the program (indicated by the "#6" label).

The next part of our solution (with which we intend to win the "*novelty flowchart of the year*" competition) is concerned with speaking the "tens" and "ones" (Figure 9.30). This is where we decide whether part of our number falls into the range 11 through 19, in which case we will have to give it special treatment.

The point to remember is that, due to the way in which we extracted the "tens" component of the number in our initial program, we know that the "tens" value will only ever contain the decimal numbers 0

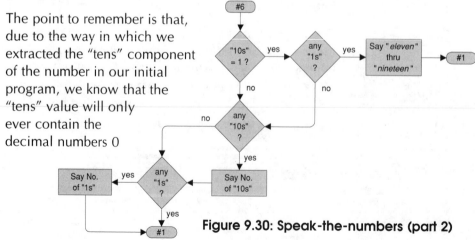

Figure 9.30: Speak-the-numbers (part 2)

through 9. Also remember that we're taking these numbers to represent "no tens" through "nine tens"; that is, 0 = "no tens," 1 = "one ten," 2 = "two tens," and so on.

Thus, the first thing we do is to check whether the "tens" value equals 1 (which actually represents 10), and if it does, we next check to see if there are any "ones." If both of these tests prove positive, then we know we're going to have to say a number in the range "eleven" through "nineteen," after which we can return to the beginning of the main body of the program. But if either of these tests fails, then we can simply proceed to say the number of "tens" followed by the number of "ones," and *then* return to the beginning of the program.

The only other point to consider is the part of the program that actually says the numbers. As we previously discussed, in order to cause the *Beboputer* to say a word, we have to send a byte to the sound card causing it to play the appropriate sound file (Figure 9.31).

Since we wish to say words at a number of different points in our program, we decided to use a subroutine, and the way in which this particular subroutine

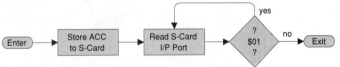

Figure 9.31: Speak-the-numbers "say word" subroutine

works is really simple.[11] The main program is ensures that the correct byte is stored in the accumulator, then it calls our "say word" subroutine. As soon as it's invoked, this subroutine immediately writes the contents of the accumulator to the output port that's connected to the sound card. The subroutine then reads the input port connected to the sound card and checks to see whether the value it receives is $00 or $01 (the sound card returns $01 if it's busy playing a sound file). So the subroutine will keep looping around checking the sound card until it reads a value of $00, at which point it knows the sound card has finished playing the current sound file (saying the current word). The subroutine then terminates and returns control to the main program at the point from which it was called.

The augmented program listing

We're champing at the bit to leap into the next chapter and sink our teeth into the subject of keyboards, but this program seems to be never-ending so

---

[11]Subroutines were introduced in Chapter 8.

we'll have to be brief.[12] The main points to note about the following listing are that it's bolted on to the end of our original program, and that it starts at address $405D, which means that it overwrites the unconditional jump instruction we originally used to return to the beginning of the program.

Address	Data	Instruction	Check "Big Red"
$405D	$91	LDA (abs)	Load the accumulator from the input port
$405E	$F0		connected to "Big Red" at address $F002
$405F	$02		
$4060	$D1	JZ (abs)	If the value is $00, then "Big Red" hasn't been
$4061	$40		pushed, so jump back to the beginning of the
$4062	$08		main body of the program at address $4008
			and do it all again

Address	Data	Instruction	Check for zero
$4063	$91	LDA (abs)	Load the accumulator from the location
$4064	$40		that we used to store the original value on
$4065	$00		the 8-bit switches at address $4000
$4066	$D6	JNZ (abs)	If the value isn't zero ($00), then jump to
$4067	$40		the "Say Hundreds" portion of the program
$4068	$6F		at address $406F, otherwise continue to
			the next instruction at $4069
$4069	$C9	JSR (abs)	Jump to the "Say Word" subroutine at
$406A	$40		address $40BB to say "zero" (because ACC
$406B	$BB		contains $00). Note that the return address
			$406C is automatically saved on the stack
$406C	$C1	JMP (abs)	Jump back to the beginning of the main
$406D	$40		body of the program at address $4008 and
$406E	$08		do it all again

Address	Data	Instruction	Say "hundreds" (if any)
$406F	$91	LDA (abs)	Load the accumulator with the contents of
$4070	$40		the "hundreds" location at address $4002
$4071	$02		
$4072	$D1	JZ (abs)	If the value is zero, then no "hundreds", so
$4073	$40		jump to the "Eleven through Nineteen" part
$4074	$8E		of the program at address $408E, otherwise
			continue to address $4075
$4075	$C9	JSR (abs)	Jump to the "Say Word" subroutine at address
$4076	$40		$40BB to say the number of "hundreds". Note
$4077	$BB		that the return address of $4078 is automatically
			saved on the stack

---

[12]"I will be so brief that, in fact, I've already finished!" — Salvador Dali, on being invited to say a "few brief words."

$4078	$90	LDA (imm)	Load the accumulator with $1E, which, when
$4079	$1E		sent to the sound card, will cause it to say the word "*hundred*"
$407A	$C9	JSR (abs)	Jump to the "Say Word" subroutine at
$407B	$40		address $40BB to say the word "*hundred*".
$407C	$BB		Note that the return address of $407D is automatically saved on the stack

Address	Data	Instruction	**Do we need to say "and" ?**
$407D	$91	LDA (abs)	Load the accumulator with the contents of
$407E	$40		the "tens" location at address $4003
$407F	$03		
$4080	$D6	JNZ (abs)	If the value isn't zero, then there are some "tens",
$4081	$40		so jump to the part of the program in charge of
$4082	$89		saying the word "*and*" at $4089, otherwise continue to $4083
$4083	$91	LDA (abs)	Load the accumulator with the contents of
$4084	$40		the "ones" location at address $4003
$4085	$04		
$4086	$D1	JZ (abs)	If the value is zero, then there aren't any "ones"
$4087	$40		either, so jump back to the beginning of the
$4088	$08		program at address $4008, otherwise continue to $4089
$4089	$90	LDA (imm)	Load the accumulator with $20, which, when
$408A	$20		sent to the sound card, will cause it to say the word "*and*"
$408B	$C9	JSR (abs)	Jump to the "Say Word" subroutine at address
$408C	$40		$40BB to say the word "*and*". Note that the
$408D	$BB		return address of $408E is automatically saved on the stack

Address	Data	Instruction	**Check for "eleven" through "nineteen"**
$408E	$91	LDA (abs)	Load the accumulator with the contents of
$408F	$40		the "tens" location at address $4003
$4090	$03		
$4091	$60	CMPA(imm)	Compare the contents of the accumulator
$4092	$01		with $01 to see whether we have one "ten"
$4093	$D6	JNZ (abs)	If the result of the comparison isn't zero, then
$4094	$40		there's either no "tens" or more than one "ten",
$4095	$A4		so jump to address $40A4, otherwise continue to address $4096
$4096	$91	LDA (abs)	Obviously we've got one "ten", so now
$4097	$40		load the accumulator with the contents of
$4098	$04		the "ones" location at address $4004

Address	Data	Instruction	
$4099	$D1	JZ (abs)	If the value of "ones" is zero, then we don't have
$409A	$40		a number between "eleven" and "nineteen", so
$409B	$A4		jump to the "tens and ones" at $40A4, else
			continue to $409C
$409C	$10	ADD (imm)	We know we've got a number between "eleven"
$409D	$0A		and "nineteen", so add $0A (decimal 10) to the
			accumulator
$409E	$C9	JSR (abs)	Jump to the "Say Word" subroutine at address
$409F	$40		$40BB to say a number between "*eleven*" and
$40A0	$BB		"*nineteen*". Note the return address $40A1 is
			automatically saved on the stack
$40A1	$C1	JMP (abs)	As the number *was* between "eleven" and
$40A2	$40		"nineteen", our job here is done, so jump
$40A3	$08		back to the beginning of the program at
			address $4008

Address	**Data**	**Instruction**	**Say "tens" and "ones"**
$40A4	$91	LDA (abs)	Load the accumulator with the contents of
$40A5	$40		the "tens" location at address $4003
$40A6	$03		
$40A7	$D1	JZ (abs)	If the value of "tens" is zero, then we don't have
$40A8	$40		any of them, so jump to the bit in charge of saying
$40A9	$AF		the "ones" at $40AF, otherwise continue to
			address $40AA
$40AA	$10	ADD (imm)	We know that we've got some number of
$40AB	$14		"tens", so add $14 (decimal 20) to the
			accumulator
$40AC	$C9	JSR (abs)	Jump to the "Say Word" subroutine at address
$40AD	$40		$40BB to say "*ten*", "*twenty*", "*thirty*", or
$40AE	$BB		whatever. Note that the return address $40AF
			is automatically saved on the stack
$40AF	$91	LDA (abs)	Load the accumulator with the contents of
$40B0	$40		the "ones" location at address $4004
$40B1	$04		
$40B2	$D1	JZ (abs)	If the value of "ones" is zero, then we don't have
$40B3	$40		any of them, so jump back to the beginning
$40B4	$08		of the program at address $4008, otherwise
			continue to address $40B5
$40B5	$C9	JSR (abs)	Jump to the "Say Word" subroutine at address
$40B6	$40		$40BB to say "*one*", "*two*", "*three*", or whatever.
$40B7	$BB		Note that the return address $40B8 is
			automatically saved on the stack
$40B8	$C1	JMP (abs)	Jump back to the beginning of the main body
$40B9	$40		of the program at address $4008, and do it all
$40BA	$08		again, and again, and ...

Address	Data	Instruction	Code for "say word" subroutine
$40BB	$99	STA (abs)	Store (send) whatever value is currently in
$40BC	$F0		the accumulator to the output port that's
$40BD	$25		connected to the sound card at address $F025
$40BE	$91	LDA (abs)	Load the accumulator from the input port that's
$40BF	$F0		connected to the sound card at address $F005
$40C0	$05		
$40C1	$D6	JNZ (abs)	If the value is not zero, then the sound card is
$40C2	$40		still busy saying a word, so jump back to address
$40C3	$BE		$40BE and try again, otherwise continue to
			address $40C4
$40C4	$CF	RTS (imp)	Automatically retrieves the return address from the
			stack (the point from which the subroutine was
			called) and returns to that address.

It's fair to say that a program listing like the one shown here can be a bit hairy the first time you see it. However, if you've diligently stuck with us from the beginning of the book, then you should be fairly comfortable with most of it. In fact the only points that might be a little puzzling occur at addresses $409C and $40AA, where we add something to the contents of the accumulator just before we call our "say word" subroutine.

As it happens, the reason for these additions is fairly simple. By the time we get to the part of the program at address $409C, we know that we're going to have to say a number between "eleven" and "nineteen," and we also know that the accumulator currently contains the number of "ones." If you glance back to the list of sound files earlier in this chapter, you'll see that the bytes that we send to the sound card for the words "eleven" through "nineteen" are numbered 11 through 19 (or $0B through $13 in hexadecimal). So, if we add $0A (decimal 10) to the contents of the accumulator, this will give us the value we need to send to the sound card.

Similarly, by the time we get to the part of the program at address $40AA, we know that we have some "tens," and we also know that the accumulator contains the number of tens in the form 1 = "one ten," 2 = "two tens," 3 = "three tens," and so on. Obviously, what we really want to do is to say a word like "ten," "twenty," "thirty," and so forth. If you glance back to the list of sound files, you'll see that the bytes we send to the sound card for the words "ten," "twenty," "thirty," ...... through "ninety" are numbered 21 through 29 (or $15 through $1D in hexadecimal). So if we add $14 (decimal 20) to the contents of the accumulator, this will give us the value we need to send to the sound card.

Entering and running the augmented program

Once again, you don't need to wear your fingers to the bone keying all of this in, because we've already written the program for you. However, it will be useful for you to enter at least the first few bytes, because this is a good example of an occasion when we actually need to modify something.

The last instruction in our original program was an unconditional jump, which occupied addresses $405D through $405F, but we no longer need this instruction and we want to overwrite these addresses with the **LDA** instruction used to read the state of "Big Red."

Click the keypad's **Address (Ad)** button, enter the address $405D, then click the keypad's **Data (Da)** button to make the data field active. Note that the data field shows a value of $C1, which is the opcode for the original **JMP** instruction we no longer require, so click the **Clear (Clr)** button to clear it. Now enter our new data of $91, which is the opcode for the **LDA** instruction, and click the **Enter (Ent)** button to load this data into the *Beboputer's* memory.

The address field automatically increments to show the next address of $405E, and the data field now shows the old data ($40) at *this* address. So click the **Clear** button, enter the new data of $F0, and click the **Enter** button to load this data. Once again the address field increments to show the next address of $405F, and the data field shows the old data ($08). One last time, click the **Clear** button, enter the new data of $02, and click the **Enter** button to load the data. As usual, the address field increments to show the next address of $4060, but this time the data field shows hyphen characters. This is because we haven't previously written any data into this location, which therefore contains random unknown values which we choose to display as hyphens.

Feel free to continue to enter the rest of our new program by hand, but if you get bored, click the **Memory** item on the project window's menu bar, then click the **Load RAM** entry in the resulting pull-down menu to invoke the appropriate dialog. As before, the scrolling list on the left-hand side of the dialog shows all of the programs that you can load. The program we're interested in at the moment is called "lab4_p2," so locate this entry in the scrolling list and double-click on it, then click the **Load** button to load the program and dismiss the dialog.

Once you've loaded the new program (and after you've checked that your real loudspeakers are plugged in and turned on), click the keypad's

Address (**Ad**) button, enter the program's start address of $4005, and click the **Run** button. Next use the 8-bit switch input device to set up an interesting number (which will be indicated on the 7-segment displays). When you're ready to hear the dulcet tones of the *Beboputer*, click "**Big Red**," gasp in awe, and amaze your family and friends. If you wish to hear the same number again simply click "**Big Red**," otherwise enter a new number on the 8-bit switches and continue on your way.

If you happen to have invoked the memory walker, then you'll probably notice a significant delay between the individual words as they are spoken. Dismissing the memory walker should result in a fairly dramatic improvement in the way the *Beboputer* speaks, because continuously updating this display occupies a lot of the *Beboputer's* time and energy.

Finally, when your adrenaline rush has spent its course, click the keypad's **ON** button (which, paradoxically, also turns it **OFF**), then exit this laboratory by clicking the **File** item on the project window's menu bar, followed by the **Exit** entry in the resulting pull-down menu.

Quick quiz #9

1) What are the advantages and disadvantages of the hex keypad compared to the switch and display panels?

2) How many diodes would be required to encode the hex keypad's buttons (excluding the **ON/OFF** and **Reset** buttons) using the mapping described in this chapter?

3) What are the advantages of using hierarchical flowcharts?

4) Why did we choose to load the stack pointer with $4FFF at the beginning of the program?

5) In the "Initializing the Variables" section of the program, we noted that it wasn't strictly necessary to initialize the variable in memory location $4004. Why is this the case?

6) Describe how a **JNC** ("*jump not carry*") instruction works.

7) When we were extracting the "hundreds" and the "tens," we compared the value in the accumulator to 99 and 9, respectively. Why didn't we compare the value in the accumulator to 100 and 10, respectively?

8) What would you expect to happen if you click on "**Big Red**" while the *Beboputer* is speaking a number? Check whether what actually happens is what you expected to happen.

9) Why is it easier to map from binary to hexadecimal than it is to map from binary to decimal?

10) The programs in this chapter assumed that the 8-bit switches represented unsigned binary numbers in the range 0_{10} through 255_{10}. How would you approach rewriting these programs such that they treated the 8-bit switches as representing signed binary numbers in the range -128_{10} through $+127_{10}$?

Chapter 10

The QWERTY Keyboard

In this chapter we will discover:

Why the first commercial typewriters looked like sewing machines

How typewriters and Morse telegraphs were combined to form early printing telegraphs

How printing telegraphs mutated into teleprinters, which themselves evolved into computer keyboards

Why keys on computer keyboards are laid out in such a user-*unfriendly* manner

What we mean by the ASCII code, and how a computer keyboard might use it

How to program computer keyboards so as to be usable by one-handed typists

Contents of Chapter 10

Why is a typewriter like a sewing machine?

One of the most ubiquitous techniques for interactively entering data into a computer is by means of a keyboard. However, although the fingers of an expert typist leap from key to key with the agility of a mountain goat and the dexterity of a concert pianist, newcomers usually spend the vast bulk of their time desperately trying to locate the next key they wish to press. It is actually not uncommon for strong words to ensue describing the way in which the keys are laid out, including the assertion that whoever came up with the scheme we employ must have been a blithering idiot. So why is it that a device we use so much is constructed in such a way that anyone who lays their hands on one is immediately reduced to uttering expletives and banging their heads against the nearest wall? Ah, there's the question and, as with so many things, the answer is shrouded in the mists of time ....

The first references to what we would call a typewriter are buried in the records of the British patent office. In 1714, by the grace of Queen Anne, a patent was granted to the English engineer Henry Mill. In a brave attempt towards the longest sentence in the English language with the minimum use of punctuation, the wording of this patent's title was: "*An artificial machine or method for the impressing or transcribing of letters singly or progressively one after another, as in writing, whereby all writing whatever may be engrossed in paper or parchment so neat and exact as not to be distinguished from print.*" Unfortunately, after all the labors of the long-suffering patent clerk (a man who could have benefited from access to a typewriter if ever there was one), Mill never got around to actually manufacturing his machine.

Following a few sporadic attempts from different parts of the globe, the first American patent for a typewriter was granted in 1829 to William Austin Burt from Detroit. However, the path of the inventor is rarely a smooth one as Burt was to discover. We may only picture the scene in the patent office:

Clark: "*Hello there, Mr. Burt, I have both good news and bad news. Which would you like first sir?*"

Burt: "*I think I'll take the good news, if it's all the same to you.*"

Clark: "*Well the good news is that you've been granted a patent for the device which you are pleased to call your Typographer.*"

Burt: "*Good grief, I'm tickled pink, and the bad news?*"

Clark: *"Sad to relate, the only existing model of your machine was destroyed in a fire at our Washington patent office!"*

To be perfectly honest, the patent office (along with the Typographer) burned down in 1836, seven years after Burt received his patent. But as we all learn at our mother's knee, one should never allow awkward facts to get in the way of a good story.

As fate would have it, the fire probably caused no great loss to civilization as we know it. Burt's first Typographer was notably ungainly, so much so that it was possible to write much faster than one could type with this device. Undaunted, Burt produced a second model the size of a present-day pinball machine, which, if nothing else, would have made an interesting conversation piece if given to a friend as a Christmas stocking-filler. Perhaps not surprisingly, no one was interested, and Burt eventually exited the stage to make room for younger contenders.

Following Burt, numerous other innovators leapt into the fray with truly Heath Robinson offerings. Some of these weird and wonderful contraptions were as difficult to use as a Church organ, while others printed by keeping the paper stationary and hurling the rest of the machine against it ...... the mind boggles.

The first practical machine was conceived by three American inventors and friends who spent their evenings tinkering together. In 1867, Christopher Latham Sholes, Carlos Glidden, and Samual W. Soule invented what they called the Type-Writer (the hyphen was discarded some years later). Soule eventually dropped out, but the others kept at it, producing close to thirty experimental models over the next five years. Unfortunately, Sholes and Glidden never really capitalized on their invention, but instead sold the rights to a smooth-talking entrepreneur called James Densmore, who, in 1873, entered into a contract with a gun and sewing machine manufacturer to produce the device.

Strangely, the manufacturers, E. Remington and Sons from the state of New York, had no experience building typewriters. This was primarily because no one had ever produced a typewriter before, but there's also the fact that (let's face it) Remington and Sons made guns and sewing machines. The first thing they did was to hunt for the best artist-mechanic they could find, and they eventually settled on William K. Jenne. However, Jenne's expertise was in the design of sewing machines, with the result that the world's first commercial typewriter, released in 1874, ended up with a foot pedal to advance the paper and sweet little flowers on the sides!

The Sholes (QWERTY) keyboard

It is commonly believed that the original layout of keys on a typewriter was intended to slow the typist down, but this isn't strictly true. Sholes and Glidden obviously wished to make their typewriters as fast as possible in order to convince people to use them. However, one problem with the first machines was that the keys jammed when the operator typed at any real speed, so Sholes invented what was to become known as the *Sholes keyboard* (Figure 10.1).

Figure 10.1: The Sholes keyboard (circa 1874)

The term *digraph* refers to combinations of two letters that represent a single sound, such as *"sh"* in *"ship,"* where these letters are frequently written or typed one after the other. What Sholes attempted to do was to separate the letters of as many common digraphs as possible. But, in addition to being a pain to use, the resulting layout also left something to be desired on the digraph front; for example, *"ed," "er," "th,"* and *"tr"* all use keys that are close to each other. Unfortunately, even after the jamming problem was overcome by the use of springs, the monster was loose amongst us — existing users didn't want to change and there was no turning back.

The original Sholes keyboard (which is known to us as the QWERTY keyboard due to the ordering of the first six keys in the third row) is interesting for at least two other reasons: first, there was no key for the number '1', because the inventors decided that the users could get by with the letter 'I'; and second, there was no shift key, because the first typewriters could only type upper case letters. [1,2] The first shift-key

---

[1] Sholes also craftily ensured that the word "Typewriter" could be constructed using only the top row of letters. This was intended to aid salesmen when they were giving demonstrations.
[2] Nothing's simple in this world. For example, instead of the top row of characters saying QWERTY, keyboards in France and Germany spell out AZERTY and QWERTZU, respectively.

typewriter (in which uppercase and lowercase letters are made available on the same key) didn't appear on the market until 1878, and it was quickly challenged by another flavor which contained twice the number of keys, one for every uppercase and lowercase character. For quite some time these two alternatives vied for the hearts and minds of the typing fraternity, but the advent of a technique known as *touch-typing* favored the shift-key solution, which thereafter reigned supreme.

Speaking of which, Figure 10.1 shows the 'A', 'S', 'D', and 'F' keys in white to indicate that these are the *home keys* for the left hand. Similarly, the other four keys shown in white are the *home keys* for the right hand. The terms *home keys* and *home row* refer to the base position for your fingers (excluding thumbs, which are used to hit the space bar) when you're practicing touch typing, which means that you type by touch without looking at the keyboard.

However, Sholes didn't invent these terms, because he actually gave very little thought to the way in which people would use his invention. The end result was that everyone was left to their own devices, effectively meaning that two-fingered typists using the "hunt-and-peck" method ruled the world. It was not until 1888 that a law clerk named Frank E. McGurrin won a highly publicized typing contest with his self-taught touch-typing technique, and a new era was born.[3]

Finally, lest you still feel that the QWERTY keyboard is an unduly harsh punishment that's been sent to try us, it's worth remembering that the early users had a much harder time than we do, not the least that they couldn't even see what they were typing! The first typewriters struck the paper from the underside, which obliged their operators to raise the carriage whenever they wished to see what had just been typed, and so-called "visible-writing" machines didn't become available until 1883.

The Dvorak keyboard

Almost anyone who spends more than a few seconds working with a QWERTY keyboard quickly becomes convinced that they could do a better job of laying out the keys. Many brave souls have attempted the task, but few came closer than efficiency expert August Dvorak in the 1930s.

---

[3]In fact, McGurrin was proficient at touch typing ten years before the contest, because he'd been practicing in the evenings since 1876 so as to gain recognition as a fast worker. However, after receiving the $2 weekly pay-raise that he'd been looking for, he neglected to tell anyone else what he'd done.

When he turned his attention to the typewriter, Dvorak spent many tortuous months analyzing the usage model of the QWERTY keyboard (now there's a man who knew how to have a good time). The results of his investigation were that, although the majority of users were right-handed, the existing layout forced the weaker left hand (and the weaker fingers on both hands) to perform most of the work. Also, thanks to Sholes' main goal of physically separating letters that are commonly typed together, the typist's fingers were obliged to move in awkward patterns and only ended up spending 32% of their time on the home row (Figure 10.1).

Dvorak took the opposite tack to Sholes, and attempted to find the optimal placement for the keys based on letter frequency and human anatomy. That is, he tried to ensure that letters which are commonly typed together would be physically close to each other, and also that the (usually) stronger right hand would perform the bulk of the work, while the left hand would have control of the vowels and the lesser-used characters. The result of these labors was the *Dvorak Keyboard*, which he patented in 1936 (Figure 10.2).

Figure 10.2: The Dvorak keyboard (circa 1936)

Note that Dvorak's keyboard had shift keys, but they are omitted here for reasons of clarity. The results of Dvorak's innovations were tremendously effective. Using his layout, the typist's fingers spend 70% of their time on the home row and 80% of this time on their home keys. Thus, as compared to the approximately 120 words that can be constructed from the home row keys of the QWERTY keyboard, it is possible to construct more than 3,000 words on Dvorak's home row (or 10,000 words if you're talking to someone who's trying to sell you one). Also, Dvorak's scheme reduces the motion of the hands by a factor of three, and improves typing accuracy and speed by approximately 50%, and 20%, respectively.

Unfortunately, Dvorak didn't really stand a chance trying to sell typewriters based on his new keyboard layout in the 1930s. Apart from the fact that existing typists didn't wish to re-learn their trade, America was in the heart of the depression, which meant that the last thing anyone wanted to do was to spend money on a new typewriter. In fact, the Dvorak keyboard might have faded away forever, except that enthusiasts in Oregon, USA, formed a club in 1978, and they've been actively promoting Dvorak's technique ever since. Coupled with the ability to re-configure computer keyboards (as discussed later in this chapter), their activities have reawakened interest in the Dvorak keyboard, to the extent that it is now used by a few businesses and educational establishments.[4]

It was the best of times ....   **.... it was the worst of times ....**

In a 1930s survey of 16 year old girls across the United States, 32% stated that they wanted to grow up to be typists (which was seen as a glamorous profession) as opposed to only 5% who wanted to be film stars.

Typewriter salesmen in the early 1900s were held in the same contempt that accident-chasing lawyers are today, because they used to pursue fire-fighters in the hope of selling new typewriters to burned-out businesses.

.... and, all things considered, there were some pretty weird times as well ....

In the early 1920s, in order to indicate that businessmen were very busy, it became common for their letters to close with the words: *"Dictated but not signed."* In an effort at one-upmanship this was soon supplanted by the words: *"Dictated but not read."* Finally, in a surrealist attempt at Monty-Python foolishness, the yuppie-equivalent of the era started to use the words: *"Dictated by transatlantic telephone and recorded on tape but not read and not signed,"* which, when you think about it, was almost a letter in itself! (Lawyers occasionally use similar terms to this day, thereby protecting themselves from inadvertent dictation and transcription errors; the result being that irrespective of how badly they do their job ...... it's not their fault.)

---

[4]For example, while penning these words, I found out that Barnaby, my co-author's son, uses a Dvorak keyboard at his junior high school (you could have knocked me down with an ostrich).

The printing telegraph

As we discussed in Chapter 4, the first telegraph machines were invented in 1837 by Sir Charles Wheatstone in England and Samuel Finley Breese Morse in America. Morse's machine was eventually adopted as the standard, because it was simpler, easier to construct, and more reliable. Morse's original machines kept a record of incoming messages using an electromechanically controlled pencil that made marks on a moving strip of paper. The paper was driven by clockwork, while the lengths of the marks corresponded to the dots and dashes used in Morse Code. However, operators quickly realized that they could recognize the message by sound alone, so Morse's recording devices returned to the nether regions from whence they came.

Throughout the rest of the 1800s there continued to be a strong interest in the idea of a printing telegraph. Much of the work toward realizing this dream was based on the concept of a wheel with characters embossed around its periphery. The idea was to use the incoming telegraph signals to spin the wheel by fixed steps until the correct character faced the paper, and to then propel that character onto an inked tape located in front of the paper. There were a variety of techniques for controlling the wheel, such as a single pulse for 'A', two pulses for 'B', three for 'C', and so on, with the wheel returning to a home position after each character, but this technique was very slow in terms of words-per-minute. Later techniques used a five-bit code created by the French inventor Jean Maurice Emile Baudot in 1880, which soon became known as the *Baudot Code*. The two-channel paper tape technique pioneered by Sir Charles Wheatstone (see Chapter 4) was subsequently extended to handle the Baudot Code (Figure 10.3).

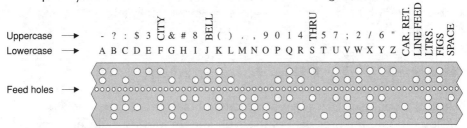

Figure 10.3: Paper tape with 5-bit Baudot Code

Using a five-bit code, it is possible to obtain $2^5 = 32$ different combinations of holes and blanks (no holes). In the case of the Baudot Code, twenty-six of these combinations were used for letters of the alphabet, leaving eight spare combinations for an idle code, a space code, a letter-shift code, and so on. The problem was that there weren't enough spare combinations left over to represent the numbers '0' through '9' or any punctuation characters. To solve this dilemma, the letter-shift code was used to emulate the shift key on a typewriter by instructing the receiver that any subsequent codes were to be treated as uppercase characters (in this context, uppercase was used to refer to numbers, punctuation, and special symbols). A second letter-shift code could subsequently be used to return the receiver to the alphabetical character set.

The five holes and blanks for each character were transmitted as a sequence of pulses and gaps, and decoded and printed at the receiving end by a variety of different techniques. Note the special characters such as BELL, which actually rang a bell on the receiver to alert the operator. We'll be seeing more of these special characters later.

The early systems required the operator to use a keypad with five separate keys, and to simultaneously push whichever keys were required to form a character. Later systems were based on a typewriter-style keyboard, whereby each typewriter key activated the five transmitting keys (or a paper tape punch) to establish the correct pattern. Unfortunately, none of these systems were tremendously robust or reliable, and they all suffered from major problems in synchronizing the transmitter and the receiver such that both knew who was doing what and when they were doing it.

The original Baudot code became known as the *International Telegraph Code No. 1*. Sometime around 1900, another 5-bit code called the *Murray Code* was invented. The Murray Code eventually displaced the Baudot Code and became known as the *International Telegraph Code No. 2*. Unfortunately, everyone was hopelessly confused by this time – Murray's name sank into obscurity, while Baudot's name became associated with almost every 5-bit code on the face of the planet, including the *International Telegraph Code No. 2*.

The advent of the teleprinter

In 1902, a young electrical engineer called Frank Pearne approached Mr. Joy Morton, the president of the well-known Morton Salt Company. Pearne had been experimenting with printing telegraphs and needed a sponsor. Morton discussed the situation with his friend, the distinguished mechanical engineer Charles L. Krum, and they eventually decided that they were interested in pursuing this project.

After a year of unsuccessful experiments, Pearne lost interest and wandered off into the sunset to become a teacher. Krum continued to investigate the problem and, in 1906, was joined by his son Howard, who had recently graduated as an electrical engineer. The mechanical and electrical talents of the Krums Senior and Junior complemented each other. After solving the problem of synchronizing the transmitter and receiver, they oversaw their first installation on postal lines between New York City and Boston in the summer of 1910. These devices, called *teleprinters*, had a typewriter-style keyboard for entering outgoing messages and a roll of paper for printing incoming communications. The Krums continued to improve the reliability of their systems over the years. By 1914, teleprinters were being used by the Associated Press to deliver copy to newspaper offices throughout America, and by the early 1920s they were in general use around the world.

Meanwhile, toward the end of the 1920s and the early 1930s, scientists and engineers began to focus their attentions on the issue of computing (see also Chapter 15). The first devices, such as Vannevar Bush's *Differential Analyzer*, were predominantly analog, but not everyone was a devotee of analog computing. In 1937, a scientist at Bell Laboratories, George Robert Stibitz, built a digital machine called the "Model K," which was based on relays, flashlight bulbs, and metal strips cut from tin-cans (the "Model K" was so-named, because Stibitz constructed most of it on his kitchen table).

Stibitz went on to create a machine called the *Complex Number Calculator* and, at a meeting in New Hampshire in September 1940, he used this machine to perform the first demonstration of remote computing. Leaving his computer in New York City, he took a teleprinter to the meeting which he connected to the computer using a telephone line. Stibitz then proceeded to astound the attendees by allowing them to pose problems which were entered on the teleprinter; within a minute, the teleprinter printed the answers generated by the computer.

By the 1950s, computers were becoming much more complex, but operators were still largely limited to entering programs using a switch panel or loading them from paper tapes or punched cards. Due to the fact that the only way for early computers to be cost-effective was for them to operate twenty-four hours a day, the time-consuming task of writing programs had to be performed off-line using teleprinters with integrated paper tape writers or card punches.

As computers increased in power, teleprinters began to be connected directly to them. This allowed the operators and the computer to communicate directly with each other, which was one of the first steps along the path toward the interactive way in which we use computers today. By the middle of the 1960s, computers had become so powerful that many operators could use the same machine simultaneously, and a new concept called *time-sharing* was born. The computer could switch between users so quickly that each user had the illusion they had sole access to the machine. (Strangely enough, time-sharing is now only practiced in large computing installations, because computers have become so powerful and so cheap that everyone can have a dedicated processor for themselves.)

However, the days of the teleprinter in the computing industry were numbered; they were eventually supplanted by the combination of computer keyboards and video displays, and the sound of teleprinters chuntering away in the back of computer rooms is now little more than a nostalgic memory.

The computer keyboard

Unlike the electro-mechanical construction of the teleprinter, a modern computer keyboard is entirely electronic (excepting the mechanical aspects of the keys themselves). When a key is pressed it generates a pattern of *logic 0s* and *logic 1s*. The keyboard may be connected to the computer via a serial interface, in which case it transmits these pattern of *logic 0s* and *logic 1s* as a series of pulses. Alternatively, the interface may be parallel, in which case each bit of the pattern is conveyed on a separate wire. In the case of the *Beboputer* we will assume a parallel interface, in which the keyboard is plugged into one of our 8-bit input ports (Figure 10.4).

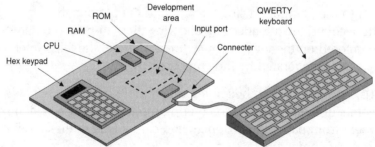

Figure 10.4: The *Beboputer's* QWERTY keyboard

There are a tremendous variety of ways in which a keyboard can be connected to a computer, but we will follow a very simple scenario. Our keyboard contains an 8-bit latch, and the outputs from this latch are fed through a cable into one of the *Beboputer's* input ports. Whenever a key on the keyboard is pressed, it generates an 8-bit code which is stored in the latch, and whenever the *Beboputer* reads a value from the input port, it also resets the latch to contain *logic 0s*. (This latch functions in a similar manner to the one we used with our Big Red Switch in the previous chapter).

Note that we will continue to use the hex keypad as our primary control device. In fact the purpose of this laboratory is to use the hex keypad to enter a simple program, which will read values from the QWERTY keyboard and display these values on our 7-segment displays. However, there are a few things we need to discuss before we plunge into this program, not the least of which is the ASCII code ...... good grief ..... I think I can feel a sub-title approaching ......

The ASCII code

We've already noted that pressing a key on the keyboard causes it to generate a pattern of *logic 0s* and *logic 1s*. Each key must generate a unique pattern, and the total set of patterns is referred to as a *code*. The question is: which patterns should we use?

In some respects this is similar to the way in which we encoded the keys on the hex keypad in the previous chapter, but in others it's quite different. The hex keypad is an integral part of a system we're designing from the ground up, so we can do anything we wish with it. By comparison, the QWERTY keyboard lives in the "outside world," so we want it to generate a standard code that will be recognized by a variety of computers and peripheral devices such as printers. There are several such codes available, but one that is very widely used is the *American Standard Code for Information Interchange (ASCII)* (Table 10.1).

In addition to the standard alphanumeric characters ('a' ... 'z', 'A' ... 'Z' and '0' ... '9'), punctuation characters (comma, period, semi-colon, ...) and special characters ('!', '#', '%', ...), there are an awful lot of strange mnemonics such as **EOT**, **ACK**, **NAK**, and **BEL**. The point is that, in addition to simple keyboards, ASCII was used for a number of purposes such as communications (and still is in some cases); hence the presence of such codes as **EOT**, meaning *"End of transmission,"* and **BEL**, which was used to ring a physical bell on old-fashioned printers. Some of these codes are still in use today, while others are, generally speaking, of historical interest only. Although many of the stranger codes are not really important to us for the purposes of this book, we will certainly be playing with some of them, so a more detailed breakdown is presented in Table 10.2.

$00	NUL	$10	DLE	$20	SP	$30	0	$40	@	$50	P	$60	`	$70	p
$01	SOH	$11	DC1	$21	!	$31	1	$41	A	$51	Q	$61	a	$71	q
$02	STX	$12	DC2	$22	"	$32	2	$42	B	$52	R	$62	b	$72	r
$03	ETX	$13	DC3	$23	#	$33	3	$43	C	$53	S	$63	c	$73	s
$04	EOT	$14	DC4	$24	$	$34	4	$44	D	$54	T	$64	d	$74	t
$05	ENQ	$15	NAK	$25	%	$35	5	$45	E	$55	U	$65	e	$75	u
$06	ACK	$16	SYN	$26	&	$36	6	$46	F	$56	V	$66	f	$76	v
$07	BEL	$17	ETB	$27	'	$37	7	$47	G	$57	W	$67	g	$77	w
$08	BS	$18	CAN	$28	(	$38	8	$48	H	$58	X	$68	h	$78	x
$09	HT	$19	EM	$29	)	$39	9	$49	I	$59	Y	$69	i	$79	y
$0A	LF	$1A	SUB	$2A	*	$3A	:	$4A	J	$5A	Z	$6A	j	$7A	z
$0B	VT	$1B	ESC	$2B	+	$3B	;	$4B	K	$5B	[	$6B	k	$7B	{
$0C	FF	$1C	FS	$2C	,	$3C	<	$4C	L	$5C	\	$6C	l	$7C	|
$0D	CR	$1D	GS	$2D	-	$3D	=	$4D	M	$5D	]	$6D	m	$7D	}
$0E	SO	$1E	RS	$2E	.	$3E	>	$4E	N	$5E	^	$6E	n	$7E	~
$0F	SI	$1F	US	$2F	/	$3F	?	$4F	O	$5F	_	$6F	o	$7F	DEL

Table 10.1: ASCII character codes

NUL	Null	DLE	Data link escape
SOH	Start of heading	DC1	Device control 1
STX	Start of text	DC2	Device control 2
ETX	End of text	DC3	Device control 3
EOT	End of transmission	DC4	Device control 4
ENQ	Enquiry	NAK	Negative acknowledge
ACK	Acknowledge	SYN	Synchronous idle
BEL	Bell	ETB	End of transmission block
BS	Backspace	CAN	Cancel
HT (TAB)	Horizontal tabulation	EM	End of medium
LF	Line feed	SUB	Substitute
VT	Vertical tabulation	ESC	Escape
FF	Form feed	FS	File separator
CR	Carriage return	GS	Group separator
SO	Shift out	RS	Record separator
SI	Shift in	US	Unit separator
SP	Space	DEL	Delete

Table 10.2: ASCII control characters

Another point is that ASCII (pronounced "*ass-key*") is a 7-bit code, which means that it only uses the binary values 00000000_2 through 01111111_2 (that is, 0 through 127 in decimal, or $00 through $7F in hexadecimal). In some systems the unused, most-significant bit of the 8-bit byte from the keyboard is simply set to *logic 0*. Alternatively, this bit might be used to implement a form of error checking known as a *parity check*, in which case it would be referred to as the *parity bit*.

There are two forms of parity checking, which are known as *even parity* and *odd parity*. In the case of even parity, special logic in the keyboard would count the number of *logic 1s* in the ASCII code for whichever key had been pressed. If there were an even number of *logic 1s*, the most-significant bit of the 8-bit byte to be transmitted to the computer would be set to *logic 0*, but if there were an odd number of *logic 1s*, the most-significant bit would be set to *logic 1*. The end result of an even parity check is to ensure that there are always an <u>even</u> number of *logic 1s* in the transmitted value. (An odd parity check ensures an <u>odd</u> number of *logic 1s* in the transmitted value.)

Similarly, when the computer receives a character code from the keyboard, it can count the number of *logic 1s* in the first seven bits to determine what the parity bit should be, and then compare this calculated parity bit against the transmitted parity bit to see if they agree. This form of parity checking is just about the simplest form of error check there is. It will only detect a single-bit error, because two errors will cancel each other out.[5] Forthermore, even if the computer does detect an error, there's no way for it to tell which bit is incorrect (indeed, the main value could be correct and the parity bit itself could have been corrupted). A variety of more sophisticated forms of error checking can be used to detect multiple errors, and even to allow the computer to work out which bits are wrong, but these techniques are outside the scope of this book.

As opposed to always forcing the most-significant bit to *logic 0* or using it to implement a parity check, we've opted for a third alternative, which is to use this bit to extend the character set. That is, if the most significant bit is *logic 0*, then the remaining bits are used to represent the standard ASCII codes $00 through $7F as shown above. However, if the most significant bit is *logic 1*, then the remaining bits are used to represent additional characters of our choosing. We will return to this point in the next chapter, but now it's time to experiment with our keyboard using the *Beboputer*.

Winding up the *Beboputer*

Make sure that the *Beboputer* CD is in the appropriate drive in your computer and summon the *Beboputer*. Once the *Beboputer's* project window has opened, click the **File** item on its menu bar, click the **Open Project** entry in the resulting pull-down menu, then select the Lab 5 project from the ensuing dialog. This will invoke our fifth lab (Figure 10.5).

---

[5]To be more precise, this form of parity check will detect an odd number of errors (one bit, three bits, five bits, and so on), but an even number of errors will cancel each other out.

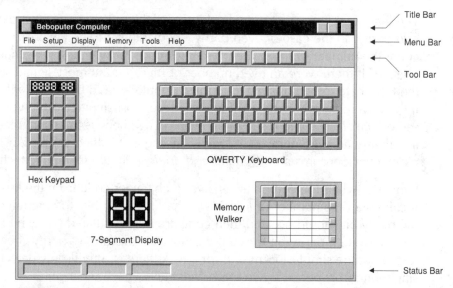

Figure 10.5: The *Beboputer* project window for Lab 5

As we see, the hex keypad and our old friends the memory walker and 7-segment displays have now been joined by the *Beboputer's* virtual QWERTY keyboard.

Program to read the QWERTY keyboard

The purpose of this lab is to create a program to read 8-bit values from the input port that's connected to the QWERTY keyboard (at address $F008), and to display these values in hexadecimal using our dual 7-segment display (at address $F023). Don't worry; compared to the program in the last chapter, this one's going to be a piece of cake (Figure 10.6).

Given that the address of the input port connected to the keyboard is $F008, the first instruction ($91 at address $4000) is a **LDA**, which loads the accumulator with whatever value is currently in the keyboard's 8-bit latch. Initially this value will be $00, which represents the ASCII code for NUL and indicates that no key has been pressed.

The second instruction ($D1 at address $4003) is a **JZ** (*"jump if zero"*), which will cause the *Beboputer* to jump back to the beginning of the program if the accumulator contains a zero value. Thus, the program will continue to loop around these first two instructions waiting for a key to be pressed on the keyboard.

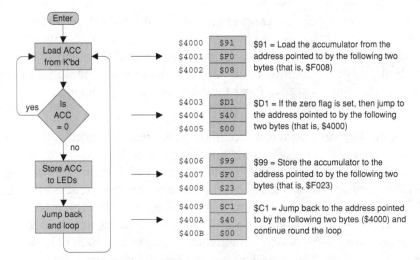

Figure 10.6: Reading from the keyboard

When a key is pressed, its non-zero ASCII code will be stored in the keyboard's 8-bit latch. The next time the program loads the accumulator from the keyboard, the **JZ** instruction at address $4003 will fail, and the program will continue on to the next instruction. This instruction ($99 at address $4006) is a **STA**, which causes the *Beboputer* to store the value in the accumulator to address $F023 (the address of the output port driving the dual 7-segment displays). The fourth and last instruction ($C1 at address $4009) is a **JMP** (*"unconditional jump"*), which causes the program to return to address $4000 and start all over again.

One of the most important points to remember with regard to this program is that the act of reading a value from the keyboard causes the latch inside the keyboard to be reset to a $00 value. Different systems work in significantly different ways, but this is how we've designed our virtual machine. Thus, once we've copied a key's hexadecimal value to our dual 7-segment display, the fact that we now have $00 stored in the keyboard's latch will once again cause the program to wait for us to press another key.

Entering the program with the hex keypad

Once again, we've arrived at the exciting part where we enter our program. Don't bother looking for a short-cut, because we haven't pre-written this program for you (this one's so short that we thought you'd like to do it yourself). First, click the **ON** button on the hex keypad to power up the *Beboputer*. As usual, the **Address (Ad)** button lights up to indicate that the address is the active field.

The first instruction in our program occurs at address $4000, so this is the address that we need to enter. Remember that the keypad automatically uses hexadecimal values, so click a '4' followed by three '0's and watch the address build up in the address field. Also remember that, should you make a mistake at any time, you can clear the address field by clicking the keypad's Clear (Clr) button.

Now click the keypad's Data (Da) button to make this field active, then click a '9' followed by a '1' and watch the data build up in the data field. To complete this operation, click the keypad's Enter (Ent) button. This causes the monitor program to load the data displayed in the data field ($91) into the memory location specified by the address field ($4000). The monitor program automatically increments the value in the address field and the Data (Da) button remains active, which allows you to alternate between inputting data and clicking the Enter button. Continue to enter the remainder of the program (from address $4001 onwards) as shown below.

Address	Data	Instruction	Read keyboard and display ASCII value
$4000	$91	LDA (abs)	Load the accumulator from the input port
$4001	$F0		connected to the keyboard at address $F008
$4002	$08		
$4003	$D1	JZ (abs)	If the value is $00, then no key has been pushed,
$4004	$40		so jump back to the beginning of the program
4005	$00		at address $4000 and do it all again
$4006	$99	STA (abs)	Store the accumulator to the output port
$4007	$F0		connected to the dual 7-segment display
$4008	$23		at address $F023
$4009	$C1	JMP (abs)	Jump back to the beginning of the program at
$400A	$40		address $4000 and do the whole thing again
$400B	$00		

Running the program with the hex keypad

Click the keypad's Address (Ad) button to make the address field active, enter the start address of the program which is $4000, then click the Run button to let the *Beboputer* rip.

Nothing appears to be happening at first, because the latch in the keyboard contains $00, so the program keeps on looping around reading this value and waiting for something more interesting to come along. You can put the program out of its misery by clicking the letter 'A' on the keyboard (the one on your screen), and noting that the 7-segment display updates to show $41. Check that this is the correct ASCII code for the uppercase letter 'A' by referring back to Table 10.1. Now click a few other letters and numbers and check that their ASCII codes are as you'd expect them to be.

As you've probably noticed by now, computer keyboards have a few more keys than their typewriter counterparts (Figure 10.7). In addition to the SHIFT key, there are the CAPS ("*Capitals*"), CTRL ("*Control*"), and ALT ("*Alternate*") keys. The annotations on each of these keys change to red on our keyboard to indicate when they are active. By default, the CAPS key on our system is active and the other keys are inactive. The CAPS key is also a "sticky" key, which means that once it's been pressed (or clicked in our case) to make it inactive or active, it will remain in that state until it's pressed again.

Figure 10.7: The *Beboputer's* keyboard "up close and personal"

Click the CAPS key and note that its annotation turns black to indicate that this key is no longer active. Note that nothing happens to the dual 7-segment display. This is because CAPS is a modifier key, which means that it doesn't generate a code of its own, but rather modifies the codes associated with some of the other keys. If the CAPS key is inactive, then the letter keys generate the codes for lowercase letters. Click the 'A' key again, and note that the 7-segment display now shows $61, which is the ASCII code for a lowercase 'a'.

SHIFT, CTRL, and ALT also act as modifier keys. On a real keyboard these keys would not be sticky, which means that you'd have to continue to hold them while you pressed another key. However, we can't emulate this on our virtual keyboard, so we've caused these keys to act like sticky keys. Click the SHIFT key and note that its annotation turns red, thereby indicating that this key is now active. Once again note that nothing happened to the dual 7-segment display, because SHIFT is a modifier key.

Click the 'A' key again and note that the 7-segment display now shows $41, which is the ASCII code for an uppercase 'A'. In this respect the **SHIFT** key acts like the **CAPS** key. However, unlike **CAPS** which only affects the letter keys, the **SHIFT** key on a real keyboard affects other characters as well. On your main computer's keyboard you will note that the key for the number '4' also shows the '$ symbol (at least it does in America; keyboards in other countries may sport different symbols). In the real world the shift key would also allow you to select between these two characters, but we didn't implement this feature on the *Beboputer's* keyboard. Now click both the **SHIFT** and **CAPS** keys to return them to their inactive and active states, respectively.

Compared to the **SHIFT** and **CAPS** keys, the actions of the **CTRL** and **ALT** keys are not quite so well defined, in that they tend to behave differently on different systems. In the case of the *Beboputer*, we've chosen to follow a reasonably intuitive scheme. Click the **CTRL** key to make it active, then click the 'A' key. The 7-segment display now shows $01, which is the ASCII value for the **SOH** control code. In fact, in our system the **CTRL** key only modifies the alphabetical keys such that 'A' generates $01, 'B' generates $02, 'C' generates $03, and so on (note that identical codes are generated for both uppercase and lowercase versions of each letter).

Now click the **CTRL** key to return it to its inactive state, then click the **ALT** key to make it active. In our system, the **ALT** key modifies all of the keys (except the cursor control keys)[6] by simply adding the value $80 (128 in decimal) to whatever codes they would have generated had the **ALT** key been inactive. For example, click on the 'A' key and note that the 7-segment display now shows $C1, which is the sum of $41 and $80.

Continue to play around, pressing various key combinations until you're comfortable with the way in which our keyboard works. When you've had enough fun, click the keypad's **ON** button (which also turns it **OFF**), then exit this laboratory by clicking the **File** item on the project window's menu bar followed by the **Exit** entry in the resulting pull-down menu.

---

[6]The *Beboputer's* cursor control keys, which are indicated as arrows in Figure 10.7, generate the codes $D2, $D3, $D0, and $D1, for "right," "left," "up," and "down," respectively (see also Chapter 11).

Programmable and one-handed keyboards

That's pretty much the end of this lab, but it's certainly not the end of the ASCII code, because we'll be using our QWERTY keyboard to drive a virtual terminal in the next chapter. But before we proceed, there are a couple of interesting points that deserve mention. First, early keyboards employed arrays of diodes to generate their codes, using similar techniques to those presented in the previous chapter. By comparison, modern keyboards are significantly more sophisticated; some of them are re-programmable and may even contain their own dedicated microprocessor. Having a re-programmable keyboard offers such capabilities as being able to change the codes that are generated by each key (for example, allowing you to reprogram your 'F' key to make it generate the code for a 'U'), and some allow a single key-press to generate an entire string of characters.

Now this may not strike you as being amazingly useful at first, but it implies all sorts of possibilities. For example, you could reprogram your entire keyboard so as to act in the Dvorak style (of course, you'd have to re-label your keys as well). Even if your keyboard is not re-programmable, you can achieve the same results by writing a program that modifies the codes as it reads them from the keyboard; in fact you can obtain such software commercially. You can also purchase software that makes your keyboard suitable for one-handed typists. One such program is called Half-QWERTY[7] and is available from the Matias Corporation, Rexdale, Ontario, Canada (Figure 10.8).

This figure only shows the half of the keyboard that would be used by a left-handed one-handed typist (and we've omitted some of the annotations for clarity). With this portion of the keyboard you use your left hand in the normal position to get the standard results. However, if you hold the space bar down while pressing another key, then you get the ASCII codes associated with the keys from the other half of the keyboard (tapping the space bar alone generates spaces as usual). This software also does the same sort of thing for the keys on the right-hand side of the board, thereby supporting right-handed one-handed typists.

Figure 10.8: The left-hand side of a Half-Qwerty keyboard

---

[7]Half-QWERTY is a trademark of the Matias Corporation.

But we've digressed again. Let's close this chapter with a few things that are really quite useful to remember, such as the fact that the ASCII code for 'A' is $41 (from which you can work out all of the other uppercase letters), and that in order to calculate the code for a lowercase letter you need only add $20 to the code for its uppercase counterpart. Similarly, it's useful to remember that the ASCII code for the number '0' is $30 (which lets you work out all of the other numbers). Of course, it would be handy to memorize the complete table, but by remembering just these three codes you can quickly work out the codes for sixty-two of the characters in your head. It also usually comes in handy to remember that the ASCII code for a space is $20 and the code for an **ESC** ("Escape") character is $1B. Try to memorize these few codes now, because we'll be using them in the next chapter.

Quick quiz #10

1) Why was the first commercial typewriter like a sewing machine?

2) Why are the keys on a typical computer keyboard arranged the way they are?

3) What are the advantages and disadvantages of a Dvorak compared to a Sholes (QWERTY) keyboard?

4) What does "ASCII" stand for?

5) Why is ASCII said to be a 7-bit code?

6) What are the ASCII codes for 'A', 'a', 'Z', and 'z' in hexadecimal, decimal, and binary?

7) What is the difference between even parity and odd parity?

8) What does the term "sticky" mean in the context of a key on a computer keyboard?

9) How can we modify our program such that, irrespective of the state of the CAPS and SHIFT keys, whenever an alpha key is pressed the program will always display the uppercase code for that character (for example, if the user clicks on 'a', the code for 'A' will be displayed)?

10) How could we write a program to cause our virtual keyboard to act like a Dvorak keyboard?

Chapter 11

The Memory-Mapped Display

In this chapter we will discover:

How and why original televisions were based on mechanical techniques

▼

Why Philo Farnsworth became a man lost in history

▼

How color vision and color television work

▼

How televisions evolved into computer monitors

▼

What memory-mapped displays are, and how they solved the problem of limited memory in early computer systems

▼

How to create a (very) simple text editing program

▼

What "chunky graphics" are, and how they relate to ASCII codes and characters

▼

How to use our memory-mapped display's medium resolution color graphics mode

▼

What we mean by "pixel," and why this can be such a slippery concept

LAB 6

Contents of Chapter 11

How to display moving pictures on a toaster

Eeeek Alors! If you think that the stuff we've already done has been interesting, then this lab is going to blow your socks off! The whole basis of the *Beboputer* is that it's a virtual machine that exists only in your physical computer's memory, and the only way to see the *Beboputer* is on the your real computer's screen. Displaying information on a screen is an incredibly efficient way for a computer to communicate with us. However, as is often the case, engineers employed an existing technology that was developed for an entirely different purpose ...... television.

Television, which comes from the Greek *tele*, meaning "distant," and the Latin *vision*, meaning "seeing" or "sight," has arguably become one of the wonders of the 20th Century, so you may be surprised to learn that television's origins are firmly rooted in the Victorian era. In fact one of the earliest examples of an image being captured, transmitted, and reproduced by electromechanical means occurred in 1842, only five years after Queen Victoria had ascended to the throne, when a Scotsman, Alexander Bain, came up with a rather ingenious idea.

Bain created an image to be transmitted by snipping it out of a thin sheet of tin, placing it on a moveable base, and connecting it to one side of a battery. He then created a pendulum using a conducting metal wire and a weight ending in a sharp point, and set this device swinging above the base. The base was slowly moved under the pendulum, where the swinging weight made periodic contact with the metal image, thereby completing the electrical circuit and converting the dark and light areas of the image (represented by the presence and absence of tin) into an electrical signal. Bain then used this signal to control a relay, which was moving back and forth in time with the pendulum. When activated, the relay pushed a pencil down onto a piece of paper mounted on a second base moving at the same rate as the first, thereby reproducing the image as a pencil drawing.

Obviously, Bain's device had little application with regard to the transmission of moving pictures, but it certainly wasn't a wasted effort, because he had essentially created the precursor to the modern Fax machine. Sometime later in 1878, one Denis Redmond of Dublin, Ireland, penned a letter to the *English Mechanic and World of Science* publication. In his letter, Redmond described creating an array of selenium photocells, each of which was connected via a voltage source to a corresponding platinum wire. As the intensity of light on a particular photocell increased it conducted more current, thereby causing its associated platinum wire to glow more brightly. Redmond's original device only contained around 10 x 10 elements, and was therefore was very limited as to what it could represent. Having said this, it could apparently reproduce moving silhouettes, which was pretty amazing for the time.

In fact Redmond's photocell-array concept was not far removed from today's semiconductor diode-array cameras, while his array of glowing platinum wires is loosely comparably to the way in which images are constructed on today's liquid-crystal and active-matrix computer screens. (Also, had Redmond continued to increase the size of his platinum-wire array to contain say 1,000 x 1,000 elements, then it would have had the added advantage of being able to double-up as a toaster!) Sadly, the large size of Redmond's photocells drastically limited the quality of the images he could display, and the ability to reproduce his efforts using semiconductors and related technologies lay some 100 years in his future, so the inventors of yesteryear were obliged to search for another approach ......

The Nipkow disk

In 1884, the German inventor Paul Gottleib Nipkow proposed a novel technique for capturing, transmitting, and reproducing pictures based on flat circular disks containing holes punched in a spiral formation (Figure 11.1).

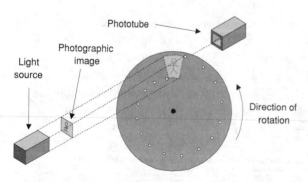

Figure 11.1: Nipkow disk for a 16-line picture

Nipkow's idea was both simple and cunning. A strong light source was used to project a photographic image onto the surface of the *Nipkow Disk*, which was spinning around.

As the outermost hole on the disk passed through the image, the light from the light source passed through the hole to hit a light-sensitive cell, such as a silver-caesium phototube. The intensity of the light was modified by the light and dark areas in the image as the hole traveled past, thereby modulating the electrical signal generated by the phototube. The holes were arranged such that as soon as the outermost hole had exited the image, the next hole began *its* trek. Since the holes were arranged in a spiral formation, each hole traversed a different slice, or line, across the image.

At the other end of the process was a brilliant lamp and a second spinning Nipkow Disk. The electrical signal coming out of the phototube was used to modulate the lamp, which was projected onto the second disk. The modulated light passed through the holes in the second disk to construct a line-by-line display on a screen. Although the resulting image was constructed as a series of lines, the speed of the disk combined with persistence of vision meant that an observer saw a reasonable (albeit low-resolution) facsimile of the original picture. (The concept of persistence of vision is discussed in a little more detail below.)

Leaping ahead to the year 1895, the Italian electrical engineer and inventor Guglielmo Marconi extended the earlier research of such notables as the British physicist James Clerk Maxwell and the German physicist Heinrich Hertz by inventing the forerunner of radio as we know it today. In the early part of the twentieth century, engineers constructed experimental systems that could transmit images using a combination of Nipkow's disks and radio signals. The electrical signal coming out of the phototube was merged with a synchronization pulse (which indicated the start of a rotation), and this combined signal was then used to modulate the carrier wave from a radio transmitter. At the other end of the process was a radio receiver and a second spinning Nipkow Disk. The receiver first separated the synchronization pulse from the video signal, and the synchronization pulse was then used to ensure that the receiver disk was synchronized to the transmitter disk. Meanwhile, the amplified video signal was once again used to modulate a brilliant lamp, which was projected through holes in the receiver disk to construct a line-by-line display on a screen.

The cathode ray tube (CRT)

Modern television systems are based on a device called a *cathode ray tube (CRT)*. Primitive cathode ray tubes had been around since 1854, when a German glass blower named Heinrich Geissler invented a powerful vacuum pump. Geissler then proceeded to use his pump to evacuate a glass tube containing electrodes to a previously unattainable vacuum. Using these *Geissler Tubes*, experimenters discovered a form of radiation which they called *cathode rays* (and which we now know to consist of electrons). The idea of using a Cathode ray tube to display television images was proposed as early as 1905, but practical television didn't really become a possibility until 1906, when the American inventor Lee de Forest invented a vacuum tube called a *triode*, which could be used to amplify electronic signals (see also Chapter 15). Even so, progress was hard fought for, and it wasn't until the latter half of the 1920s that the first rudimentary television systems based on cathode ray tubes became operational in the laboratory.

The principles behind the cathode ray tube are quite simple (although actually building one is less than trivial). The tube itself is formed from glass, from which the air is evacuated to leave a strong vacuum (Figure 11.2a). In the rear of the tube is a device called an *electron gun*, which generates electrons. A positively charged grid mounted a little way in front of the electron gun focuses the electrons into a beam and accelerates them towards the screen. Thus, the name "cathode ray tube" is derived from the electron gun (which forms the negative terminal, or *cathode*), the electron beam (or *ray*), and the glass enclosure (or *tube*).

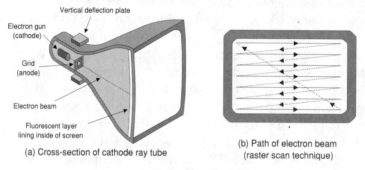

Vertical deflection plate

Electron gun (cathode)

Grid (anode)

Electron beam

Fluorescent layer lining inside of screen

(a) Cross-section of cathode ray tube

(b) Path of electron beam (raster scan technique)

Figure 11.2: Cathode ray tube

The inside face of the screen is lined with a layer of material called a *phosphor*, which has the ability to *fluoresce*. Hmmm, this is going to take a moment to explain. Phosphors are distinguished by the fact that when they absorb energy from some source such as an electron beam, they release a portion of this energy in the form of light. Depending on the material being used, the time it takes to release the energy can be short (less than one-hundred-thousandth of a second) or long (several hours). The effect from a short-duration phosphor is known as *fluorescence*, while the effect from a long-duration phosphor is referred to as *phosphorescence*. Televisions use short-duration phosphors, and their screens' lining is therefore known as the *fluorescent layer*.

The end result is that the spot where the electron beam hits the screen will glow. By varying the intensity of the electron beam, it's possible to make the spot glow brightly or hardly at all. Now on its own this would not be particularly useful (there's only so much you can do with an individual spot), but, of course, there's more. Note the two plates referred to as *vertical deflection plates* in Figure 11.2a. If an electrical potential is applied across these two plates, the resulting electric field will deflect the electron beam. If the upper plate is more positive than the lower, it will attract the negatively charged electrons forming the beam and the spot will move up the screen. Conversely, if the lower plate is the more positive the spot will move down the screen. Similarly, two more plates mounted on either side of the tube can be used to move the spot to the left or the right of the screen (these *horizontal deflection plates* are not shown here for clarity).

By combining the effects of the vertical and horizontal deflection plates, we are able to guide the spot to any point on the screen. There are several ways in which we can manipulate our spot to create pictures on the screen, but by far the most common is the *raster scan* technique (Figure 11.2b). Using this technique, the electron beam commences in the upper-left corner of the screen and is guided across the screen to the right. The path the beam follows as it crosses the screen is referred to as a *line*. When the beam reaches the right-hand side of the screen it undergoes a process known as *horizontal flyback*, in which its intensity is reduced and it is caused to "fly back" across the screen. While the beam is flying back it is also pulled a little way down the screen.[1]

The beam is now used to form a second line, then a third, and so on until it reaches the bottom of the screen. The number of lines affects the resolution of the resulting picture (that is, the amount of detail that can be displayed).[2] When the beam reaches the bottom right-hand corner of the screen it undergoes *vertical flyback*, in which its intensity is reduced, it "flies back" up the screen to return to its original position in the upper left-hand corner, and the whole process starts again. Thus, in a similar manner to Nipkow's technique, we can create pictures by varying the intensity of the beam as it scans across the screen. For example, consider how we'd draw a simple triangle (Figure 11.3).

In the real world the lines forming the picture would be very close together, so this would actually be a very small triangle, but it serves to illustrate the concept. When they are first introduced to this technique for creating pictures, many people wonder why they can't see the lines being drawn and why the image doesn't appear to flicker. The answer has three parts:

   a) The electrons forming the electron beam travel at a tremendous
      speed, and the beam itself can be manipulated very quickly. The

---

[1] This description is something of a simplification, but it will serve our purposes
[2] British television is based on 625 glorious lines, while American television only uses a measly 405!

beam used in a television set can scan the entire picture in a fraction of a second, and the entire picture is actually redrawn approximately thirty times a second.

b) The phosphor lining the inside of the screen is carefully chosen to fluoresce for exactly the correct amount of time, such that any particular point has only just stopped fluorescing by the time the electron beam returns to that point on its next scan.

c) The combination of our eyes and nervous system exhibit *persistence of vision*, which means we continue to see an image for a fraction of a second. For example, if you look at a bright light for a short time and then turn your head, an after-image of the light persists for a while.

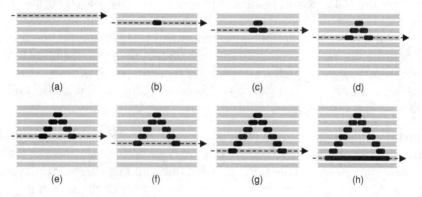

Figure 11.3: Drawing a picture (a triangle) on a cathode ray tube

All of these effects combine to form a seemingly substantial picture. However, if you ever look at a television program where the scene contains a television set, you'll often see bands of light and dark areas moving up or down that television's screen. This is because the camera taking the picture and the television *in* the picture are not synchronized together, resulting in a kind of stroboscopic effect (much like wagon wheels appearing to rotate backwards in old cowboy films). Thus, if producers of television programs wish to include a television in the scene, the engineers have to go to great lengths to ensure that the systems are synchronized to each other.

Philo Farnsworth – a man lost in history

There are two primary requirements for a functional television system: a technique for capturing an image and a way to display it. Following Nipkow's experiments, other inventors tried to move things forward with limited success. The history books mention several names in this regard, such as John Logie Baird, a Scotsman who used a derivation of Nipkow's disks for capturing and displaying pictures during the latter half of the 1920s and the early 1930s. The British Broadcasting Corporation (BBC) allowed Baird to transmit his pictures on their unused radio channels in the evening. By 1934, even though he could only transmit simple pictures with a maximum resolution of around 50 lines, Baird had sold thousands of his "Televisor" receivers around Europe in the form of do-it-yourself kits. Meanwhile, on the other side of the Atlantic, the Radio Corporation of America (RCA) experimented with a system consisting of a mechanical-disk camera combined with a cathode ray tube

As a point of interest, the reason we use the phrase "television set" derives from the early days of radio. The first radio systems for home use essentially consisted of three stages: the receiver to detect and preamplify the signal, the demodulator to extract the audio portion of the signal, and the main amplifier to drive the speaker. Each of these stages were packaged in individual cabinets, which had to be connected together; hence the user had to purchase all three units which formed a "wireless set." The term "set" persisted even after all of the radio's components were packaged in a single cabinet, and was subsequently applied to televisions when they eventually arrived on the scene.

display device. Using this system, RCA transmitted a picture of a model of Felix the Cat endlessly rotating on the turntable of a record player in the early 1930s.

Strange as it may seem, relatively few reference sources seem to be aware of the real genius behind television as we know it today – a farmboy named Philo T. Farnsworth from Rigby, Idaho. In 1922, at the age of 14, with virtually no knowledge of electronics, Philo conceived the idea for a fully electronic television system. Flushed with enthusiasm, he sketched his idea on a blackboard for his high school science teacher, a circumstance that was to prove exceedingly fortuitous in the future. Over the years, Philo solved the problems that had thwarted other contenders. He invented a device called an *Image Dissector*, which was the forerunner to modern television cameras, and he also designed the circuitry to implement horizontal and vertical flyback blanking signals on his cathode ray tube, which solved the problems of ghosting images. By the early 1930s, Philo could transmit moving pictures with resolutions of several hundred lines, and all subsequent televisions are directly descended from his original designs.

The reason Philo has been lost to history is almost certainly attributable to RCA. The corporation first attempted to persuade Philo to sell them his television patents, but he informed them in no uncertain terms that he wasn't interested. In 1934, RCA adopted another strategy by claiming that the Russian émigré Vladimir Zworkin, who was working for them at that time, had actually invented everything to do with televisions back in 1923. Eventually the case went to the patent tribunal, at which time Zworkin's claim was shown to leak like a sieve. The final nail in the coffin came when Philo's old science teacher reconstructed the sketch Philo had drawn on the blackboard back in 1922. This picture was recognizably that of the television system that Philo had subsequently developed, and the tribunal had no hesitation in awarding him the verdict. Unfortunately, by this time the waters had been muddied to the extent that Philo never received the recognition he deserved. Almost every standard reference continues to cite Zworkin (and his camera called an Iconoscope) as initiating modern television. In fact it was only towards the end of the 1970s that Philo's achievements began to be truly appreciated, and, although it's still rare to find references to him, Philo's name is gradually coming to the fore.

As video historian Paul Schatzkin told the authors: *"Many engineers and scientists contributed to the emergence of the television medium, but a careful examination of the record shows that no one really had a clue until Philo Farnsworth set up shop in San Francisco at the age of 20 and said: We'll do it this way!"*

The video tube

The tubes used in television sets and computer monitors (which we might call *video tubes*) are very similar to cathode ray tubes with some additional refinements. First, in place of the deflection plates discussed above, video tubes tend to use electromagnetic coils, but the end result is much the same, so we don't really need to go into that here. More importantly, video tubes have a second grid called the *shadow mask*, which is mounted a fraction of an inch from the screen's fluorescent coating (Figure 11.4a).

Like the grid, the shadow mask is positively charged, so it helps accelerate the electrons forming the electron beam, thereby giving them more energy which results in a brighter picture. More importantly the shadow mask helps to focus the beam, because any electrons that deviate even slightly from the required path hit the mask and are conducted away, thereby producing a sharper image.[3] Note that Figure 11.4a is greatly magnified and not to scale; in reality the shadow mask is only slightly thicker than aluminum foil and the holes are barely larger than pin-pricks.

---

[3]The shadow mask also has a role with regard to protecting the image from the effects of magnetic fields such as the Earth's, but this is beyond the scope of this book.

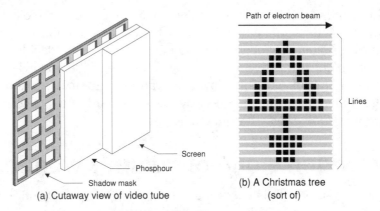

(a) Cutaway view of video tube

(b) A Christmas tree (sort of)

Figure 11.4: The shadow mask

If you approach your television at home and get really close to the screen, you'll see that the picture is formed from individual dots (much like our Christmas tree in Figure 11.4b). A "black-and-white" television only contains one electron gun, and the phosphor lining its screen is chosen to fluoresce with white light. In this case, each dot on the screen corresponds to a hole in the shadow mask, and each dot may be referred to as a picture element, or *pixel* for short. By comparison, if you own a color television, you'll see that the picture is composed of groups of three dots, where each dot corresponds to one of the primary colors: *red*, *green*, and *blue*. Each of these dots has its own hole in the shadow mask, and each dot is formed from a different phosphor, which is chosen to fluoresce with that color. In this case each group of three dots would equate to a single pixel (Figure 11.5).

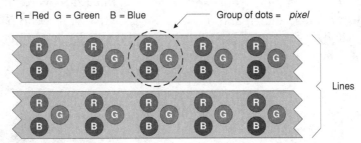

Figure 11.5: Groups of dots on a colour television screen

A color television also contains three electron guns, one to stimulate the red dots, one for the green, and one for the blue. The three electron beams scan across the screen together, but the intensity of each beam can be varied independently. Thus, by making only one of the beams active we can select which color in a group will be stimulated (we can also specify how brightly the dot should glow by varying the strength of that electron beam).

Now this is the clever bit. We might decide to make two of the electron beams active and stimulate two of the dots in the group at the same time: red-green, red-blue, or green-blue. Alternatively, we might decide to make all three of the beams active and stimulate all three of the dots. The point is that we can form different colors by using various combinations and intensities of the three dots. In one way this is similar to mixing colored paints, but in another way it's quite different ……

Color vision – one of nature's wonders

Actually this can be a little confusing at first, so sit up, pay attention, and place your brain into its turbo-charged mode. What we refer to as light is simply the narrow portion of the electromagnetic spectrum that our eyes can see, ranging from violet at one end to red at the other, and passing through blue, green, yellow, and orange on the way (Figure 11.6).[4]

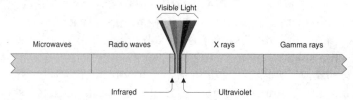

Figure 11.6: The visible portion of the electromagnetic spectrum

Just outside the visible spectrum above violet is *ultraviolet*, the component of the sun's rays that gives us a suntan. Similarly, just below red is *infrared*, which we perceive as heat. Strange as it may seem, white light is a mixture of all of the colors in the visible spectrum, a fact first discovered in 1666 by the English mathematician and physicist Sir Isaac Newton, who passed a beam of sunlight through a glass prism to find that it separated into what he called *"a spectrum of colors"* (Figure 11.7).

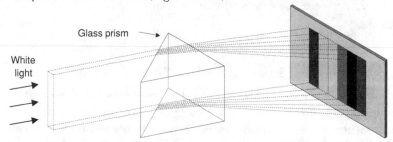

Figure 11.7: Newton's experiment splitting white light into a spectrum

[4]At one time indigo was recognized as a distinct spectral color, but this is typically no longer the case.

We're used to seeing the same effect in the form of a rainbow, which is caused by sunlight passing through droplets of water, each of which acts like a tiny prism. The point is that if we take beams of all of the different colors and merge them together, we'll end up with white light again. Thus, in the context of our color television, if all three of the electron beams are active when they pass a particular group of dots, the individual dots will fluoresce red, green, and blue, but from a distance we'll perceive the group as a whole as being white. (If we looked really closely we'd still see each dot as having its own individual color.) Similarly, if we stimulate just the red and green dots we'll see yellow; combining the green and blue dots will give us cyan (a green-ish, light-ish blue); while mixing the red and blue dots will result in magenta (a sort of purple).[5]

Now, this may seem counter-intuitive at first, because it doesn't seem to work the way we recall being taught at school, which was that mixing yellow and blue paints together would give us green, mixing all of the colored paints together would result in black (not white as discussed above), and so on. The reason for this is that mixing light is additive (Figure 11.8a), while mixing paint is subtractive (Figure 11.8b).

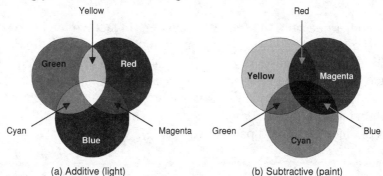

(a) Additive (light)   (b) Subtractive (paint)

Figure 11.8: Additive and subtractive color combinations

In the case of light, the *primary colors* are red, green, and blue, which are therefore known as the *additive primaries* (where primary colors are those which can be combined to form all of the other colors). In the case of paint, the primary colors are yellow, magenta, and cyan, which are therefore known as the *subtractive primaries*.[6]

---

[5]The color magenta was named after the dye of the same name, which, in turn, was named after the Battle of Magenta which occurred in Italy in 1859, the year in which the dye was first discovered.

[6]It is also common to refer to red, yellow, green, blue, white, and black as being the *psychological primaries*, because we subjectively and instinctively believe that these are the basis for all of the other colors.

So why does mixing light work one way while mixing paint works another? Gosh, we were hoping you wouldn't ask us that one. Well, here's a question right back to you — what colors come to mind when you hear the words "tomato," "grass," and "sky"? You almost certainly responded with red, green, and blue, respectively. Why? The main reason is that when you were young, your mother told you that *Tomatoes are red, grass is green, and the sky is blue*," and you certainly had no cause to doubt her word. However, the terms "red," "green," and "blue" are just labels that we have collectively chosen to assign to certain portions of the spectrum. If our mothers had told us that "*Tomatoes are blue, grass is red, and the sky is green*," then we'd all quite happily use those labels instead. What we can say is that, using an instrument called a spectrometer, we can divide the visible part of the spectrum into different bands, and we've collectively agreed to call certain of these bands "red," "green," and "blue." Of course everyone's eyes are different, so there's no guarantee that your companions are seeing exactly the same colors that you are. Also, as we shall see, our brains filter and modify the information coming from our eyes, so a number of people looking at exactly the same scene will almost certainly perceive the colors forming that scene in slightly different ways.

Here's another question: "*Why is grass green?*" In fact we might go so far as to ask: "*Is grass really green at all?*" Surprisingly, this isn't as stupid a question it seems, because from one point of view we might say that grass is a mixture of red and blue; that is, anything and everything except green! When we look at something like grass, what we actually see are the colors that it didn't absorb. Consider what happens when we shine white light on patches of different colored paint (Figure 11.9).

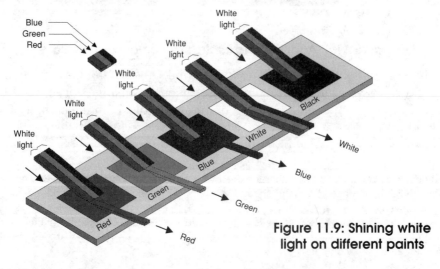

Figure 11.9: Shining white light on different paints

The red paint absorbs the green and blue light, but it reflects the red light, which is what we end up seeing. Similarly, the green paint absorbs the red and blue light and reflects the green, while the blue paint absorbs the red and green and reflects the blue. The white paint reflects all of the colors and the black paint absorbs them all, which means that black is really an absence of any color. So returning to our original question about the color of grass: We could say that grass is green, because that's the color that it reflects for us to see, or we could say that grass is both blue and red, because those are the colors it absorbs.

This explains why mixing paints is different from mixing light. If we start off with two tins of paint, say cyan and yellow, and shine white light at them, then each of the paints absorbs some of the colors from the white light and reflects others. If we now mix the two paints together, they each continue to absorb the same colors that they did before, so we end up seeing whichever colors neither of them absorbed, which is green in this case. This is why we say mixing paints is subtractive, because the more paints we mix together, the greater the number of colors the combination subtracts from the white light.

Actually, there is a point to all of this (well, most ...... well, some of it), although we won't find out what that point is until later in this chapter. But before we move on, it is perhaps appropriate to note that although colors themselves are reasonably simple (being merely sub-bands in the visible spectrum), color vision is amazingly complex. Our visual systems, which engage our eyes, brains, and nervous systems, have evolved to such a sophisticated level that for a long time we didn't even begin to comprehend the problems that nature had been compelled to overcome. In fact it was only when we (the human race, not the authors) constructed the first television cameras and television sets, and discovered they didn't work as expected, that we began to realize there was a problem in the first place.

First of all, it is commonly accepted (though not necessarily correct — see the sidebar) that we have five senses: touch, taste, smell, hearing, and sight. Of these senses, sight accounts for approximately 80% of the information we receive, so our brains are particularly well-adapted at processing this information and making assumptions based on it. For example, if you give someone yellow jello, they will automatically assume that it will taste of lemon; similarly for green jello and lime and red jello and strawberry.[7] This association is so strong that if you give people yellow jello with a strawberry

---

[7] What the Americans call "jello" would be referred to as "jelly" in England. (Also, what the Americans call "jelly" would translate to "jam" in the mother-tongue.)

Actually, there is a great deal of evidence that we have more than five senses (and we're not talking about extra-sensory perception); for example, the ability to detect magnetic fields. In a series of experiments performed in the early 1980s, groups of students who had lived in the same area for a number of years were blindfolded and driven out into the country on coaches that followed a bafflingly random, twisted route. When they reached their destination (still blindfolded), they were asked to point in the direction they thought home to be. Although some pointed exactly the wrong way, the average of all of the students was within 5% of the true direction! Subsequent refinements to the experiment revealed that the subjects were unconsciously using the earth's magnetic field as a reference.

flavor, they often continue to believe it tastes of lemon. This is because their brains give more weight to what their eyes are telling them compared to what their taste buds are trying to say.

When we use our eyes to look at something, the data is pre-processed by an area of the brain called the *visual cortex*, followed by the rest of the brain, which tries to make sense of what we're seeing. The brain's ability to process visual information is nothing short of phenomenal. For example, in a famous series of experiments, subjects donned special glasses which made everything appear to be upside down.

Amazingly, within a few days their brains began to automatically correct for the weird signals coming in and caused objects to appear to be the right way up again. Similarly, when the subjects removed their special glasses, things initially appeared to be upside down, because their brains were locked into the new way of doing things. Once again, within a short period of time their brains adapted and things returned to normal. (Actually, the way in which the lenses in our eyes function means that the images we see are inverted by the time they strike the retina at the back of the eye, so our brains start off by having to process "upside-down" data.)

This exemplifies the brain's processing capabilities, but doesn't begin to illustrate how well we handle color. As a starting point, human eyes have three different types of color receptors; some for red light, some for green, and some for blue.[8] This is why we use red, green, and blue dots on our television screens to generate all of the colors, because this directly maps onto the way in which our eyes work. However, this physical portion of our visual system is supplemented by an incredibly sophisticated color-processing component within our brains.

Assume for the sake of argument that you particularly like the shade of green you see in your lawn – so much so that you instruct a carpet manufacturer

---

[8]Several forms of color blindness are caused by deficiencies in one or more of these receptors.

to make you a rug in exactly that color. The great day arrives and your new rug is delivered. The first thing you do is to lay it next to your grass and confirm that they are, in fact, the same color. Next you take the rug into your house and place it on your recreation-room floor. Not surprisingly it remains the same color ...... or at least, it *appears* to.

The fact that an object generally looks much the same color-wise irrespective of where we put it and, within certain constraints, regardless of ambient lighting, is something we tend to take for granted. We can therefore only imagine the surprise of the creators of the first color television cameras when they discovered that objects appeared to have strikingly different colors according to whether they were filmed inside a building or outside. While engineers worked to correct the problem, people started to question why the same effect didn't occur with our eyes. Eventually it was realized that this effect did indeed occur, but our brains were correcting for it without our even noticing. One of the most effective ways to demonstrate exactly what it is our brains are doing to handle this color problem is illustrated in Figure 11.10.

To perform this experiment, we commence by painting a board with a wide variety of colors in various interlocking geometric shapes. Next, three light sources, which generate pure red, green, and blue light, are all set to the same intensity and used to light up the board. The combination of these pure sources effectively illuminates the board with white light.

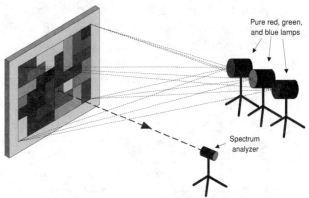

Figure 11.10: Experiment to determine the brain's method of correcting for color variations

Now a spectrum analyzer is pointed at the board. The analyzer is able to separate and distinguish the various bands of the spectrum that it's receiving. The analyzer also has a telescopic lens, such that it can be focused on individual colored shapes on the board. Consider a shape that's painted primary red. In this case the paint will reflect most of the light from the red light source and it will absorb the majority of the light from the green and blue sources. Thus, if we were to point the spectrum analyzer at this red area, the light received by the analyzer will show a large red component, along with relatively small green and blue components

(Figure 11.11a). Similarly, if we point the analyzer at areas that are painted primary green or primary blue, it will see large green or blue components, respectively (Figures 11.11b and 11.11c). .

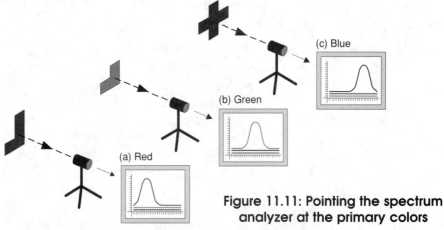

Figure 11.11: Pointing the spectrum analyzer at the primary colors

Now suppose we consider two shapes on the board that aren't painted in primary colors. Let's say that one of these shapes is painted a light-ish brown, while the other has a pink-ish sort of hue, and that both colors reflect some amount of red, green, and blue light, but in different proportions. Thus, if we pointed our spectrum analyzer at these two shapes in turn, we'd be able to detect the differences in their color components (Figures 11.12a and 11.12b).

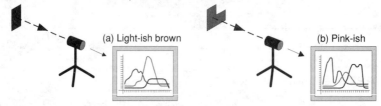

Figure 11.12: Pointing the spectrum analyzer at non-primary colors

Our obvious reaction is that the differences between the amount of red, green, and blue light being reflected from these shapes gives each of them their own distinctive color, and that's certainly true to an extent, but there's more to it than this. Suppose we point our spectrum analyzer at the pink-ish shape, and then vary the intensities of our three light sources until the light that's reflected from this shape has exactly the same characteristics we recorded from the brown-ish shape. The question is: *"What color is the pink-ish shape now?"*

Common sense would dictate that if we're now receiving exactly the same color components from the pink-ish shape that we originally received from the brown-ish shape, then the pink-ish shape should look exactly the same color as the brown-ish shape used to (and also that all of the other shapes on the board will have changed color to one degree or another). Well, take a firm grip on your seats, because here comes the amazing part ...... it does and it doesn't and they do and they don't. (If you think that this is difficult to follow, just wait until you try to explain it to someone else!)

Assume that we take a large piece of white card, lay it over the top of the board, and cut out a piece exactly the same size, shape, and position as our original pink-ish area. In this case, our shape that was originally pink-ish would now appear to be a light-ish brown-ish color. Similarly, if we did the same thing for any of the other shapes, they would all appear to have changed color to some extent. However, if we were to remove the white paper so that we could see the entire board, the pink-ish shape would once again appear to be, well ...... pink-ish, and all of the other colors would appear to be pretty much as we'd expect.

As we said, this is pretty amazing. What's actually happening is that if you can only see the one shape, then your brain has no other recourse than to assume that its color is determined by the different proportions of red, blue, and green light that are being reflected from that shape. However, if you can see that shape's color in the context of all of the other shapes' colors, then your brain does some incredibly nifty signal processing, determines what colors the various shapes *should* be, and corrects all of the colors before handing the information over to the conscious portion of your mind. To put this another way, your brain maintains a 3-dimensional color-map in which every color is weighted in relation to every other color. Thus, when you can see the whole board, your brain automatically calculates all of the color relationships and adjusts what you're *actually* seeing to match what it thinks you *should* be seeing.

Now all of this is quite impressive, but you're probably asking yourself: *"Why bother?"* After all, does it really matter if your lawn-colored rug looks a slightly different shade of green when it's inside the house? In fact it's possible to set up a television camera to emulate what we'd see if our brains weren't performing all of their "behind the scenes" activity, and the results are pretty staggering. For example, if you were to take such a camera and film a yellow taxi-cab as it progressed down the street, you would see it dramatically changing color as it passed through different lighting conditions such as shadows.

Thus we see that the signal processing performed by our brains actually has survival value. For example, life wouldn't be too much fun if you were to find yourself reincarnated as a small rodent of a type that happens to be a favorite after-dinner snack for saber-tooth parrots.[9] As bad as this may seem, life could quickly get to be an awful lot harder if everything in the jungle assumed new colors every time a cloud passed by, and if the parrots themselves were constantly changing color as they passed through shadows during the process of swooping down on you from above. Similarly, if you were a prehistoric hunter, explaining the local flora and fauna to a friend who was visiting for a long weekend could pose some problems. We might imagine a conversation along the lines of: *"One thing you've got to watch out for around here is lions. That's a lion over there, the big yellow thing ...... the big blue thing ...... the thing that's stood next to the parrot that just turned from violet to emerald green ..... good grief, where did that cloud come from?"*

Visual display units (VDUs)

Today's computer monitors have smaller pixels and more pixels per inch than a television set, which means that they have a higher resolution and can display images with greater precision. (Note that the concept of pixels is somewhat slippery when we come to computers – we'll discuss this in more detail later). Modern computers typically contain a circuit board called a graphics card, which contains a substantial amount of memory and its own on-board microprocessor. All that your main system has to do is to send an instruction to the processor on the graphics card saying something like *"Draw me a purple circle with 'this' diameter at 'that' location on the screen."* The graphics processor then slogs away completing the task, while the system's main processor is left free to work on something else.

The combination of high-resolution monitors and graphics cards endows today's computer screens with millions of pixels, each of which can be individually set to thousands or even millions of colors. We require this level of sophistication because we often wish to display large amounts of graphical data, such as three-dimensional animations. This wasn't possible until recently, because it requires a huge amount of computing power and memory. In fact it's only because today's computers are incredibly fast and memory is reasonably inexpensive that we are in a position to display images at this level of sophistication.

By comparison, computers in the early 1960s were relatively slow, memory was extremely expensive, and there weren't any dedicated computer

---

[9]This once happened to a friend of ours and it's no laughing matter, let us tell you.

monitors as we know them today. On the bright side, very few people had access to computers, and those who did were generally only interested in being able to see textual data, which was typically printed out on a teleprinter or some comparable device. However, at some stage it struck someone that it would be useful to be able to view and manipulate their data on something similar to a television screen, and the first *visual display unit (VDU)* was born.

By 1977, a few lucky souls were the proud possessors of rudimentary home computers equipped with simple VDUs. A reasonably typical system at that time would probably have resembled the one shown in Figure 11.13.

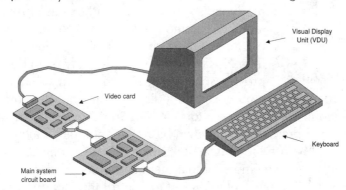

Figure 11.13: Home computer with VDU circa 1977

Even though these computers were slow and had hardly any memory by today's standards, their owners were immensely proud of them and justly so, because most of these devices were hand-built from kits or from the ground up. Similarly, although their rudimentary monitors could only display a few rows of "black-and-white" text, anyone who was fortunate enough to own one was deliriously happy to actually see words appearing on their screen.

The professional VDUs (which we shall return to calling monitors henceforth) typically offered between 20 and 24 rows, each containing 80 characters. Why 80? Because there wasn't much point in displaying fewer characters than could fit on IBM punched cards, which were used to store a large proportion of the world's computer data at that time. Similarly, there didn't seem to be much point in being able to display more characters than were on these cards.[10] By comparison, monitors for home use were less expensive, less sophisticated, and generally only capable of displaying around 16 rows of 32 characters.

---

[10]IBM punched cards are discussed in Chapters 4 and 15

A major consideration for the designers of these early monitors was the amount of memory they required, because, unlike a television which receives its pictures from afar, a computer needs somewhere to store everything that it's displaying. From our discussions on video tubes earlier in this chapter, you may recall that images are created as a series of lines containing "dots," and this is the way in which a monitor displays characters. For example, consider how a monitor could be used to display the letter 'E' (Figure 11.14).

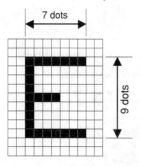

Figure 11.14: An 'E'

One configuration common in early monitors was a matrix of 9 x 7 dots per character as illustrated here (another common style was based on a 7 x 5 matrix, but the resulting characters were "clunky" and difficult to read). So ignoring any extra dots used to provide spaces between rows and columns, each character would require 63 dots, and a display containing 16 rows of 32 characters would therefore use a total of 32,256 dots. This means that if each dot were represented by its own bit in the computer's memory (where a *logic 0* could be used to indicate the dot is off and a *logic 1* to indicate the dot is on), then remembering that there are 8 bits in a byte, the system would require 4,032 bytes of RAM just to control the monitor.

Now although this doesn't seem like a lot of memory today, in 1977 you considered yourself fortunate indeed to have 2 K-bytes (2,048 bytes) of RAM, and you were the envy of your street if you had as much as 4 K-bytes (4,096 bytes). Obviously this was a bit of a conundrum, because even if you were the proud possessor of a system with a 4 K-byte RAM, there wouldn't have been much point in running a monitor that required 4,032 bytes, because you would only have 64 bytes left to write your programs in!

In those days of yore, programmers prided themselves in writing efficient code that occupied as little memory as possible, but this would have been pushing things above and beyond the call of duty. A measly 64 bytes certainly wouldn't have been enough to have written a program that could

The first memory-mapped display was developed around 1976 by Lee Felsenstein, who, in addition to designing the *Pennywhistle modem* and the *Osborne One* (one of the earliest successful microcomputers), also found the time to moderate the famous Homebrew Computer Club and act as the system administrator of the pioneering *Community Memory* wide-area network.

do anything particularly useful with the monitor, which would defeat the purpose of having a monitor in the first place. What was needed was a cunning ploy, and electronics engineers are nothing if not ingenious when it comes to cunning ploys (in fact the term *engineer* is derived from the Latin *ingeniator*, meaning "a creator of ingenious devices"). The solution to the problem was a concept known as a *memory-mapped display*.

The memory-mapped display

To honor the pioneers of home computing, the *Beboputer* is equipped with a virtual memory-mapped display that supports 16 rows of 32 characters. However, to improve on the early devices, each of our characters is going to be formed from a matrix of 15 dots by 10 dots, which will give us nicer-looking images (why suffer if you don't have to?) (Figure 11.15).

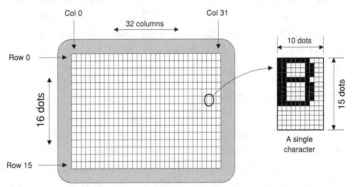

Figure 11.15: The *Beboputer's* memory-mapped screen

When you magnify one of our characters (the letter 'B' in this example), it may seem that we've carelessly wasted a lot of our dots. But remember that we require some way to form spaces between the rows and columns. Also, some of the lowercase characters such as 'q', 'y', and 'p' have "tails" that extend downward, and we have to reserve some space to accommodate these as well.

Be this as it may, the problem remains that we've got 16 x 32 = 512 characters, each of which occupies 15 x 10 = 150 dots (which would require 9,600 bytes if we used one bit to store each dot), yet we want to use the smallest amount of our computer's memory as possible. The solution to our problem lies in that fact that the patterns of dots for each character are pre-defined and relatively immutable (at least they were in the early days). To put this another way, if we wish to display several 'B' characters at different positions on the screen, then we know that each of them will use exactly the same pattern of dots. This means that we can divide our problem into three distinct parts:

a) We need some way to remember which characters are being displayed at each location on the screen; for example, *"The character in column 6 of row 3 is a letter 'B'."* Due to the fact that we want to be able to change the characters displayed at each location, this information will have to be stored in our RAM.

b) We need some way to store a single master pattern of dots for each character we wish to be able to display (for example, 'A', 'B', ... 'Z', and so on). Assuming that we don't wish to change the way our characters look, then these master patterns can be stored in some flavor of read-only memory (ROM) device.[11]

c) We need some mechanism to combine the information from points (a) and (b). That is, if the system knows that the character in column 6 of row 3 should be a letter 'B', then it requires the ability to access the master pattern of dots associated with this letter and display them on the screen at the appropriate location.

The first thing we have to decide is which types of characters we wish to use. Obviously we'll want to be able to display the uppercase letters 'A' through 'Z', and it's not beyond the bounds of possibility that we'd like to use their lowercase counterparts 'a' through 'z'. Similarly, we'd appreciate the numbers '0' through '9', punctuation characters such as commas and semi-colons, and special symbols such as '$', '&', and '#'. Just a moment, doesn't all of this seem strangely familiar? Are you experiencing a feeling of deja-vu? Didn't somebody just say that? Well you can flay us with wet noodles if this isn't beginning to sound like the specification for ASCII that we introduced in the previous chapter (we love it when a plan comes together).

ASCII is a 7-bit code and, as we tend to store our information in 8-bit bytes, this means that we've got a spare bit in each byte to play with (but you can bet your little cotton socks that we'll find a use for these bits in the not-so-distant future). The main point is that if we use ASCII codes to indicate the characters that we wish to display at each location on the screen, then we'll only need to reserve 512 bytes (16 x 32 characters) of our RAM for the entire screen, which is pretty efficient usage of our limited resources when you come to think about it.

---

[11]We will discuss ways in which we *can* modify these master patterns in Chapter 13

The next thing we need to consider is how we map locations in the *Beboputer's* memory to rows and columns on the screen. As you may recall, the *Beboputer* perceives its world as consisting of 64 K-bytes of memory (we've provided you with far more memory than the early home users could hope for in their wildest dreams) (Figure 11.16).

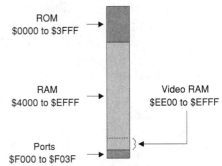

In the case of our virtual system, addresses $0000 through $3FFF are occupied by ROM, addresses $4000 through $EFFF are occupied by RAM, and addresses $F000 through $F03F are used for our input and output ports. (Of course the *Beboputer* doesn't really know anything about this, and treats every location as being identical.)

Figure 11.16: The *Beboputer's* memory map (video RAM)

So all we need to do is to reserve 512 bytes of our RAM to store the codes for the characters that are going to be displayed on our virtual screen (henceforth we'll refer to these locations as the *Video RAM*). In reality any contiguous set of 512 bytes would do, but as we typically place our programs in the low-order locations commencing at $4000, we decided to keep the video memory as far away as possible and to use the last 512 RAM locations that occupy addresses $EE00 through $EFFF (just before our input and output ports).

Note that we haven't altered anything in a physical sense and the *Beboputer* hasn't changed in any way; all we've done is to make the intellectual decision that we're going to regard the last 512 bytes in our RAM as being reserved for use by our memory-mapped display. Also remember that the *Beboputer* doesn't know anything about any of this – it just does what it's told. So if we instruct the *Beboputer* to load a value of $42 into memory location $EE00, it will happily do so without any understanding that, in this case, we're treating $42 as the ASCII code for the letter 'B', and that we're hoping the corresponding pattern of dots will somehow wend their way to the correct position on the screen.

In fact the video card (which is connected to the main circuit board by a cable) performs most of the work, by slipping in to read the *Beboputer's* Video RAM while the *Beboputer* isn't looking and displaying the appropriate characters on the screen. When we constructed our virtual video card, we hard-wired it to understand that our memory-mapped display supports 16 rows of 32 columns, and we also hard-wired the fact that address $EE00 is defined as the start address of the Video RAM. Thus, the video card knows that whichever ASCII character occupies address $EE00 is supposed to appear at row 0 column 0 on the screen, that the character at address $EE01 is supposed to appear at row 0 column 1, and so on. Similarly, because the video card knows how many rows and columns our display supports, it understands that the character at address $EE1F is supposed to appear at row 0 column 31 (since $1F = 31_{10}), while the character at address $EE20 is supposed to appear at the beginning of the next line at row 1 column 0 (Figure 11.17).

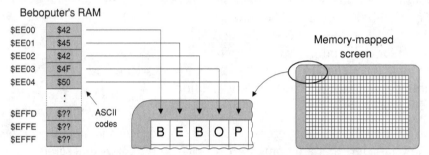

Figure 11.17: Mapping the *Beboputer's* video RAM to the screen

The fact that certain memory locations are mapped to particular character positions on the screen is why this technique is referred to as "memory-mapped." The final problem is to use the ASCII codes from the *Beboputer's* RAM to generate the patterns of dots that are displayed on the screen. In order to do this, the video card uses a device called a *Character ROM*. Remember that ROM is a form of memory containing hard-coded patterns of *logic 0s* and *logic 1s*. In the case of the Character ROM, these *logic 0s* and *logic 1s* are used to represent the absence or presence of dots on the screen. Assume that the video card is commencing a new pass to refresh the screen commencing at row 0 column 0 (Figure 11.18).

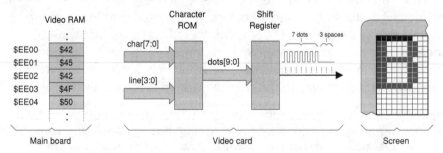

Figure 11.18: Using the character ROM to generate the dots

One thing we have to remember is that each character is formed from fifteen lines of dots, but that the electron beam scans all the way across the screen to form each line. As we see, our Character ROM has twelve input signals;

eight of these inputs are used to indicate which character we're interested in (char[7:0]), while the other four are used to indicate a particular line of that character (line[3:0]). Thus, the video card commences by peeking into location $EE00 of the *Beboputer's* memory to see what's there (for the purposes of this example we're assuming that it's going to find the ASCII code $42, which corresponds to the letter 'B'). The video card passes this ASCII code to the character ROM's char[7:0] inputs, and it also sets the line[3:0] inputs to binary 0000 (thereby indicating that it's interested in line 0).

Using this data, the character ROM's ten outputs, dot[9:0], return the pattern of *logic 0s* and *logic 1s* that correspond to the first line of the character 'B' (binary 1111111000 in this case). This pattern is then loaded into a shift register, which converts it into a sequence of pulses that are used to control the electron beam (a *logic 1* turns the beam on to form a dot, while a *logic 0* turns it off to leave a space).

However, the video card can't complete the rest of this character yet, because the electron beam is continuing its scan across the screen. So the video card peeks into location $EE01 of the *Beboputer's* memory to see what's there, and finds the ASCII code $45, which corresponds to the letter 'E'. The video card passes this new ASCII code to the character ROM's char[7:0] inputs and keeps the line[3:0] inputs set to binary 0000 (thereby indicating that it's still interested in line 0). Once again, the character ROM responds with the pattern of dots required to construct the first line of the letter 'E', and once again this pattern is loaded into the shift register, which converts it into the pulses required to control the electron beam.

The video card continues this process for addresses $EE02 through $EE1F, at which time it has completed the first line of the first row of the display. It then repeats the process for the same set of characters in addresses $EE00 through $EE1F, but this time it sets the character ROM's line[3:0] inputs to binary 0001, thereby indicating that it's now interested in line 1 of these characters. Ultimately, the video card has to go through the process fifteen times (incrementing the line[3:0] inputs each time) until it finally manages to complete all of the lines required to form the first row of characters.

Now the video card has to perform another fifteen scans to construct the second row of characters from the ASCII codes stored in addresses $EE20 through $EE3F, and so on for the remaining fourteen rows. This may seem to be a dreadfully complicated process involving a lot of work, but it really isn't too bad. Transistors can switch millions of times a second, so what seems to be a horrendous amount of effort to us actually leaves them with a lot of time on their hands waiting around for something interesting to happen. More importantly, as users we aren't really affected by any of this. All we really need to know is that if we create a program that stores an ASCII code into one of the RAM locations we've designated as the Video RAM, then our video card will automatically cause the corresponding character to appear on our virtual screen at the appropriate location. OK, enough of the theory ...... now it's time to rock and roll.

Winding up the *Beboputer*

Make sure the *Beboputer* CD is in the appropriate drive in your computer and summon the *Beboputer*. Once the *Beboputer's* project window has opened, click the File item on its menu bar, click the **Open Project** entry in the resulting pull-down menu, then select the Lab 6 project from the ensuing dialog. This will invoke our sixth lab (Figure 11.19).

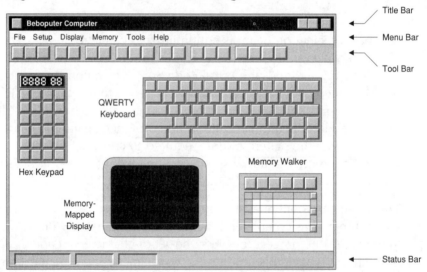

Figure 11.19: The *Beboputer's* project window for Lab 6

As usual, most of the tools that appear in the project working area are familiar to us: the memory walker, the hex keypad, and the QWERTY keyboard. In fact the only new addition to the team is our memory-mapped display. Note that this display is initially black, because we haven't powered the *Beboputer* up yet.

Program to clear the screen

Click the **ON** button on the hex keypad to power the *Beboputer* up (this also applies power to the memory-mapped display). Eeeek, why has the screen filled with weird characters? The reason is that the *Beboputer's* RAM initially contains random *logic 0s* and *logic 1s*, but the video card doesn't know this, so it just does its job, which is to treat locations $EE00 through $EFFF as valid ASCII codes and display them on the screen. This means that the first thing we need to do is to write a program to clear the screen. For reasons of our own, we're going to create this program in two parts. First we've going to specify a top-level program that sets things up the way we wish. This top-level program will then call a subroutine to actually perform all of the work (Figure 11.20).

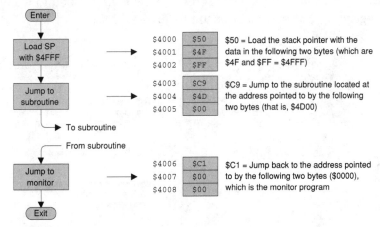

Figure 11.20: Top level program to clear the screen

The first instruction ($50 at address $4000) is a **BLDSP** (*"big load stack pointer"*), which we use to initialize the stack pointer. We call this a "big load" because the stack pointer requires two bytes of data (the use of the stack pointer and subroutines was introduced in Chapter 8). As you may recall, we could initialize the stack pointer to point almost anywhere in the RAM (with the exception of addresses $EE00 through $EFFF, which we've now designated as being reserved for use as the Video RAM). In fact it's generally considered to be good practice to locate the stack pointer as far away from our programs as possible, because programs grow in the opposite direction to the stack (see also Chapter 8). However, in this case we know that both our programs and our stack are going to be relatively small, so we've arbitrarily decided to initialize the stack pointer to address $4FFF, which is the end of the first 4K block of RAM.

The second instruction ($C9 at address $4003) is a **JSR** (*"jump to subroutine"*). Once again, we could have placed the subroutine almost anywhere in the memory, but we've made another arbitrary decision that the first instruction of this subroutine will be at address $4D00. Remember that when the subroutine finishes its task, it will automatically return control to the instruction following the one that called it. Thus, in this case our subroutine will return control to address $4006. The last instruction ($C1 at address $4006) is a **JMP** (*"unconditional jump"*) to address $0000, which is the first address in our monitor program. This is the first time we've done anything like this, but the effect will be the same as if we'd clicked the **Reset** button on the hex keypad to reset the *Beboputer*.

Now we come to the subroutine itself. There are myriad ways in which we could write a routine to clear the screen, but we've decided to feature the index register in this particular example (Figure 11.21).

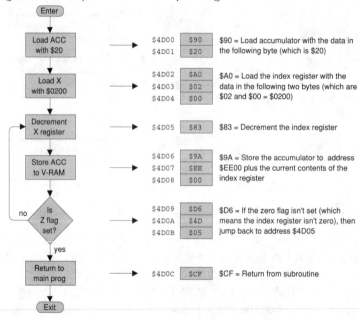

Figure 11.21: The clear screen subroutine

The first thing we do upon entering the subroutine is to load the accumulator with $20, which happens to be the ASCII code for a space character. The second thing we do is to load our 16-bit index register with the value $0200 (or 512 in decimal). Perhaps surprisingly, we immediately decrement the index register in the next instruction, which means that it will now only contain $01FF (or 511 in decimal). Now this may seem a little counter-intuitive at first, but there's method behind our madness.[12]

For reasons that will become apparent, we actually want to commence with $01FF in the index register, but our subroutine is based on a loop that commences by decrementing the index register. Thus, we start off by loading the index register with $0200, and then drop straight into our loop, which decrements the index register to leave the value we required in the first place.

The cunning part of the subroutine occurs at address $4D06, which contains a **STA** ("*store accumulator*") instruction using the indexed addressing mode (the concept of indexed addressing was introduced in Chapter 8). This instruction tells the CPU to store the contents of the accumulator to the address pointed to by the next two bytes (which form the address $EE00) *plus* the current contents of the index register. Now you will remember that $EE00 is the address of the first location in our Video RAM, so the first time around the loop we actually store the contents of the accumulator (the $20 ASCII space code) to address $EE00 + $01FF = $EFFF, which is the address of the last location in the Video RAM.

Now here's another cunning point. The instruction that decrements the index register at address $4D05 also updates the zero flag; that is, if the index register's contents are zero after it's been decremented, then the zero flag will be set to a *logic 1*, otherwise it will be cleared to a *logic 0*. However, the instruction that stores the contents of the accumulator at address $4D06 does *not* have any effect on the zero flag. Thus, even after we've stored the contents of the accumulator, the zero flag still indicates the current state of the index register. This is useful to us because the next instruction at address $4D09 is a **JNZ** ("*jump if not zero*"), which instructs the CPU to jump back to the beginning of the loop at address $4D05 if the zero flag is not set. Of course, the index register contains $01FF at the end of the first pass around the loop, so the zero flag won't be set and the program will jump back to the beginning of the loop.

The second iteration of the loop commences by decrementing the index register again, such that it now contains $01FE. Once again, the next instruction at address $4D06 tells the CPU to store the contents of the accumulator to address $EE00 plus the current contents of the index register. Thus, on this second trek around the loop we actually store the contents of the accumulator (the $20 ASCII space code) to address $EE00 + $01FE = $EFFE, which is the address of the next-to-last location in the Video RAM.

---

[12]"*There is only one difference between a madman and me. I am not mad.*" – Salvador Dali

The end result of all this is that our subroutine will load all 512 bytes of the Video RAM with space characters, commencing at the last location in the Video RAM and working its way up to the first location. Eventually, the index register will be decremented to zero, the **JNZ** instruction at address $4D09 will fail, and the program will continue on to the last instruction ($CF at address $4D0C), which is an **RTS** (*"return from subroutine"*). This last instruction instructs the CPU to return control to the top-level program that called it. While you're entering this program as discussed below, take a few moments to ponder two questions:

   a) What do you expect to occur on the memory-mapped display when we come to run this program?

   b) Why on earth did we write the program to load the Video RAM from the bottom up instead of from the top down?

Entering the program with the hex keypad

Once again, we've arrived at the exciting part where we enter our program. Don't bother looking for a short-cut, because we haven't pre-written this program for you. As we've already powered up the *Beboputer*, the **Address (Ad)** button on the hex keypad is lit up to indicate that the address is the active field.

The first instruction in our program occurs at address $4000, so this is the address that we need to enter. Remember that the keypad automatically uses hexadecimal values, so click a '4' followed by three '0's, and watch the address build up in the address field. Also remember that if you make a mistake at any time, you can clear the address field by clicking the keypad's **Clear (Clr)** button.

Now click the keypad's **Data (Da)** button to make this field active, click a '5' followed by a '0', and watch the data build up in the data field. To complete this operation, click the keypad's **Enter (Ent)** button. This causes the monitor program to load the data displayed in the data field ($50) into the memory location specified by the address field ($4000). The monitor program automatically increments the value in the address field and the **Data (Da)** button remains active, which allows you to alternate between inputting data and clicking the **Enter** button. So, continue to enter the remainder of the program from address $4001 onwards as follows:

Address	Data	Instruction	Clear screen top-level program
$4000	$50	BLDSP (imm)	Load the stack pointer with $4FFF (the stack
$4001	$4F		pointer is a 16-bit register, so it requires two bytes)
$4002	$FF		
$4003	$C9	JSR (abs)	Jump to the subroutine that's located at
$4004	$4D		address $4D00
$4005	$00		
$4006	$C1	JMP (abs)	On returning from the subroutine, jump
$4007	$00		immediately to address $0000, which is the
$4008	$00		start of our monitor program in ROM (just like
			hitting a reset)

This completes the top level program, so now we've got to change the
address in order to enter the subroutine. Click the **Address (Ad)** button on
the hex keypad to make this the active field. The first instruction in our
subroutine occurs at address $4D00, so click a '4', a 'D', and two '0's. Now
click the **Data (Da)** button again to make this field active, click a '9' and a
'0', then click the keypad's **Enter (Ent)** button. As usual, the monitor
program automatically increments the value in the address field and the
Data (Da) button remains active, so continue to enter the remainder of the
subroutine from address $4D01 onwards as follows:

Address	Data	Instruction	Clear screen top-level program
$4D00	$90	LDA (imm)	Load the accumulator with $20 (which is the
$4D01	$20		ASCII code for a space)
$4D02	$A0	BLDX (imm)	Load the index register with $0200 (the index
$4D03	$02		register is a 16-bit register, so it requires two bytes)
$4D04	$00		
$4D05	$83	DECX (imp)	Decrement the index register
$4D06	$9A	STA (abs-x)	Store the contents of the accumulator to the
$4D07	$EE		address $EE00 plus the current contents of the
$4D08	$00		index register
$4D09	$D6	JNZ (abs)	If the zero flag isn't set to logic 1 (which means
$4D0A	$4D		that the index register doesn't contain zero), then
$4D0B	$05		jump back to address $4D05
$4D0C	$CF	RTS (imp)	Return to the main program

Running the program with the hex keypad

Click the keypad's **Address (Ad)** button to make the address field active,
enter the start address of the program which is $4000, then click the **Run**
button to let the *Beboputer* rip.

Following our in-depth discussions above, we know that our subroutine loads $20 values into the area of the *Beboputer's* RAM that we've designated as the Video RAM. As $20 is the ASCII code for a space, this means that our video card will display spaces on the screen. We also know that, due to the way in which we wrote it, the subroutine loads the first $20 character into location $EFFF and then works its way down to location $EE00. Thus, the space characters start to appear at the bottom right-hand corner of the screen and work their way back to the top left-hand corner.

Why did we do it this way? Wouldn't it have been more intuitive to have commenced in the top left-hand corner of the screen and wend our way towards the bottom right? The simple answer is that it really doesn't matter, because the screen ended up being cleared, which is all we set out to do. However, the real reason we did it this way is that we can test to see whether the index register contains a zero value, which provides an easy way to recognize when to terminate our subroutine.

Finally, after clearing the screen, the subroutine returns control to the main program, which immediately jumps to address $0000. This address is the first location of our monitor program in the ROM, which is where the CPU is forced to go when we click the **Reset** (Rst) button on the hex keypad. Thus, our top level program voluntarily returns control to the monitor once the screen has been cleared, and the *Beboputer* returns to its *reset mode*.

Program to display all characters

Now that we know how to clear our screen, we'd like to do something really interesting with it, but we've got to learn how to take small steps before we enter the 50-yard sprint. As a simple exercise, we're going to modify our top-level program such that, after it's called the subroutine to clear the screen, it displays all of the characters that are available to us. This means that we're going to have to overwrite the JMP instruction at address $4006, which originally returned us to the tender care of our monitor program (Figure 11.22).

By now you should be reaching the stage where you don't actually recoil in horror when you see a flowchart like this, and rightly so — after all, it's only seven instructions long. The first of our new instructions ($A0 at address $4006) is a BLDX ("*big load index register*"). This is the same instruction we used in our subroutine, except that this time we're loading the index register with $0000.

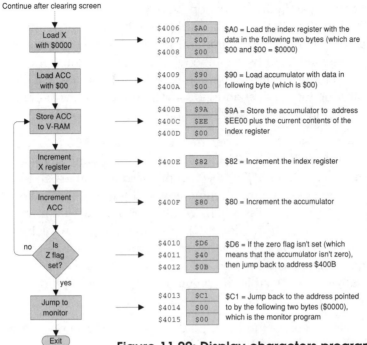

Continue after clearing screen

Load X with $0000	→	$4006	$A0	$A0 = Load the index register with the data in the following two bytes (which are $00 and $00 = $0000)
		$4007	$00	
		$4008	$00	

| Load ACC with $00 | → | $4009 | $90 | $90 = Load accumulator with data in following byte (which is $00) |
| | | $400A | $00 | |

Store ACC to V-RAM	→	$400B	$9A	$9A = Store the accumulator to address $EE00 plus the current contents of the index register
		$400C	$EE	
		$400D	$00	

| Increment X register | → | $400E | $82 | $82 = Increment the index register |

| Increment ACC | → | $400F | $80 | $80 = Increment the accumulator |

Is Z flag set? (no)	→	$4010	$D6	$D6 = If the zero flag isn't set (which means that the accumulator isn't zero), then jump back to address $400B
		$4011	$40	
		$4012	$0B	

Jump to monitor (yes)	→	$4013	$C1	$C1 = Jump back to the address pointed to by the following two bytes ($0000), which is the monitor program
		$4014	$00	
		$4015	$00	

Exit

Figure 11.22: Display characters program

The second instruction ($90 at address $4009) loads the accumulator with $00, while the third instruction ($9A at address $400B) is a **STA** ("*store accumulator*") using the indexed addressing mode. Once again, this instruction (which is identical to the one we used in our subroutine) tells the CPU to store the contents of the accumulator to the address pointed to by the next two bytes (which is $EE00) *plus* the current contents of the index register. Now we know that $EE00 is the address of the first location in our Video RAM, and we know that the index register starts off containing $0000, so the first time around the loop we store the accumulator to address $EE00 + $0000 = $EE00; that is, row 0 col 0.

Next we increment the index register using an **INCX** instruction ($82 at address $400E), then we increment the

If you're alert (the world needs more "lerts"), you'll realize that this first instruction to load the index register with $0000 is superfluous in this case, because the clear screen subroutine already leaves the index register containing $0000. However, unless you're trying to use as few memory locations as possible or make your program run as fast as possible, it's generally considered to be good practice to explicitly initialize any registers you're going to use at the time you're going to use them. For example, at some time in the future we might decide to rewrite the clear screen subroutine in a way that doesn't use the index register, in which case we wouldn't have a clue what that register contained.

accumulator using an INCA instruction ($80 at address $400F). Now we perform a test to see whether the act of incrementing the accumulator left it containing zero. Although we started off loading the accumulator with $00, we just incremented it, so by the time we reach this test on our first pass round the loop the accumulator will contain $01. Thus, the JNZ ("*jump if not zero*") instruction ($D6 at address $4010) will cause the program to jump back to address $400B and continue around the loop.

To cut a long story short, this program is going to load $00 into the first location in our Video RAM, $01 into the second location, $02 into the third location, and so on up to $FF in the two-hundred and fifty-sixth location. At this point, incrementing the accumulator will return it to a value of $00, the JNZ instruction at address $4010 will fail, and the program will continue on to the last instruction ($C1 at address $4013), which is a JMP ("*unconditional jump*") back into the monitor program. While you're entering this program as discussed below, cast your mind back to the ASCII character set we introduced in the previous chapter and consider another two questions:

a) What do you expect to be displayed for the ASCII codes $00 through $1F, and also code $7F?

b) Remembering that ASCII is a 7-bit code that only occupies the values $00 through $7F, what do you expect to be displayed for the remaining codes of $80 through $FF?

Entering the program with the hex keypad

The following listing covers our entire new top-level program, but don't forget that we want to keep the first six bytes from our earlier program, so we actually wish to start entering data at address $4006. Click the Address (Ad) button on the hex keypad to make this the active field, enter the address $4006, then click the Data (Da) button to make this the active field. The data field initially displays our old data of $C1, so click the Clear (Clr) button to dismiss this data, enter our new data of $A0, and click the Enter (Ent) button.

As usual, the monitor program automatically increments the value in the address field to $4007 and the Data (Da) button remains active. The data field contains the old data $00 which was stored in this location. By some happy quirk of fate, this is the same value that we need for our new program, so simply click the Enter (Ent) button to accept this data and move onto location $4008. As we see, the data that used to be stored at location

$4008 is $00, which we also require for our new program, so click the Enter (Ent) button to accept this data and move onto location $4009.

Our luck just ran out, because this is the point where our original program ended, so continue to enter the remainder of the program from address $4009 onwards as shown below.

Address	Data	Instruction	Display characters top-level program
$4000	$50	BLDSP (imm)	Load the stack pointer with $4FFF (the stack
$4001	$4F		pointer is a 16-bit register so it requires two bytes)
$4002	$FF		
$4003	$C9	JSR (abs)	Jump to the subroutine that's located at address
$4004	$4D		$4D00
$4005	$00		
$4006	$A0	BLDX (imm)	On returning from the subroutine, load the index
$4007	$00		register with $0000
$4008	$00		
$4009	$90	LDA (imm)	Load the accumulator with $00
$400A	$00		
$400B	$9A	STA (abs-x)	Store the contents of the accumulator to the
$400C	$EE		address $EE00 plus the current contents of
$400D	$00		the index register
$400E	$82	INCX (imp)	Increment the index register
$400F	$80	INCA (imp)	Increment the accumulator
$4010	$D6	JNZ (abs)	If the zero flag isn't set to logic 1 (which means
$4011	$40		that the accumulator doesn't contain zero),
$4012	$0B		then jump back to address $400B
$4013	$C1	JMP (abs)	Jump immediately to address $0000, which is
$4014	$00		the start of our monitor program in ROM (just
$4015	$00		like hitting a reset)

Running the program with the hex keypad

Before we run this new program, use the memory walker to view address $4D01 in our "clear screen" subroutine. This location currently contains $20, which is the ASCII code for a space. Unfortunately, as we saw in the previous exercise, it takes a while to clear the screen using this particular subroutine, so in order to add a little variety to our lives, double-click on this data in the memory walker and change it to $2E, which is the ASCII code for a period.

Now click the keypad's Address (Ad) button to make the address field active, enter the start address of the program, which is $4000, then click the Run button to let the *Beboputer* run wild and free (Figure 11.23).

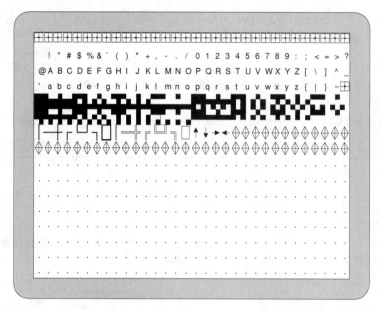

Figure 11.23: Displaying all of the available characters

Why is the resulting screen only half filled (ignoring the periods in the bottom half of the screen, which are left over from our clear screen subroutine)? The answer is that our screen can contain 512 characters, but our program only wrote out 256 different codes, $00 through $FF, because this is the maximum number of values that can be represented by each 8-bit byte in our Video RAM.

As we see, the entire first row contains copies of a strange character. This first row equates to the ASCII control codes $00 through $1F, which are referred to as *non-printable characters*; for example, how would you display the **BEL** code, which was originally intended to actually ring a bell? In fact the character we display for these control codes could be anything we choose, but we decided to use something unusual so that it would be easily recognized.

The second, third, and fourth rows are predominantly filled with the alphanumeric, punctuation, and special symbol characters that we know and love. Note the first character on the second row, which is a space (ASCII code $20). Also note the last character on the fourth row, which is a **DEL** (ASCII code $7F), and which is represented by the same strange character we used for the other control codes on the first row.

That takes care of the ASCII characters, but we've still got another four rows of characters on the screen. Where did these come from? Well as we previously discussed, ASCII is a 7-bit code, which only uses the values $00 through $7F, but we're storing these characters in 8-bit bytes, so we've still got values $80 through $FF to play with. Many of the early computers used these spare characters to implement simple graphics and, as the resulting images were somewhat "chunky," these were often referred to as *chunky graphics* (Table 11.1).

$80		$90		$A0		$B0		$C0		$D0		$E0		$F0	
$81		$91		$A1		$B1		$C1		$D1		$E1		$F1	
$82		$92		$A2		$B2		$C2		$D2		$E2		$F2	
$83		$93		$A3		$B3		$C3		$D3		$E3		$F3	
$84		$94		$A4		$B4		$C4		$D4		$E4		$F4	
$85		$95		$A5		$B5		$C5		$D5		$E5		$F5	
$86		$96		$A6		$B6		$C6		$D6		$E6		$F6	
$87		$97		$A7		$B7		$C7		$D7		$E7		$F7	
$88		$98		$A8		$B8		$C8		$D8		$E8		$F8	
$89		$99		$A9		$B9		$C9		$D9		$E9		$F9	
$8A		$9A		$AA		$BA		$CA		$DA		$EA		$FA	
$8B		$9B		$AB		$BB		$CB		$DB		$EB		$FB	
$8C		$9C		$AC		$BC		$CC		$DC		$EC		$FC	
$8D		$9D		$AD		$BD		$CD		$DD		$ED		$FD	
$8E		$9E		$AE		$BE		$CE		$DE		$EE		$FE	
$8F		$9F		$AF		$BF		$CF		$DF		$EF		$FF	

Table 11.1: Chunky graphics codes

Note that there is no standard for this sort of thing, so computer designers typically make up their own set as they go along (the sneaky ones copy someone else's). Remember that each of these codes will be represented as some pattern of dots and spaces on the screen. Also remember that the size of each character on the screen is 15 dots by 10 dots. In the case of codes $80 through $BF, we decided to divide their associated characters into six chunks, and to walk through every possible permutation of these chunks being white and black; for example, consider the dots forming the character associated with code $99 (Figure 11.24a).

Similarly, in the case of codes $C0 through $CF, we decided to create some "line-art" characters (Figure 11.24b), and we also used the codes $D0 through $D3 to create "arrow" characters. We couldn't think of anything that we particularly wanted to do with the remaining codes, $D4 through $FF, so we simply assigned another unusual character to them in order to allow us to differentiate them from space characters.

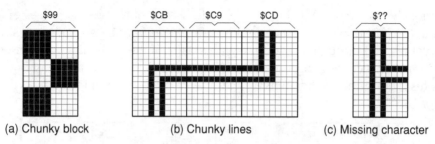

(a) Chunky block   (b) Chunky lines   (c) Missing character

Figure 11.24: Some chunky characters

Returning to our line-art, we created two sets of characters: thick single lines ($C0 through $C7) and thin double lines ($C8 through $CF). In both cases we've got vertical lines ($C0 and $C8), horizontal lines ($C1 and $C9), crossed lines ($C2 and $CA), right-angled corners ($C3 through $C6 and $CB through $CE), and simple boxes ($C7 and $CF). However, we unaccountably forgot to include any "T-junction" characters such as the one shown in Figure 11.24c. These characters can be very useful when creating formatted displays or mazes or whatever, so you might want to employ some of the unused codes ($D4 through $FF) to create them yourself when we describe how you can "burn" your own character ROM in Chapter 13.

Program to display characters from the QWERTY keyboard

Our next task is to read a single character from our QWERTY keyboard and display it on the screen. Purely for the sake of argument, let's say that we wish to display our character in the sixth column of the sixth row (six is our lucky number). In order to do this, we need to know the address in the Video RAM that corresponds to this position on the screen, which we calculate as follows:

a) We know that the base address of our Video RAM (the address of the character at row 0 column 0) is $EE00.

b) We know that we have sixteen rows numbered from 0 through 15, which means that the first row is actually referred to as *row 0*, the second row is *row 1*, the third row is *row 2*, and so on.

c) We know that each row contains thirty-two columns numbered from 0 through 31, which means that the first column is actually referred to as *column 0*, the second column is *column 1*, and so on.

d) This means that we can quickly calculate the address of column 0 on any row 'n' using the formula: *address = base address of Video RAM + ('n' x $20)*, where $20 is the hexadecimal equivalent of 32 in decimal. It's easy to see how this works by looking at the following examples:

Row ('n')	Formula	Resulting address
0	$EE00 + (0 x $20)	= $EE00 (row 0 col 0)
1	$EE00 + (1 x $20)	= $EE20 (row 1 col 0)
2	$EE00 + (2 x $20)	= $EE40 (row 2 col 0)
3	$EE00 + (3 x $20)	= $EE60 (row 3 col 0)
4	$EE00 + (4 x $20)	= $EE80 (row 4 col 0)
5	$EE00 + (5 x $20)	= $EEA0 (row 5 col 0)
:	:	:

Thus, as the sixth row is actually referred to as row 5, we know that the address of the first column on this row is going to be $EEA0.

e) Similarly, for any column 'm', we know that the address of that column is going to be equal to the address of column 0 on that row plus 'm'. Once again, it's easy to see how this works by looking at the following examples for the sixth row (*row 5*):

Column ('m')	Formula	Resulting address
0	$EEA0 + 0	= $EEA0 (row 5 col 0)
1	$EEA0 + 1	= $EEA1 (row 5 col 1)
2	$EEA0 + 2	= $EEA2 (row 5 col 2)
3	$EEA0 + 3	= $EEA3 (row 5 col 3)
4	$EEA0 + 4	= $EEA4 (row 5 col 4)
5	$EEA0 + 5	= $EEA5 (row 5 col 5)
:	:	:

Thus, as the sixth column is actually referred to as column 5, we know that the address of the sixth column on the sixth row is going to be $EEA5.

In the previous chapter we wrote a program to read a character from the keyboard and display its ASCII code on our dual 7-segment display. The program we're about to create is very similar, except for the additional instructions that call our clear screen subroutine, and the fact that we are going to store the character in our Video RAM instead of writing it to our dual 7-segment display (Figure 11.25).

The first instruction ($91 at address $4006) is an **LDA**, which loads the accumulator with a value from the input port that's connected to the

QWERTY keyboard (this port is located at address $F008). The second instruction ($D1 at address $4009) is a JZ ("*jump if zero*"), which will cause the program to jump back to the beginning of the loop if the accumulator contains $00 (which means that no key has been pressed on the keyboard).

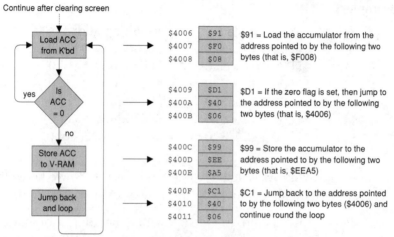

Figure 11.25: Reading and displaying a character from the keyboard

If a key has been pressed, the program will continue on to the third instruction ($99 at address $400C), which is a STA ("*store accumulator*"). This stores the contents of the accumulator to address $EEA5 which, as we discussed above, is the location in our Video RAM that corresponds to the sixth column on the 6th row. The last instruction ($C1 at address $400F) is a JMP ("*jump unconditionally*"), which returns the program to the start of the loop to wait for another key to be pressed.

Entering the program with the hex keypad

Due to the way in which our keypad and monitor program operate, the easiest way to enter our new program is to remove the old one first. Click the **Memory** item in the project window's menu bar, then click the **Purge Memory** entry in the resulting pull-down menu. Set the **Start Address** and **End Address** fields in the ensuing dialog box to $4006 and $4015, respectively; then click the **OK** button to purge these addresses and dismiss the form. Note that this will not affect the first part of our existing program in addresses $4000 through $4005 (the part that calls our clear screen subroutine), and it will also preserve the subroutine which occupies addresses $4D00 through $4D0C.

To enter the new program, click the **Address (Ad)** button on the hex keypad to make this field active, then enter the address $4006. Next click the keypad's **Data (Da)** button to make this field active, enter the data $91, and click the keypad's **Enter (Ent)** button. Continue to enter the remainder of the program from address $4007 onwards as shown below.

Address	Data	Instruction	Read keyboard and display ASCII value
$4000	$50	BLDSP (imm)	Load the stack pointer with $4FFF (the stack
$4001	$4F		pointer is a 16-bit register so it requires two
$4002	$FF		bytes)
$4003	$C9	JSR (abs)	Jump to the subroutine that's located at address
$4004	$4D		$4D00
$4005	$00		
$4006	$91	LDA (abs)	Load the accumulator from the input port
$4007	$F0		connected to the keyboard at address $F008
$4008	$08		
$4009	$D1	JZ (abs)	If the zero flag is set, then no key has been
$400A	$40		pressed, so jump to address $4006, otherwise
$400B	$06		continue to address $400C
$400C	$99	STA (abs)	Store the accumulator to the Video RAM at
$400D	$EE		address $EEA5 (the address corresponding to
$400E	$A5		the 6th column on the 6th row)
$400F	$C1	JMP (abs)	Jump back to the beginning of the loop at
$4010	$40		address $4006 and wait for another key to be
$4011	$06		pressed

Running the program with the hex keypad

Before we run this program, use the memory walker once again to view address $4D01 in our "clear screen" subroutine. Due to our previous modification, this location currently contains $2E, which is the ASCII code for a period. In order to stave off the boredom while our subroutine leisurely clears the screen, double-click on this data in the memory walker and change it back to $20, which is the ASCII code for a space. (Note that we'll introduce a much faster technique for clearing the screen in a little while.)

Click the keypad's **Address (Ad)** button to make the address field active, enter the start address of the program which is $4000, then click the **Run** button to let the *Beboputer* rip. The program first calls our clear screen subroutine, which works its way back from address $EFFF to address $EE00 loading $20 values, which are the ASCII codes for space characters. After clearing the screen, the program starts the loop that reads from the input port connected to the QWERTY keyboard.

Now click the Step (Stp) button on the hex keypad to place the *Beboputer* in it's step mode, then use the scroll bar on the memory walker to center address $EEA5 in the middle of the display (this is the location in the Video RAM that corresponds to row 6 column 6). Note that this location currently contains $20, which is the ASCII code for a space. Next click the Run (Ru) button on the hex keypad to return the *Beboputer* to it's run mode, then click the letter 'A' on the *Beboputer's* QWERTY keyboard and watch the corresponding character appear on the screen. Return the *Beboputer* to its step mode by clicking the Step (Stp) button on the hex keypad once again, and note that address $EEA5 in the memory walker now contains $41, which is the ASCII code for the letter 'A'. Finally, return the *Beboputer* to its run mode, then spend a while clicking keys on the keyboard and watching them appear on the screen. Continue to experiment until you're sated, then click the Reset (Rst) button on the hex keypad to return us to the monitor program.

Creating a very simple text editing program

Almost everyone who owns a contemporary computer employs a program called a wordprocessor to create documents ranging from letters to books. Today's wordprocessors are extremely sophisticated, providing us with the ability to change the size and style of the characters we use and to include pictures and charts in our documents, but they weren't always this way. In the not-so-distant past, the term "wordprocessor" was rarely used; instead we called these programs "text editors," because that was pretty much all they did.

Creating even a simple text editor with any degree of useful functionality is a far from trivial task. But just to give us a taste, we're going to write a rudimentary program that will allow us to add and delete characters on our screen. What we wish to do is to use some symbol to indicate the point where characters will be inserted (Figure 11.26a), and to add appropriate letters and advance the insertion point when a key is pressed on the keyboard (Figures 11.26b through 11.26f). Additionally, we wish to remove a character and cause the insertion point to fall back each time the Bspace ("Back-space") key is pressed (Figure 11.26g), thereby allowing us to correct mistakes (Figure 11.26h).

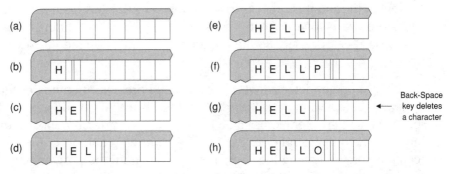

Figure 11.26: Simple text editing

The symbol we've decided to use to indicate the insertion point is one of our chunky line-art characters with a code of $C8, but you may feel free to change this to any of the other chunky graphics characters we looked at earlier in Table 11.1. The flowchart for this program may appear a bit scary at first, but it's really quite easy to understand (Figure 11.27).

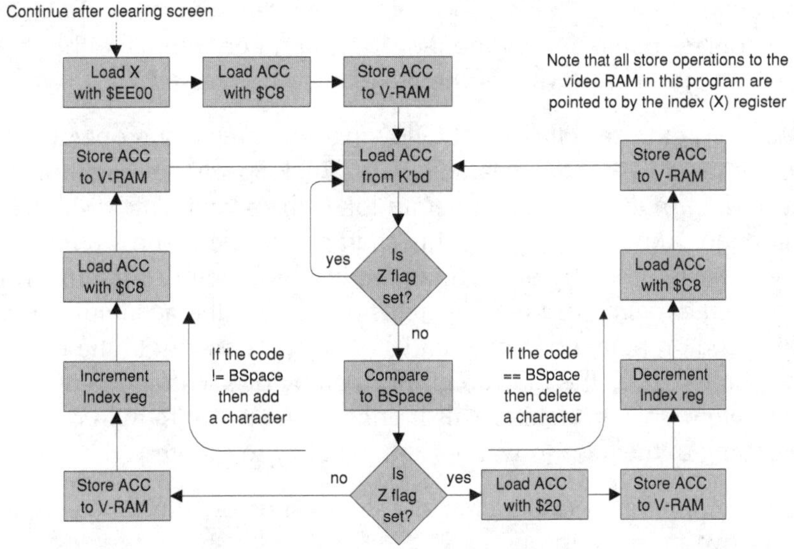

Figure 11.27: Flowchart for (very) rudimentary text editor

The first thing the program does after calling the clear screen subroutine is to load the index register with $EE00, which is the base address of our Video RAM. Next we load the accumulator with $C8, which is the ASCII code for the character we're using to indicate our insertion point, and we store this character to the address pointed to by the index register.

Now the program enters the loop that actually performs the editing function. The program first loads the accumulator from the input port connected to the keyboard, and then checks to see if the zero flag has been set to *logic 1*. If the zero flag is *logic 1*, then the accumulator contains $00 implying that no key has been pressed, so the program loops back to read the keyboard again.

Once the program detects that a key *has* been pressed, it compares the contents of the accumulator with $08, which is the ASCII code for a "Back Space" character. (Remember that a comparison instruction updates the carry and zero flags, but does not affect the current contents of the accumulator.) Following the comparison instruction, the program checks to see if the zero flag is set, which would indicate that the value in the accumulator is equal to the $08 "Back Space" character.

If the zero flag isn't set, the program knows that this character should be displayed (the left branch in our flowchart), so it stores the character to the address pointed to by the index register, thereby overwriting the insertion point character. The program then *increments* the index register, reloads the accumulator with the $C8 insertion point character, stores this character to the new address pointed to by the index register, and returns to the beginning of the loop to wait for the next key to be pressed.

Alternatively, if the zero flag is set following the comparison operation, then the program knows that this character is a "Back Space" (the right branch in our flowchart). In this case the program loads the accumulator with $20 (the ASCII code for a space) and saves this character to the address pointed to by the index register, thereby overwriting the insertion point character. The program then *decrements* the index register, reloads the accumulator with the $C8 insertion point character, and stores this character to the new address pointed to by the index register, thereby overwriting the original character we wished to delete. This branch of the program than returns to the beginning of the loop to wait for the next key to be pressed.

While you're entering this program as discussed below, take a few moments to ponder two more questions:

a) What do you expect to occur if you click more than thirty-two keys, which will fill the first row on the memory-mapped display?

b) What do you expect to occur if you click the **Bspace** ("Back Space") key more times than the number of characters you've entered?

Entering the program with the hex keypad

Once again, the easiest way to enter our new program is to first remove the old one. We'll start by clicking the RAM icon in the memory walker's toolbar, which returns us to the beginning of our program at address $4000. Now click the Memory item in the project window's menu bar, then click the Purge Memory entry in the resulting pull-down menu. Set the Start Address and End Address fields in the ensuing dialog box to $4006 and $4011, respectively, then click the OK button to purge these addresses and dismiss the form. Note that this will not affect the first part of our existing program in addresses $4000 through $4005 (the part that calls our clear screen subroutine), and it will also leave our subroutine intact. Also note that the memory walker now shows $XX values in the purged locations.

In order to enter the new program, click the Address (Ad) button on the hex keypad to make this field active, then enter the address $4006. Next click the keypad's Data (Da) button to make this field active, enter the data $A0, and click the keypad's Enter (Ent) button. Continue to enter the remainder of the program from address $4007 onwards as shown below.

Address	Data	Instruction	Read keyboard and display ASCII value
$4000	$50	BLDSP (imm)	Load the stack pointer with $4FFF (the stack
$4001	$4F		pointer is a 16-bit register, so it requires two
$4002	$FF		bytes)
$4003	$C9	JSR (abs)	Jump to the subroutine that's located at
$4004	$4D		address $4D00
$4005	$00		
$4006	$A0	BLDX (imm)	Load the index register with $EE00, the base
$4007	$EE		address of our Video RAM
$4008	$00		
$4009	$90	LDA (imm)	Load the accumulator with $C8, the ASCII
$400A	$C8		code for our insertion point character
$400B	$9A	STA (abs-x)	Store the contents of the accumulator (the
$400C	$00		insertion point character) to address $0000
$400D	$00		plus the current contents of the index register
$400E	$91	LDA (abs)	Load the accumulator from the input port
$400F	$F0		connected to the keyboard at address $F008
$4010	$08		
$4011	$D1	JZ (abs)	If the zero flag is set, then no key has been
$4012	$40		pushed, so jump back to address $400E;
$4013	$0E		otherwise continue to address $4014
$4014	$60	CMPA (imm)	Compare the contents of the accumulator to
$4015	$08		$08, the ASCII code for a "Back Space"

$4016	$D1	JZ (abs)	If the zero flag is set, then this was a "Back
$4017	$40		Space" character, so jump to address $4025;
$4018	$25		otherwise continue to address $4019
$4019	$9A	STA (abs-x)	Store the contents of the accumulator (the
$401A	$00		character to be added) to address $0000 plus
$401B	$00		the current contents of the index register
$401C	$82	INCX (imp)	Increment the contents of the index register
$401D	$90	LDA (imm)	Load the accumulator with $C8, the ASCII
$401E	$C8		code for our insertion point character
$401F	$9A	STA (abs-x)	Store the contents of the accumulator (the
$4020	$00		insertion point character) to address $0000
$4021	$00		plus the current contents of the index register
$4022	$C1	JMP (abs)	Jump back to the beginning of the loop at
$4023	$40		address $400E and wait for another key to
$4024	$0E		be pressed
$4025	$90	LDA (imm)	Load the accumulator with $20, which is
$4026	$20		the ASCII code for a space character
$4027	$9A	STA (abs-x)	Store the contents of the accumulator (the
$4028	$00		space character) to address $0000 plus the
$4029	$00		current contents of the index register
$402A	$83	DECX (imp)	Decrement the contents of the index register
$402B	$90	LDA (imm)	Load the accumulator with $C8, the ASCII
$402C	$C8		code for our insertion point character
$402D	$9A	STA (abs-x)	Store the contents of the accumulator (the
$402E	$00		insertion point character) to address $0000
$402F	$00		plus the current contents of the index register
$4030	$C1	JMP (abs)	Jump back to the beginning of the loop at
$4031	$40		address $400E and wait for another key to
$4032	$0E		be pressed

Running the program with the hex keypad

Before we run this program, use the memory walker to once again view
address $4D01 in our "clear screen" subroutine. As before, in order to make
things more interesting while our subroutine clears the screen, we want you
to change the contents of this location from $20 (space) back to $2E
(period).

Now click the keypad's **Address (Ad)** button to make the address field active,
enter the start address of the program, which is $4000, then click the **Run**
button. After clearing the screen (or filling it with periods, depending on
your point of view), the program writes the $C8 code for the insertion
character to location $EE00 in the Video RAM, which corresponds to row 0

column 0 on the screen. The program then starts the loop that reads from the input port connected to the QWERTY keyboard.

Make sure that the **ALT** and **CRTL** keys on the keyboard are inactive (their annotations should be black; if not, click these keys to make them inactive). Similarly ensure that the **CAPS** key is active. Now click the letter 'H', which will appear at row 0 column 0 on the screen, while the insertion character moves to row 0 column 1.

Click the letters 'E', 'L', 'L', 'O' in turn to complete the word "HELLO", and observe their characters appearing on the screen. Keep clicking on letters and spaces to form a message to yourself until the $C8 insertion character appears in the rightmost column of the first row, then pause for a moment of thought.

What do you expect to happen if you add more characters? Click another letter on the keyboard. The corresponding character appears in the last column on row 0, while the insertion character moves to the first column on row 1. Similarly, if you click yet another letter, *it* appears at row 1 column 0 and the insertion point character moves one column to the right.

The point is that our program doesn't understand anything about the rows and columns on the screen – it's only purpose it to store each ASCII code it reads from the keyboard into the next free memory location in the Video RAM. Meanwhile, our virtual video card knows enough to take whatever codes it finds in locations $EE00 through $EE1F and display the corresponding characters on the first row of the screen; then to take whatever codes it finds in locations $EE20 through $EE3F and display the corresponding characters on the second row, and so on.

Now click the **BSpace** key on the keyboard and observe the last character being deleted from the screen. Keep clicking the **BSpace** key until all of the characters have been deleted and the insertion character once again occupies row 0 column 0.

What do you expect to happen if you click the **BSpace** key again? Try it. As you'll see, the insertion character disappears from the screen. What just happened? Well once again, our program doesn't understand anything about the Video RAM – all it's doing when it sees a BSpace code is to overwrite the memory location currently being pointed to by the index register with a $20 ASCII space code, and to relocate the insertion point character to the previous memory location. Thus, when we clicked the **BSpace** key, the $C8 code for our insertion character was stored into location $EDFF.

Now try clicking the letter 'H' again, and see the insertion character reappear on the screen. In this case, clicking the 'H' key caused the $48 ASCII code associated with this key to be written into location $EDFF, while the $C8 code associated with the insertion point was stored into location $EE00, at which point it reappeared on the screen.

In this case no harm was done, because we weren't using location $EDFF anyway. But had we been using this location for something like the beginning of our stack, the results could have been catastrophic (in programming terms). Thus, if this had been a real text editor, we would have included some error checking instructions to ensure that a user couldn't do this sort of thing.

Continue to experiment until you're bored, then click the Reset (Rst) button on the hex keypad to return us to the monitor program.

The medium-resolution color graphics mode

Thus far we've been treating our video card as a fairly simple device that monitors a selected portion of the *Beboputer's* memory and blindly translates the ASCII codes it finds there into characters that it displays on the screen. But there's a bit more to it than this, because the video board also has a medium-resolution color graphics mode.

The way in which you access this mode is discussed in more detail in the next section of this chapter. Suffice it to say that, in its medium-resolution mode, the screen contains 48 rows x 64 columns of square "blocks," each of which can be individually set to its own color (Figure 11.28).

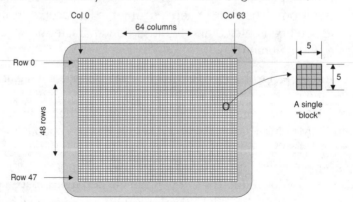

Figure 11.28: Rows and columns of "blocks" in color graphics mode

As a point of interest, each block in this medium-resolution mode is 5 x 5 of our pixels, which means that six of these blocks could be combined to form one of the "chunky graphics" characters we used in the text mode. However, this relationship is more by chance than by design (and if you believe that you'll believe anything).

Having 48 rows x 64 columns results in a grand total of 3,072 blocks. There are several different techniques we could use to map the *Beboputer's* memory to these blocks. Some of these techniques would be more efficient than others (in terms of memory usage), but these efficient techniques can be difficult to understand and use. Thus, we decided to employ a somewhat inefficient scheme, which uses one byte for each block, meaning that we will require 3,072 bytes of the *Beboputer's* memory (Figure 11.29).

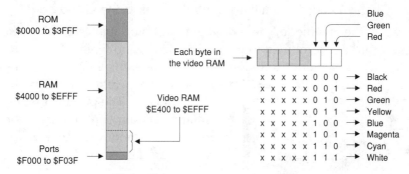

Figure 11.29: The video RAM for medium-resolution graphics mode

In turn, this means that when the video card is in its medium-resolution graphics mode, the base address for the Video RAM is $E400. The reason our mapping scheme is somewhat inefficient is that we're only using the three least-significant bits of each byte in the Video RAM (the video card simply ignores the contents of the five most-significant bits). In the case of the bits we're using, each bit corresponds to a different primary color, where a *logic 0* means the color is OFF and a *logic 1* means it's ON.

The video card's control codes

When power is first applied to the video card, it "wakes up" in its default configuration, which is text mode, black characters on a white background, and assuming the Video RAM occupies addresses $EE00 through $EFFF in the *Beboputer's* memory. As we've already seen, we can use the video card in this default mode without doing anything more than writing ASCII codes or our chunky graphics codes into the appropriate part of the RAM. But the

Beboputer can also send instructions to the video card in the form of control codes through the output port at address $F028 (Figure 11.30).

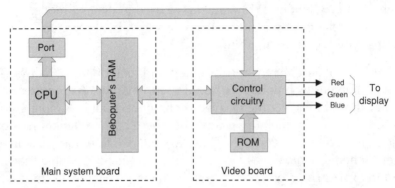

Figure 11.30: Transmitting control codes to the video card

Note that in the text mode, the red, green, and blue signals coming out of the video card are combined to give us our black and white characters. Also note that in the medium-resolution graphics mode, the video card's control circuitry ignores the character ROM and simply generates our colored blocks on-the-fly. The point is that by transmitting certain control codes, the *Beboputer* can modify the way in which the video card functions (Table 11.2)

Code	Description
$02	Text mode (default)
$03	Graphics mode
$04	Default video
$05	Inverse video
$08	Default base address
$09	Alternate base address
$10	Clear screen

Table 11.2: Control codes

As we've already noted, the default mode for the video card is to treat the 512 bytes of data in memory locations $EE00 through $EFFF as ASCII codes, and (in conjunction with the character ROM) to display the corresponding characters for these codes on the screen.

If the *Beboputer* writes a control code of $03 to the output port at address $F028, this will instruct the video card to switch to its graphics mode (writing a code of $02 will instruct the video card to return to its text mode).

Similarly, writing a control code of $05 to the output port will instruct the video card to change to its inverse video mode, which will cause it to display white characters on a black background[13] (writing a code of $04 will instruct the video card to return to its default mode of black text on a white background). Note that if the video card is in its graphics mode, then

---

[13]This can be easily achieved by passing the output from the shift register in Figure 11.18 to one input of an XOR gate whose other input is presented with a *logic 1* value.

the inverse video mode will cause any color that is normally ON to be turned OFF, and vice versa.

To further extend the video card's repertoire, the *Beboputer* can instruct it to use an alternate base address for the Video RAM by transmitting a control code of $09 (a control code of $08 returns the video card to the default base address). As for the "inverse video" control code, the "base address" control codes are context-sensitive, depending on whether the video card is in text mode or graphics mode. In text mode the default base address is $EE00 and the alternate base address is $EC00; in graphics mode the default base address is $E400 and the alternate base address is $D800 (Figure 11.31).

One advantage of being able to change the Video RAM's base address in this manner is that the *Beboputer* can construct an entire screen of information in whichever area of memory the video card isn't currently using, and then quickly display this new data by simply instructing the video card to switch its base address.

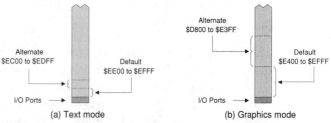

Figure 11.31: Default versus alternate video RAM configurations

Finally, the "clear screen" control code of $10 instructs the video card to take control of the *Beboputer's* RAM for a short time, and to clear all of the memory locations (thereby saving us the effort of having to write a clear screen subroutine). Once again, this control code is context-sensitive:

a) It will only clear the Video RAM that is currently in use. For example, if the video card is in text mode and using the default base address, then the clear screen control code will clear addresses $EE00 through $EEFF. Similarly, if the video card is in graphics mode and using the alternate base address, then the clear screen control code will clear addresses $D800 through $E3FF.

b) If the video card is in text mode, the clear screen control code will cause it to load the appropriate video RAM locations with $20 characters (which are ASCII codes for spaces). However, if the video card is in graphics mode, then the clear screen control code will cause it to load the appropriate Video RAM locations with $00 characters (which will set all of the graphics blocks to the color black).

Program to flaunt the medium-resolution mode

To close this lab, we're going to create a simple program that uses our screen's medium-resolution mode. This program is based on a software implementation of an 8-bit *linear-feedback shift register (LFSR)*, which we can use to generate pseudo-random numbers in the range 1 to 255.[14]

What we intend to do is to use this number generator to randomly select blocks on our screen, and to load these blocks with random colors (excluding white). Our program will also highlight whichever block it's currently playing with by making it turn white, and then set it to whatever color has been selected.

To keep this program as simple as possible, we're only going to play with the four rows (256 blocks) at the top of the screen, which occupy addresses $E400 through $E4FF in the Video RAM (assuming the default base address). However, just to make life interesting, we're *not* going to provide a flowchart, because this is one of the tasks we've set for you in the quiz at the end of the chapter.

Entering the program with the hex keypad

Before we enter this program, we wish to remove all traces of our previous exercises. Click the **Memory** item in the project window's menu bar, then click the **Purge Memory** entry in the resulting pull-down menu. Select the **Purge All** option, then click the **OK** button to purge the entire memory and dismiss the form. (Note that the memory-mapped display fills with random characters again, because we've just randomized all of the *Beboputer's* memory, including the Video RAM.)

Click the **Address (Ad)** button on the hex keypad, enter the address $4000, click the keypad's **Data (Da)** button, enter the data $90, click the keypad's **Enter (Ent)** button to load this data, then continue to enter the remainder of the program from address $4001 onwards as shown below.

Address	Data	Instruction	Initialize the video card
$4000	$90	LDA (imm)	Load the accumulator with the $03 control
$4001	$03		code, which sets the video card into graphics mode
$4002	$99	STA (abs)	Store the contents of the accumulator to

[14]The theory of linear-feedback shift registers was introduced in this book's companion volume: *Bebop to the Boolean Boogie (An Unconventional Guide to Electronics)*.

Address	Data	Instruction	
$4003	$F0		address $F028, which is the address of the
$4004	$28		output port that's connected to the video card.
$4005	$90	LDA (imm)	Load the accumulator with the $10 control
$4006	$10		code, which tells the video card to clear the screen
$4007	$99	STA (abs)	Store the contents of the accumulator to
$4008	$F0		address $F028, which is the address of the
$4009	$28		output port that's connected to the video card.
Address	**Data**	**Instruction**	**Generate a pseudo-random number**
$400A	$90	LDA (imm)	Load the accumulator with an initial value of $01
$400B	$01		
$400C	$70	SHL (imp)	Shift the contents of the accumulator left one bit
$400D	$E6	JNC (abs)	If the carry bit isn't set, then jump to address
$400E	$40		$4012, otherwise continue to address $4010
$400F	$12		
$4010	$40	XOR (imm)	XOR the contents of the accumulator with $1D
$4011	$1D		
$4012	$99	STA (abs)	Store the contents of the accumulator to
$4013	$40		address $4035. This location is going to form
$4014	$35		the least significant byte of our target address
Address	**Data**	**Instruction**	**Highlight the selected block (set it to white)**
$4015	$90	LDA (imm)	Load the accumulator with $07, which equates
$4016	$07		to a white block
$4017	$9B	STA (ind)	Store the contents of the accumulator to the
$4018	$40		address pointed to by the two bytes at $4034
$4019	$34		and $4035 (note that this instruction uses the indirect addressing mode)
Address	**Data**	**Instruction**	**Set the selected block to a random color**
$401A	$91	LDA (abs)	Load the accumulator with the contents of
$401B	$40		address $4035 (the least-significant byte of our
$401C	$35		target address and also our random number)
$401D	$30	AND (imm)	AND the contents of the accumulator with $07
$401E	$07		(to extract the three least-significant bits)
$401F	$60	CMPA (imm)	Compare the contents of the accumulator with
$4020	$07		$07 to see if the random color is white
$4021	$D6	JNZ (abs)	If the zero flag isn't set (which means that the
$4022	$40		color isn't white), then jump to address $4026,
$4023	$26		otherwise continue to address $4024
$4024	$90	LDA (imm)	The color was white, so load the accumulator
$4025	$01		with $01, which equates to a color of red

Address	Data	Instruction	
$4026	$9B	STA (ind)	Store the contents of the accumulator to the address pointed to by the two bytes at $4034 and $4035 (note that this instruction uses the indirect addressing mode)
$4027	$40		
$4028	$34		
$4029	$91	LDA (abs)	Load the accumulator with the contents of address $4035 (the least-significant byte of our target address and also our random number)
$402A	$40		
$402B	$35		
$402C	$60	CMPA (imm)	Compare the contents of the accumulator with $01 to see if we've returned to our starting point
$402D	$01		
$402E	$D6	JNZ (abs)	If the zero flag isn't set (which means that there are more random numbers), then jump to address $400C, otherwise continue to address $4031
$402F	$40		
$4030	$0C		
$4031	$C1	JMP (abs)	Jump immediately to address $0000, which is the start address of our monitor program in ROM (just like hitting a reset)
$4032	$00		
$4033	$00		
Address	**Data**	**Instruction**	**Save two bytes to be used as indirect address**
$4034	$E4	-------	Don't bother loading anything into address $4035, because our program will do this for us (see below)
$4035	$XX	-------	

The only really unusual aspect to this program (compared to those in earlier labs) is the use of the indirect addressing mode for some of the load and store instructions (indirect addressing was introduced in Chapter 8). Let's look at this in a little more detail. When we key in the program, we leave the memory location at address $4035 containing unknown values (indicated by $XX).

The first thing our program does is to write two control codes to our video card. These codes instruct the video card to enter its medium-resolution graphics mode and to clear the Video RAM. Next we generate a pseudo-random number between 1 and 255 (or between $01 and $FF in hexadecimal). Our program then stores this value to the location at address $4035 using a **STA** instruction with the absolute addressing mode ($99 at address $4012) (Figure 11.32a).

In this figure we've used $?? to indicate the fact that location $4035 has now been loaded with some value (our pseudo-random number), but that we aren't particularly concerned as to exactly what this value is. The program then loads the accumulator with $07, which equates to a color of white ($90 at address $4015), and then stores this value using a **STA** instruction with the indirect addressing mode ($9B at address $4017) (Figure 11.32b).

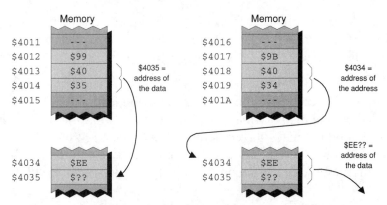

Figure 11.32: Use of absolute and indirect addressing

As usual, the *Beboputer* recognizes this instruction's operands ($40 and $34 at addresses $4018 and $4019) as representing the address $4034. Furthermore, due to the fact that this store instruction uses the indirect addressing mode, the *Beboputer* understands that this location actually contains the most-significant byte of the address that it's really looking for. Thus, the *Beboputer* next reads the $EE and $?? at addresses $4034 and $4035, uses these as its real target address of $EE??, and stores the contents of the accumulator to the location at *this* address. Now remembering that we're using $?? to represent a pseudo-random number between $01 and $FF, this means that we've just loaded the code for a white block into our Video RAM at one of the addresses between $EE01 and $EEFF; that is, to one of the blocks on the first four rows of our screen.

The program then generates a random color (excluding white), and stores this color to the same location in the Video RAM (search through the program listing to find the second store using the indirect addressing mode). The program continues to loop around, loading random locations with random colors, until it's cycled through every value of $01 through $FF, at which point it terminates by jumping back to our monitor program.

Running the program with the hex keypad

Use the memory walker to zoom up to the start of the Video RAM for the graphics screen at location $E400. Note the random values in the Video RAM, then return the memory walker to the start of our program at location $4000.

Now click the keypad's **Address (Ad)** button to make the address field active and enter the start address of the program at $4000, then click the **Step (Stp)** button on the hex keypad. This executes the first instruction, which loads the accumulator with the control code that will place our memory-mapped display into its graphics mode. Note the chevrons that appear in the memory walker at address $4002, which contains the opcode for our next instruction.

Click the Step button again, thereby executing the instruction that writes our control code to the memory-mapped display. As soon as the display enters its graphics mode, it reads the contents of the Video RAM (which currently contains random values) and draws the corresponding colored blocks on the screen. This may take a few seconds, so sit back and watch the blocks appear.

Now click the Step button once more, which causes the accumulator to be loaded with our clear code, then click Step one more time to write this code to the memory-mapped display. As we see, the screen clears almost immediately, because this time our virtual graphics card is doing all of the work. Use the memory walker to return to address $E400, and observe that the Video RAM now contains $00 values, which were placed there by the video card when it received the clear code.

Now click the Run button and watch our program do its cunning stuff. As you will see, although our program does write the colored blocks to random locations, the actual result consists of vertical colored lines, but this is just a by-product of the particular shift-register algorithm we used.

When all of the blocks on the first four rows have been loaded with colored blocks, our program will automatically return the *Beboputer* to its reset mode. You can run this program again if you wish, although this time you might decide to make greater use of the Step button, so as to examine what the program is doing in more detail. When you've had your fill, click the keypad's ON button (which also turns it OFF), then exit this laboratory by clicking the File item on the project window's menu bar followed by the Exit entry in the resulting pull-down menu.

Memory-mapped displays versus modern monitors

Although we've been talking about memory-mapped displays as though they're historical curiosities, these devices are still found in some "cheap and cheerful" applications such as automatic teller machines at banks. Of course, we don't use these displays in our home computers anymore, because we've grown to expect, nay demand, sophisticated user-interfaces and high-resolution graphics.[15]

However, simply demanding something doesn't necessarily mean that you're going to get it – a number of developments had to occur and technologies had to mature for us to reach the present state-of-play. First of all manufacturing techniques improved, allowing computer monitors to have smaller pixels and more pixels-per-inch than was previously achievable. This means that today's monitors have high resolutions and can display images with great precision. Perhaps more importantly, the amount of memory we can squeeze into a single silicon chip has increased enormously, while the cost of such devices has plummeted dramatically. Finally, modern computers are tremendously faster and more powerful than their predecessors.

As we previously discussed, modern computers typically contain a circuit board called a graphics card, which contains a substantial amount of memory and its own on-board microprocessor. Thus, all your main system has to do is to send an instruction to the processor on the graphics card saying something like *"Draw me a purple circle with 'this' diameter at 'that' location on the screen."* The graphics processor then slogs away completing the task while the system's main processor is left free to work on something else.

The combination of high-resolution monitors and graphics cards means that today's computer screens can have millions of pixels, each of which can be individually set to thousands or even millions of colors. The fact that the graphics card can individually address each pixel means we can create all sorts of sophisticated effects, such as changing the size and font of characters on a character-by-character basis and dynamically varying the spacing between characters, because each character can be individually drawn pixel-by-pixel. Furthermore, these high-resolution displays support today's graphical user interfaces, such as the one employed by the *Beboputer*, which both enhance and simplify the human-machine interface.

So, just what is a pixel anyway?

As we previously noted, the term "pixel" is a somewhat slippery customer when it comes to computers. For example, many home computers arrive

---

[15]Note that we're only considering terminals based on video tubes here; other technologies such as liquid crystal and active matrix displays play by a different set of rules (and these technologies are outside the scope of this book).

with a default setting of 640 x 480 pixels. However, when you installed the *Beboputer* (as discussed in Appendix A), we recommended that you change this setting to a minimum of 800 x 600 pixels. Similarly, while you were instigating this change, you may have noticed other options such as 720 x 512 pixels, 1024 x 768 pixels, and so on.

Obviously the number of physical dots on your screen remains constant, but you can instruct your computer to use larger or smaller groups of these dots to represent a pixel. Increasing the number of pixels that you're using (by using more groups, each of which contains fewer dots) means that you can display finer details, but it also means that you require more memory on your video card.

Quick quiz #11

1) Summarize the process of reproducing images using Nipkow disks.

2) Summarize the functions of the electron gun, grid, deflection plates, and shadow mask in a video tube.

3) Considering the raster scan technique shown in Figure 11.2, can you suggest an alternative path we could make the spot (electron beam) follow?

4) Describe the difference between the additive, subtractive, and psychological primary colors.

5) Summarize the main features of a memory-mapped display.

6) Why did the early memory-mapped displays commonly support 80 columns of characters?

7) Assuming that the video card is in its graphics mode and using its default base address for this mode, how would you calculate the Video RAM address for the graphic block in the mth column of the nth row?

8) Create a flowchart that illustrates the major actions performed by the last program in this chapter (the one that randomly places colored blocks on the memory-mapped display).

9) With regard to the previous question, how could we modify this program such that it never generates a black color?

10) With regard to the previous question, why would it be such a pain to actually perform these modifications?

Chapter 12

Assembly Language and Stuff

In this chapter we will discover:

What is the difference between machine code and
assembly language

How we defined the *Beboputer's* assembly language

How to assemble programs by hand

Whether you should hand-edit your first assembler or
hand-assemble your first editor

How to use the *Beboputer's* CPU Register display and
messaging utility

How to use the *Beboputer's* breakpoint capability

Cross-assemblers, macro assemblers, meta-
assemblers, and disassemblers

Linkers, loaders, and relocatable code

Contents of Chapter 12

---

[1]Etch-A-Sketch is a registered trademark of the Ohio Art Company.

Machine code is a pain

Thus far we've entered all of our programs as a motley collection of numerical values. This style of representation is known as *machine language* or *machine code*, because this is the form that is directly understood and executed by the machine (computer). It probably hasn't escaped your notice that working with machine code is only slightly more fun than banging your head against a wall. Whenever we wish to use an instruction like an **LDA** (load accumulator), we first have to decide which addressing mode we wish to use and then spend an inordinate amount of time rooting around to determine the opcode corresponding to that particular flavor of the instruction (Figure 12.1).

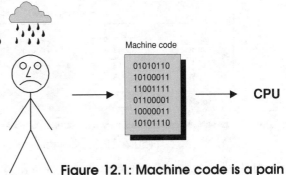

Working with machine code is time-consuming and prone to error, and programs written using this technique can be extremely difficult to understand and modify.

Figure 12.1: Machine code is a pain

One of the main problems with machine code is that humans tend to find it difficult to conceptualize things purely in terms of numbers; we much prefer to describe things using symbolic representations consisting of words and symbols. Thus, we would ideally prefer to describe our programs at a high level of abstraction (along the lines of "*First do this, then do that, then do….*") and then translate them into machine code for the computer to ruminate on (Figure 12.2).

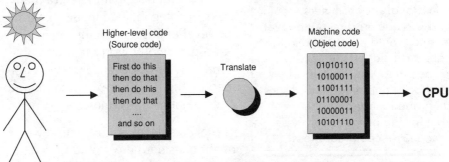

Figure 12.2: Higher-level code turns your frown upside down

Note the use of the terms *source* and *object* in this illustration. We previously introduced these terms in relation to teleprinters and paper tapes way back in Chapter 4. However, in the context of our current discussions, *source language* or *source code* refers to programs represented in a textual-symbolic form amenable to being understood by human beings.

Varying levels of language abstraction

Having decided that we would like to escape from the machine code maze, we must determine the type of source language we wish to use. One way of categorizing computer languages is by the level of abstraction they can represent (Figure 12.3).

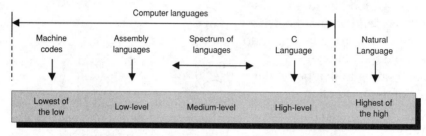

Figure 12.3: Varying levels of abstraction

At the lowest level of the hierarchy we find machine codes, in which everything is represented in terms of numbers. One step up the evolutionary ladder are assembly languages, which are to be the focus of this chapter. In some respects assembly languages may be considered only a small improvement over machine codes, but in other respects we may regard them as being a quantum leap. Purely for the sake of comparison, we might consider the C programming language as being fairly representative of a high-level computer language. But we should note that there are a whole slew of programming languages (some of which are far more sophisticated than C), and also that there are many ways of categorizing languages besides the level of abstraction they can represent. (Don't worry if you're not familiar with C, because we won't be mentioning it again, except for a couple of concept-level examples.)

Many professional programmers would only regard C as being a medium-level language, and would point to object-oriented and artificial-intelligence (AI) languages as being truly high-level. We could spend days debating these issues and grading one language against another, but for the purposes of these discussions ...... we could care less!

The highest level of abstraction we might consider here would be a *natural language*, such as written English. Unfortunately, the present state of our technology does not allow us to use a natural language for programming purposes, because such languages contain numerous ambiguities and logical inadequacies. For this reason we use symbolic languages, which are similar in concept to natural languages, but which are highly formalized in terms of their *syntax* and *semantics*. In this context, the term "syntax" refers to the grammar of the language, such as the *ordering* of the words and symbols in relation to each other, while the term "semantics" refers to the underlying *meaning* of the words and symbols and the relationships between the things they denote. Good grief, you're looking awfully serious all of a sudden – stop worrying and consider a simple example (Table 12.1).

Machine code	Assembly code	C code	Natural language
$4000 $91	LDA [i]	i = i + j;	Add the contents
$4001 $??	ADD [j]		of the variable 'j' to
$4002 $??	STA [i]		the existing contents
			of the variable 'i'
$4003 $11			
$4004 $??			
$4005 $??			
	Note that the " $400x " values in the machine code example indicate		
$4006 $99	hexadecimal addresses. Similarly, the "??" values would actually be		
$4007 $??	used to point to the memory locations of the 'i' and 'j' variables		
$4008 $??			

Table 12.1: Varying levels of abstraction

Note that these examples are assumed to be segments of a larger program. Also note that the variables 'i' and 'j' are assumed to refer to 1-byte quantities that have been declared elsewhere in the program (these quantities equate to memory locations that have been set aside to hold numbers in the machine code example).

Besides the fact that machine code is difficult to understand and you tend to have to enter a lot of it in order to get anything done, this code is also machine-dependent, which means that it will only run on the specific type of computer for which it was created. Similarly, although the assembly version is easier to understand and more compact, it also is machine-dependent, because each assembly instruction is directly related to a machine-code counterpart (there are higher-level assembly languages that don't strictly follow this rule, but we aren't concerned with those here). By comparison, the C version is both concise and easy to understand, and has the added advantage that it's portable between different types of computers, because each type of computer has its own special translator (Figure 12.4).

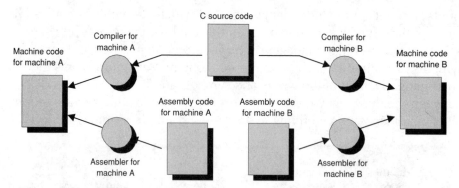

Figure 12.4: Unlike assembly code, C code is machine independent

If your source code is in assembly language, then the translator program that converts it into machine code is called an *assembler* (because it "assembles" the statements into machine code). By comparison, if your source code is in a high-level language like C, then the translator program is called a *compiler* (because it "compiles" the C statements into machine code). In reality, assemblers and compilers are just special flavors of translators which function in slightly different ways. Note that the machine code generated by an assembler and a compiler would rarely be byte-for-byte identical; we just illustrated it this way for simplicity. The reason that the resulting machine code may differ is because the source code fed into the C compiler is specified at a high level of abstraction, and the compiler may well make different decisions to the ones you make whilst creating your assembly source. In fact some compilers actually generate assembly source code as their output, which is then fed into an assembler to be translated into machine code. Irrespective of the route taken, the resulting machine code should ultimately generate the same functional results.

To place this in perspective, let's consider a simple analogy that's reasonably close to home. If you happen to be a devotee of American football (and who amongst us isn't?), you'll know that each team has a set of special codes they use to call or modify plays. For example, the quarterback may shout something like *"Red 32, Gold 57, Green 26, Hup"* (where the "Hup" sounds like a loud burp and signifies that he's voiced all the wisdom he wishes to impart at this time). In certain respects we might compare the play to a program, while the team might be a machine whose task it is to execute that program (Figure 12.5).

The point is that the codes above are team (machine) dependent. If we magically dropped our quarterback in the midst of another team, either they wouldn't understand anything he said, or, as a worse-case scenario, they might recognize some of the codes, but they would actually have been trained to respond to these codes in different ways than the first team. By comparison, consider what would happen if the quarterback had specified his play (program) at a higher level of abstraction;

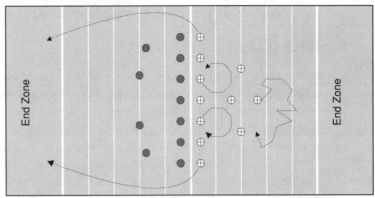

Figure 12.5: American football baffles the unwary

for example: *"I want the wide receivers to run towards the other team's end zone, I want the guards to confuse the issue by running around in ever-decreasing circles, and I want the full back to wander around in an aimless sort of way."* Irrespective of whether such a play actually makes sense (and remembering that any analogy is suspect and this one doubly so), the fact is that specifying the play at this high level of abstraction means that it's now portable across teams (machines).

All of the above would lead us to assume that high-level languages are more efficacious in every way than assembly-level representations. However, learning a high-level language like C to the extent that you'd be considered dangerous isn't something you tend to do over the weekend, and writing a compiler for such a language is a non-trivial task. Also, creating programs in assembly teaches you an awful lot about how computers work, and can be a whole bunch of fun in its own self-effacing way. The upshot of this is that the remainder of this chapter is devoted to specifying an assembly language for the *Beboputer*, and then using said language to create programs.

For those readers who aren't familiar with American football, the following gems of wisdom will hopefully serve to clarify the situation. American football bears a passing resemblance to English Rugby, except that the Americans have a penchant for excessive amounts of body armor and tend to pass the ball forwards (they also spend an inordinate amount of time performing Monty Python-style walks when they actually score).

By some strange quirk of fate, neither of these games in any way resembles Australian Rules football, which is played on an elliptical pitch and has more goal-posts than you can swing a stick at. In what many regard as one of the finest examples of Antipodean humor, Australian Rules football is distinguished by the fact that it doesn't appear to have any rules at all!

A few examples before we plunge into the fray

Before we delve into the depths, we should point out that programming in assembly language isn't going to be anywhere as difficult as you probably fear. There's nothing magical about any of this (except, of course, the fact that it works). This is *our* assembly language that *we're* specifying, so the way it looks and the things it is capable of are absolutely in our hands.[1] We should also note that the act of defining the language does not directly dictate the way in which we eventually go about translating it into machine code (we'll return to consider this point a little later). Perhaps the easiest way to kick things off is by means of a few simple examples, commencing with the program shown in Figure 12.6.

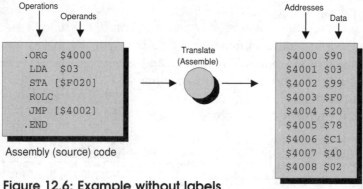

Figure 12.6: Example without labels

Note that we're showing the machine code on the right in hexadecimal for our convenience, but the computer would actually see this in binary. Also note that the object file wouldn't actually contain any addresses in the way they're shown here — we just added them for purposes of clarity. Bearing these points in mind, the resulting machine code is identical to the very first program you created for the *Beboputer*, way back in those mists of time we used to call Chapter 3. Thus, the assembly code on the left is also identical to our first program, it's just presented in a slightly different way. First, the .ORG $4000 statement informs us that this program will commence at location $4000 (where **ORG** is an abbreviation for "origin"). Similarly, the **.END** statement is used to let everyone know when we've finished the program.

---

[1]At some stage in the future you may decide that you can create a much better assembly language and assembler program for the *Beboputer* than we did — and why not?

LDA is the mnemonic we decided we'd use to represent the *load accumulator* instruction back in Chapter 8, but this is where things start to get a little crafty. As you will recall, we have several flavors of the load accumulator instruction, depending on the addressing mode we wish to use (such as *immediate*, *absolute*, *indexed*, and so on). One way we could handle this would be to create different mnemonics for each flavor of instruction, such as LDA_imm, LDA_abs, and so forth, but this would be something of a pain to use. One very common alternative is to employ only a single mnemonic such as LDA, and to then qualify the flavor we want to use by the way in which we specify the operand. In the case of our language, we decided that if an instruction mnemonic is simply followed by a number, then this will be understood to mean that we wish to use the immediate addressing mode. Thus, LDA $03 means: *"Load the accumulator with the hexadecimal value $03."* However, if we decide to use the absolute addressing mode to load the accumulator with the contents of a particular memory location (for example, from address $F000, which is the input port that's connected to our 8-bit switch device), then we will say LDA [$F000], where the square brackets indicate that the operand is actually an address.

This explains the STA [$F020] statement, which translates to: *"Store the accumulator to the memory location at address $F020"* (where you may recognize address $F020 as being the output port that's connected to our 8-bit LED display). Of course, the ROLC instruction doesn't have an operand, because this instruction only has an implied addressing mode and means: *"Rotate the contents of the accumulator one bit to the left and through the carry flag."*

Last but not least, the JMP [$4002] instruction means: *"Jump unconditionally to address $4002."* Why address $4002? ...... because this is the address of the first byte in the STA instruction (and this is what we did in Chapter 3). We can work out the address of this instruction from the fact that the .ORG $4000 statement tells us that the program starts at address $4000, and we know that the LDA $03 instruction will only occupy two bytes (at addresses $4000 and $4001), so the STA instruction has to start at address $4002.

What a pain and what a swizz! This is scarcely easier than entering the program in machine code. If this is all assembly code has to offer, then we may as well pack everything up and stop now. In reality this only serves to emphasize the fact that this was a rudimentary example, because there is, of course, a lot more to our assembly language than this.

Now consider an alternative version of our program using an address label, which you should find more pleasing to your palate (Figure 12.7).

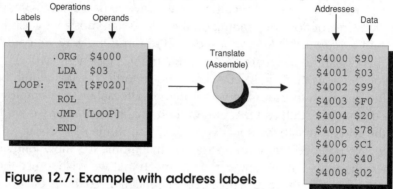

Figure 12.7: Example with address labels

Although we've modified the source, the resulting machine code is identical to that of our previous example. Also note that when a label is first declared, it is terminated by a colon ':' character, but this character doesn't form part of the label's name and is not used thereafter. When the assembler is wandering through our source file we say that it's *parsing the file*, where the term "parse" comes from the Latin *pars*, meaning "part." In this context, "parsing the file" means that the assembler analyses each of our source statements and splits them into their component parts, then determines the grammatical function of each part and its syntactic relationship to each of the other parts. Now all of this may sound a bit highfalutin, but the point is that when our assembler sees the label **LOOP**, it understands that we're associating this label with the **STA** instruction. Furthermore, the assembler understands that we want to associate **LOOP** with the address of the first byte in the **STA** instruction and remember that address for future reference. (When we say the assembler "*understands this*" and "*understands that,*" we actually mean that we've created it in such a way that this is what it will do.)

The assembler can work out the address of the first byte of the **STA** instruction in exactly the same way that we calculated it by hand. Like us, the assembler knows that the program starts at address $4000 (from the .ORG $4000 statement), and it knows that the LDA $03 instruction will only occupy two bytes (at addresses $4000 and $4001), so it knows that the **STA** instruction has to start at address $4002. Thus, when the assembler sees the JMP [LOOP] statement later in the program, it will automatically replace the label **LOOP** with the address $4002.

Obviously this saves us from the tedium of having to calculate the jump address ourselves, which is a major step forward whichever way you look at it, but there's a lot more to address labels than this. For example, if we suddenly decided to add a few more statements between the **LDA** and the **STA** instructions, then the address of the **STA** would change. If we hadn't used the label **LOOP**, then we'd have to manually recalculate this address and modify the jump instruction. But as we did use a label, all that would be required would be to reassemble the program and our assembler would take care of the rest. In the case of modifications to a larger program, this can save you hours, days, or even weeks of effort, with the cream-on-the-cake advantage that you'd still have a high degree of confidence (or at least a batting chance) that your program would continue to work as planned.

But wait, there's more! The label we used above was of a type called an "address label," because it's intimately associated with the address of a particular instruction. For your delectation and delight, we've also decided to provide entities called "constant labels," to which you can assign constant values for later use. Consider a further incarnation of our program that makes use of a constant label (Figure 12.8).

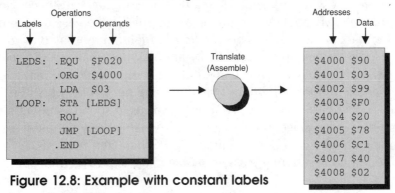

Figure 12.8: Example with constant labels

Once again, although we've modified the source, the resulting machine code is identical to that of our previous examples. The first thing you'll notice is that we've added a new statement to our repertoire – the .EQU on the first line (where **EQU** is an abbreviation for "equates to"). Thus, this particular example states that the constant label named LEDS is equated to the hexadecimal number $F020, which just happens to be the address of the output port connected to our 8-bit LED display. This means that when we come to our **STA** instruction, we can replace the **STA** [$F020] from our original program with **STA** [LEDS], and our assembler will automatically substitute the LEDS label with $F020 when it comes to do its cunning stuff.

Even in a simple case like this, in which we only employ the label **LEDS** once in the body of the program, the fact that we used this label certainly increases the program's readability; but once again there's a lot more to these entities than this. Consider a more complex program containing a large number of store instructions that refer to this output port. Now consider what would happen if we suddenly decided that we'd prefer to store our data to the dual decoded 7-segment display, whose output port is located at address $F023. In this case, assuming that we'd used the label **LEDS** throughout, we would only have to make a single modification to the value assigned to the **.EQU** statement, reassemble the program, and our assembler would take care of the rest. Pretty neat, huh? ...... and you ain't seen nothing yet!

Assembly language specification

Hopefully the above examples will have served to illustrate that writing programs in assembly code really isn't all that difficult. In fact assembly code is so much easier to understand than machine code that, before long, you'll be wondering how you managed to perform the earlier labs without it. However, as with any language (natural or computer), it's necessary to understand the vocabulary and the linguistic rules, otherwise an attempt at a casual remark along the lines of: "*Hello old friend, may I say that your toupee looks particularly dapper today and it almost matches the color of your mustache,*" may actually come out: "*It is my conjecture that you are dweeb and a dimbox, for whom I have nothing but contempt .*" This would be unfortunate to say the least, so it behooves us to spend some little time examining our language in detail (where any particularly pertinent points will be proffered with a pointing finger 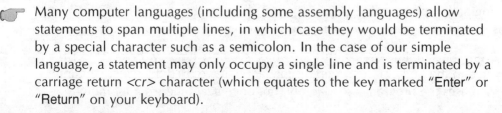 character). (A formal syntax definition of the *Beboputer's* assembly language is provided in Appendix F.)

Statements

Just as one of the fundamental building blocks of a natural language is the sentence, the equivalent construct in a computer language is called a *statement*, which, for the purposes of our language, we may regard as encompassing a single thought or idea. An assembly source file is composed of a series of these statements, each of which nominally consists of four fields (Figure 12.9).

Many computer languages (including some assembly languages) allow statements to span multiple lines, in which case they would be terminated by a special character such as a semicolon. In the case of our simple language, a statement may only occupy a single line and is terminated by a carriage return <cr> character (which equates to the key marked "Enter" or "Return" on your keyboard).

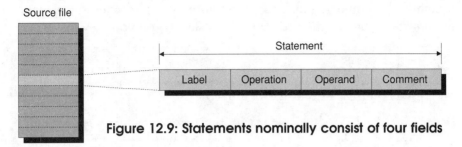

Figure 12.9: Statements nominally consist of four fields

The majority of the early assembly languages had extremely restrictive rules, such as specifying exactly on which column each field must commence. By comparison, our syntax is relatively free-format – you can use as many whitespace (*<tab>* and *<space>*) characters and be as messy as you wish. Having said this, we strongly recommend that you keep your source as neat and tidy as possible. You can follow the style we use in our examples or feel free to develop your own, but whatever you do, try to be as consistent as possible – you'll find that consistency pays dividends in the long run when you return to blow the dust off a neglected source file some time in the future.

Many assemblers only allow you to create source files using uppercase characters. In the case of our language, you may use uppercase, lowercase, or a mixture of both. However, for the purposes of its machinations, our assembler internally converts everything to uppercase, which means that it will consider labels such as *fred*, *Fred*, *FrEd* and *FRED* to be identical.

Comments and blank lines

Generally speaking it's a good idea to liberally sprinkle your assembly source with comments, and to distinguish logically distinct portions of your program with blank lines. Hopefully this will mean that when you return to your source code in the future you will have a clue as to what's going on. Some authorities hold that it isn't possible to have too many comments, but if you're too extravagant it can be difficult to locate your program amongst the commentary. Ultimately it's a matter of personal choice – it's up to you to find a style you like and stick to it (Figure 12.10).

A comment can occur anywhere on a source line and commences with a hash '#' character (this character is also often referred to as a *number sign*, *pound sign*, or a *sharp*). The hash character may be followed by any printable text characters (including spaces, tabs, and other hashes).

A comment is terminated by a carriage return <cr> character (once again, this equates to the key marked "Enter" or "Return" on your keyboard).

```
# This is a program wot wos wrote on 3rd day of Grunge in
# the year of the lesser-spotted Mugwump. (If we're lucky
# it will flash our 8-bit LED display).

LEDS:    .EQU   $F020    # $F020 is the address of the output
                        # port driving the 8-bit LED display


         .ORG   $4000    # Start of program is address $4000
         LDA    03       # Initialize the ACC
```

Figure 12.10: Comments and blank lines

Label names

As we discussed in our introductory examples, our language supports two kinds of labels, called *constant* and *address* labels. We will examine the differences in the way these labels are used in a little while; for the nonce we need only note that they have identical naming conventions (Figure 12.11).

```
LEDS:    .EQU   $F020    # "LEDS" is a constant label
         .ORG   $4000    # Start of program is address $4000
         LDA    $03      # Intialize the ACC
LOOP:    STA    [LEDS]   # "Loop" is an address label
```

Figure 12.11: Label names

☞ Both types of label can consist of a mixture of alphabetic, numeric, and underscore '_' characters, but the first character *must* be either an alpha or an underscore (not a numeric). Note that we actually recommend that you *don't* start your labels with an underscore, because this is how we distinguish the labels in the pre-defined subroutines we've prepared for you (see also Appendix G).

☞ When a label is declared it is terminated with a colon ':' character, but this character doesn't form part of the label's name, and is not used thereafter.

☞ The maximum length of a label name is eight characters. This includes any underscores, but excludes the colon ':' character used to terminate the label.

☞ Labels can include both uppercase and lowercase characters, but the assembler internally converts everything to uppercase, so it will consider labels such as *fred*, *Fred*, *FrEd* and *FRED* to be identical.

```
RET_ADDR:  # Legal and useful, because just by reading it
           # you get the picture "return address"

 BIG_BOY:  # Legal, but not very indicative of its function

  _LOOP1:  # Legal, but we recommend that you don't start
           # your labels with underscore characters

1ST_LOOP:  # Illegal, can't start with a numeric character

LOOP_FIVE: # Illegal, can't have more than 8 characters

     LDA:  # Illegal, this is one of our reserved words
```

Figure 12.12: Legal and illegal label names

☞ In this last example, note that labels cannot be the same as any of our reserved words. These include directive mnemonics, instruction mnemonics, and also the special reserved word "X". A complete list of reserved words is provided in Appendix F.

The .ORG and .END directives

In addition to standard instructions, our assembly language supports special instructions to direct the assembler to do certain things. These special instructions may be called *directives* (because they direct the assembler) or *pseudo-instructions*. As we've already seen, every program must contain at least two directives: the .ORG and the .END (Figure 12.13).

```
# Any declaration statements come here (before the .ORG)


     .ORG  $4000   # Start of program is address $4000


# The statemants forming the body of the program go here


  .END              # Tells the assembler to stop here


# Anything appearing after the .END will be ignored
```

Figure 12.13: The .ORG and .END directives

☞ The .ORG directive instructs the assembler as to the origin of the program; that is, the memory location into which it should place the program's first byte. Thus, this directive must have an operand in the form of a number (as shown here) or a constant label from a declaration statement (as described below).

☞ The .END directive simply informs the assembler that it's reached the end of the program. Thus, this directive does not require any operand.

☞ Neither .ORG or .END directives are allowed to have labels.

The .EQU directive

Another directive we saw in our earlier examples is .EQU, which means "*equates to.*" This directive appears in *declaration statements*, which are used to declare constant values for later use (Figure 12.14).

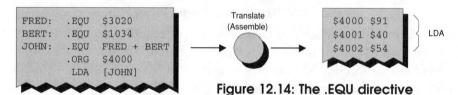

Figure 12.14: The .EQU directive

☞ If declaration statements are used, they *must* appear before the .ORG directive at the beginning of the program.

☞ Each .EQU directive *must* have a label assigned to it. These constant labels may be used in the body of the program instead of literal (numerical) values. When the assembler is assembling the program, it will automatically substitute any constant labels in the body of the program with their numerical equivalents. For example, the assembler will automatically substitute JOHN in the LDA instruction above for the address $4054.

☞ With regard to the previous point, note that constant labels are only used by the assembler, and they don't appear in (or occupy any space in) the resulting machine code. Also note that constant labels can be used to represent addresses, data, or both (this will be discussed in more detail a little later).

☞ The assignment to an .EQU statement may be presented in the form of an expression, as is illustrated by the assignment to JOHN in the above example (expressions are introduced in more detail below). However, it is important to note that forward-referencing is not allowed; that is, JOHN is allowed to reference FRED and BERT, because they've already been declared, but BERT isn't allowed to reference JOHN, while FRED isn't allowed to reference either BERT or JOHN.

The .BYTE, .2BYTE, and .4BYTE directives

The .BYTE, .2BYTE, and .4BYTE directives are used in *reserve statements* to set aside (reserve) memory locations for later use. Not surprisingly, the .BYTE directive reserves a single byte, the .2BYTE directive reserves two bytes, and the .4BYTE directive reserves ...... well, we'll leave that as an exercise for the reader (Figure 12.15).

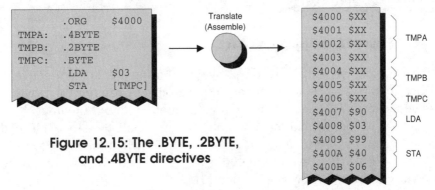

Figure 12.15: The .BYTE, .2BYTE, and .4BYTE directives

☞ If reserve statements are used they *must* appear in the body of the program; that is, between the .ORG and .END directives. In this example we've shown the reserve statements as appearing immediately after the .ORG directive. However, although this is perfectly legal, it means that we can't run the program from address $4000, but instead have to remember to run from address $4007. Thus, it is very common to find reserve statements hanging around the end of the program instead of the beginning.

☞ Each reserve statement may have an *optional* label assigned to it. These address labels may be used in the body of the program instead of literal (numerical) values. When the assembler is assembling the program, it will automatically substitute numerical equivalents for any address labels in the body of the program. For example, the assembler will automatically substitute **TMPC** in the **STA** instruction for the address $4006, which is the location the assembler decided to reserve for this byte.

☞ Note that if a label is used with a **.2BYTE** or a **.4BYTE** directive, then the address that the assembler associates with that label corresponds to the first byte of that field. Thus, in the case of this example, the assembler associates the labels **TMPA**, **TMPB**, and **TMPC** with addresses $4000, $4004, and $4006, respectively.

☞ With regard to the previous points, labels are optional with these directives, because you may not always require the ability to individually reference every location set aside by a reserve statement. This is due to the fact that you can reference one location as an offset from another location (Figure 12.16).

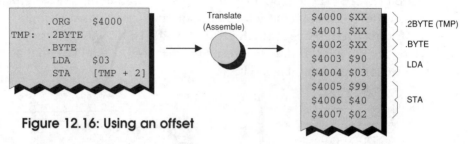

Figure 12.16: Using an offset

In this example we first reserved a 2-byte field using a .2BYTE directive with a label of **TMP**, and we immediately followed this by reserving a 1-byte field reserved using a .BYTE directive without a label. From our previous discussions, we know that the assembler will associate the label **TMP** with the address of the first location in the 2-byte field (which happens to be address $4000). Thus, even though the 1-byte field doesn't have a label of its own, we can still reference it using "TMP+2".

When writing a program it is often necessary to reserve a number of consecutive memory locations. As an alternative to painstakingly reserving locations individually, the .BYTE, .2BYTE, and .4BYTE directives support an optional operand in the form "*n", where 'n' is any expression that resolves into a positive integer. For example, suppose that we wished to reserve three 1-byte fields and two 2-byte fields (Figure 12.17).

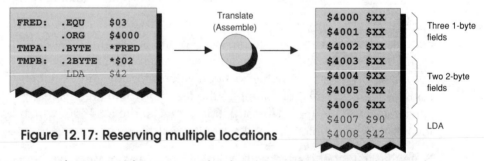

Figure 12.17: Reserving multiple locations

In this case we first assign the numerical value $03 to the constant label **FRED**. Thus, when the assembler comes to consider the reserve statement associated with the address label **TMPA**, it will replace the "*FRED" with "*$03" and reserve three 1-byte fields. Similarly, when the assembler comes to consider the reserve statement associated with **TMPB**, it will understand that we're instructing it to reserve two 2-byte fields (it's just that we're a bit more explicit in this case). Note that the labels will be associated with the first byte in their corresponding groups; thus, the assembler will associate

TMPA with address $4000 and TMPB with address $4003. Also, although we've not illustrated this point here, note that the 'n' in "*n" can be a full-blown expression. Assuming that we're still using FRED from the previous example, the statement ".BYTE *(FRED + 5)" would reserve eight bytes of memory.

All of the machine code resulting from the reserve statement examples we've considered so far has contained $XX values, which indicate that we have not defined the contents of these locations. As it happens, our assembler will automatically cause these undefined locations to contain zero values, but that's largely beside the point. In fact our assembly language allows us to associate values with these locations as a comma-separated list (Figure 12.18).

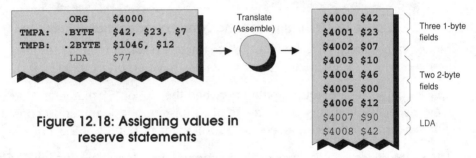

**Figure 12.18: Assigning values in
reserve statements**

Once again, the labels will be associated with the first byte in their corresponding groups; thus, the assembler will associate **TMPA** with address $4000 and **TMPB** with address $4003. Additionally, as we promised, the assembler accepts the values in the comma separated lists and inserts them into the appropriate locations. Note that the assembler will automatically zero-fill numbers to the requisite size, so the $7 in this example is automatically coerced to $07, because it's being assigned to a 1-byte field, while the $12 is automatically coerced to $0012, because *it's* being assigned to a 2-byte field (we'll return to consider this aspect of things in more detail in a little while). Also note that any numbers assigned to multi-byte fields associated with .2BYTE and .4BYTE directives will be stored with their most-significant byte first. For reasons more fully discussed in Chapter 15, this style of storage is referred to as *big-endian* (because we're storing the numbers "big end" first). Finally, although we've not illustrated this point here, note that each of the values in these comma-separated lists could be a full-blown expression.

Literals (binary, decimal, and hexadecimal values)

Thus far, all of our examples have employed hexadecimal numbers, because this is the base we've used predominantly throughout our book. But it is sometimes more appropriate to use numbers with other bases to better clarify the intent of the program. For this reason, we decided our assembly language should support binary, decimal, and hexadecimal values (Figure 12.19).

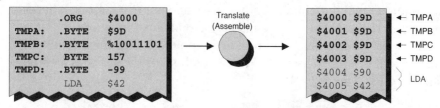

Figure 12.19: Binary, decimal, and hexadecimal values

☞ Binary values are prefixed with a '%' character; hexadecimal values are prefixed with a '$' character; decimal values have no prefix at all.

☞ Space characters are not permitted between the '%' or '$' characters and their respective numbers. Also, decimal values are not permitted to contain commas or any other characters, so 32565 is legal, but 32,565 is not.

The example above commences by reserving four 1-byte fields called **TMPA**, **TMPB**, **TMPC**, and **TMPD**, and assigning them values in hexadecimal, binary, decimal, and decimal (again), respectively. You will note that all of these values actually result in identical bit-patterns when they are translated into machine code (which is, of course, why we selected them in the first place). Note especially the negative value assigned to **TMPD**, where the unary minus operator instructs the assembler to take the twos complement of 99, resulting in the same value as all of the other *1-byte fields*.

The reason why we emphasized "1-byte fields" in the preceding paragraph is that the assembler actually represents every number as a 4-byte field internally, and it only considers them as being 1-byte or 2-byte fields when it comes to assign them to reserve statements or use them as operands for instructions (Figure 12.20).

The first **LDA** instruction passes the assembler's scrutiny without any problems, because the constant **BERT** being loaded into the accumulator was only assigned an 8-bit value, which fits into our 8-bit accumulator. The second **LDA** instruction is more interesting, because **FRED** was originally assigned a 16-bit value. However, this is an example of an expression using the logical AND operator '&', in which the $FF is used as a mask to extract

FRED's least-significant byte (this is discussed in more detail below). Finally, the third **LDA** would cause the assembler to issue an error message, because it can't squeeze the un-masked 16-bit value assigned to FRED into our 8-bit accumulator.

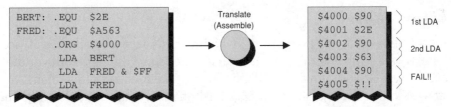

```
BERT:  .EQU   $2E
FRED:  .EQU   $A563
       .ORG   $4000
       LDA    BERT
       LDA    FRED & $FF
       LDA    FRED
```

Translate (Assemble)

```
$4000  $90      1st LDA
$4001  $2E
$4002  $90      2nd LDA
$4003  $63
$4004  $90      FAIL!!
$4005  $!!
```

Figure 12.20: The assembler checks the size of the target destination

The concept of expressions will be introduced shortly, but, as we've opened this can of worms here, it behooves us to explain why the second **LDA** in the above example passed muster. Remember that the assembler internally regards every number as a 4-byte field, and it's only when the assembler comes to assign a value to a target destination that it checks to see whether the value will fit. (Note that we'll be discussing the assembler itself in more detail later on.) Also, don't forget that *we're* the ones who are defining what *our* assembly language looks like, and we've decided that our language should support simple expressions. So in the case of the second **LDA** instruction, we've decided that when our assembler sees an expression like "FRED & $FF", it will perform a logical AND operation between the two values (Figure 12.21).

First, the 2-byte value assigned to FRED is zero-filled by the assembler to boost it up to its 4-byte value of $0000A563, while the $FF value is zero-filled to its 4-byte value of $000000FF. The logical AND operator ('&' in our assembly language) is a bit-wise operator (it performs its actions on a bit-

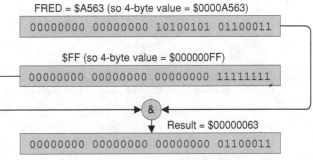

FRED = $A563 (so 4-byte value = $0000A563)

`00000000 00000000 10100101 01100011`

$FF (so 4-byte value = $000000FF)

`00000000 00000000 00000000 11111111`

&

Result = $00000063

`00000000 00000000 00000000 01100011`

Figure 12.21: The assembler performing a logical AND on 4-byte values

by-bit basis) that functions in a similar manner to the logical AND in the *Beboputer's* instruction set. To put this another way, the least-significant bit of the first number is AND'ed with the least-significant bit of the second number to give the least-significant bit of the result, and so on for all of the other bits. Remember the way in which an AND works is that its output is only *logic 1* if both of its the inputs are *logic 1*, so the three most-significant bytes of the result are forced to zero by the six 0's in the $000000FF value. The outcome of all of this is that only the least-significant eight bits of the result contain a value, which will therefore fit into our 8-bit accumulator.

Expressions

Ah, so here we are at expressions, which can be exceptionally useful, so long as you quickly establish who's in charge ...... you (hopefully) or the expressions (if you turn your back on them). The trick is to look them straight in the eye and show no fear! First of all, we have decided that our assembly language should support the following selection of *binary operators*:

Arithmetic:	+	Add	Logical:	&	AND
	−	Subtract		|	OR
	*	Multiply		^	Exclusive-OR
	/	Divide			

☞ We call these "binary operators," because each of them requires two operands to work with; for example, in the expression "6 + 3" we see two operands (numbers), one on either side of the operator.

☞ The operands in expressions can be a mixture of numbers (binary, decimal, and hexadecimal) and labels; for example, assuming that **BERT** is a label, the expression "**BERT** & %11001100" is perfectly acceptable.

☞ Our language only supports integer expressions, which are expressions involving whole numbers. Thus, "**BERT** * 3" is legal, while "**BERT** * 3.5" is not.

☞ Any remainder from a division operation will be automatically discarded by the assembler without any error messages being issued. Similarly, the assembler will not report any errors if the actions from addition, subtraction, and multiplication operations overflow or underflow the 4-byte fields it uses to store the results. However, the assembler will make its feelings known in no uncertain terms should you try to divide anything by zero.

☞ Expressions can be of arbitrary length and employ any mixture of arithmetic and logical operators, so long as they fit on a single line of source code; for example, "**BERT** ^ 2 * **JOHN** & $A5 / **HARRY**" is a legal expression (assuming that **BERT**, **JOHN**, and **HARRY** are labels that have been declared elsewhere in the program).

With regard to the previous point, all of our binary operators have *equal precedence,* and expressions are evaluated from *left to right*. What does this mean? Consider the following example:

At school we're taught that: 6 * 3 + 5 * 4 = 38

But, in our assembly language: 6 * 3 + 5 * 4 = ~~98~~ 92

Eeeek, how can this be? Well, at school we were taught that multiplication and division have a higher precedence (are more powerful) than addition or subtraction. This means that we normally evaluate expressions by performing any multiplications and divisions first, followed by any additions and subtractions. Thus, in the first portion of this example, we'd multiply 6 by 3 to get 18, multiply 5 by 4 to get 20, then add the 18 and 20 to generate the final result of 38. Had we so wished, we could easily have decided to make our language (and therefore our assembler) work in just this way. However, we decided that you need to broaden your horizons, because it's common for simple programs (like our assembler) to treat all of the binary operators as having equal precedence (being equally powerful) and, as we already noted, to evaluate expressions from left to right. This means that in the case of our language, we would solve this expression by multiplying 6 by 3 to get 18, then adding 5 to get 23, and then multiplying by 4 to generate a final result of ~~98~~ 92 .

Although this may seem to be a pain, it's really just another way of looking at the world and you'll soon learn to get used to it – let's face it, what other choice do you have? Actually, there are options open to you, because you can use parenthesis to force your expressions to evaluate in any order you like; for example, if you were to write your expression as "(6 * 3) + (5 * 4)", then the assembler will evaluate the contents of any parenthesis before moving on to the rest of the expression. Also note that it's possible to nest parenthesis within each other, but each '(' must have a corresponding ')'. For example, in addition to being legal, "(((6 * 3) + 5) * 4)" would force the assembler to evaluate the expression in exactly the same order as if the parenthesis weren't there at all (from left to right), while "(6 * (3 + (5 * 4)))" would force the assembler to evaluate the expression in reverse order (from right to left).

Generally speaking you'll find that most of the expressions you create will be short, sweet, and to the point; but even simple expressions can be incredibly useful. Expressions can be employed in a variety of roles, including assignments to .EQU statements, modifying data values, and calculating addresses. First consider an example involving expressions in .EQU statements (Figure 12.22).

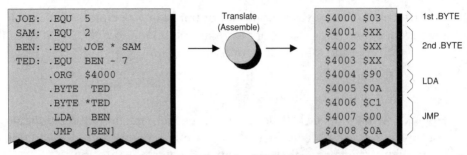

Figure 12.22: Expressions in .EQU statements

☞ Remember that our language doesn't support forward-referencing in .EQU statements, which means that BEN can reference JOE and SAM because they've already been declared; TED can reference BEN because that's already been declared; but BEN could not reference TED, SAM could not reference BEN or TED, and JOE could not reference SAM, BEN, or TED.

It shouldn't take you too long to work out that the value assigned to BEN is 10 (or $A in hexadecimal), while the value assigned to TED is 3 (or $3 in hexadecimal). As we see, we directly assign the value represented by TED to our first .BYTE statement, so the assembler will store $03 in address $4000 (note that the assembler adds a leading zero to pad the value to 8 bits). In the second .BYTE statement we use TED in a different role, because the construct "*TED" instructs the assembler to set aside a number of bytes equal to TED, which appear at addresses $4001 through $4003. Note that the assembler would actually load these bytes with default $00 values, but we've shown them as containing $XXs to indicate that we didn't explicitly assign these values.

Next we use BEN as the data to be loaded into the accumulator from the LDA instruction in its immediate addressing mode. The $90 at address $4004 is the opcode for the LDA, while the $0A at address $4005 is the value that was in BEN. As usual, the assembler adds a leading zero to pad this data value to eight bits. Finally, we use BEN as the target address for a JMP instruction in its absolute addressing mode. The $C1 at address $4006 is the opcode for the JMP, while the $000A stored in addresses $4007 and $4008 is the value that was in BEN. Note that in this case, the assembler automatically added three leading zeros to pad the address value to sixteen bits.

In the example above, we used the results from a previously-calculated expression in the role of data and an address, but we didn't actually use expressions directly in the data and address fields, so let's remedy that right here and now (Figure 12.23).

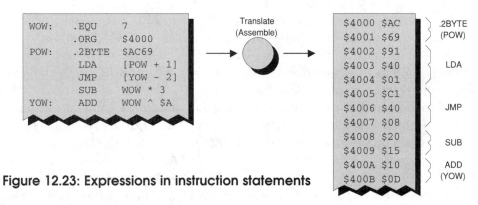

Figure 12.23: Expressions in instruction statements

Unlike the expressions in .**EQU** statements, expressions in instructions are allowd to make forward references to future address labels, such as the "JMP [YOW - 2]" statement in this example.

Note that this is an artificial test case whose sole purpose is to illustrate some simple concepts, so don't spend an inordinate amount of time trying to wring some hidden meaning from it, or saying "*I wonder why they did it that way; wouldn't it have been simpler to .....?*" Yes it would and no we didn't!

The first thing we do in this program is to declare a 2-byte field called **POW**, and load it with the number $AC69 (the value that appears in addresses $4000 and $4001). As we know, our assembler will consider **POW** to be associated with $4000, which is the address of the first byte in this 2-byte field. Thus, the statement "**LDA [POW + 1]**," which is an **LDA** using its absolute addressing mode, is understood by the assembler to mean "**LDA [$4000 + 1]**," or "**LDA [$4001]**." This means "*Load the accumulator with the contents of address $4001,*" so when we run the program, the accumulator will be loaded with $69.

Now glance at the end of this program segment, where we associate the label **YOW** with an **ADD** instruction. As usual, our assembler will consider **YOW** to be associated with $400A, which is the address of the first byte in this 2-byte instruction. Thus, the "JMP [YOW - 2]" statement is understood by the assembler to mean "JMP [$400A - 2], or "JMP [$4008]," which, by some strange quirk of fate, happens to be the address of the first byte in the **SUB** instruction. (This means that our program would do exactly the same things (functionally speaking) if we chopped the **JMP** statement right out of it!)[2]

---

[2]Note the cunning use of nested parenthesis in this sentence. Your English teachers might not approve, but did they ever?

At the bottom of this program come the SUB and ADD instructions, which are both using their immediate addressing modes, and which employ expressions to calculate their data values. The "SUB WOW * 3" statement is understood by the assembler to mean "SUB 7 * 3," or "SUB 21" ("*subtract 21 from the current contents of the accumulator*"). The $20 at address $4008 is the opcode for this instruction, while the $15 at address $4009 is the hexadecimal equivalent of 21. Similarly, the "ADD WOW ^ $A" statement is understood by the assembler to mean "ADD 7 ^ $A" (where '^' is the exclusive OR operator), which boils down to "ADD $0D" ("*add $0D to the current contents of the accumulator*"). Thus, the $10 at address $400A is the opcode for this instruction, while the $0D at address $400B is the value to be added.

In common with many other assembly languages, ours includes a special symbol in its syntax that allows you (well, the assembler, really) to access the value that the *Beboputer's* program counter would contain at any particular point in the code. The symbol we decided to use is the '@' character, and an example of its use is illustrated in Figure 12.24.

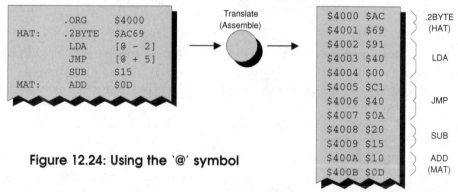

Figure 12.24: Using the '@' symbol

The way in which this works is that when the assembler sees the '@' character, it substitutes this character with the address of the first byte (the opcode byte) in that instruction. Thus, as the first byte of the LDA instruction occurs at address $4002, the assembler will understand the statement "LDA [@ - 2]" to mean "LDA [$4002 - 2]," or "LDA [$4000]." Similarly, as the first byte of the JMP instruction occurs at address $4005, the assembler will understand "JMP [@ + 5]" to mean "LDA [$4005 + 5]," or "LDA [$400A]." Note that the '@' symbol can only be used in expressions in the body of the program, but it has no meaning in declaration (.EQU) statements.

Last but not least, it would be extremely remiss of us if we failed to mention that our language supports two *unary operators*: the unary minus '-' and the unary negation '!'. (The exclamation mark we used to represent the unary negation is often referred to as a *bang, ping,* or *shriek*.) The reason we call these "unary operators" is that they only require a single operand to work with (Figure 12:25).

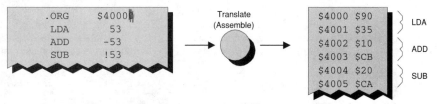

Figure 12.25: The unary operators `-` and `!`

☞ The unary operators are associated with the value immediately to their right, where said value can be a numeric literal (in binary, decimal, or hexadecimal) or a label. Note that space characters are not allowed between a unary operator and its related value.

☞ Both of the unary operators have a higher precedence than the binary operators. This means that in expressions containing a mixture of unary and binary operators, the effects of the unary operators will be evaluated first. For example, in the expression "TOM + !BERT," the unary negation will be applied to BERT and the result will be added to TOM. Similarly, in the expression "!TOM + BERT," the unary negation will be applied to TOM and the result will be added to BERT. Of course, you can use parenthesis to force the issue, so if you wanted to add TOM to BERT and then negate the result, you could do so using "!(TOM + BERT)."

By some weird and wonderful coincidence, the $35 in address $4001 is the hexadecimal equivalent of 53 in decimal, which is the data value associated with the LDA instruction. In the case of the ADD, the unary minus '–' takes the two's complement of 53, resulting in the $CB value at address $4001. By comparison, in the case of the SUB, the unary negation takes the one's complement of 53, resulting in the $CA value at address $4003.[3] This leads to an interesting point, which is related to the fact that the assembler stores all of its values in 4-byte fields. Consider how the assembler views these three values as it's manipulating them (Figure 12.26).

We know that the ADD and SUB instructions expect 8-bit data values for their immediate addressing modes. We also know that the assembler will issue an error message if a number is too big to fit into its target destination. However, although both of the values resulting from the unary operations in this example leave the three most-significant bytes of the assembler's 4-byte

---

[3]The concepts of one's and two's complements were introduced in Chapter 7.

fields packed to bursting with 1s, we seem to be implying that the assembler will let them slip past without so much as raising a metaphorical eyebrow. Strange things are afoot indeed.

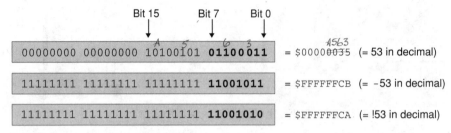

Figure 12.26: How the assembler views the effects of the unary operators

In fact there's a reasonably simple explanation for all of this (thank goodness). Like the heroes who paved the way before us, we decided that we wish to be able to assign negative numbers as data values in our language, but we also recognized that this might cause the assembler to "throw a wobbly." To solve this conundrum, we wrote the assembler in such a way that we might imagine it using the following reasoning:

> "Hmmm, I'm supposed to assign this value to an 8-bit field, but the three most-significant bytes of my internal 4-byte field contain non-zero values, which suggests that these numbers are too big. Perhaps I ought to issue a warning message ......? Just a moment, let's rein in them thar horses and look at this from another point of view. If the most-significant bit of the least significant byte (bit 7) is a logic 1, and if all of the bits in the three most significant bytes are also logic 1s, then I'd be justified in assuming that this is a negative number, in which case I can just use the least-significant byte, and a nod's as good as a wink to a blind fruitbat."

And, in fact, this is just what our assembler does. Of course things can mess up sometimes, but that's a case of "Let the programmer beware!" Finally, note that if the assembler is trying to assign one of these values to a 16-bit field, it essentially follows the same procedure, except that it looks to see if bit 15 is a *logic 1* and if all of the bits in the *two* most-significant bytes are *logic 1s*.

Instructions and addressing modes

Cease those nervous twitches and sit up straight, because this is the last section in our language specification and it's quite possibly the easiest one of all. As you know, our *Beboputer* supports a variety of addressing modes. Thus, our language requires some way of distinguishing which mode we're trying to use, especially since certain instructions can employ more than one mode.

The implied addressing mode: The simplest mode of all is the *implied* addressing mode, in which the instruction only requires a single byte for the opcode and there are no operand bytes. For example, consider a **SHL** (*"shift left"*), which instructs the CPU to shift the contents of the accumulator left by one bit (Figure 12.27).

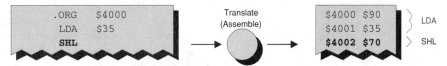

Figure 12.27: The implied addressing mode

Note that we only included an **LDA** in this example because we need something to be the accumulator before we can do anything with it. The point we're trying to make here is that instructions like **SHL** that use the implied addressing mode don't have an operand in the source (assembly) code and only occupy a single byte in the object (machine) code.

☞ Instructions that use the implied addressing mode are CLRIM, DECA, DECX, HALT, INCA, INCX, NOP, POPA, POPSR, PUSHA, PUSHSR, ROLC, RORC, RTI, RTS, SETIM, SHL, and SHR.

The immediate addressing mode: In the case of the *immediate* addressing mode, the data to be used is directly associated with the instruction. Such instructions occupy two bytes: one for the opcode and one for the data (Figure 12.28).

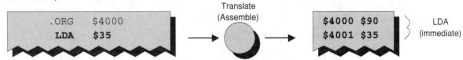

Figure 12.28: The immediate addressing mode

☞ Instructions that can use the immediate addressing mode are ADD, ADDC, AND, CMPA, LDA, OR, SUB, SUBC, and XOR.

The "big immediate" addressing mode: This mode is very similar to the standard immediate mode, in that the data to be used is directly associated with the instruction. We decided to distinguish between these modes because, unlike the **LDA** which loads an 8-bit accumulator, certain instructions are used to load 16-bit registers, such as the stack pointer, the index register, and the interrupt vector. Thus, these instructions occupy three bytes, one for the opcode and two for the data (Figure 12.29).

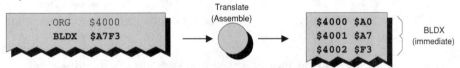

Figure 12.29: The "big immediate" addressing mode

☞ All of the "big" instructions (those that involve 16-bit registers) are distinguished by the fact that the first letter in their mnemonics is 'B' for "Big" – how subtle can you get? Instructions that can use the "big immediate" addressing mode are **BLDSP**, **BLDX**, and **BLDIV**.

The absolute addressing mode: Unlike the immediate addressing mode, in which the instruction's operand represents a data value, the operand for an absolute instruction is a 2-byte address. Thus, these instructions occupy three bytes, one for the opcode and two for the address (Figure 12.30).

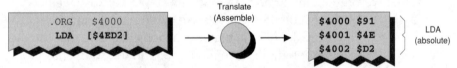

Figure 12.30: The absolute addressing mode

☞ The absolute mode is distinguished from the immediate mode in the assembly source file by enclosing the operand in square brackets '[' and ']'. We decided to use square brackets because they visually imply a memory location. Thus, "LDA [$4ED2]" means *"Load the accumulator with the data value that will be found in the memory location at address $4ED2."*

☞ Note that "big" absolute instructions, such as **BLDX**, use the same format as do standard absolute instructions, such as **LDA**. However, in the case of the "big" instructions, the *Beboputer* understands that the address actually points to the first byte of data in a 2-byte field.

☞ Instructions that can use the absolute (and "big" absolute) addressing mode are **ADD, ADDC, AND, BLDSP, BLDX, BLDIV, BSTSP, BSTX, CMPA, JC, JNC, JN, JNN, JO, JNO, JZ, JNZ, JMP, JSR, LDA, OR, STA, SUB, SUBC,** and **XOR**.

The indexed addressing mode: The indexed addressing mode is very similar to the absolute mode, especially since these instructions also occupy three bytes, one for the opcode and two for the address (Figure 12.31).

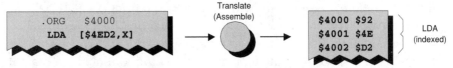

Figure 12.31: The indexed addressing mode

☞ The indexed mode is distinguished from the absolute mode in the assembly source file by including the special keyword "X" in the square brackets; where the "X", which is separated from the address by a comma, is a shorthand mnemonic for "inde<u>X</u> register." As you may recall, we previously noted that you couldn't use "X" as the name for a label because it was one of our reserved words ...... now you know "Y" ("why" – get it? – come on, work with us on this).

☞ Note that apart from the opcode bytes, the machine code generated by the assembler is identical for both the absolute and indexed addressing modes in our examples (this is because we used the same address in both sources of courses). However, when the *Beboputer* sees the $91 opcode associated with our indexed **LDA** instruction, it understands that after reading the 2-byte address in the following two bytes, it has to internally add the current contents of the index register to this address, and to then use this modified address to point to the target location containing the data (or into which it should write the data in the case of a store instruction). Thus, "LDA [$4ED2,X]" means *"Load the accumulator with the data value that will be found in the memory location generated by adding the current contents of the index register to address $4ED2."*

☞ Instructions that can use the indexed addressing mode are ADD, ADDC, AND, CMPA, JMP, JSR, LDA, OR, STA, SUB, SUBC, and XOR.

The indirect addressing mode: When we play with the indirect addressing mode, we're really starting to cook on a hot stove (Figure 12.32).

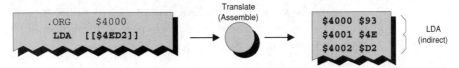

Figure 12.32: The indirect addressing mode

☞ The whole point of an instruction using the indirect mode is that its operand is not an address that points to the data, but rather an address that's pointing to a second address, and this second address is the one that points to the data. Purely for aesthetic reasons, we decided to describe this in our source file using pairs of square brackets ("[[" and "]]"), which we understand to mean *"an address pointed to by an address."* Thus, "LDA [[$4ED2]]" means *"Load the accumulator with the data value that will be found in the memory location that's pointed to by a 2-byte address, whose first byte is at address $4ED2"* (try saying that ten times without taking a breath).

☞ Instructions that can use the indirect addressing mode are JMP, JSR, LDA, and STA. Note that there's no reason why other instructions such as ADD, SUB, AND, and OR should not be equipped with an indirect addressing mode (other than the fact that we decided not to bother implementing this mode for these instructions).

The pre-indexed indirect addressing mode: (Don't worry, we're almost done). As its name might suggest, the pre-indexed indirect addressing mode is a combination of the indexed and indirect addressing modes that we've already seen (Figure 12.33).

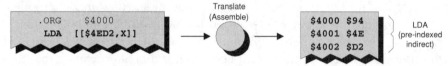

Figure 12.33: The pre-indexed indirect addressing mode

☞ In this case, the *Beboputer* first adds the current contents of the index register to the address it finds in the operand bytes, and it uses this generated address to point to a second address that actually points to the data. Thus, "LDA [[$4ED2,X]]" means *"Load the accumulator with the data value that will be found in the memory location that's pointed to by a 2-byte address, whose first byte is at the address generated by adding the current contents of the index register to address $4ED2."*

☞ Instructions that can use the pre-indexed indirect addressing mode are: JMP, JSR, LDA, and STA.

The indirect post-indexed addressing mode: Settle down and cease your whimpering ...... this is the very last one. Once again, as its name might suggest, the indirect post-indexed addressing mode is a combination of the indirect and indexed addressing modes that we've already seen (Figure 12.34).

☞ Note that the previous *pre-indexed indirect* mode and this *indirect post-indexed* mode are distinguished in the assembly source file by the positioning of the "X" keyword. In this post-indexed case, the *Beboputer* uses the address it finds in the instruction's operand bytes to point to a second address, it internally adds the current contents of the index register to this second address, and it uses the result to point to the data. Thus,

"LDA [[$4ED2],X]" means "*Load the accumulator with the data value that will be found in the memory location that's pointed to by a 2-byte address, where this address is determined by adding the current contents of the index register to the address whose first byte is located at address $4ED2.*"

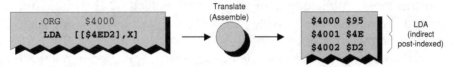

Figure 12.34: The indirect post-indexed addressing mode

☞ Instructions that can use the indirect post-indexed addressing mode are: JMP, JSR, LDA, and STA.

These last two modes are fairly esoteric and you might not find much use for them in the normal course of your routine. You can actually write any program using just the implied, immediate, and absolute addressing modes (or just the implied and absolute modes at a pinch) – the other modes are simply there to make our lives easier and our programs smaller and faster. On the other hand, should you become enamored of creating your own programs, you might be pleasantly surprised to discover just how frisky the more sophisticated modes can be.

Motley miscellaneous musings on assembling in general

In the discussions above, we were wont to wantonly wield words along the lines of: "*Our assembler will look at this type of statement and grungle-groil its dingle-frolls.*" The point is that we've happily assumed the presence of an assembly program without pausing to wonder from whence it came. But these things don't just sprout up like mushrooms in the dead of night, so before we delve deep into the depths of the *Beboputer's* assembler utility, let's pause to ponder a few miscellaneous musings about the concept of assembling in general.

Although use of symbolic representations such as assembly languages (and higher-level languages) seems obvious to us today, this was not always the case. Many of the teams designing the original computers believed that, to achieve optimal results, it was necessary to get as close to the machine as possible (in intellectual terms – not sitting on top of the thing). To put this another way, their philosophy was to write programs in a form as close as possible to the machine's internal representations.

However, some groups did advocate symbolic programming (albeit in small doses), such as the team at Cambridge University in England who designed EDSAC in the late 1940s.[4] EDSAC employed a rudimentary assembler called *Initial Orders*, which was implemented in a primitive form of read-only memory constructed out of telephone uniselectors. This embryonic utility allowed operators to write machine-level instructions using a single letter to represent the opcode followed by a decimal address. This address could then be followed by a second letter, which was used to reference one of twelve constant values (each of which was preset by the programmers) to be added to the address at assembly time.

By today's standards, Initial Orders was extremely elementary. The first assembler that we'd really credit as such was the *Symbolic Optimizer and Assembly Program (SOAP)*, which was created for the IBM 650 computer in the mid-1950s. Following SOAP came the *United Aircraft Symbolic Assembly Program (UASAP)*, later abbreviated to SAP, which was designed by programmers at the United Aircraft Corporation to run on IBM 704 computers. SAP was to prove pivotal in the history of assemblers, because it essentially defined the external form that was to become the basis of such programs to this day.

Starting at ground zero

Purely for the sake of argument, let's assume that you've just designed and built the first computer on the face of the planet. Initially this computer consists of a CPU, some form of random-access (read-write) memory, and a switch panel. (Note that your computer isn't equipped with any form of read-only memory, because you haven't got around to inventing this yet.) There you stand, jaw jutting out, staring your creation straight in the facia-panel, both of you determined not to be the first to blink – so what do you do now? Although you are the proud possessor of your own computer, it doesn't have an operating system, you don't have any programs to run on it, and there aren't any other computers to help you out.

Hmmm, this is obviously a poser. Well if you've designed your system in the same way that the computer pioneers did in the real world, it won't yet have a monitor program (because you don't have any read-only memory to store one in) and your switch panel will be hard-wired directly into the guts of the computer. This means that you can specify an address and its associated data using the appropriate switches on the switch panel, and

---

[4]EDSAC is discussed in more detail in Chapter 15.

then press the Enter button to force-load this data into the target address in your random-access memory. You can repeat this process for different addresses and data values indefinitely (or until you run out of physical addresses) to load a program in machine code, should you so desire.

Now let us suppose that your mother and a gaggle of her friends are visiting on the morrow to see your latest invention. Not unnaturally, you determine to put on a bit of a show. The problem is that watching a computer performing calculations is intrinsically rather boring, so you decide to add a display panel with flashing lights that reflect the current values on the address and data busses. (Actually, this isn't as weird an idea as it sounds — the display panels on some of the early computers were primarily added to give journalists something visual to "Ooh" and "Aah" about.) Next you jot down a simple program on a piece of paper, where this program will perform some cunning calculations and, eventually, present the result on your display panel. (Naturally you're writing your program in machine code, because the concept of assembly language hasn't dawned on you yet).

Having designed your program, you spend some considerable time entering the little rascal using your switch panel (Figure 3.35). The hour hand sweeps around the clock in grand Hollywood style until, suddenly, the birds start their dawn chorus outside your window and you realize that you've finished. With trembling hands you enter your program's start address on the switch panel and press the Run button, thereby handing control over to your creation. **It works!** (We decided to be charitable and give you the benefit of the doubt.) Your mother and her cohorts duly arrive and ferret around, praising your accomplishments in strident tones (whilst surreptitiously running fingers across every available surface to check for dust), and eventually depart in a maelstrom of missing purses and misplaced umbrellas ...... sweet silence falls, and you take a few moments to bask in the glow of a job well done.

However, apart from the fact that entering your program via the switch panel was tedious and error-prone, you now have another major problem on your hands, in that turning your computer off will cause it to forget everything you've done. This means that the next time you wish to show off your computer to your friends, you're going to have to enter your program into the system all over again (and it wasn't all that much fun the first time around). One solution would be to throw a tantrum; alternatively, you could add a paper tape reader/writer to your computer, and then design a subroutine that could copy a selected portion of your memory onto a paper tape. In order to create this subroutine, you would employ the same technique that you used for your first program; that is, writing the machine code down on a piece of paper and entering it into the computer by hand.

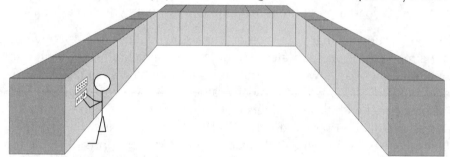

Figure 12.35: Oh, the joy of programming your first computer

Once you've entered this subroutine, you can use it to copy your program from the random-access memory onto paper tape. In fact, you can even use this subroutine to copy itself from the memory onto another paper tape. Overcome with enthusiasm, you might develop a second subroutine that can read data from the paper tape and load it back into memory, and then use your first subroutine to save this second subroutine onto yet another paper tape. Finally, flushed with success, you might put your precious paper tapes in a safe place and turn your computer off for the night.

{Did you spot the obvious flaw in the preceding sequence?}

The following morning, feeling relaxed and refreshed, you turn on your computer, load your first paper tape into the reader, and ...... gnash your teeth, rent your garb, and utter strange and wondrous oaths as you realize that the subroutine to read data from a paper tape is on a paper tape, but you can't read that paper tape without first having a subroutine that reads data from a paper tape, but ...... Fortunately, your simple subroutine to read data from a paper tape would be relatively small, so it wouldn't take too long to enter it again. In fact this was a typical procedure with the early computers. The first thing one did after switching the computer on was to use the switch panel to enter a subroutine referred to as a *Bootstrap Loader* – so-named from the concept of *"pulling oneself up by ones' bootstraps"*. The Bootstrap Loader was then used to load more-sophisticated programs from an external storage device such as a paper tape reader.

A few days (or years) later, you might get around to inventing some form of read-only memory. Modern computers use special integrated circuits for this purpose, but you could achieve the same effect by hard-wiring specific memory locations to the requisite patterns of *logic 0s* and *logic 1s*, and then forcing your computer to commence operations by reading the first of these locations when you turned it on. You might then decide to establish your paper-tape-reader subroutine in this read-only memory, so that you only have to set up a single address on the switch panel (the start address of the subroutine) and hit the Run button to load your first program from the paper tape reader.

Some further time down the road, you might come to the conclusion that having a switch panel hard-wired into the guts of your computer doesn't exactly reflect the high-tech image you're trying to portray to your cohorts. On this basis, you might decide to add a simple switch-panel monitor program into your read-only memory, and replace your predominantly mechanical switch panel with a sleek little chrome-plated number festooned with "go-faster stripes" and similar paraphernalia.

Assembling programs by hand

Now let's assume that you're eager to start creating a more advanced program; for example, a more sophisticated monitor that could be used to control a hexadecimal keypad (which you just happen to have designed, built, and connected to your computer the night before). Of course, this will require substantially more instructions than the existing monitor for your simple switch panel, but you are swept away with visions of how easy life is going to be when you no longer have to enter programs in binary using your accursed switch panel.

So, armed with a family-sized box of pencils and reams of paper, you grit your teeth and prepare yourself for the ordeal to come. However, just as your pencil is poised to pen its first stroke, you reel back in the sway of overpowering inspiration. Is it possible? Yes ...... No ...... Yes ...... No......
Yes, Yes, **Yes!** You've just realized how efficacious it would be to describe your programs at a higher level of abstraction, and to then assemble them into machine code later. It all seems so clear to you now – if you're going to assemble your programs, then you might as well call the high level representation "assembly language," while the process of translating the source program into machine code can be referred to as "assembling."

Naturally, these things are easier to say than they are to do, but after several false starts you might end up with something akin to the formal specification for the *Beboputer's* assembly language in Appendix F. Once you've completed this specification, you're all set to describe a hex keypad monitor in this language and assemble it by hand (Figure 2.36).

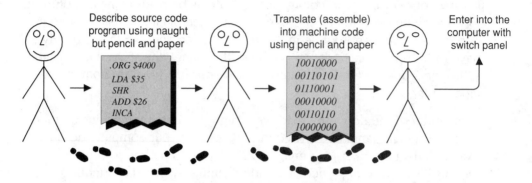

Figure 12.36: Assembling programs by hand

As we discussed at the beginning of this chapter, it's a lot easier to work with the limited number of mnemonics and symbols in an assembly language than it is to remember opcodes and write your programs in machine code. When you're writing a program you're trying to capture ideas, and it's easy to lose your train of thought if you're constantly having to look up the opcodes associated with all of the various instructions and their addressing modes. Also, when you're trying to read and debug a program, it's much easier to understand in assembly language that it would be in machine code. The bottom line is that, even if you're doing everything by hand, it is generally much more productive to describe any program larger than a few bytes in assembly language and translate it into machine code than it would be to create the machine code directly.

One-pass versus two-pass assembly processes

Assuming that you do have to assemble your source code by hand, then the next point to ponder would be exactly how you would set about doing this. Your first reaction might be: "*Duh, I'd start at the top, stroll through the middle, amble in the vague direction of the end, then stop.*" Oh, the innocence of bright-eyed youth. In fact there are two main strategies you might employ, which are referred to as *one-pass* and *two-pass* processes. Let's consider an example source file (Figure 12.37).

One-pass assembly processes: First let's assume that, in addition to the parchment bearing your hand-written source code, you have two more pieces of paper at your disposal. On one of these pieces of paper you might pen the title "*Machine Code*," while the other might be identified as the "*Symbol Table*." One approach would then be to look at the first statement (which is an .EQU declaration) and jot down the name SWITCHES and its associated value of $F000 on your *"Symbol Table"* paper. The next statement in this example is your .ORG, which doesn't really require any action on your part, except to note that the program commences at address $4000.

SWITCHES:	.EQU	$F000	# Address of 8-bit switch panel	Line 1
	.ORG	$4000	# Start of program	Line 2
LOOP:	LDA	[SWITCHES]	# Load ACC with value on switches	Line 3
	JZ	[LOOP]	# If value = 0 then try again	Line 4
	JSR	[GROK]	# If value ! = 0 call subroutine grok	Line 5

GROK:	SHL		# Shift ACC left 1 bit	Line 942
	AND	$0F	# AND with $0F to mask LS Nybble	Line 943

Figure 12.37: Hand-written source file to be hand-assembled

The first statement in the body of the program is the "LOOP: LDA [SWITCHES]." On your *"Symbol Table"* paper you would add the name LOOP and its associated value of $4000 (remember that the value of this type of label is the address of the first byte in its corresponding instruction). When you come to consider the "LDA [SWITCHES]"portion of this statement, you realize that this is a *"load accumulator"* instruction using the absolute addressing mode, so you would use a "cheat sheet" to look up the related opcode of $91. On your *"Machine Code"* paper you would now write the line "$4000 $91", meaning address $4000 is to contain the value $91. Finally, you recognize that the address for this absolute instruction is presented in the form of the label **SWITCHES**, so you turn to your *"Symbol Table"* paper to retrieve the value associated with this label, which is $F000, and then add two more lines to your *"Machine Code"* paper: "$4001 $F0" and "$4002 $00."

Similarly, the "JZ [LOOP]" statement poses no problems, because you can easily look up the opcode for this *"jump if zero"* instruction using absolute addressing mode (which is $D1), retrieve the value of **LOOP** (which is $4000) from your *"Symbol Table"* paper, and then add three more lines to your *"Machine Code"* paper: "$4003 $D1," "$4004 $40," and "$4005 $00."

Unfortunately, you do run into a problem when you come to the "JSR [GROK]" statement, because although you can look up the opcode for this *"jump to subroutine"* instruction using absolute addressing mode (which is $C9), you realize that you don't know what the value of GROK is, because when you come to consult your *"Symbol Table"* you discover that GROK hasn't been declared yet. Hmmm, what are you going to do now? Well one thing you do know is that GROK is going to be an address that requires two bytes, so you can still add three lines to your *"Machine Code"* paper: "$4006 $C9," "$4007 $??," and "$4008 $??," where the question marks indicate that you aren't sure what values should go into addresses $4007 and $4008 at this moment in time. Similarly, in your *"Symbol Table"* paper you can add the name GROK, indicate that you don't actually know its value yet, and note that when you do eventually determine the value of GROK you'll need to copy it into locations $4007 and $4008 (Figure 12.38).

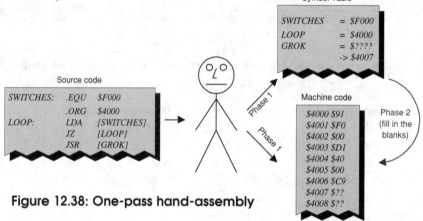

Figure 12.38: One-pass hand-assembly

Thus, even though this is called a "one-pass" process, it still requires a number of phases. In phase one, you generate the symbol table and the machine code as best you can (figure 12.38 reflects the state of the code during the middle of this phase). By the time you reach the end of the source program you'll know the values of all of the labels, so phase 2 consists of retrofitting any values that you didn't know at the time you needed them. Hence, the reason this is referred to as a "one pass" process is that it involves only a single pass through the source code.

Before moving on, we should note that the above description is something of a simplification, because a label like GROK may be used many times both *before* and *after* its value is revealed. In reality, every label on your *"Symbol Table"* paper would be annotated with a record of where the label was declared, along with a list of all of the locations in which the label was used, and you'd also maintain a "fix-up" list of any locations that need to be updated in phase two.

Two-pass assembly processes: Perhaps not surprisingly, a *two-pass process* requires you to stroll through the source file twice. The primary role of the first pass is to check the syntax of the source file and to determine the values associated with the labels (which obliges you to keep a running total of how

many bytes will be occupied by the instructions). After ascertaining the
values of the labels, you take a second pass through the source file to
assemble it into machine code, which is relatively easy in this case because
you already know the values of all of the labels (assume for the sake of
argument that the address associated with the label GROK eventually turns
out to be $4933) (Figure 12.39).

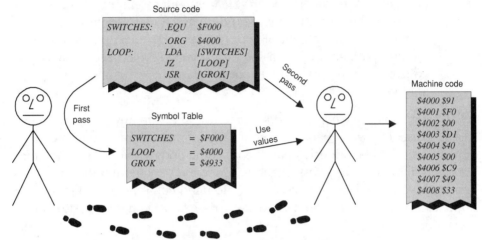

Figure 12.39: Two-pass hand-assembly

As you might expect, the one-pass and two-pass processes each have
distinct advantages and disadvantages. For example, the one-pass process
only requires you to wander through the source code a single time, but
you end up doing a lot of things all "mushed" together. By comparison,
although the two-pass process requires you to revisit the source code,
it also allows you to partition the assembly problem into two relatively
well-defined and well-bounded chunks.[5]

Before we continue our headlong plunge into the unknown, let's pause for a
moment to remind ourselves of exactly what you've achieved and where
you're heading:

a) We're assuming that you are a genius of heroic proportions, and that
   you've single-handedly constructed the first computer on the face of
   the planet.

b) Over a period of time, you invented some form of read-only memory
   and created an extremely simple switch-panel monitor program in
   machine code. You then decided to hard-wire your monitor program

[5]The decision as to whether to use a one-pass or a two-pass process may be influenced by
hardware considerations, such as the amount of memory you have available.

(including your Bootstrap Loader subroutine) into your read-only memory.

c) Next you added a hexadecimal keypad to your computer and single-handedly invented the concept of assembly language. You then created a formal definition for your language, which, by some strange quirk of fate, is identical to the *Beboputer's* assembly language (go figure the odds). Finally, you designed a more sophisticated monitor program to control your hex keypad. You captured this new monitor program in your assembly language on a piece of paper, and you've just hand-assembled your program into machine code on another piece of paper.

It all seems so easy when you look back, doesn't it? In any case, you now have to use the switch panel and your original monitor program in read-only memory to laboriously enter the machine code for your new monitor program into random-access memory. Once the new monitor has been entered, you can direct the old monitor to hand control over to the new one, at which point you are free to use your hex keypad with gusto and abandon.

Of course, you continue to be faced with the problem that turning your computer off will cause it to forget your new monitor program. However, you've still got a paper tape containing a copy of the "save" subroutine that can save data to a paper tape. Thus, you can use your "read" subroutine (that you hard-wired into your read-only memory along with your switch-panel monitor) to load the "save" subroutine from paper tape into some free area in the computer's memory, and then use this "save" subroutine to save your new hex keypad monitor to yet another paper tape …… phew!

This means that the next time you turn your computer on, you only need to use your switch panel and the first monitor program long enough to invoke your paper tape reader subroutine, which you then use to load the new hex keypad monitor from paper tape. In fact, once you are satisfied that your new monitor performs its duties to the standard you expect, you might feel moved to add this program into your read-only memory (along with the subroutine that writes data to paper tape).

Which comes first, the chicken or the egg?

If you think that the previous discussions on using your first monitor program to enter your second monitor program were somewhat circular and involved …… you ain't seen nothing yet! Although having a hex keypad monitor certainly goes some way toward making your tiny corner of the universe a better place to live, it hasn't altered the fact that you still have to write the source code for any new program on paper, assemble it into machine code by hand, and enter this machine code via the hex keypad. Thus, unless you actually enjoy the mindless tedium of endlessly juggling numbers (or you happen to know an accountant), it probably wouldn't be long before you started to cast a reflective gaze upon your computer, which is skulking in the corner desperately trying to look inconspicuous and failing miserably.

Smitten with your latest brain wave, you decide that henceforth you would like your computer to assemble your programs for you. This means that you need to write a program that you decide to call an "assembler," which will read other programs written in assembly language and assemble them into machine code. Unfortunately, although this sounds easy if you say it quickly, there's a bit more to it than meets the eye. For example, even if you already had such an assembler program, how would you present a source file to it? Currently, the only technique available to you would be to write the source on paper, hand-translate each of the characters into some form of numerical codes, and then enter these codes into another area of the memory using your hex keypad. Once you'd entered the source in this coded form, you could give your assembler the scent by pointing it in the direction of the first character in the source program and letting it roam wild and free. Although we [the authors] haven't actually tried this methodology, we would happily bet our wives' life savings that it would take longer to hand-translate your source programs into numerical codes than it would to assemble the little scamps by hand in the first place.

Let's approach this problem from a different angle. First, let's assume that you've already invented the concept of the ASCII code, along with a teleprinter, a QWERTY keyboard, and a memory-mapped display, all of which you proceed to connect to your computer (it's fair to say that this has been one of your better years).[6] Now let's take a step back and consider what you actually want to do, because knowing what you want to do invariably makes it easier to decide how you're going to set about doing it (Figure 12.40).

After some little thought, you decide that you'd like to be able to use some sort of editor program to manipulate your source code, and to then use an assembler program to translate this machine-readable source into its

---

[6]ASCII, QWERTY keyboards, and memory-mapped displays were introduced in Chapters 10 and 11.

machine-code equivalent. But, returning to earth with a stomach-churning thump, you realize that you haven't actually got either an editor or assembler at this time. Thus, you find yourself in a classic "chicken and egg" situation: is it better to hand-assemble an editor and use this to create your assembler, or would it be preferable to hand-edit an assembler and use this to create your editor? Fortunately, you decide to do us all a favor by spurning both courses (because the resulting tautological circumlocutions would add several more chapters to this book). Instead, you determine to create both editor and assembler completely by hand.

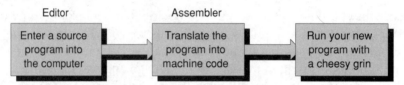

Figure 12.40: The process you'd like to follow in the fullness of time

Line editors versus screen editors

The main trick at this stage of the game is not to set your sights too high. What you have to do is to consider the minimum set of capabilities that you want your editor to have – you can add any "bells and whistles" later. As it happens, your minimum requirements are actually quite reasonable; all you really need is:

a) The ability to start editing a new source file, or to load an existing source file from paper tape.

b) The ability to interactively view selected lines or portions of your source file.

c) The ability to interactively delete unwanted lines and add new lines.

d) The ability to save a source file back onto a paper tape.

Note the use of the qualifier "interactively" in points (b) and (c), which immediately eliminates some alternatives and automatically channels your energies in certain ways. Also, with regard to point (c), it would obviously be nice to be able to modify an existing line in the source file, but you can ill-afford to add any unnecessary complexity, so you sensibly decide to follow the KISS principle (*"Keep it simple, stupid!"*) and stick with your original list of features.

The next point to consider is how you intend to use your resulting editor. In one of the many possible scenarios, you may decide to perform all of your data entry using the teleprinter (Figure 12.41).

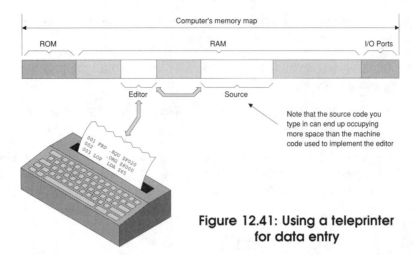

**Figure 12.41: Using a teleprinter
for data entry**

As we see, your editor program (when you got around to creating it, and assuming this is the sort of editor you decided to create in the first place) would reside somewhere in the RAM portion of your computer's memory map (which, as the fates would have it, looks remarkably similar to our *Beboputer's* memory map). The editor would loop around reading an input port connected to the teleprinter and waiting for you to press a key on the keyboard. Whenever you pressed a key, the editor would store the corresponding ASCII value somewhere in the RAM, gradually building up a machine-readable copy of your source file (or any other type of text file you cared to create, such as a letter to your great-aunt).

Also, remember that the keyboard and printer portions of the teleprinter are logically and physically distinct, which means that pressing a key on the keyboard does not, of itself, cause that character to be printed out. Thus, in addition to storing your characters in the RAM, it would also make sense for your editor program to write their ASCII codes to an output port driving the teleprinter (this process may be referred to as "echoing" the characters).

In addition to simply entering characters, you also need to be able to give your editor commands, such as *"save my source file to paper tape"* or *"load a source file from paper tape."* Also, according to our original specification, you need the ability to interactively view selected lines or portions of your source file, add new lines, and delete unwanted lines. There are several ways in which you could achieve this, but one of the simplest would be to use control sequences. As you may recall from Chapter 10, when we designed our keyboard we said that our **CTRL** key would modify the alphabetical keys such that 'A' would generate ASCII code $01, 'B' would generate ASCII $02, 'C' would generate ASCII $03, and so forth. Assuming that you designed your teleprinter in the same way, your editor could keep a watchful eye open for the following codes:

    a) The code $01, which equates to <CTRL-A>, could instruct the editor to **add** a line.

    b) The code $04, which equates to <CTRL-D>, could instruct the editor to **delete** one or more lines.

    c) The code $0C, which equates to <CTRL-L>, could instruct the editor to **list** lines (in the context of this editor, "listing lines" means causing the teleprinter to print them out).

    d) The code $13, which equates to <CTRL-S>, could instruct the editor to **save** the file to paper tape.

    e) The code $15, which equates to <CTRL-U>, could instruct the editor to **upload** a file from paper tape.

Each of these commands would require additional qualifiers known as "arguments"; for example, after pressing "<CTRL-L>", you would have to tell the editor which lines you would like to list. Once again, there are many possible alternatives, but a simple option in the case of the list command would be to follow the control sequence with two colon-separated numbers. Thus, "<CTRL-L>14:22" could instruct your editor to list lines fourteen through twenty-two.

Since the editor we just described functions in a line-oriented manner, it is, not surprisingly, referred to as a *line editor*. Editors of this type were very common in the early days, largely because they were just about the only such tool you could use in conjunction with a teleprinter. However, they also have advantages in their own right, such as being reasonably simple to create, not requiring much memory, and being very efficient in terms of CPU resources (which means that they don't place much demand on the computer). Thus, even after the combination of keyboards and memory-mapped displays flounced onto the stage, line editors still managed to find a role to play (in fact there are modern variants around to this day). Even so, the advent of memory-mapped displays also threw open the doors to another style of editor called a *screen editor* (Figure 12.42).

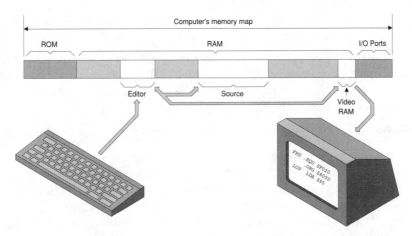

Figure 12.42: Using a keyboard and memory-mapped display for data entry

Once again, your editor program (when you got around to creating it) would reside somewhere in the RAM portion of your computer's memory map, looping around reading an input port connected to the keyboard and waiting for you to press a key. Whenever you pressed a key, the editor would again store the corresponding ASCII value somewhere in the RAM, gradually building up a machine-readable copy of your new source file. However, if your editor were a screen editor, it would also copy a portion of your source file into the Video RAM, from whence it would subsequently appear on your memory-mapped display. One way to visualize the way in which this type of editor works is to consider the memory-mapped display's screen as a window, through which one can view a portion of your source file (Figure 12.43).

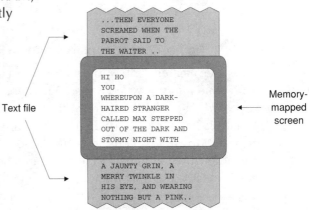

A screen editor requires different commands to those of a line editor. For example, it needs techniques to navigate around the screen and the file. In order

Figure 12.43: Viewing the screen as a window into the source file

to navigate around the screen, you might design the editor to check for the codes associated with the arrow keys on the keyboard. (Note that, in the case of the *Beboputer's* keyboard, we associated the codes $D0 through

$D3 with these keys — see also Table 11.1 in the previous chapter.) When one of these keys is pressed, the editor could move some sort of cursor character around the screen. Similarly, to navigate around the file you might use control sequences such as <CTRL-T> or <CTRL-B> to instruct the editor to display the **top** or **bottom** of the file, respectively (and so forth for a variety of other commands that *you* might decide would be of use in *your* editor).

Remember that Figure 12.43 is just a convenient way to visualize what's happening, but you must not allow this illustration to mislead you. Flick back to Figure 12.42 to remind yourself that the source (or text) file is stored in one section of the computer's RAM, and it's up to your editor to copy a selected portion of the file into the Video RAM. A little thought reveals that the editor is going to have quite a lot of work on its hands (Figure 12.44).

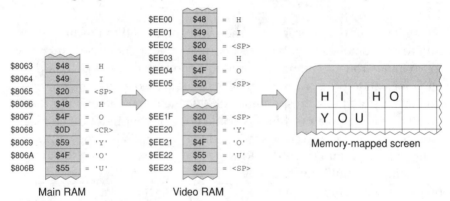

Figure 12.44: Mapping the main RAM into the video RAM

As we see, the editor has to do more than simply copy a portion of the source file into the Video RAM. When you're entering a source file from the keyboard, every key has an ASCII code associated with it, such as $20 for a space (<SP>) and $0D for a carriage return (<CR>). However, if your editor were to copy a $0D code into the Video RAM, all you would see would be a weird symbol at the corresponding position on the screen. Instead, your editor must know how many rows and columns can be displayed on your memory-mapped screen, it has to keep track of the number of characters that are already being displayed on each line, and it has to replace any $0D carriage return codes with as many $20 space codes as are required to fill the remaining columns on those lines.

All of this means that, although screen editors are user-friendly, they are significantly harder to design and build than line editors, they require more of the system's memory, and they make much greater demands on the computer's processing resources. Before moving on to the next section, spend a few moments contemplating the tasks a screen editor would have to perform if you instructed it to add or delete a single character from a portion of your source file that was currently being displayed in the middle of the screen.

Pulling yourself up by your bootstraps

Once again, it's time to return to earth with a sickening thump, because you haven't actually got an editor yet – all you've done is think about it a lot. However, you can certainly see the benefits that would ensue if you did have an such a program, so you decide to construct one forthwith.

As we previously noted, your first editor should be as simple as you can possibly make it, because you're going to have to build it by hand. First of all you'd determine which features you considered to be vital and which you could live without for a while. Then you'd draw your flowcharts, write down your source code on a piece of paper, hand-assemble this source code into machine code on another piece of paper, and then enter your machine code into the computer using your hex keypad.

At this point you might consider running your editor to see whether or not it works as planned. Good grief ...... have you learnt nothing? There are a number of rules that it's well worth taking to heart, and the first is: *"Anything that can go wrong usually does."* Based on this insight, we can extrapolate a second rule which is: *"Always back everything up."* Make this your mantra as you wend your weary way through the day – start by saying it aloud: *"Always back everything up."* That was pathetic. Let's try it again ...... all together now: *"Always back everything up."* That was a little better. Now, once more, but this time just the ladies in the upper circle: ***"Always back everything up."*** By George, I think they've got it (although the lesson won't really sink in until you forget to follow our advice and something malapropos happens).[7]

Why are we being so hard on you? Well, let's just say that there's a million-to-one chance you made a teensy-weensy mistake somewhere in the process: either in your original concept, or when you were describing the flowcharts, or while you were jotting down the source code, or during the process of hand assembling, or even, just maybe, while you were entering the machine code with the hex keypad. Assuming that an error did slip in,

[7] And when it does, as it undoubtedly will, the annoying whisper in your ear will be us saying: *"We told you so ...... we told you so ......"*

what do you think might happen? Well as a best case your editor might just sit there, in which case you'd quickly realize that there was a problem and leap into the fray to start sorting it out. As a worse case, your program could wreak havoc throughout the system, writing data where it wasn't supposed to and quite possibly trashing your hex keypad monitor and the editor itself, before finally giving up the ghost and withdrawing into the nether regions from whence it came. Thus, the first thing you'd do after entering your editor's machine code is to back it up by copying it onto a paper tape (or a similar mechanism).

Once you've debugged your rudimentary editor and persuaded it to work, your next task would be to create an equally simple assembler. Once again, you would first determine which features you considered to be vital and which you could live without for a while. For example, you don't really need the ability to use both uppercase and lowercase letters in your source file, so you might decide that your first assembler will accept uppercase letters only. Similarly, a minimum requirement would be to support address labels, but you could restrict each label to consist of say only four alphabetic characters (no more and no less). Having .ORG, .END, and .BYTE directives would probably be a minimum requirement, but you could get by without having any form of .EQU directives or equations (you'd have to use more labels, but "so what?"). As usual, you'd now draw your flowcharts, write your source code down on a piece of paper, hand-assemble this source code into machine code on another piece of paper, enter your machine code into the computer using your hex keypad, and *back it up onto a paper tape.*

One of the tasks we didn't mention earlier, but which you would hopefully have undertaken before creating either the editor or the assembler, is to define your proposed *usage model,* by which we mean a high-level specification describing the way in which you anticipate using these tools and the way in which they are going to interact. For example, if your computer has only a limited amount of RAM, you may be forced to adopt a somewhat disjoint usage model (Figure 12.45).

As you can imagine, this usage model would have its painful aspects, not the least that it could take an awful long time to debug a program of any size. On the other hand, if your computer doesn't have much memory then you may not have any choice, and this model certainly wouldn't have raised too many eyebrows in the early days.

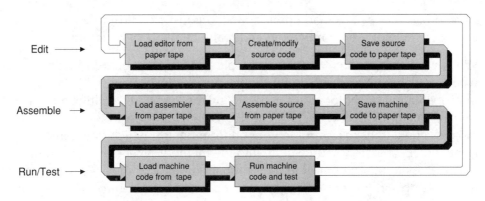

Figure 12.45: A somewhat disjoint usage model

The amount of memory available on your system may also dictate the way in which you implement tools such as the assembler. For example, if you have enough memory, you may opt for a one-pass assembly process in which you assemble all of the machine code into memory and then save it to paper tape. However, if your memory is a little thin on the ground but you have two paper tape devices, then you may decide to use a two-pass assembly process: the first pass would be used to build a symbol table in memory, while the second pass could re-read the source file line-by-line from one paper tape and write out the corresponding machine code byte-by-byte onto the second tape.

As time passed and you found yourself able to afford greater quantities of memory, your usage model would probably change to reflect this. For example, you may decide to keep both your editor and assembler resident in memory at the same time (Figure 12.46).

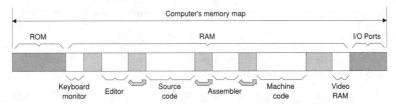

Figure 12.46: A more sophisticated usage model based on the ability to have multiple tools resident in memory simultaneously

Rather than constantly running your programs from the hex keypad, you might decide to implement a simple QWERTY keyboard monitor. Of course, you would initially have to use the hex keypad to run the editor to enter your source, and then use it again to run the assembler in order to generate the machine code for your keyboard monitor. However, once you had created this new monitor (and saved it to paper tape), you would only have to use your hex keypad one last time to transfer control to your keyboard monitor, and then you would really be ready to rock and roll.

When you come to think about it, a simple QWERTY keyboard monitor would actually be ..... well, quite simple. For example, your first implementation might loop around checking the keyboard, waiting for you to press one of three keys: 'E', 'A', or 'R'. When you pressed the 'E' key the monitor could transfer control to your editor program, which you could then use to enter some new source code into the memory. When you exited the editor it would return control to the keyboard monitor. Similarly, pressing the 'A' key could instruct the keyboard monitor to hand control over to your assembler program, which could read the source code in memory and generate the associated machine code. Once the assembler had done its deed, it also could return control back to the keyboard monitor. Finally, pressing the 'R' key could cause the keyboard monitor to run your new machine code. Obviously we've simplified certain things in this description, such as how the keyboard monitor knows where to find the editor and the assembler, and how these tools know where to locate the source and machine code. However, it wouldn't take you much effort to solve these problems, and one of the fun things about computers is that everyone can come up with their own ideas and techniques.

Anyway, let's assume that you're now in possession of an editor and an assembler. Irrespective of their simplicity, they will greatly ease the task of creating any future programs. Furthermore, it probably wouldn't take long before you started contemplating ways in which you could improve these tools. For example, you might decide that life would be a great deal sweeter if your assembler could support labels with up to eight characters, and that you really, *really* need the ability to use .**EQU** directives and rudimentary expressions in your source code.

Improving things in this way is like an itch that you've got to scratch, and before long you would come to believe that life is meaningless without these enhancements. You would find yourself using your existing editor to create the source code for your new assembler, and then use your existing assembler to assemble this source code and generate the machine code for your new assembler. Next, you might use your existing editor and your new assembler to create a better editor, and then ...... carry on around and around the circle, using your existing tools to create better tools and using these tools to create still-better tools, which, once again, is why we refer to the process as: *"Pulling yourself up by your bootstraps."*[8]

Creating a cross-assembler

Assume that you awake one morning with a song in your heart, fire in your belly, and a brilliant idea for a brand new computer. Flushed with enthusiasm, you immediately set sail on your latest voyage of discovery. The days fly by, and before long your new masterpiece stands before you in all its glory. As for your first computer, this new beast initially hangs around waiting for you to come up with the software tools required for it to do its cunning stuff. Do you have to go through the entire frustrating process of creating new monitors, editors, and assemblers from the ground up? "*No,*" you cry, "*a thousand times no!*" In fact, you can use the existing tools on your first computer to create a fresh set for your new computer.

Of course there are certain complications, but aren't there always? Possibly the biggest consideration is that you've learnt a lot from your original project, so your new computer will almost certainly have a different architecture and instruction set than your old machine. This doesn't pose insurmountable problems, but it can, as usual, involve some convoluted thinking.

One of the first tasks you might set yourself is to create an assembler for your new computer, but this is where things start to get a little tricky. Assuming that your new computer does have a different instruction set (which may well include different addressing modes), then you're going to have to specify a new assembly language with its own mnemonics, syntax, and semantics. Once you've defined your new language, the next stage is to write an assembly program that will accept this language and generate your new machine code (Figure 12.47).

In this scenario, you have to write this new assembler in your original source code (Figure 12.47a) and assemble it through your original assembler (Figure 12.47b); the resulting machine code is your new assembler. Note that your new assembler will only actually run on your original computer, because its machine code was generated by your original assembler. However, you can now create the source code for some other program in your new assembly language (Figure 12.47c) and assemble it through your new assembler (Figure 12.47d). Interestingly enough, the resulting machine code won't run on your original computer, because your new assembler

---

[8]One of the interesting quirks about pulling yourself up by your bootstraps in this manner is that you end up riding the crest of a wave and, although you know where you are, you can't quite remember how you got there. To put this another way, it's quite common for earlier incarnations of your tools to become lost in the mists of time, to the extent that it becomes well-nigh impossible to re-create your path through the labyrinth.

generated the machine code used by your new computer, which means that you now have to copy this machine code over to your new computer in order to run it (Figure 12.47e).

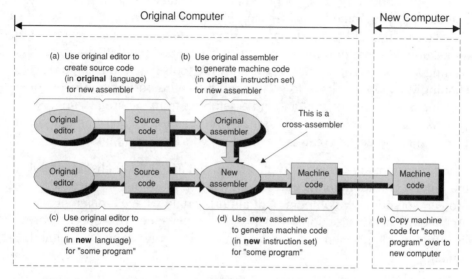

Figure 12.47: Creating a cross-assembler

Due to the way in which it works, your new assembler is referred to as a *cross-assembler*, which does not imply that it's dissatisfied with its lot in life – a cross-assembler is simply an assembler that runs on one computer and produces machine code for another. To obtain a version of your new assembler that will run on your new computer, you could hand-translate its source code (which you created in your original assembly language) into your new assembly language, pass this through your cross-assembler, and copy the resulting machine code over to your new computer. Similarly, you could dig out the source code for the editor on your original computer, hand-translate it into your new assembly language, pass this through your cross-assembler, and copy the resulting machine code over to your new computer, thereby giving you an editor on that computer. Alternatively, as opposed to hand-translating these (and other) source programs into your new assembly language, you may well consider writing a special translator program that can do the job for you.

Introducing the *Beboputer's* cross-assembler

This must be your lucky day, because rather than make you design everything from the ground up, we've taken the trouble to provide your *Beboputer* with a combined editor and cross-assembler. As you will see, the usage model for our humble offering is somewhat more sophisticated than the models we discussed above, but the basic principles are pretty much the same. The only novel aspect of our scenario is that both of your computers (your real computer and your virtual *Beboputer*) actually inhabit the same physical machine, but it will be advantageous if you can persuade yourself to regard them as two totally distinct entities (Figure 12.48).

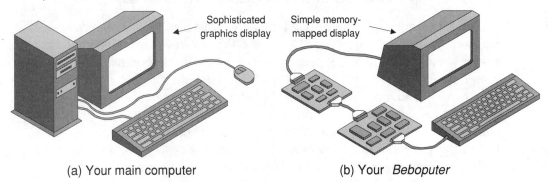

Sophisticated graphics display

Simple memory-mapped display

(a) Your main computer   (b) Your *Beboputer*

Figure 12.48: Visualizing your main computer and *Beboputer* as distinct entities

The combined editor and cross-assembler runs on your main computer, and you can use it to create source programs in the *Beboputer's* assembly language and translate these programs into the *Beboputer's* machine code. In the real world, it would then be necessary to transport this machine code to the *Beboputer* using some mechanism such as a paper tape, but our virtual environment provides for some short cuts. So let's not dilly-dally and shilly-shally talking about it – instead, let us fling the gates asunder and behold the glory that is ...... **the *Beboputer's* cross-assembler!**

Winding up the Beboputer

Make sure the *Beboputer* CD is in the appropriate drive in your computer and summon the *Beboputer*. Once the *Beboputer's* project window has opened, click the File item on its menu bar, click the Open Project entry in the resulting pull-down menu, then select the Lab 7 project from the ensuing dialog. This will invoke our seventh lab (Figure 12.49).

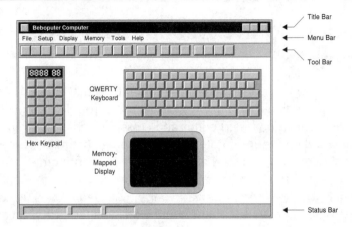

Figure 12.49: The *Beboputer* **project window for Lab 7**

The tools that appear in the working area are familiar to us: the memory-mapped display, the hex keypad, and the QWERTY keyboard. Note that the memory-mapped display is initially black, because the *Beboputer* hasn't been powered up yet. To rectify this situation, click the **ON** button on the hex keypad, which powers up the *Beboputer* and the memory-mapped display. As we observed in the previous lab, the display powers up to show random characters, which reflect the uninitialized contents of the *Beboputer's* video RAM. Now rather than using the hex keypad to enter a machine code program to clear the display, we are going to use our cross-assembler to create this machine code for us.

Invoking and running the assembler

There are several ways for you to access the *Beboputer's* cross-assembler. For example, if you hadn't already launched the *Beboputer*, you could use the assembler as a standalone utility by clicking the Windows 95™ **Start** button, followed by the **Programs** entry, then the *Beboputer* entry, and finally the **Assembler** item. However, as you are already in **Lab 7**, you can call the assembler directly from the *Beboputer's* project window. One way to invoke the assembler would be to click the **Tools** item on the project window's menu bar, then click the **Assembler** entry in the resulting pull-down menu. Alternatively, you can achieve the same effect by simply clicking the **Assembler** icon in the project window's toolbar, resulting in our combined editor and cross assembler manifesting itself before your very eyes (Figure 12.50).

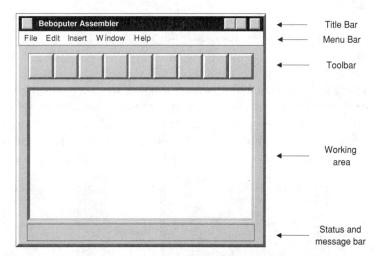

Figure 12.50: The *Beboputer's* combined editor and cross-assembler

Use your mouse to drag the assembler by its title bar and position it wherever you like in the project window. It doesn't matter if the assembler obscures any of the other tools – we'll handle that problem when we come to it. Now you're going to use the assembler to create a simple program to clear the memory-mapped display's screen. The flowchart for this program is short, sharp, and sweet (as is its title) (Figure 12.51).

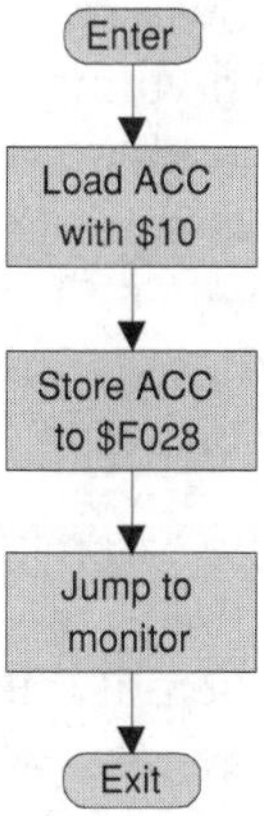

This program loads the accumulator with a value of $10, which is the code that instructs the memory-mapped display to clear the screen. The program then writes this code to the output port at address $F028, which is the port that drives the memory-mapped display's control circuitry. Finally, the program performs an unconditional jump back to the start of our hex keypad's monitor program at address $0000.

Figure 12.51: Flowchart

Entering this program would be a trivial matter, but we actually want you to load some source code that we prepared earlier. Click the File item on the *assembler's* menu bar (**not** the project window's menu bar), then click the Open entry in the resulting pull-down menu. Select the "lab7_p1b.asm" entry from the resulting dialog, then click the Open button to open this file and dismiss the dialog.

Now, before you do anything else, use the assembler's File → Save As command to save this file under the new name of "lab7_p1.asm," thereby ensuring that an unmodified version of our original file will be available to you in the future. The reason we required you to use our existing source code is that, for some inexplicable reason, it contains two errors that we'd like you to correct (Figure 12.52). Both of these errors are fairly obvious, but play along with us for a while. The first error occurs in the second line, where the .EQU directive is spelt incorrectly. Let's assume that you spot this error on your own. Our editor works in the standard way for such tools, so move your mouse cursor to the left of the 'U', press-and-hold the left mouse button and drag the cursor to the right to highlight both the 'U' and the 'Q', then release the mouse button and type "QU" to correct the problem.

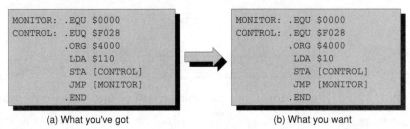

```
MONITOR:  .EQU  $0000          MONITOR:  .EQU  $0000
CONTROL:  .EUQ  $F028          CONTROL:  .EQU  $F028
          .ORG  $4000                    .ORG  $4000
          LDA   $110                     LDA   $10
          STA   [CONTROL]                STA   [CONTROL]
          JMP   [MONITOR]                JMP   [MONITOR]
          .END                          .END
```

(a) What you've got   (b) What you want

Figure 12.52: Errors to be corrected in our source file

Our second error occurs on the fourth line, where a careless slip of the finger has caused us to enter "$110" rather than the "$10" we required. However, let's assume that we all miss this one, and truly believe that everything is as it should be. As we honestly feel that the source code is "good-to-go," our next step would be to assemble it. To do this, click the 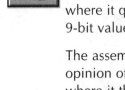 **Assemble** icon on the *assembler's* toolbar (**not** the project window's toolbar). This instructs the assembler to rummage through our source code, where it quickly locates the problem, which is that we're trying to assign a 9-bit value to our 8-bit accumulator.

The assembler displays a message in its status bar informing us as to its opinion of what went wrong, places its cursor at the beginning of the line where it thinks the error is most likely to be found, beeps in an annoying way, and waits for us to do something about it (muttering to itself how programmers these days aren't what they used to be). In this instance the assembler correctly identified the problem and resolved it to the value "$110," so all that is required is for you to replace this with the correct value of $10. Once you've made the correction, click the **Assemble** icon again: this time the status area displays a message informing you that your assembly was successful.

Note that our assembler is a relatively simple tool on the scale of things; sometimes it will tightly focus on an error and issue a really useful message, but on other occasions it may be somewhat cryptic and only vaguely indicate the problem area (if you're generous, you'll assume that we carefully engineered our tool in just this way so as to emulate the early assemblers). Also, an assembler intended for use by professional programmers would typically proceed all the way through the source code and generate an output file documenting multiple errors. However, presenting information in this form can be a little disconcerting for beginners, so we decided that our assembler would only identify errors individually and give you the opportunity to correct them one at a time.

The fact that the assembly process has now succeeded has some important ramifications, not the least that, while your back was turned, the assembler created two output files: "lab7_p1.lst" (a list file) and "lab7_p1.ram" (a RAM file). We will return to consider the list file a little later; for the nonce we will concentrate our attentions on the RAM file, which contains the machine code for our program. As we've finished with the assembler for the moment, iconize it by clicking the appropriate button in its title bar, and you'll see the assembler disappear from the screen and reappear in the main window's task bar. Now

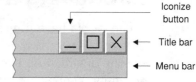

Iconize button

Title bar

Menu bar

use your mouse to click the **Memory** item on the project window's menu bar, then click the **Load RAM** entry in the resulting pull-down menu. Double-click the "lab7_p1.ram" file in the scrolling list on the left-hand side of the dialog, which selects this file and adds it to the right-hand list. The entry in the right-hand list informs us that the machine code in this file will occupy addresses $4000 through $4007 (where $4000 is the start address from our .ORG directive, and the three instructions in our program occupy eight bytes).

Click the **Load** button to load this machine code into the *Beboputer's* RAM and dismiss the form. Finally, ensure that the hex keypad's **Address (Ad)** button is active, enter the program's start address of $4000, then click the **Run** button. It should come as no great surprise that our program causes the memory-mapped display to clear the screen and then returns control to the monitor. Although this program was quite trivial, it's the process that we're interested in here, which can be summarized as follows:

a) Use the assembler to create the source code for a new program or modify an existing program.

b) Use the assembler to debug the source code and generate the associated machine code.

c) Use the Memory → Load RAM pull-down menu to load the machine code into the *Beboputer's* RAM.

d) Use the hex keypad to run the machine code program.

In the real world the machine code generated from step (b) would have to be transported to the *Beboputer* by some means. In the past this would probably have involved paper tapes or punched cards, whilst today we might use something akin to a floppy disk or a direct network connection between the two machines. However, in our virtual world, we're making the assumption that step (c) encompasses the act of copying the machine code from your main computer to the *Beboputer*.

Introducing the CPU register display

As fate would have it, your highly versatile *Beboputer* comes equipped with some extremely useful tools and utilities that we haven't even mentioned yet, one of which is called the *CPU register display*. Before we examine this utility, we need to create a more interesting program to demonstrate its capabilities. First, click the **assembler** item on the Windows 95™ task bar to return it to its former glory. Next click the **File** item on the *assembler's* menu bar (**not** the project window's menu bar), then save your current program by clicking on the **Save** entry in the resulting pull-down menu. (Actually, you didn't really need to save this file at all, because the act of running the assembler automatically saves whichever source file is currently active, but it's a good idea to get into the habit of saving things.) Now create a new file by clicking the **File** item on the assembler's menu bar and clicking the **New** entry in the resulting pull-down menu; then edit the file such that it looks like Figure 12.53.

```
CTRLPORT: .EQU $F028    # O/P port driving mem-map display
CLEARSCR: .EQU $10      # Code to clear the mem-map display
KEYBOARD: .EQU $F008    # I/P port connected to keyboard
ROW6COL6: .EQU $EEA5    # Video RAM address for row=6 col=6
          .ORG $4000
          LDA  CLEARSCR  # Load ACC with code to clear screen
          STA [CTRLPORT] # Clear the screen
LOOP:     LDA [KEYBOARD] # Load ACC from keyboard
          JZ  [LOOP]     # If no key pressed jump back and loop
          STA [ROW6COL6] # Write character to the screen
          JMP [LOOP]     # Jump back and do it again
          .END
```

Figure 12.53: Reading and displaying a character from the keyboard

Once you've entered this source code, save it by clicking the File item on the assembler's menu bar and clicking the **Save As** entry in the resulting pull-down menu. Use the ensuing dialog to name your file "lab7_p2.asm," then click the **Save** button to save this file and dismiss the dialog. Now click the **assemble** icon (the one on the assembler's toolbar) to process this file and debug any errors that may have crept in along the way. As we've finished with the assembler for the moment, iconize it by clicking the appropriate button in its title bar; as before, you'll see the assembler appear in the Windows 95™ task bar.

Iconize button

Title bar

Menu bar

Use your mouse to click the **Memory** item on the project window's menu bar, then click the **Load RAM** entry in the resulting pull-down menu. As you scroll through the list on the left-hand side of the dialog window, you will find the new "lab7_p2.ram" file which you just created. Double-click this entry to select this file and add it to the right-hand list, then click the **Load** button to load this machine code into the *Beboputer's* RAM and dismiss the form.

Now click the **Display** item on the main project window's menu bar, then click the **CPU Register Display** entry in the resulting pull-down menu. This results in a new form of display appearing as shown in Figure 12.54. Use your mouse to drag this display by its title bar to a convenient location on your main computer's screen.

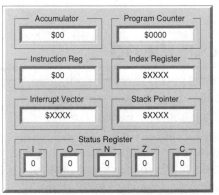

Figure 12.54: CPU register display

Not surprisingly, the CPU register display shows the contents of the internal registers in the *Beboputer's* CPU. Some of these registers initially display zero values, which is the way they're initialized following a power-on reset or a hard reset. By comparison, some of the registers display "X" characters indicating unknown values, which is just a trick on our part to show that we haven't loaded anything into these registers yet. In order to activate the display, ensure that the hex keypad's Address (**Ad**) button is active, enter the program's start address of $4000, then click the **Step** button.

Understanding this display takes a bit of practice, but once you've got the hang of it you will find it to be an incredibly useful tool. The main thing to get used to is the fact that the *program counter (PC)* field is always left pointing at the first byte of the *next* instruction to be executed, while all of the other fields reflect the state of registers after the *previous* instruction was executed. Thus, as you've just stepped through the first instruction (the "**LDA CLEARSCR**"), the *accumulator (ACC)* field shows $10, which is the value you just loaded. Meanwhile, any of the status flags that were affected by this instruction are set to the appropriate values, and the program counter field updates to show $4002, which is the address of the next instruction. Note that any "X" values that remain in the display indicate registers that have not been initialized yet (such as the *stack pointer (SP)*), but we'll look at these in a little while.

You may have noticed that the assembly program you just entered is almost identical to the program we wrote in Chapter 11 (Figure 11.25), but it was a lot easier this time around. As you may recall, this program first clears the memory-mapped screen, then loops around reading the QWERTY keyboard until you press a key. Click the hex keypad's **Step** button a few times and watch the program reading $00 values from the QWERTY keyboard. Now click a key on the keyboard, then continue to click the **Step** button until the corresponding character appears in the sixth column of the sixth row on the memory-mapped display. Keep on stepping through this program until you're relatively happy with your understanding of the way in which the CPU register display operates, then click the **Run** button and play some more. Finally, click the **Reset (Rst)** button to return us to the monitor program.

The stack wants to be your friend

In earlier chapters we've mentioned the stack and even used it to a limited extent (mostly in the context of subroutine calls), but now we need to become more familiar with its wily ways. As we know, the *Beboputer's* CPU contains a 16-bit register called the stack pointer. When the *Beboputer* is powered-up, this register contains a random pattern of 0s and 1s, but we can use a **BLDSP** ("*big load stack pointer*") instruction to load it with a value of our choice. For example, assume that we decide to load the stack pointer with a value of $4FFF (Figure 12.55).

Let's further assume that during the course of writing our program we realize we'd like to temporarily store the current value in the accumulator. For example, we may be poised to modify the accumulator's contents and do something with this new value, but in a while we'll need to access the accumulator's original value again. Of course, we could declare a temporary 1-byte location called something like TEMP, and then use a "STA [TEMP]" instruction to store the value in the accumulator. Later on, when we wished to access the value that used to be in the accumulator, we could use a "LDA [TEMP]" instruction to retrieve our value from its temporary location. Alternatively, we could simply use a PUSHA instruction to copy ("*push*") the contents of the accumulator onto the stack (Figure 12.56).

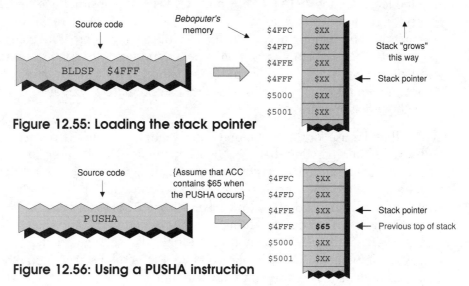

Figure 12.55: Loading the stack pointer

Figure 12.56: Using a PUSHA instruction

Note that there's no significance to our assumption that the accumulator contains a value of $65 when the PUSHA instruction occurs, we just needed some value to use in this illustration. After the PUSHA has copied the contents of the accumulator onto the stack, the CPU automatically decrements the stack pointer, thereby causing it to point to the next free location. Remember that the reason the stack pointer is decremented is that the stack "grows" towards address $0000 (as was discussed in Chapter 8). This is why we have to be careful when choosing the initial value for the stack pointer and when using the stack, because we have to ensure that it doesn't "grow" so big as to overwrite our program. If we so wished, we could continue to push values onto the stack, and each time we did the CPU would automatically decrement the stack pointer to point to the next free location. Thus, the reason we refer to this entity as "the stack" is because words of data are "stacked" on top of each other.

Be this as it may, the act of pushing the accumulator onto the stack doesn't affect the accumulator's contents, so we can continue to use the accumulator howsoever we desire. Sometime later we can use a POPA instruction to retrieve ("*pop*") the value off the top of the stack and load it back into the accumulator. When the CPU sees a **POPA** instruction, it first increments the stack pointer to point to the last value placed on top of the stack, and then copies this value back into the accumulator.

There are several reasons why we might prefer to use this push and pop technique as opposed to storing the accumulator to a temporary location, not the least that the "**STA [TEMP]**" and "**LDA [TEMP]**" instructions we considered earlier each require three bytes, while **PUSHA** and **POPA** instructions only require a single byte. This means that a program using the push-and-pop approach will be both smaller and faster than the store-and-load alternative. Also, the push-and-pop method saves us from littering our program with temporary locations, which can be more advantageous than it might at first appear.

We will find a use for this technique and variations of it in the next section. Also, we should mention that a **PUSHSR** instruction can be used to copy the contents of the status register onto the stack, while a **POPSR** instruction can be used to retrieve the value on the top of the stack and load it into the status register. Apart from anything else, using a **PUSHA** followed by a **POPSR** allows us to copy the contents of the accumulator into the status register (which allows us to play cunning tricks like setting and clearing status flags), while a **PUSHSR** followed by a **POPA** allows us to copy the contents of the status register into the accumulator.[9]

The subterranean world of subroutines

As we've previously discussed, the stack is a key element when it comes to implementing subroutines. When our program uses a JSR ("*jump to subroutine*") instruction to call a subroutine, the CPU automatically stores the return address on the top of the stack (Figure 12.57).

This program isn't particularly meaningful, but it will serve to illustrate a couple of interesting points. First we use a **BLDSP** instruction to initialize the stack pointer to point to location $4FFF; then we use an **LDA** instruction to load the accumulator with $65 (for no apparent reason beyond the purposes of this example). The interesting part of our tale occurs when we execute the **JSR** instruction to jump to the subroutine called **CLEAR**. At this point, the CPU will automatically store the address of the instruction following the JSR (that is, the address of the **INCA**) on the top of the stack

---

[9]See also Appendix D for examples of these PUSHSR-POPA and PUSHA-POPSR combinations used in the context of interrupt handling.

and cause the stack pointer to be decremented by two memory locations. This address is referred to as the "return address," because this is the address that the program will return to when the subroutine terminates itself. Since the **BLDSP**, **LDA**, and **JSR** instructions require three, two, and three bytes, respectively; the return address (which is the address of the **INCA** instruction) will be $4008, and this is the value that's stored on the stack.

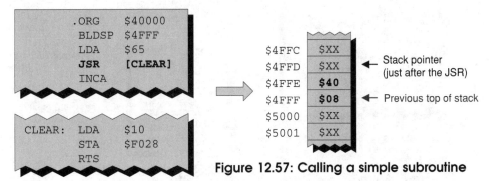

```
        .ORG    $40000
        BLDSP   $4FFF
        LDA     $65
        JSR     [CLEAR]
        INCA


CLEAR:  LDA     $10
        STA     $F028
        RTS
```

$4FFC	$XX
$4FFD	$XX
$4FFE	$40
$4FFF	$08
$5000	$XX
$5001	$XX

Stack pointer (just after the JSR)

Previous top of stack

Figure 12.57: Calling a simple subroutine

When we enter the subroutine itself, the first thing it does is to load the accumulator with $10 and store this value to address $F028. You may recognize this sequence as being the one we use to clear the memory-mapped display. The last instruction in the subroutine is the **RTS** (*"return from subroutine"*), which instructs the CPU to reload the program counter with the return address from the top of the stack (during which process the stack pointer is automatically incremented by two memory locations).

Pushing the accumulator <u>before</u> calling a subroutine

One reason why we might wish to create a subroutine is to allow us to call it several times during the course of the program. Besides speeding the writing of the program, this makes the body of the program smaller and increases its legibility.[10] However, the subroutine described above overwrote the original contents of our accumulator ($65), which would be unfortunate if we wished to use this value after returning from the routine. Of course, we already know a technique to overcome this problem, which would be to push the accumulator onto the stack before the subroutine was called, and then pop the accumulator off the stack after the subroutine was finished (Figure 12.58).

Remember that pushing the accumulator onto the stack causes the stack pointer to be decremented by one memory location, so that when we call the subroutine the return address is automatically stacked on top of this

---

[10]There are also overheads involved in using subroutines; these are discussed in Appendix G.

value. Similarly, when the RTS instruction causes the CPU to retrieve the return address from the stack, it automatically leaves the stack pointer in the right place for the POPA instruction to be able to retrieve the original value in the accumulator. (Note that the addition of the 1-byte PUSHA instruction causes the return address (the address of the POPA instruction) to be modified to $4009.)

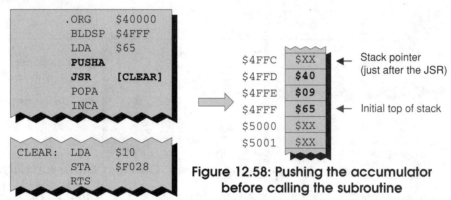

Figure 12.58: Pushing the accumulator
before calling the subroutine

Pushing the accumulator _after_ calling a subroutine

The problem with our latest solution is that we have to use the PUSHA and POPA instructions every time we call the subroutine. This means that the program will take longer to write, its body will be larger, and it will be less legible, which rather negates the factors that made us interested in using a subroutine in the first place. As an alternative, we could move the PUSHA and POPA instructions out of the body of the program and into the subroutine itself (Figure 12.59).

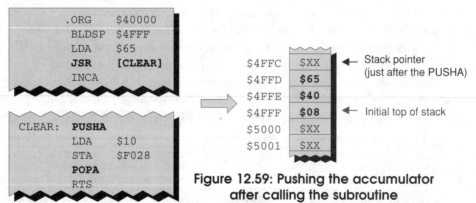

Figure 12.59: Pushing the accumulator
after calling the subroutine

In this case, the first two bytes on the stack are the $4008 return address associated with the JSR instruction, while the byte on the top of the stack is the $65 value from the accumulator, which was put there by the PUSHA instruction. Following the PUSHA instruction, the subroutine is free to modify the contents of the accumulator as it wishes, the only requirement being that it executes a POPA instruction before the RTS instruction. If we neglected to include the POPA instruction, the RTS instruction would use the value $6540 as its return address and pandemonium would ensue.

Passing parameters into subroutines

Thus far our subroutines have been relatively simple affairs, in that they have been logically divorced from the main body of the program. By this we mean that when we've called a subroutine, it's done whatever it was we designed it to do with minimal interfacing to the main program; but this is only scratching the surface of subroutines. Assume that we wish to create a subroutine that will compare two numbers and return the one with the largest value. Further assume that we want to be able to call this subroutine at different points in the main program and ask it to compare different numbers. One technique for doing this is based on ...... you guessed it ...... the stack. First, consider the preparations we'll have to make in the body of the program before calling the subroutine (Figure 12.60).

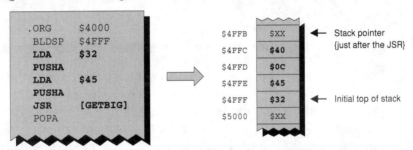

Figure 12.60: Passing parameters into subroutines (the program body)

Note that in the case of this particular example, we are explicitly defining the two numbers to be compared as being $32 and $45. Your first reaction may be that this program is pretty meaningless, because we already know which of these two numbers is the larger. You're right. However, in the real world the numbers under consideration would typically be the results of previous calculations, so their values at any particular time would be unknown to the programmer.

This program works in a reasonably straightforward fashion. After initializing the stack pointer with the BLDSP instruction, we load the accumulator with $32 and push this value onto the stack. Next we load the accumulator with $45 and push *this* value onto the stack. Then we call a subroutine named

BIGONE, which will determine which of these numbers is the larger and return it to us. The act of calling the subroutine automatically causes its return address of $400C to be put on top of the stack, where this is the address of the POPA instruction immediately following the JSR. Now let's turn our attention to the subroutine itself (Figure 12.61).

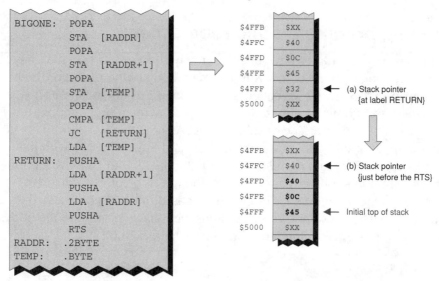

```
BIGONE:   POPA
          STA   [RADDR]
          POPA
          STA   [RADDR+1]
          POPA
          STA   [TEMP]
          POPA
          CMPA  [TEMP]
          JC    [RETURN]
          LDA   [TEMP]
RETURN:   PUSHA
          LDA   [RADDR+1]
          PUSHA
          LDA   [RADDR]
          PUSHA
          RTS
RADDR:    .2BYTE
TEMP:     .BYTE
```

$4FFB	$XX
$4FFC	$40
$4FFD	$0C
$4FFE	$45
$4FFF	$32	◄ (a) Stack pointer {at label RETURN}
$5000	$XX

$4FFB	$XX
$4FFC	$40	◄ (b) Stack pointer {just before the RTS}
$4FFD	**$40**
$4FFE	**$0C**
$4FFF	**$45**	◄ Initial top of stack
$5000	$XX

Figure 12.61: Passing parameters into subroutines (the subroutine itself)

Take a firm grip on your seats, because this might appear to be a little bit scary at first, but it really isn't as bad as it seems. The first thing the subroutine does is to pop the top byte off the stack (the most-significant byte of the return address) into the accumulator. Next we store this byte into a temporary location called RADDR (meaning *"return address"*). Note that RADDR is a 2-byte field and, as usual, the label is associated with the first byte. We continue by popping the least-significant byte of the return address off the stack, and storing this into RADDR+1 (the second byte of the RADDR field).

Next we pop the first number ($45) off the stack and store it into a temporary location called TEMP, then we pop the second number ($32) off the stack and leave it in the accumulator. Now we use a CMPA instruction to compare the value in the accumulator to the value in TEMP. Remember that a CMPA will set the carry flag to *logic 1* if the value in the accumulator is the larger; otherwise, it will clear the carry flag to a *logic 0*. Thus, the JC (*"jump if carry"*) instruction following the CMPA says: *"If the value in the accumulator is the larger, then jump to the label RETURN."* In this particular example, the value in the accumulator is actually the smaller of the two, so the jump never occurs and we end up loading the value in **TEMP** back into the accumulator. Thus, whichever path we follow to reach **RETURN**, we know that the accumulator now contains the larger value.[11]

If you return to consult Figure 12.61a, you'll see the state of the stack at this stage in the game. As we've popped all of the values off the stack, the stack pointer has returned to its initial value. Note that the act of popping a value off the stack doesn't physically erase that value from the memory, which is why these values continued to be displayed. The fact that the data values are still hanging around can be of use in certain circumstances, but we aren't particularly interested in this aspect of things here.

In any case, we're currently at the label **RETURN**, and we know that the accumulator contains the larger of our two numbers, so we use a **PUSHA** instruction to copy this value back onto the stack. Next we load the accumulator with the least-significant byte of the return address (which we previously stored in our temporary location **RADDR+1**), and we push this value back onto the stack. Now we load the accumulator with the most-significant byte of the return address (which we previously stored in the temporary location **RADDR**) and push *this* value onto the stack. Thus, Figure 12.61b shows the state of the stack just before we use the **RTS** instruction to return from the subroutine. Now consider the state of the stack upon our return to the main body of the program (Figure 12.62).

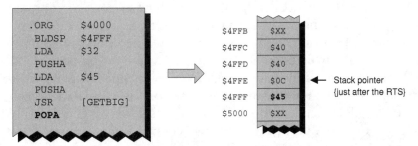

Figure 12.62: Retrieving results from subroutines (the program body)

When the CPU executes the **RTS** instruction, it automatically retrieves the return address from the top of the stack and increments the stack pointer by two memory locations, which leaves the result that we're interested in (the largest number) as the next value on the stack. This means that on returning to the main body of our program, we can simply use a **POPA** instruction to copy this value off the stack into the accumulator, after which we can do whatever we want with it.

---

[11]Unless both values are equal of course, in which case it doesn't really matter which one ends up in the accumulator.

Multiple RTS's

One point that may not be self-evident to a beginner is that a subroutine is allowed to contain multiple RTS instructions. This can be very useful because, depending on the results from a test, we may decide to return to the main body of the program immediately or wander off to perform other actions and then return (Figure 12.63).

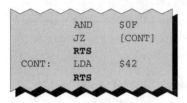

Figure 12.63: Subroutines can have multiple RTS instructions

In this particular example, we AND the contents of the accumulator with $0F, and then perform a test to see if the result is zero. If the contents of the accumulator are zero the JZ ("*jump if zero*") instruction will cause the CPU to jump to the label CONT; otherwise, the test will fail and the program will execute the first RTS instruction to exit the subroutine. However, if the program does jump to the CONT label, it will first load the accumulator with $42, then execute the second RTS instruction and exit the subroutine. (Note that none of the data values shown here have any particular meaning beyond the scope of this example.)

Nested subroutines

Another point to consider is that there's nothing to stop one subroutine calling another, where we refer to this situation as *nesting* or *nested* subroutines. For example, suppose that we want to call a subroutine called PANIC from the main body of the program, where the purpose of PANIC is to display a warning message on our memory-mapped display. The first task we might wish the PANIC subroutine to perform is to clear the screen. We could include the code to do this in PANIC itself, or we could simply ask PANIC to call the CLEAR subroutine we created earlier (Figure 12.64).

When the main body of the program calls the PANIC subroutine, the return address for PANIC is automatically pushed onto the top of the stack. In this example, the first thing PANIC does is call the CLEAR subroutine, which causes the return address for CLEAR to be pushed onto the new top of the stack. After CLEAR has done its stuff, its RTS instruction will pop its return address off the top of the stack and return us to the location in the PANIC subroutine which called it. Similarly, when PANIC has completed its remaining actions, *its* RTS instruction will pop *its* return address off the top of the stack and return us to the location in the main body of the program which called *it*. In the case of the *Beboputer*, you can nest subroutines to any convenient depth, limited only by your stamina and the space available for your stack; that is, subroutine "A" can call subroutine "B," which can call subroutine "C," ad infinitum, until you begin to run out of memory and your stack starts to overwrite your main program.

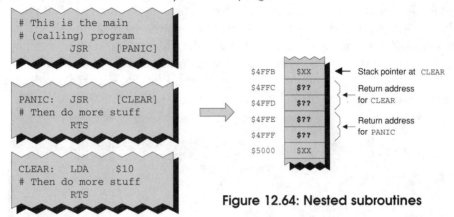

Figure 12.64: Nested subroutines

Recursion can make your brain ache

In addition to the fact that one subroutine can call another, it is also possible for a subroutine to call itself! This technique, which is referred to as *recursion*, can become so convoluted that it makes your brain ache. To provide a simple example of recursion, let's create a program to calculate factorials. As you may recall from school, factorials are represented using a shriek '!' character and are evaluated thus:

```
1! =                           1  =    1
2! =                   2  x  1  =    2
3! =             3  x  2  x  1  =    6
4! =       4  x  3  x  2  x  1  =   24
5! = 5  x  4  x  3  x  2  x  1  =  120
   :                 :               :
```

If we were to work out a factorial by hand, we would probably perform the operation in much the same way as shown above; that is, to evaluate factorial eight (8!), we would multiply eight by seven, then multiply the result by six, then multiply this result by five, and so on down to one. We could use the same technique in a computer program, but as we will see, it may be more efficacious to work the problem from the other end; that is, to multiply one by two, then multiply the result by three, then multiply this result by four, and so on up to eight.

In a moment we'll create a program to illustrate this process, but first we need a way to multiply two numbers together. You may have noticed that the *Beboputer* doesn't actually have a multiply instruction, which means we have to achieve the same effect using whatever instructions *are* available to us. As it happens, we've created a small number of useful subroutines, which are fully documented in Appendix G. One of these subroutines, which is called _UMULT8, accepts two 8-bit unsigned numbers, multiplies them together, and returns a 16-bit unsigned result. (Note that we distinguish our "official" subroutines by commencing their names with an underscore character.) For the moment you don't need to know how _UMULT8 works, but you do have to understand how to use it. Consider an example program that could be used to call this subroutine (Figure 12.65).

```
.ORG      $4000
BLDSP     $4FFF        # Initialize the stack pointer
LDA       $73          # Load ACC with 1st 8-bit number
PUSHA                  # and push it onto the stack
LDA       $16          # Load ACC with the 2nd 8-bit number
PUSHA                  # and push it onto the stack
JSR       [_UMULT8]    # Call the _UMULT8 subroutine
```

Figure 12.65: Example program to call the_UMULT8 subroutine

In this simple example, we first push the 8-bit number $73 onto the stack, then we push $16 onto the stack, and then we call the _UMULT8 subroutine. Irrespective of how this subroutine actually performs its machinations, it will multiply our two 8-bit numbers together and return the 16-bit result on the top of the stack (Figure 12.66).

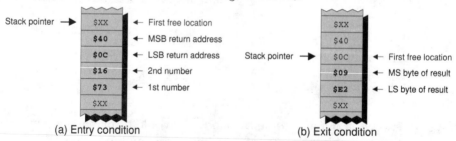

(a) Entry condition   (b) Exit condition

Figure 12.66: The stack's entry and exit conditions for the_UMULT8 subroutine

When we first enter the subroutine, the stack contains our two 8-bit numbers followed by the return address $400C, which is the address of whatever instruction follows the JSR in the main program (Figure 12.66a). After the subroutine has completed its task and executed its RTS instruction, it will leave the 16-bit result ($73 x $16 = $09E2) on the top of the stack (Figure 12.66b). The main program can then do whatever it wants to with this result. For example, it could use POPA instructions to retrieve the result from the stack, or it could simply leave the result on the stack in the anticipation of calling another subroutine to further process this value.

In the case of our program to calculate factorials, we're going to limit ourselves to only being able to calculate factorials up to five; that is, 1!, 2!, 3!, 4!, or 5!. The reason for this restriction is that 5! = 120, which will fit into an 8-bit field, but anything larger (such as 6! = 720) would require a 2-byte field, which would, before we knew it, require us to start multiplying 16-bit numbers together. We could certainly manage to multiply larger numbers, but we don't want to introduce any confusing side-issues at this stage. The effect of limiting ourselves to 5! as our largest factorial is that we know our result will never require more than one byte, which allows us to always discard the most-significant byte of the result returned from our _UMULT8 subroutine (which makes the following easier to explain and understand). Armed with this wealth of knowledge, let's move on to consider our factorial program itself (Figure 12.67).

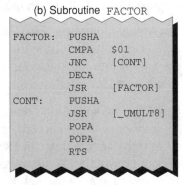

(a) Main program

```
VALUE:  .EQU    $03
        .ORG    $4000
        BLDSP   $4FFF
        LDA     VALUE
        JSR     [FACTOR]
# The result is now
# in the accumulator
```

(b) Subroutine FACTOR

```
FACTOR:  PUSHA
         CMPA    $01
         JNC     [CONT]
         DECA
         JSR     [FACTOR]
CONT:    PUSHA
         JSR     [_UMULT8]
         POPA
         POPA
         RTS
```

Figure 12.67: Recursion can make your brain ache

Purely for the sake of this discussion, we will make the assumption that the first instruction in the **FACTOR** subroutine occurs at address $4100. Also, although we haven't shown the code for the _UMULT8 subroutine here, you may assume that it's hanging around somewhere in the program.

Note the declaration statement at the beginning of the main program, in which we assign $03 to the label **VALUE**. This is the number for which we intend to calculate the factorial (that is, 3!). Thus, by simply changing this assignment to $01, $02, $04 or $05, we can make our program calculate 1!, 2!, 4!, or 5!, respectively. The first instruction in the program is a **BLDSP**, which we use to initialize the stack pointer to $4FFF. Next we load the accumulator with the value for which we wish to calculate the factorial, then we call the subroutine **FACTOR**, which will actually perform the calculations. When this subroutine returns control to the main program in the fullness of time, it will leave the result of its calculations in the accumulator. However, we are getting a little ahead of ourselves – let's consider the activity on the stack as we plunge into the bowels of our program (Figure 12.68).

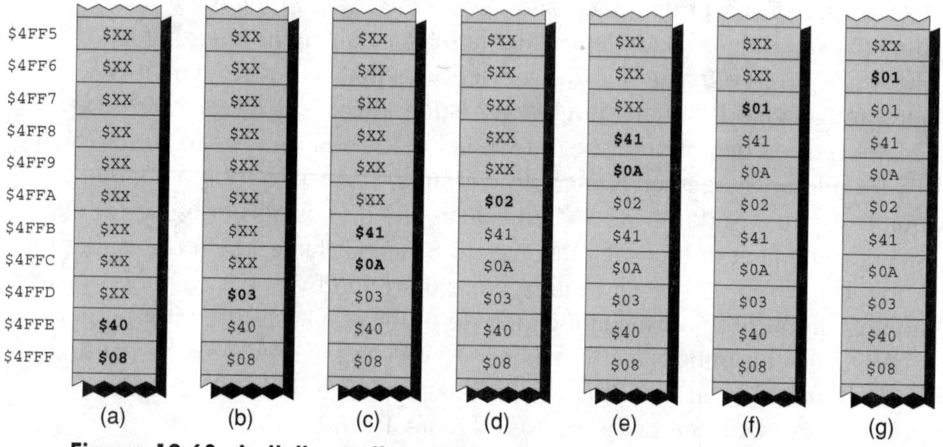

	(a)	(b)	(c)	(d)	(e)	(f)	(g)
$4FF5	$XX	$XX	$XX	$XX	$XX	$XX	$XX
$4FF6	$XX	$XX	$XX	$XX	$XX	$XX	$01
$4FF7	$XX	$XX	$XX	$XX	$XX	$01	$01
$4FF8	$XX	$XX	$XX	$XX	$41	$41	$41
$4FF9	$XX	$XX	$XX	$XX	$0A	$0A	$0A
$4FFA	$XX	$XX	$XX	$02	$02	$02	$02
$4FFB	$XX	$XX	$41	$41	$41	$41	$41
$4FFC	$XX	$XX	$0A	$0A	$0A	$0A	$0A
$4FFD	$XX	$03	$03	$03	$03	$03	$03
$4FFE	$40	$40	$40	$40	$40	$40	$40
$4FFF	$08	$08	$08	$08	$08	$08	$08

Figure 12.68: Activity on the stack as we plunge into the bowels

The first time we enter the **FACTOR** subroutine is when it's called from the main program, at which time the CPU automatically pushed the return address $4008 into the stack (Figure 12.68a), where this is the address of whichever instruction follows the JSR in the main program.

The first thing the subroutine does is to push the current value in the accumulator onto the stack (Figure 12.68b). This value is the $03 that we loaded into the accumulator in the main program. The second instruction in the subroutine is a **CMPA**, which compares the value in the accumulator to $01. Remember that, if the value in the accumulator is greater than the value we're comparing it to, then the carry flag will be set to *logic 1*, otherwise the carry flag will be cleared to *logic 0*. Thus, the JNC ("*jump if not carry*") instruction is effectively saying: "*If the value in the accumulator is not bigger than $01, then jump to the label CONT.*" As the value in the accumulator is $03, this test will fail, so the subroutine uses a **DECA** instruction to decrement the contents of the accumulator, leaving it containing $02. This is followed by a **JSR** instruction, in which the subroutine calls itself! Remember that we are assuming the first instruction in the **FACTOR** subroutine occurs at address $4100. Thus, when our subroutine calls itself, the return address that is pushed onto the stack is $410A, which would be the address of the PUSHA instruction associated with the label CONT (Figure 12.68c).

As before, the first thing the subroutine does is to push the current value in the accumulator onto the stack (Figure 12.68d). This value is the $02 that was left in the accumulator by the previous iteration of the subroutine. Once again, the subroutine compares the value in the accumulator to $01. As the value in the accumulator is $02, this test will fail again, so the subroutine decrements the contents of the accumulator, thereby leaving it containing $01. As before, the subroutine uses its **JSR** instruction to call itself, so the CPU once more pushes a return address of $410A onto the stack (Figure 12.68e).

Once again, the first thing the subroutine does is to push the current value in the accumulator onto the stack (Figure 12.68f). This value is the $01 that was left in the accumulator by the previous iteration of the subroutine. The subroutine next compares the value in the accumulator to $01, and this is where things really start to happen. As the value in the accumulator is $01, it *isn't* bigger than the $01 we're comparing it to, which means that the carry flag will be cleared to *logic 0*. In turn, this means that the **JNC** test will pass, thereby causing the subroutine to jump to the label **CONT**. At this point, the subroutine pushes the value in the accumulator onto the stack a second time (Figure 12.68g), and then calls the **_UMULT8** subroutine.

When we introduced the **_UMULT8** subroutine, we noted that it takes the two unsigned 8-bit numbers it finds on the top of the stack, multiplies them together, and returns a 16-bit result, which it leaves on the top of the stack. Keep this in mind as we consider the activity on the stack as we rise towards the light at the end of the tunnel (Figure 12.69).

	(a)	(b)	(c)	(d)	(e)	(f)	(g)	(h)	(i)
$4FF5	$??	$??	$??	$??	$??	$??	$??	$??	$??
$4FF6	**$00**	$??	$??	$??	$??	$??	$??	$??	$??
$4FF7	**$01**	$??	$??	$??	$??	$??	$??	$??	$??
$4FF8	$41	**$41**	$??	$??	$??	$??	$??	$??	$??
$4FF9	$0A	**$0A**	$??	**$01**	**$00**	$??	$??	$??	$??
$4FFA	$02	$02	**$02**	**$02**	**$02**	$??	$??	$??	$??
$4FFB	$41	$41	$41	$41	$41	**$41**	$??	$??	$??
$4FFC	$0A	$0A	$0A	$0A	$0A	**$0A**	$??	**$02**	**$00**
$4FFD	$03	$03	$03	$03	$03	$03	**$03**	**$03**	**$06**
$4FFE	$40	$40	$40	$40	$40	$40	$40	$40	$40
$4FFF	$08	$08	$08	$08	$08	$08	$08	$08	$08

Figure 12.69: Activity on the stack as we rise towards the light

The **_UMULT8** subroutine takes the two $01 bytes that we left on the top of the stack (Figure 12.68g), multiplies them together, and replaces them with the 16-bit result $0001 (Figure 12.69a). Remembering that data isn't physically obliterated from the stack, the $?? entries in Figure 12.69 are used to indicate that we're no longer particularly concerned as to what these bytes contain. Earlier we made the decision that we were only going to consider factorials that could fit into a single byte, which means that we aren't interested in the most-significant byte of the result returned by _UMULT8. Thus, the first POPA instruction in the FACTOR subroutine retrieves the most-significant byte of the result (in which we have no interest), while the second POPA overwrites the accumulator with the byte in which we *are* interested (whose value is $01). At this stage, the stack pointer is left pointing at the return address $410A (Figure 12.69b).

When the subroutine executes its RTS instruction, this retrieves the return address $410A from the top of the stack (Figure 12.69c), which returns us to the CONT label in the previous iteration of the subroutine. The PUSHA instruction at the CONT label pushes the contents of the accumulator ($01) onto the top of the stack (Figure 12.69d), then the JSR calls _UMULT8 again. The _UMULT8 subroutine takes the $01 and $02 bytes it finds on the top of the stack (Figure 12.69d), multiplies them together, and replaces them with the 16-bit result $0002 (Figure 12.69e). Once again, on returning from _UMULT8, the first POPA instruction in the FACTOR subroutine retrieves the most-significant byte of the result (in which we have no interest), while the second POPA overwrites the accumulator with the byte in which we *are* interested (whose value is $02). As before, this leaves the stack pointer pointing at the return address $410A (Figure 12.69f).

This earlier iteration of the subroutine now executes *its* RTS instruction, which retrieves the return address $410A from the top of the stack (Figure 12.69g) and returns us to the CONT label in our very first iteration of the subroutine. The PUSHA instruction at the CONT label pushes the contents of the accumulator ($02) onto the top of the stack (Figure 12.69h), then we call _UMULT8 one last time. The _UMULT8 subroutine takes the $02 and $03 bytes it finds on the top of the stack (Figure 12.69h), multiplies them together, and replaces them with the 16-bit result $0006 (Figure 12.69i). Once again, on returning from _UMULT8, the first POPA instruction in the FACTOR subroutine retrieves the most-significant byte of the result (of no interest to us here), while the second POPA overwrites the accumulator with the byte in which we *are* interested (whose value is $06). This leaves the stack pointer pointing to the return address $4008. Thus, when we execute the RTS instruction from this iteration of the subroutine, we will be returned to the main body of the program, with the final result of the factorial stored safe and snug in our accumulator ..... phew!

Explaining how this works is actually much more difficult that writing the code itself. Return to take a peek at Figure 12.67 to remind yourself just how little code was actually involved here. The main trick with recursion is knowing when to use it and when not to. Anything you can do recursively can also be done some other way, but some tasks lend themselves to a recursive solution while others don't. Recursive techniques can result in very compact code which is easy to write and understand (or, in some cases, a swine to write and a pain to understand). Also, while recursive code may be compact in and of itself, every time a subroutine calls itself it stores parameters and its return address onto the stack, so the net result may not yield any saving in terms of the memory required by the program when its running.

Last but not least, recursion does not necessarily imply that a subroutine calls itself directly. For example, subroutine "A" could call subroutine "B," which could, in turn, call subroutine "A," and so on and so forth. Also, it is possible to write recursive code that doesn't employ subroutines at all, although this would be somewhat less common.

Self-modifying code

Before we commence this topic, we should note that self-modifying code really has no relation to subroutines per se, but we couldn't think of anywhere else to stick it (which may explain why so few books get around to mentioning it at all).

By now we're familiar with the concept that a program can modify its own *data*, but one point that many newbies don't intuitively grasp is that a program can also modify its own *instructions*! Consider the simple example in Figure 12.70.

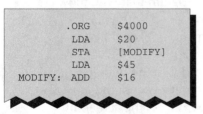

```
          .ORG   $4000
          LDA    $20
          STA    [MODIFY]
          LDA    $45
MODIFY:   ADD    $16
```

Figure 12.70: Self-modifying code

If we ignore the first **LDA** and the **STA** for the moment, you will see that the second **LDA** in the source code directs the computer to load the accumulator with $45, then an **ADD** instruction directs the computer to add $16 to this value. However, if we were to run this program, we would find that the computer would actually *subtract* $16 from the value in the accumulator. This is because the first **LDA** loaded the accumulator with $20, then the **STA** stored this value into the location associated with the label **MODIFY**. As it happens, $20 is the opcode for a **SUB** instruction in its immediate addressing mode. Thus, our program will replace the opcode for an **ADD** with the opcode for a **SUB**, and then proceed to execute this new instruction.

Note that we're in no way recommending this as an everyday practice. Generally speaking this sort of coding would be considered to be very, very naughty, and programmers who use this technique usually deserve to be soundly and painfully chastised (unfortunately we live in strange times, and this may actually be an inducement to some of them).

However, now that we've opened this Pandora's box, we may as well mention that there are several different flavors of self-modifying code. One flavor is a program which changes existing instructions as discussed above, while another is "on-the-fly code generation," whereby a program may generate new instructions (and possibly data) in some free area of the memory and then transfer control to these new instructions. Although this may seem a little weird, it is actually not uncommon in such things as graphical applications, in which the programmer is striving for extreme speed. In this case, it may be possible to generate a routine to perform a specific graphical operation and then execute this routine faster than it would be to use a pre-created general-purpose routine, because a general-purpose routine may be carrying a lot of "baggage" around to make it "general-purpose."

Creating an "Etch-A-Sketch-like" program[12]

As we begin to move toward the close of this chapter (they said hopefully), we are going to create a slightly more sophisticated program that will allow us to demonstrate some additional utilities that are provided with your *Beboputer*. What we are going to do is to design an Etch-a-Sketch-like program that responds to the cursor-control keys on your virtual QWERTY keyboard. This program will commence by placing a dot in the middle of your screen, and then loop around waiting for you to click one of the cursor-control keys, at which time it will place a new dot on the screen in the direction corresponding to whichever cursor-control key you selected. Pause for a moment to consider how you would implement such a program, then perform the following actions.

First, click the **Assembler** item on the Windows 95™ task bar to return it to its former glory. Next click the **File** item on the *assembler's* menu bar (**not**

---

[12]Etch-A-Sketch is a registered trademark of the Ohio Art Company.

the project window's menu bar), click the **New** entry in the resulting pull-down menu, then enter the following source code. Feel free to perform a **Save As** operation at any time during the process of entering the code and save this program as "lab7_p3.asm." Once you've performed the initial **Save As**, you can use standard Save operations as and when you see fit (you can also cut down on the comments if you wish).

```
# Etch-a-sketch-like program created by a very tired guy called
# Max who can't wait to get to the end of this chapter :-)

# Declare any constants we want to use throughout the course of
# the program
MMSPORT:    .EQU    $F028      # O/P port to mem-mapped screen
KEYBOARD:   .EQU    $F008      # I/P port from QWERTY keyboard

CLRCODE:    .EQU    $10        # Code to clear mem-mapped
                               # screen
GPHCODE:    .EQU    $03        # Code to place the mem-mapped
                               # screen in medium-resolution
                               # graphics mode

UP:         .EQU    $D0        # Our keyb'd code for up arrow key
DOWN:       .EQU    $D1        # Our keyb'd code for down arrow
                               # key
RIGHT:      .EQU    $D2        # Our keyb'd code for right arrow
                               # key
LEFT:       .EQU    $D3        # Our keyb'd code for left arrow
                               # key

            .ORG    $4000      # Start of program is address
                               # $4000

# Initialize the memory-mapped screen into the state we require
START:      BLDSP   $4FFF      # Initialize the stack pointer
            LDA     GPHCODE    # Load ACC with code to put
                               # screen in
            STA     [MMSPORT]  # graphics mode and write to
                               # O/P port
            LDA     CLRCODE    # Load ACC with code to clear
                               # screen
            STA     [MMSPORT]  # and write it to the O/P port

# Place an initial dot/square around the middle of the
# screen
            LDA     [COLOR]    # Load ACC with the color to use
            STA     [[SQUARE]] # Store ACC to the address
                               # pointed to by the address
                               # stored in "SQUARE" (which ends
                               # up in the Video RAM)
```

```
# This is the start of the main program loop - hurrah!
# Start off by sticking the current target address on the
# mem-mapped screen onto the stack (saves time/effort later)
GETNEXT:    LDA      [SQUARE+1] # Load ACC with LS byte of address
            PUSHA              # and hurl it onto the stack
            LDA      [SQUARE]   # Load ACC with MS byte of
                               # address and hurl it
            PUSHA              # onto the stack

GETCHAR:    LDA      [KEYBOARD] # Load ACC from keyboard - if NUL
            JZ       [GETCHAR]  # code ($00) jump back to
                               # "GETCHAR"

# Now we've got a character (hopefully an arrow key), so we work
# out which one it is (up/north, down/south, left/west,
# right/east)Remember that CMPA instructions set the zero
# flag if values are equal - also that they don't affect the
# current value in ACC
            CMPA     UP         # Compare ACC to code for up arrow
            JZ       [NORTH]    # If yes jump to label"NORTH" ...
                               # ... if no continue to next test


            CMPA     DOWN       # Compare ACC to code for down
                               # arrow
            JZ       [SOUTH]    # If yes jump to label"SOUTH" ...
                               # ... if no continue to next test


            CMPA     RIGHT      # Compare ACC to code for right
                               # arrow
            JZ       [EAST]     # If yes jump to label "EAST" ...
                               # ... if no continue to next test


            CMPA     LEFT       # Compare ACC to code for left
                               # arrow
            JZ       [WEST]     # If yes jump to label "WEST" ...
                               # if no continue on to whatever


            JMP      [RESTORE]  # There is no other test at
                               # this time which means that
                               # the user selected a key he/
                               # she wasn't supposed to.
                               # Doesn't matter - jump to
                               # "RESTORE"

# Note that, if we decided to add the facility for the user
# to be able to change the color of the dots, this is where
# we would add the extra code.
```

```
# Now we know which arrow key was pressed, so we need to modify
# the target Video RAM address accordingly (remember that we left
# it on the stack at the beginning of the main loop at label
# "GETNEXT"
NORTH:      LDA       $40           # Load ACC with $40 (64 in decimal)
                                    # which is the number of locations
                                    # to the dot above on the screen
                                    # then push this onto the stack

            PUSHA
            LDA       $00           # Load ACC with zero and push
                                    # this onto stack as MSB
            PUSHA                   # of 2-byte pair
            JSR       [_SUB16]      # Call predefined subroutine
                                    # (see notes at end of listing)
            JMP       [RESTORE]     # Jump to label "RESTORE"


SOUTH:      LDA       $40           # Load ACC with $40 (64 in decimal)
                                    # which is the number of locations
                                    # to the dot below on the screen
                                    # then push this onto the stack

            PUSHA
            LDA       $00           # Load ACC with zero and push
                                    # this onto stack as MSB
            PUSHA                   # of 2-byte pair
            JSR       [_ADD16]      # Call predefined subroutine
                                    # (see notes at end of listing)
            JMP       [RESTORE]     # Jump to label "RESTORE"


EAST:       LDA       $01           # Load ACC with $01 which is the
                                    # number of locations to the dot to
                                    # the right on the screen then push
                                    # this onto the stack

            PUSHA
            LDA       $00           # Load ACC with zero and push
                                    # this onto stack as MSB
            PUSHA                   # of 2-byte pair
            JSR       [_ADD16]      # Call predefined subroutine
                                    # (see notes at end of listing)
            JMP       [RESTORE]     # Jump to label "RESTORE"


WEST:       LDA       $01           # Load ACC with $01 which is
                                    # the number of locations to
                                    # the dot to the left on the
                                    # screen then push this onto
            PUSHA                   # the stack
            LDA       $00           # Load ACC with zero and push
                                    # this onto stack as MSB
            PUSHA                   # of 2-byte pair
            JSR       [_SUB16]      # Call predefined subroutine
```

```
                              # (see notes at end of listing)
          JMP       [RESTORE]   # Jump to label "RESTORE"


# The "_ADD16" and "_SUB16" subroutines above add or subtract two
# 16-bit numbers and leave a 16-bit result on # top of stack See
# the notes on these subroutines in the book
RESTORE:  POPA                  # Pop the MS byte of new address
                              # and save it
          STA       [SQUARE]    # Pop the LS byte of new address
          POPA                  # and save it
          STA       [SQUARE+1]


# Draw a dot at the new location on the memory-mapped screen then
# jump back to the beginning of the loop and do it all again
          LDA       [COLOR]     # Load ACC with the color to use
                              # Store ACC to the address pointed
                              # to by the address stored in
          STA       [[SQUARE]]  # "SQUARE" (which ends up in the
                              # Video RAM)
          JMP       [GETNEXT]   # Jump back to start of main loop


# Reserve some temporary locations in which to store things
# and, in this particular case, initialize them with certain
# values
COLOR:    .BYTE     $07         # Original color = White
SQUARE:   .2BYTE    $E9E0       # Original square around middle of
                              # the mem-mapped screen (24th row
                              # 32nd col)


# This is where we're going to insert any pre-defined
# subroutines see the notes in the book.
          .END
```

If you can't be bothered to enter all of this program by hand, at least take the time to read through it carefully, then use the assembler's File pull-down and the Open entry to load the "lab7_p3b.asm" file that we've already created for you. Ooops, perhaps we should have mentioned this earlier, but it's too late now and there's no use crying over spilt milk. If you do use this technique, then use the assembler's File → Save As pull-down menu to rename this code to "lab7_p3.asm," thereby ensuring that you won't accidentally overwrite our original source code.

Whilst perusing this program, you may have noticed a number of subroutine calls to _ADD16 and _SUB16. As we previously mentioned, Appendix G documents a number of useful subroutines that we've pre-defined for you, and these are two of them. The problem is that you have to incorporate them into your program before you assemble it. First, scroll through the source code to the bottom of the file, add a blank line before the .END directive, and position the cursor at the beginning of this line. Next click the Insert item in the menubar, which will reveal three options: Directive, Instruction, and Insert File. The first two options can be used to aid you in the process of creating assembly programs, but you can return to play with these later (see also the *Beboputer's* online help for more information on these commands). For the moment we're only interested in the Insert File option, so click this now. The resulting dialog offers a scrolling list showing any files with ".asm" extensions. Use this scrolling list to locate the file called "add16.asm" and double-click it, which causes the contents of this file to be automatically inserted into your main program at the point where you left your cursor (which is usually referred to as the "*insertion point*").

Without pausing for breath, use the Insert File technique to insert the contents of the "sub16.asm" file into your program. Now click on the Assemble icon to initiate the assembly process and debug your code (hopefully the fates will smile upon you and there won't be any errors, especially if you cheated and used our existing code).

As we've finished with the assembler for the moment, iconize it by clicking the appropriate button in its title bar; as usual, you'll see the assembler appear in the Windows 95™ task bar. Use your mouse to click the Memory item on the project window's menu bar, then click the Load RAM entry in the resulting pull-down menu. As you scroll through the list on the left-hand side of the dialog window, you will find the new "lab7_p3.ram" file which you just created. Double-click this entry to select this file and add it to the right-hand list, then click the Load button to load this machine code into the *Beboputer's* RAM and dismiss the form.

Iconize button

Title bar

Menu bar

Ensure that the hex keypad's **Address (Ad)** button is active, enter the program's start address of $4000, then click the **Run** button. Our program first instructs the memory-mapped display to enter its medium-resolution mode, which may take a few seconds while the display loads all of the random colored blocks to the screen (see also the discussions in the previous chapter). The program then clears the screen (to black), places a white dot in the middle of the display, and starts to loop around reading the QWERTY keyboard waiting for you to click one of the cursor-control keys (LE = left, RI = right, UP = up, DO = down). Try clicking a single time on the UP key and wait for a second dot to appear above the first, then click the RI key and wait for a third dot to appear. The amount of time it takes for the dot to appear will depend on the speed of your real computer – please be patient if your computer is a little slow (emulating the *Beboputer* is a lot of work for the poor little rapscallion), and try to wait for each dot to appear before clicking another key.

While the program is still running, close the CPU Register display (also close the memory walker if it's active) and note the improvement in the *Beboputer's* response. When you're ready to continue, click the hex keypad's Reset (Rst) button to return us to the *Beboputer's* reset mode.

Introducing the list file

Click the assembler item in the Windows 95™ task bar to return it to the screen. Previously we noted that, upon setting its shoulder to the wheel, the assembler generates two files, one of which is called a "*list file.*" When the list file is combined with the additional *Beboputer* utilities and capabilities that we shall come to shortly, it can be an incredibly useful tool for understanding the way in which your program is working (or not, as the case might be).

As the source code for the program you just assembled was called "lab7_p3.asm," the assembler will automatically name its corresponding list file "lab7_p3.lst." One way to access this list file is to click the Window item in the assembler's menubar, then click the List File entry in the resulting pull-down menu (you can use the same technique to return to your source code; also note that there are icons on the toolbar for both of these operations). Should you wish to obtain a *hard-copy*, or *printout*, of your list file (and assuming that you actually have a printer connected to your computer), you can do so by using the Print entry under the File pull-down menu, or by clicking the appropriate toolbar icon. If you do have a printer, we recommend that you generate a printout now.

By default, the *Beboputer's* assembler uses a font called *Courier*, because each of the characters in this font occupy exactly the same amount of space (unlike the proportional fonts we tend to use on today's systems, in which each character occupies whatever amount of space it requires). The reasons we decided to use the Courier font are twofold: first, because this was pretty much all that was available in the early years; and second, because it's easier to align text in files such as our list file. Should you wish, you can modify the font using the Font entry under the File pull-down menu, but you will find that this can result in your list file being well-nigh impossible to read (you have been warned).

When you are first presented with a list file, a lot of it may seem to be incomprehensible gibberish, but it's actually quite easy to read when you know the rules. In fact the list file contains three sections: the body of the program and two cross-reference tables. First consider the body of the program (Figure 12.71).

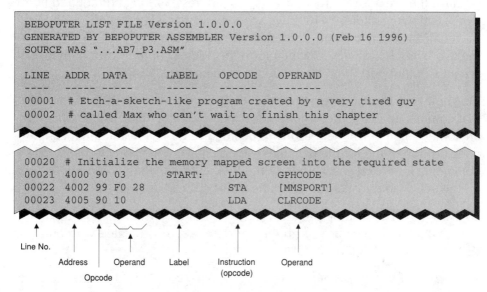

Figure 12.71: List file body

Following a few lines of introductory preamble, we enter the list file proper. During the process of reading the source file the assembler assigns a number to every line, and this number is displayed (*in decimal*) in the left-hand column of the list file. The original source code is displayed on the right-hand side of the list file; thus, we see that the body of our program commenced on line 21 when we loaded our accumulator with the value assigned to **GPHCODE** (note that the line numbers you see on your screen may vary from those in these discussions).

Of particular interest is the fact that the machine code relating to each line of source code appears between the line number and the source code. The first value after the line number is the hexadecimal address of the instruction. Following this address we may see one, two, or three values depending on the instruction and its addressing mode, where the first value is always an opcode (except in the case of .BYTE, .2BYTE, and .4BYTE statements). For example, on line 21 we used a **LDA** instruction with an immediate addressing mode; the $90 value is the opcode for this instruction, while the $03 value is the immediate data (which, in this case, was the value we assigned to **GPHCODE**). (Note that '$' characters are omitted from the values in the list file to save space, but that only *line numbers* are displayed in decimal.)

Moving on to line 22, we see that the address has jumped to $4002; this is because the previous instruction started at address $4000 and required two bytes. Following address $4002 we see $99, which is the opcode for a **STA** instruction with an absolute addressing mode. This opcode is followed by the two bytes $F0 and $28, which form the address of the memory-mapped screen's output port (from the value we assigned to **MMSPORT**).

One point we should note here is that the list file will only show comments that commence in the first column of a line – the assembler will gobble up any other comments. The reason we decided to do this is that the machine code portion of the list file occupies a lot of space. Had we left the comments in, they'd wrap around onto the next line when you printed the file, which would make it an absolute swine to read.

Following the body of the program you will find the first cross-reference table, which concerns itself with the constant labels associated with our .EQU statements (Figure 12.72).

```
CONSTANT LABELS CROSS-REFERENCE

  NAME      VALUE    LINE NUMBERS WHERE USED (* = DECLARATION)
--------  --------   ---------------------------------------------
CLRCODE   00000010   00009* 00023
DOWN      000000D1   00014* 00051
```

Figure 12.72: Constant labels cross-reference table

The first column contains the names of the labels sorted alpha-numerically. Following the name of the label is its hexadecimal value – the reason these values are shown with eight characters is twofold: first, the assembler internally stores and manipulates every constant as a 4-byte field; and second, the .4BYTE directive supports 4-byte assignments, which therefore require eight hexadecimal characters to display their values.

To the right of the value field appears a list of the line numbers (in decimal) which use this label. A number annotated with a star '*' character indicates the line on which the label was actually declared, while the other line numbers are the ones in which this label was used. In the case of constant labels, the star character will always be associated with the first line number in the list, because our language specification dictates that constant labels have to be declared before they can be used.

Finally, at the bottom of the list file, we find the cross-reference table for any address labels you may have used (Figure 12.73).

```
ADDRESS LABELS CROSS-REFERENCE

  NAME      VALUE    LINE NUMBERS WHERE USED (* = DECLARATION)
--------  --------   ----------------------------------------------------
COLOR     ....4076   00027   00125   00133*
EAST      ....404D   00056   00095*
GETCHAR   ....4018   00040*  00041
```

Figure 12.73: Address labels cross-reference table

Once again, the first column contains the label's name, followed by its value (in hexadecimal), followed by the line numbers (in decimal) on which it appears. In the case of the values, these can only ever be two-byte fields (because we only have a 16-bit address bus), so we decided to insert four periods for the purposes of lining up the two cross-reference tables and making them look pretty.

Note that our language specification does allow address labels to be forward-referenced, which means that they can be used before they've been declared. This explains why the label COLOR has a star '*' character associated with line 133 – if you look at the body of the list file you'll see that COLOR was referenced in lines 27 and 125, but it wasn't actually declared until line 133 (remember that the line numbers in your list file may differ from those shown here). When you start to write your own *Beboputer* programs, you will quickly find that the list file is an invaluable resource and that you refer to these cross-reference tables much more than you might think.

Introducing the *Beboputer's* breakpoint capability

Well, we've finished with the assembler for the moment, so you might as well close it down by clicking the Exit button in its title bar (**not** the main project window's title bar). Throughout much of this book, we've employed the memory walker to root around in the *Beboputer's* memory, but now we're going to reveal some hitherto unsuspected tricks that this display has been cunningly hiding up its sleeves.

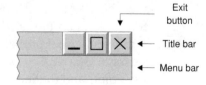

Click the **Display** item on the *project window's* menu bar, then click the **Memory Walker** entry in the resulting pull-down menu. Next use your mouse to drag this display by its title bar to a convenient location on the screen (trying not to obscure the other tools and displays as far as possible). Now look at this display as if it were for the very first time, and note the left-hand column of boxes which have thus far remained empty – the *breakpoint column* (Figure 12.74).

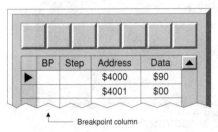

Breakpoint column

Figure 12.74: Memory-walker display

Let's assume that the program you entered above isn't working exactly as planned, and that you're trying to work out exactly what's going on. One option would be to run the program and try to understand what it's doing by puzzling over its communications with the outside world. However, this may not prove to be a particularly useful technique if the program "crashes-and-burns" in a catastrophic manner. Similarly, this approach falters at the first fence if your program gets itself locked up in a loop and sits there not doing much of anything.

As an alternative, you might consider single-stepping through the program, using both the memory walker and the CPU register display to try to determine exactly what the program is doing. The problem here is that you might have to step through hundreds or even thousands of instructions before reaching the point in the program where the problem may lie. Yet another option would be to start off by running the program, and then dropping back into the step mode by clicking the **Step** button in the faint hope that you'll end up somewhere useful. Strange as it may seem, this technique occasionally works to your favor, particularly if your problem involves the program getting stuck in a loop, but most of the time this approach leaves something to be desired.

For the sake of discussion, let's assume that when you run your program it displays the initial dot on the memory-mapped display, but nothing happens after this point and the program doesn't respond to your clicking the cursor-control keys on the QWERTY keyboard. Glancing through your source code, you would probably decide that everything is running smoothly until the label **GETNEXT**; so what you'd like to do is to run the program up to this point, and to then start single-stepping through the instructions to see what's going on.

Unfortunately, there's no way to tell the address of the **GETNEXT** label from your source code (unless you want to work it out by hand), so this is where the list file starts to prove its worth. You can find the address of the instruction at **GETNEXT** by simply looking this label up in the cross-reference table at the end of the list file. Alternatively, you could scan the body of the list file to find the appropriate section, which reveals that the required address is $4010 (Figure 12.75)

```
00035 4010 91 40 78   GETNEXT:   LDA      [SQUARE+1]
00036 4013 B2                    PUSHA
00037 4014 91 40 77              LDA      [SQUARE]
00038 4017 B2                    PUSHA
```

Figure 12.75: Determing the address of GETNEXT

Once you've determined that $4010 is the address of interest, scroll down through the memory walker to bring this address into view. Now click the **Breakpoint** icon in the memory walker's toolbar. This invokes a dialog that allows you to set or clear breakpoints. Use this dialog to specify a breakpoint at address $4010, and then apply it by means of the **Apply** button. Don't dismiss this form just yet, because we'll be using it later. The characters "BP" appear in the appropriate box in the memory walker's breakpoint column to show you that a breakpoint has been set. To find out how we can use this breakpoint, ensure that the hex keypad's **Address (Ad)** button is active, enter the program's start address of $4000, then click the **Run** button. The *Beboputer* starts at the beginning of the program and charges merrily ahead until it runs headfirst into the breakpoint, at which point it comes to a grinding halt and automatically drops into its step mode. Now you can start to single-step through the instructions using the memory walker display, the CPU display, and your list file to determine why the program isn't performing up to par. Of course, in this case your program doesn't actually have a problem, but step through a few instructions anyway to get into the swing of things. When you're ready to move on, click the hex keypad's **Reset (Rst)** button to return the *Beboputer* to its reset mode.

You can sprinkle breakpoints throughout the memory walker display like confetti. This means that you can enter the run mode and execute the program up to the first breakpoint, single-step for a while as you wish, and then click the **Run** button again to let the *Beboputer* race on to the next breakpoint. (**Very important:** The *Beboputer* will only honor breakpoints that occur on the first byte (the opcode byte) of an instruction — if you foolishly try to set breakpoints on operand bytes, the *Beboputer* will simply ignore these "pseudo breakpoints" in its frantic desire to reach the next instruction.)

Once you're happy with the portion of the code you've been scrutinizing, you can use the breakpoint dialog window to clear specific breakpoints, or you can clear them all in one fell swoop by clicking the Clear All option on the form followed by the Apply button. Last but not least, when you turn the *Beboputer* off, it will promptly forget any and all breakpoints from the current session (but don't turn it off just yet).

Introducing the *Beboputer's* message display system

In addition to the memory walker and CPU register displays, there's one more display utility that's been bashfully hiding in the wings waiting for its time in the limelight. Make sure that the *Beboputer* is in its reset mode, then clear any breakpoints you may have inserted in the memory walker display excepting the original one at address $4010. Now ensure that the hex keypad's Address (Ad) button is active, enter the program's start address of $4000, then click the Run button. As before, the *Beboputer* skips through the program until it reaches the breakpoint, at which point it automatically falls back into the step mode.

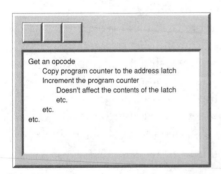

Get an opcode
   Copy program counter to the address latch
   Increment the program counter
      Doesn't affect the contents of the latch
         etc.
    etc.
etc.

Figure 12.76: The message system

To invoke the messaging display you can click the Display item in the menu bar, and then click the Message System entry in the resulting pull-down menu. Alternatively, you can click the appropriate icon in the project window's tool bar. Either method will result in the message system appearing on your screen (Figure 12.76). You can use your mouse to drag this display by its title bar to move it to a convenient location on your screen, and also to re-size the display by stretching its corners or edges.

Click the hex keypad's Step button to execute the next instruction. If it's active, the CPU register display updates to show the current contents of the *Beboputer's* registers. However, although the CPU register display is a very useful device, it does tend to operate in a rather coarse-grained manner, which means that it doesn't tell us a great deal about what actually went through the *Beboputer's* mind while it was performing the instruction.

By comparison, the message system provides a wealth of information – use its scroll bar (not shown here) to wander through all of the messages that were generated during the execution of this instruction.

As you will see, the messages in this display have different colors (on the screen) and indentations. The left-most text indicates a macro-action, such as acquiring an opcode, decoding the opcode, and so on. The first level of indented text reflects micro-actions, such as copying the program counter into the address latch, while the second level of indented text describes any additional points of interest, such as the fact that incrementing the program counter doesn't affect the contents of the address latch.

New messages will be added to the bottom of the list every time you click the hex keypad's **Step** button. You can use the icons in this display's tool bar to print the current contents of the file or to clear the display. Note that the message system is automatically deactivated whenever you enter the *Beboputer's* run mode. When you've finished playing with this display, click the hex keypad's **ON** button (which also turns it **OFF**), then exit this laboratory by clicking the **File** item on the project window's menu bar followed by the **Exit** entry in the resulting pull-down menu.

Macro assemblers, meta-assemblers, disassemblers, and stuff

In the same way that there is a spectrum of computer languages, with assembly language at the lower end of abstraction, there is also a spectrum of assembly languages. In fact our assembly language is relatively simple in the scheme of things, and there are several ways in which it could be augmented. Note that the following discussions are hypothetical in nature; we haven't actually implemented any of this stuff in our language or assembler (but you could write your own if you wanted to.....).

Conditional assembly

One way in which we could extend our capabilities would be to add the concept of conditional assembly, whereby the assembler decides whether or not to process portions of the source code "on-the-fly." There are numerous techniques we could use to achieve this; for example, we could add some new directive statements: .IFT (*"if true"*), .IFF (*"if false"*), and .ENDIF (*"end if"*) (Figure 12.77).

Remember that we're discussing how *we* could enhance *our* language – other languages may use many different variations on this theme. In our case, we could decide that a "true" condition (or result from an expression) is any non-zero value, while a "false" condition is represented by a zero value. Thus, as we assigned the constant label TEST a value of zero, the ".IFT TEST" ("*if TEST is true*") statement would fail, and the assembler would ignore any statements up to the .ENDIF. Thus, the only instruction that

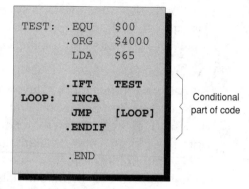

```
TEST:   .EQU    $00
        .ORG    $4000
        LDA     $65

        .IFT    TEST
LOOP:   INCA
        JMP     [LOOP]
        .ENDIF

        .END
```
Conditional part of code

Figure 12.77: Conditional assembly

would actually be assembled in this particular program would be the LDA $65, and we'd end up with a 2-byte program that didn't do much of anything at all. But this is only an example; in a larger program we might have a number of conditional sections scattered throughout the code, and we could decide what to assemble and what not to assemble by simply modifying the value of one or more constants.

Macro assemblers

Another way in which we could augment our assembly language would be to add a macro capability, which essentially allows the user to extend the language by adding new instructions. Assume that we introduce two new directives .SMACRO ("*start macro*") and .EMACRO ("*end macro*") into our language, and consider how we might use these directives to create a macro to compare two unsigned 8-bit numbers and leave the larger value in the accumulator (Figure 12.78).

In the case of our hypothetical language extensions, we've decided that any macros have to be defined before the .ORG statement. This particular example only contains one macro definition called BIGONE. The syntax we're using is that the .SMACRO directive would instruct the

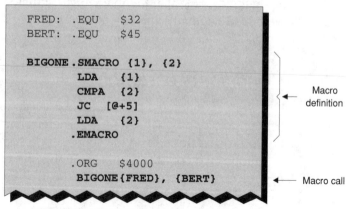

```
FRED:   .EQU    $32
BERT:   .EQU    $45

BIGONE .SMACRO {1}, {2}
        LDA     {1}
        CMPA    {2}
        JC      [@+5]
        LDA     {2}
        .EMACRO

        .ORG    $4000
        BIGONE{FRED}, {BERT}
```
Macro definition

Macro call

Figure 12.78: Defining macros

assembler that this is the start of a macro definition, while the label associated with the directive will become the name of the macro.

Following the .SMACRO directive are a number of comma-separated arguments in squiggly parenthesis "{}." In the case of our BIGONE macro, we have two arguments: "{1}" and "{2}." These arguments instruct the assembler as to the number of values this macro will expect and the order it will expect them in. The body of the macro definition contains standard assembly-language instructions; however, in addition to any standard arguments, our macro arguments are also allowed to form the operands for these instructions. Finally, the .EMACRO directive informs the assembler when it reaches the end of the macro definition.

The important point to understand is that the assembler doesn't actually generate any machine code from the macro definition *per se*, all it does is memorize the macro's contents. Only if this macro name subsequently appears in the main body of the program will the assembler use a process called *macro expansion* to insert the macro into the code. In our example, we actually use the BIGONE macro immediately following the .ORG statement. The assembler will replace this statement with the series of instructions in the macro definition, and it will substitute the appropriate arguments in the macro for the labels FRED and BERT ($32 and $45, respectively).

Once a macro has been defined, it can be used multiple times in the body of the program. Macros allow the user to extend the language by defining new instructions, and they can reduce the size of the source code and improve its legibility. Also, the code for a macro will run faster than the code for a subroutine performing an equivalent function, because we don't have the overhead of pushing parameters onto the stack and popping them back off again (see the subroutine corresponding to this macro in the "*Passing parameters into subroutines*" section of this chapter). On the other hand, macros don't do anything towards reducing the size of the resulting machine code, because they're always expanded into in-line instructions during the assembly process.

Not surprisingly, an assembler with the ability to handle macros is called a *macro assembler*. The example we just discussed was a relatively simple representative of the macro fraternity; there is nothing to prohibit macros calling other macros (that is, *nested macros*) or even macros calling themselves. Also, note that we are just introducing concepts here, while desperately trying to avoid becoming enmeshed in the complexities. For example, we used the "JC [@+5]" statement in our macro which means:

"If the carry flag is logic 1, jump to the current address plus five locations" (where the "current address", which is indicated by the @ operator, is the address of the first byte in the **JC** instruction). The reason we employed this technique was to avoid using a label inside our macro, because calling the macro multiple times in the body of the program would result in multiple copies of the same label, which isn't allowed. Of course there are ways around this, such as instructing the assembler to replace any macro labels with automatically generated versions, in which case it would be the assembler's responsibility to ensure that each instantiation of the macro had its own unique labels.

Meta-assemblers

Earlier in this chapter we introduced the concept of a *cross-assembler*, which is an assembler that runs on one computer but generates machine code for use on another. We can extend this concept in a number of ways; for example, by creating a tool known as a *meta-assembler*, which can assemble programs for multiple systems. Of course, the world being what it is, there are a variety of alternative meta-assembly techniques, which can serve to make life somewhat confusing. For our purposes here, we will only introduce two such approaches: *adaptive* and *generative*.

Adaptive meta-assemblers: A key concept underlying meta-assemblers is that they support a *meta-syntactic language*, which allows you to define your own instruction set. Assume that we wished to use a meta-assembler to generate machine code for our *Beboputer*. The first thing we would do would be to create a file defining our instruction set: mnemonics, addressing modes, opcodes, and so on (Figure 12.79).

```
MNEMONIC = "AND", ADDRESSING_MODE = IMMEDIATE, OPCODE = $30
MNEMONIC = "AND", ADDRESSING_MODE = ABSOLUTE,  OPCODE = $31
MNEMONIC = "AND", ADDRESSING_MODE = INDEXED,   OPCODE = $32

MNEMONIC = "LDA", ADDRESSING_MODE = IMMEDIATE, OPCODE = $90
MNEMONIC = "LDA", ADDRESSING_MODE = ABSOLUTE,  OPCODE = $91
MNEMONIC = "LDA", ADDRESSING_MODE = IMMEDIATE, OPCODE = $92
```

Figure 12.79: Defining an instruction set for a mata-assembler

The keywords *"Mnemonic," "Addressing_mode," "Immediate," "Absolute," "Indexed," "Opcode,"* and others not shown here are all ones that the meta-assembler will understand. The purpose of this file is to inform the meta-assembler that there is an instruction whose mnemonic is "AND," which supports an immediate addressing mode, and whose opcode is $30; and so on for all of our other instructions and addressing modes. Note that the above syntax is offered as an example only – the format for a real meta-assembler would be substantially different and harder to describe, but, once again, the purpose of this portion of our discussions is to introduce concepts rather than details of actual implementations.

One interesting point to consider is that our *Beboputer* only supports a simple instruction set with a limited number of addressing modes. Other computers can easily offer a richer instruction set with more diverse addressing modes, which means that the meta-assembler has to provide a superset of all of the different target systems' capabilities.

Another major point is that the meta-assembler will have its own source code syntax that is independent of the language definition. For example, in our *Beboputer*-specific assembly language we decided to use a single set of square parenthesis "[ ]"to indicate an instruction using the absolute addressing mode, but the creators of the meta-assembler may have decided that they preferred to use round parenthesis "( )." Similarly, we decided to use a hash '#' character it indicate the start of a comment, while they may have opted for a semi colon ';'. For example:

LDA [FRED]   # This is our original assembly language syntax

LDA (FRED)   ; This might be the meta-assembler's language syntax

Thus, the fact that we've used the meta-assembler's language definition capability to describe our *Beboputer*-specific instruction set doesn't alter the fact that we will still have to use the meta-assembler's syntax when creating a new source file, it just means that we are able to employ our own mnemonics as part of this syntax.

Once we've created a language definition that the meta-assembler can understand, the next step is to create a source program that we wish to assemble. Every time the assembler is run, it has to be provided with both the language definition file and the source code file (Figure 12.80).

The meta-assembler first reads the language definition file in order to learn the instructions we wish to use, the addressing modes they support, and the opcodes that are associated with them. The meta-assembler then reads the source code program and uses its newfound knowledge of the language to assemble it into the target machine code.

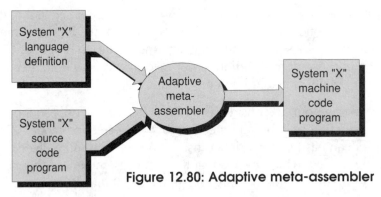

Figure 12.80: Adaptive meta-assembler

Generative meta-assemblers: In certain respects generative meta-assemblers are similar to their adaptive cousins, in that they also support a meta-syntactic language allowing you to define your own instruction set. However, the generative meta-assembler doesn't assemble source code itself; instead, it uses the language definition to generate the machine code for an assembler, which is then used to assemble source code in the usual manner (Figure 12.81).

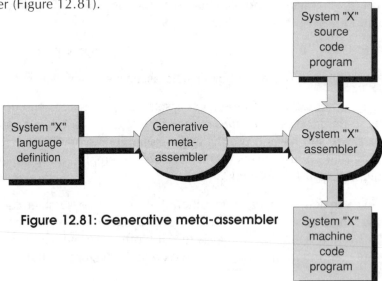

Figure 12.81: Generative meta-assembler

Once again, the fact that we've used the meta-assembler's language definition capability to describe a system-specific instruction set doesn't alter the fact that we will still have to use the meta-assembler's syntax when it comes to creating our source code programs; it just means that we can now use our own mnemonics as part of this syntax.

Disassemblers

A disassembler, as its name might suggest, performs the complementary function to an assembler, in that it accepts a machine code program as input and regenerates a source code equivalent as output (Figure 12.82).

Figure 12.82: Using a disassembler

Since the *Beboputer* has a relatively unsophisticated instruction set, creating a disassembler for it would be a fairly simple task. The disassembler would read an opcode from the machine code file and use a lookup table to find its associated mnemonic and addressing mode. Based on this addressing mode, the disassembler would then know how many operand bytes it would have to read and the way in which to "package" them in the output file. The disassembler would then output a line of source code and continue onto the next instruction.

There are a number of reasons for using a disassembler, one of the most common being that you've misplaced the source code for a particularly useful program that you'd like to modify in some way. However, disassemblers may also be employed for more nefarious purposes, such as rooting around in a program that someone else has spent a lot of time creating to find out how they did it, and then using the same techniques to create your own program and pretending that it was all your own work. Needless to say, this tends to be frowned upon by the program's original creators and the legal system.

Although disassemblers can be very useful, there are several things they cannot do. For instance, the original source code probably contained informative comments, but these aren't saved in the machine code, so the disassembler has no way of regenerating them. Similarly, the original source code probably employed address labels with meaningful names, but the disassembler has no knowledge of these, so it ends up creating its own labels along the lines of L00001, L00001, L00003, and so on. The same thing applies to constant labels used in .EQU statements – the disassembler doesn't know anything about them, so it just incorporates the appropriate numerical values directly into the source code. Last but not least, the disassembler wouldn't recognize a macro if one bit it on the leg;

the disassembler regards just about anything (apart from subroutines) as in-line code and disassembles it accordingly.

Linkers, loaders, and relocatable code

In the world of assembly language programs, there are two main processes required to get the program in a state that's ready for the computer to use: assembling the program into machine code using an *assembler,* and loading the machine code into the computer's memory using a *loader.* In certain respects we've simplified the process *you* use to load machine code into the *Beboputer*; for example, when we load the machine code into the *Beboputer's* memory, it will always start to load into the address we specified with the .ORG statement in the source code.

In fact our simplifications go somewhat deeper than this, because the *Beboputer* doesn't have its own virtual hard disk on which it can store programs. Instead, we are using the real hard disk on your main system, and we've glossed over a lot of the fiddly details. If the *Beboputer* were a real computer, we would have to provide it with a physical storage device such as a hard disk, and we would have to offer a real mechanism by which machine code programs were loaded into its memory. In fact, for the purposes of the following discussions, we will assume that the *Beboputer is* a real computer and that it does indeed have its own hard disk.

Different types of loaders

Assemble-go loaders: The simplest type of loader isn't really a loader at all. In the case of *assemble-go* loaders, the act of loading is simply a function of the assembler, which loads the machine code it generates directly into the computer's memory.

Absolute loaders: The next step up the hierarchy is an *absolute* loader, which reads a machine code program off the hard disk (or other storage device) and loads it into the computer's memory. The reason this is called an absolute loader is because it can only load the program to an absolute area of memory, commencing with the address specified by the .ORG statement in the source code. Thus, the *Beboputer's* loader (which we access using the Load Ram option under the Memory pull-down menu) is an absolute loader.

Relocating loaders: It can be inconvenient to have to load a program into the same area of memory every time we desire to use it. For example, we may wish to have several programs in memory at the same time, in which case we'd like to be able to load our program into whatever area of memory is currently available. Thus, although we might use a .ORG statement to set the program's start address to $4000 in the source code, when we come to use the program we may well wish to use a relocating leader to load it into the memory locations commencing at $6000 or whatever. Unfortunately, changing the start address of a program can be a non-trivial matter; consider the few lines of code shown in Figure 12.83.

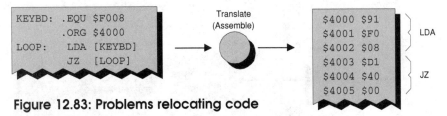

Figure 12.83: Problems relocating code

As we see, this program segment makes use of two addresses: the input port connected to the keyboard at address $F008 and the label **LOOP** at address $4000. Now assume that we want our loader to take this machine code, which was intended to start at address $4000, and actually load it starting at address $6000. We obviously don't want to loader to do anything to the address $F008 stored in locations $4001 and $4002, because the port connected to the keyboard isn't going anywhere; on the other hand, we do want the loader to change the address stored in locations $4004 and $4005 from $4000 to $6000. But how is the loader supposed to know which values to change and which it should leave alone?

One technique for achieving this is to modify our assembler such that it generates an extra byte for every opcode. If the assembler recognizes an absolute address that must not be changed (such as a constant label), then it could set this extra byte to zero. Similarly, if the assembler recognizes an address that that would need to be changed if the program were relocated (such as an address label), then it could set the extra byte to a specific non-zero value. Now when we come to run the relocating loader, we could design it to strip out these extra bytes and throw them away, but first it would use them to decide whether or not to modify the their associated operands by adding the difference between the original start address and the new start address. (It probably doesn't need to be said that this technique causes the output from the assembler to be bloated and ungainly, but we'll say it anyway: *"This technique causes the ......"*).[13]

---

[13]See also the discussion on relocatable code later in this chapter.

Linking loaders: The *Beboputer's* assembler only accepts a single "flat" source file containing everything that has to go into a particular program. Unfortunately, this can be really painful if you're creating a large program, not least because it can take a long time to assemble. One alternative is to partition the source code into logical "chunks" based on major functions, and assemble these chunks into individual machine-code files. Obviously, you would then require a loader that could handle multiple chunks of machine code (Figure 12.84).

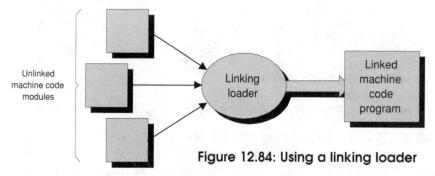

Figure 12.84: Using a linking loader

The linking loader (or link-loader) reads all of the machine code modules, links them together into a single machine code program, and loads the resulting program into the system's memory. Generally speaking this technique only makes sense if the link-loader can relocate all of the modules as and where it sees fit, so link-loaders require all of the capabilities of relocating loaders and then some.

There are also other considerations, such as the fact that a link-loader needs to be able to recognize the main module that starts the program. Also, the individual modules need the ability to pass data between themselves. This means that we need to modify our source language to differentiate between local labels and constants that can only be used within a particular module, as opposed to global labels and constants that can be accessed by multiple modules. For example, we might decide to have a .GLOBAL directive that can be used to make specific labels available to the outside world. This would then entail modifying our assembler such that it appended each machine code module with additional information as to any of its attributes that could be accessed by other modules. The link-loader would then use this information during the process of constructing the final machine code program.

In fact, the concept of differentiating between label and constant names that are local to a module versus names that are visible to other modules has a number of implications, one of them being the opportunity to come up with a whole new set of terms such as *scope* (meaning the extent to which a name is visible) and *namespace* (meaning much the same thing). More importantly, it allows us to use the same name for local labels in multiple modules without confusion, because their scope is limited to the module in which they are declared. Unfortunately, the *Beboputer* doesn't support the concept of modules, which means that we are obliged to use a somewhat painful naming convention to prevent multiple subroutines having the same label (you'll discover more about this when you start to rummage through the pre-defined subroutines we've provided in Appendix G).

Linkage editors: In many respects a linkage editor is similar to a linking loader, except that once it has assembled the sub-modules into a single machine code program, it then saves that program to a storage device instead of loading it into memory. In fact link-loaders often have the ability to save their output to disk, while linkage editors often have the ability to load their output into memory, so the boundary between the two can be rather fuzzy and gray.

Relocatable code

Apart from the implied and immediate addressing modes, the *Beboputer's* instructions are all based on some form of absolute addressing. For example, when we use a statement like "JMP [FRED]" in the *Beboputer's* source code, the resulting machine code effectively says: *"Jump immediately to address $4065"* (assuming of course that the label FRED is declared at address of $4065). As we discussed in the *"Relocating Loaders"* section above, this means that it's difficult to change the start address of the machine code program, because we have to "tweak" any references to this type of address within the program.

However, some computers support *relative addressing modes*, which involves special opcodes whose operands are *offsets* from their current position. To illustrate this, assume that we have a computer with both standard and relative instructions, such as JMP (*"jump immediate"*) and JMPR (*"jump relative"*). Further assume that the address of the opcode for the JMP instruction in the "JMP [FRED]" statement we discussed previously occurred at address $4053. If our language supported relative instructions, our assembler could automatically translate this instruction into the opcode for a "JMPR [$0012]," meaning: *"Jump forward $0012 bytes from your current location."* Using this technique, the loader could simply load the program into another area of the memory …. and it would still work!

That's it, we're done (with assemblers)

You didn't know how long this chapter was going to be when you started reading it and, to be frank, we had no idea of its size until we started writing the little rascal. But now it's time to break out the party supplies and deck the halls with streamers, because we've all survived the experience. As the old saying goes: *"Anything that doesn't kill you makes you stronger"* (so our muscles should have muscles on their muscles by now)!

Quick quiz #12

1) Summarize the advantages of writing programs in assembly language as opposed to writing them in machine code.

2) What do the terms "syntax" and "semantics" mean in the context of computer languages?

3) What are the differences between unary and binary operators?

4) Summarize the differences between one-pass and two-pass assemblers.

5) What is a nested subroutine?

6) If you've just created a computer, is it better to hand-edit your first assembler and use it to assemble your first editor, or is it preferable to hand-assemble your first editor and use it to create your first assembler?

7) Summarize the differences between a standard assembler and a cross-assembler.

8) What are the main problems with disassemblers?

9) How would you go about modifying our "Etch-A-Sketch-like" program to allow you to interactively change the color of the dots?

10) Create an assembly language program that can write the phrase "Hello World" to our memory-mapped display, and that could be easily modified to write a different phrase.

Chapter 13

Burning Character and Monitor EEPROMs

In this chapter we will discover:

The difference between ROMs, PROMs, EPROMs, and EEPROMs

How to use the character editor tool to create a file containing new character patterns

How to use our character patterns to burn a new Character EEPROM device

How to plug our new Character EEPROM into the *Beboputer*'s virtual video card

How to create a new system EEPROM

Contents of Chapter 13

ROMs, PROMs, EPROMs, and ...... wait for it ...... EEPROMs

When we first introduced our memory-mapped display in Chapter 11, we noted that the patterns of 0s and 1s used to generate the characters on the screen are stored in an integrated circuit called a *Character ROM*. In reality this is just a standard read-only memory (ROM) device; the only reason we call it a "Character ROM" is that ...... well you can work it out for yourself (Figure 13.1).

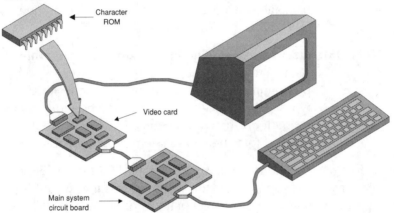

Character
ROM

Video card

Main system
circuit board

Figure 13.1: The memory-mapped display's character ROM

Now, hold onto your hat, because in this chapter you're going to learn how to modify the patterns stored in the Character ROM, thereby allowing you to create your own set of characters. But before we start, it's important to note that there are a number of different flavors of ROM devices:[1]

ROM: **Read-Only Memory**
The patterns of 0s and 1s in a ROM are formed when the device is constructed and they cannot be modified by the user.

PROM: **Programmable Read-Only Memory**
In the case of a PROM, the device is delivered to the user containing all 0s or all 1s. By means of a special programming tool used to apply certain signals to the device's pins, the user can program the contents of a PROM. Once programmed the contents cannot be

---

[1]All of the memory devices introduced here are discussed in greater detail in this book's companion volume: *Bebop to the Boolean Boogie (An Unconventional Guide to Electronics).*

changed, so these devices are referred to as being *one-time programmable (OTP)*.

EPROM: Erasable Programmable Read-Only Memory
Like PROMs, these devices can be programmed by the user, but they have the added advantage that they can subsequently be erased and reprogrammed. An EPROM has a small quartz "window" in the top of its package (this window is usually covered by a piece of opaque tape). To erase the device the tape is removed and the package is exposed to an intense source of ultraviolet (UV) light.

EEPROM: Electrically-Erasable Programmable Read-Only Memory
As its name might suggest, an EEPROM can be both programmed and erased using electrical signals. Some types of EEPROM can be programmed while remaining resident on the circuit board, in which case they may be referred to as being *in-system programmable (ISP)*.

As fate would have it, the *Beboputer*'s Character ROM is an EEPROM device (in our virtual world of course), which means that we have the ability to erase it and load it with new patterns of 0s and 1s. (If we wanted to be pedantic we should really refer to our Character ROM as a "Character EEPROM," but this would get real old real fast, so we'll continue to refer to it using our original designation.)

Winding up the *Beboputer*

Make sure the *Beboputer* CD is in the appropriate drive in your computer and summon the *Beboputer*. Once the *Beboputer*'s project window has opened, click the File item on its menu bar, click the Open Project entry in the resulting pull-down menu, then select the Lab 8 project from the ensuing dialog. This will invoke our eighth (and penultimate) lab (Figure 13.2).

Initially the only tools on the screen are the hex keypad and the memory-mapped display. As usual, the memory-mapped display is black, because the *Beboputer* isn't powered up yet. Just for a change we'll leave things this way for the moment.

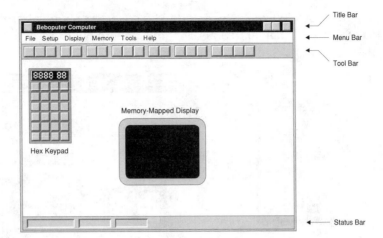

Figure 13.2: The *Beboputer* project window for Lab 8

Creating a file containing our new patterns

Our first task is to create a text file containing a description of the patterns of 0s and 1s that we want to program into our new Character ROM. To do this we will employ a tool we dubbed the *character editor*. You can invoke this tool by clicking the **Tools** item on the project window's menu bar, then clicking the **Character Editor** entry in the resulting pull-down menu. Alternatively, you can simply click the **Character Editor** icon on the tool bar.

The character editor is initially blank, because we haven't loaded a file into it yet. You could create a new file by clicking the **File** item on the <u>character editor's</u> menu bar, then clicking the **New** entry in the resulting pull-down menu. However, it can take a long time to create a complete character set (trust us on this, for we know whereof we speak), so instead you can use our existing character set as a starting point. In order to do this, click the **File** item on the <u>character editor's</u> menu bar, then click the **Open** entry in the resulting pull-down menu. This will bring up a dialog box which, for the moment, only contains a single entry called "**defchar.jed**" (we'll explain the rational behind the ".jed" file extension later). Double-click this entry to select it and load the file into the character editor (Figure 13.3).

Note that the file you've just loaded actually resides on your <u>main system's</u> hard disk (we haven't started to play with the *Beboputer* itself yet). Also note that this file contains the patterns for each of the 256 characters in our character set. Once the file has been loaded, the character editor shows the pattern associated with ASCII code $00. As you may recall from our earlier discussions in Chapters 10 and 11, this pattern is just something that we made up to represent the NULL control code.

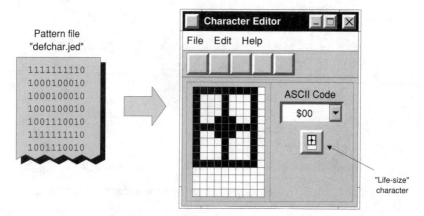

Figure 13.3: Loading an existing pattern file into the character editor

Before you do anything else, click the character editor's **File** pull-down menu and select the **Save As** option. Then save this file our under a new name such as "mychar.jed," thereby ensuring that you can't do anything to mess up our default character set.

Now click on the **arrow** button next to the character's ASCII code, then use the resulting scrolling list to select ASCII code $41. The pattern that appears in the character editor is obviously that of a letter 'A', which is what we'd expect for this code.

Note that five lines of dots are left blank under the letter 'A'. These blank lines are used to form a gap between this letter and any other character that may be located under it when we eventually replicate them on the memory-mapped display. You may wish to take a few moments to glance back to Table 10.1 in Chapter 10 to refresh your memory as to the characters associated with the various ASCII codes, then pick a few of these characters at random and check the patterns of dots we

Remember that the ASCII code is simply a convention that we've all decided to live with. Instead of having a pattern of dots forming a letter 'A' associated with ASCII code $41, you could modify this pattern to form another letter. This means that when you send the code $41 to the memory-mapped display you'd see your new letter. However, you would no longer be using the ASCII code, but just another home-brewed code of which the world has more than enough already, and the end result would be confusion for all concerned.

used to represent them. After we've finished this lab, you may decide that you can improve on our character set – maybe you'll think that the "curly" letters should be just a bit more curly (or a bit less so) – and why not? Feel free to have at it with gusto and abandon, and be sure to email us to let us know how well you did.[2]

Now glance back to Table 11.1 in Chapter 11, which shows our "chunky graphics" codes. Once again, pick a few of these characters at random and check the patterns of dots we used to represent them. In particular, note that the characters with codes of $D4 and above all contain the same "dummy pattern," because we couldn't think of anything else to put in them ...... but you're about to change all that.

Click the arrow button next to the ASCII code in the character editor, then use the resulting scrolling list to select character $D4, which is the first of the characters we didn't know what to do with. Once again, this initially contains the dummy character that we employed to differentiate the unused characters from a space character. One way to clear this character is to click the Edit item on the *character editor's* menu bar, then click the Clear entry in the resulting pull-down menu (there's also an icon on the Character editor's toolbar for this purpose).

Move your mouse cursor over one of the squares in the grid and click the left mouse button to turn that square black. As an alternative to clicking on the squares individually, you can hold the left mouse button down and drag the cursor over a number of squares. If you wish to change squares back from black to white, you can do so using the *right* mouse button.

Now clear the grid again, then use all of your artistic skill to create an image of the Mona Lisa. If you can't handle this, just do your best to achieve a smiley face (it really doesn't matter how good it is). When you've finished, click the character editor's File pull-down menu followed by the Save option, thereby saving your edits in the "mychar.jed" file (Figure 13.4).

Once you've generated your new file, dismiss the character editor using the rightmost button in its title bar, or click the File item on its menu bar then click the Exit entry in the resulting pull-down menu.

---

[2]If you're feeling particularly frisky, why not try your hand at creating an *italic* character set?

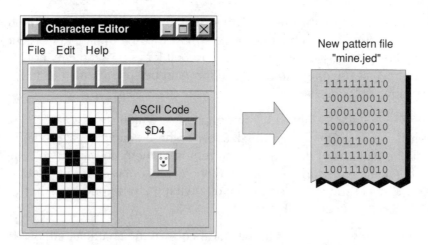

Figure 13.4: Generating a new pattern file from the character editor

Burning a new Character ROM

It's important to note that you haven't actually created a new Character ROM yet. All you've done is to use the character editor utility to generate a text file containing the patterns of 0s and 1s you wish to program into the ROM device. (Once again, we should really be using the term "EEPROM," but this gets to be a bit of a mouthful after a while.)

In order to program a new ROM, you need to employ another tool called an **EPROM Burner.** You can invoke this tool by clicking the **Tools** item on the project window's menu bar, then clicking the **EPROM Burner** entry in the resulting pull-down menu.

Alternatively, you can simply click the **EPROM Burner** icon on the tool bar. The resulting utility promptly appears on your screen, where it sits waiting for you to decide what type of device you wish to program: a new Character ROM or a new System ROM (Figure 13.5).

At this time we're only interested in programming a new Character ROM, so click the appropriate integrated circuit package on the form. This will invoke a standard dialog for you to select the pattern file you wish to use. Select the

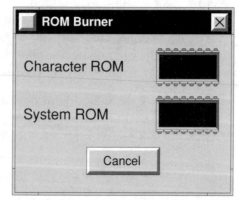

Figure 13.5: The ROM burner utility

pattern file called "mychar.jed" that you just created, then click the Open button to accept this file. At this point you will be presented with a new form. Click the Burn button on this form, then sit back while the EPROM Burner programs your new device.

Once you've initiated the device programmer, a new form will appear to illustrate your progress. The entire process of programming the device may take a few minutes, so you'll just have to sit back and be patient. Note that we are playing a few tricks in our virtual environment, not the least that in the real world you would have to use a physical tool to program your device (Figure 13.6).

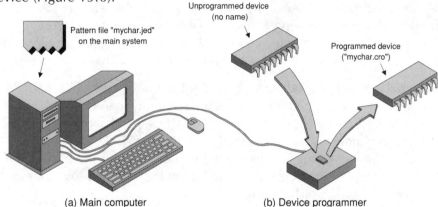

(a) Main computer   (b) Device programmer

Figure 13.6: Physically programming your new Character ROM

After creating your pattern file, you would have to connect your main · computer to a device programmer. Next you'd pluck a new device off the shelf and insert it into a special socket on top of the programmer, then you'd instruct your main computer to download your pattern file to the programmer, which would treat the file's contents as instructions as to how to program the device. This process may be referred to as *programming* the device, *burning* the device, or *blowing* the device.

There are a variety of standard formats that one might use to represent the contents of the pattern file, one of the more common ones being known as JEDEC (for reasons that we're not particularly concerned with here). This explains why we gave our pattern file the extension ".jed" – to indicate that we're pretending it's a JEDEC file.[3,4]

---

[3]We're not really using a JEDEC format, but rather one of our own devising (see also Appendix B).

[4]To be perfectly honest, JEDEC files are rarely used with programmable memory devices, but are more commonly associated with other flavors of programmable components (pattern files for memory devices are typically represented using Intel Hex or Motorola S-Record formats).

Having programmed a physical device in the real world, you would probably attach a label to it to prevent your confusing it with other such devices. In the case of our virtual world the EPROM Burner does this for you. Due to the fact that your pattern file was called "mychar.jed," the EPROM Burner automatically calls your programmed device "mychar.cro" (where the ".cro" stands for "Character ROM").

Using your new Character ROM

Earlier on (while you weren't looking) we created an assembly source program called "lab8_p1.asm," and we even took the time to run the assembler, thereby generating a machine code file called "lab8_p1.ram." (When you have a few minutes you may wish to invoke the assembler and look at our source program, but we haven't got time for that now.)

Power up the *Beboputer* by clicking the **ON** button on the hex keypad. As usual, the memory-mapped display fills with random characters reflecting the uninitialized contents of the Video RAM. Click the **Memory** item on the main project window's menu bar, then click the **Load RAM** entry in the resulting pull-down menu. Double-click the "lab8_p1.ram" program in the ensuing dialog form, then click the **Load** button to load this program into the *Beboputer's* RAM and dismiss the form.

Ensure that the **Address (Ad)** button on the hex keypad is active, enter the program's start address (which is $4000), and click the hex keypad's **Run** button. As you will see, this program first clears the memory-mapped display, then draws a "checkerboard" pattern of characters that alternate between ASCII $20s (spaces) and $D4s. Once the program has finished it jumps back to address $0000, which returns the *Beboputer* to its reset mode.

But wait! What is this? Where is your smiley face? Why is the display showing the old "dummy" character associated with the $D4 code? The problem is that although you've burnt a new Character ROM, you haven't inserted it into the *Beboputer's* video card yet.

First click the **ON/OFF** button on the hex keypad to power-down the *Beboputer*, because it's extremely unwise to play around with any electronic equipment when the power is still on (even in our virtual world). Now click the **Setup** item on the main project window's menu bar, then click the **Swap EPROM** entry in the resulting pull-down menu. Select the **Character ROM** option in the ensuing form, then select the "mychar.cro" entry in the resulting dialog and click the **Open** button, which will pull our tired old Character ROM out of the video card and replace it with your new shiny device.

Now let's try running our program again. Power up the *Beboputer* by clicking the **ON** button on the hex keypad, click the **Memory** item on the main project window's menu bar, click the **Load Ram** entry in the resulting pull-down menu, double-click the "lab8_p1.ram" program in the ensuing dialog form, then click the **Load** button to load this program into the *Beboputer's* RAM and dismiss the dialog. Ensure that the **Address (Ad)** button on the hex keypad is active, enter the program's start address of $4000, and click the hex keypad's **Run** button. This time the checkerboard pattern of characters shows the smiley face that you created for the $D4 code. You've done it, you've burnt and installed a new Character ROM and survived to tell the tale!

Creating a new System ROM

You may recall that, in addition to the Character ROM, our **EPROM Burner** tool also had a System ROM option. Unfortunately, you can't create a new monitor program for the hex keypad, because we've subsumed these activities into our interface, but you can produce a new System ROM containing any programs to which you've become particularly attached.

When using our assembler in the previous chapter, we always employed the .ORG directive to set our programs' start addresses to $4000 or higher, because $4000 is the first address in our RAM. Thus, when we ran the assembler, it always generated a ".ram" file. However, if you so desire, you can use the .ORG directive to set a program's start address to be in the ROM area, in which case the assembler will generate a ".rom" file.

There are only two main rules. First, you can't set the start address to be lower than $1000, because we've reserved the first 4 K-bytes of ROM (addresses $0000 through $0FFF) for our own nefarious purposes, but this still leaves you 12 K-Bytes (addresses $1000 through $3FFF) in which to romp around wild and free. The second rule is that the body of your machine code program can't cross the boundary from ROM into RAM. Also, we should note that if a program you intend to burn into your System ROM requires any memory locations in which to store intermediate values, then you must use .EQU directives to ensure that these locations appear in the RAM area (otherwise you'd never be able to write to them).

If you do create any programs you'd like to load into your System ROM, then you can use the appropriate entry on the **EPROM Burner** tool to select these programs and burn a new device. Once you've created this device, you then have to click the **Setup** item on the main project window's menubar followed by the **Swap EPROM** entry in the resulting pull-down menu, and then follow a similar path to that used to create a Character ROM. To actually invoke one of the programs in a System ROM, you have to use the hex keypad to specify that program's start address, and then select the **Step** or **Run** options.

Important! Note that the effects of exchanging the default Character ROM or System ROM for a user-defined version will only persist for the duration of the current session. To put this another way, whenever you invoke the *Beboputer* or open a new project, the *Beboputer* will automatically initialize containing its original Character and System ROM devices.

Quick quiz #13

1) Summarize the differences between ROMs, PROMs, EPROMs, and EEPROMs.

2) To what does the phrase *"in-system programmable"* refer?

3) What is a JEDEC file?

4) What is a Character ROM?

5) How does a Character ROM differ from a normal ROM?

6) Summarize the process of creating a new Character ROM.

7) Why do we associate our character patterns with ASCII codes when creating a Character ROM ?

8) Summarize the process of creating a new System ROM.

9) Why might you wish to create a new System ROM?

10) Why do you think that we (the authors) decided that the effects of exchanging the default Character and System ROMs would only persist for the duration of the current session?

Chapter 14

Calculator Sign-Off Project

In this chapter we will discover:

How to write the program for a simple
four-function calculator

How much you've actually understood thus far

How much you thought you'd understood.....
but didn't

What it feels like when a program finally works
after you've slaved over it for hours

▼

What the ancient Incas had to say about this
sort of thing

LAB 9

Contents of Chapter 14

Using everything you've learned thus far

As we noted at the beginning of this book, computers really aren't as difficult to understand as many people believe – it's largely a case of learning the basic concepts and building on them one piece at a time. On the other hand there are a lot of fiddly bits to remember and it can be quite a lot of effort to learn them sufficiently to grasp the big picture. So if you've worked your way through the preceding chapters and performed all of the labs, then we'd like to extend our congratulations for a job well done!

In this, the penultimate chapter, we're going to present you with a sign-off project that will allow you to use everything that you've learnt thus far, add a large dollop of your own imagination, stir it all together, and create a real-world application: a four-function calculator.

Winding up the *Beboputer*

Make sure the *Beboputer* CD is in the appropriate drive in your computer and summon the *Beboputer*. Once the *Beboputer's* project window has opened, click the File item on its menu bar, click the Open Project entry in the resulting pull-down menu, then select the Lab 9 project from the ensuing dialog. This will invoke our final lab (Figure 14.1).

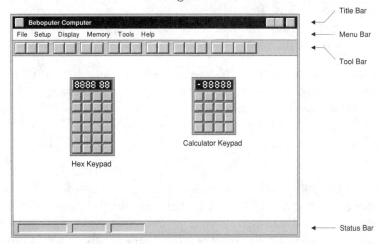

Figure 14.1: The *Beboputer* project window for Lab 9

This project window may seem to be a little sparsely furnished compared to our previous laboratories, because the only tools we've launched for you are the hex keypad and the calculator keypad. We've done this to emphasize the fact that we haven't prejudged how you are to implement this project –

you're free to employ any and all of the *Beboputer's* tools, but it's up to you to decide which ones to use.

The calculator shell

The calculator shell is a very simple device with almost no intelligence of its own. This device features a keypad area containing sixteen buttons, along with a display area that can contain an optional minus sign and up to five decimal digits (Figure 14.2).

The calculator's keypad contains an 8-bit latch that's connected to one of the *Beboputer's* input ports (the port at address $F007). By default this latch will contain $FF (or 1111 1111 in binary) to indicate that no buttons have been pressed. When one of the buttons *is* pressed (that is, clicked by the mouse), an associated 8-bit code is loaded into the latch, where it will be stored until the *Beboputer* is ready to read the input port (Figure 14.3a). When the *Beboputer* does get around to reading the data from this port, the latch will be automatically reset to contain $FF.

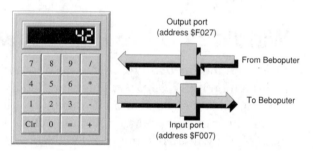

Figure 14.2: The calculator shell

The buttons on the keypad are logically and physically distinct from the display area. To put this another way, clicking a button on the keypad does not, of itself, affect the display area. The only way to modify the contents of the display is for the *Beboputer* to write codes to the output port at address $F027 (Figure 14.3b). For example, writing a value of $10 to this port will clear the display.

Note that the codes we chose to assign to the calculator's buttons are somewhat arbitrary. It obviously makes sense to use codes $00 through $09 to represent the '0' through '9' buttons (because it will make processing numbers easier), but we could have used other codes for these buttons had we so desired. Similarly, we could have assigned any unused codes we wished to the 'Clr', '–', '+', '/', '*', and '=' buttons, we just happened to decide that the ones shown in Figure 14.3a were the ones our calculator would use. Also, there is no overwhelming reason why the codes that are used to drive the display should be the same as the codes associated with the corresponding buttons, except that it is aesthetically pleasing and more intuitive to do so.

Button	Code (%=Bin, $=Hex)	
0	%0000 0000	$00
1	%0000 0001	$01
2	%0000 0010	$02
3	%0000 0011	$03
4	%0000 0100	$04
5	%0000 0101	$05
6	%0000 0110	$06
7	%0000 0111	$07
8	%0000 1000	$08
9	%0000 1001	$09
Clr	%0001 0000	$10
-	%0010 0000	$20
+	%0011 0000	$30
/	%0100 0000	$40
*	%0101 0000	$50
=	%0110 0000	$60
Nothing	%1111 1111	$FF

Figure 14.3: Calculator codes

Display	Code (%=Bin, $=Hex)	
0	%0000 0000	$00
1	%0000 0001	$01
2	%0000 0010	$02
3	%0000 0011	$03
4	%0000 0100	$04
5	%0000 0101	$05
6	%0000 0110	$06
7	%0000 0111	$07
8	%0000 1000	$08
9	%0000 1001	$09
Clr	%0001 0000	$10
-	%0010 0000	$20
Bell	%0111 0000	$70

(a) Input Port (to *Beboputer*)   (b) Output Port (from *Beboputer*)

Also note that the calculator's display does have a limited amount of hardware-assist to make your life a little easier. For example, assume that you've cleared the display by writing $10 (the 'Clr' code) to the output port driving the calculator, and that you now wish to display the number "42." If you first write $04 to this port, the number '4' will appear in the right-hand column of the display. If you next write $02 to the port, the number '4' will automatically move one place to the left and the number '2' will appear in the right-hand column. (Writing the $20 code to the port will cause a minus sign to appear in the display, while a $70 code will make the calculator "beep" in an annoying way.)

Finally, note that the calculator keypad doesn't have an **ON/OFF** button of its own, because it's powered by the main *Beboputer*. Thus, when you click the **ON** button on the hex keypad, this will also serve to power up the calculator.

Your mission ...... should you decide to accept it

So your mission (should you decide to accept it) is to write a program that uses the calculator keypad to add, subtract, multiply, and divide numbers. Note that, for the sake of simplicity, your calculator is only required to work with numbers in the range -32,767 through +32,767.

For your interest we've offered one possible solution to this problem in Appendix I. However, we <u>strongly</u> recommend that you don't take even the briefest peek at our example until you've created your own (working) version, because you will learn far more by struggling with your own specification and implementation than you ever will by looking at what someone else has done; you might even come up with a much better solution that we did (if so, please drop us a line to let us know).

So, that's your lot ...... good luck ...... and while you're slaving away, be sure you don't forget the ancient Inca saying: *"Pthwesa nwe nimegos vah yubetha"* – words we're sure you'll agree are as profound and relevant in today's world as when they were originally voiced deep in the mists of time.

Quick quiz #14

1) Why did we (the authors) decide to assign the calculator keys '0' through '9' to the codes $00 through $09?

2) Why does the calculator return a value of $FF when no key has been pressed (as opposed to the QWERTY keyboard which returns $00 in the absence of a key being pressed)?

3) Why did we decide that your calculator was only required to work with numbers in the range -32,767 through +32,767?

4) With regard to the previous question, why didn't we allow your calculator to work with numbers in the range -32,768 through +32,767?

5) What do we mean when we say that the keys on the calculator are logically and physically distinct from its display area?

6) How should one approach a programming task such as this calculator?

7) What result would you expect if you entered "243 - 382 x 14 =" on your calculator (after you've created the program of course)?

8) How should your calculator respond to the sequence "- 243 =" (as opposed to the sequence "0 - 243 =") ?

9) Assuming that you've just entered the sequence "0 - 243 =", what should occur if you now enter the sequence "+ 10 ="?

10) How should your calculator respond to the sequence "10 + + 42 =" ?

Chapter 15

A Sort of History of Computers

In this chapter we will discover:

The first aids to calculation

Where the concepts of zero and negative
numbers came from

The first mechanical calculators

The first mechanical computers

The first electromechanical computers

The first electronic computers

The first and worst computer bugs

The first personal computers

How Johnathan Swift (author of *Gulliver's Travels*)
and Lewis Carroll (author of *Alice's Adventures
in Wonderland*) fit into the picture

Contents of Chapter 15

Taking a cruise through history

In this, the closing chapter, we take a cruise through history to discover some of the key developments that have brought us to our present state of computing, including the development of numbers, the introduction of mechanical aids to calculation, the evolution of electronics, and the impact of electronics on computing. No one person may be credited with the invention of computers, but several names stand proud in the crowd. The following offers some of the more notable developments and individuals, with great regret for any omissions.

The first aids to calculation

The first tools used as aids to calculation were almost certainly man's own fingers, and it is not simply a coincidence that the word "*digit*" is used to refer to a finger (or toe) as well as a numerical quantity. As the need to represent larger numbers grew, early man employed readily available materials for the purpose. Small stones or pebbles could be used to represent larger numbers than fingers and toes, and had the added advantage of being able to easily store intermediate results for later use. Thus, it is also no coincidence that the word "*calculate*" is derived from the Latin word for pebble.

The oldest objects known to represent numbers are bones with notches carved into them. These bones, which were discovered in western Europe, date from the Aurignacian period 20,000 to 30,000 years ago and correspond to the first appearance of Cro-Magnon man.[1] Of special interest is a wolf's jawbone more than 20,000 years old with fifty-five notches in groups of five, which was discovered in Czechoslovakia in 1937. This is the first evidence of the tally system, which

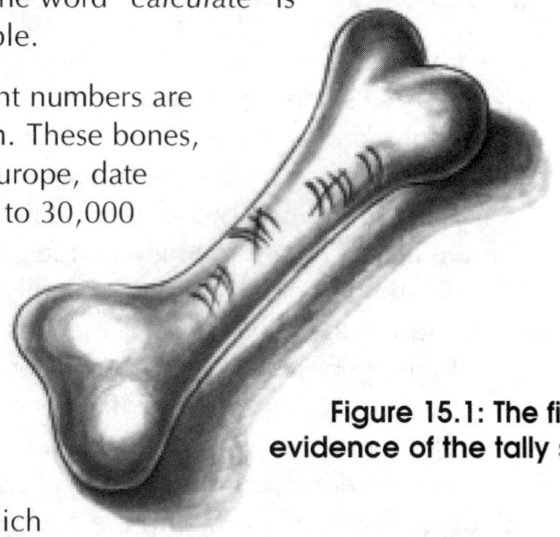

Figure 15.1: The first evidence of the tally system

is still used occasionally to the present day and could therefore qualify as one of the most enduring of human inventions (Figure 15.1).

---

[1]The term "Cro-Magnon" comes from caves of the same name in Southern France, in which the first skeletons of this race were discovered in 1868.

Also of interest is a piece of bone dating from around 8,500 BC, which was discovered in Africa, and which appears to have notches representing the prime numbers 11, 13, 17, and 19. Prime numbers are those that are only wholly divisible by the number one and themselves, so it is not surprising that early man would have attributed them with a special significance. What *is* surprising is that someone of that era had the mathematical sophistication to recognize this quite advanced concept and took the trouble to write it down – not the least that prime numbers had little relevance to everyday problems of gathering food and staying alive.

Tally sticks – the hidden dangers

The practice of making marks on, or cutting notches into, things to represent numbers has survived to the present day, especially among school children making tally marks on their desks to signify the days of their captivity. In the not-so-distant past, storekeepers, who often could not read or write, used a similar technique to keep track of their customer's debts. For example, a baker might make cuts across a stick of wood equal to the number of loaves in the shopper's basket. This stick was then split lengthwise, with the baker and the customer keeping half each, so that both could remember how many loaves were owed and neither of them could cheat.

Similarly, the British government used wooden tally sticks until the early 1780s. These sticks had notches cut into them to record financial transactions and to act as receipts. Over the course of time these tally sticks were replaced by paper records, leaving the cellars of the Houses of Parliament full to the brim with pieces of old wood. Rising to the challenge with the inertia common to governments around the world, Parliament dithered around until 1834 before finally getting around to ordering the destruction of the tally sticks. There was some discussion about donating the sticks to the poor as firewood, but wiser heads prevailed, pointing out that the sticks actually represented "top secret" government transactions. The fact that the majority of the poor couldn't read or write and often couldn't count was obviously of no great significance, and it was finally decreed that the sticks should be burned in the courtyard of the Houses of Parliament. However, fate is usually more than willing to enter the stage with a pointed jape – gusting winds caused the fire to break out of control and burn the House of Commons to the ground (although they did manage to save the foundations)!

The decimal number system

The number system we use on a day-to-day basis is the decimal system, which is based on ten digits: zero through nine. The name decimal comes from the Latin *decem* meaning ten, while the symbols we use to represent these digits arrived in Europe around the thirteenth century from the Arabs who, in turn, acquired them from the Hindus. As the decimal system is based on ten digits, it is said to be *base-10* or *radix-10*, where the term *radix* comes from the Latin word meaning "root."

Outside of specialist requirements such as computing, base-10 numbering systems have been adopted almost universally. This is almost certainly due to the fact that we happen to have ten fingers (including our thumbs). If mother nature had decreed six fingers on each hand, we would probably be using a base-twelve numbering system. In fact this isn't as far-fetched as it may at first seem. The term *terapod* refers to an animal which has four limbs, along with hips and shoulders and fingers and toes. In the mid-1980s, paleontologists discovered *Acanthostega* who, at approximately 350 million years old, is the most primitive terapod known – so primitive in fact that these creatures still lived exclusively in water and had not yet ventured onto land.

After the dinosaurs (who were also terapods) exited the stage, humans were one branch of the terapod tree that eventually inherited the earth (along with hippopotami, hedgehogs, aardvarks, frogs, ... and all of the other vertebrates). Ultimately, we're all descended from *Acanthostega* or one of her cousins. The point is that *Acanthostega* had <u>eight</u> fully evolved fingers on each hand (Figure 15.2), so if evolution hadn't taken a slight detour, we'd probably have ended up using a base-sixteen numbering system (which would have been jolly handy when we finally got around to inventing computers, let me tell you).[2]

Figure 15.2: The first terapod, Acanthostega, had eight fully developed fingers on each hand

If we were to take a plunge into the unknown (as is our wont), we might speculate about the existence of multiple universes. Suppose that in some

---

[2]As a point of interest, the Irish hero Cuchulain was reported as having seven fingers on each hand (but this would have been no help in computing whatsoever).

reverse-Polish parallel universe,[3] eight-fingered counterparts of the authors are penning their version of this book, which might perhaps be called *Pobeb Setyb Kcab (Olleh Elttil Rehtorb Werdna)*. In *their* book, this undoubtedly handsome duo might well be noting the serendipity of having a base-16 number system that so well matched their computing applications. Indeed, they may go so far as to point out that, but for some small quirk of fate, terapods in *their* universe might have ended up with only five fingers on each hand: "*In which case*," they would conclude, "*we would probably be using a base-10 numbering system — and can you imagine how awful that would be?*"

But let us curb our metaphysical speculations and return to the point at hand (assuming, for the sake of charity, that there is one). The decimal system with which we are fated is a place-value system, which means that the value of a particular digit depends both on the digit itself and on its position within the number. For example, a '4' in the right-hand column simply means four — in the next column it means forty — one more column over means four-hundred — then four thousand, and so on.

Unfortunately, although base-ten systems are anatomically convenient they have few other advantages to recommend them. In fact, depending on your point of view, almost any other base (with the possible exception of nine) would be as good as, or better than, base-ten. This is because, for many arithmetic operations, the use of a base that is wholly divisible by many numbers, especially the smaller values, conveys certain advantages. A base-ten system is only wholly divisible by two or five, so, given the choice, we might prefer a base-twelve system on the basis that twelve is wholly divisible by two, three, four, and six. By comparison, for their own esoteric purposes, some mathematicians would ideally prefer a system with a prime number as a base; for example, seven or eleven.

> Quite apart from anything else, man has been interested in the properties of odd numbers since antiquity, often ascribing mystical and magical properties to them — for example, "lucky seven" and "unlucky thirteen." As Pliny the Elder (AD 23-79) said: "*Why is it that we entertain the belief that for every purpose odd numbers are the most effectual?*"

---

[3]For your edification, *Reverse Polish Notation (RPN)* is a style of data entry favored by some calculators, in which the operators and operands are input in a backwards sort-of fashion (we kid you not).

The ancient Egyptians

Number systems with bases other than ten have sprouted up throughout history. For example, the ancient Egyptians experimented with duo-decimal (base-12) systems, because they counted finger-joints instead of fingers. Each of our fingers has three joints (at least they do in my branch of the family), so if you use your thumb to point to the joints of the other fingers on the same hand, you can count one-two-three on the first finger, four-five-six on the next, and so on up to twelve on your little finger.

If a similar technique is used with both hands, you can represent values from one through twenty-four. This explains why the ancient Egyptians divided their days into twenty-four periods, which is, in turn, why we have twenty-four hours in a day. Strangely enough, an Egyptian hour was only approximately equal to one of our hours. This was because the Egyptians liked things to be nice and tidy, so they decided to have twelve hours of daylight and twelve hours of nighttime. Unfortunately, as the amount of daylight varies throughout the year, they were obliged to adjust the lengths of their hours according to the seasons.

One of the methods that the Egyptians used to measure time was the water clock, or *Clepsydra*,[4] which consisted of a container of water with a small hole in the bottom through which the water escaped. Units of time were marked on the side of the container, and the length of the units corresponding to day and night could be adjusted by varying the distance between the markings or by modifying the shape of the container; for example, by having the top wider than the bottom.

> In addition to the Egyptians, many other people experimented with water clocks and some interesting variations sprouted forth. For example, in some cases a float was connected to a wheel and, as the float changed its level, the wheel turned to indicate the hour on a dial.
>
> Water clocks were also a standard means of keeping time in Korea as early as the "Three Kingdoms" period, and it was here that one of the first known automatic water clocks was devised in 1434. This clock was called *Chagyongnu*, which literally translates as "*self-striking water clock.*" When the water reached a certain level, a trigger device released a metal ball, which rolled down a chute into a metal drum to "gong the hour."

In addition to their base-twelve system, the Egyptians also experimented with a sort-of-base-ten system. In this system the numbers 1 through 9 were

---

[4]The term "Clepsydra" is derived from the Greek *klepto*, meaning "thief," and *hydro*, meaning "water." Thus, Clepsydra literally means "water thief."

drawn using the appropriate number of vertical lines; 10 was represented by a circle; 100 was a coiled rope; 1,000 a lotus blossom; 10,000 a pointing finger; 100,000 a tadpole; and 1,000,000 a picture of a man with his arms spread wide in amazement. So to represent a number like 2,327,685, they would have been obliged to use pictures of two amazed men, three tadpoles, two pointing fingers, seven lotus blossoms, six coiled ropes, eight circles, and five vertical lines. It only requires a few attempts to divide tadpoles and lotus blossoms by pointing fingers and coiled ropes to appreciate why this scheme didn't exactly take the world by storm.

Actually, it's easy for us to rest on our laurels and smugly criticize ideas of the past with the benefit of hindsight (the one exact science), but the Egyptians were certainly not alone. As an example we might consider Roman numerals, in which I = 1, V = 5, X = 10, L = 50, C = 100, D = 500, M = 1,000, and so forth. Now try to multiply CCLXV by XXXVIII as quickly as you can. In fact Roman numerals were used extensively in England until the middle of the 17th century, and are still used to some extent to this day; for example, the copyright notice on films and television programs often indicates the year in Roman numerals!

The ancient Babylonians

Previously we noted that, for many arithmetic operations, the use of a number system whose base is wholly divisible by many numbers, especially the smaller values, conveys certain advantages. And so we come to the Babylonians, who were famous for their astrological observations and calculations, and who used a sexagesimal (base-60) numbering system. Although sixty may appear to be a large value to have as a base, it does convey certain advantages. Sixty is the smallest number that can be wholly divided by two, three, four, five, and six ...... and

> Although the Babylonian's sexagesimal system may seem unwieldy to us, one cannot help but feel that it was an improvement on the Sumerians who came before them. The Sumerians had three distinct counting systems to keep track of land, produce, and animals, and they used a completely different set of symbols for each system!

of course it can also be divided by ten, fifteen, twenty, and thirty. In addition to using base sixty, the Babylonians also made use six and ten as sub-bases.

The Babylonian's sexagesimal system, which first appeared around 1900 to 1800 BC, is also credited as the first known place-value number system, in which the value of a particular digit depends both on the digit itself and its position within the number. This was an extremely important development, because prior to place-value systems people were obliged to use different symbols to represent different powers of a base. As was illustrated by the Egyptian and Roman systems discussed above, having unique symbols for ten, one-hundred, one thousand, and so forth makes even rudimentary calculations very difficult to perform.

The concept of zero and negative numbers

Interestingly enough, the idea of numbers like one, two, and three developed a long time before the concept of zero. This was largely because the requirement for a number "zero" was less than obvious in the context of the calculations that early man was trying to perform. For example, suppose that a young man's father had instructed him to stroll up to the top field to count their herd of goats and, on arriving, the lad discovered the gate wide open and no goats to be seen. First, his task on the counting front had effectively been done for him. Second, on returning to his aged parent, he probably wouldn't feel the need to say: *"Oh revered one, I regret to inform you that the result of my calculations lead me to believe that we are the proud possessors of zero goats."* Instead, he would be far more inclined to proclaim something along the lines of: *"Father, some drongo left the gate open and all of our goats have wandered off."*

In the case of the original Babylonian system, a zero was simply represented by a space. Imagine if, in our decimal system, instead of writing 104 (one-hundred-and-four) we were to write 1 4 (one-space-four). It's easy to see how this can lead to a certain amount of confusion, especially when multiple zeros occur next to each other. The problems can only be exacerbated if, like the Babylonians, one is using a base-sixty system and writing on clay tablets in a thunderstorm.

After more than 1,500 years of potentially inaccurate calculations the Babylonians finally began to use a special sign for zero. Many historians believe that this sign, which first appeared around 300 BC, was one of the most significant inventions in the history of mathematics. However, the Babylonians only used their symbol as a place holder and they didn't have the concept of zero as an actual value. Thus, clay tablet accounting records of the time couldn't say something like *"zero fish,"* but instead they had to write out in full: *"We don't have any fish left."*

The use of zero as an actual value, along with the concept of negative numbers, first appeared in India around 600 AD. Although negative numbers appear reasonably obvious to us today, they were not well-understood until modern times. As recently as the eighteenth century, the great Swiss mathematician Leonhard Euler (pronounced "Oiler" in America) believed that negative numbers were greater than infinity, and it was common practice to ignore any negative results returned by equations on the assumption that they were meaningless!

Aztecs, Eskimos, and Indian merchants

Other cultures, such as the Aztecs, developed vigesimal (base-20) systems, because they counted using both fingers and toes. The Ainu of Japan and the Eskimos of Greenland are two of the peoples who make use of vigesimal systems to the present day. For example, to say thirty-three, the Greenland Eskimos would use the expression *"Of the second man, three on the first foot."* This means that the first person contributes twenty (ten fingers and ten toes), and the second person contributes thirteen (ten fingers and three toes).

Another system that is relatively easy to understand is quinary (base-5), which uses five digits: 0, 1, 2, 3, and 4. This system is particularly interesting, in that a quinary finger-counting scheme is still in use today by Indian merchants near Bombay. This allows them to perform calculations on one hand while serving their customers with the other.

Jobs abound for time-travelers

To this day we bear the legacies of almost every number system our ancestors experimented with. From the duo-decimal systems we have twenty-four hours in a day, twelve inches in a foot, and special words such as dozen (meaning 12) and gross (meaning 12 x 12 = 144). Similarly, the Chinese have twelve hours in a day (each equal to two of our hours) and twenty-four seasons in a year (each approximately equal to two of our weeks). From the Babylonian's sexagesimal system we have sixty seconds in a minute, sixty minutes in an hour, and 360 degrees in a circle, where 360 degrees is derived from the product of the Babylonian's main base (sixty) and their sub-base (six); that is, 60 x 6 = 360. And from the vigesimal systems we have special words like score (meaning 20), as in Lincoln's famous Gettysburg Address, in which he said: *"Four score and seven years ago....."* This all serves to illustrate that number systems with bases other than ten are not only possible, but positively abound throughout history.

Because we're extremely familiar with using numbers, we tend to forget the tremendous amounts of mental effort that have been expended to raise us to our present level of understanding. In the days of yore when few people knew how to count, anyone who was capable of performing relatively rudimentary mathematical operations could easily achieve a position of power. For example, if you could predict an eclipse that actually came to pass you were obviously someone to be reckoned with. Similarly, if you were a warrior chieftain, it would be advantageous to know how many fighting men and women you had at your command, and the person who could provide you with this information would obviously rank highly on your summer-solstice card list.[5] So should you ever be presented with the opportunity to travel back through time, you can bask in the glow of the knowledge that there are numerous job opportunities awaiting your arrival.

The first mechanical calculators

The first actual calculating mechanism known to us is the abacus, which is thought to have been invented by the Babylonians sometime between 1,000 BC and 500 BC (although some pundits are of the opinion that it was actually invented by the Chinese). The word *abacus* comes to us by way of Latin as a mutation of the Greek word *abax*. In turn, the Greeks may have adopted the Phoenician word *abak*, meaning "sand," although some authorities lean toward the Hebrew word *abhaq*, meaning "dust." Irrespective of the source, the original concept referred to a flat stone covered with sand (or dust) into which numeric symbols were drawn. The first abacus was almost certainly based on such a stone, with pebbles being placed on lines drawn in the sand. Over time the stone was replaced by a wooden frame supporting thin sticks, braided hair, or leather thongs, onto which clay beads or pebbles with holes were threaded. A variety of different types of abacus were developed, but the most popular became those based on the bi-quinary system, which utilizes a combination of two bases (base-2 and base-5) to represent decimal numbers. Although the abacus does not qualify as a mechanical calculator, it certainly stands proud as one of first mechanical aids to calculation.

In the early 1600s, a Scottish mathematician called John Napier (Figure 15.3) invented a tool called *Napier's Bones*, which were multiplication tables inscribed on strips of wood or bone (Figure 15.4). Napier, who was the Laird of Merchiston, also invented logarithms, which

---

[5]You wouldn't have a Christmas card list, because the concept of Christmas cards wasn't invented until 1843 (try finding this nugget of trivia in another computer book).

greatly assisted in arithmetic calculations. In 1621, an English mathematician and clergyman called William Oughtred used Napier's logarithms as the basis for the slide rule (Oughtred invented both the standard rectilinear slide rule and the less commonly used circular slide rule). However, although the slide rule was an exceptionally effective tool that remained in common use for over three hundred years, it also does not qualify as a mechanical calculator.

Figure 15.3: John Napier

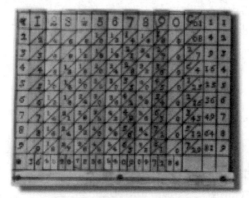

Figure 15.4: Napier's Bones
(Courtesy of IBM)

In fact determining who did invent the first mechanical calculator is somewhat problematical. Many references cite the French mathematician, physicist, and theologian, Blaise Pascal (Figure 15.5) as being credited with the invention of the first operational calculating machine. In 1640, Pascal started developing a device to help his father add sums of money. The first operating model, the *Arithmetic Machine*, was introduced in 1642, and Pascal created fifty more devices over the next ten years (Figure 15.6).[6] However, Pascal's device could only add and subtract, while multiplication and division operations were implemented by performing a series of additions or subtractions. In fact the

Figure 15.5: Blaise Pascal

Arithmetic Machine could really only add, because subtractions were performed using complement techniques, in which the number to be subtracted is first converted into its complement, which is then added to the first number. Interestingly enough, modern computers employ similar complement techniques.[7]

Figure 15.6: Pascal's Arithmetic Machine (Courtesy of IBM)

Pascal's claim to fame notwithstanding, the German astronomer and mathematician Wilhelm Schickard wrote a letter to his friend Johannes Kepler[8] about fifteen years before Pascal started developing his Arithmetic Machine. In this letter, Schickard wrote that he had built a machine that *"...immediately computes the given numbers automatically; adds, subtracts, multiplies, and divides."* Unfortunately, no original copies of Schickard's machine exist, but working models have been constructed from his notes.

In fact it now appears that the first mechanical calculator may have been conceived by Leonardo da Vinci (Figure 15.7) almost one hundred and fifty years earlier than Schickard's machine. Da Vinci was a genius: painter, musician, sculptor, architect, engineer, and so forth. However, his contributions to mechanical calculation remained hidden until the rediscovery of two of his notebooks in 1967. These notebooks, which date from sometime

Figure 15.7: Leonardo da Vinci

---

[6]In 1658, Pascal created a scandal when, under the pseudonym of Amos Dettonville, he challenged other mathematicians to a contest and then awarded the prize to himself!
[7]Complement techniques were introduced in Chapter 7.
[8]Kepler, a German astronomer and natural philosopher, was the first person to realize (and prove) that the planets travel around the sun in elliptical orbits.

around the 1500s, contained drawings of a mechanical calculator (Figure 15.8), and working models of da Vinci's device have since been constructed (Figure 15.9).

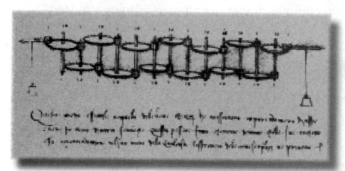

Figure 15.8: One of da Vinci's original sketches for a mechanical calculator (Courtesy of IBM)

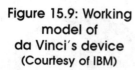

Figure 15.9: Working model of da Vinci's device (Courtesy of IBM)

In the 1670s, a German Baron called Gottfried von Leibniz (Figure 15.10) took mechanical calculation a step further. Leibniz, who entered university at fifteen years of age and received his bachelor's degree at seventeen, said:

"It is unworthy of excellent men to lose hours like slaves in the labor of calculation which could be safely relegated to anyone else if machines were used." Leibniz developed Pascal's ideas and, in 1671, introduced the *Step Reckoner*, a device which, as well as performing additions and subtractions, could multiply, divide, and evaluate square roots by series of stepped additions (Figure 15.11). Leibniz also strongly advocated the use of the binary number system, which is fundamental to the operation of modern computers.

Figure 15.10: Gottfried von Leibniz

Figure 15.11: Leibniz's Step Reckoner
(Courtesy of IBM)

Pascal's and Leibniz's devices were the forebears of today's desk-top computers, and derivations of these machines continued to be produced until their electronic equivalents finally became readily available and affordable in the early 1970s.

The first mechanical computers

In the early 1800s, a French silk weaver called Joseph-Marie Jacquard invented a way of automatically controlling the warp and weft threads on a silk loom by recording patterns of holes in a string of cards. In the years to come, variations on Jacquard's punched cards would find a variety of uses, including representing the music to be played by automated pianos and the storing of programs for computers.

The first device that might be considered to be a computer in the modern sense of the word was conceived by the eccentric British mathematician and inventor Charles Babbage (Figure 15.12). In Babbage's time, mathematical tables, such as logarithmic and trigonometric functions, were generated by teams of mathematicians working day and night on primitive calculators. Due to the fact that these people performed computations they were referred to as *computers*. Over the course of time,

Figure 15.12: Charles Babbage

the term *computer* became associated with machines that could perform the computations on their own.[9] In 1822, Babbage proposed building a machine called the *Difference Engine* to automatically calculate these tables.

The Difference Engine was only partially completed when Babbage conceived the idea of another, more sophisticated machine called an *Analytical Engine*. (Some texts refer to this machine as an *Analytical Steam Engine*, because Babbage intended that it would be powered by steam.) The Analytical Engine was intended to use loops of Jacquard's punched cards to control an automatic calculator, which could make decisions based on the results of previous computations. This machine was also intended to employ several features subsequently used in modern computers, including sequential control, branching, and looping.

Working with Babbage was Augusta Ada Lovelace (Figure 15.13),[10] the daughter of the English poet Lord Byron. Ada, who was a splendid mathematician and one of the few people who fully understood Babbage's vision, created a program for the Analytical Engine. Had the machine ever actually worked, this program would have been able to compute a mathematical sequence known as *Bernoulli numbers*. Based on this work, Ada is now credited as being the first computer programmer and, in 1979, a modern programming language was named ADA in her honor.

Babbage worked on his Analytical Engine from around 1830 until he died, but sadly it was never completed. It is often said that Babbage was a hundred years ahead of his time, and

Figure 15.13: Ada Lovelace

that the technology of the day was inadequate for the task. Refuting this is the fact that, in 1834, two Swedish engineers called Georg and Edward Scheutz built a small Difference Engine based on Babbage's description. In his book, *Engines of the Mind*, Joel Shurkin stated that:

---

[9]In fact the term *computer* was used as a job description (rather than referring to the machines themselves) well into the 1940s.

[10]In their spare time, Babbage and Ada also attempted to create a system for predicting the winners of horse races, but it is said that they lost a lot of money!

"One of Babbage's most serious flaws was his inability to stop tinkering. No sooner would he send a drawing to the machine shop than he would find a better way to perform the task and would order work stopped until he had finished pursuing the new line. By and large this flaw kept Babbage from ever finishing anything."

Further supporting this theory is the fact that, in 1876, only five years after Babbage's death, an obscure inventor called George Barnard Grant exhibited a full-sized difference engine of his own devising at the Philadelphia Centennial Fair. Grant's machine was 8 feet wide, 5 feet tall, and contained over 15,000 moving parts.

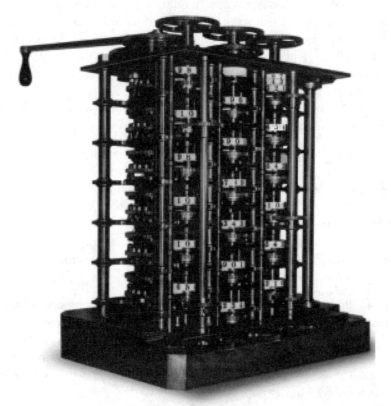

Figure 15.14: Part of one of Babbage's Difference Engines

Interestingly enough, more than one hundred and fifty years after its conception, one of Babbage's earlier Difference Engines was eventually constructed from original drawings by a team at London's Science Museum. The final machine, which was constructed from cast iron, bronze and steel, consisted of 4,000 components, weighed three tons, and was 10 feet wide and 6½ feet tall. It performed its first sequence of calculations in the early 1990's and returned results to 31 digits of accuracy, which is far more accurate than the standard pocket calculator. However, each calculation requires the user to turn a crank hundreds, sometimes thousands of times, so anyone employing it for anything more than the most rudimentary calculations is destined to become one of the fittest computer operators on the face of the planet!

Boolean algebra

Around the time that Babbage was struggling with his Analytical Engine, one of his contemporaries, a British mathematician called George Boole, was busily inventing a new form of mathematics. Boole made significant contributions in several areas of mathematics, but was immortalized for two works in 1847 and 1854, in which he represented logical expressions in a mathematical form now known as *Boolean Algebra*. Boole's work was all the more impressive because, with the exception of elementary school and a short time in a commercial school, he was almost completely self-educated.

In conjunction with Boole, another British mathematician, Augustus DeMorgan, formalized a set of logical operations now known as *DeMorgan transformations*. As the Encyclopedia Britannica says: "*A renascence of logical studies came about almost entirely because of Boole and DeMorgan.*" In fact the rules we now attribute to DeMorgan were known in a more primitive form by William of Ockham in the 14th Century. To celebrate Ockham's position in history, the *OCCAM* computer programming language was named in his honor.[11]

Unfortunately, with the exception of students of philosophy and symbolic logic, Boolean Algebra was destined to remain largely unknown and unused for the better part of a century. It was not until 1938 that Claude E. Shannon published an article based on his master's thesis at MIT. (Shannon's thesis has been described as: "*Possibly the most important Master's thesis of the twentieth century.*") In his paper, which was widely circulated, Shannon showed how Boole's concepts of TRUE and FALSE could be used to represent the functions of switches in electronic circuits. Shannon is also credited with the invention of the rocket-powered Frisbee, and is famous for riding down the corridors at Bell Laboratories on a unicycle while simultaneously juggling four balls.[12]

---

[11]OCCAM is the native programming language for the British-developed INMOS transputer.
[12]One of the authors can (almost) ride a unicycle, and both can juggle five china plates ......
but only for a very short period of time!

The American census of 1890

It is often said that necessity is the mother of invention, and this was certainly true in the case of the American census. Following the population trends established by previous surveys, it was estimated that the census of 1890 would be required to handle data from more than 62 million Americans. In addition to being prohibitively expensive, the existing system of making tally marks in small squares on rolls of paper and then adding the marks together by hand was extremely time consuming. In fact it was determined that, if the system remained unchanged, there was no chance of collating the data from the 1890 census into any useful form until well after the 1900 census had taken place, by which time the 1890 data would be of little value.

The solution to this problem was developed during the 1880s by an American inventor called Herman Hollerith (Figure 15.15). Hollerith's idea was to use Jacquard's punched cards to represent the census data, and to then read and collate this data using an automatic machine. While he was a lecturer at MIT, Hollerith developed a simple prototype which employed cards he punched using a tram conductor's ticket punch, where each card was intended to contain the data associated with a particular individual. From this prototype, he evolved a mechanism that could read the presence or absence of holes in the cards by using spring-mounted nails that passed through the holes to make electrical connections.

Many references state that Hollerith originally made his punched cards the same size as dollar bills of that era, because he realized that it would be convenient and economical to buy existing office furniture, such as desks and cabinets, that already contained receptacles to accommodate stacks of bills. However, some other sources are of the opinion that this is no more than a popular fiction.

Figure 15.15: Herman Hollerith

Hollerith's final system included an automatic electrical tabulating machine with a large number of clock-like counters that accumulated the results. By means of switches, operators could instruct the machine to examine each card for certain characteristics, such as profession, marital status, number of children, and so on. When a card was detected that met the specified criteria, an electrically controlled sorting mechanism could gather those cards into a separate container. Thus, for the first time, it was possible to extract information such as the number of engineers living in a particular state who owned their own house and were married with two children. Although this may not tickle *your* fancy, having this capability was sufficient to drive the statisticians of the time into a frenzy of excitement and data collation.

In addition to solving the census problem, Hollerith's machines proved themselves to be extremely useful for a wide variety of statistical applications, and some of the techniques they used were to be significant in the development of the digital computer. In February 1924, Hollerith's company changed its name to International Business Machines, or IBM.

The invention of the vacuum tube

Now here's a bit of a poser for you — who invented the first electric light bulb? If your immediate response was "*The legendary American inventor, Thomas Alva Edison,*" then you'd certainly be in the majority, but being in the majority doesn't necessarily mean that you're right. It's certainly true that Edison did invent the light bulb (or at least a light bulb), but he wasn't the first (Figure 15.16).

In 1860, an English physicist and electrician, Sir Joseph Wilson Swan, produced his first experimental light bulb using carbonized paper as a filament. Unfortunately, Swan didn't have a strong enough vacuum or sufficiently powerful batteries and his prototype didn't achieve complete incandescence, so he turned his attentions to other pursuits. Fifteen years later, in 1875, Swan returned to consider the problem of the light bulb and, with the aid of a better vacuum and a carbonized thread as a filament (the same material Edison eventually decided upon), he successfully demonstrated

Figure 15.16: Thomas Alva Edison

a true incandescent bulb in 1878 (a year earlier than Edison). Furthermore, in 1880, Swan gave the world's first large-scale public exhibition of electric lamps at Newcastle, England.

So it's reasonable to wonder why Edison received all of the credit, while Swan was condemned to obscurity. The more cynical among us may suggest that Edison was thrust into the *limelight* because many among us learn their history through films, and the vast majority of early films were made in America by patriotic Americans. However, none of this should detract from Edison who, working independently, experimented with thousands of filament materials and expended tremendous amounts of effort before discovering carbonized thread. It is also probably fair to say that Edison did produce the first *commercially viable* light bulb.

> The term *limelight* comes from the incandescent light produced by a rod of lime bathed in a flame of oxygen and hydrogen. At the time it was invented, limelight was the brightest source of artificial light known. One of it's first uses was for lighting theater stages, and actors and actresses were keen to position themselves "*in the limelight*" so as to be seen to their best effect.

In 1879, Edison publicly exhibited his incandescent electric light bulb for the first time.[13] Edison's light bulbs employed a conducting filament mounted in a glass bulb from which the air was evacuated leaving a vacuum. Passing electricity through the filament caused it to heat up enough to become incandescent and radiate light, while the vacuum prevented the filament from oxidizing and burning up. Edison continued to experiment with his light bulbs and, in 1883, found that he could detect electrons flowing through the vacuum from the lighted filament to a metal plate mounted inside the bulb. This discovery subsequently became known as the *Edison Effect*.

Edison did not develop this particular finding any further, but an English physicist, John Ambrose Fleming, discovered that the Edison Effect could also be used to detect radio waves and to convert them to electricity. Fleming went on to develop a two-element vacuum tube known as *diode*.

In 1906, the American inventor Lee de Forest introduced a third electrode called the *grid* into the vacuum tube. The resulting *triode* could be used as both an amplifier and a switch, and many of the early radio transmitters were built by de Forest using these triodes (he also presented the first live opera broadcast and the first news report on radio). De Forest's triodes revolutionized the field of broadcasting and were destined to do much more, because their ability to act as switches was to have a tremendous impact on digital computing.

---

[13]If you ever happen to be in Dearborn, Michigan, you should take the time to visit the Henry Ford Museum, which happens to contain the world's largest collection of light bulbs.

Another device that was to prove useful in early computers was the relay, which is formed from a metal bar surrounded by a coil. When current is passed through the coil, the resulting electromagnetic field causes the metal bar to move (a spring is used to return the bar to its original position when the current is removed). The bar can be used to activate switches, which can be used to control other devices; for example, to apply current to the coils of other relays.

As a nugget of trivia, in 1921, the Czech author Karel Capek produced his best known work, the play *R.U.R. (Rossum's Universal Robots)*, which featured machines created to simulate human beings. Some references state that term *robot* was derived from the Czech word *robota*, meaning "work," while others propose that *robota* actually means "forced workers" or "slaves." This latter view would certainly fit the point that Capek was trying to make, because his robots eventually rebelled against their creators, ran amok, and tried to wipe out the human race. However, as is usually the case with words, the truth of the matter is a little more convoluted. In the days when Czechoslovakia was a feudal society, "robota" referred to the two or three days of the week that peasants were obliged to leave their own fields to work without remuneration on the lands of noblemen. For a long time after the feudal system had passed away, *robota* continued to be used to describe work that one wasn't exactly doing voluntarily or for fun, while today's younger Czechs and Slovaks tend to use *robota* to refer to work that's boring or uninteresting.

The first electromechanical computers

In 1927, with the assistance of two colleagues at MIT, the American scientist, engineer, and politician Vannevar Bush designed an analog computer that could solve simple equations. This device, which Bush dubbed a *Product Intergraph*, was subsequently built by one of his students.

Bush continued to develop his ideas and, in 1930, built a bigger version which he called a *Differential Analyzer*. The Differential Analyzer was based on the use of mechanical integrators that could be interconnected in any desired manner. To provide amplification, Bush employed torque amplifiers which were based on the same principle as a ship's capstan. The final device used its integrators, torque amplifiers, drive belts, shafts, and gears to measure movements and distances (not dissimilar in concept to an automatic slide rule).

Although Bush's first Differential Analyzer was driven by electric motors, its internal operations were purely mechanical. In 1935, Bush developed a second version, in which the gears were shifted electro-mechanically and which employed paper tapes to carry instructions and to set up the gears.

In our age, when computers can be constructed the size of postage stamps, it is difficult to visualize the scale of the problems that these early pioneers faced. To provide some sense of perspective, Bush's second Differential Analyzer weighed in at a whopping 100 tons! In addition to all of the mechanical elements, it contained 2000 vacuum tubes, thousands of relays, 150 motors, and approximately 200 miles of wire. As well as being a major achievement in its own right, the Differential Analyzer was also significant because it focused attention on analog computing techniques, and therefore detracted from the investigation and development of digital solutions for quite some time.

However, not everyone was enamored by analog computing. In 1937, George Robert Stibitz, a scientist at Bell Laboratories built a digital machine based on relays, flashlight bulbs, and metal strips cut from tin-cans. Stibitz's machine, which he called the "Model K" (because the majority of it was constructed on his kitchen table), worked on the principle that if two relays were activated they caused a third relay to become active, where this third relay represented the sum of the operation. For example, if the two relays representing the numbers 3 and 6 were activated, this would activate another relay representing the number 9. (A replica of the Model K is on display at the Smithsonian.)

Stibitz went on to create a machine called the *Complex Number Calculator*, which, although not tremendously sophisticated by today's standards, was an important step along the way. In 1940, Stibitz performed a spectacular demonstration at a meeting in New Hampshire. Leaving his computer in New York City, he took a teleprinter to the meeting and proceeded to connect it to his computer via telephone. In the first example of remote computing, Stibitz astounded the attendees by allowing them to pose problems which were entered on the teleprinter; within a short time the teleprinter presented the answers generated by the computer.

Many consider that the modern computer era commenced with the first large-scale automatic digital computer, which was developed between 1939 and 1944. This device, the brainchild of a Harvard graduate, Howard H. Aiken (Figure 15.17), was officially known as the IBM *automatic sequence controlled calculator (ASCC)*, but is more commonly referred to as the *Harvard Mark I* (Figure 15.18). The Mark I was constructed out of switches,

Figure 15.17: Howard Aiken

relays, rotating shafts, and clutches, and was described as sounding like a *"roomful of ladies knitting."* The machine contained more than 750,000 components, was 50 feet long, 8 feet tall, and weighed approximately 5 tons!

Although the Mark I is considered to be the first digital computer, its architecture was significantly different from modern machines. The device consisted of many calculators which worked on parts of the same problem under the guidance of a single control unit. Instructions were read in on paper tape, data was provided separately on punched cards, and the device could only perform operations in the sequence in which they were received. This machine was based on numbers that were 23 digits wide – and it could add or subtract two of these numbers in three-tenths of a second, multiply them in four seconds, and divide them in ten seconds.

Figure 15.18: IBM *automatic sequence controlled calculator* (ASCC)
(Courtesy of IBM)

Aiken was tremendously enthused by computers, but like so many others he didn't anticipate the dramatic changes that were to come. For example, in 1947 he predicted that only six electronic digital computers would be required to satisfy the computing needs of the entire United States. Although this may cause a wry chuckle today, it is instructive, because it accurately reflects the general perception of computers in that era. In those days computers were typically only considered in the context of scientific calculations and data processing for governments, large industries, research establishments, and educational institutions. It was also widely believed that computers would only ever be programmed and used by experts and intellectual heroes (if only they could see us now).

In the aftermath of World War II, it was discovered that a program controlled calculator called the Z3 had been completed in Germany in 1941, which means that the Z3 pre-dated the Harvard Mark I. The Z3's architect was a German engineer called Konrad Zuse, who developed his first machine, the Z1, in his parents' living room in Berlin in 1938. Although based on relays, the Z3 was very sophisticated for its time; for example, it utilized the binary number system and could handle floating-point arithmetic. (Zuse had considered employing vacuum tubes, but he decided to use relays because they were more readily available and also because he feared that tubes were unreliable.)

In 1943, Zuse started work on a general-purpose relay computer called the Z4. Sadly, his original Z3 was destroyed by bombing in 1944 and therefore didn't survive the war (although a new Z3 was reconstructed in the 1960s). However, the Z4 did survive – in a cave in the Bavarian Alps – and by 1950 it was up and running in a Zurich bank. It is interesting to note that paper was in short supply in Germany during to the war, so instead of using paper tape, Zuse was obliged to punch holes in old movie film to store his programs and data. We may only speculate as to the films Zuse used for his hole-punching activities; for example, were any first-edition Marlene Dietrich classics on the list?[14]

Zuse was an amazing man, who, in many respects, was well ahead of his time. For example, in 1958 he proposed a parallel processor called a field computer, years before parallel computing became well understood. He also wrote (but never implemented) *Pkankalk I*, which is a strong contender as the first high-level programming language. To fully appreciate Zuse's achievements, it is necessary to understand that his background was in construction engineering. Also, Zuse was completely unaware of any computer-related developments in Germany or in other countries until a very late stage. In 1957, Zuse received the honorary degree of Dr.techn. in Berlin, and he was subsequently showered with many other honors and awards.

---

[14]Marlene Dietrich fell out of favor with the Hitler regime when she emigrated to America in the early 1930s, but copies of her films would still have been around during the war.

Logic diagrams and machines

Although this book is predominantly concerned with computers, we should also note that there has historically been a great deal of fascination in logic in general. This fascination was initially expressed in the form of logic diagrams, and later in the construction of special-purpose machines for manipulating logical expressions and representations.

Diagrams used to represent logical concepts have been around in one form or another for a very long time. For example, Aristotle was certainly familiar with the idea of using a stylized tree figure to represent the relationships between (and successive sub-divisions of) such things as different species. Diagrams of this type, which are known as the *Tree of Porphyry*, are often to be found in medieval pictures.

Following the *Tree of Porphyry*, there seems to have been a dearth of activity on the logic diagram front until 1761, when the brilliant Swiss mathematician Leonhard Euler introduced a geometric system that could generate solutions for problems in class logic. However, Euler's work in this area didn't really catch on because it was somewhat awkward to use, and it was eventually supplanted in the 1890s by a more polished scheme proposed by the English logician John Venn. Venn was heavily influenced by the work of George Boole, and his *Venn Diagrams* very much complemented Boolean Algebra.

Venn Diagrams were strongly based on the interrelationships between overlapping circles or ellipses. The first logic diagrams based on squares or rectangles were introduced in 1881 by Allan Marquand, a lecturer in logic and ethics at John Hopkins University. Marquand's diagrams spurred interest by a number of other contenders, including one offering by an English logician and author, the Reverend Charles Lutwidge Dodgson. Dodgson's diagrammatic technique first appeared in his book *The game of Logic*, which was published in 1886, but he is better known to us by his pen-name, Lewis Carroll, and as being the author of *Alice's Adventures in Wonderland*. Apart from anything else, these rectangular diagrams are of interest to us because they were the forerunners of a more modern form known as *Karnaugh Maps*. Karnaugh Maps, which were invented by Maurice Karnaugh in the 1950s, quickly became one of the mainstays of the digital logic designer's tool-chest.[15]

---

[15]The use of Karnaugh Maps is discussed in this book's companion volume: *Bebop to the Boolean Boogie (An Unconventional Guide to Electronics)*.

Possibly the first person in the history of formal logic to use a mechanical device to generate (so-called) logical proofs was the Spanish theologian Ramon Lull. In 1274, Lull climbed Mount Randa in Majorca in search of spiritual sustenance. After fasting and contemplating his navel for several days, Lull experienced what he believed to be a divine revelation, and he promptly rushed back down the mountain to pen his famous *Ars Magna*. This magnum opus described a number of eccentric logical techniques, but the one of which Lull was most proud (and which received the most attention) was based on concentric disks of card, wood, or metal mounted on a central axis.

Lull's idea was that each disk should contain a number of different words or symbols, which could be combined in different ways by rotating the disks (Figure 15.19). In the case of our somewhat jocular example, we can achieve 4 x 4 x 4 = 64 different sentences along the lines of *"I love mice," "You hate cats,"* and *"They eat frogs."*

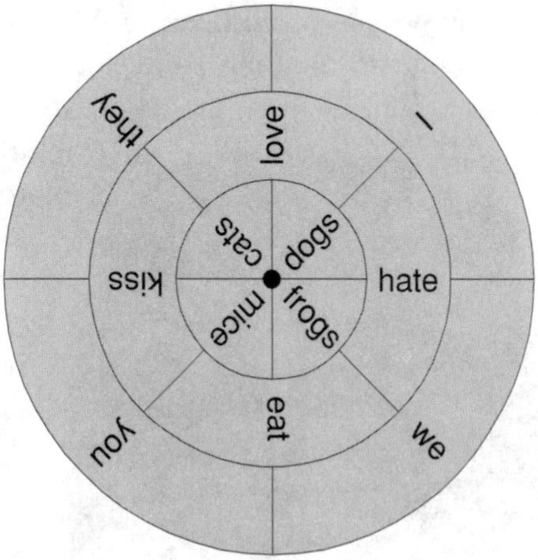

Figure 15.19: Ramon Lull's disks

Of course, Lull had a more serious purpose in mind, which was to prove the truth of everything contained within the Bible. For example, he used his disks to show that *"God's mercy is infinite," "God's mercy is mysterious," "God's mercy is just,"* and so forth.

Lull's devices were far more complex than our simple example might suggest, with several containing as many as sixteen different words or symbols on each disk. His masterpiece was the *figura universalis*, which consisted of fourteen concentric circles – the mind boggles at the range of combinations that could be generated by this device. Strange as it may seem to us, Lull's followers (called Lullists) flourished in the late middle ages and the renaissance, and Lullism spread far and wide across Europe.

Why is all of this of interest to us? Well by some strange quirk of fate, Lull's work fired the imagination of several characters with whom we are already familiar, such as Gottfried von Leibniz who invented the Step Reckoner. Although Leibniz had little regard for Lull's work in general, he believed there was a chance it could be extended to apply to formal logic. In a rare flight of fancy, Leibniz conjectured that it might be possible to create a universal algebra that could represent just about everything under the sun, including (but not limited to) moral and metaphysical truths. In 1666, at the age of 19, Leibniz wrote his *Dissertio de Arte Combinatoria*, from which comes a famous quote describing the way in which he believed the world could be in the future: "*If controversies were to arise,*" said Leibniz, "*there would be no more need of disputation between two philosophers than between two accountants. For it would suffice to take their pencils in their hands, and say to each other: Let us calculate.*"

Of course Lull also has his detractors (which is a kind way of saying that many people considered him to be a raving lunatic). In 1726, the Anglo-Irish satirist Jonathan Swift (Figure 15.20) wrote *Gulliver's Travels*,[16] which was originally intended as an attack on the hypocrisy of the establishment

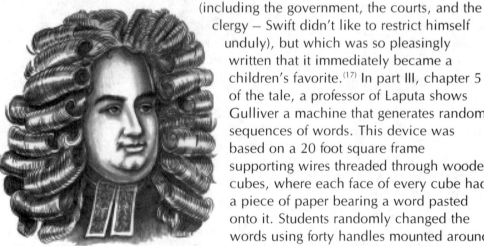

(including the government, the courts, and the clergy – Swift didn't like to restrict himself unduly), but which was so pleasingly written that it immediately became a children's favorite.[17] In part III, chapter 5 of the tale, a professor of Laputa shows Gulliver a machine that generates random sequences of words. This device was based on a 20 foot square frame supporting wires threaded through wooden cubes, where each face of every cube had a piece of paper bearing a word pasted onto it. Students randomly changed the words using forty handles mounted around the frame. The students then examined the cubes, and if three or four adjacent words

Figure 15.20: Johnathan Swift

formed part of a sentence that made any sense, they were immediately written down by scribes. The professor told Gulliver that by means of this technique: "*The most ignorant person at a reasonable charge, and with little bodily labor, may write books in philosophy, poetry, law, mathematics, and theology, without the least assistance from genius or study.*" The point is that Swift is believed to have been mocking Lull's art when he penned this part of his story. (Having said this, computer programs have been used to create random poetry and music ...... which makes you wonder what Swift would have written about *us*.)

---

[16]On the off chance you were wondering, Swift penned his great work nine years before the billiard que was invented. Prior to this, players used to strike the balls with a small mace.
[17]It's a funny old world when you come to think about it.

In fact Swift continues to affect us in strange and wondrous ways to this day. When a computer uses multiple bytes to represent a number, there are two main techniques for storing those bytes in memory: either the most-significant byte is stored in the location with the lowest address (in which case we might say it's stored "big-end-first"), or the least-significant byte is stored in the lowest address (in which case we might say it's stored "little-end-first"). Not surprisingly, some computer designers favor one style while others take the opposite tack. This didn't really matter until people became interested in creating heterogeneous computing environments, in which multiple diverse machines were connected together, at which point many acrimonious arguments ensued. In 1980, a famous paper written by Danny Cohen entitled *"On Holy Wars and a Plea for Peace"* used the terms *big-endian* and *little-endian* to refer to the two techniques for storing data. These terms, which are still in use today, were derived from that part of Gulliver's tale whereby two countries go to war over which end of a hard-boiled egg should be eaten first – the little end or the big end!

Leaping from one subject to another with the agility of a mountain goat, we might also note that Lewis Carroll (Figure 15.21) enjoyed posing logical conundrums in many of his books, such as *Alice's Adventures in Wonderland* (1865), *Through the Looking-Glass* (1872), and *The Hunting of the Snark* (1876). For example, consider this scene from the Mad Hatter's tea party in Chapter 7 of *Alice's Adventures in Wonderland*:[18]

Figure 15.21: Lewis Carroll

> *"Take some more tea,"* the March Hare said to Alice, very earnestly.
>
> *"I've had nothing yet,"* Alice replied in an offended tone: *"so I can't take more."*
>
> *"You mean you can't take <u>less</u>,"* said the hatter: *"it's very easy to take more than nothing."*

---

[18]The phrase *"As mad as a Hatter"* comes from the fact that, in ye olden tymes, the manufacturers of men's top hats used mercury compounds as part of the process. Over time the mercury accumulated in their bodies causing severe impairment to their mental functions.

And we would have to chastise ourselves soundly if we neglected the scene involving Tweedledum and Tweedledee in Chapter 4 of *Through the Looking-Glass*:

> *"I know what you're thinking about,"* said Tweedledum; *"but it isn't so, nohow."*

> *"Contrariwise,"* continued Tweedledee, *"if it was so, it might be; and if it were so, it would be; but as it isn't, it ain't. That's logic."*

You have to admit, these gems of information aren't to be found in your average computer book, are they? But once again we've wandered off the beaten path (*"No,"* you cry, *"tell me it isn't so!"*). The world's first real logic machine – in the sense that it could actually be used to solve formal logic problems; as opposed to Lull's, which tended to create more problems than it solved – was invented in the early 1800s by the British scientist and statesman Charles Stanhope (third Earl of Stanhope). A man of many talents, the Earl designed a device called the *Stanhope Demonstrator*, which was a small box with a window in the top, along with two different colored slides that the user pushed into slots in the sides. Although this doesn't sound like much it was a start,[19] but Stanhope wouldn't publish any details and instructed his friends not to say anything about what he was doing. In fact it wasn't until around sixty years after his death that the Earl's notes and one of his devices fell into the hands of the Reverend Robert Harley, who subsequently published an article on the Stanhope Demonstrator in 1879.

Working on a somewhat different approach was the British logician and economist William Stanley Jevons, who, in 1869, produced the earliest model of his famous *Jevons' Logic Machine*. This device is notable because it was the first machine that could solve a logical problem faster than that problem could be solved without using the machine! Jevons was an aficionado of Boolean logic, and his solution was something of a cross between a logical abacus and a piano (in fact it was sometimes referred to as a *"Logic Piano"*). This device, which was about 3 feet tall, consisted of keys, levers, and pulleys, along with letters that could be either visible or hidden. When the operator pressed keys representing logical variables and operations, the appropriate letters appeared to reveal the result.

The next real advance in logic machines was made by Allan Marquand, whom we previously met in connection with his work on logic diagrams. In 1881, by means of the ingenious use of rods, levers, and springs, Marquand extended Jevons' work to produce the *Marquand Logic Machine*.

---

[19]There was more to the Stanhope Demonstrator than we can cover here.

Like Jevons' device, Marquand's machine could only handle four variables, but it was smaller and significantly more intuitive to use.[20]

Things continued to develop apace. In 1936, the American psychologist Benjamin Burack from Chicago constructed what was probably the world's first electrical logic machine. Burack's device used light bulbs to display the logical relationships between a collection of switches, but for some reason he didn't publish anything about his work until 1949. In fact the connection between Boolean algebra and circuits based on switches had been recognized as early as 1886 by an educator called Charles Pierce, but nothing substantial happened in this area until Claude E. Shannon published his 1938 paper (as was discussed earlier in this chapter).

Following Shannon's paper, a substantial amount of attention was focused on developing electronic logic machines. Unfortunately, interest in special-purpose logic machines waned in the 1940s with the advent of general-purpose computers, which proved to be much more powerful and for which programs could be written to handle formal logic.[21]

The first electronic computers

It is said that history is written by the victors.[22] However, when one is considering events that occurred only a few decades in the past, it would not be unreasonable to expect said events to be fairly well-documented, thereby allowing one to report: *"This person definitely invented this thing at this time."* Unfortunately, this is not always the case as we shall see.

We now turn our attention to an American mathematician and physicist, John Vincent Atanasoff, who has the dubious honor of being known as the man who either did or did not construct the first truly electronic special-purpose digital computer. A lecturer at Iowa State College (now Iowa State University), Atanasoff was disgruntled with the cumbersome and time-consuming process of solving complex equations by hand. Working alongside one of his graduate students (the brilliant Clifford Berry), Atanasoff commenced work on an electronic computer in early 1939, and had a prototype machine by the autumn of that year.

---

[20]Following the invention of his logic machine, Marquand abandoned logical pursuits to become a professor of art and archeology at Princeton University.
[21]An example of one such program is a logic synthesizer, which can be used to translate high-level descriptions of circuits into optimized gate-level representations.
[22]It is also said that those who fail to learn the lessons of history are doomed to repeat them (this is particularly true in the case of history courses at high school).

In the process of creating the device, Atanasoff and Berry evolved a number of ingenious and unique features. For example, one of the biggest problems for computer designers of the time was to be able to store numbers for use in the machine's calculations. Atanasoff's design utilized capacitors to store electrical charge that could represent numbers in the form of *logic 0s* and *logic 1s*. The capacitors were mounted in rotating bakelite cylinders, which had metal bands on their outer surface. These cylinders, each approximately 12 inches tall and 8 inches in diameter, could store thirty binary numbers, which could be read off the metal bands as the cylinders rotated.

Input data was presented to the machine in the form of punched cards, while intermediate results could be stored on other cards. Once again, Atanasoff's solution to storing intermediate results was quite interesting – he used sparks to burn small spots onto the cards. The presence or absence of these spots could be automatically determined by the machine later, because the electrical resistance of a carbonized spot varied from that of the blank card.

Some references report that Atanasoff and Berry had a fully working model of their machine by 1942. However, while some observers agreed that the machine was completed and did work, others reported that it was almost completed and would have worked, while still others stated that it was just a collection of parts that never worked. So unless more definitive evidence comes to light, it's a case of: *"You pays your money and you takes your choice."*

Many of the people who designed the early computers were both geniuses and eccentrics of the first order, and the English mathematician Alan Turing was first among equals (Figure 15.22). In 1937, while a graduate student, Turing wrote his ground-breaking paper *"On Computable Numbers with an Application to the Entscheidungsproblem."* One of the premises of Turing's paper was that some classes of mathematical problems do not lend themselves to algorithmic representations, and are therefore not amenable to solution by automatic computers. Since Turing did not have access to a real computer (not unreasonably as they didn't exist at the time), he invented his own as an abstract "paper

Figure 15.22: Alan Turing

exercise." This theoretical model, which became known as a *Turing Machine*, was both simple and elegant, and subsequently inspired many "thought experiments."

During World War II Turing worked as a cryptographer, decoding codes and ciphers at one of the British government's top-secret establishments located at Bletchley Park. During this time, Turing was a key player in the breaking of the German's now-famous ENIGMA code. However, in addition to ENIGMA, the Germans had another cipher that was employed for their ultra-top-secret communications. This cipher, which was vastly more complicated than ENIGMA, was generated by a machine called a *Geheimfernschreiber* (secret telegraph), which the allies referred to as the "Fish."

In January 1943, along with a number of colleagues, Turing began to construct an electronic machine to decode the *Geheimfernschreiber* cipher. This machine, which they dubbed COLOSSUS, comprised 1,800 vacuum tubes and was completed and working by December of the same year! By any standards COLOSSUS was one of the world's earliest working programmable electronic digital computers. But it was a special-purpose machine that was really only suited to a narrow range of tasks (for example, it was not capable of performing decimal multiplications). Having said this, although COLOSSUS was built as a special-purpose computer, it did prove flexible enough to be programmed to execute a variety of different routines.

By the mid-1940s, the majority of computers were being built out of vacuum tubes rather than switches and relays. Although vacuum tubes were fragile, expensive, and used a lot of power, they were much faster than relays (and much quieter). If we ignore Atanasoff's machine and COLOSSUS, then the first true general-purpose electronic computer was the *electronic numerical integrator and computer (ENIAC)*, which was constructed at the University of Pennsylvania between 1943 and 1946. ENIAC, which was the brainchild of John William Mauchly and J. Presper Eckert Jr., was a monster — it was 10 feet tall, occupied 1,000 square feet of floor-space, weighed in at approximately 30 tons, and used more than 70,000 resistors, 10,000 capacitors, 6,000 switches, and 18,000 vacuum tubes. The final machine required 150 kilowatts of power, which was enough to light a small town.

One of the greatest problems with computers built from vacuum tubes was reliability; 90% of ENIAC's down-time was attributed to locating and replacing burnt-out tubes. Records from 1952 show that approximately

19,000 vacuum tubes had to be replaced in that year alone, which averages out to about 50 tubes a day!

During the course of developing ENIAC, Mauchly and Eckert recognized a variety of improvements and new techniques, which they determined to use in any subsequent machines. For example, one of the main problems with ENIAC was that it was hard-wired; that is, it did not have any internal memory as such, but needed to be physically programmed by means of switches and dials. Around the summer of 1943, Mauchly and Eckert discussed the concept of creating a *stored-program computer*, in which an internal read-write memory would be used to store both instructions and data. This technique would allow the program to branch to alternate instruction sequences based on the results of previous calculations, as opposed to blindly following a pre-determined sequence of instructions.

Eckert's idea was to use mercury delay lines (which he already knew a great deal about) for the memory. These delay lines were constructed using a thin tube of mercury sealed with quartz crystals at each end. Applying an electric current to a quartz crystal causes it to vibrate. Similarly, vibrating a quartz crystal causes it to generate an electric current. The principle behind the mercury delay line was to briefly apply a current to the crystal at one end of the tube, which generated a pulse that propagated through the mercury at a known speed. When the pulse reached the far end of the delay line, it caused the crystal at that end to generate a corresponding current.

By amplifying the output from the second crystal and feeding it back to the first crystal, a continuous loop could be established. Moreover, a number of individual pulses could be maintained in a single delay line, similar in concept to a column of people marching down a corridor in single file. In fact 1000 bits could be stored in a delay line 5 feet long. Around the beginning of 1944, Eckert wrote an internal memo on the subject and, in August 1944, Mauchly and Eckert proposed the building of another machine called the *electronic discrete variable automatic computer (EDVAC)*. As we will see, the dates associated with these activities are of some significance.

In June 1944, the Hungarian-American mathematician Johann (John) von Neumann (Figure 15.23) first became aware of ENIAC. Von Neumann, who was a consultant on the Manhattan Project, immediately recognized the role that could be played by a computer like ENIAC in solving the vast arrays of complex equations involved in designing atomic weapons. A brilliant mathematician, von Neumann crossed mathematics with subjects such as philosophy in ways that had never previously been conceived; for example, he was a pioneer of *Game Theory*, which continues to find numerous and diverse applications to this day.

Von Neumann was tremendously excited by ENIAC, and quickly became a consultant to both the ENIAC and EDVAC projects. In June 1945, he published a paper entitled *"First Draft of a report to the EDVAC,"* in which he presented all of the basic elements of a stored-program computer:

a) *A memory* containing both data and instructions. Also to allow both data and instruction memory locations to be read from, and written to, in any desired order.

b) *A calculating unit* capable of performing both arithmetic and logical operations on the data.

c) *A control unit*, which could interpret an instruction retrieved from the memory and select alternative courses of action based on the results of previous operations.

The key point made by the paper was that the computer could modify its own programs, in much the same way as was originally suggested by Babbage. The computer structure resulting from the criteria presented in this paper is popularly known as a *von Neumann Machine*, and virtually all digital computers from that time forward have been based on this architecture.

The "First Draft" was a brilliant summation of the concepts involved in stored-program computing; indeed, many believe it to be one of the most important documents in the history of computing. It is said that the paper was written in a way that possibly only von Neumann could have achieved at that time.

Figure 15.23: John von Neumann

However, although there is no doubt that von Neumann made major contributions to the EDVAC design, the result of the "First Draft" was that he received almost all of the credit for the concept of stored-program computing, while Mauchly and Eckert received almost none. But Mauchly and Eckert discussed stored-program computers a year before von Neumann arrived on the scene, and Eckert wrote a memo on the subject six months before von Neumann had even heard about ENIAC. It has to be said that there is no evidence that von Neumann intended to take all of the credit (not the least that his paper was titled *"First Draft ...."*), but it also cannot be denied that he didn't go out of his way to correct matters later.

Unfortunately, although the conceptual design for EDVAC was completed by 1946, several key members left the project to pursue their own careers, and the machine did not become fully operational until 1952. When it was finally completed, EDVAC contained approximately 4,000 vacuum tubes and 10,000 crystal diodes. A 1956 report shows that EDVAC's average error-free up-time was approximately 8 hours.

In light of its late completion, some would dispute EDVAC's claim-to-fame as the first stored-program computer. A small experimental machine based on the EDVAC concept consisting of 32 words of memory and a 5-instruction instruction set was operating at Manchester University, England, by June 1948. Another machine called EDSAC (Electronic Delay Storage Automatic Calculator) performed its first calculation at Cambridge University, England, in May 1949. EDSAC contained 3,000 vacuum tubes and used mercury delay lines for memory. Programs were input using paper tape and output results were passed to a teleprinter. Additionally, EDSAC is credited as using one of the first assemblers called *Initial Orders*, which allowed it to be programmed symbolically instead of using machine code. Last but not least, the first commercially available computer, UNIVAC I (Universal Automatic Computer), was also based on the EDVAC design. Work started on UNIVAC I in 1948, and the first unit was delivered in 1951, which therefore predates EDVAC's becoming fully operational.

Apropos of nothing at all, a jazz style known as *Bebop* became highly popular in the decade following World War II. Charlie Parker, Dizzy Gillespie and Thelonius Monk were especially associated with this form of music, which is known for its fast tempos and agitated rhythms. We may only speculate if it was but a coincidence that many of the most significant ideas and discoveries in the history of computing occurred alongside the flourishing *Bebop*.

The first `bug" and the worst `bug"

The term *bug* is now universally accepted by computer users as meaning an error or flaw — either in the machine itself or, perhaps more commonly, in a program (hence the phrase *"debugging a program"*). The first official record of the use of the word "bug" in the context of computing is associated with a relay-based Harvard Mark II computer, which was in service at the Naval Weapons Center in Dahlgren, Virginia. On September 9th, 1945, a moth flew into one of the relays and jammed it. The offending moth was taped into the log book alongside the official report, which stated: *"First actual case of a bug being found."*

It has now become a popular tradition that it was the legendary Grace Hopper who found the offending insect, but Grace is on the record as stating that she wasn't there when it happened. It is also widely believed that this incident was the origin of the term "bug," but this is also not the case. If you read the wording of the report carefully, you can see that the writer is really saying: *"Hey, we actually found a bug that was a _real_ bug!"* In fact the word "bug" was already being used in Thomas Edison's time to imply a glitch, error, or defect in a mechanical system or an industrial process. Furthermore, "bug" was used as far back as Shakespearean times to mean a frightful object (derived from a Welsh mythological monster called the *"Bugbear"*).

As to the worst computer bug, there are obviously many contenders, some of which are tragic (they cost lives) and some of which are humorous, such as the 1989 case of the court computer in Paris, France, which targeted over 41,000 traffic offenders and issued them with summons for a variety of crimes, including drug trafficking, extortion, prostitution, and deviant sexual practices. However, there is one bug which certainly caught the popular imagination and which stands proud in the crowd. On 28th July, 1962, the Mariner I space probe was launched from Cape Canaveral on the beginning of its long voyage to Venus.[23] The flight plan stated that after thirteen minutes a booster engine would accelerate the probe to 25,820 mph; after eighty days the probe's on-board computer would make any final course corrections; and after one hundred days,

> An American Naval Officer and mathematician, Grace Murray Hopper was a pioneer in data processing and legend in her own lifetime. Hopper is credited with developing the first *compiler* (a program that translates a high-level human-readable language into machine code), and was also a supervisor on the project that eventually produced *COBOL* (*Common Business-Oriented Language*). In 1983, Grace became the first woman to achieve the rank of Rear Admiral in the United States Navy.

> Although some references say that Mariner 1 was heading for Mars, its itinerary definitely had Venus penned in at the top of the list (NASA does try to keep track of where they're attempting to send these things) – trust us on this one, for we know whereof we speak. Mariners 1 and 2 were intended for Venus (only Mariner 2 made it there); Mariners 3 and 4 were aimed at Mars (only Mariner 4 got there); Mariner 5 returned to Venus, Mariners 6, 7, and 9 returned to Mars (Mariner 8 ended up at the bottom of the Atlantic Ocean); and Mariner 10 wended its way to Mercury by way of Venus.

[23]From 1963 to 1973, Cape Canaveral was known as Cape Kennedy in honor of president John F. Kennedy.

Mariner 1 would be in orbit around Venus taking radar pictures of the planet's surface through its thick cloud cover.

However, only four minutes into the flight, Mariner I did an abrupt U-turn and plunged into the Atlantic ocean. The investigating team found that a logical negation operator had been accidentally omitted from the computer program in charge of controlling the rocket's engines. On the basis that the launch, including the probe, cost in the region of $10,000,000, this has to rank as one of the more expensive (and visible) bugs in the history of computing.[24]

The first transistors

The transistor and subsequently the integrated circuit must certainly qualify as two of the greatest inventions of the twentieth century. These devices are formed from materials known as semiconductors, whose properties were not well-understood until the 1950s. However, as far back as 1926, Dr. Julius Edgar Lilienfield from New York filed for a patent on what we would now recognize as an NPN junction transistor being used in the role of an amplifier (the title of the patent was *"Method and apparatus for controlling electric currents"*).

Unfortunately, serious research on semiconductors didn't really commence until World War II. At that time it was recognized that devices formed from semiconductors had potential as amplifiers and switches, and could therefore be used to replace the prevailing technology of vacuum tubes, but that they would be much smaller, lighter, and would require less power. All of these factors were of interest to the designers of the radar systems which were to play a large role in the war.

Bell Laboratories in the United States began research into semiconductors in 1945, and physicists William Shockley, Walter Brattain and John Bardeen succeeded in creating the first point-contact germanium transistor on the 23rd December, 1947 (they took a break for the Christmas holidays before publishing their achievement, which is why some reference books state that the first transistor was created in 1948). In 1950, Shockley invented a new device called a bipolar junction transistor, which was more reliable, easier and cheaper to build, and gave more consistent results than point-contact devices. (Apropos of nothing at all, the first TV dinner was marketed by the C.A. Swanson company three years later.)

---

[24]I'm glad I wasn't that programmer!

By the late 1950s, bipolar transistors were being manufactured out of silicon rather than germanium (although germanium had certain electrical advantages, silicon was cheaper and easier to work with). Bipolar junction transistors are formed from the junction of three pieces of doped silicon called the collector, base, and emitter. The original bipolar transistors were manufactured using the mesa process, in which a doped piece of silicon called the mesa (or base) was mounted on top of a larger piece of silicon forming the collector, while the emitter was created from a smaller piece of silicon embedded in the base.

In 1959, the Swiss physicist Jean Hoerni invented the planar process, in which optical lithographic techniques were used to diffuse the base into the collector and then diffuse the emitter into the base. One of Hoerni's colleagues, Robert Noyce, invented a technique for growing an insulating layer of silicon dioxide over the transistor, leaving small areas over the base and emitter exposed and diffusing thin layers of aluminum into these areas to create wires. The processes developed by Hoerni and Noyce led directly to modern integrated circuits.

In 1962, Steven Hofstein and Fredric Heiman at the RCA research laboratory in Princeton, New Jersey, invented a new family of devices called *metal-oxide semiconductor field-effect transistors* (MOS FETs for short). Although these transistors were somewhat slower than bipolar transistors, they were cheaper, smaller and used less power. Also of interest was the fact that modified metal-oxide semiconductor structures could be made to act as capacitors or resistors.

The first integrated circuits

To a large extent the demand for miniaturization was driven by the demands of the American space program. For some time people had been thinking that it would be a good idea to be able to fabricate entire circuits on a single piece of semiconductor. The first public discussion of this idea is credited to a British radar expert, G.W.A. Dummer, in a paper presented in 1952. However, it was not until the summer of 1958, that Jack Kilby, working for Texas Instruments, succeeded in fabricating multiple components on a single piece of semiconductor. Kilby's first prototype was a phase shift oscillator and, although manufacturing techniques subsequently took different paths to those used by Kilby, he is still credited with the creation of the first true integrated circuit.

By 1961, Fairchild and Texas Instruments had announced the availability of the first commercial planar integrated circuits comprising simple logic functions. This announcement marked the beginning of the mass production of integrated circuits. In 1963, Fairchild produced a device called the 907 containing two logic gates, each of which consisted of four bipolar transistors and four resistors. The 907 also made use of isolation layers and buried layers, both of which were to become common features in modern integrated circuits.

In 1967, Fairchild introduced a device called the *Micromosaic*, which contained a few hundred transistors. The key feature of the Micromosaic was that the transistors were not initially connected to each other. The designer used a computer program to specify the function the device was required to perform, and the program determined the necessary transistor interconnections and constructed the photo-masks required to complete the device. The Micromosaic is credited as the forerunner of the modern *application-specific integrated circuit (ASIC),* and also as the first real application of computer aided design. In 1970, Fairchild introduced the first 256-bit static RAM called the 4100, while Intel announced the first 1024-bit dynamic RAM, called the 1103, in the same year.

The first microprocessors

With the benefit of hindsight, the advent of the microprocessor appears to have been an obvious development. However, this was less than self-evident at the time for a number of reasons, not the least that computers of the day were big, expensive, and a complete pain to use. Although these reasons would appear to support the development of the microprocessor, by some strange quirk of fate they actually worked to its disfavor.

Due to the fact that computers were so big and expensive, only large institutions could afford them and they were only used for computationally intensive tasks. Thus, following a somewhat circular argument, popular opinion held that only large institutions needed computers in the first place. Similarly, due to the fact that computers were few and far between, only the chosen few had any access to them, which meant that only a handful of people had the faintest clue as to how they worked. Coupled with the fact that the early computers were difficult to use in the first place, this engendered the belief that only heroes (and heroines) with size-sixteen turbo-charged brains had any chance of being capable of using them at all. Last but not least, computers of the day required many thousands of transistors, and the thrust was toward yet more powerful computers in terms of raw number-crunching capability, but integrated circuit technology was in its infancy and it wasn't possible to construct even a few thousand transistors on a single integrated circuit until the late 1960s.

The end result was that the (potential) future of the (hypothetical) microprocessor looked somewhat bleak, but fortunately other forces were afoot. Although computers were somewhat scarce in the 1960s, there was a large and growing market for electronic desktop calculators. In 1970, the Japanese calculator company Busicom approached Intel with a request to design a set of twelve integrated circuits for use in a new calculator. The task was presented to one Marcian "Ted" Hoff, a man who could foresee a somewhat bleak and never-ending role for himself designing sets of special-purpose integrated circuits for one-of-a-kind tasks. However, during his early ruminations on the project, Hoff realized that rather than design the special-purpose devices requested by Busicom, he could create a single integrated circuit with the attributes of a simple-minded, stripped-down, general-purpose computer processor.

The result of Hoff's inspiration was the world's first microprocessor, the 4004, where the '4's were used to indicate that the device had a 4-bit data path. The 4004 was part of a four-chip system, which also consisted of a 256-byte ROM, a 32-bit RAM, and a 10-bit shift register. The 4004 itself contained approximately 2,300 transistors and could execute 60,000 operations per second. The advantage (as far as Hoff was concerned) was that by simply changing the external program, the same device could be used for a multitude of future projects.

Knowing how pervasive microprocessors were to become, you might be tempted to imagine that there was a fanfare of trumpets and Hoff was immediately acclaimed to be the master of the known universe, but such was not to be the case. The 4004 was so radically different from what Busicom had requested that they didn't immediately recognize its implications (much as if they'd ordered a Chevy Cavalier, which had suddenly transmogrified itself into an Aston Martin), so they politely said that they weren't really interested and could they please have the twelve-chip set they'd originally requested (they did eventually agree to use the fruits of Hoff's labors).

In November 1972, Intel introduced the 8008, which was essentially an 8-bit version of the 4004. The 8008 contained approximately 3,300 transistors, and was the first microprocessor to be supported by a high-level language compiler called PL/M. The 8008 was followed by the 4040, which extended the 4004's capabilities by adding logical and compare instructions, and by supporting subroutine nesting using a small internal stack. However, the 4004, 4040, and 8008 were all designed for specific applications, and it was not until April 1974 that Intel presented the first true general-purpose microprocessor, the 8080. This 8-bit device, which contained around 4,500 transistors and could perform 200,000 operations per second, was destined for fame as the central processor of many of the early home computers.

Following the 8080, the microprocessor field exploded with devices such as the 6800 from Motorola in August 1974, the 6502 from MOS Technology in 1975, and the Z80 from Zilog in 1976 (to name but a few). Unfortunately, documenting all of the different microprocessors would require a book in its own right, so we won't even attempt the task here. Instead, we'll create a cunning diversion that will allow us to leap gracefully into the next topic ...... Good grief! Did you see what just flew past your window?

The first personal computers (PCs)

Given that the 8008 was not introduced until November 1972, the resulting flurry of activity was quite impressive. Only six months later, in May 1973, the first computer based on a microprocessor was designed and built in France. Unfortunately the 8008-based Micral, as this device was known, did not prove to be tremendously successful in America. However, in June of that year, the term "microcomputer" first appeared in print in reference to the Micral.

In the same mid-1973 time-frame, the Scelbi Computer Consulting Company presented the 8008-based Scelbi-8H microcomputer, which was the first microprocessor-based computer kit to hit the market (the Micral wasn't a kit – it was only available in fully assembled form). The Scelbi-8H was advertised at $565 and came equipped with 1 K-byte of RAM.

In June 1974, Radio Electronics magazine published an article by Jonathan Titus on building a microcomputer called the Mark-8, which, like the Micral and the Scelbi-8H, was based on the 8008 microprocessor. The Mark-8 received a lot of attention from hobbyists, and a number of user groups sprang up around the US to share hints and tips and disseminate information.

Around the same time that Jonathan Titus was penning his article on the Mark-8, a man called Ed Roberts was pondering the future of his failing calculator company known as MITS (which was located next to a laundromat in Albuquerque, New Mexico). Roberts decided to take a gamble with what little funds remained available to him, and he started to design a computer called the Altair 8800 (the name "Altair" originated in one of the early episodes of Star Trek).[25] Roberts based his system on the newly-released 8080 microprocessor, and the resulting do-it-yourself kit was advertised in Popular Electronics magazine in January 1975 for the then unheard-of price of $439. In fact, when the first unit shipped in April of that year, the price had fallen to an amazingly low $375. Even though it only contained a miserly 256 bytes of RAM, and the

> As is true of many facets in computing, the phrase "Personal Computer" can be something of a slippery customer. For example, the IBM 610 Auto-Point Computer (1957) was described as being *"IBM's first personal computer"* on the premise that it was intended for use by a single operator, but this machine was not based on the stored program concept and it cost $55,000! Other contenders include MIT's LINC (1963), CTC's Datapoint 2200 (1971), the Kenbak-1 (1971), and the Xerox Alto (1973), but all of these machines were either cripplingly expensive, relatively unusable, or only intended as experimental projects. For the purposes of this book, we understand "Personal Computer" to refer to an affordable, general-purpose, microprocessor-based computer intended for the consumer market.

only way to program it was by means of a switch panel, the Altair 8800 proved to be a tremendous success. (These kits were supplied with a steel cabinet sufficient to withstand most natural disasters, which is why a remarkable number of them continue to lurk in their owner's garages to this day.)

Also in April 1975, Bill Gates and Paul Allen founded Microsoft (which was to achieve a certain notoriety over the coming years), and in July of that year, MITS announced the availability of BASIC 2.0 on the Altair 8800. This BASIC interpreter, which was written by Gates and Allen, was the first reasonably high-level computer language program to be made available on a home computer — MITS sold 2,000 systems that year, which certainly made Ed Roberts a happy camper, while Microsoft had taken its first tentative step on the path toward world domination.

In June 1975, MOS Technology introduced their 6502 microprocessor for only $25 (an Intel 8080 would deplete your bank account by about $150 at that time). A short time later, MOS Technology announced their 6502-based KIM-1 microcomputer, which boasted 2 K-bytes of ROM (for the monitor program), 1 K-byte of RAM, an octal keypad, a flashing LED display, and a

---

[25]The authors don't have the faintest clue why the Altair 8800 wasn't named the Altair 8080, but we would be delighted to learn the answer to this conundrum if anyone out there knows.

cassette recorder for storing programs. This unit, which was only available in fully-assembled form, was initially priced at $245, but this soon fell to an astoundingly $170.

The introduction of new microcomputers proceeded apace. Sometime after the KIM-1 became available, the Sphere Corporation introduced its Sphere 1 kit, which comprised a 6800 microprocessor, 4 K-bytes of RAM, a QWERTY keyboard, and a video interface (but no monitor) for $650.

In March 1976, two guys called Steve Wozniak and Steve Jobs (who had been fired with enthusiasm by the Altair 8800) finished work on a home-grown 6502-based computer which they called the Apple 1 (a few weeks later they formed the Apple Computer Company on April Fools day). Although it was not tremendously sophisticated, the Apple 1 attracted sufficient interest for them to create the Apple II, which many believe to be the first personal computer that was both affordable and usable. The Apple II, which became available in April 1977 for $1,300, comprised 16 K-bytes of ROM, 4 K-bytes of RAM, a keyboard, and a color display. Apple was one of the great early success stories – in 1977 they had an income of $700,000 (which was quite a lot of money in those days), and just one year later this had soared tenfold to $7 million! (which was a great deal of money in those days).

In 1975, an IBM mainframe computer that could perform 10,000,000 instructions per second[26] cost around $10,000,000. In 1995 (only twenty years later), a computer video game capable of performing 500,000,000 million instructions per second was available for approximately $500!

Also in April 1977, Commodore Business Machines presented their 6502-based Commodore PET, which contained 14 K-bytes of ROM, 4 K-bytes of RAM, a keyboard, a display, and a cassette tape drive for only $600. Similarly, in August of that year, Tandy/Radio Shack announced their Z80-based TRS-80, comprising 4 K-bytes of ROM, 4 K-bytes of RAM, a keyboard, and a cassette tape drive for $600.

One point that may seem strange today is that there were practically no programs available for these early machines (apart from the programs written by the users themselves). In fact it wasn't until late in 1978 that commercial software began to appear. Possibly the most significant tool of that time was the VisiCalc spreadsheet program, which was written for the

---

[26]Due to the fact that the amount a computer can do with an "average" instruction depends strongly on its architecture, many engineers believe that MIPS, which is officially the abbreviation of *millions of instructions per second*, should more properly stand for *meaningless interpretation of processor speed*.

Apple II by a student at the Harvard Business School, and which appeared in 1979. It is difficult to overstate the impact of this program, but it is estimated that over a quarter of the Apple machines sold in 1979 were purchased by businesses solely for the purpose of running VisiCalc. In addition to making Apple very happy, the success of VisiCalc spurred the development of other applications such as wordprocessors.

When home computers first began to appear, existing manufacturers of large computers tended to regard them with disdain (*"It's just a fad ..... it will never catch on"*). However, it wasn't too long before the sound of money changing hands began to awaken their interest. In 1981, IBM[27] launched their first PC for $1,365, which, if nothing else, sent a very powerful signal to the world that personal computers were here to stay.

Unfortunately, we've only been able to touch on a few systems here, but hopefully we've managed to illustrate both the public's interest in, and the incredible pace of development of, the personal computer. The advent of the general-purpose microprocessor heralded a new era in computing – microcomputer systems small enough to fit on a desk could be endowed with more processing power than monsters weighing tens of tons only a decade before. The effects of these developments are still unfolding, but it is not excessive to say that digital computing and the personal computer have changed the world more significantly than almost any other human invention, and many observers believe that we've only just begun our journey into the unknown!

---

[27]Many people refer to IBM affectionately as "Big Blue," but for some reason IBM never bothered to trademark this sobriquet. In 1995, another enterprising company did just that, which probably caused a certain amount of consternation in the corridors of power!

Further reading

There are a great number of books available on the history of computers and computing, so many in fact that it can be difficult to know where to begin. Fortunately, Kip Crosby, the president of the *Computer History Association of California (CHAC)*, was kind enough to provide his personal "top ten" titles and commentary for your delectation and delight.

Survey Histories

Engines of the Mind: A History of the Computer
By Joel Shurkin,
W. W. Norton, 1984

> *A lively, anecdotal history of computers and computing, essentially from the sixteenth century to the 1960s. Quirky and partisan in spots, but magnificently inclusive and a great read.*

The Dream Machine: Exploring the Computer Age
By Jon Palfreman and Doron Swade
BBC Press (UK), 1991

> *A computer history coffee-table book! Based on the BBC-TV series, with useful and engaging emphasis on computer history in Europe. Odd typography, good quotes, and great pictures.*

"Big-Iron" Histories

Father, Son, and Co.
By T.J. Watson Jr. and Peter Petre
Bantam Books, New York, 1991

> *If the history of IBM appeals to you, this is the book to get it from, because the man who knew it best was also a really good writer. Candid, compelling, unsparing, and important.*

Alan Turing: The Enigma
By Andrew Hodges
Simon and Schuster, 1983

> *Not only computer history, of course; yet this one rockets into the "Ten Best" on its technical content alone. Add in meticulous biography and penetrating character study, and the result is a permanent classic.*

The Computer from Pascal to von Neumann
By Herman H. Goldstine
Princeton University Press, 1972

> *Primarily the story of ENIAC and its immediate successors, and probably the best book on early computer history in the United States. (Unless you understand calculus you may have to skip around a bit).*

IBM's Early Computers
By C.J. Bashe, L.R. Johnson, J.H. Palmer, and E.W. Pugh
MIT Press, 1986 (Vol. 3 in the *History of Computing* series)

> *Make no mistake: this is solid, unadorned technical history, and a real slog. Yet no other book can match this description of the agony and glory of computer design at a time when even its most basic principles were still topics of conjecture.*

The Computer Establishment
By Katharine Davis Fishman
McGraw-Hill, 1982

> *A fine-grained portrait of a special time – the few years when the IBM hegemony slipped and the so-called "Seven Dwarfs" and the plug-compatible manufacturers rushed in to make fortunes. Packed with illuminating detail and scathing war stories.*

Micro Histories

Hackers
By Steven Levy
Doubleday, 1984

> *The rise and maturity of the Hacker Ethic, from the Tech Model Railroad Club to the Free Software Foundation. Sometimes exalted, sometimes dismissed, always argued over, this remains a seminal work in the social history of computing.*

Fire in the Valley: The Making of the Personal Computer
By Paul Freiberger and Michael Swaine
Osborne/McGraw-Hill, 1984

> *Yes, the desktop computer was invented by fanatics in garages. Written not long after the fact, this is the most vivid rendering of a heart-warming story, even if some of the details will be disputed forever.*

Accidental Empires
By Robert X. Cringely
Addison-Wesley, 1992

> ....and the titans moved from garages to tilt-ups, got rich, and still wore
> jeans. How Silicon Valley startled the world, as written by an insider
> with plenty of opinions. A good read by itself, and fascinating when
> read back-to-back with "Fire In The Valley."

As a point of interest, Kip Crosby is also the publisher of the *Analytical
Engine*, which is the official magazine of CHAC. The *Analytical Engine* is
replete with nuggets of historical information and trivia, and contains some
outstandingly interesting interviews with those people who designed or used
the great machines of the past. Should you wish to know more about CHAC
or the *Analytical Engine*, you can email Kip at engine@chac.org

Quick quiz #15

1) What were *"Napier's Bones"*?

2) Who invented the first mechanical calculator?

3) Who invented the first mechanical computer?

4) When were punched cards first used in a data-processing role and by
    whom?

5) When was the *Jevons' Logic Machine* invented and why was it so
    notable?

6) What is a *"Turing Machine"*?

7) What are the basic elements of a stored program computer as described
    by von Neumann?

8) Who invented the first transistor?

9) Who invented the first integrated circuit?

10) Who invented the first microprocessor and why?

Appendix A

Installing your
Beboputer

Contents of Appendix A

Mandatory system requirements

In order to use the *Beboputer* Computer Simulator V1.00 for Windows 95™, you will need:

- Microsoft® Windows 95™

- 8 MB RAM (16 MB recommended).

- A Windows 95™ compatible mouse.

- A VGA or higher graphics adapter capable of displaying resolutions of a 800 x 600 or better.

- 15 MB of available space on your hard drive.

Optional system features:

- An 8-bit sound card or better.

- A printer installed under Windows 95™.

Installation guide

The installation program (setup.exe) decompresses and copies the *Beboputer* and associated files to a directory on your hard drive (some program and multimedia files will remain on the CD-ROM).

When you are ready to install your *Beboputer*, ensure Windows 95™ is up and running, insert the *Beboputer* CD-ROM into your CD-ROM drive, then complete the following steps (note that only the main dialog windows are shown below; in the case of any other dialogs, simply click the **Next** button to proceed):

1) Click the **Start** button on the Windows 95™ taskbar, then select the **Settings** entry, followed by the **Control Panel** entry, followed by the **Add/ Remove Programs** item, which will result in the following **Add/Remove Program Properties** dialog:

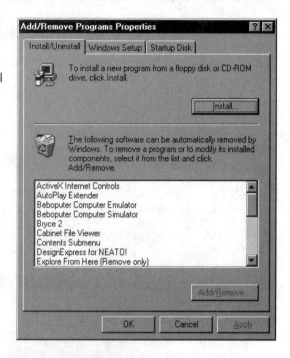

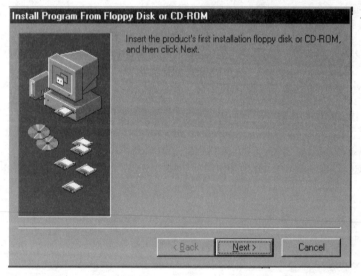

2) Click the **Install** button on the **Add/ Remove Program Properties** dialog, which will result in the **Install From Floppy Disk** or **CD-ROM** dialog:

3) Click the Next
button on the
Install From Floppy
Disk or CD-ROM
dialog, which will
result in the
following Run
Installation Program
dialog:

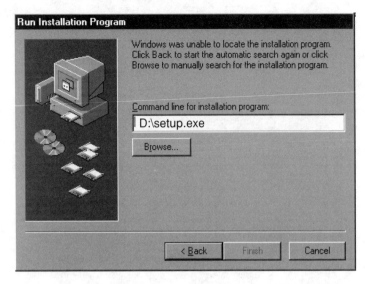

4) Click the Finish button to move on, then click the Next buttons of any
subsequent forms to complete the installation.

Note that before running your *Beboputer*, we strongly recommend that your
screen resolution is set to 800 x 600 or higher.

Important: If you know that you don't have Microsoft's "Video for
Windows" loaded on your system (or if you do have it loaded, but you only
receive sound without any video when you attempt to play our multimedia
lab introductions), then:

a) Recommence the installation process as described above, but ….

b) Once you've invoked the Run Installation Program dialog as
discussed in point 3) above, use the Browse button on the form to
locate the file called either "setup.exe" or "install.exe" in the d:\vfm
directory (substitute d: for the drive letter of your CD-ROM as
necessary).

c) Keep clicking the Next or Finish buttons to complete the installation
as required.

Appendix B

File Formats and Stuff

Contents of Appendix B

Directory structure

As described in Appendix A, during the process of installing your *Beboputer*, the installation program will create the following directory structure on your hard disk (Figure B.1).

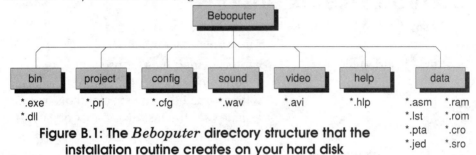

Figure B.1: The *Beboputer* directory structure that the installation routine creates on your hard disk

As we see, the installation program created a top-level *Beboputer* directory, under which are located seven sub-directories as follows:

a) **bin:**   Contains executables (programs), including those for the *Beboputer*, the assembler, the calculator, and the character editor. Also contains any dynamic link libraries.

b) **project:**   Contains the project files specifying the contents of our laboratories, along with any user-defined projects you care to create.

c) **config:**   Contains any configuration files.

d) **sound:**   Contains any sound files for use with the *Beboputer's* virtual sound card.

e) **video:**   Contains any video files for use with the *Beboputer's* virtual video card.

f) **help:**   Contains any help files.

g) **data:**   Contains all of the data files generated by the assembler, the paper tape writer, the character editor, and so forth. Also contains any general-purpose assembly-language subroutines and other such goodies provided with the *Beboputer*.

Generally speaking many of these files will be of limited interest in the course of your average day (excepting the fact that they are there and they work of course). But once you start to know your way around the

Beboputer, you may be overtaken by the desire to create your own utility programs (say a disassembler), in which case you will need to know the internal formats of certain files as discussed below.

Common file extensions

*.asm	Assembly source	Created when you use the *Beboputer's* assembler.
*.avi	Video file	Standard video files for use with the *Beboputer's* video card. (These files have to be generated using special tools that are designed for the task. Note that no such tools are provided with the *Beboputer*).
*.cfg	Configuration data	Used to configure the *Beboputer's* sound and video cards.
*.cro	Character ROM	Generated when you "burn" a new Character ROM.
*.dll	Dynamic link library	Contains linkable objects
*.exe	Executable	Program files such as the *Beboputer* and the assembler.
*.jed	JEDEC data	Generated by the character editor.
*.lst	Assembly listing	Generated by the assembler.
*.prj	Project data	Project/laboratory-specific configuration data.
*.pta	Paper tape	Generated by the paper tape reader/writer.
*.ram	RAM file	Generated by the assembler (if .ORG is greater than $3FFF).
*.rom	ROM file	Generated by the assembler (if .ORG is less than $4000).
*.sro	System ROM	Generated when you "burn" a new System ROM.
*.wav	Sound file	Standard waveform files for use with the *Beboputer's* sound card. (These files have to be generated using special tools that are designed for the task. Note that no such tools are provided with the *Beboputer*).

Assembler source and list files

Assembler source (*.asm) and list (*.lst) files are located in the \data directory on your hard disk. These files are generated by the *Beboputer's* assembler (Figure B.2).

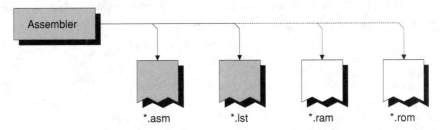

Figure B.2: Assembler source (*.asm) and (*.list) files

The formats of the source and list files are fully discussed in Chapter 12, while the formats of the RAM and ROM files are discussed later in this appendix.

Configuration files

Excepting project-specific data, any configuration files are located in the \config directory on your hard disk. Two such files of particular interest are sound.cfg and video.cfg, which are used by the *Beboputer's* sound and video cards, respectively.

The sound.cfg file: The sound configuration file is used to associate sound (*.wav) files with any data values that the *Beboputer* outputs to its virtual sound card (Figure B.3).

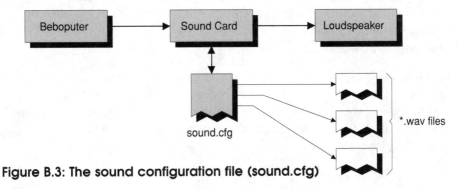

Figure B.3: The sound configuration file (sound.cfg)

When one of your programs requires the *Beboputer* to play a sound, it writes a byte of data to the output port at address $F025, which is the port that drives the sound card (remember to use the **Output Ports** dialog to activate the sound card first). The sound card uses its **sound.cfg** file to determine the name of the *.wav file associated with this particular data value (all of the *.wav files are stored in the *Beboputer's* \sound directory). The format of the **sound.cfg** file is as follows:

```
'The Beboputer sound card configuration file
'Comments start with a single quote
'Data values must be in the range 0 to 255 ($00 to $FF)
'Directory paths are not supported in *.wav file names
[Wave_files]
    0 = num_0.wav
    1 = num_1.wav
    2 = num_2.wav
    3 = num_3.wav
    :       :
    :       :
    100 = klaxon1.wav
    132 = droopy.wav
    164 = error.wav
    128 = ahoo.wav
    255 = whistle.wav
```

Comment lines start with a single quote and you may add as many comments as you wish, but only at the beginning of the file. The field **[Wave_files]** is a keyword that must be present in the file, and the data value to sound file associations follow this keyword. The files **num_0.wav**, **num_1.wav**, **num_2.wav**, and so forth are the ones that we (the authors) created for use in lab 4 (Chapter 9), while the others are just extra sounds we threw in for you to play with. Thus, if your program writes a value of $FF (255 in decimal) to the sound card, it will play the **whistle.wav** file located in the \sound directory. Note that it isn't necessary to reference every possible data value in the **sound.cfg** file ...... only the ones for which you wish to associate *.wav files.

Feel free to add your own *.wav files to the \sound directory and to modify the **sound.cfg** file accordingly. There are a lot of free data bytes left over for you to use, so we strongly recommend that you don't change any of the associations that we've already made, because you could mess up existing and future laboratories.

The video.cfg file: The video configuration file is used to associate video (*.avi) files with any data values that the *Beboputer* outputs to its virtual video card (Figure B.4).

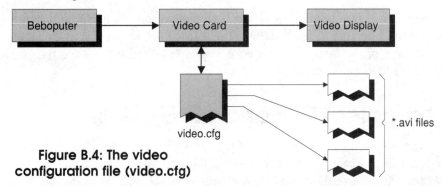

Figure B.4: The video configuration file (video.cfg)

When one of your programs requires the *Beboputer* to display a video, it writes a byte of data to the output port at address $F026, which is the port that drives the video card (remember to use the Output Ports dialog to activate the video card first). The video card uses its video.cfg file to determine the name of the *.avi file associated with this particular data value (all of the *.avi files are stored in the *Beboputer's* \video directory). The format of the video.cfg file is as follows:

```
'The Beboputer video card configuration file
'Comments start with a single quote
'Data values must be in the range 0 to 255 ($00 to $FF)
'Directory paths are not supported in *.avi file names
[Video_files]
   0 = to2160.avi
   1 = to2160.avi
   2 = to2160.avi
   3 = to2160.avi
           :
           :
 128 = to2160.avi
 255 = to2160.avi
```

Once again, comment lines start with a single quote and you may add as many comments as you wish, but only at the beginning of the file. The field [Video_files] is a keyword that must be present in the file, and the data value to video file associations follow this keyword. As for the sound.cfg file, it isn't necessary to reference every possible data value...... only the ones for which you wish to associate *.avi files.

In the example above we've associated a video file called to2160.avi with multiple data values, just to illustrate that fact that this can be done (to2160.avi is just a video we threw in for you to play with). Thus, if your program writes a value of $80 (128 in decimal) to the video card, it will display the to2160.avi video located in the \video directory.

As before, feel free to add your own *.avi files to the \video directory and to modify the video.cfg accordingly. In this case it doesn't really matter if you change any of the associations we've already made, because we haven't used the video card in any of our labs.

Character ROM and JEDEC files

Any user-defined Character ROM (*.cro) and JEDEC (*.jed) files are located in the \data directory on your hard disk. In the real world, a *.jed file would contain a textual description in the standard JEDEC format of the patterns of 0s and 1s that are to be programmed into a physical device using an EPROM programmer. However, in the *Beboputer's* virtual world, these files use a format of our own devising as discussed below.

The process used to create these files is as follows. First, the *Beboputer's* character editor utility is employed to generate a *.jed file. This file is then used by the *Beboputer's* EPROM programmer to generate an equivalent *.cro file, which represents a physical Character ROM containing the patterns of 0s and 1s that are used to form symbols on the *Beboputer's* memory-mapped display (Figure B.5).

Figure B.5: Character ROM (*.cro) files

Once you've created a *.cro file, you have to use the Setup → Swap EPROM pull-down to "plug" your new Character ROM device into the *Beboputer*. In reality, the *Beboputer's* *.cro files actually contain bit-maps that we BitBlit to the screen, so their internal format is that of a standard bit-map, which is beyond the scope of this book. (Note that the use of the character editor, the EPROM Programmer, and the Swap EPROM pull-down are fully discussed in Chapter 13).

With exception of *.cro files, the format of our *.jed files is the most complicated of all of the *Beboputer's* data files, which isn't saying much, because it's really quite simple as you will see from the following:

```
BEBOPUTER JEDEC FILE Version 1.0.0.0
Character Code 0
 511
 273
 273
 273
 313
 511
 313
 273
 273
 273
 511
 0
 0
 0
 0
Character Code 1
 511
 273
  :
  :
 etc
  :
  :
END OF DATA
```

The first line identifies this as being one of our pseudo JEDEC files[1] and indicates the version of the *Beboputer* that generated it, while the last line ("**END OF DATA**") is self-explanatory. The body of the file consists of 256 blocks of data describing the patterns of 0s and 1s associated with each character. Each of these blocks comprises a line of text indicating the character's code (**in hexadecimal**), followed by fifteen **decimal** numbers, where each number relates to a row in that character. For example, on the following page, consider the contents associated with Character Code 41 (that is, ASCII code $41, which equates to an uppercase letter 'A') in the default defchar.jed file we provided with your *Beboputer* (the defchar.jed file is located in the \data directory, along with it's corresponding Character ROM file defchar.cro) (Figure B.6).

Each column in the character has a weight associated with it, where these weights are powers of two, commencing with 1 for the left-most column and ending with 512 for the right-most column. The decimal value for each row is determined by adding all the weights associated with any black squares

---

[1]Remember that these files are in a format of our devising, and that this is not the real JEDEC format.

on that row. A little thought reveals that these weights are the exact opposite to their standard binary counterparts (hence the appellation "*Reverse binary equivalent*" in Figure B.6). This format does requires a little "lateral thinking," but it's easy to follow once you've got the hang of it.[2]

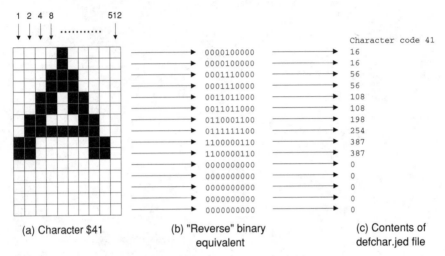

(a) Character $41 (b) "Reverse" binary equivalent (c) Contents of defchar.jed file

Figure B.6: Format of the *Beboputer's* *.jed files

Paper tape files

Paper tape (*.pta) files are located in the \data directory. These files are generated by the paper tape writer, which is activated when the *Beboputer* is instructed to jump to address $0030 in the System ROM. The paper tape writer automatically copies the contents of the 512 bytes occupying locations $4000 to $41FF in the *Beboputer's* RAM onto a paper tape with a name of your choosing (Figure B.7a).

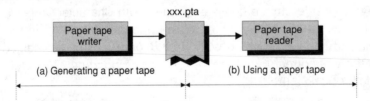

(a) Generating a paper tape (b) Using a paper tape

Figure B.7: Generating and using paper tape (*.pta) files

---

[2]Max would like to make it absolutely clear that Alvin bears full responsibility for the *Beboputer's* data file formats in general (and this one in particular). Alvin has assured Max that this "*Reverse Binary Notation*" was painstakingly conceived and conveys innumerable benefits of an imponderable nature, and who amongst us would doubt the word of an English gentleman?

Similarly, paper tape files are used by the paper tape reader, which is activated when the *Beboputer* is instructed to jump to address $0050 in the System ROM. The paper tape reader copies the contents of a named paper tape back into the *Beboputer's* RAM (Figure B.7b). The format of a paper tape file is as follows:

```
BEBOPUTER PAPER TAPE FILE Version 1.0.0.0
 16384
 16895
Paper Tape File C:\work\BOOK\DATA\Test1.pta
Paper Tape File
START OF DATA
 144
 3
 153
 240
  :
  :
 etc
  :
  :
END OF DATA
```

The first line identifies this as being a paper tape file and indicates the version of the *Beboputer* that generated it. The second and third lines of the file reflect the start and end RAM addresses (in decimal) of the data that was written to the file, while the fourth and fifth lines are comments that will be ignored by the *Beboputer*. Note that the start and end address values are used by the paper tape reader to determine where to load the data back into the *Beboputer's* RAM. The data itself consists of a series of decimal values (one for each address) prefixed by the "**START OF DATA**" line and terminated by the "**END OF DATA**" line. The data values are typically in the range 0 through 255 ($00 through $FF in hexadecimal). However, data values may also be set to 256 ($100 in hexadecimal), which the *Beboputer* will interpret and display as unknown 'X' values.

You may think that the format of paper tape files is somewhat bulky and inefficient (similarly for the other *Beboputer* data files discussed below). You are correct; we could have employed much more efficient techniques. However, our formats have the benefit of being simple, easy to understand, and easy to replicate with any tools you might wish to create for yourself.

RAM files

Any *.ram files are located in the \data directory. These files are generated by the *Beboputer's* assembler when the .ORG statement in the assembly source program is specified as being greater than or equal to $4000, which is the start of the *Beboputer's* RAM (Figure B.8).

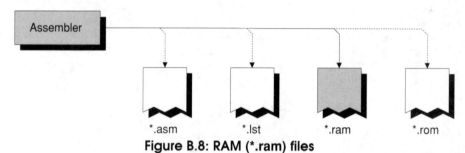

Figure B.8: RAM (*.ram) files

Note that *.ram files may also be generated by means of the Memory → Save RAM pull-down menu, in which case the resulting dialog will prompt you for the name of the file and the addresses of the start and end locations in the RAM, where these addresses define the block of locations you wish to save. An example *.ram file is shown below:

```
BEBOPUTER RAM FILE Version 1.0.0.0
24576
24584
C:\work\BOOK\COMPUTER\DATA\testab.asm
GENERATED BY BEBOPUTER ASSEMBLER Version 1.0.0.0
START OF DATA
144
  0
153
240
 32
128
193
 96
  0
END OF DATA
```

The format of a *.ram file is almost identical to that of a paper tape file as discussed in the previous section. The first line identifies this as being a RAM file and indicates the version of the *Beboputer* that generated it. The second and third lines of the file reflect the start and end RAM addresses (in decimal) of the data that was written to the file, while the fourth and fifth lines are comments that will be ignored by the *Beboputer*. Note that the start and end address values are used by the Memory → Load RAM command to determine where to load the data back into the *Beboputer's* RAM (Figure B.9).

Note that the Memory → Load RAM command allows you to load multiple *.ram files at the same time if you so desire. The data in each *.ram file consists of a series of decimal values (one for each address) prefixed by the "START OF DATA" line and terminated by "END OF DATA" line. The data values are typically in the range 0 through 255 ($00 through $FF in hexadecimal). However, data values may also be set to 256 ($100 in hexadecimal), which the *Beboputer* will interpret and display as unknown 'X' values.

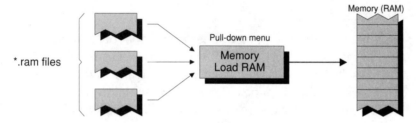

Figure B.9: RAM Loading *.ram files

ROM files

Any *.rom files are located in the \data directory. These files are generated by the *Beboputer's* assembler when the .ORG statement in the assembly source program is specified as being in the range $1000 to $3FFF, which is the user-definable area of the *Beboputer's* ROM (Figure B.10).

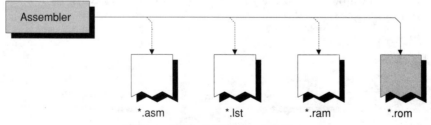

Figure B.10: RAM (*.rom) files

Note that we (the authors) have reserved ROM locations $0000 through $0FFF for our own nefarious purposes, so the assembler won't allow you to set a .ORG in this region. Also note that the only way that you (the reader) can employ *.rom files is to generate a System ROM as discussed in the next section. Meanwhile, an example *.rom file follows:

```
BEBOPUTER ROM FILE Version 1.0.0.0
4096
4104
C:\Program Files\Beboputer\data\testrom1.asm
GENERATED BY BEBOPUTER ASSEMBLER Version 1.0.0.0
START OF DATA
144
  0
153
240
 32
128
193
 16
  2
END OF DATA
```

Apart from the title and various comment lines, the format of *.rom files is almost identical to that of paper tape and RAM files as discussed above. However, note that although *.rom data values are typically in the range 0 through 255 ($00 through $FF in hexadecimal), these data values may also be set to 257 ($101 in hexadecimal), which the *Beboputer* will interpret and display as '#' values (indicating that these are unused locations in the ROM).

System ROM files

System ROM (*.sro) files are stored in the \data directory. To generate a System ROM, you first have to use the *Beboputer's* assembler to create one or more *.rom files as discussed in the previous section, then you use the EPROM programmer tool to read these files and burn a new System ROM (Figure B.11).

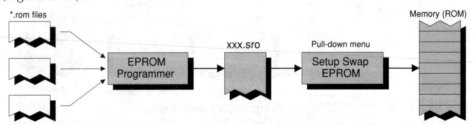

Figure B.11: Generating and using a System ROM (*.sro) file

Once you've generated a new System ROM, it is necessary to use the Setup → Swap EPROM command to instruct the *Beboputer* to remove it's default system ROM and replace it with your new one. Note that the effects of inserting a new System ROM will only persist for the duration of the current lab/session (see Chapter 13 for more details). The format for an example *.sro file follows:

```
BEBOPUTER EPROM FILE Version 1.0.0.0
 4096
 16383
START OF DATA
 144
 0
 153
 240
 32
 128
 193
 16
 2
 257
  :
  :
etc
  :
  :
END OF DATA
```

Note that *.sro files always cover the address range 4,096 through 16,383 ($1000 through $3FFF in hexadecimal), which represents the full range of user-definable ROM locations. As for standard *.rom files, data values are typically in the range 0 through 255 ($00 through $FF in hexadecimal), but some data values may also be set to 257 ($101 in hexadecimal), which the *Beboputer* will interpret and display as '#' values (indicating that these are unused locations in the ROM).

Files delivered with the *Beboputer* in the \data directory

The following files are delivered with the *Beboputer* in the \data directory:

General

defchar.jed	Default JEDEC file used to generate the Character ROM
defchar.cro	Default Character ROM

Paper tapes

lab3_p1.pta	Paper tape of program that loops around reading the 8-bit switches and writing to the 8-bit LEDs.
lab3_p6.pta	Paper tape of program that loops around incrementing the accumulator and writing to the 8-bit LEDs and the dual 7-segment displays.

Ram files

lab4_p1.ram	Program that loops around reading from the 8-bit switches and displaying the result in decimal using the solo and dual 7-segment displays
lab4_p2.ram	As for lab4_p1 but also speaks the numbers out loud
lab8_p1.ram	Program to display a new character in the Character ROM

Subroutines (assembly source)

add16.asm	16-bit add. (Appendix G)
sub16.asm	16-bit subtract. (Appendix G)
smult8.asm	8-bit signed multiplication. (Appendix G)
smult16.asm	16-bit signed multiplication. (Appendix G)
umult8.asm	8-bit unsigned multiplication. (Appendix G)
umult10.asm	10-bit unsigned multiplication. (Appendix I)
umult16.asm	16-bit unsigned multiplication. (Appendix G)
sdiv16.asm	16-bit signed division. (Appendix G)
udiv10.asm	10-bit unsigned division. (Appendix I)
udiv16.asm	16-bit unsigned division. (Appendix G)

Programs (assembly source)

lab1_p1.asm	Loops around rotating the accumulator and displaying on 8-bit LEDs
lab1_p2.asm	Loops around incrementing the accumulator and displaying on 8-bit LEDs
lab2_p1.asm	Loops around reading 8-bit switches and writing to 8-bit LEDs
lab3_p1.asm	Identical to lab2_p1 (only included for completeness)
lab3_p2.asm	Loops around reading 8-bit switches and writing to the undecoded 7-segment display
lab3_p3.asm	As for lab3_p2 but writes to 8-bit LEDs and undecoded 7-segment display
lab3_p4.asm	As for lab3_p3 but writes to 8-bit LEDs and solo decoded 7-segment display
lab3_p5.asm	As for lab3_p4 but writes to 8-bit LEDs and dual decoded 7-segment display
lab3_p6.asm	As for lab1_p2 but writes to 8-bit LEDs and dual decoded 7-segment display
lab4_p1.asm	Loops around reading binary numbers from the 8-bit switches and displaying them in decimal on the solo and dual 7-segment displays
lab4_p2.asm	As for lab4_p1 but also uses Big Red and speaks the numbers aloud
lab5_p1.asm	Loops around reading keys from the QWERTY keyboard and displaying their ASCII codes on the dual 7-segment display

lab6_p1.asm	Program (and subroutine) to clear the memory-mapped display
lab6_p2.asm	Program to display all the characters on the memory-mapped display
lab6_p3.asm	Loops around reading keys from the QWERTY keyboard and display the corresponding characters in row 6, column 6 of the memory-mapped display
lab6_p4.asm	Very simple text editor program
lab6_p5.asm	Tests the medium-resolution color mode of the memory-mapped display
lab7_p1b.asm	Test program containing errors in assembly language
lab7_p2b.asm	Identical to lab5_p1 (only included for completeness)
lab7_p3b.asm	Etch-A-Sketch-type program[3]
lab8_p1.asm	Displays the new character we create in the Character ROM
lab9_p1.asm	Reads and displays numbers on the calculator (Appendix I)
lab9_p2.asm	Converts numbers to internal 16-bit representation (Appendix I)
lab9_p3.asm	Converts numbers from internal 16-bit representation and displays them (Appendix I)
lab9_p4.asm	Full solution for calculator sign-off project (Appendix I)
irupt_1b.asm	First test of interrupt servicing (Appendix D)
irupt_2b.asm	Service an interrupt and then disable it (Appendix D)
irupt_3b.asm	Nested interrupt service routines (Appendix D)
quiz_12.asm	Solution to assembly question in quick quiz #12 (Appendix H)

---

[3]Etch-A-Sketch is a registered trademark of the Ohio Art Company.

Appendix C

Addressing Modes and Instruction Set

Contents of Appendix C

Addressing modes

The phrase *"addressing modes"* refers to the way in which the CPU determines or resolves the addresses of any data to be used in the execution of its instructions. Different computers can support a wide variety of addressing modes, where the selection of such modes depends both on the computer's architecture and the whims of the designer.

Some computers employ very few addressing modes, while others boast enough to make your eyes water. Due to its educational nature, the *Beboputer* supports far more modes than it really needs, although these are only a subset of all possible modes. The seven addressing modes supported by the *Beboputer* are as follows:

a) Implied   e) Indirect

b) Immediate   f) Pre-indexed indirect

c) Absolute   g) Indirect post-indexed

d) Indexed (or *absolute-indexed*)

The majority of instructions in your programs will predominantly employ the implied, immediate, or absolute addressing modes, with a smattering of indexed instructions (which are particularly useful for manipulating arrays and tables of values) and a sprinkling of indirect instructions wherever the situation demands. Also, should you succumb to the thrill of program writing, you'll almost certainly find occasion to use the other modes, at which time you'll be jolly glad we made them available.

Implied addressing (imp)

The implied addressing mode refers to instructions that only comprise an opcode without an operand; for example, INCA (*"increment accumulator"*). In this case, any data required by the instruction and the destination of any result from the instruction are implied by the instruction itself (Figure C.1).

Registers			Flags			Addressing Modes			Other		
ACC	=	Accumulator	Z	=	Zero	imp	=	Implied	LS	=	Least-significant
PC	=	Program Counter	N	=	Negative	imm	=	Immediate	MS	=	Most-significant
IR	=	Instruction Register	C	=	Carry	abs	=	Absolute	Addr	=	Address
X	=	Index Register	O	=	Overflow	abs-x	=	Indexed			
SP	=	Stack Pointer	I	=	Interrupt Mask	ind	=	Indirect			
IV	=	Interrupt Vector				x_ind	=	Pre-indexed indirect			
						ind-x	=	Indirect post-indexed			

An implied sequence commences when the PC reaches the opcode for an implied instruction (a), loads that opcode into the IR (b), and increments the PC (c). Recognizing that this is an implied instruction, the CPU executes it and continues on to the next instruction.

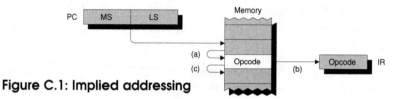

Figure C.1: Implied addressing

Instructions that use implied addressing are: CLRIM, DECA, DECX, HALT, INCA, INCX, NOP, POPA, POPSR, PUSHA, PUSHSR, ROLC, RORC, RTI, RTS, SETIM, SHL, and SHR.

Standard immediate addressing (imm)

An instruction using standard immediate addressing has one data operand byte following the opcode; for example, ADD $03 (*"add $03 to the contents of the accumulator"*) (Figure C.2).

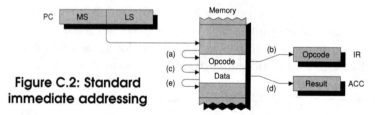

Figure C.2: Standard immediate addressing

The sequence commences when the PC reaches the opcode for an immediate instruction (a), loads that opcode into the IR (b), and increments the PC (c). Recognizing that this is an immediate instruction, the CPU reads the data byte pointed to by the PC, executes the instruction using this data, stores the result in the accumulator (d), and increments the PC to look for the next instruction (e).

Instructions that use standard immediate addressing are: ADD, ADDC, AND, CMPA, LDA, OR, SUB, SUBC, and XOR.

Registers		Flags		Addressing Modes		Other	
ACC	= Accumulator	Z	= Zero	imp	= Implied	LS	= Least-significant
PC	= Program Counter	N	= Negative	imm	= Immediate	MS	= Most-significant
IR	= Instruction Register	C	= Carry	abs	= Absolute	Addr	= Address
X	= Index Register	O	= Overflow	abs-x	= Indexed		
SP	= Stack Pointer	I	= Interrupt Mask	ind	= Indirect		
IV	= Interrupt Vector			x_ind	= Pre-indexed indirect		
				ind-x	= Indirect post-indexed		

Big immediate addressing (imm)

The big immediate addressing mode is very similar to the standard mode, but it refers to instructions that are used to load our 16-bit **X**, **SP**, and **IV** registers. An instruction using big immediate addressing has two data operand bytes following the opcode; for example, **BLDSP $01C4** (*"load $01C4 into the stack pointer"*) (Figure C.3).

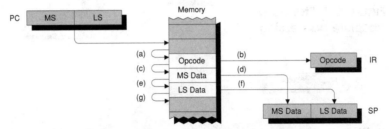

Figure C.3: Big immediate addressing (using BLDSP as example)

The sequence commences when the PC reaches the opcode for an immediate instruction (a), loads that opcode into the IR (b), and increments the PC (c). Recognizing that this is a big immediate instruction, the CPU reads the MS data byte from memory, stores it in the MS byte of the target register (d), and increments the PC (e). The CPU then reads the LS data byte from memory, stores it in the LS byte of the target register (f), and increments the PC to look for the next instruction (g).

Instructions that use big immediate addressing are: **BLDSP**, **BLDX**, and **BLDIV**.

Standard absolute addressing (abs)

An instruction using standard absolute addressing has two address operand bytes following the opcode, and these two bytes are used to point to a byte of data (or to a byte in which to store data); for example, **ADD [$4B06]** (*"add the data stored in location $4B06 to the contents of the accumulator"*) (Figure C.4).

The sequence commences when the PC reaches the opcode for an absolute instruction (a), loads that opcode into the IR (b), and increments the PC (c). Recognizing that this is a standard absolute instruction, the CPU reads the MS address byte from memory, stores it in the MS byte of one of our temporary PCs (d), and increments the main PC (e). The CPU then reads the LS address byte from memory, stores it in the LS byte of the temporary PC (f), and increments the main PC (g).

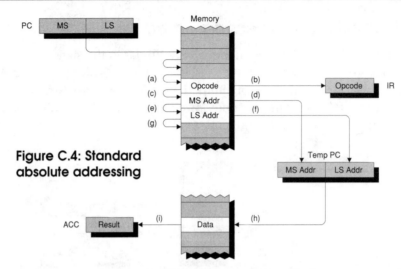

Figure C.4: Standard absolute addressing

The main PC is now "put on hold" while the CPU uses the temporary PC to point to the target address containing the data (h). The CPU executes the original instruction using this data, stores the result into the accumulator (i), and returns control to the main PC to look for the next instruction.

Instructions that use standard absolute addressing are: ADD, ADDC, AND, CMPA, LDA, OR, STA, SUB, SUBC, and XOR. Note that, in the case of a STA (*"store accumulator"*), the contents of the accumulator would be copied (stored) *into* the data byte in memory. Also note that the jump instructions JMP, JC, JNC, JN, JNN, JO, JNO, JZ, JNZ, and JSR can use absolute addressing. However, in this case, the address operand bytes point to the target address which will be loaded into the main PC (see Chapter 8 for more details on the jump instructions).

Big absolute addressing (abs)

The big absolute addressing mode is very similar to the standard mode, but it refers to instructions that affect our 16-bit X, SP, and IV registers. An instruction using big absolute addressing has two address operand bytes following the opcode, and these two bytes are used to point to a *pair* of

Registers			Flags			Addressing Modes			Other		
ACC	=	Accumulator	Z	=	Zero	imp	=	Implied	LS	=	Least-significant
PC	=	Program Counter	N	=	Negative	imm	=	Immediate	MS	=	Most-significant
IR	=	Instruction Register	C	=	Carry	abs	=	Absolute	Addr	=	Address
X	=	Index Register	O	=	Overflow	abs-x	=	Indexed			
SP	=	Stack Pointer	I	=	Interrupt Mask	ind	=	Indirect			
IV	=	Interrupt Vector				x_ind	=	Pre-indexed indirect			
						ind-x	=	Indirect post-indexed			

bytes from which to load or store data; for example, BLDSP [$4B06] (*"load the two bytes of data starting at location $4B06 into the stack pointer"*) (Figure C.5).

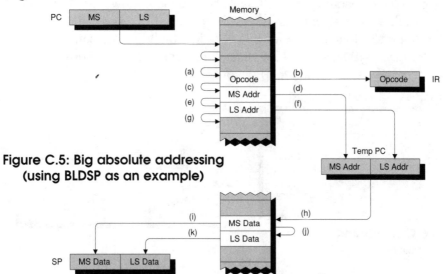

Figure C.5: Big absolute addressing (using BLDSP as an example)

The sequence commences when the PC reaches the opcode for an absolute instruction (a), loads that opcode into the IR (b), and increments the PC (c). Recognizing that this is a big absolute instruction, the CPU reads the MS address byte from memory, stores it in the MS byte of one of our temporary PCs (d), and increments the main PC (e). The CPU then reads the LS address byte from memory, stores it in the LS byte of the temporary PC (f), and increments the main PC (g).

The main PC is now "put on hold" while the CPU uses the temporary PC to point to the target address containing the MS data byte (h) and store it in the MS byte of our target register (i). The CPU then increments the temporary PC so as to point to the LS data byte (j) and store it in the LS byte of our target register (k). The CPU now returns control to the main PC to look for the next instruction.

Remember that the above sequence described a "big load" of one of our 16-bit registers (the stack pointer in this example). In the case of a "big store", the contents of the 16-bit register in question would be copied (stored) *into* the two data bytes in memory.

Instructions that use big absolute addressing are: BLDSP, BLDX, BLDIV, BSTSP, and BSTX.

Indexed addressing (abs-x)

An indexed instruction is very similar to its absolute counterpart, in that it has two address operand bytes following the opcode. However, these two bytes are added to the contents of the index register (X), and the result is used to point to a byte of data (or to a byte in which to store data); for example, ADD [$4B06,X] ("*add the data stored in location ($4B06 + X) to the contents of the accumulator*") (Figure C.6).

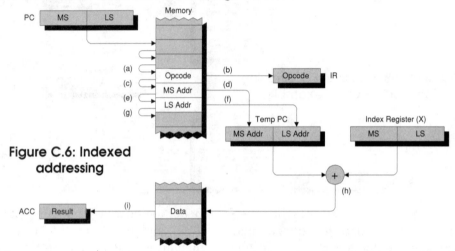

Figure C.6: Indexed addressing

The sequence commences when the PC reaches the opcode for an indexed instruction (a), loads that opcode into the IR (b), and increments the PC (c). Recognizing that this is an indexed instruction, the CPU reads the MS address byte from memory, stores it in the MS byte of one of our temporary PCs (d), and increments the main PC (e). The CPU then reads the LS address byte from memory, stores it in the LS byte of the temporary PC (f), and increments the main PC (g).

The main PC is now "put on hold" while the CPU adds the contents of the temporary PC to the contents of the index register and uses the result to point to the target address containing the data (h). The CPU now executes the original instruction using this data and stores the result into the accumulator (i). Finally, the CPU returns control to the main PC to look for

Registers		Flags			Addressing Modes			Other		
ACC	= Accumulator	Z	=	Zero	imp	=	Implied	LS	=	Least-significant
PC	= Program Counter	N	=	Negative	imm	=	Immediate	MS	=	Most-significant
IR	= Instruction Register	C	=	Carry	abs	=	Absolute	Addr	=	Address
X	= Index Register	O	=	Overflow	abs-x	=	Indexed			
SP	= Stack Pointer	I	=	Interrupt Mask	ind	=	Indirect			
IV	= Interrupt Vector				x_ind	=	Pre-indexed indirect			
					ind-x	=	Indirect post-indexed			

the next instruction. (Note that the act of adding the temporary PC to the index register does not affect the contents of the index register. Also note that the index register must have been loaded with a valid value prior to the first indexed instruction).

Instructions that use indexed addressing are: ADD, ADDC, AND, CMPA, LDA, OR, STA, SUB, SUBC, and XOR. Note that, in the case of a STA ("*store accumulator*"), the contents of the accumulator would be copied (stored) *into* the data byte in memory. Also note that the jump instructions JMP and JSR can use indexed addressing; however, in this case, the result of adding the contents of the temporary program counter to the index register forms the target jump address, which is loaded into the main PC (see Chapter 8 for more details on the jump instructions).

Indirect addressing (ind)

As for an absolute instruction, an indirect instruction has two address operand bytes following the opcode. However, these two bytes do not point to the target data themselves, but instead point to the first byte of another pair of address bytes, and it is *these* address bytes that point to the data (or to a byte in which to store data). Thus, an indirect instruction is so-named because it employs a level of indirection. For example, consider an LDA [[$4B06]] ("*load the accumulator with the data stored in the location pointed to by the address whose first byte occupies location $4B06*") (Figure C.7).

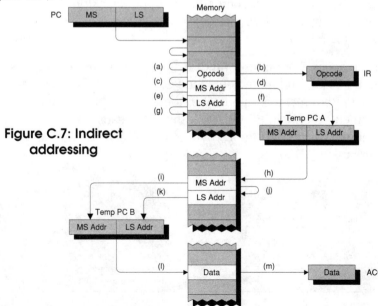

Figure C.7: Indirect addressing

When the PC reaches an indirect opcode (a), the CPU loads that opcode into the IR (b), and increments the PC (c). Now the CPU reads the MS address byte from memory, stores it in the MS byte of temporary PC A (d), and increments the main PC (e). Next the CPU reads the LS address byte from memory, stores it in the LS byte of temporary PC A (f), and increments the main PC (g).

The CPU now employs temporary PC A to read the MS byte of the second address (h), store it in the MS byte of temporary PC B (i), and increment temporary PC A (j). Next the CPU reads the LS byte of the second address, stores it in the LS byte of temporary PC B (k), uses temporary PC B to point to the target data (l), and loads this data into the accumulator (m). Finally, the CPU returns control to the main PC to look for the next instruction.

Instructions that use indirect addressing are **LDA** and **STA**. Also, the jump instructions **JMP** and **JSR** can use indirect addressing; however, in this case, the second address is the target jump address which is loaded into the main PC (see Chapter 8 for more details on the jump instructions).

Pre-indexed indirect addressing (x-ind)

Pre-indexed indirect addressing is a combination of the indexed and indirect modes. This form of addressing is so-named because the address in the opcode bytes is first added to the contents of the index register, and the result points to the first byte of the second address. For example, consider an **LDA [[$4B06,X]]** (*"load the accumulator with the data stored in the location pointed to by the address whose first byte occupies location ($4B06 + X)"*) (Figure C.8).

When the PC reaches a pre-indexed indirect opcode (a), the CPU loads that opcode into the IR (b), and increments the PC (c). Next the CPU reads the MS address byte from memory, stores it in the MS byte of temporary PC A (d), and increments the main PC (e). Now the CPU reads the LS address byte from memory, stores it in the LS byte of temporary PC A (f), and increments the main PC (g).

Registers		Flags			Addressing Modes			Other		
ACC	= Accumulator	Z	=	Zero	imp	=	Implied	LS	=	Least-significant
PC	= Program Counter	N	=	Negative	imm	=	Immediate	MS	=	Most-significant
IR	= Instruction Register	C	=	Carry	abs	=	Absolute	Addr	=	Address
X	= Index Register	O	=	Overflow	abs-x	=	Indexed			
SP	= Stack Pointer	I	=	Interrupt Mask	ind	=	Indirect			
IV	= Interrupt Vector				x_ind	=	Pre-indexed indirect			
					ind-x	=	Indirect post-indexed			

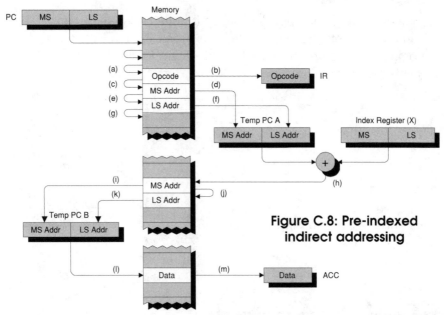

Figure C.8: Pre-indexed indirect addressing

The CPU now adds the contents of temporary PC A to the contents of the index register, uses the result to point to the MS byte of the second address (h), and stores this byte in the MS byte of temporary PC B (i). The CPU then points to the LS byte of the second address (j), stores it in the LS byte of temporary PC B (k), uses temporary PC B to point to the target data (l), and loads this data into the accumulator (m). Finally, the CPU returns control to the main PC to look for the next instruction.

Instructions that use pre-indexed indirect addressing are **LDA** and **STA**. Also, the jump instructions **JMP** and **JSR** can use this form of addressing; however, in this case, the address pointed to by the combination of temporary PC A and the index register is the target jump address which is loaded into the main PC (see Chapter 8 for more details on the jump instructions).

Indirect post-indexed addressing (ind-x)

Indirect post-indexed addressing is similar in concept to pre-indexed indirect addressing. However, in this case, the address in the opcode bytes points to a second address, and it is this second address that is added to the contents of the index register to generate the address of the target data. For example, consider an **LDA [[$4B06],X]** (Figure C.9).

When the PC reaches an indirect post-indexed opcode (a), the CPU loads that opcode into the IR (b), and increments the PC (c). Now the CPU reads the MS address byte from memory, stores it in the MS byte of temporary PC A (d), and increments the main PC (e). Next the CPU reads the LS address byte from memory, stores it in the LS byte of temporary PC A (f), and increments the main PC (g).

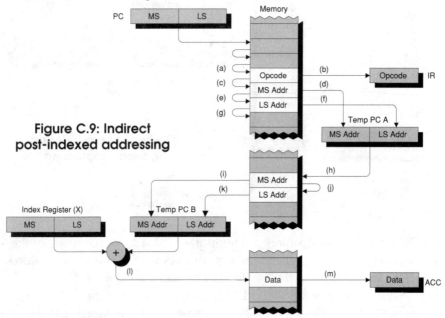

Figure C.9: Indirect post-indexed addressing

The CPU uses the contents of temporary PC A to point to the MS byte of the second address (h), and stores this byte in the MS byte of temporary PC B (i). The CPU then increments temporary PC A to point to the LS byte of the second address (j), and stores this byte in the LS byte of temporary PC B (k). Now the CPU adds the contents of temporary PC B to the contents of the index register, uses the result to point to the target data (l), and loads this data into the accumulator (m). Finally, the CPU returns control to the main PC to look for the next instruction.

Instructions that use indirect post-indexed addressing are **LDA** and **STA**. Also, the jump instructions **JMP** and **JSR** can use this form of addressing; (see Chapter 8 for more details on the jump instructions).

Registers		Flags		Addressing Modes		Other	
ACC =	Accumulator	Z =	Zero	imp =	Implied	LS =	Least-significant
PC =	Program Counter	N =	Negative	imm =	Immediate	MS =	Most-significant
IR =	Instruction Register	C =	Carry	abs =	Absolute	Addr =	Address
X =	Index Register	O =	Overflow	abs-x =	Indexed		
SP =	Stack Pointer	I =	Interrupt Mask	ind =	Indirect		
IV =	Interrupt Vector			x_ind =	Pre-indexed indirect		
				ind-x =	Indirect post-indexed		

Instruction set summary

Category		
Control	NOP	No-operation, CPU doesn't do anything.
	HALT	Generate internal NOPs until an interrupt occurs.
	SETIM	Set the interrupt mask flag in the status register.
	CLRIM	Clear the interrupt mask flag in the status register.
Arithmetic	ADD	Add data in memory to the accumulator.
	ADDC	Like an ADD, but include contents of the carry flag.
	SUB	Subtract data in memory from the accumulator.
	SUBC	Like a SUB, but include contents of the carry flag.
Logical	AND	AND data in memory to the accumulator.
	OR	OR data in memory to the accumulator.
	XOR	XOR data in memory to the accumulator.
Comparison	CMPA	Compare data in memory to the accumulator.
Shifts & Rotates	SHL	Shift the accumulator left 1 bit (arithmetic shift).
	SHR	Shift the accumulator right 1 bit (arithmetic shift).
	ROLC	Rotate the accumulator left 1 bit (through carry flag).
	RORC	Rotate the accumulator right 1 bit (through carry flag).
Increments & Decrements	INCA	Increment the accumulator.
	DECA	Decrement the accumulator.
	INCX	Increment the index register.
	DECX	Decrement the index register.
Loads & Stores	LDA	Load data in memory into the accumulator.
	STA	Store data in the accumulator into memory.
	BLDX	Load data in memory into the index register.
	BSTX	Store data in the index register into memory.
	BLDSP	Load data in memory into the stack pointer.
	BSTSP	Store data in the stack pointer into memory.
	BLDIV	Load data in memory into the interrupt vector,
Push & Pop	PUSHA	Push the accumulator onto the stack.
	POPA	Pop the accumulator from the stack.
	PUSHSR	Push the status register onto the stack.
	POPSR	Pop the status register from the stack.
Jumps	JMP	Jump to a new memory location.
	JSR	Jump to a subroutine.
	JZ	Jump if the result was zero.
	JNZ	Jump if the result wasn't zero.
	JN	Jump if the result was negative.
	JNN	Jump if the result wasn't negative.
	JC	Jump if the result generated a carry.
	JNC	Jump if the result didn't generate a carry.
	JO	Jump if the result generated an overflow.
	JNO	Jump if the result didn't generate an overflow.
Returns	RTS	Return from a subroutine.
	RTI	Return from an interrupt.

Table C.1: *Beboputer* instructions by categories

	imp		imm		abs		abs-x		ind		x-ind		ind-x		flags				
	op	#	op	#	op	#	op	#	op	#	op	#	op	#	I	O	N	Z	C
ADD			$10	2	$11	3	$12	3							-	O	N	Z	C
ADDC			$18	2	$19	3	$1A	3							-	O	N	Z	C
AND			$30	2	$31	3	$32	3							-	-	N	Z	-
BLDIV			$F0	3	$F1	3									-	-	-	-	-
BLDSP			$50	3	$51	3									-	-	-	-	-
BLDX			$A0	3	$A1	3									-	-	-	-	-
BSTSP					$59	3													
BSTX					$A9	3									-	-	-	-	-
CLRIM	$09	1													0	-	-	-	-
CMPA			$60	2	$61	3	$62	3							-	-	-	≥	≥
DECA	$81	1													-	-	N	Z	-
DECX	$83	1													-	-	-	Z	-
HALT	$01	1													-	-	-	-	-
INCA	$80	1													-	-	N	Z	-
INCX	$82	1													-	-	-	Z	-
JC					$E1	3									-	-	-	-	-
JMP					$C1	3	$C2	3	$C3	3	$C4	3	$C5	3	-	-	-	-	-
JN					$D9	3									-	-	-	-	-
JNC					$E6	3									-	-	-	-	-
JNN					$DE	3									-	-	-	-	-
JNO					$EE	3									-	-	-	-	-
JNZ					$D6	3									-	-	-	-	-

Figure C.2: *Beboputer* instruction set summary (standard format)

Registers			Flags			Addressing Modes			Other		
ACC	=	Accumulator	Z	=	Zero	imp	=	Implied	LS	=	Least-significant
PC	=	Program Counter	N	=	Negative	imm	=	Immediate	MS	=	Most-significant
IR	=	Instruction Register	C	=	Carry	abs	=	Absolute	Addr	=	Address
X	=	Index Register	O	=	Overflow	abs-x	=	Indexed			
SP	=	Stack Pointer	I	=	Interrupt Mask	ind	=	Indirect			
IV	=	Interrupt Vector				x_ind	=	Pre-indexed indirect			
						ind-x	=	Indirect post-indexed			

	imp		imm		abs		abs-x		ind		x-ind		ind-x		flags				
	op	#	op	#	op	#	op	#	op	#	op	#	op	#	I	O	N	Z	C
JO					$E9	3									-	-	-	-	-
JSR					$C9	3	$CA	3	$CB	3	$CC	3	$CD	3	-	-	-	-	-
JZ					$D1	3									-	-	-	-	-
LDA			$90	2	$91	3	$92	3	$93	3	$94	3	$95	3	-	-	N	Z	-
NOP	$00	1													-	-	-	-	-
OR			$38	2	$39	3	$3A	3							-	-	N	Z	-
POPA	$B0	1													-	-	N	Z	-
POPSR	$B1	1													Φ	Φ	Φ	Φ	Φ
PUSHA	$B2	1													-	-	-	-	-
PUSHSR	$B3	1													-	-	-	-	-
ROLC	$78	1													-	-	N	Z	↔
RORC	$79	1													-	-	N	Z	↔
RTI	$C7	1													Φ	Φ	Φ	Φ	Φ
RTS	$CF	1													-	-	-	-	-
SETIM	$08	1													1	-	-	-	-
SHL	$70	1													-	-	N	Z	↔
SHR	$71	1													-	-	N	Z	↔
STA					$99	3	$9A	3	$9B	3	$9C	3	$9D	3	-	-	-	-	-
SUB			$20	2	$21	3	$22	3							-	O	N	Z	C
SUBC			$28	2	$29	3	$2A	3							-	O	N	Z	C
XOR			$40	2	$41	3	$42	3							-	-	N	Z	-

Legend

op	=	Opcode
$	=	Hexadecimal number
#	=	Number of bytes
-	=	No change
≥	=	Magnitude comparison (special case)
↔	=	Shift or rotate through carry bit
Φ	=	Restored by popping status register

ADD (Add without carry)

Description:

This instruction adds the contents of a byte of data in memory to the current contents of the accumulator and stores the result in the accumulator (the contents of the memory are not affected). Note that the result is not affected by the contents of the carry flag, because the carry-in to the ALU is forced to *logic 0*. See also the corresponding **ADDC** instruction.

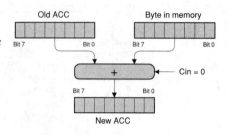

Addressing modes:

Mode	#Bytes	Opcode	Assembly example	Comments
imm	2	$10	ADD $03	Add $03 to the ACC.
abs	3	$11	ADD [$4C76]	Add the contents of memory location $4C76 to the ACC
abs-x	3	$12	ADD [$4C76,X]	Add the contents of a memory location to the ACC, where the address of the memory location is $4C76 plus the contents of the X register

Flags affected:

O   Set to 1 if the result overflows, otherwise cleared to 0
N   Set to 1 if the MS bit of the result is 1, otherwise cleared to 0
Z   Set to 1 if all of the bits in the result are 0, otherwise cleared to 0
C   Set to 1 if there is a carry out from the addition, otherwise cleared to 0

Registers			Flags			Addressing Modes			Other		
ACC	=	Accumulator	Z	=	Zero	imp	=	Implied	LS	=	Least-significant
PC	=	Program Counter	N	=	Negative	imm	=	Immediate	MS	=	Most-significant
IR	=	Instruction Register	C	=	Carry	abs	=	Absolute	Addr	=	Address
X	=	Index Register	O	=	Overflow	abs-x	=	Indexed			
SP	=	Stack Pointer	I	=	Interrupt Mask	ind	=	Indirect			
IV	=	Interrupt Vector				x_ind	=	Pre-indexed indirect			
						ind-x	=	Indirect post-indexed			

ADDC (Add with carry)

Description:

This instruction adds the contents of a byte of data in memory (along with the current contents of the carry flag) to the current contents of the accumulator and stores the result in the accumulator (the contents of the memory are not affected). See also the corresponding **ADD** instruction.

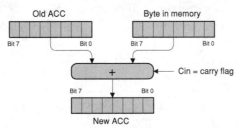

Addressing modes:

Mode	#Bytes	Opcode	Assembly example	Comments
imm	2	$18	ADDC $03	Add $03 to the ACC
abs	3	$19	ADDC [$4C76]	Add the contents of memory location $4C76 to the ACC
abs-x	3	$1A	ADDC [$4C76,X]	Add the contents of a memory location to the ACC, where the address of the memory location is $4C76 plus the contents of the X register

Flags affected:

O	Set to 1 if the result overflows, otherwise cleared to 0
N	Set to 1 if the MS bit of the result is 1, otherwise cleared to 0
Z	Set to 1 if all of the bits in the result are 0, otherwise cleared to 0
C	Set to 1 if there is a carry out from the addition, otherwise cleared to 0

AND (Logical operation)

Description:

This instruction logically ANDs the contents of a byte of data in memory with the current contents of the accumulator and stores the result in the accumulator (the contents of the memory are not affected). Note that this is a bit-wise operation, which means that bit 0 of the old ACC is AND-ed with bit 0 of the memory to generate bit 0 of the new ACC. Similarly, bit 1 is AND-ed with bit 1, bit 2 with bit 2, and so forth. See also the OR and XOR instructions.

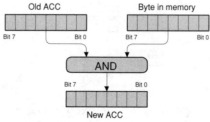

Addressing modes:

Mode	#Bytes	Opcode	Assembly example	Comments
imm	2	$30	AND $03	Logically AND $03 with the ACC
abs	3	$31	AND [$4C76]	Logically AND the contents of memory location $4C76 with the ACC
abs-x	3	$32	AND [$4C76,X]	Logically AND the contents of a memory location with the ACC, where the address of the memory location is $4C76 plus the contents of the X register

Flags affected:

N   Set to 1 if the MS bit of the result is 1, otherwise cleared to 0

Z   Set to 1 if all of the bits in the result are 0, otherwise cleared to 0

Registers		Flags		Addressing Modes		Other	
ACC = Accumulator		Z = Zero		imp = Implied		LS = Least-significant	
PC = Program Counter		N = Negative		imm = Immediate		MS = Most-significant	
IR = Instruction Register		C = Carry		abs = Absolute		Addr = Address	
X = Index Register		O = Overflow		abs-x = Indexed			
SP = Stack Pointer		I = Interrupt Mask		ind = Indirect			
IV = Interrupt Vector				x_ind = Pre-indexed indirect			
				ind-x = Indirect post-indexed			

BLDIV ("Big" load the interrupt vector)

Description:

This instruction loads two contiguous bytes of memory into the 16-bit interrupt vector, MS byte first (the contents of the memory are not affected). Note that, unlike the **BLDSP** and **BLDX** instructions which have corresponding store instructions (**BSTSP** and **BSTX**), there is no **BSTIV**. This is because the contents of the IV register can only be changed explicitly using a **BLDIV**, which means that the programmer always knows what it contains (a programmer who doesn't is a *"silly-billy"*).

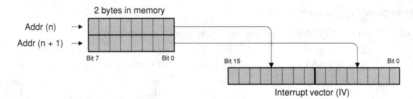

Addressing modes:

Mode	#Bytes	Opcode	Assembly example	Comments
imm	3	$F0	BLDIV $6100	Load the IV with $6100
abs	3	$F1	BLDIV [$4C76]	Load the IV with two bytes from memory, where the first (MS) byte is located at address $4C76

Flags affected:

None

BLDSP ("Big" load the stack pointer)

Description:

This instruction loads two contiguous bytes of memory into the 16-bit stack pointer, MS byte first (the contents of the memory are not affected).

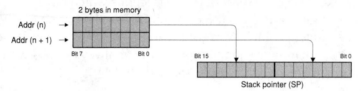

Addressing modes:

Mode	#Bytes	Opcode	Assembly example	Comments
imm	3	$50	BLDSP $4FFF	Load the SP with $4FFF
abs	3	$51	BLDSP [$4C76]	Load the SP with two bytes from memory, where the first (MS) byte is located at address $4C76

Flags affected:

None

Registers		Flags		Addressing Modes			Other		
ACC	= Accumulator	Z	= Zero	imp	=	Implied	LS	=	Least-significant
PC	= Program Counter	N	= Negative	imm	=	Immediate	MS	=	Most-significant
IR	= Instruction Register	C	= Carry	abs	=	Absolute	Addr	=	Address
X	= Index Register	O	= Overflow	abs-x	=	Indexed			
SP	= Stack Pointer	I	= Interrupt Mask	ind	=	Indirect			
IV	= Interrupt Vector			x_ind	=	Pre-indexed indirect			
				ind-x	=	Indirect post-indexed			

BLDX ("Big" load the index register)

Description:

This instruction loads two contiguous bytes of memory into the 16-bit index register, MS byte first (the contents of the memory are not affected).

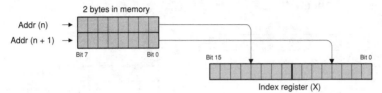

Addressing modes:

Mode	#Bytes	Opcode	Assembly example	Comments
imm	3	$A0	BLDX $0C64	Load the X register with $0C64
abs	3	$A1	BLDX [$4C76]	Load the X register with two bytes from memory, where the first (MS) byte is located at address $4C76

Flags affected:

None

BSTSP ("Big" store the stack pointer)

Description:

This instruction stores the current contents of the 16-bit stack pointer into two contiguous bytes of memory, MS byte first (the contents of the stack pointer are not affected).

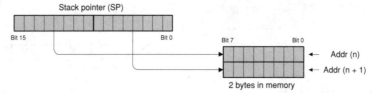

Addressing modes:

Mode	#Bytes	Opcode	Assembly example	Comments
abs	3	$59	BSTSP [$4C76]	Store the SP into two bytes of memory, where the first (MS) byte is located at address $4C76

Flags affected:

None

BSTX ("Big" store the index register)

Description:

This instruction stores the current contents of the 16-bit index register into two contiguous bytes of memory, MS byte first (the contents of the index register are not affected).

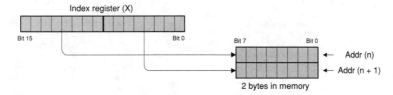

Addressing modes:

Mode	#Bytes	Opcode	Assembly example	Comments
abs	3	$A9	BSTX [$4C76]	Store the X register into two bytes of memory, where the first (MS) byte is located at address $4C76

Flags affected:

None

CLRIM (Clear the interrupt mask)

Description:

This instruction clears the interrupt mask bit in the status register to *logic 0*, thereby preventing the *Beboputer* from seeing any future interrupts. See also the SETIM instruction in this appendix and the discussions on interrupts in Appendix D.

Addressing modes:

Mode	#Bytes	Opcode	Assembly example	Comments
imp	1	$09	CLRIM	Load the interrupt mask with 0

Flags affected:

I	Loaded with *logic 0*

Registers		Flags		Addressing Modes		Other		
ACC	= Accumulator	Z	= Zero	imp	= Implied	LS	=	Least-significant
PC	= Program Counter	N	= Negative	imm	= Immediate	MS	=	Most-significant
IR	= Instruction Register	C	= Carry	abs	= Absolute	Addr	=	Address
X	= Index Register	O	= Overflow	abs-x	= Indexed			
SP	= Stack Pointer	I	= Interrupt Mask	ind	= Indirect			
IV	= Interrupt Vector			x_ind	= Pre-indexed indirect			
				ind-x	= Indirect post-indexed			

CMPA (Compare accumulator to byte in memory)

Description:

This instruction compares the contents of the accumulator to a byte in memory. The instruction assumes that both quantities represent unsigned binary values. Based on this assumption, the carry flag is set to *logic 1* if the value in the accumulator is the greater (otherwise it's cleared to *logic 0*), while the zero flag is set to *logic 1* if the values are equal (otherwise it's cleared to *logic 0*). The original values in the accumulator and memory are not modified in any way.

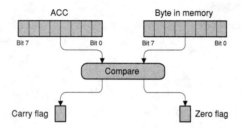

Addressing modes:

Mode	#Bytes	Opcode	Assembly example	Comments
imm	2	$60	CMPA $03	Compare the contents of the ACC with $03
abs	3	$61	CMPA [$4C76]	Compare the contents of the ACC with the contents of memory location $4C76
abs-x	3	$62	CMPA [$4C76,X]	Compare the contents of the ACC with the contents of a memory location, where the address of the memory location is $4C76 plus the contents of the X register

Flags affected:

Z   Set to 1 if the two values are equal, otherwise cleared to 0
C   Set to 1 if the (unsigned) value in the accumulator is the greater, otherwise cleared to 0

DECA (Decrement the contents of the accumulator)

Description:

This instruction decrements (subtracts 1 from) the contents of the accumulator. See also the counterpart to this instruction, INCA, and the somewhat similar instructions DECX and INCX.

Addressing modes:

Mode	#Bytes	Opcode	Assembly example	Comments
imp	1	$81	DECA	Decrement (subtract 1 from) the contents of the ACC

Flags affected:

N   Set to 1 if the MS bit of the result is 1, otherwise cleared to 0

Z   Set to 1 if all of the bits in the result are 0, otherwise cleared to 0

Registers		Flags		Addressing Modes		Other	
ACC	= Accumulator	Z =	Zero	imp	= Implied	LS	= Least-significant
PC	= Program Counter	N =	Negative	imm	= Immediate	MS	= Most-significant
IR	= Instruction Register	C =	Carry	abs	= Absolute	Addr	= Address
X	= Index Register	O =	Overflow	abs-x	= Indexed		
SP	= Stack Pointer	I =	Interrupt Mask	ind	= Indirect		
IV	= Interrupt Vector			x_ind	= Pre-indexed indirect		
				ind-x	= Indirect post-indexed		

DECX (Decrement the contents of the index register)

Description:

This instruction decrements (subtracts 1 from) the contents of the 16-bit index register. See also the counterpart to this instruction, **INCX**, and the somewhat similar instructions **DECA** and **INCA**. Note that this instruction only modifies the Z flag (unlike **DECA** which modifies both the Z and N flags).

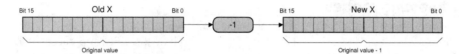

Addressing modes:

Mode	#Bytes	Opcode	Assembly example	Comments
imp	1	$83	DECX	Decrement (subtract 1 from) the contents of the X register

Flags affected:

Z   Set to 1 if all of the bits in the result (the new contents of the X register) are 0, otherwise cleared to 0.

HALT (Halt the CPU)

Description:

This instruction instructs the CPU to cease processing instructions from the memory, and to start performing *internal* NOP (no-operation) instructions. Left to its own devices, the CPU will continue to perform internal NOPs until the end of time, and the only way to override the HALT is for the CPU to receive an interrupt (or for it to be reset). See also the NOP instruction in this appendix and the discussion on interrupts in Appendix D.

Addressing modes:

Mode	#Bytes	Opcode	Assembly example	Comments
imp	1	$01	HALT	Halts the CPU and causes it to perform internal NOP instructions

Flags affected:

None

Registers		Flags		Addressing Modes		Other	
ACC	= Accumulator	Z =	Zero	imp	= Implied	LS	= Least-significant
PC	= Program Counter	N =	Negative	imm	= Immediate	MS	= Most-significant
IR	= Instruction Register	C =	Carry	abs	= Absolute	Addr	= Address
X	= Index Register	O =	Overflow	abs-x	= Indexed		
SP	= Stack Pointer	I =	Interrupt Mask	ind	= Indirect		
IV	= Interrupt Vector			x_ind	= Pre-indexed indirect		
				ind-x	= Indirect post-indexed		

INCA (Increment the contents of the accumulator)

Description:

This instruction increments (adds 1 to) the contents of the accumulator. See also the counterpart to this instruction, **DECA**, and the somewhat similar instructions **DECX** and **INCX**.

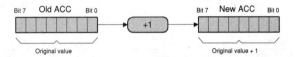

Addressing modes:

Mode	#Bytes	Opcode	Assembly example	Comments
imp	1	$80	INCA	Increment (add 1 to) the contents of ACC

Flags affected:

N   Set to 1 if the MS bit of the result is 1, otherwise cleared to 0.

Z   Set to 1 if all of the bits in the result are 0, otherwise cleared to 0.
    Note that the reason incrementing the ACC can result in it containing zero is if its original value were all 1s; that is, $FF in hexadecimal.

INCX (Increment the contents of the index register)

Description:

This instruction increments (adds 1 to) the contents of the 16-bit index register. See also the counterpart to this instruction, **DECX**, and the somewhat similar instructions **DECA** and **INCA**. Note that this instruction only modifies the **Z** flag (unlike **INCA** which modifies both the **Z** and **N** flags).

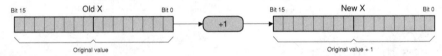

Addressing modes:

Mode	#Bytes	Opcode	Assembly example	Comments
imp	1	$82	INCX	Increment (add 1 to) the contents of the X register

Flags affected:

Z   Set to 1 if all of the bits in the result (the new contents of the X register) are 0, otherwise cleared to 0. Note that the reason incrementing the X register can result in it containing zero is if its original value were all 1s; that is, $FFFF in hexadecimal.

Registers			Flags			Addressing Modes			Other		
ACC	=	Accumulator	Z	=	Zero	imp	=	Implied	LS	=	Least-significant
PC	=	Program Counter	N	=	Negative	imm	=	Immediate	MS	=	Most-significant
IR	=	Instruction Register	C	=	Carry	abs	=	Absolute	Addr	=	Address
X	=	Index Register	O	=	Overflow	abs-x	=	Indexed			
SP	=	Stack Pointer	I	=	Interrupt Mask	ind	=	Indirect			
IV	=	Interrupt Vector				x_ind	=	Pre-indexed indirect			
						ind-x	=	Indirect post-indexed			

JC (Jump if carry)

Description:

This instruction is used to change the "flow" of the program by causing the CPU to jump to a new address if the carry status flag is TRUE (contains a *logic 1*, thereby indicating that the previous instruction generated a carry), otherwise the CPU ignores the operand and continues to the next instruction. See also the corresponding **JNC** instruction.

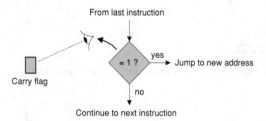

Addressing modes:

Mode	#Bytes	Opcode	Assembly example	Comments
abs	3	$E1	JC [$4C76]	If the carry flag contains a *logic 1*, then jump to address $4C76, otherwise continue to the next instruction

Flags affected:

None

JMP (Jump unconditionally)

Description:

This is the instruction that occupies the memory location(s) before the JMP.

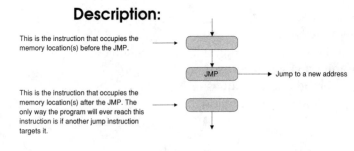

JMP → Jump to a new address

This is the instruction that occupies the memory location(s) after the JMP. The only way the program will ever reach this instruction is if another jump instruction targets it.

This instruction is used to change the "flow" of the program by causing the CPU to unconditionally jump to a new address. See also the somewhat related JSR instruction.

Addressing modes:

Mode	#Bytes	Opcode	Assembly example	Comments
abs	3	$C1	JMP [$4C76]	Jump to address $4C76
abs-x	3	$C2	JMP [$4C76,X]	Add $4C76 to the contents of the X register to form the target address $xxxx and jump to this target address
ind	3	$C3	JMP [[$4C76]]	Read the target address $xxxx stored in the two bytes starting at address $4C76, and then jump to this target address
x-ind	3	$C4	JMP [[$4C76,X]]	Add $4C76 to the contents of the X register to form a new address $zzzz. Read the target address $xxxx stored in the two bytes starting at address $zzzz and jump to this target address
ind-x	3	$C5	JMP [[$4C76],X]	Read the address $zzzz stored in the two bytes starting at address $4C76, then add $zzzz to the contents of the X register to form the target address $xxxx and jump to this target address

Flags affected:

None

Registers		Flags		Addressing Modes		Other	
ACC =	Accumulator	Z =	Zero	imp =	Implied	LS =	Least-significant
PC =	Program Counter	N =	Negative	imm =	Immediate	MS =	Most-significant
IR =	Instruction Register	C =	Carry	abs =	Absolute	Addr =	Address
X =	Index Register	O =	Overflow	abs-x =	Indexed		
SP =	Stack Pointer	I =	Interrupt Mask	ind =	Indirect		
IV =	Interrupt Vector			x_ind =	Pre-indexed indirect		
				ind-x =	Indirect post-indexed		

JN (Jump if negative)

Description:

This instruction is used to change the "flow" of the program by causing the CPU to jump to a new address if the negative status flag is TRUE (contains a *logic 1*, thereby indicating that the result from the previous instruction was negative), otherwise the CPU ignores the operand and continues to the next instruction. See also the corresponding **JNN** instruction.

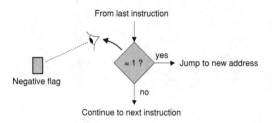

Addressing modes:

Mode	#Bytes	Opcode	Assembly example	Comments
abs	3	$D9	JN [$4C76]	If the negative flag contains a *logic 1*, then jump to address $4C76, otherwise continue to the next instruction

Flags affected:

None

JNC (Jump if not carry)

Description:

This instruction is used to change the "flow" of the program by causing the CPU to jump to a new address if the carry status flag is **FALSE** (contains a *logic 0*, thereby indicating that the previous instruction did not generate a carry), otherwise the CPU ignores the operand and continues to the next instruction. See also the corresponding **JC** instruction.

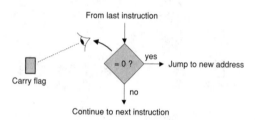

Addressing modes:

Mode	#Bytes	Opcode	Assembly example	Comments
abs	3	$E6	JNC [$4C76]	If the carry flag contains a *logic 0*, then jump to address $4C76, otherwise continue to the next instruction

Flags affected:

None

Registers		Flags		Addressing Modes			Other		
ACC	= Accumulator	Z	= Zero	imp	=	Implied	LS	=	Least-significant
PC	= Program Counter	N	= Negative	imm	=	Immediate	MS	=	Most-significant
IR	= Instruction Register	C	= Carry	abs	=	Absolute	Addr	=	Address
X	= Index Register	O	= Overflow	abs-x	=	Indexed			
SP	= Stack Pointer	I	= Interrupt Mask	ind	=	Indirect			
IV	= Interrupt Vector			x_ind	=	Pre-indexed indirect			
				ind-x	=	Indirect post-indexed			

JNN (Jump if not negative)

Description:

This instruction is used to change the "flow" of the program by causing the CPU to jump to a new address if the negative status flag is **FALSE** (contains a *logic 0*, thereby indicating that the result from the previous instruction was positive (not negative)), otherwise the CPU ignores the operand and continues to the next instruction. See also the corresponding **JN** instruction.

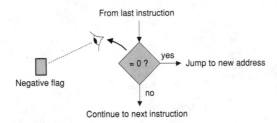

Addressing modes:

Mode	#Bytes	Opcode	Assembly example	Comments
abs	3	$DE	JNN [$4C76]	If the negative flag contains a *logic 0*, then jump to address $4C76, otherwise continue to the next instruction

Flags affected:

None

JNO (Jump if not overflow)

Description:

This instruction is used to change the "flow" of the program by causing the CPU to jump to a new address if the overflow status flag is **FALSE** (contains a *logic 0*, thereby indicating that the previous instruction did not generate an overflow), otherwise the CPU ignores the operand and continues to the next instruction. See also the corresponding **JO** instruction.

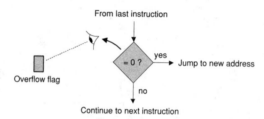

Addressing modes:

Mode	#Bytes	Opcode	Assembly example	Comments
abs	3	$EE	JNO [$4C76]	If the overflow flag contains a *logic 0*, then jump to address $4C76, otherwise continue to the next instruction

Flags affected:

None

Registers		Flags		Addressing Modes		Other	
ACC = Accumulator		Z = Zero		imp = Implied		LS = Least-significant	
PC = Program Counter		N = Negative		imm = Immediate		MS = Most-significant	
IR = Instruction Register		C = Carry		abs = Absolute		Addr = Address	
X = Index Register		O = Overflow		abs-x = Indexed			
SP = Stack Pointer		I = Interrupt Mask		ind = Indirect			
IV = Interrupt Vector				x_ind = Pre-indexed indirect			
				ind-x = Indirect post-indexed			

JNZ (Jump if not zero)

Description:

This instruction is used to change the "flow" of the program by causing the CPU to jump to a new address if the zero status flag is **FALSE** (contains a *logic 0*, thereby indicating that result from the previous operation was non-zero), otherwise the CPU ignores the operand and continues to the next instruction. See also the corresponding **JZ** instruction.

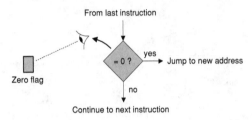

Addressing modes:

Mode	#Bytes	Opcode	Assembly example	Comments
abs	3	$D6	JNZ [$4C76]	If the zero flag contains a *logic 0*, then jump to address $4C76, otherwise continue to the next instruction

Flags affected:

None

JO (Jump if overflow)

Description:

This instruction is used to change the "flow" of the program by causing the CPU to jump to a new address if the overflow status flag is TRUE (contains a *logic 1*, thereby indicating that the previous instruction generated an overflow), otherwise the CPU ignores the operand and continues to the next instruction. See also the corresponding **JNO** instruction.

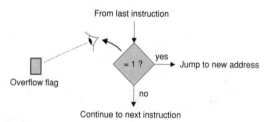

Addressing modes:

Mode	#Bytes	Opcode	Assembly example	Comments
abs	3	$E9	JO [$4C76]	If the overflow flag contains a *logic 1*, then jump to address $4C76, otherwise continue to the next instruction

Flags affected:

None

Registers		Flags		Addressing Modes			Other		
ACC	= Accumulator	Z	= Zero	imp	=	Implied	LS	=	Least-significant
PC	= Program Counter	N	= Negative	imm	=	Immediate	MS	=	Most-significant
IR	= Instruction Register	C	= Carry	abs	=	Absolute	Addr	=	Address
X	= Index Register	O	= Overflow	abs-x	=	Indexed			
SP	= Stack Pointer	I	= Interrupt Mask	ind	=	Indirect			
IV	= Interrupt Vector			x_ind	=	Pre-indexed indirect			
				ind-x	=	Indirect post-indexed			

JSR (Jump to a subroutine)

Description:

This instruction is used to change the "flow" of the program by causing the CPU to jump to a subroutine. Note that the CPU automatically places a 2-byte return address on the top of the stack before jumping to the subroutine. See also the related **RTS** instruction.

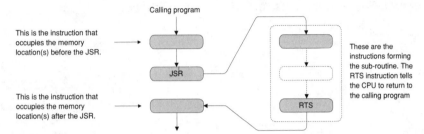

Addressing modes:

Mode	#Bytes	Opcode	Assembly example	Comments
abs	3	$C9	JSR [$4C76]	Jump to the subroutine at address $4C76
abs-x	3	$CA	JSR [$4C76,X]	Add $4C76 to the contents of the X register to form the target address of the subroutine ($xxxx) and jump to this target address
ind	3	$CB	JSR [[$4C76]]	Read the target address of the subroutine ($xxxx) stored in the two bytes starting at address $4C76, and then jump to this target address
x-ind	3	$CC	JSR [[$4C76,X]]	Add $4C76 to the contents of the X register to form a new address $zzzz. Read the target address of the subroutine ($xxxx) stored in the two bytes starting at address $zzzz and jump to this target address
ind-x	3	$CD	JSR [[$4C76],X]	Read the address $zzzz stored in the two bytes starting at address $4C76, then add $zzzz to the contents of the X register to form the target address of the subroutine ($xxxx) and jump to this target address

Flags affected:

None

JZ (Jump if zero)

Description:

This instruction is used to change the "flow" of the program by causing the CPU to jump to a new address if the zero status flag is **TRUE** (contains a *logic 1*, thereby indicating that the result from the previous instruction was zero), otherwise the CPU ignores the operand and continues to the next instruction. See also the corresponding **JNZ** instruction.

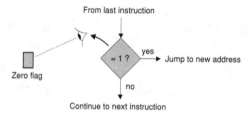

Addressing modes:

Mode	#Bytes	Opcode	Assembly example	Comments
abs	3	$D1	JZ [$4C76]	If the zero flag contains a *logic 1*, then jump to address $4C76, otherwise continue to the next instruction

Flags affected:

None

Registers		Flags		Addressing Modes			Other		
ACC	= Accumulator	Z	= Zero	imp	=	Implied	LS	=	Least-significant
PC	= Program Counter	N	= Negative	imm	=	Immediate	MS	=	Most-significant
IR	= Instruction Register	C	= Carry	abs	=	Absolute	Addr	=	Address
X	= Index Register	O	= Overflow	abs-x	=	Indexed			
SP	= Stack Pointer	I	= Interrupt Mask	ind	=	Indirect			
IV	= Interrupt Vector			x_ind	=	Pre-indexed indirect			
				ind-x	=	Indirect post-indexed			

LDA (Load the accumulator)

Description:

This instruction loads the contents of a byte of data in memory into the accumulator (the contents of the memory are not affected). See also the corresponding STA instruction.

Byte in memory

Bit 7   Bit 0   Bit 7   Bit 0

ACC

Addressing modes:

Mode	#Bytes	Opcode	Assembly example	Comments
imm	2	$90	LDA $03	Load the ACC with $03.
abs	3	$91	LDA [$4C76]	Load the ACC with the contents of address $4C76
abs-x	3	$92	LDA [$4C76,X]	Add $4C76 to the contents of the X register to form the target address $xxxx, then load the ACC with the contents of the target address
ind	3	$93	LDA [[$4C76]]	Read the target address $xxxx stored in the two bytes starting at address $4C76, then load the ACC with the contents of the target address
x-ind	3	$94	LDA [[$4C76,X]]	Add $4C76 to the contents of the X register to form a new address $zzzz. Read the target address $xxxx stored in the two bytes starting at address $zzzz, then load the ACC with the contents of the target address
ind-x	3	$95	LDA [[$4C76],X]	Read the address $zzzz stored in the two bytes starting at address $4C76, then add $zzzz to the contents of the X register to form the target address $xxxx, then load the ACC with the contents of the target address

Flags affected:

N   Set to 1 if the MS bit of the ACC is 1, otherwise cleared to 0

Z   Set to 1 if all of the bits in the ACC are 0, otherwise cleared to 0

NOP (No operation)

Description:

This instruction is a little strange in that it doesn't do anything at all, which may prompt the question: *"why bother having it in the first place?"* The point is that executing a **NOP** takes a finite amount of time, which makes it useful for creating delay loops in a program. See also the **HALT** instruction, which causes the CPU to generate internal NOPs.

Addressing modes:

Mode	#Bytes	Opcode	Assembly example	Comments
imp	1	$00	NOP	Doesn't do a thing

Flags affected:

None

Registers		Flags		Addressing Modes			Other		
ACC	= Accumulator	Z	= Zero	imp	=	Implied	LS	=	Least-significant
PC	= Program Counter	N	= Negative	imm	=	Immediate	MS	=	Most-significant
IR	= Instruction Register	C	= Carry	abs	=	Absolute	Addr	=	Address
X	= Index Register	O	= Overflow	abs-x	=	Indexed			
SP	= Stack Pointer	I	= Interrupt Mask	ind	=	Indirect			
IV	= Interrupt Vector			x_ind	=	Pre-indexed indirect			
				ind-x	=	Indirect post-indexed			

OR (Logical operation)

Description:

This instruction logically ORs the contents of a byte of data in memory with the current contents of the accumulator and stores the result in the accumulator (the contents of the memory are not affected). Note that this is a bit-wise operation, which means that bit 0 of the old ACC is OR-ed with bit 0 of the memory to generate bit 0 of the new ACC. Similarly, bit 1 is OR-ed with bit 1, bit 2 with bit 2, and so forth. See also the **AND** and **XOR** instructions.

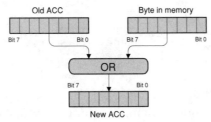

Addressing modes:

Mode	#Bytes	Opcode	Assembly example	Comments
imm	2	$38	OR $03	Logically OR $03 with the ACC
abs	3	$39	OR [$4C76]	Logically OR the contents of memory location $4C76 with the ACC
abs-x	3	$3A	OR [$4C76,X]	Logically OR the contents of a memory location with the ACC, where the address of the memory location is $4C76 plus the contents of the X register

Flags affected:

N   Set to 1 if the MS bit of the result is 1, otherwise cleared to 0

Z   Set to 1 if all of the bits in the result are 0, otherwise cleared to 0

POPA (Pop the accumulator off the top of the stack)

Description:

This instruction first increments the stack pointer such that it points to the last byte placed onto the stack, then it copies this byte into the accumulator. See also the corresponding PUSHA instruction and the related POPSR and PUSHSR instructions.

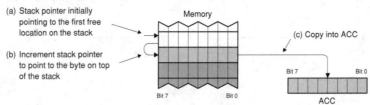

(a) Stack pointer initially pointing to the first free location on the stack

(b) Increment stack pointer to point to the byte on top of the stack

Memory

(c) Copy into ACC

Bit 7   Bit 0

Bit 7   Bit 0

ACC

Addressing modes:

Mode	#Bytes	Opcode	Assembly example	Comments
imp	1	$B0	POPA	Pops the byte on the top of the stack into the ACC (I'm a poet and I never knew-it)

Flags affected:

N	Set to 1 if the MS bit of the ACC is 1, otherwise cleared to 0
Z	Set to 1 if all of the bits in the ACC are 0, otherwise cleared to 0

Registers		Flags			Addressing Modes			Other		
ACC	= Accumulator	Z	=	Zero	imp	=	Implied	LS	=	Least-significant
PC	= Program Counter	N	=	Negative	imm	=	Immediate	MS	=	Most-significant
IR	= Instruction Register	C	=	Carry	abs	=	Absolute	Addr	=	Address
X	= Index Register	O	=	Overflow	abs-x	=	Indexed			
SP	= Stack Pointer	I	=	Interrupt Mask	ind	=	Indirect			
IV	= Interrupt Vector				x_ind	=	Pre-indexed indirect			
					ind-x	=	Indirect post-indexed			

POPSR (Pop the status register off the top of the stack)

Description:

This instruction first increments the stack pointer such that it points to the last byte placed onto the stack, then it copies this byte into the status register. Note that as the status register is only five bits wide, the three most-significant bits from the byte on top of the stack are discarded. See also the corresponding PUSHSR instruction and the related POPA and PUSHA instructions.

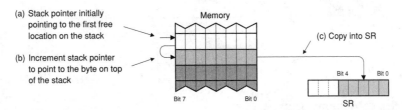

Addressing modes:

Mode	#Bytes	Opcode	Assembly example	Comments
imp	1	$B1	POPSR	Pops the byte on top of the stack into the SR

Flags affected:

I	Loaded with whatever was in bit 4 of the byte on top of the stack
O	Loaded with whatever was in bit 3 of the byte on top of the stack
N	Loaded with whatever was in bit 2 of the byte on top of the stack
Z	Loaded with whatever was in bit 1 of the byte on top of the stack
C	Loaded with whatever was in bit 0 of the byte on top of the stack

PUSHA (Push the accumulator onto the top of the stack)

Description:

This instruction first copies the contents of the accumulator onto the top of the stack, then decrements the stack pointer such that it points to the next free location (the contents of the accumulator are not affected). See also the corresponding POPA instruction and the related POPSR and PUSHSR instructions.

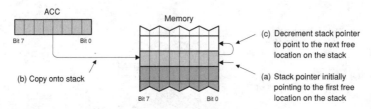

Addressing modes:

Mode	#Bytes	Opcode	Assembly example	Comments
imp	1	$B2	PUSHA	Pushes the ACC onto the stack

Flags affected:

None

Registers		Flags		Addressing Modes		Other		
ACC	= Accumulator	Z	= Zero	imp	= Implied	LS	=	Least-significant
PC	= Program Counter	N	= Negative	imm	= Immediate	MS	=	Most-significant
IR	= Instruction Register	C	= Carry	abs	= Absolute	Addr	=	Address
X	= Index Register	O	= Overflow	abs-x	= Indexed			
SP	= Stack Pointer	I	= Interrupt Mask	ind	= Indirect			
IV	= Interrupt Vector			x_ind	= Pre-indexed indirect			
				ind-x	= Indirect post-indexed			

PUSHSR (Push the status register onto the top of the stack)

Description:

This instruction first copies the contents of the status register onto the top of the stack, then decrements the stack pointer such that it points to the next free location (the contents of the status register are not affected). Note that as the status register is only five bits wide, the three most-significant bits in the byte on top of the stack are coerced to *logic 0s*. See also the corresponding POPSR instruction and the related POPA and PUSHA instructions.

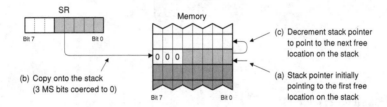

Addressing modes:

Mode	#Bytes	Opcode	Assembly example	Comments
imp	1	$B3	PUSHSR	Pushes the SR onto the stack

Flags affected:

None

ROLC (Rotate accumulator left through the carry flag)

Description:

This instruction rotates the contents of the accumulator 1 bit left and through the carry status flag. The original contents of the carry flag are loaded into bit 0 of the ACC, while the original contents of bit 7 of the ACC are loaded into the carry flag. See also the corresponding RORC instruction and the related SHL and SHR instructions.

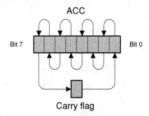

Addressing modes:

Mode	#Bytes	Opcode	Assembly example	Comments
imp	1	$78	ROLC	Rotates the ACC 1 bit left and through the carry flag

Flags affected:

N	Set to 1 if the MS bit of the ACC is 1, otherwise cleared to 0
Z	Set to 1 if all of the bits in the ACC are 0, otherwise cleared to 0
C	Loaded with whatever was in bit 7 of the ACC

Registers		Flags		Addressing Modes		Other	
ACC = Accumulator		Z = Zero		imp = Implied		LS = Least-significant	
PC = Program Counter		N = Negative		imm = Immediate		MS = Most-significant	
IR = Instruction Register		C = Carry		abs = Absolute		Addr = Address	
X = Index Register		O = Overflow		abs-x = Indexed			
SP = Stack Pointer		I = Interrupt Mask		ind = Indirect			
IV = Interrupt Vector				x_ind = Pre-indexed indirect			
				ind-x = Indirect post-indexed			

RORC (Rotate accumulator right through the carry flag)

Description:

This instruction rotates the contents of the accumulator 1 bit right and through the carry status flag. The original contents of the carry flag are loaded into bit 7 of the ACC, while the original contents of bit 0 of the ACC are loaded into the carry flag. See also the corresponding ROLC instruction and the related SHL and SHR instructions.

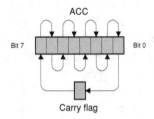

Addressing modes:

Mode	#Bytes	Opcode	Assembly example	Comments
imp	1	$79	RORC	Rotates the ACC 1 bit right and through the carry flag

Flags affected:

N   Set to 1 if the MS bit of the ACC is 1, otherwise cleared to 0
Z   Set to 1 if all of the bits in the ACC are 0, otherwise cleared to 0
C   Loaded with whatever was in bit 0 of the ACC

RTI (Return from an interrupt)

Description:

This instruction is used to terminate an interrupt service routine and return control back to the main program. Remember that when an interrupt occurs, the CPU completes the instruction it's currently working on, automatically pushes a return address onto the stack followed by the current contents of the status register, then jumps to the interrupt service routine located at the address contained in the interrupt vector.

By comparison, when the CPU sees an RTI instruction, it automatically pops the topmost byte off the stack into the status register (much like a POPSR instruction). The CPU then retrieves the 2-byte address from the top of the stack and uses this address as the entry point for its return to the main program. Note that an interrupt service routine can contain a number of RTI instructions. See also the somewhat related RTS instruction and the discussions on interrupts in Appendix D.

Addressing modes:

Mode	#Bytes	Opcode	Assembly example	Comments
imp	1	$C7	RTI	Exits the interrupt service routine and returns control to the main program

Flags affected:

All   The SR is reloaded with whatever its contents were when the interrupt caused it to be pushed onto the stack (assuming the programmer hasn't used the interrupt service routine to modify the copy of the SR on the stack)

Registers		Flags		Addressing Modes		Other	
ACC	= Accumulator	Z	= Zero	imp	= Implied	LS	= Least-significant
PC	= Program Counter	N	= Negative	imm	= Immediate	MS	= Most-significant
IR	= Instruction Register	C	= Carry	abs	= Absolute	Addr	= Address
X	= Index Register	O	= Overflow	abs-x	= Indexed		
SP	= Stack Pointer	I	= Interrupt Mask	ind	= Indirect		
IV	= Interrupt Vector			x_ind	= Pre-indexed indirect		
				ind-x	= Indirect post-indexed		

RTS (Return from a subroutine)

Description:

This instruction is used to terminate a subroutine and return control to the calling program. The CPU automatically retrieves a 2-byte address from the top of the stack and uses this address as the entry point for its return to the calling program. Note that a subroutine can contain a number of RTS instructions. See also the related JSR instruction and the somewhat related RTI instruction.

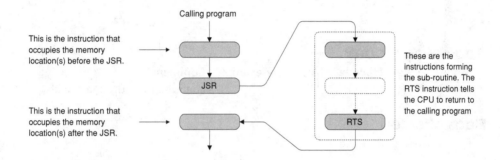

Calling program

This is the instruction that occupies the memory location(s) before the JSR.

JSR

This is the instruction that occupies the memory location(s) after the JSR.

These are the instructions forming the sub-routine. The RTS instruction tells the CPU to return to the calling program

RTS

Addressing modes:

Mode	#Bytes	Opcode	Assembly example	Comments
imp	1	$CF	RTS	Exits the subroutine and returns control to the calling program

Flags affected:

None

SETIM (Set the interrupt mask)

Description:

This instruction sets the interrupt mask bit in the status register to *logic 1*, thereby allowing the *Beboputer* to see any future interrupts. See also the CLRIM instruction in this appendix and the discussions on interrupts in Appendix D.

Addressing modes:

Mode	#Bytes	Opcode	Assembly example	Comments
imp	1	$08	SETIM	Load the interrupt mask with 1

Flags affected:

I   Loaded with *logic 1*

Registers		Flags			Addressing Modes			Other		
ACC	= Accumulator	Z	=	Zero	imp	=	Implied	LS	=	Least-significant
PC	= Program Counter	N	=	Negative	imm	=	Immediate	MS	=	Most-significant
IR	= Instruction Register	C	=	Carry	abs	=	Absolute	Addr	=	Address
X	= Index Register	O	=	Overflow	abs-x	=	Indexed			
SP	= Stack Pointer	I	=	Interrupt Mask	ind	=	Indirect			
IV	= Interrupt Vector				x_ind	=	Pre-indexed indirect			
					ind-x	=	Indirect post-indexed			

SHL (Shift accumulator left)

Description:

This instruction shifts the contents of the accumulator 1 bit to the left. A *logic 0* is shifted in to the least-significant bit of the ACC, while the bit that "falls off the end" (bit 7 in this case) is stored in the carry status flag. See also the corresponding **SHR** instruction and the related **ROLC** and **RORC** instructions.

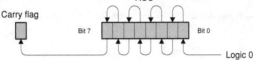

Addressing modes:

Mode	#Bytes	Opcode	Assembly example	Comments
imp	1	$70	SHL	Shifts the accumulator 1 bit left

Flags affected:

N   Set to 1 if the MS bit of the ACC is 1, otherwise cleared to 0

Z   Set to 1 if all of the bits in the ACC are 0, otherwise cleared to 0

C   Loaded with whatever was in bit 7 of the ACC

SHR (Shift accumulator right)

Description:

This instruction shifts the contents of the accumulator 1 bit to the right. This is an arithmetic shift right (as opposed to a logical shift right, for which the *Beboputer* doesn't have an instruction), which means that the most-significant bit of the ACC is copied back into itself, while the bit that "falls off the end" (bit 0 in this case) is stored in the carry status flag. See also the corresponding SHL instruction and the related ROLC and RORC instructions.

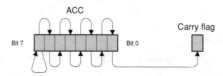

Addressing modes:

Mode	#Bytes	Opcode	Assembly example	Comments
imp	1	$71	SHR	Shifts the accumulator 1 bit right (arithmetic shift)

Flags affected:

N   Set to 1 if the MS bit of the ACC is 1, otherwise cleared to 0
Z   Set to 1 if all of the bits in the ACC are 0, otherwise cleared to 0
C   Loaded with whatever was in bit 0 of the ACC

Registers		Flags		Addressing Modes		Other	
ACC	= Accumulator	Z	= Zero	imp	= Implied	LS	= Least-significant
PC	= Program Counter	N	= Negative	imm	= Immediate	MS	= Most-significant
IR	= Instruction Register	C	= Carry	abs	= Absolute	Addr	= Address
X	= Index Register	O	= Overflow	abs-x	= Indexed		
SP	= Stack Pointer	I	= Interrupt Mask	ind	= Indirect		
IV	= Interrupt Vector			x_ind	= Pre-indexed indirect		
				ind-x	= Indirect post-indexed		

STA (Store the accumulator)

Description:

This instruction stores the contents of the accumulator to a byte in the memory (the contents of the accumulator are not affected). See also the corresponding **LDA** instruction.

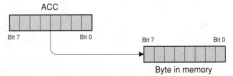

Addressing modes:

Mode	#Bytes	Opcode	Assembly example	Comments
abs	3	$99	STA [$4C76]	Stuff the contents of the ACC into address $4C76
abs-x	3	$9A	STA [$4C76,X]	Add $4C76 to the contents of the X register to form the target address $xxxx, then stuff the contents of the ACC into the target address
ind	3	$9B	STA [[$4C76]]	Read the target address $xxxx stored in the two bytes starting at address $4C76, then stuff the contents of the ACC into the target address
x-ind	3	$9C	STA [[$4C76,X]]	Add $4C76 to the contents of the X register to form a new address $zzzz. Read the target address $xxxx stored in the two bytes starting at address $zzzz, then stuff the contents of the ACC into the target address
ind-x	3	$9D	STA [[$4C76],X]	Read the address $zzzz stored in the two bytes starting at address $4C76, then add $zzzz to the contents of the X register to form the target address $xxxx, then stuff the contents of the ACC into the target address

Flags affected:

None

SUB (Subtract without carry)

Description:

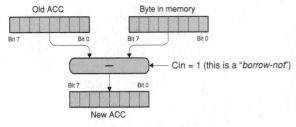

Old ACC

Byte in memory

Bit 7   Bit 0

Bit 7   Bit 0

— ◄— Cin = 1 (this is a *"borrow-not"*)

Bit 7   Bit 0

New ACC

This instruction subtracts the contents of a byte of data in memory from the current contents of the accumulator and stores the result in the accumulator (the contents of the memory are not affected). Note that the result is not affected by the contents of the carry flag, because the carry-in to the ALU is forced to *logic 1* (the carry-in is really a *"borrow-not"* in this case). See also the corresponding SUBC instruction.

In particular, note that the diagram above is a stylized representation of the action of the SUB instruction. In reality, the CPU doesn't have a "subtractor block," so the actual operation that is performed to achieve the desired result is as follows:

$$new\_ACC[7:0] = old\_ACC[7:0] + NOT(byte\_in\_memory[7:0]) + 1$$

Addressing modes:

Mode	#Bytes	Opcode	Assembly example	Comments
imm	2	$20	SUB $03	Subtract $03 from the ACC.
abs	3	$21	SUB [$4C76]	Subtract the contents of memory location $4C76 from the ACC
abs-x	3	$22	SUB [$4C76,X]	Subtract the contents of a memory location from the ACC, where the address of the memory location is $4C76 plus the contents of the X register

Flags affected:

O   Set to 1 if the result overflows, otherwise cleared to 0
N   Set to 1 if the MS bit of the result is 1, otherwise cleared to 0
Z   Set to 1 if all of the bits in the result are 0, otherwise cleared to 0
C   Set to 1 if there is a carry out (really a *"borrow-not"*) from the subtraction, otherwise cleared to 0 (indicating a *"borrow"*)

Registers		Flags		Addressing Modes		Other		
ACC	= Accumulator	Z	= Zero	imp	= Implied	LS	=	Least-significant
PC	= Program Counter	N	= Negative	imm	= Immediate	MS	=	Most-significant
IR	= Instruction Register	C	= Carry	abs	= Absolute	Addr	=	Address
X	= Index Register	O	= Overflow	abs-x	= Indexed			
SP	= Stack Pointer	I	= Interrupt Mask	ind	= Indirect			
IV	= Interrupt Vector			x_ind	= Pre-indexed indirect			
				ind-x	= Indirect post-indexed			

SUBC (Subtract with carry)

Description:

This instruction subtracts the contents of a byte of data in memory (along with the current contents of the carry flag) from the current contents of the accumulator and stores the result in the accumulator (the contents of the memory are not affected). See also the corresponding SUB instruction.

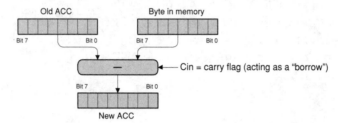

In particular, note that the diagram above is a stylized representation of the action of the SUBC instruction. In reality, the CPU doesn't have a "subtractor block," so the actual operation that is performed to achieve the desired result is as follows:

$$new\_ACC[7:0] = old\_ACC[7:0] + NOT(byte\_in\_memory[7:0]) + Cin$$

Addressing modes:

Mode	#Bytes	Opcode	Assembly example	Comments
imm	2	$28	SUBC $03	Subtract $03 from the ACC
abs	3	$29	SUBC [$4C76]	Subtract the contents of memory location $4C76 from the ACC
abs-x	3	$2A	SUBC [$4C76,X]	Subtract the contents of a memory location from the ACC, where the address of the memory location is $4C76 plus the contents of the X register

Flags affected:

O   Set to 1 if the result overflows, otherwise cleared to 0
N   Set to 1 if the MS bit of the result is 1, otherwise cleared to 0
Z   Set to 1 if all of the bits in the result are 0, otherwise cleared to 0
C   Set to 1 if there is a carry out (really a "*borrow-not*") from the subtraction, otherwise cleared to 0 (indicating a "*borrow*")

XOR (Logical operation)

Description:

This instruction logically XORs the contents of a byte of data in memory with the current contents of the accumulator and stores the result in the accumulator (the contents of the memory are not affected). Note that this is a bit-wise operation, which means that bit 0 of the old ACC is XOR-ed with bit 0 of the memory to generate bit 0 of the new ACC. Similarly, bit 1 is XOR-ed with bit 1, bit 2 with bit 2, and so forth. See also the AND and OR instructions.

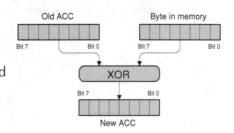

Addressing modes:

Mode	#Bytes	Opcode	Assembly example	Comments
imm	2	$40	XOR $03	Logically XOR $03 with the ACC
abs	3	$41	XOR [$4C76]	Logically XOR the contents of memory location $4C76 with the ACC
abs-x	3	$42	XOR [$4C76,X]	Logically XOR the contents of a memory location with the ACC, where the address of the memory location is $4C76 plus the contents of the X register

Flags affected:

N	Set to 1 if the MS bit of the result is 1, otherwise cleared to 0
Z	Set to 1 if all of the bits in the result are 0, otherwise cleared to 0

Registers		Flags		Addressing Modes		Other		
ACC	= Accumulator	Z	= Zero	imp	= Implied	LS	=	Least-significant
PC	= Program Counter	N	= Negative	imm	= Immediate	MS	=	Most-significant
IR	= Instruction Register	C	= Carry	abs	= Absolute	Addr	=	Address
X	= Index Register	O	= Overflow	abs-x	= Indexed			
SP	= Stack Pointer	I	= Interrupt Mask	ind	= Indirect			
IV	= Interrupt Vector			x_ind	= Pre-indexed indirect			
				ind-x	= Indirect post-indexed			

Appendix D

Interrupts and Interrupt Handling

Contents of Appendix D

Just another one of those days

Before we commence, we should note that there are a multitude of strategies for handling interrupts, so we can only hope to cover some of the more common techniques here. Also note that we'll start by discussing these techniques at a generic level, then we'll return to consider how the *Beboputer* handles interrupts.

Let's begin our discussions by considering a (hopefully) fictitious scenario. Suppose that you've just taken possession of a brand-new car equipped with an on-board computer, whose tasks include closing the windows (when instructed to do so) and activating the airbag (in the event of a crash). Now assume that you're merrily cruising down the highway and you flick the "Close Window" button, which causes the computer to enter a loop saying *"Is the window closed yet? If not, I'll keep on closing it."*

Suddenly, as if from nowhere, a herd of rampaging grockles appear! Swerving to avoid them you rocket off the road, screech across a farmyard, and collide rather forcibly with an extremely large pile of manure (don't you hate it when that happens?). It's fortunate indeed that you're wearing your seat belt, because your airbag sadly fails to make an appearance (your computer is still looping around saying *"Is the window closed yet? ...."*). Thanking your lucky stars,[1] you reach for the steaming-hot coffee that you recently acquired from a well-known purveyor of fast foods. But at the self-same moment that you raise the coffee to your lips, the window finishes closing and the computer finally gets around to check what's happening in the outside world. Realizing that there's a problem, the computer immediately activates the airbag, you unexpectedly find yourself taking a somewhat larger gulp of coffee than was your original intent, and you're well on the way to having another *"one of those days"*.

Unfortunately, this scenario is not as uncommon (in general terms) as you might think, because it can be tricky to ensure that a computer is made aware of external events in a timely manner so as to handle them appropriately.

Using a polling strategy

If you cast your mind back to Chapter 10, you may recall that we created a simple program to loop around reading characters from our QWERTY keyboard and writing them to our dual 7-segment displays. Now assume

---

[1] *"If it wasn't for my bad luck, I wouldn't have any luck at all!"* - Anon

that, whilst performing this task, we also want our computer to act as a burglar alarm that monitors the state of a switch connected to the front door of our house. For the purposes of these discussions, let's assume that opening the door will cause the switch to close, in which case we want the computer to respond by ringing a bell.

Thus far, we've considered the CPU's primary mechanism for "seeing" things occurring in the outside world as being via its input ports. On this basis, we might decide to connect our burglar alarm switch to a bit on one of these ports, say bit[0], and to connect the other bits to *logic 0* (Figure D.1).

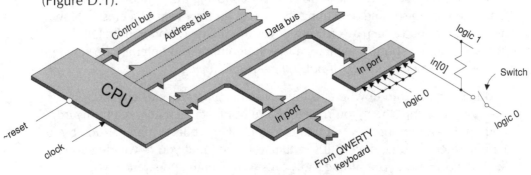

**Figure D.1: Connecting an external signal
(such as a burglar alarm switch) to an input port**

Note that we've omitted the circuitry that generates the input port ~read_enable signals from the address and control busses for simplicity. The way in which we've wired this particular circuit means that when the switch is **OPEN** (meaning the door is closed), bit[0] of the input port will be presented with a *logic 1* value via the pull-up resistor. By comparison, when the switch is **CLOSED** (meaning the door is open), bit[0] of the port will be presented with a *logic 0* value.[2] We now have to modify our program to check the status of our burglar alarm switch, but this may not be quite as simple as it first appears, because even a rudimentary task like this one offers opportunities for mistakes (Figure D.2).

Our original program (Figure D.2a) loops around reading from the input port connected to the keyboard until it sees a non-zero value indicating that a key has been pressed. When a non-zero value is detected, the program writes that value to the 7-segment displays and then returns to look for the next key (remember that the act of reading a value from this particular input port automatically clears the latch in the keyboard).

---

[2]We could easily have wired the switch such that its OPEN and CLOSED positions were represented by *logic 0* and *logic 1* values, respectively ...... but we didn't.

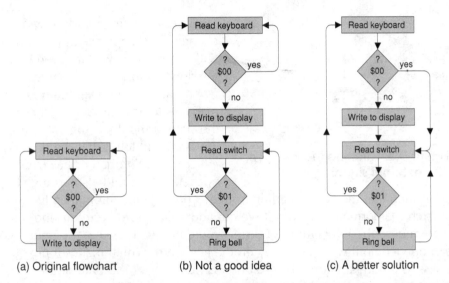

Figure D.2: Augmenting our program to monitor the switch and ring bell

In our first-pass solution (Figure D.2b), we might simply add the test to read the alarm switch onto the end of our original program, but this isn't a particularly good idea ...... can you see why? The problem is that this version of the program only checks the state of the switch *after* you activate a key on the keyboard. So while you're pondering which key to press, a burglar could have entered your abode and be creeping up behind you ......

Imagine the scene when you eventually press a key on the keyboard: the bell rings, you leap to your feet shouting *"Don't panic, we've got a burglar, don't panic,"* you turn around, and there he is! (This may well be the time when you contemplate investing in a better alarm system). As an alternative scenario, the burglar could slip into your house and close the door while you're contemplating the keyboard. In this case, the alarm won't be sounded even after you've pressed a key, because the door will be closed by the time the computer finally comes to look at it. So now you've got a burglar roaming wild and free throughout your house, while your computer is essentially saying: *"Don't worry about a thing my little fruit-bat, because the front door is safely closed."*

Jocularity aside, this latter point is quite important. A key aspect of external signals, such as the switch forming our burglar alarm, is that they're typically asynchronous. This means that they can occur at any time and are not synchronized to the computer system's clock, which therefore means that we usually have to latch such signals. In this particular scenario, we could place a latch between the switch and the port (Figure D.3).

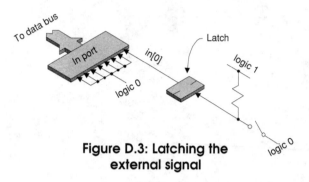

Figure D.3: Latching the external signal

The act of opening the door will change the state of the latch, which will retain this new state even when the door is closed again. Thus, when our program eventually manages to limp around to check the state of the door, the value in the latch will tell it that the door is either currently open or has been opened. (We could also arrange the circuit such that the act of reading from this port would automatically reset the latch). Unfortunately, even if we did add a latch to our circuit, the program described in Figure D.2b still would not warn us that the door has been opened until we press a key on the keyboard, which makes it next to useless as a burglar alarm. The solution is to check for the state of the door every time we go around the loop that tests to see if a key has been pressed (Figure D.2c).

Thus we see that ensuring the CPU recognizes the door's opening in a timely manner does require a little thought, and the problems can only become more pronounced as we increase the number of signals from the outside world. For example, we might decide to add burglar alarm switches to all of the doors and windows in our house. We might also decide to connect a few smoke detectors to our computer, and perhaps even add a sensor to warn us if the Jacuzzi in the master bedroom starts to overflow. Thus, we now have to perform a process known as *polling* (meaning surveying or sampling), which requires us to modify our program to check for each of these signals in turn (Figure D.4).

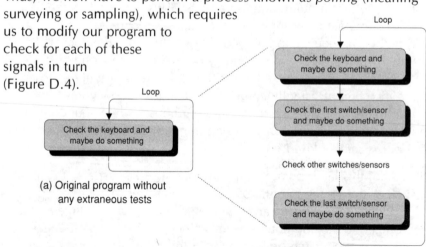

(a) Original program without any extraneous tests

(b) New program that checks lots of external signals

Figure D.4: Polling external signals

One thing we now have to consider is the relative priority of the various signals. For example, unlike the outline presented in Figure D.4b, we might decide that checking whether or not the house was on fire takes precedence over testing to see if a key had been pressed on the keyboard. In fact, we have to prioritize all of our external signals and determine the order in which they should be evaluated.

Another consideration is that our original program only contained one simple loop, but this could be a small portion of a larger program containing a multitude of loops and sub-loops (Figure D.5). In this case we'd probably bundle all of the switch/sensor tests into a subroutine, and then ensure that we called this subroutine at the appropriate point (or points) from within each loop.

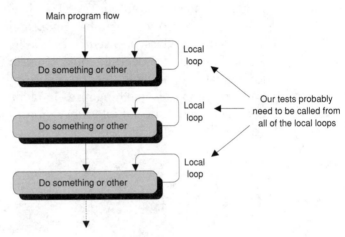

The end result is that, if we're not careful, we might spend more time thinking about when to call the tests for the external signals than we do creating the rest of the program. Also, if we decide to add any new switches or sensors (or remove any existing ones), then we will have to re-prioritize everything

Figure D.5: Larger program containing multiple loops

and update all of the programs that include these tests. Last but not least, our programs might expend more effort checking the switches and sensors than they do performing the tasks for which they are predominantly intended, which can be extremely inefficient, especially in those cases when the external conditions occur infrequently (how many times do we really expect the house to catch fire on an average day?). Thus, we have two somewhat contradictory requirements, in that we don't want our programs to spend the bulk of their time checking for conditions that will rarely transpire, but when something important does arise (such as a smoke detector being activated), then we want the computer to respond quickly and effectively.

The interrupt request (IRQ) input

Let's take a step back and re-think exactly what it is we're trying to do. We wish to create a program that can concentrate on the task for which it was intended, without being obliged to constantly check to see what's happening in the outside world. However, when an external situation meriting action does arise, then we want the computer's response to be fast and furious.

Bearing this in mind, let's return to our original program that loops around reading characters from our QWERTY keyboard and writing them to our display. Let's also regress to having a single external signal to worry about, such as the burglar alarm switch on the front door. What we really want is for our program to spend the bulk of its time dealing with the keyboard, and for the act of opening the door to interrupt whatever the computer is doing and force it to do something else. To facilitate this sort of thing, CPUs are equipped with a special *interrupt request* input, or IRQ for short (some CPUs have multiple IRQs, but we'll leave this point for later) (Figure D.6).

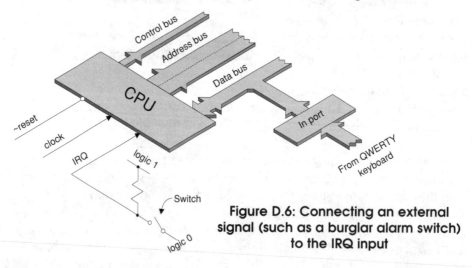

Figure D.6: Connecting an external signal (such as a burglar alarm switch) to the IRQ input

When the IRQ enters its active state, this fact is stored in a special latching circuit inside the CPU, thereby circumventing the problem of the IRQ going inactive before the CPU manages to check it (this is similar to the external latch we considered in Figure D.3, except that this one's inside the CPU). In some CPUs this interrupt latch can be programmed to look for active-high (*logic 1*) or active-low (*logic 0*) signals, but many simply assume that the IRQ's active state is a *logic 0*.

The CPU also contains a special status flag called the *interrupt mask*,[3] which is used to enable or disable interrupts, and which can be set or cleared under program control. For example, the *Beboputer* has two instructions, **SETIM** and **CLRIM**, which set or clear its interrupt mask, respectively. By default, the CPU powers up with the interrupt mask in its inactive state (which is typically a *logic 0*). Thus, in order for the CPU to be able to "see" an IRQ, the programmer has to use a **SETIM** ("*set interrupt mask*") instruction to place the mask in its active state. Similarly, if the programmer subsequently wishes to prevent the CPU from responding to IRQs, then he or she can use a **CLRIM** ("*clear interrupt mask*") instruction to return the mask to its inactive state.

The CPU checks the state of the interrupt mask every time it completes a machine-code level instruction. If the mask is inactive the CPU simply proceeds to the next instruction; but if the mask is active, then the CPU takes a peek inside the interrupt latch to determine whether or not an interrupt has been requested (Figure D.7).

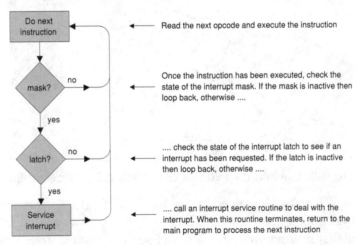

Figure D.7: High-level flowchart for interrupt handling

When the CPU does decide to service an interrupt it has to perform a sequence of tasks. At a minimum it has to push a copy of the current contents of the program counter onto the top of the stack, followed by a copy of the contents of the status register. The CPU next places the interrupt mask into its inactive state, thereby preventing any subsequent activity on the IRQ input from confusing the issue (we'll discuss this in more detail later). Some CPUs also push copies of one or more of the other internal

[3]The status register and the interrupt mask were introduced in Chapter 8.

registers onto the stack, such as the accumulator and the index register, because there's a good chance that the act of servicing the interrupt will modify the contents of these registers. If the CPU doesn't do this automatically, then it's up to the programmer to save the contents of any registers he or she deems to be important as soon as the interrupt service routine is entered.

But what is an interrupt service routine and where might one be found? In fact this routine, which is very similar to a subroutine, is a sequence of instructions that has been created by the programmer and stored somewhere in the computer's memory. As soon as the CPU has placed copies of the program counter and status register (and any other registers) on the top of the stack, it loads a hard-wired address into the program counter, then uses this address to point to a location in memory (Figure D.8).

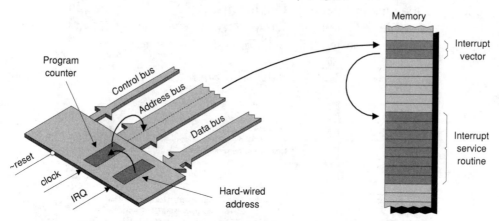

Figure D.8: The interrupt vector and interrupt service routine

The location in memory identified by the hard-wired address contains the first byte of yet another address called the interrupt vector, which, in turn, points to the first instruction in the interrupt service routine. Thus, the CPU effectively uses its hard-wired address to perform an unconditional jump using the indirect addressing mode, which eventually leaves it at the beginning of the interrupt service routine. Note that the interrupt vector may be stored in either the RAM or the ROM, as can the interrupt service routine; it all depends on how the system is being used.

Once the interrupt service routine has performed whatever actions are required to deal with the interrupt, it can be terminated using an RTI ("*return from interrupt*") instruction. This is similar to an RTS ("*return from subroutine*") instruction, except that it reloads the status register with whatever byte is residing on the top of the stack before loading the program counter with the return address from the stack. Also, if the CPU is of a type that automatically pushes the contents of any other registers onto the stack following an interrupt request, then these registers would also be restored from the stack before loading the program counter with the return address.

One advantage of using this sort of interrupt strategy is that (to a large extent) the interrupt service routine is distinct from main program, so it's conceptually much simpler to develop, maintain, and update. Also, we are now in a position to design the body of our program to concentrate on a certain task without explicitly having to monitor what's going on in the outside world. When an external event occurs that requires attention, the CPU automatically hands control over to the interrupt service routine; and when this routine has finished dealing with the interrupt it returns control to the main program, which picks up the main program where it left off.

Non-maskable interrupts (NMIs)

In addition to the interrupt request input discussed above, many processors also sport a *non-maskable interrupt (NMI)*, which has its own latch within the CPU (Figure D.9).

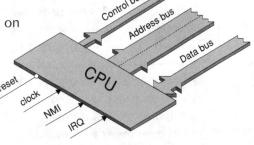

As it's name might suggest, an active event on the NMI will always cause the CPU to respond, irrespective of the state of the interrupt mask. Thus, the flowchart shown in Figure D.7 would now be modified to include a test for the NMI before the test for the interrupt mask, and the NMI therefore has a higher precedence than an IRQ. Apart from the fact that it can't be masked, the system

Figure D.9: The non-maskable interrupt (NMI) input

responds to an NMI in much the same way that it handles an IRQ, the only difference being that the NMI has its own hard-wired address inside the CPU; this new hard-wired address points to a separate interrupt vector in the system's memory; and this second interrupt vector points to its own interrupt service routine.

The non-maskable interrupt tends to be used in mission-critical circumstances. For example, we might decide that an alert from a smoke detector takes priority over a warning that the Jacuzzi is overflowing. For the sake of discussion, let's assume your Jacuzzi does begin to overflow, and a short time later the resulting deluge shorts out a power point and starts a fire (yes, it's turning out to be yet another "*one of those days*"). The problem is that when the CPU "sees" the IRQ generated by the Jacuzzi, it will immediately leap into action and start performing the appropriate interrupt service routine. But, as you may recall, one of the first things the CPU does when it responds to an IRQ is to disable the interrupt mask, thereby preventing any other IRQs from being seen (we'll consider ways to get around this later). So if the smoke detector also generated an IRQ, the computer wouldn't see it because it would be too busy working on the Jacuzzi problem. However, if the smoke detector generates an NMI, then this will take precedence over anything else that the computer is doing, including servicing an IRQ.[4]

Software interrupts (SWIs)

Generally speaking we regard an interrupt as being caused by an external event as discussed above. However, some CPU instruction sets include special instructions to trigger an interrupt from within the program, and these are known as *software interrupts (SWIs)*. If the CPU supports both IRQs and NMIs, then there may be equivalent SWI instructions for each type.

SWIs have a variety of uses, not the least that they allow the programmer to perform some level of testing on the interrupt service routines without having to physically trigger an external interrupt (such as burning the house down). Also, these instructions may find application in debugging the body of a program. For example, we could create an interrupt service routine whose only task was to display the current values of the CPU's registers on some form of output device (such as our memory mapped display). We could then insert SWI instructions at strategic locations within our program, such that whenever the CPU sees one of these instructions it will leap to the interrupt service routine, display the current contents of the registers, then return to the body of the program.

The HALT instruction

All of the program examples in this book have required the CPU to be constantly doing something, such as looping around reading an input port and waiting until it sees a certain value. However, it sometimes happens that the only thing we actually want the CPU to do is to wait for an interrupt to occur and then service it. Of course, we could achieve this in our

---

[4]If CPU has NMI input but we're not using it, then we can just "tie it off" to its inactive state.

program by creating some sort of a dummy loop; consider the following assembly statement (Figure D.10a).

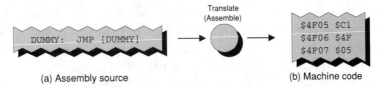

(a) Assembly source   (b) Machine code

Figure D.10: Creating a dummy loop

Once this has been assembled into machine code (Figure D.10b), it will cause the CPU to continuously perform unconditional jumps back to itself. In this example we're assuming that the DUMMY label occurs at address $4F05, so the resulting machine code contains a $C1 opcode at $4F05, where $C1 equates to a **JMP** (*"unconditional jump"*) instruction. The two operand bytes $4F and $05 cause the CPU to return to address $4F05, from whence it reads the $C1 opcode again, and ...... so it goes.

The only way to break out of this loop is to call an interrupt or reset the computer (where the latter option is a somewhat stern measure). Unfortunately, when we do call an interrupt, the CPU will automatically push the return address $4F05 onto the top of the stack. So once the interrupt service routine has completed its task, it will return control to address $4F05 and the CPU will return to mindlessly looping around, which means that it will never be able to proceed to the instruction following the loop. We could get around this by causing the interrupt service routine to finagle the return address on the top of the stack, but this is both aesthetically unpleasing and intellectually unsatisfying.

The solution is to replace our dummy loop with a **HALT** instruction, which uses the implied addressing mode and only occupies a single byte in memory. When the CPU sees a **HALT**, it stops executing the program and commences to generate internal **NOP** (*"no-operation"*) instructions. Once again, the only way to break out of the **HALT** is to call an interrupt or to reset the computer. However, during the process of reading the **HALT** opcode, the CPU automatically increments the program counter to point to the next instruction. Thus, when an interrupt occurs, the return address placed on the stack will be for the instruction following the **HALT** (pretty cunning, huh?).

The interrupt acknowledge (IACK) output

Until now we've been considering the source of our interrupt requests to be simple devices such as switches and sensors, but this is not necessarily the case. In some circumstances the interrupt request may come from a more sophisticated device, and this device may have more than a passing interest in knowing when the CPU begins to respond to its request. Thus, CPUs are typically equipped with an *interrupt acknowledge (IACK)* output (Figure D.11).

Assuming that all of our control signals are active-low (which is usually the case), the game commences when the external device places a *logic 0* value on either the IRQ or the NMI inputs. In turn, as soon as it starts to respond to the interrupt request, the CPU drives a *logic 0* onto its IACK output, thereby informing the external device that its plea for attention has been heard and is being acted upon. Once the CPU has finished servicing the interrupt, it returns the IACK output to a *logic 1*, which tells the external devices that the CPU is now willing and able to accept a new interrupt.

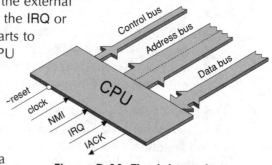

Figure D.11: The interrupt acknowledge (IACK) output

Interrupt-driven Input/Output

During our investigations of devices such as a QWERTY keyboard (Chapter 10), we've tended to handle them using a polling strategy. For example, we've created programs that loop around reading the port connected to the keyboard until a key has been pressed; then we've passed the code for this key to an output device (such as our memory-mapped display) and returned to looping around waiting for the next key.

But a modern computer can execute many millions of instructions a second, which means that 99.9% of the time our CPU is just hanging around twiddling its metaphorical thumbs. This is not to say that there's anything particularly wrong with this technique, providing we only want to perform simple tasks like copying characters from the keyboard to the display. However, instead of recklessly squandering all of this processing power, we might wish to employ it in a gainful way. For example, while the CPU is waiting for us to press the next key, we could be using it to perform some useful task like reformatting the contents of the display to line all of the words up nicely.

The problem is that if we do create a routine to reformat the screen, then this routine will need to keep on checking the keyboard to see if we've pressed another key. What we'd really like is to leave the reformatting routine free to perform its machinations, and break in as soon as a key is pressed on the keyboard. Just a moment, doesn't this sound suspiciously like a task for an interrupt? In fact, that's exactly where we're leading, in that we could easily equip our keyboard with the ability to generate an interrupt whenever a key is pressed (Figure D.12).

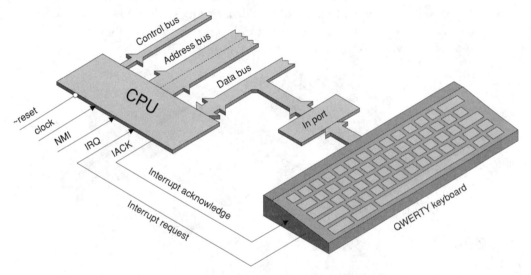

Figure D.12: Interrupt-driven I/O

In this scenario, the CPU can be happily performing some task or other without having to monitor the state of the keyboard. Whenever a key is pressed, the keyboard would issue an interrupt request, which would cause the CPU to hand control over to the associated interrupt service routine. In turn, this routine would read the input port connected to the keyboard, copy the resulting value to the display, then return control to the main program. Also, when the CPU starts to respond to the interrupt request, it would activate its interrupt acknowledge output, thereby informing the keyboard that things were on the move. As soon as the service routine had terminated, the CPU would return the interrupt acknowledge to its inactive state, which would inform the keyboard that it is now free to clear its internal latch.

This type of interrupt-driven input control is quite common with devices such as the keyboard and the mouse. Similarly, output devices might generate interrupts to inform the CPU when they are ready to accept more data. Of course, this implies that multiple devices might be generating interrupt requests, but our example CPU only supports a single IRQ input, which means that we need to come up with a cunning ruse ....

Handling multiple interrupt request signals

Let's assume that our CPU only has a single IRQ input, but that we have two external devices that wish to generate interrupt requests. One technique we can use to achieve this is to connect both of these signals together in what is referred to as a wired-AND configuration (Figure D.13).

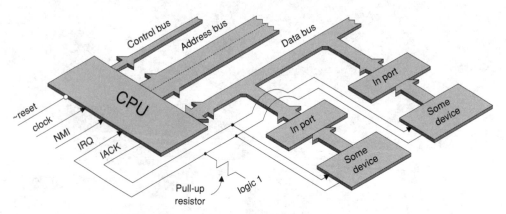

Figure D.13: Connecting multiple devices to the IRQ input

The idea here is to modify each of the external devices such that when they aren't calling for an interrupt, they effectively disconnect themselves from the IRQ signal, which is therefore coerced to a weak *logic 1* value (it's inactive state) by the pull-up resistor. However, if one of the devices does wish to call an interrupt, it can overpower the pull-up resistor by driving a strong *logic 0* onto the wire. Also, the interrupt acknowledge output from the CPU can be connected to both of the external devices, thereby allowing each of them to tell if one of their number has already called an interrupt.

The advantage of this scheme is that it's relatively easy to hook additional devices up to the interrupt request signal. The disadvantage is that when the CPU receives an interrupt request, it doesn't actually know which of the devices called it, so the interrupt service routine's first task is to check each device in turn to determine which device is attempting to gain the CPU's attention (using some type of polling strategy as discussed at the beginning of this appendix).

An alternative technique for handling multiple interrupts is to simply equip the CPU with more IRQ inputs, each with its own interrupt latch, hard-wired address, interrupt vector, and interrupt service routine. In this case, the CPU's status register would now contain individual interrupt mask flags for each of the IRQ inputs.

Priority encoding

As we noted early in this chapter, there are many different strategies for handling interrupts and it isn't possible to cover them all here. However, it would be remiss of us to neglect the topic of priority encoding, if only because it's quite an interesting subject. We commence by attaching a special device called a priority encoder to the data bus (Figure D.14).

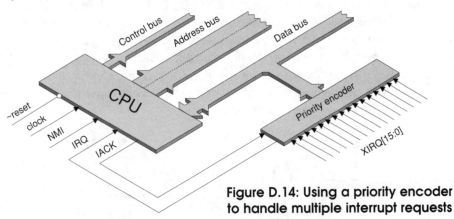

**Figure D.14: Using a priority encoder
to handle multiple interrupt requests**

In this particular example our priority encoder accepts sixteen external interrupt request inputs called XIRQ[15:0] (where 'X' stands for "external") and, if any of these signals becomes active, the encoder generates a master interrupt request which is fed to the CPU. One of the first things the CPU does when it receives a master interrupt request is to read a value from the priority encoder which, in this instance, acts in a similar manner to an input port. (As for a standard input port, the priority encoder would have an ~read_enable input which would be decoded from the address and control busses, but this isn't shown here for reasons of clarity).

Now here's one of the clever bits. The priority encoder converts its sixteen inputs into a 4-bit binary code (the most-significant four bits of the data byte can be set to *logic 0*), and it's this code the CPU sees when it reads a value from the encoder (Figure D.15).

XIRQ[15:0]	data[7:0]
0000000000000001	00000000
0000000000000010	00000001
0000000000000100	00000010
0000000000001000	00000011
0000000000010000	00000100
0000000000100000	00000101
0000000001000000	00000110
0000000010000000	00000111
0000000100000000	00001000
0000001000000000	00001001
:	:
etc	etc

Figure D.15: Codes generated by priority encoder

Note that this figure only illustrate those cases in which a single external interrupt request is activated; we'll consider what happens when multiple interrupts occur in a little while (also note that we're going to simplify things just a tad for the sake of understandability). Somewhere in the system's memory are sixteen interrupt vectors organized as a table, and the hard-wired address in the CPU points to the "base" interrupt vector in this table (Figure D.16a). When the CPU receives an interrupt request and reads the value from the priority encoder, it adds this value to its hard-wired address, thereby generating a new address which points to the appropriate interrupt vector in the table (Figure D.16b). This combined address is then loaded into the program counter and used by the CPU to retrieve an interrupt vector, which in turn points to the appropriate interrupt service routine.

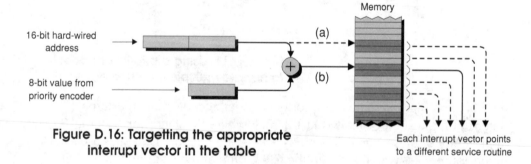

16-bit hard-wired address

8-bit value from priority encoder

(a)

(b)

Memory

Each interrupt vector points to a different service routine

Figure D.16: Targetting the appropriate interrupt vector in the table

One small point to consider is that, if we assume that our CPU has a 16-bit address bus and an 8-bit data word, then each interrupt vector will occupy two bytes in memory, which means that the CPU has to multiply the value from the priority encoder by two before adding it to the hard-wired address (it can easily achieve this by automatically shifting the value left by one bit).

All of this can be a little tricky to understand at first, so let's walk through a simple example. Purely for the sake of discussion, we'll assume that the base address of the interrupt vector table is located at address $9000, which is therefore the value represented by the CPU's hard-wired address. This means that the first interrupt vector occupies addresses $9000 and $9001, the second interrupt vector occupies $9002 and $9003, the third occupies $9004 and $9005, and so forth.

Now assume that the external device connected to the XIRQ[2] signal requests an interrupt, which causes the priority encoder to activate the main interrupt request signal to the CPU. After completing its current instruction, the CPU pushes the values in its program counter and status register onto the stack, and then reads a value from the priority encoder. As XIRQ[2] was the signal that called the interrupt, the code generated by the encoder will be $02 (or 00000010 in binary). The CPU multiplies this value by two (by shifting it one bit to the left) to generate $04 (or 00000100 in binary). The CPU then adds this value to the hard-wired address to generate a new address of $9004, which it loads into the program counter in order to point to the appropriate interrupt vector. Finally, the CPU performs an unconditional jump to address $9004 using the indirect addressing mode, which causes it to end up at the first instruction in the relevant interrupt service routine.

Let's now return to consider what happens if the priority encoder receives multiple requests on its sixteen XIRQ[15:0] inputs, of which there are 2^{16} = 65,536 potential combinations. By some strange quirk of fate, the reason this device is called a priority encoder is that it prioritizes things. Let's assume that, by default, XIRQ[0] is considered to have a higher priority than XIRQ[1], which, in turn, has a higher priority than XIRQ[2], and so forth. Thus, if the priority encoder should happen to simultaneously receive interrupt requests on XIRQ[15], XIRQ[12], and XIRQ[9], the value it eventually hands over to the CPU will be the $09 (or 00001001 in binary) corresponding to XIRQ[9], because this input has the higher priority.

Also, if the system is already dealing with an interrupt when another, higher-priority interrupt occurs, then there are techniques we can use to permit this new signal to interrupt the first (but you'll forgive us if we don't go into that here). Another interesting point is that the CPU can *write* values to the priority encoder, because, in addition to acting like an input port, this device can also behave in a similar fashion to an output port. Why would we wish to do this? Well, one common scenario is that the priority encoder would contain its own 16-bit interrupt mask register (completely distinct from the interrupt mask in the CPU), thereby giving it the power to enable or disable the external interrupt requests on an individual basis. For example, if we loaded this interrupt mask register to contain 0000 0100 0000 1001 in binary, then the priority encoder would only respond to interrupt requests on the XIRQ[10], XIRQ[3], and XIRQ[0], signals. The next problem relates to how the CPU can address this 2-byte field in order to write to it when our data bus is only 8-bits wide. As is usually the case, there are a number of alternatives; for example, we could trick the system into thinking that the priority encoder was actually two separate output ports, one for each byte in its interrupt mask register, where each of these "ports" would have it's own address in the memory map and its own ~write_enable input on the device.[5]

The *Beboputer's* interrupt capability

The *Beboputer* has a relatively simple interrupt structure, in that it only sports a single IRQ input (with an associated interrupt latch and interrupt mask bit in the status register), but it doesn't support an NMI input and it doesn't provide an IACK output. Also, the *Beboputer* doesn't employ a hard-wired interrupt address pointing to an interrupt vector in the system's memory. Instead, it contains a 16-bit interrupt vector (IV) register, which has to be loaded under program control using a BLDIV instruction. Having the interrupt vector inside the *Beboputer* isn't a particularly common technique, but there's no rule book that says a CPU cannot be implemented this way.

The *Beboputer's* IRQ input is controlled by the interrupt icon on the toolbar. Every time you click this icon with your mouse, it generates an active pulse on the IRQ signal, and this event is stored in the interrupt latch inside the CPU. When the *Beboputer* powers-up or is reset, its interrupt mask is cleared to a *logic 0*, thereby disabling the CPU's ability to see an interrupt. This means that if we want the *Beboputer* to respond to an interrupt, we first have to use a SETIM ("*set interrupt mask*") instruction, which loads the interrupt mask with a *logic 1*.

Ensure that the CD-ROM accompanying this book is in the CD drive, then invoke the *Beboputer* in the usual way. We haven't provided a special laboratory project for this, so you'll have to bring up the appropriate tools and devices yourself. First call up the hex keypad and the CPU register

---

[5]Another common programmable option is the ability to individually configure each interrupt latch in the priority encoder to look for active-high or active-low interrupt request signals. Yet another alternative is the ability to re-prioritize the interrupts on the fly.

display, then use the output ports form to invoke the single and dual decoded 7-segment displays (which are located at addresses $F022 and $F023, respectively). Now activate the *Beboputer's* assembler and enter the following program:

```
# Program to test the Beboputer's interrupt capability
# First define addresses for the two output displays
SOLO7SEG:  .EQU    $F022     # Define addr for solo display
DUAL7SEG:  .EQU    $F023     # Define addr for dual display

# Here's the main body of the program
           .ORG    $4000     # Specify the program's origin
           BLDSP   $4FFF     # Load the stack pointer
           BLDIV   SERVICE   # Load the interrupt vector
           SETIM             # Enable interrupts
           LDA     $00       # Load accumulator with zero
MAINLOOP:  STA     [DUAL7SEG]  # Store accumulator to dual
                             # display
           INCA              # Increment the accumulator
           JMP     [MAINLOOP]  # Jump back and continue

# Here's the interrupt service routine
SERVICE:   PUSHA             # Push accumulator onto the
                             # stack
           LDA     $0F       # Load accumulator with
                             # decimal 15
SUBLOOP:   STA     [SOLO7SEG]  # Store accumulator to solo
                             # display
           DECA              # Decrement the accumulator
           JNN     [SUBLOOP] # If accumulator >= 0 loop back
           POPA              # Retrieve the original value
                             # in the accumulator off the
                             # stack
           RTI               # Return to the main program
# This is the end of the interrupt service routine

           .END              # End of the program
```

As we see, the main body of the program is quite simple. First we define a couple of constant labels called SOLO7SEG and DUAL7SEG, which we assign to the port addresses of our output displays. After defining the origin of the program to be $4000, we load the stack pointer with $4FFF and we initialize the interrupt vector by assigning the label SERVICE to it (the assembler will automatically substitute this label for the start address of our interrupt service routine which is defined later in the program). The final step in the initialization is to use a SETIM instruction to load the interrupt mask with a *logic 1*, thereby permitting the CPU to see an interrupt (the SETIM also clears the CPU's interrupt latch, so as to ensure that the CPU only responds to any new interrupt request).

The remainder of the main body of the program initializes the accumulator to contain zero, and then enters a loop which copies the contents of the accumulator to the dual 7-segment display, increments the accumulator, then jumps back to do it again. Thus, we expect to see our dual display counting up from $00 to $FF, at which point it will automatically wrap around to $00 (because the accumulator can't contain a value bigger than $FF) and start the count again.

The main body of the program will continue to loop around forever, unless the *Beboputer* is reset or an interrupt happens to disturb it. Remember that the CPU checks the state of the interrupt mask after every instruction and, as we've loaded the mask with a *logic 1* (using our **SETIM** instruction), it will then proceed to check the state of the interrupt latch. Thus, whenever we click the interrupt icon in the toolbar, the CPU will see the interrupt as soon as it finishes whatever instruction it's currently working on. At this point, the CPU will push the current contents of the program counter onto the stack, followed by the current contents of the status register. The CPU will then automatically load the interrupt mask with a *logic 0* to prevent additional interrupts from having any effect.

The first thing we do upon entering our interrupt service routine is to use a **PUSHA** instruction to push a copy of the current contents of the accumulator onto the stack. We do this because we know that this particular routine is going to modify the accumulator, which would interfere with the main body of the program when we eventually return to it. Purely for the sake of this example, the only task performed by our interrupt service routine is to count down from $0F to $00 on the solo 7-segment display. Once this has been completed, we use a **POPA** instruction to restore the contents of the accumulator to their original value when we entered the routine, followed by an **RTI** instruction to terminate the interrupt service routine and return us to the main body of the program. The RTI causes the CPU to pop the original value of the status register back off the stack, and to then restore the program counter from the stack. Note that the act of popping the status register off the stack will return the interrupt mask to a *logic 1* (which was its value when the status register was originally pushed onto the stack), thereby re-enabling the CPU's ability to see any future interrupts. Also, the other status flags will be returned to whatever states they were in at the point when the interrupt was first activated.

But enough of this idle chit-chat, let's run the program to see what happens first hand. Click the File pull-down in the assembler window followed by the Save As option, save this file under the name irupt_1.asm, then assemble it to generate the resulting irupt_1.ram file. Next click the **ON** button on the hex keypad to power up the *Beboputer*, then use the **Memory** pull-down to load the irupt_1.ram file into the *Beboputer's* RAM.

Ensure that the hex keypad's **Ad** (**Address**) button is active, enter the program's start address of $4000, and click the **Ru** (**Run**) button. This will cause the *Beboputer* to start counting and displaying the result on the dual 7-segment display. Whenever you're ready, click the interrupt icon in the tool bar. Observe that the dual display ceases counting, while the solo display commences to count down. As soon as the solo display reaches zero, the interrupt service routine returns control to the main body of the program, which resumes counting on the dual display.

There are two points we should note in regard to this interrupt service routine example. First, clicking the interrupt icon has no significant effect whilst we're currently servicing an interrupt, because the interrupt mask was automatically disabled (loaded with a *logic 0*) by the CPU when it began to respond to the first interrupt. Second, the act of returning from the interrupt service routine automatically re-enables the CPU's ability to respond to future interrupts, because the status register's original contents are restored from the stack, and these contents include the fact that the interrupt mask originally contained a *logic 1*. Test both of these features for yourself, then break out of this program by clicking the *Beboputer's* **Rst** (**Reset**) button.

Two last tricks before we close

The behavior presented in the previous paragraph reflects the way in which CPUs typically handle interrupts by default, but we can modify this behavior if we wish. For example, suppose that we only want the *Beboputer* to respond to the first interrupt it sees, but for any subsequent interrupts to be ignored. To achieve this requires us to modify the value of the interrupt mask that is stored on the top of the stack when the interrupt service routine is called the first time. To illustrate this process, consider a new version of our interrupt service routine as follows:

```
# Second version of the interrupt service routine (this
# one only services one interrupt then disables itself).
SERVICE:    STA     [TEMPACC]  # Store accumulator to temp
                               # location
            POPA               # Retrieve status contents from
                               # stack
            AND     $EF        # Clear the interrupt mask
            PUSHA              # Return status contents to the
                               # stack
```

```
               LDA     $0F          # Load accumulator with decimal 15
   SUBLOOP:    STA     [SOLO7SEG]   # Store accumulator to solo
                                    # display
               DECA                 # Decrement the accumulator
               JNN     [SUBLOOP]    # If accumulator >= 0 loop back
               LDA     [TEMPACC]    # Retrieve the original value
                                    # in the accumulator off the stack
               RTI                  # Return to the main program
   TEMPACC:    .BYTE                # Reserve a temporary location
        # This is the end of the interrupt service routine
```

In this version, the first instruction in the service routine stores the contents of the accumulator to a temporary location called TEMPACC. The reason we don't want to push the accumulator onto the stack as we did before is that we wish to have access to the original contents of the status register, which are presently on the top of the stack. The second instruction is a POPA, which retrieves the old contents of the status register from the top of the stack and copies them into the accumulator. Next we AND the contents of the accumulator with $EF, which has the effect of clearing bit[4], the interrupt mask, to a *logic 0*. Finally, we use a PUSHA to place the new contents of the accumulator back onto the top of the stack.

The remainder of the routine is almost identical to our first version, except that before executing the RTI instruction, we restore the original contents of the accumulator from our temporary location instead of from the top of the stack.

All of this means that when we do eventually execute the RTI instruction, and the CPU reloads the status register with the byte on the top of the stack, the interrupt mask bit will now contain a *logic 0*, thereby preventing any future interrupts from being seen. You can test this by modifying the original program to reflect our changes, saving it to irupt_2.asm, assembling it, and loading the resulting irupt_2.ram file into the RAM as before. When you run this new version, the dual display begins to count as usual. Similarly, when you click the interrupt icon, the interrupt service routine counts down from $0F to $00 on the solo display, and then returns control to the main program. However, nothing will happen if you click the interrupt icon again, because our machinations have caused the interrupt service routine to leave the interrupt mask containing a *logic 0*. Before moving on, break out of the program by clicking the *Beboputer's* Rst (Reset) button.

Finally, let's suppose that we wish to be able to respond to a second interrupt whilst we're already in the process of responding to an interrupt.

The easiest way to explain this is to look at an example assembly program as follows:

```
# Yet another program to test the Beboputer's interrupt
# capability. This one supports a nested interrupt
SOLO7SEG:  .EQU   $F022        # Define addr for solo display
DUAL7SEG:  .EQU   $F023        # Define addr for dual display
EIGHTLED:  .EQU   $F020        # Define addr of 8-bit LED display
# Here's the main body of the program
           .ORG   $4000        # Specify the program's origin
           BLDSP  $4FFF        # Load the stack pointer
           BLDIV  SERVICEA     # Load the first interrupt
                               # vector
           SETIM               # Enable interrupts
           LDA    $00          # Load accumulator with zero
MAINLOOP:  STA    [DUAL7SEG]   # Store accumulator to dual
                               # display
           INCA                # Increment the accumulator
           JMP    [MAINLOOP]   # Jump back and continue
# Here's the first interrupt service routine
SERVICEA:  PUSHA               # Push accumulator onto the stack
           BLDIV  SERVICEB     # Load the second interrupt vector
           SETIM               # Re-enable interrupts
           LDA    $0F          # Load accumulator with decimal 15
SUBLOOPA:  STA    [SOLO7SEG]   # Store accumulator to solo
                               # display
           DECA                # Decrement the accumulator
           JNN    [SUBLOOPA]   # If accumulator >= 0 loop back
           CLRIM               # Disable interrupts
           BLDIV  SERVICEA     # Reload the first interrupt
                               # vector
           POPA                # Retrieve the original value
                               # in the accumulator off the
                               # stack
           RTI                 # Return to the main program
# This is the end of the first interrupt service routine
# Here's the second interrupt service routine
SERVICEB:  PUSHA               # Push accumulator onto the stack
           LDA    $0F          # Load accumulator with decimal 15
SUBLOOPB:  STA    [EIGHTLED]   # Store accumulator to 8-bit
                               # display
           DECA                # Decrement the accumulator
           JNN    [SUBLOOPB]   # If accumulator >= 0 loop back
           POPA                # Retrieve the original value
                               # in the accumulator off the stack
           RTI                 # Return to first service routine
# This is the end of the second interrupt service routine
           .END                # End of the program
```

Now this is going to require a little thought, but it's really not too difficult. As usual, the main body of the program uses a BLDIV instruction to load the interrupt vector with the start address of our first interrupt service routine, which we've called SERVICEA in this program. The main body of the program then uses a SETIM instruction to enable the CPU to see an interrupt request, and it then starts to count on the dual 7-segment display.

When an interrupt occurs, the CPU responds as usual, by placing a copy of the program counter and status register onto the stack, clearing the interrupt mask to disable any future interrupts, copying the current contents of the interrupt vector into the program counter, and handing control off to the SERVICEA interrupt service routine.

The first action in the SERVICEA routine is to push the current contents of the accumulator onto the stack, so that when we eventually return to the main body of the program it will be able to continue counting from the point at which it left off. However, we now come to something interesting, in that we use a new BLDIV instruction to reload the interrupt vector with the start address or our second interrupt service routine, which we've called SERVICEB. This is followed by a new SETIM instruction which re-enables the CPU's ability to see an interrupt request.

Let's assume for the moment that no additional interrupt request is forthcoming (that is, no one clicks the interrupt icon until we return to the main body of the program), then SERVICEA will count down from $F to $0 on the solo 7-segment display as before. Once this count has finished, we use a CLRIM instruction to clear the interrupt mask followed by a BLDIV to re-load the interrupt vector with the start address of SERVICEA. Finally, we use a POPA to retrieve the original value of the accumulator off the stack and an RTI to return to the main body of the program.

Now let's consider what will happen if an interrupt request *does* occur while we're in the process of executing SERVICEA (assuming that it occurs after the BLDIV and SETIM instructions). In this case, the CPU will respond by placing a copy of the program counter and status register onto the *current* top of the stack, clearing the interrupt mask to disable any future interrupts, copying the current contents of the interrupt vector into the program counter, and handing control off to the SERVICEB routine.

Interestingly enough, our first task upon entering SERVICEB is to push the current contents of the accumulator onto the stack, so that when we eventually return to the SERVICEA routine it will be able to continue *its* count from the point at which it left off. Next we perform a simple count sequence using our 8-bit LED display (just to show that we're doing something), then we pop the accumulator off the stack and use an **RTI** to terminate **SERVICEB** and return us to **SERVICEA**, which will continue from the point at which it was interrupted.

All of this can seem a little convoluted at first, so it may be easier to understand when you see it actually happening. Use the assembler to enter our latest program, save it to irupt_3.asm, assemble it, and load the resulting irupt_3.ram file into the RAM as before. Remember that this new program requires the use of our 8-bit LED display, so use the output ports form to add this display to our ensemble.

> **Important:** Note that the reason we use the CLRIM before the BLDIV and POPA in the SERVICEA routine is to prevent the CPU from responding to an interrupt while we're preparing to return to the main body of the program. For example, consider what would happen if we omitted the CLRIM, and an interrupt occurred while we're in the middle of executing the BLDIV. In this case, the CPU would complete the BLDIV, and then respond to the interrupt request by jumping to SERVICEA whilst it's *still in* SERVICEA (not that there would be anything terribly wrong with this if it was what we were trying to do, but it's not).

When you first run this latest version of the program, the dual 7-segment display starts counting as before. Click once on the interrupt icon, which causes the main program to hand control to **SERVICEA**, which performs its count sequence on the solo display and then hands control back to the main program.

Now here's the clever part. Click the interrupt icon to invoke the **SERVICEA** routine, but this time, as soon as the solo display has commenced its count, click the interrupt icon again. This causes **SERVICEA** to pass control to **SERVICEB**, which performs *its* count sequence on the 8-bit display before returning control to **SERVICEA**, which in turn completes its actions before handing the baton back to the main program.

This concept of enabling a second interrupt to be attended to whilst another interrupt is already in the process of being serviced is referred to as *nested interrupts*. Note that the example above only showed a simple case of nesting, but we could extend this such that **SERVICEB** enabled another routine called **SERVICEC**, which in turn enabled **SERVICED**, and so forth.

Appendix E

The ASCII and EBCDIC
Character Sets

Contents of Appendix E

The ASCII character set

During the course of this book, we have repeatedly encountered the *American Standard Code for Information Interchange (ASCII)* (pronounced "ass-key") character set, particularly in regard to our discussions on the QWERTY keyboard and the memory-mapped display. This character set is summarized below, followed by illustrations showing the patterns we used to realize these characters for our memory-mapped display.[1] The meaning of the special control codes $00 through $1F are detailed in Chapter 10, while Chapter 11 explains the strange pattern we use to display these characters on the screen.

$00	NUL	$10	DLE	$20	SP	$30	0	$40	@	$50	P	$60	`	$70	p
$01	SOH	$11	DC1	$21	!	$31	1	$41	A	$51	Q	$61	a	$71	q
$02	STX	$12	DC2	$22	"	$32	2	$42	B	$52	R	$62	b	$72	r
$03	ETX	$13	DC3	$23	#	$33	3	$43	C	$53	S	$63	c	$73	s
$04	EOT	$14	DC4	$24	$	$34	4	$44	D	$54	T	$64	d	$74	t
$05	ENQ	$15	NAK	$25	%	$35	5	$45	E	$55	U	$65	e	$75	u
$06	ACK	$16	SYN	$26	&	$36	6	$46	F	$56	V	$66	f	$76	v
$07	BEL	$17	ETB	$27	'	$37	7	$47	G	$57	W	$67	g	$77	w
$08	BS	$18	CAN	$28	(	$38	8	$48	H	$58	X	$68	h	$78	x
$09	HT	$19	EM	$29	)	$39	9	$49	I	$59	Y	$69	i	$79	y
$0A	LF	$1A	SUB	$2A	*	$3A	:	$4A	J	$5A	Z	$6A	j	$7A	z
$0B	VT	$1B	ESC	$2B	+	$3B	;	$4B	K	$5B	[	$6B	k	$7B	{
$0C	FF	$1C	FS	$2C	,	$3C	<	$4C	L	$5C	\	$6C	l	$7C	|
$0D	CR	$1D	GS	$2D	-	$3D	=	$4D	M	$5D	]	$6D	m	$7D	}
$0E	SO	$1E	RS	$2E	.	$3E	>	$4E	N	$5E	^	$6E	n	$7E	~
$0F	SI	$1F	US	$2F	/	$3F	?	$4F	O	$5F	_	$6F	o	$7F	DEL

Table E.1: ASCII character codes

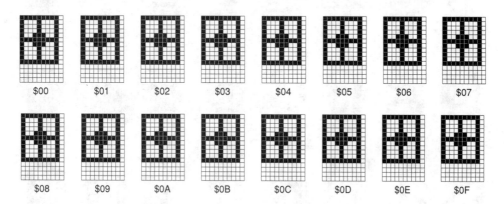

$00 $01 $02 $03 $04 $05 $06 $07

$08 $09 $0A $0B $0C $0D $0E $0F

---

[1]Don't forget that you have the ability to create your own character set for the memory-mapped display, as described in Chapter 13.

$10 $11 $12 $13 $14 $15 $16 $17

$18 $19 $1A $1B $1C $1D $1E $1F

$20 $21 $22 $23 $24 $25 $26 $27

$28 $29 $2A $2B $2C $2D $2E $2F

$30 $31 $32 $33 $34 $35 $36 $37

$38 $39 $3A $3B $3C $3D $3E $3F

$40 $41 $42 $43 $44 $45 $46 $47

$48 $49 $4A $4B $4C $4D $4E $4F

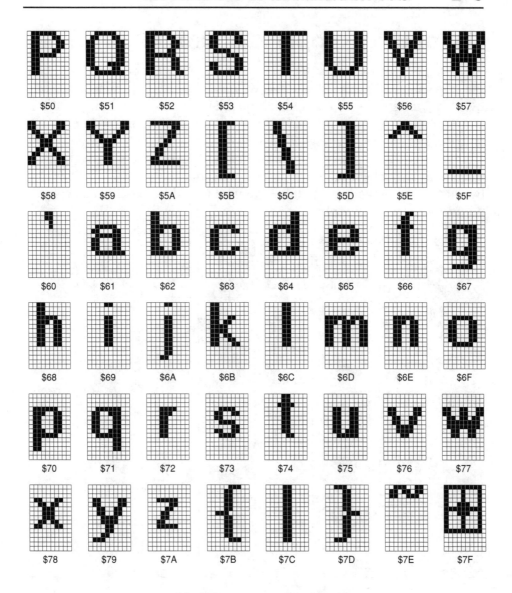

$50	$51	$52	$53	$54	$55	$56	$57
$58	$59	$5A	$5B	$5C	$5D	$5E	$5F
$60	$61	$62	$63	$64	$65	$66	$67
$68	$69	$6A	$6B	$6C	$6D	$6E	$6F
$70	$71	$72	$73	$74	$75	$76	$77
$78	$79	$7A	$7B	$7C	$7D	$7E	$7F

The chunky graphics character set

As we know from Chapters 10 and 11, ASCII is a 7-bit code, which only uses the values $00 through $7F. But we're storing these characters in 8-bit bytes, so we've still got values $80 through $FF to play with. Many of the early computers employed these spare characters to implement simple graphics and, as the resulting displays were somewhat "chunky," these were often referred to as *chunky graphics*. For your delectation and delight, the *Beboputer's* chunky graphic character set is summarized below, followed by illustrations showing the patterns we used to realize these characters for our memory-mapped display.[2]

$80	$90	$A0	$B0	$C0	$D0	$E0	$F0
$81	$91	$A1	$B1	$C1	$D1	$E1	$F1
$82	$92	$A2	$B2	$C2	$D2	$E2	$F2
$83	$93	$A3	$B3	$C3	$D3	$E3	$F3
$84	$94	$A4	$B4	$C4	$D4	$E4	$F4
$85	$95	$A5	$B5	$C5	$D5	$E5	$F5
$86	$96	$A6	$B6	$C6	$D6	$E6	$F6
$87	$97	$A7	$B7	$C7	$D7	$E7	$F7
$88	$98	$A8	$B8	$C8	$D8	$E8	$F8
$89	$99	$A9	$B9	$C9	$D9	$E9	$F9
$8A	$9A	$AA	$BA	$CA	$DA	$EA	$FA
$8B	$9B	$AB	$BB	$CB	$DB	$EB	$FB
$8C	$9C	$AC	$BC	$CC	$DC	$EC	$FC
$8D	$9D	$AD	$BD	$CD	$DD	$ED	$FD
$8E	$9E	$AE	$BE	$CE	$DE	$EE	$FE
$8F	$9F	$AF	$BF	$CF	$DF	$EF	$FF

Table E.2: Chunky graphics codes

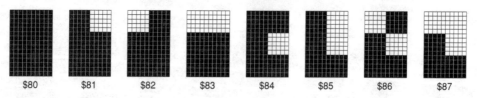

$80 $81 $82 $83 $84 $85 $86 $87

---

[2]Once again, don't forget that you have the ability to create your own character set for the memory-mapped display, as described in Chapter 13.

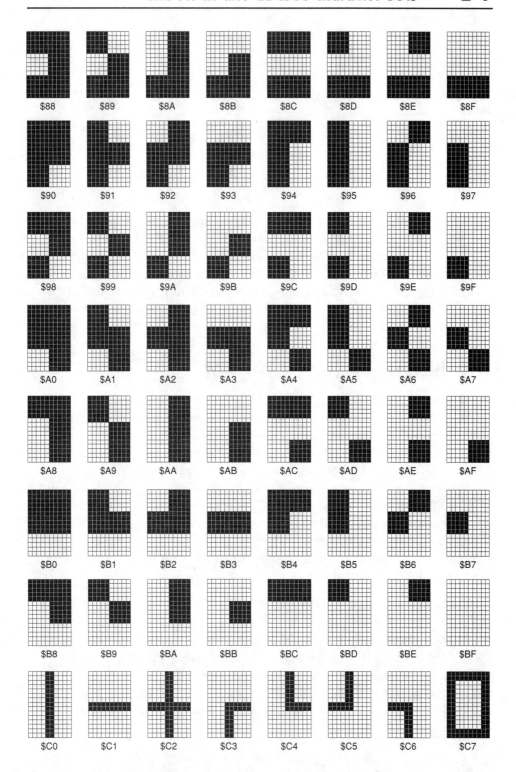

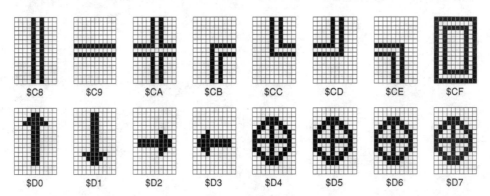

| $C8 | $C9 | $CA | $CB | $CC | $CD | $CE | $CF |

| $D0 | $D1 | $D2 | $D3 | $D4 | $D5 | $D6 | $D7 |

Note that the remaining characters occupying codes $D8 through $FF have identical patterns to those shown for codes $D4 through $D7 above. We used this distinctive pattern to distinguish these characters from spaces, in order to make them easy to recognize when they appear on your memory-mapped display. As we have created all of the chunky graphics that are of interest to us, we left these codes free for you to create your own characters (as discussed in Chapter 13).

The EBCDIC character set

The *Extended Binary Coded Decimal Interchange Code (EBCDIC)* (pronounced "ebb-sid-ick") was originally developed for use on the IBM 360 and 370 systems. A number of other systems subsequently adopted this code in order to remain compatible with IBM. EBCDIC has the advantage of being a true 8-bit code, but the discontinuities in the character set have brought many a bright-eyed programmer to the brink of despair. If the fates smile upon you, you'll never meet EBCDIC face to face. On the other hand, it's not completely beyond the bounds of possibility that you'll one day be obliged to tackle this monster in its lair, so the full EBCDIC character set is summarized in Table E.3 (although we offer our fervent hope that you'll never actually be forced to use it).

A brief glance at this table shows just why EBCDIC can be such a pain to use – the alphabetic characters don't have sequential codes. That is, the letters 'A' through 'I' occupy codes $C1 to $C9, 'J' through 'R' occupy codes $D1 to $D9, and 'S' through 'Z' occupy codes $E2 to $E9 (and similarly for the lowercase letters). With ASCII you can play a variety of programming tricks, such as using the expression ('A' + 23) and having a reasonable expectation of ending up with the letter 'X', but this type of ruse is a real pain with EBCDIC.[3]

1st hex digit

2nd hex digit	0	1	2	3	4	5	6	7	8	9	A	B	C	D	E	F
0	NUL	DLE	DS		SP	&	-									0
1	SOH	DC1	SOS			/			a	j			A	J		1
2	STX	DC2	FS	SYN					b	k	s		B	K	S	2
3	ETX	TM							c	l	t		C	L	T	3
4	PF	RES	BYP	PN					d	m	u		D	M	U	4
5	HT	NL	LF	RS					e	n	v		E	N	V	5
6	LC	BS	ETB	UC					f	o	w		F	O	W	6
7	DEL	IL	ESC	EOT					g	p	x		G	P	X	7
8		CAN							h	q	y		H	Q	Y	8
9		EM							i	r	z	`	I	R	Z	9
A	SMM	CC	SM		¢ CENT	!		:								
B	VT	CU1	CU2	CU3		$	,	#								
C	FF	IFS		DC4	<	*	%	@								
D	CR	IGS	ENQ	NAK	(	)	_	'								
E	SO	IRS	ACK		+	;	>	=								
F	SI	IUS	BEL	SUB	|	--	?	"								

Table E.3: EBCDIC character codes

As with ASCII, in addition to the standard alphanumeric characters ('A' … 'Z' and '0' … '9'), punctuation characters (comma, period, semi-colon, …), and special characters ('!', '#', '%', …), EBCDIC includes an awful lot of strange mnemonics, such as **ACK**, **NAK**, and **BEL**, which were designed for communications purposes. Some of these codes are still used today, while others are, generally speaking, of historical interest only. A slightly more detailed breakdown of these codes is presented in Table E.4 for your edification.

---

[3]Someone (who shall remain nameless) once told the authors that, for various unfathomable reasons, there were several versions of EBCDIC, but the methods of translating among them were kept a tip-top secret by IBM for decades.

ACK	Acknowledge		IGS	Interchange group separator
BEL	Bell		IL	Idle
BS	Backspace		IRS	Interchange record separator
BYP	Bypass		IUS	Interchange unit separator
CAN	Cancel		LC	Lowercase
CC	Cursor control		LF	Line feed
CR	Carriage return		NAK	Negative acknowledge
CU1	Customer use 1		NL	New line
CU2	Customer use 2		NUL	Null
CU3	Customer use 3		PF	Punch off
DC1	Device control 1		PN	Punch on
DC2	Device control 2		RES	Restore
DC4	Device control 4		RS	Reader stop
DEL	Delete		SI	Shift in
DLE	Data link escape		SM	Set mode
DS	Digit select		SMM	Start of manual message
EM	End of medium		SO	Shift out
ENQ	Enquiry		SOH	Start of heading
EOT	End of transmission		SOS	Start of significance
ESC	Escape		SP	Space
ETB	End of transmission block		STX	Start of text
ETX	End of text		SUB	Substitute
FF	Form feed		SYN	Synchronous idle
FS	Field separator		TM	Tape mark
HT (TAB)	Horizontal tab		UC	Uppercase
IFS	Interchange file separator		VT	Vertical tab

Table E.4: EBCDIC control characters

Harking back to our discussions on "perforated paper products" in Chapter 4, you may find codes such as PN ("Punch on") and PF ("Punch off") to be of particular nostalgic interest, because these codes were used to control devices such as readers and writers for paper tapes and punched cards.

Appendix F

The *Beboputer's* Assembly Language

Contents of Appendix F

Backus-Naur notation

The *Beboputer's* assembly language is defined using style of notation known as *Backus-Naur*. This allows us to represent the language using a combination of syntactic entities and meta-syntactic symbols, where the meta-syntactic symbols are used to define how the syntactic entities can be combined. An individual syntactic definition is composed of a name in *italic font*, followed by the definition symbol '≡' (meaning "*is defined as*"), followed by the definition itself; for example:

alpha_char ≡ '*A*' through '*Z*' and '*a*' through '*z*'

num_char ≡ '*0*' through '*9*'

alphanum_char ≡ *alpha_char* | *num_char*

These statements define three syntactic entities: *alpha_char*, *num_char*, and *alphanum_char*. The approach we employ is bottom-up, with fundamental items being defined in advance of any constructs that use them. Note that syntactic entities are only ever defined once, but they may be used multiple times in the definitions of subsequent entities. Also note the use of the | symbol in the third example. This is one of the meta-syntactic symbols, which are used to define how syntactic entities can be combined. The meanings of the meta-syntactic symbols are as follows:

| | Indicates alternative choices; for example:

alphanum_char ≡ *alpha_char* | *num_char*

This means that an *alphanum_char* can be either an *alpha_char* or a *num_char*.

{ ...... } Indicates part of a definition that can be repeated zero or many times; for example:

dec_literal ≡ *num_char*{*num_char*}

The first part of this definition means that a *dec_literal* must consist at least one *num_char*, while the second part enclosed by the {} symbols means that it may also contain zero or more additional instances of *num_char*.

(......) Indicates part of a definition that contains options separated by the | symbol; only one of the options can be selected;

also one of the options <u>must</u> be selected; for example:

$$address\_label \equiv (\_ \mid alpha\_char)\{label\_char\}$$

The first part of this definition enclosed by the ( ) symbols means that an *address_label* must commence with either an underscore character or an *alpha_char*, while the second part enclosed by the **{}** symbols means that it may also contain zero or more instances of *label_char*.

[......]   Indicates part of a definition that is optional; for example:

$$implied\_instruction \equiv [address\_label:]$$
$$implied\_mnemonic\ [comment]$$

This means that an implied_instruction consists of an optional *address_label*; followed by a mandatory *implied_mnemonic*; followed by an optional *comment*.

Note that you've got to be careful with some of the definitions, because in addition to being meta-syntactic, symbols such as **|**, **[ ]**, and **( )** are also part of the assembly language itself; for example:

$$absolute\_instruction \equiv [address\_label:]\ immediate\_mnemonic$$
$$[\ integer\_expression\ ]\ [comment]$$

Here we see that the *[ ]* characters used to delimit the *integer_expression* are part of the syntax of our assembly language, and are therefore presented in *10-point italic font*. This distinguishes them from their meta-syntactic cousins **[ ]**, which are presented in 14-point bold font.

Formal syntax summary

The remainder of this appendix is devoted to a syntactic summary of the *Beboputer's* assembly language described in the Backus-Naur representation introduced above. In an ideal world our Backus-Naur description would fully and completely define our language without requiring any augmentation; but in practice we discover that a few well-placed notes tend to ease the way considerably, and these notes are indicated by ☞ pointing finger characters.

Names (Labels)

alpha_char ≡ 'A' through 'Z' and 'a' through 'z'

num_char ≡ '0' through '9'

alphanum_char ≡ *alpha_char* | *num_char*

label_char ≡ *alphanum_char* | _

constant_label ≡ (_ | *alpha_char*){*label_char*}

address_label ≡ (_ | *alpha_char*){*label_char*}

any_label ≡ *constant_label* | *address_label*

☞ Both types of labels (*address_labels* and *constant_labels*) must commence with either an underscore '_' character or an alpha character. However, we recommend that *you* don't use an underscore as the first character in any of your labels, because this is how we distinguish labels in the pre-defined subroutines that we created for you (see also Appendix G).

☞ Although our syntax doesn't impose a limit on the length of labels, our current implementation restricts these entities to a maximum of eight characters including any underscores. Also, labels are not allowed to be one of our language's keywords (which are listed at the end of this appendix).

☞ Although the syntactic entity *alpha_char* includes both uppercase and lowercase characters, our assembler internally converts all characters to uppercase for the purposes of its machinations. Thus, *fred, Fred, FrEd,* and *FRED* will be considered to be identical.

Text, comments, and blank lines

horizontal_whitespace ≡ <tab> | <space>

vertical_whitespace ≡ <cr> | <lf> | <ff> {Carriage return, Line feed, Form feed}

blank_line ≡ {*horizontal_whitespace*} *vertical_whitespace*

extra_char ≡ ' | ' | " | ~ | ! | @ | # | $ | % | ^ | & | * | (|) | - | _ | = | + | \ | / | | | [|] | { | } | ; | : | . | , | < | > | ?

$$text\_char \equiv alphanum\_char \mid extra\_char \mid horizontal\_whitespace$$

$$comment \equiv \#\{text\_char\} \ vertical\_whitespace$$

☞ The *horizontal_whitespace* characters *<tab>* and *<space>* are equivalent to the keyboard keys of the same name, and they equate to the ASCII codes $09 and $20, respectively.

☞ The *vertical_whitespace* characters *<cr>*, *<lf>*, and *<ff>* ("carriage return," "line feed," and "form feed") equate to the ASCII codes $0D, $0A, and $0C, respectively. Note that *<cr>* may be called "return" or "enter" on your keyboard, while the other *vertical_whitespace* characters typically don't have keyboard equivalents.

☞ Comments can commence anywhere on an input line. A comment starts with a '#' character followed by any *text_chars*, and is terminated by any *vertical_whitespace* character.

Literals

$$bin\_num\_char \equiv \text{'0' through '1'}$$

$$hex\_num\_char \equiv \text{'0' through '9' and 'A' through 'F' (or 'a' through 'f')}$$

$$dec\_literal \equiv num\_char\{num\_char\}$$

$$bin\_literal \equiv \%bin\_num\_char\{bin\_num\_char\}$$

$$hex\_literal \equiv \$hex\_\ num\_char\{hex\_num\_char\}$$

$$integer\_ref \equiv dec\_literal \mid bin\_literal \mid hex\_literal \mid any\_label$$

☞ An *integer_ref* is either a *dec_literal* (decimal literal), *bin_literal* (binary literal), *hex_literal* (hexadecimal literal), or a label that's been assigned to such a literal or which equates to an address.

☞ Decimal literals are formed from one or more decimal digits with no spaces or commas between them (e.g. 32565 and not 32,565). Binary literals are formed from one or more binary digits, which must be prefixed by a '%' character (e.g. %00110101). Hexadecimal literals are formed from one or more hexadecimal digits, which must be prefixed by a '$' character (e.g. $E0A2). Note that no whitespace characters are permitted between the '%' and '$' characters and their associated arguments.

☞ All *integer_refs* are automatically padded with zeros to occupy four bytes within the assembler. An *integer_ref* (or the result of an expression using *integer_refs*) can be used as a data value, an address value, or both. In these cases the assembler will issue a warning if the value is too large for its intended purpose (this point is discussed in more detail in Chapter 12).

Expressions

arithmetic_operator ≡ + | – | * | / {Add, Subtract, Multiply, Divide}

logical_operator ≡ & | | | ^   {AND, OR, Exclusive-OR}

unary_ operator ≡ – | !   {Unary minus, Unary NOT)

any_operator ≡ *arithmetic_operator* | *logical_operator*

integer_primary ≡ *integer_ref* | *integer_expression* | @ |
          unary_operator integer_primary

integer_expression ≡ [( ] *integer_primary* {*any_operator*
          integer_primary} [ )]

☞ Note that *integer_primaries* are self-referential, in that they may be generated as a combination of a *unary_operator* (– or !) and another *integer_primary*. Also note that *integer_primaries* and *integer_expressions* are recursively defined in that they each refer to the other.

☞ The unary minus operator (which appears in the form –*integer_primary*) generates the two's complement of the *integer_primary* with which it is associated. The unary NOT operator (which would appear in the form !*integer_primary*) generates the one's complement of the *integer_primary* with which it is associated (that is, it inverts all of the bits in the *integer_primary*). Note that no space characters are allowed between a *unary_operator* and its *integer_primary*.

☞ Expressions in *declaration_statements* (see the directive statements section below) may not employ forward-referencing, but may only employ literals (binary, decimal, hexadecimal) and previously declared *constant_labels*. By comparison, expressions in *reserve_statements* or *instruction_statements* may use any type of label, including forward-references to *address_labels* (these points are discussed in more detail in Chapter 12).

☞ The *Beboputer's* assembler supports only a simple expression syntax, in which the binary operators +, −, *, /, &, |, and ^ all have equal precedence (the unary operators ! and − have a higher precedence than the binary operators). By default expressions are evaluated from left to right, so you have to use parenthesis ( ) to force particular ordering of any sub-expression evaluations.

☞ Although not apparent from the syntax above, parenthesis must be balanced. That is, any open bracket '(' must have a matching close bracket ')'.

☞ The results from any integer divisions will be truncated without warning (e.g., 8 / 3 will return 2); however, any attempt to divide by zero will cause the assembler to flag an error.

☞ The '@' character directs the assembler to substitute whatever value the program counter will contain at this point in the program. For example, consider the statement "JMP [@ + 6]", in which the "[@ + 6]" will be translated into the address of the JMP instruction's opcode plus 6.

Instruction mnemonics

> *implied_mnemonic* ≡ CLRIM | SETIM | INCA | DECA | INCX |
> DECX | HALT | NOP | PUSHA | POPA |
> PUSHSR | POPSR | SHL | SHR | ROLC |
> RORC | RTI | RTS

> *immediate_mnemonic* ≡ ADD | ADDC | SUB | SUBC | AND |
> OR | XOR | CMPA | LDA

> *big_immediate_mnemonic* ≡ BLDIV | BLDSP | BLDX

> *absolute_mnemonic* ≡ ADD | ADDC | SUB | SUBC | AND |
> OR | XOR | CMPA | LDA | STA | BLDIV |
> BLDSP | BLDX | BSTSP | BSTX | JC | JNC |
> JN | JNN | JO | JNO | JZ | JNZ | JMP | JSR

> *indexed_mnemonic* ≡ ADD | ADDC | SUB | SUBC | AND |
> OR | XOR | CMPA | LDA | STA | JMP |
> JSR

indirect_mnemonic ≡ LDA | STA | JMP | JSR

preindexed_indirect_mnemonic ≡ LDA | STA | JMP | JSR

indirect_postindexed_mnemonic ≡ LDA | STA | JMP | JSR

☞ We distinguish between *immediate_mnemonics* and *big_immediate_mnemonics*, because the former only require a single byte of data while the latter require two bytes of data. Thus, differentiating between these two groups allows our assembler to perform additional error checking.

Instruction statements

instruction_statement ≡ implied_instruction | immediate_instruction
    | big_immediate_instruction
    | absolute_instruction | indexed_instruction
    | indirect_instruction
    | preindexed_indirect_instruction
    | indirect_postindexed_instruction

implied_instruction ≡ [address_label:] implied_mnemonic [comment]

immediate_instruction ≡ [address_label:] immediate_mnemonic
    integer_expression [comment]

big_immediate_instruction ≡ [address_label:]
    big_immediate_mnemonic
    integer_expression [comment]

absolute_instruction ≡ [address_label:] immediate_mnemonic
    [integer_expression] [comment]

indexed_instruction ≡ [address_label:] indexed_mnemonic
    [integer_expression , X] [comment]

indirect_instruction ≡ [address_label:] indirect_mnemonic
    [[integer_expression]] [comment]

preindexed_indirect_instruction ≡ [*address_label:*]
 preindexed_indirect_mnemonic
 [[*integer_expression , X*]]
 [*comment*]

indirect_postindexed_instruction ≡ [*label:*]
 indirect_postindexed_mnemonic
 [[*integer_expression*] *, X*]
 [*comment*]

☞ In the absence of a comment, any instruction can have trailing *horizontal_whitespace* characters. Also, every instruction is terminated by a *vertical_whitespace* character.

☞ An *integer_expression* in an *instruction_statement* may employ forward-referencing. That is, these expressions may employ both *constant_labels* and *address_labels* (and, of course, literal values).

☞ The '*X*' character in the *indexed, preindexed indirect,* and *indirect postindexed* instruction statements is a special keyword that is understood by the assembler to refer to the index register, thereby causing the assembler to select the appropriate opcode for that instruction (see also the "Reserved words" section at the end of this appendix).

Directive statements

origin_statement ≡ *.ORG integer_ref* [*comment*]

end_statement ≡ *.END* [*comment*]

declaration_statement ≡ *constant_label: .EQU integer_expression*
 [*comment*]

reserve_statement ≡ [*address_label:*] (*.BYTE* | *.2BYTE* | *.4BYTE*)
 [**integer_expression* | *integer_expression*
 {*, integer_expression*}] [*comment*]

☞ An *integer_expression* in a *declaration_statement* may not employ any forward-referencing, but may only employ previously declared *integer_refs*. To put this another way, these expressions may only employ literal values or previously declared *constant_labels*.

☞ A ".BYTE" statement without an associated operand will reserve a single byte of memory for the program's future use. By comparison, a ".BYTE *n" will reserve 'n' bytes, where 'n' can either be a literal value (for example, ".BYTE *10", which will reserve ten bytes), or an integer expression (for example, ".BYTE *(FRED + 3)", which, assuming FRED equals 7, will also reserve ten bytes).

☞ By default, any locations set aside by *reserve_statements* will be initialized by the assembler to contain zero values. Alternatively, they may be explicitly initialized as part of the statement; for example, the statement ".BYTE 2, 32, 14, 42" will cause the assembler to reserve four bytes and initialize these bytes with the values 2, 32, 14, and 42, respectively. Additionally, any of the values in this comma-separated list could be full-blown *integer_expressions*.

☞ The ".2BYTE" and ".4BYTE" versions of *reserve_statements* work in a similar way to their ".BYTE" counterpart, except that (not surprisingly) they reserve two and four bytes, respectively. For example, the statement ".2BYTE $A42" will reserve a single 2-byte field and initialize that field to contain $0A42 (the assembler will automatically zero-extend the value to fit the 2-byte field). Note that our assembly language is based on a "big-endian" approach, in that multi-byte numbers are stored with their most-significant byte in the lowest address.[1]

File structure

declaration_section ≡ {declaration_statement | blank_line | comment}

body_statement ≡ reserve_statement | instruction_statement

body_section ≡ origin_statement {body_statement | blank_line | comment} end_statement

assembly_source_file ≡ declaration_section body_section
[{comment | blank_line}]

---

[1]See Chapters 12 and 15 for further discussions of the "big-endian" and "little-endian" concepts.

Reserved words

Although all of the reserved words are shown below in uppercase, they are in fact case-insensitive. Our assembler internally converts all characters to uppercase for the purposes of its machinations, and will therefore consider reserved words such as *add*, *Add*, and *ADD* to be identical.

Directive keywords

.ORG   .END   .EQU   .BYTE   .2BYTE   .4BYTE

Instruction keywords

ADD	ADDC	AND	BLDSP	BLDX	BLDIV	BSTSP	BSTX
CLRIM	CMPA	DECA	DECX	HALT	INCA	INCX	JC
JNC	JN	JNN	JO	JNO	JZ	JNZ	JMP
JSR	LDA	NOP	POPA	POPSR	PUSHA	PUSHSR	ROLC
RORC	RTI	RTS	SETIM	SHL	SHR	STA	SUB
SUBC	XOR						

Special keywords

The only special keyword is 'X', which is used when an instruction is employing one of the indexed addressing modes. There is no theoretical reason why a label could not be named 'X', or indeed given the same name as any of the instruction keywords. However, in practice, prohibiting such label names reduces confusion on the part of both the user and the assembler.

Appendix G

Assembly Language Subroutines

Contents of Appendix G

General-purpose subroutines

The concept of subroutines was first introduced in Chapter 8, and these little rascals have reappeared sporadically throughout subsequent chapters. But the examples we discussed during the course of the book have primarily been "one-of-a-kind" subroutines that we created on the fly to address particular requirements for specific programs. To remedy this situation, this appendix presents a small selection of general-purpose subroutines that are applicable to a wide variety of programs.

For your delectation and delight, we've created the routines introduced below and delivered them with the *Beboputer*. As we discussed in Chapter 12, you can insert these routines into your programs by means of the *Beboputer's* assembler (or indeed, any editor of your choice). If you have a modem and can access the Internet, you can also use the Web button on the *Beboputer's* toolbar to bounce over to our Web pages. Amongst myriad other goodies on these pages, you will also find additional subroutines that we'll be creating over the course of time. Also, if you feel moved to create any interesting programs or subroutines of your own, you can email the assembly source code to us at ***bebopbb@aol.com***. If we agree that your offerings will be of general interest, we will gladly add them to our web pages for other *Beboputer* users to peruse and download (see also the "*Subroutine label naming conventions*" section below).

Note that it will be to your advantage to wander through the following subroutines sequentially – starting at the beginning and strolling through the middle until you reach the end. The reason for this is that we've written copious notes for the earlier examples, but we've tried to avoid repeating the same discussions for identical points in later examples.

Finally, remember that nothing comes for free in this world. Although subroutines can be incredibly useful, there are always compromises involved in their deployment. So once you've waded through the examples, it would be well worth your while to spend a few moments glancing at the "*Tradeoffs involved in using subroutines*" section at the end of this appendix.

Subroutine label naming conventions

Before we start juggling without a safety-net, there's one more point we have to discuss, which revolves around the fact that our subroutines are going to have labels in them and so are your programs. Now some label names are really common, such as **LOOP**, **START**, or **RETADDR** ("*Return Address*"). Imagine the confusion if you included one of our subroutines in your main program, and both of us had used the same label name – the assembler would start frothing at its metaphorical mouth and it would be a pain to sort out. To avoid this problem, all of the labels in our subroutines commence with the underscore '_' character, which is why we recommended that you don't use this character for your own labels.

But wait, there's more. Some of our subroutines will be performing similar functions; for example _ADD16 and _SUB16, which add or subtract two 16-bit numbers, respectively. If we weren't careful, we might use the same label in both routines, which would mean that your program could only call one routine or the other, but not both. In the introduction above, we noted that you might wish to create your own subroutines and email them to us so that we can add them to our web pages for others to use, but this means that the potential for duplicate label names has just been magnified horrendously.

The answer to this conundrum is to establish some sort of naming convention we can all follow. The convention we've decided upon is that every label inside the body of our first subroutine will commence with the same four characters, which will be "_AA_". We can then use the last four characters in each label to distinguish between them; for example, _AA_VALA ("*Value A*"), _AA_VALB ("*Value B*"), _AA_RADD ("*Return Address*"). Similarly, every label inside the body of our second subroutine will commence with the characters "_AB_", every label in our third subroutine will commence with the characters "_AC_", and so on.

As there are 26 characters in the alphabet, we can happily create 26 x 26 = 676 different subroutines without any problems – we will call this "*Plan A*" to avoid confusion. In the unlikely event that we actually ever get around to creating so many subroutines that we start to run out of unique labels, then we'll adopt "*Plan B*" (we don't know what "*Plan B*" is yet, but you can bet that it will be a corker).

The main beauty of this scheme is that, now that you know it, you can use any labels you like in your own subroutines without fear that they'll clash with ours, so long as your labels don't commence with "_AA_", "_AB_", "_AC_", through "_ZZ_", which shouldn't unduly restrict your creative potential. In fact the only thing that we ask is that, if you do decide to email one of your subroutines to us for possible inclusion on our web pages, then please make sure that all of its labels have the same four characters, irrespective of what those characters may be. This will allow us to quickly modify your labels to adopt the next unique code in our sequence.

Last but not least, you should note that similar problems can occur when using higher level languages, and that the solution with modern systems is to limit the scope of names by declaring whether they're *local* (only available to a particular module) or *global* (available to multiple modules). (See also the discussions on the concepts of scope and namespaces in the *"Linking, loading, and relocatable code"* section of Chapter 12.)

16-bit Addition (_ADD16)

This subroutine retrieves two 16-bit numbers from the stack, adds them together, and places the 16-bit result on the top of the stack. It works for both signed and unsigned numbers, and assumes that all of the numbers are stored in the *Beboputer* style with the most significant byte "on top" of the least significant byte. Before considering _ADD16 itself, let's examine an example of a program that might call this subroutine:

```
# The following program declares two 16-bit numbers called VALUEA
# and VALUEB. The program sets things up in such a way that, when
# it calls the subroutine, VALUEA is added to VALUEB

            .ORG    $4000       # Start of program is address $4000

VALUEA:     .2BYTE  $3024       # Here's a 16-bit number
VALUEB:     .2BYTE  $8150       # Here's another 16-bit number
ANSWER:     .2BYTE              # Save a 16-bit field for the result
                                # Set everything up so that the
                                # subroutine will add VALUEA to
                                # VALUEB

            LDA     [VALUEB+1]  # Load ACC with the LS byte of
                                # VALUEB
            PUSHA               # Push this byte onto the stack
            LDA     [VALUEB]    # Load ACC with the MS byte of
                                # VALUEB
            PUSHA               # Push this byte onto the stack
            LDA     [VALUEA+1]  # Load ACC with the LS byte of
                                # VALUEA
            PUSHA               # Push this byte onto the stack
            LDA     [VALUEA]    # Load ACC with the MS byte of
                                # VALUEA
            PUSHA               # Push this byte onto the stack
            JSR     [_ADD16]    # Jump to the "_ADD16" subroutine
                                # and add VALUEA to VALUEB (the code
                                # for the subroutine would be
```

```
                                # somewhere else in the program)
         POPA                   # Retrieve the MS byte of the result
         STA      [ANSWER]      # from the stack and store it
         POPA                   # Retrieve the LS byte of the result
         STA      [ANSWER+1]    # from the stack and store it
          :        :                                :
```

Before calling the subroutine, we have to place the two 16-bit numbers that we want to add together on the stack ($3024 and $8150 in this example). The order in which the numbers are put on the stack doesn't particularly matter in the case of an addition, but both numbers must be placed on the stack with their least-significant bytes first, because this is the way in which the subroutine will expect them to arrive. After the subroutine has done its cunning stuff, we can retrieve the 16-bit result ($B174 in this example) from the top of the stack and do whatever we wish with it. Note that the first byte to be retrieved will be the most-significant byte of the result. In the case of this particular program, we simply stored the result in two bytes that we reserved under the name of **ANSWER**, but we could easily have done something else. For example, if we had wished to add three 16-bit numbers together, we could have left the result from the first addition on the stack, placed our third 16-bit number on the stack, and then called our _ADD16 subroutine again. The way in which the subroutine receives the numbers and returns the result is illustrated in Figure G.1.

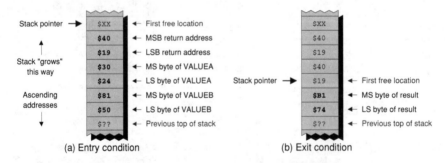

(a) Entry condition   (b) Exit condition

Figure G.1: The stack's entry and exit conditions for the _ADD16 subroutine

Remember that the stack "grows" in the direction of address $0000. Thus, every time we PUSH a value onto the stack, that value is stored at the location pointed to by the stack pointer, which is then modified (decremented) to point to the next free location. Similarly, every time we POP a value off the stack, the stack pointer is first modified (incremented) to point to the last piece of data that was stored on the stack, and this value is then copied into the appropriate register.

Also remember that when the main program calls the subroutine, the *Beboputer* automatically stores the return address on the top of the stack and modifies the stack pointer accordingly. Thus, when we enter our subroutine, the two bytes at the top of the stack will contain the return address $4019, which happens to be the location of the first POPA instruction following the JSR (*"jump to subroutine"*).

Finally, note that popping a value off the stack doesn't physically obliterate that value, which is why we've shown these old values as persisting in Figure G.1b. Of course, this raises an interesting question, which is: *"Why does the return address of $4019 now appear on the stack twice?"* Take a few moments to see whether you can solve this brain-teaser before plunging into the body of the subroutine as follows:

```
##################################################################
# Name:    _ADD16                                                #
#                                                                #
# Function: Adds two 16-bit signed or unsigned numbers together  #
#          and returns a 16-bit signed or unsigned result.       #
#                                                                #
# Entry:   Top of stack                                          #
#          Most-significant byte of return address               #
#          Least-significant byte of return address              #
#          Most-significant byte of first number                 #
#          Least-significant byte of first number                #
#          Most-significant byte of second number                #
#          Least-significant byte of second number               #
#                                                                #
# Exit:    Top of stack                                          #
#          Most-significant byte of result                       #
#          Least-significant byte of result                      #
#                                                                #
# Modifies: Accumulator                                          #
#                                                                #
# Size:    Program = 41 bytes                                    #
#          Data    =  5 bytes                                    #
##################################################################


_ADD16:    POPA               # Retrieve MS byte of return
           STA  [_AA_RADD]    # address from stack and store it
           POPA               # Retrieve LS byte of return
           STA  [_AA_RADD+1]  # address from stack and store it

           POPA               # Retrieve MS byte of 1st number
           STA  [_AA_NUMA]    # from stack and store it
           POPA               # Retrieve LS byte of 1st number
           STA  [_AA_NUMA+1]  # from stack and store it
           POPA               # Retrieve MS byte of 2nd number
           STA  [_AA_NUMB]    # from stack and store it
```

```
            POPA                # Retrieve LS byte of 2nd number
                                # from stack & leave it in the ACC
            ADD   [_AA_NUMA+1]  # Add LS byte of 1st number to ACC
            PUSHA               # and stick LS result on stack
            LDA   [_AA_NUMB]    # Load ACC with MS byte of 2nd
                                # number from temp location
            ADDC  [_AA_NUMA]    # Add MS byte of 1st number to ACC
            PUSHA               # and stick MS result on stack
            LDA   [_AA_RADD+1]  # Load ACC with LS byte of return
                                # address from temp location and
            PUSHA               # stick it back on the stack
            LDA   [_AA_RADD]    # Load ACC with MS byte of return
                                # address from temp location and
            PUSHA               # stick it back on the stack
            RTS                 # That's it, exit the subroutine
_AA_RADD:  .2BYTE               # Reserve 2-byte temp location for
                                # the return address
_AA_NUMA:  .2BYTE               # Reserve 2-byte temp location for
                                # the 1st number
_AA_NUMB:  .BYTE                # Reserve 1-byte temp location for
                                # the MS byte of the 2nd number
```

☞ Note that we reserve the locations for our temporary variables **_AA_RADD**, **_AA_NUMA**, and **_AA_NUMB** at the end of the subroutine where they won't get in the way.

☞ Also note that when we add the least-significant bytes of our numbers together we use an **ADD** instruction, because this automatically forces a *logic 0* to be used for the "carry" into this addition. By comparison, when we add the most-significant bytes of our numbers together we use an **ADDC** instruction, because this employs the value stored in the *carry flag* (which was set by the first addition) as the "carry" into this addition.

☞ Remember that the stack pointer "grows" toward address $0000 and dwindles in the opposite direction. This means that "pushing" a value onto the stack causes the stack pointer to decrement to point to the next free location, while "popping" a value off the stack causes the stack pointer to increment to point to the previous location.

This means that once we've retrieved and stored the six bytes of data at the beginning of the subroutine (the two return address bytes and the four data bytes), the stack pointer is left pointing to the same location that it was before the main (calling) program placed the data on the stack in the first place. During the process of performing the addition, the subroutine stores the 2-byte result on the stack. Finally, the subroutine retrieves the return address from its temporary location, places it on the stack, and then returns to the main program.

The **RTS** instruction, which terminates the subroutine, automatically retrieves the return address from the stack and increments the stack pointer by two bytes, leaving it in the right position for the main program to be able to retrieve the result. (All of this explains why the subroutine's exit condition illustrated in Figure G.1 shows two copies of the return address on the stack.)

☞ Pay attention to the way in which we commented this subroutine. Some programmers might consider this to be over-enthusiastic, while others might feel that we were on the stingy side. We feel that this is a pretty reasonable median level that you should aim at if you expect people to be able to understand whatever it is you are trying to do.

16-bit Subtraction (_SUB16)

This subroutine retrieves two 16-bit numbers from the stack, subtracts one from the other, and places the 16-bit result on the top of the stack. The subroutine works for both signed and unsigned numbers, and assumes that all of the numbers are stored in the usual *Beboputer* style with the most significant byte "on top" of the least significant byte. Before considering _SUB16 itself, let's examine an example of a program that might call this subroutine:

```
# The following program declares two 16-bit numbers called VALUEA
# and VALUEB. The program sets things up in such a way that, when
# it calls the subroutine, the second value to be pushed onto the
# stack is subtracted from the first value on the stack
            .ORG    $4000          # Start of program is address $4000
VALUEA:     .2BYTE  $3024          # Here's a 16-bit number
VALUEB:     .2BYTE  $8150          # Here's another 16-bit number
ANSWER:     .2BYTE                 # Save a 16-bit field for the result

                                   # Set everything up so that the
                                   # subroutine will subtract VALUEA
                                   # from VALUEB
            LDA     [VALUEB+1]     # Load ACC with the LS byte of VALUEB
            PUSHA                  # Push this byte onto the stack
            LDA     [VALUEB]       # Load ACC with the MS byte of VALUEB
            PUSHA                  # Push this byte onto the stack
            LDA     [VALUEA+1]     # Load ACC with the LS byte of VALUEA
            PUSHA                  # Push this byte onto the stack
```

```
        LDA     [VALUEA]      # Load ACC with the MS byte of VALUEA
        PUSHA                 # Push this byte onto the stack
        JSR     [_SUB16]      # Jump to the "_SUB16" subroutine and
                              # subtract VALUEA from VALUEB (the
                              # code for the subroutine would be
                              # somewhere else in the program)

        POPA                  # Retrieve the MS byte of the result
        STA     [ANSWER]      # from the stack and store it
        POPA                  # Retrieve the LS byte of the result
        STA     [ANSWER+1]    # from the stack and store it
        :        :                             :
```

Before calling the subroutine, we first have to place the two 16-bit numbers that we want to subtract on the stack ($3024 and $8150 in this example). Note that the order in which the numbers are put on the stack *does* matter in the case of a subtraction. Also, as before, both numbers must be placed on the stack with their least-significant bytes first, because this is the way in which the subroutine will expect them to arrive (Figure G.2).

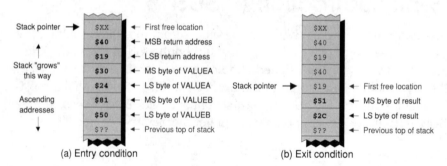

(a) Entry condition   (b) Exit condition

**Figure G.2: The stack's entry and exit
conditions for the _SUB16 subroutine**

After the subroutine has done its minor magic, we can retrieve the 16-bit result ($512C in this example) from the stack and do whatever we wish with it. See also the discussions on _ADD16 above for more details on the way the stack is used for both of these subroutines.

```
###################################################################
# Name:     _SUB16                                                #
#                                                                 #
# Function: Subtracts two 16-bit signed or unsigned numbers       #
#           and returns a 16-bit signed or unsigned result.       #
#                                                                 #
# Entry:    Top of stack                                          #
#           Most-significant byte of return address               #
#           Least-significant byte of return address              #
#           Most-significant byte of first number   } Sub this No.#
```

```
#           Least-significant byte of first number } from 2nd No.#
#           Most-significant byte of second number            #
#           Least-significant byte of second number           #
#                                                             #
# Exit:     Top of stack                                      #
#           Most-significant byte of result                   #
#           Least-significant byte of result                  #
#                                                             #
# Modifies: Accumulator                                       #
#                                                             #
# Size:     Program = 41 bytes                                #
#           Data    = 5 bytes                                 #
###############################################################

_SUB16:    POPA               # Retrieve MS byte of return
           STA   [_AB_RADD]    # address from stack and store it
           POPA               # Retrieve LS byte of return
           STA   [_AB_RADD+1]  # address from stack and store it

           POPA               # Retrieve MS byte of 1st number
           STA   [_AB_NUMA]    # from stack and store it
           POPA               # Retrieve LS byte of 1st number
           STA   [_AB_NUMA+1]  # from stack and store it
           POPA               # Retrieve MS byte of 2nd number
           STA   [_AB_NUMB]    # from stack and store it

           POPA               # Retrieve LS byte of 2nd number
                              # from stack & leave it in the ACC
           SUB   [_AB_NUMA+1]  # Subtract LS byte of 1st number
                              # from ACC and stick LS result
           PUSHA              # on stack
           LDA   [_AB_NUMB]    # Load ACC with MS byte of 2nd
                              # number from temp location
           SUBC  [_AB_NUMA]    # Subtract MS byte of 1st number
                              # from ACC and stick MS result
           PUSHA              # on stack
           LDA   [_AB_RADD+1]  # Load ACC with LS byte of return
                              # address from temp location and
           PUSHA              # stick it back on the stack
           LDA   [_AB_RADD]    # Load ACC with MS byte of return
                              # address from temp location and
           PUSHA              # stick it back on the stack
           RTS                # That's it, exit the subroutine
_AB_RADD:  .2BYTE             # Reserve 2-byte temp location for
                              # the return address
_AB_NUMA:  .2BYTE             # Reserve 2-byte temp location for
                              # the 1st number
_AB_NUMB:  .BYTE              # Reserve 1-byte temp location for
                              # the MS byte of the 2nd number
```

☞ Note that when we subtract the least-significant bytes we use a **SUB** instruction, because this automatically forces a *logic 1* to be used for the "borrow" into this subtraction. By comparison, when we subtract the most-significant bytes we use a **SUBC** instruction, because this employs the value stored in the *carry flag* (which was set by the first subtraction) as the "borrow" into this subtraction.

8-bit Unsigned Multiplication (_UMULT8)

Before we hurl ourselves into the bowels of this subroutine, we need to introduce a few basic concepts. Modern computers typically have special instructions and employ dedicated logic (either inside or outside the central processor) to perform multiplication operations, but the early microcomputers didn't have this capability and neither does the *Beboputer*. This means that we have a choice: either we make do without the ability to multiply numbers together (which would limit our ability to write useful programs to the point of absurdity), or we have to come up with some technique to perform multiplication using whatever instructions are available to us.

One technique for performing multiplication in any number base is by means of repeated addition; for example, 6 x 4 = 6 + 6 + 6 + 6 = 24 in decimal, (similarly, 4 x 6 = 4 + 4 + 4 + 4 + 4 + 4 = 24). However, although modern computers can perform millions operations every second, this technique can be extremely time-consuming when the values to be multiplied are large. In the case of this particular subroutine, we are going to multiply two unsigned 8-bit numbers together. An unsigned 8-bit number can be used to represent values in the range 0 through 255 in decimal ($00 through $FF in hexadecimal), so the worst case for a subroutine based on this technique would be to have to perform 255 additions. Now, this might not seem too dire, but consider the case of the _UMULT16 subroutine which we will be looking at a little later. Our _UMULT16 subroutine will be used to multiply two 16-bit numbers together, so its worst-case scenario would require it to perform 65,535 additions, which would be less than amusing. As an alternative, we can multiply binary numbers using a "shift-and-add" technique to generate partial products (Figure G.3).

Using this algorithm, a partial product is generated for each bit in the multiplier (note that the dash '-' characters in this figure would actually be 0s used to pad the partial products to the necessary width). If the value of the multiplier bit is 0, its corresponding partial product consists only of 0s, but if the value of the multiplier bit is 1, its corresponding partial product is a copy of the multiplicand. Also, each partial product is left-shifted as a function of the multiplier bit with which it is associated; for example, the partial product associated with bit 0 in the multiplier is left-shifted zero bits, while the partial product associated with bit 1 in the multiplier is left-shifted one bit, and so on. Once all of the partial products have been generated, they are added together to generate the result, whose width is equal to the sum of the widths of the multiplicand and the multiplier.

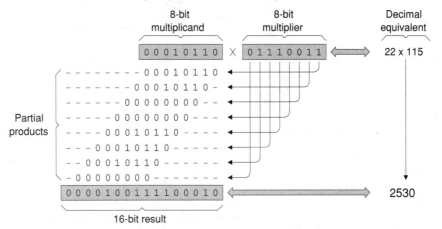

Figure G.3: Binary multiplication using a shift-and-add technique

As was illustrated in Figure G.3, multiplying two 8-bit numbers together generates a 16-bit result. As each of our unsigned 8-bit numbers can carry values in the range 0 through 255 in decimal ($00 through $FF in hexadecimal), the result will be in the range 0 through 65,025 in decimal ($0000 through $FE01 in hexadecimal). Our shift-and-add approach can be implemented in hardware or software. If we were considering a hardware implementation, then we could use a dedicated block of logic to generate all of the partial products simultaneously and add them together. However, in our case we're obliged to use a software solution, which means that we have to generate each partial product individually and add it into the result. Still, the beauty of this scheme is that it only requires the same number of additions as there are bits in the multiplier, which means eight additions for this particular subroutine.

But there are several considerations here that we need to ponder. For example, if our solution directly mapped onto Figure G.3, then each of our partial products would be 16 bits wide (including the 0s used for padding), and we would have to perform eight 16-bit additions. Also, we would have to expend a substantial amount of effort splitting our multiplicand into the various 8-bit quantities required to form each 16-bit partial product.

To illustrate the situation, consider the partial product associated with bit 4 of the multiplier (remember that we number bits from right to left starting at 0) (Figure G.4).

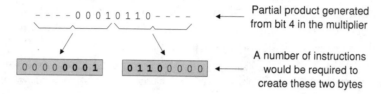

Partial product generated from bit 4 in the multiplier

A number of instructions would be required to create these two bytes

Figure G.4: Problems associated with generating 16-bit partial products

The problem is that we would have to perform a number of operations to split our 8-bit multiplicand across these two bytes. Also, we'd have to split the multiplicand in a different place for each partial product. This isn't to say that we couldn't use this technique, but that we would prefer a method that could achieve the same effect with fewer instructions and less hassle. In fact, by some strange quirk of fate, there is indeed a rather cunning ploy that we can use (Figure G.5).

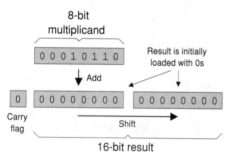

Figure G.5: A rather cunning ploy

Initially, the two bytes we're using to represent our result are loaded with 0s. Next we look at bit 0 in the multiplier to see if it contains a 0 or a 1. If bit 0 of the multiplier contains a 0, we add a byte of 0s to the most-significant byte of the result, but if bit 0 of the multiplier contains a 1, then we add a copy of the multiplicand into the most-significant byte of the result. Note that, in both cases, we're interested in the resulting state of the carry flag.

Next we shift both bytes of the result one bit to the right. When we shift the most-significant (left hand) byte of the result, it is important that we shift the carry flag into its most-significant bit, and also that we remember the value of the original least-significant bit that "drops off the end." Similarly, when we shift the least-significant (right hand) byte of the result, it is important that whatever bit "dropped off the end" from the most-significant byte is shifted into the most-significant bit of the least-significant byte (hmmm, you might need to ruminate on that last sentence for a while).

The point is that we can repeat this procedure for each of the bits in the multiplier, either adding a byte of 0s or a copy of the multiplicand into the most significant byte of the result, and then shifting both bytes of the result one bit to the right. If you sketch this out on a piece of paper, you'll find that performing this sequence for each of the bits in the multiplier ultimately generates the same result as the technique based on 16-bit partial products – but this method has the advantage of requiring far fewer computer instructions.

Sad to relate, there's still one more problem before we continue – the task of extracting and testing the bits in the multiplier. One approach would be to individually mask out the bits. For example, to determine the value in bit 0 of the multiplier we could **AND** it with $01 (or %00000001 in binary), and then use a **JZ** (*"jump if zero"*) instruction to vary our actions depending on the result (alternatively, we could use a **JNZ** (*"jump if not zero"*) if that better served our purposes). Similarly, to determine the value in bit 1 of the multiplier we could **AND** it with $02 (or %00000010 in binary); to determine the value in bit 2 of the multiplier we could **AND** it with $04 (or %00000100 in binary); and so forth. However, if you actually try to implement this technique, you will again discover that it requires a lot of instructions and muddling around.

As an alternative, we could simply shift the multiplier one bit to the right (which would result in its least-significant bit falling off the end and dropping into the carry flag), and then use a **JC** (*"jump if carry"*) instruction to vary our actions depending on the result (as usual, we could use a **JNC** (*"jump if not carry"*) instruction if that better served our purposes). Finally, we might note that we already have to shift our 16-bit result one bit to the right for each bit in our multiplier,
which means that whatever is initially loaded into the least-significant byte of the result will ultimately be thrown away anyway. Thus, we can save ourselves considerable effort by initializing the result such that its most-significant byte contains 0s, while its least-significant byte contains the multiplier (Figure G.6).

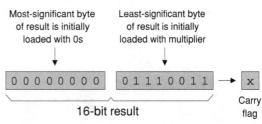

Figure G.6: Another cunning ploy

This means that every time we stroll around the main loop, which involves shifting both bytes of the result one bit to the right, the next bit of interest in the multiplier will automatically end up in the carry flag, ready and waiting for the following iteration of the loop.

Don't worry if you find the above to be a bit mind-boggling at first — after a while you'll find that this sort of "wheels-within-wheels" thinking starts to come naturally (and this would be the time to start worrying). So with these words of comfort, let's proceed to our subroutine , which retrieves two 8-bit numbers from the stack, multiplies them together, and places the 16-bit result on the top of the stack. The subroutine only works for unsigned numbers (see also _SMULT8 later on), and assumes that any 16-bit values are stored in the usual *Beboputer* style with the most-significant byte "on top" of the least-significant byte. Before considering _UMULT8 itself, let's first examine an example of a program that might call this subroutine:

```
# The following program declares two 8-bit unsigned numbers called
# VALUEA and VALUEB. The program sets things up in such a way
# that,when it calls the subroutine, VALUEA is multiplied by
# VALUEB
            .ORG    $4000       # Start of program is address $4000
VALUEA:     .BYTE   $16         # First  8-bit number ( 22 in
                                # decimal)
VALUEB:     .BYTE   $73         # Second 8-bit number (115 in
                                # decimal)
ANSWER:     .2BYTE              # Save a 16-bit field for the result

                                # Set everything up so that the
                                # subroutine will multiply VALUEA
                                # by VALUEB
            LDA     [VALUEB]    # Load ACC with VALUEB and push it
            PUSHA               # onto the stack
            LDA     [VALUEA]    # Load ACC with VALUEA and push it
            PUSHA               # onto the stack

            JSR     [_UMULT8]   # Jump to the "_UMULT8" subroutine
                                # and multiply VALUEA by VALUEB (the
                                # code for the subroutine would be
                                # somewhere else in the program)

            POPA                # Retrieve the MS byte of the result
            STA     [ANSWER]    # from the stack and store it
            POPA                # Retrieve the LS byte of the result
            STA     [ANSWER+1]  # from the stack and store it
            :       :                   :
```

Before calling the subroutine, we first have to place the two 8-bit numbers that we want to multiply together on the stack ($16 and $73 in this example). Note that the order in which the numbers are put on the stack doesn't particularly matter in the case of a multiplication (Figure G.7).

After the subroutine has performed its curious machinations, we can retrieve the 16-bit result ($09E2 in this example) from the stack and do whatever we wish with it. Alternatively, we could leave it on the stack and use it as one of the values to be passed into another subroutine, such as the _ADD16 we introduced earlier.

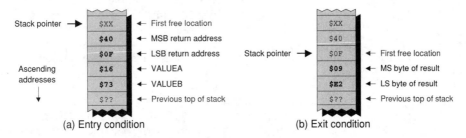

(a) Entry condition   (b) Exit condition

Figure G.7: The stack's entry and exit conditions for the _UMULT8 subroutine

```
####################################################################
# Name:      _UMULT8                                               #
#                                                                  #
# Function: Multiplies two 8-bit unsigned numbers and returns a    #
#           16-bit unsigned result.                                #
#                                                                  #
# Entry:    Top of stack                                           #
#           Most-significant byte of return address                #
#           Least-significant byte of return address               #
#           First 8-bit number (multiplicand)                      #
#           Second 8-bit number (multiplier)                       #
#                                                                  #
# Exit:     Top of stack                                           #
#           Most-significant byte of result                        #
#           Least-significant byte of result                       #
#                                                                  #
# Modifies: Accumulator                                            #
#           Index register                                         #
#                                                                  #
# Size:     Program = 67 bytes                                     #
#           Data    =  5 bytes                                     #
####################################################################
_UMULT8:   BLDX   9           # Load the index register with 9,
                              # which equals the number of times
                              # we want to go around the loop +1

           POPA               # Retrieve MS byte of return
           STA  [_AC_RADD]     # address from stack and store it
           POPA               # Retrieve LS byte of return
           STA  [_AC_RADD+1]   # address from stack and store it

           POPA               # Retrieve multiplicand from stack
           STA  [_AC_MAND]     # and store it
           POPA               # Retrieve multiplier from stack
           STA  [_AC_RES+1]    # and store it in LS byte of result
           LDA    0           # Load the accumulator with 0 and
```

```
                STA   [_AC_RES]      # store it in the MS byte of result

_AC_DUMY:  ADD   0          # Add zero to the accumulator (dummy
                            # instruction whose sole purpose is
                            # to set the carry flag to 0)
####
#### Hold tight - this is the start of the main multiplication
#### loop
####
_AC_LOOP:  LDA   [_AC_RES]      # Load ACC with MS byte of result
                               # (doesn't affect the carry flag)
           JNC   [_AC_SHFT]     # If carry=0, jump to start shifting
           ADD   [_AC_MAND]     # otherwise add the multiplicand
                               # (which may modify the carry flag)
_AC_SHFT:  RORC              # Rotate the accumulator (MS byte of
                            # result) 1-bit right. This shifts
                            # the carry flag into the MS bit and
                            # also updates the carry flag with
                            # the bit that "falls off the end"
           STA   [_AC_RES]      # Now store the MS byte of result
                               # (doesn't affect the carry flag)
           LDA   [_AC_RES+1]    # Load ACC with LS byte of result
                               # (doesn't affect the carry flag)
           RORC              # Rotate the LS byte of the result
                            # 1-bit right. This shifts the carry
                            # flag into the MS bit and also
                            # updates
                            # the carry flag with the multiplier
                            # bit that "falls off the end"
           STA   [_AC_RES+1]    # Now store the LS byte of result
                               # (doesn't affect the carry flag)
           DECX              # Decrement the index register (which
                            # doesn't affect the carry flag). If
           JNZ   [_AC_LOOP]     # the index register isn't 0 then
                               # jump back to the beginning of the
                               # loop
####
#### Breathe out - this is the end of the main multiplication loop
####
           LDA   [_AC_RES+1]    # Load ACC with LS byte of result
           PUSHA             # and stick it on the stack
           LDA   [_AC_RES]      # Load ACC with MS byte of result
           PUSHA             # and stick it on the stack
           LDA   [_AC_RADD+1]   # Load ACC with LS byte of return
                               # address from temp location and
           PUSHA             # stick it back on the stack
           LDA   [_AC_RADD]     # Load ACC with MS byte of return
                               # address from temp location and
           PUSHA             # stick it back on the stack
```

```
              RTS                 # That's it, exit the subroutine
_AC_RADD: .2BYTE                  # Reserve 2-byte temp location for
                                  # the return address
_AC_MAND: .BYTE                   # Reserve 1-byte temp location for
                                  # the multiplicand
_AC_RES:  .2BYTE                  # Reserve 2-byte temp location for
                                  # the result
```

☞ Note that, when we shift the two byte result 1-bit to the right, we actually use **RORC** ("*rotate through carry*") instructions. This is because an **RORC** shifts the carry flag into the most-significant bit of the accumulator and also updates the carry flag with the bit that "falls off the end" (the least-significant bit of the accumulator in this case). This feature of the **RORC** is key to facilitating multi-byte shifts.

☞ We load the index register with 9 at the beginning of this subroutine, because we have to go around the loop one more time that we really want to; the first pass around the loop has no other purpose than to shift the LS bit of the LS byte of the result out into the carry flag (remember that the LS byte actually contains the multiplier). This also explains why we performed the dummy **ADD** instruction at label **_AC_DUMY**, because we had to ensure that the carry flag was set to 0 the first time around the loop, thereby ensuring that we wouldn't add anything we didn't want to into the result.

8-bit Signed Multiplication (_SMULT8)

Unfortunately, the _UMULT8 subroutine we just looked at can only handle unsigned numbers; if we consider our 8-bit numbers to be signed values, then sometimes this routine will work and sometimes it won't. Thus, if we wish to multiply signed 8-bit numbers with any level of confidence, we will need to use the _SMULT8 subroutine presented here.

The idea behind _SMULT8 is rather simple. We already know that we can multiply positive (unsigned) numbers together, so all we need to do in this subroutine is to convert any negative numbers into their positive equivalents, multiply them together, and then correct the sign of the result if necessary. For some reason it's usually easier to visualize the way in which this sort of thing works in terms of a hardware implementation (Figure G.8).

First we know that the most-significant bit of a signed binary number is called the *sign bit*, and that this bit will be *logic 0* if the value is positive and *logic 1* if it's negative (the sign bit would be bit 7 in the case of an 8-bit number).

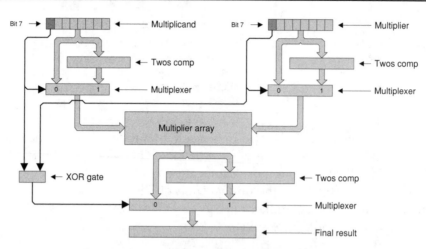

**Figure G.8: Hardware implementation for
multiplying signed binary numbers**

Now consider the multiplicand, which is fed directly into a multiplexer and
also into a twos complementor. The twos complementor automatically
generates the negative equivalent of whatever value is fed to its inputs. This
means that, if the multiplicand is a positive value, the output from the twos
complementor will be its negative equivalent, and vice versa. The output
from the twos complementor is also connected to the multiplexer, whose
select input is driven from the multiplicand's sign bit. This is the clever part,
because if the sign bit is logic 0 (indicating a positive value), this instructs
the multiplexer to select the multiplicand. Conversely, if the sign bit is a
logic 1 (indicating a negative value), this instructs the multiplexer to select
the output from the twos complementor, which is the positive equivalent of
the multiplicand.

Similar actions are performed in the case of the multiplier; thus, the
multiplier array is presented with two positive numbers, which it proceeds
to multiply together. If we assume that the multiplier array is based on the
shift-and-add technique introduced in the previous subroutine, then this
array will generate all of the partial products, add them together, and
present the 16-bit result at its outputs.

Now we come to another ingenious legerdemain, in which we decide
whether or not to negate the output from the multiplier array. If both the
multiplicand and the multiplier were positive we don't have to invert the
output from the array, because a positive times a positive equals a positive.
Similarly, we don't have to invert the output from the array if both the
multiplicand and the multiplier were negative, because a negative times a
negative equals a positive. Thus, it is only when the multiplicand and the

multiplier have different signs that the result should be negative, in which case we need to invert the output from the array. As we see in Figure G.8, the output from the array is fed into a multiplexer and twos complementor arrangement similar to the ones we used earlier for the multiplicand and the multiplier. However, in this case, the multiplexer is controlled by the output from an XOR gate, whose inputs are the sign bits from the multiplicand and the multiplier.[1] If both of the sign bits have the same value, then the output from the XOR will be *logic 0* and the multiplexer will select the multiplier array. Alternatively, if the sign bits have different values, then the output from the XOR will be *logic 1*, thereby causing the multiplexer to select the outputs from the twos complementor.

Of course, we are not going to implement our solution in hardware, but the same general principles also apply to a software implementation. On the other hand, you should be aware that software guys keep tricks of their own up their sleeves; for example, to generate the twos complement of a number, we can simply subtract that number from zero (see the _SMULT16 subroutine for an example of this); alternatively, we can achieve the same effect by inverting all of the bits in the number and then adding 1 (you will see this technique used in the code for the subroutine below).

The technique presented above does raise one slight problem, in that signed 8-bit numbers can carry values in the range -128 through +127 in decimal ($80 through $7F in hexadecimal). The problem lies in the fact that we can't convert any -128 values into their positive equivalents, because our 8-bit fields simply cannot represent a value of +128. This means we have to introduce a rule that says we can only guarantee the results returned by our subroutine if it is presented with values in the range -127 through +127 in decimal ($81 through $7F in hexadecimal). (Note that it's the user's responsibility to ensure that this condition is met.) Thus, the most-negative result we can receive will be -127 x +127 (or +127 x -127) = -16,129, while the most-positive will be +127 x +127 (or -127 x -127) = +16,129, so our 16-bit result will be in the range -16,129 through +16,129 in decimal ($C0FF through $3F01 in hexadecimal).

Now let's proceed to our subroutine, which retrieves two 8-bit signed numbers from the stack, multiplies them together, and places the 16-bit signed result on the top of the stack. As usual, the subroutine assumes that any 16-bit numbers are stored *Beboputer*-style with the most-significant byte "on top" of the least-significant byte. Before considering _SMULT8 itself, let's examine an example of a program that might call this subroutine:

---

[1]XOR gates were introduced in Chapter 6.

```
# The following program declares two 8-bit signed numbers called
# VALUEA and VALUEB. The program sets things up in such a way
# that, when it calls the subroutine, VALUEA is multiplied by
# VALUEB.
            .ORG      $4000       # Start of program is address $4000
VALUEA:     .BYTE     $EA         # First  8-bit number ( -22 in
                                  # decimal)
VALUEB:     .BYTE     $73         # Second 8-bit number (+115 in
                                  # decimal)
ANSWER:     .2BYTE                # Save a 16-bit field for the result

                                  # Set everything up so that the
                                  # subroutine will multiply VALUEA
                                  # by VALUEB
            LDA       [VALUEB]    # Load ACC with VALUEB and push it
            PUSHA                 # onto the stack
            LDA       [VALUEA]    # Load ACC with VALUEA and push it
            PUSHA                 # onto the stack

            JSR       [_SMULT8]   # Jump to the "_SMULT8" subroutine
                                  # and multiply VALUEA by VALUEB (the
                                  # code for the subroutine would be
                                  # somewhere else in the program)

            POPA                  # Retrieve the MS byte of the result
            STA       [ANSWER]    # from the stack and store it
            POPA                  # Retrieve the LS byte of the result
            STA       [ANSWER+1]  # from the stack and store it
            :         :                      :
```

Before calling the subroutine, we have to place the two 8-bit numbers that
we want to multiply together on the stack ($EA and $73 in this example). As
usual, the order in which the numbers are put on the stack doesn't
particularly matter in the case of multiplication (Figure G.9).

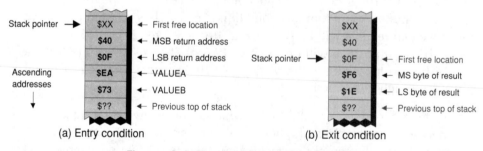

(a) Entry condition   (b) Exit condition

**Figure G.9: The stack's entry and exit
conditions for the _SMULT8 subroutine**

After the subroutine has done its clever turn, we can retrieve the 16-bit
signed result ($F61E in this example) from the stack and do whatever we

wish with it. Alternatively, we could leave it on the stack and use it as one of the values to be passed into another subroutine, such as the _ADD16 we introduced earlier.

```
###############################################################
# Name:     _SMULT8                                           #
#                                                             #
# Function: Multiplies two 8-bit signed numbers (in the range #
#           -127 to +127) and returns a 16-bit signed result. #
#                                                             #
# Entry:    Top of stack                                      #
#           Most-significant byte of return address           #
#           Least-significant byte of return address          #
#           First 8-bit number (multiplicand)                 #
#           Second 8-bit number (multiplier)                  #
#                                                             #
# Exit:     Top of stack                                      #
#           Most-significant byte of result                   #
#           Least-significant byte of result                  #
#                                                             #
# Modifies: Accumulator                                       #
#           Index register                                    #
#                                                             #
# Size:     Program = 128 bytes                               #
#           Data    =   6 bytes                               #
###############################################################
_SMULT8:    BLDX  9           # Load the index register with 9,
                              # which equals the number of times
                              # we want to go around the loop +1

            POPA              # Retrieve MS byte of return
            STA  [_AD_RADD]   # address from stack and store it
            POPA              # Retrieve LS byte of return
            STA  [_AD_RADD+1] # address from stack and store it

            POPA              # Retrieve multiplicand from stack
            STA  [_AD_MAND]   # and store it
            POPA              # Retrieve multiplier from stack
            STA  [_AD_RES+1]  # and store it in LS byte of result
            LDA  0            # Load the accumulator with 0 and
            STA  [_AD_RES]    # store it in the MS byte of result
####
#### Invert input values if necessary and load the output flag
####
_AD_TSTA:   LDA [_AD_MAND]    # Load the multiplicand and save
            STA [_AD_FLAG]    # it to the flag
            JNN [_AD_TSTB]    # If multiplicand is positive then
                              # jump to '_AD_TSTB', otherwise ..
            XOR $FF           # ..invert the contents of the ACC
            INCA              # ..add 1 to ACC
            STA [_AD_MAND]    # ..store now-positive multiplicand
```

```
_AD_TSTB:   LDA  [_AD_FLAG]       # Load the flag,
            XOR  [_AD_RES+1]      # XOR it with the multiplier,
            STA  [_AD_FLAG]       # then store the flag again

            LDA  [_AD_RES+1]      # Load the multiplier into the ACC
            JNN  [_AD_DUMY]       # If multiplier is positive then
                                  # jump to '_AD_DUMY', otherwise ..
            XOR  $FF              # ..invert the contents of the ACC
            INCA                  # ..add 1 to ACC
            STA  [_AD_RES+1]      # ..store now-positive multiplier
_AD_DUMY:   ADD  0               # Add zero to the accumulator (dummy
                                  # instruction whose sole purpose is
                                  # to set the carry flag to 0)
####
#### Hold tight - this is the start of the main multiplication
#### loop
####
_AD_LOOP:   LDA  [_AD_RES]        # Load ACC with MS byte of result
                                  # (doesn't affect the carry flag)
            JNC  [_AD_SHFT]       # If carry=0, jump to start shifting
            ADD  [_AD_MAND]       # otherwise add the multiplicand
                                  # (which may modify the carry flag)
_AD_SHFT:   RORC                  # Rotate the accumulator (MS byte of
                                  # result) 1-bit right. This shifts
                                  # the carry flag into the MS bit and
                                  # also updates the carry flag with
                                  # the bit that "falls off the end"
            STA  [_AD_RES]        # Now store the MS byte of result
                                  # (doesn't affect the carry flag)
            LDA  [_AD_RES+1]      # Load ACC with LS byte of result
                                  # (doesn't affect the carry flag)
            RORC                  # Rotate the LS byte of the result
                                  # 1-bit right. This shifts the carry
                                  # flag into the MS bit and also
                                  # updates
                                  # the carry flag with the multiplier
                                  # bit that "falls off the end"
            STA  [_AD_RES+1]      # Now store the LS byte of result
                                  # (doesn't affect the carry flag)
            DECX                  # Decrement the index register
                                  # (which doesn't affect the carry
                                  # flag). If the index register
            JNZ  [_AD_LOOP]       # isn't 0 then jump back to the
                                  # beginning of the loop
####
#### Breathe out - this is the end of the main multiplication loop
#### Now check the flag and negate the output result if necessary
####
_AD_TSTC:   LDA  [_AD_FLAG]       # Load ACC with the flag
```

```
            JNN   [_AD_SAVE]      # If MS bit of flag is 0 then
                                  # jump to '_AD_SAVE', otherwise ..
            LDA   [_AD_RES+1]     # ..load ACC with LS byte of result
            XOR   $FF             # ..invert the contents of the ACC
            INCA                  # ..add 1 to ACC (updates carry
                                  # flag)
            STA   [_AD_RES+1]     # ..store negated LS byte (doesn't
                                  #    affect carry flag)
            LDA   [_AD_RES]       # ..load ACC with MS byte of result
                                  #    (doesn't affect carry flag)
            XOR   $FF             # ..invert the contents of the ACC
                                  #    (doesn't affect carry flag)
            ADDC  $00             # ..propagate any carry from LS byte
            STA   [_AD_RES]       # ..store negated MS byte
####
#### Save the result on the stack and then let's bug out of
#### here
####
_AD_SAVE:   LDA   [_AD_RES+1]     # Load ACC with LS byte of result
            PUSHA                 # and stick it on the stack
            LDA   [_AD_RES]       # Load ACC with MS byte of result
            PUSHA                 # and stick it on the stack
            LDA   [_AD_RADD+1]    # Load ACC with LS byte of return
                                  # address from temp location and
            PUSHA                 # stick it back on the stack
            LDA   [_AD_RADD]      # Load ACC with MS byte of return
                                  # address from temp location and
            PUSHA                 # stick it back on the stack
            RTS                   # That's it, exit the subroutine
_AD_RADD:   .2BYTE                # Reserve 2-byte temp location for
                                  # the return address
_AD_MAND:   .BYTE                 # Reserve 1-byte temp location for
                                  # the multiplicand
_AD_RES:    .2BYTE                # Reserve 2-byte temp location for
                                  # the result
_AD_FLAG:   .BYTE                 # Reserve 1-byte to be used as a
                                  # flag for negating the result
                                  # (or not as the case might be)
```

☞ The way in which the flag, _AD_FLAG, works is as follows ...... In the
_AD_TSTA part of the routine, this flag is loaded with all eight bits of the
multiplicand. Later, in the _AD_TSTB part of the routine, the flag (which
now contains a copy of the multiplicand) is XOR-ed with all eight bits of
the multiplier. In reality, we could care less about the least-significant
seven bits of the flag, because we're only interested in the most-significant
bit (the sign bit). However, we don't have to worry about the other bits,
because when we come to actually use the flag at the beginning of the

_AD_TSTC part of the routine, we can use a JNN ("*jump if not negative*") instruction, which only considers the state of the sign bit.

16-bit Unsigned Multiplication (_UMULT16)

This _UMULT16 subroutine is very similar to the _UMULT8 subroutine that we considered earlier, the main difference being that this routine can be used to multiply two unsigned 16-bit numbers together, where said numbers must be in the range 0 through +65,535.

Beware! As we know from our previous discussions, the width of the result of a binary multiplication is the sum of the widths of the multiplicand and the multiplier, so multiplying two 16-bit numbers together will return a 32-bit result. This subroutine does indeed generate a 32-bit bit value, but, to maintain consistency with our other 16-bit subroutines, we will only return the least-significant 16-bits, which means that the product of any numbers you multiply together must fall in the range 0 through +65,535. (Note that this is a reasonably common practice, and also that you could easily modify this subroutine to return the full 32-bit result, should you so desire.)[2]

Now let's proceed to our subroutine, which retrieves two 16-bit unsigned numbers from the stack, multiplies them together, and places the least-significant sixteen bits of the 32-bit result on the top of the stack. As usual, the subroutine assumes that any 16-bit numbers are stored *Beboputer* style with the most-significant byte "on top" of the least-significant byte. Before considering _UMULT16 itself, let's first examine an example of a program that might call this subroutine:

```
# The following program declares two 16-bit unsigned numbers
# called VALUEA and VALUEB. The program sets things up in such a
# way that when it calls the subroutine, VALUEA is multiplied by
# VALUEB
            .ORG    $4000       # Start of program is address $4000
VALUEA:     .2BYTE  $0056       # 1st 16-bit number ( 86 in decimal)
VALUEB:     .2BYTE  $0171       # 2nd 16-bit number (369 in decimal)
ANSWER:     .2BYTE              # Save a 16-bit field for the result
```

---

[2]You should not actually modify our subroutine, because any programs that use it would become confused. The correct approach would be to make a copy of our subroutine, give it a new name, modify the names of all of the labels, and then modify the size of the value returned by the subroutine.

```
                                # Set everything up so that the
                                # subroutine will multiply VALUEA
                                # by VALUEB

        LDA     [VALUEB+1]      # Load ACC with LS byte of VALUEB
        PUSHA                   # and push it onto the stack
        LDA     [VALUEB]        # Load ACC with MS byte of VALUEB
        PUSHA                   # and push it onto the stack
        LDA     [VALUEA+1]      # Load ACC with LS byte of VALUEA
        PUSHA                   # and push it onto the stack
        LDA     [VALUEB]        # Load ACC with MS byte of VALUEA
        PUSHA                   # and push it onto the stack

        JSR     [_UMULT16]      # Jump to the "_UMULT16" subroutine
                                # to multiply VALUEA by VALUEB (the
                                # code for the subroutine would be
                                # somewhere else in the program)

        POPA                    # Retrieve the MS byte of the result
        STA     [ANSWER]        # from the stack and store it
        POPA                    # Retrieve the LS byte of the result
        STA     [ANSWER+1]      # from the stack and store it
         :       :                           :
```

Before calling the subroutine, we first have to place the two 16-bit numbers that we want to multiply together on the stack ($0056 and $0171 in this example). As usual, the order in which the numbers are put on the stack doesn't particularly matter in the case of a multiplication. Once the subroutine has finished its task, we can retrieve the least-significant 2 bytes of the 4-byte result from the stack and do whatever we wish with them (these least-significant 2 bytes will contain $7BF6 in this example). Alternatively, we could leave this value on the stack and use it as one of the values to be passed into another subroutine, such as the _ADD16 we introduced earlier.

```
##################################################################
# Name:      _UMULT16                                            #
#                                                                #
# Function: Multiplies two 16-bit unsigned numbers (in the range #
#           0 to 65,535) and returns a 16-bit unsigned result.   #
#                                                                #
# Entry:    Top of stack                                         #
#           Most-significant byte of return address              #
#           Least-significant byte of return address             #
#           MS Byte of 1st 16-bit number (multiplicand)          #
#           LS Byte of 1st 16-bit number (multiplicand)          #
#           MS Byte of 2nd 16-bit number (multiplier)            #
#           LS Byte of 2nd 16-bit number (multiplier)            #
#                                                                #
```

```
# Exit:     Top of stack                                        #
#           Most-significant byte of result                     #
#           Least-significant byte of result                    #
#                                                               #
# Modifies: Accumulator                                         #
#           Index register                                      #
#                                                               #
# Size:     Program = 107 bytes                                 #
#           Data    =   8 bytes                                 #
################################################################
_UMULT16:  BLDX  17          # Load the index register with 17,
                             # which equals the number of times
                             # we want to go around the loop +1

           POPA              # Retrieve MS byte of return
           STA   [_AE_RADD]  # address from stack and store it
           POPA              # Retrieve LS byte of return
           STA   [_AE_RADD+1] # address from stack and store it

           POPA              # Retrieve MS byte of multiplicand
           STA   [_AE_MAND]  # from stack and store it
           POPA              # Retrieve LS byte of multiplicand
           STA   [_AE_MAND+1] # from stack and store it

# Note that the result is 4 bytes in size (_AE_RES+0, +1, +2,
# and +3), where _AE_RES+0 is the most-significant byte
           POPA              # Retrieve MS multiplier from stack
           STA   [_AE_RES+2] # and store it in byte 2 of result
           POPA              # Retrieve LS multiplier from stack
           STA   [_AE_RES+3] # and store it in byte 3 of result
           LDA   0           # Load the accumulator with 0 and
           STA   [_AE_RES]   # store it in byte 0 of result then
           STA   [_AE_RES+1] # in byte 1 of result
_AE_DUMY:  ADD   0           # Add zero to the accumulator (dummy
                             # instruction whose sole purpose is
                             # to set the carry flag to 0)
####
#### Hold tight - this is the start of the main multiplication
#### loop
####
_AE_LOOP:  JNC   [_AE_SHFT]  # If carry=0, jump to start shifting
           LDA   [_AE_RES+1] # otherwise add 16-bit multiplicand
           ADD   [_AE_MAND+1] # to the 16 MS bits of the result.
           STA   [_AE_RES+1] # Add LS 8-bits first and store
           LDA   [_AE_RES]   # Now add MS 8-bits (with carry)
           ADDC  [_AE_MAND]  # and store (note we're interested
           STA   [_AE_RES]   # in any carry out)
_AE_SHFT:  LDA   [_AE_RES]   # Might not already be loaded
           RORC              # Rotate the accumulator (MS byte of
                             # result) 1-bit right. This shifts
                             # the carry flag into the MS bit and
```

```
                          # also updates the carry flag with
                          # the bit that "falls off the end"
        STA   [_AE_RES]   # Now store the MS byte of result
                          # (doesn't affect the carry flag)

        LDA   [_AE_RES+1] # Load ACC with next byte of result
                          # (doesn't affect the carry flag)
        RORC              # Rotate this byte of the result
                          # 1-bit right. This shifts the carry
                          # flag into the MS bit and also
                          # updates the carry flag with the
                          # bit that "falls off the end"
        STA   [_AE_RES+1] # Now store this byte of result
                          # (doesn't affect the carry flag)

        LDA   [_AE_RES+2] # Load ACC with next byte of result
                          # (doesn't affect the carry flag)
        RORC              # Rotate this byte of the result
                          # 1-bit right. This shifts the carry
                          # flag into the MS bit and also
                          # updates the carry flag with the
                          # bit that "falls off the end"
        STA   [_AE_RES+2] # Now store this byte of result
                          # (doesn't affect the carry flag)

        LDA   [_AE_RES+3] # Load ACC with LS byte of result
                          # (doesn't affect the carry flag)
        RORC              # Rotate the LS byte of the result
                          # 1-bit right. This shifts the carry
                          # flag into the MS bit and also
                          # updates the carry flag with the
                          # multiplier bit that "falls off the
                          # end"
        STA   [_AE_RES+3] # Now store the LS byte of result
                          # (doesn't affect the carry flag)

        DECX              # Decrement the index register(which
                          # doesn't affect the carry flag). If
        JNZ   [_AE_LOOP]  # the index register isn't 0 then
                          # jump back to the beginning of the
                          # loop
####
#### Breathe out - this is the end of the main multiplication loop
#### Save the result on the stack and let's bug out of here
#### Remember we're only returning LS 16 bits of 32-bit result
####
_AE_SAVE:  LDA   [_AE_RES+3]  # Load ACC with LS byte of result
           PUSHA             # and stick it on the stack
           LDA   [_AE_RES+2]  # Load ACC with next byte of result
           PUSHA             # and stick it on the stack

           LDA   [_AE_RADD+1] # Load ACC with LS byte of return
                             # address from temp location and
```

```
            PUSHA                  # stick it back on the stack
            LDA   [_AE_RADD]       # Load ACC with MS byte of return
                                   # address from temp location and
            PUSHA                  # stick it back on the stack
            RTS                    # That's it, exit the subroutine
_AE_RADD:   .2BYTE                 # Reserve 2-byte temp location for
                                   # the return address
_AE_MAND:   .2BYTE                 # Reserve 2-byte temp location for
                                   # the multiplicand
_AE_RES:    .4BYTE                 # Reserve 4-byte temp location for
                                   # the result
```

☞ If we did wish to return all 4 bytes of the result, all we would have to do would be to add two more pairs of **LDA** and **PUSHA** instructions in the **_AE_SAVE** section of the subroutine (just before we push the return address onto the stack).

16-bit Signed Multiplication (_SMULT16)

This _SMULT16 subroutine is very similar to the _SMULT8 subroutine we considered earlier, the main difference being that this routine can be used to multiply two signed 16-bit numbers together, where said numbers must be in the range -32,767 through +32,767.

Beware! As we know from previous discussions, the width of the result of a binary multiplication is the sum of the widths of the multiplicand and the multiplier, so multiplying two 16-bit numbers together will return a 32-bit result. This subroutine does indeed generate a 32-bit bit value, but to maintain consistency with our other 16-bit subroutines, we will only return the least-significant 16-bits, which means that the product of any numbers you multiply together must fall in the range -32,767 through +32,767. (Note that this is reasonably common practice, and that you could easily modify this subroutine to return the full 32-bit result, should you so desire.)[3]

Now let's proceed to our subroutine, which retrieves two 16-bit signed numbers from the stack, multiplies them together, and places the least-significant sixteen bits of the 32-bit result on the top of the stack. As usual, the subroutine assumes that any 16-bit numbers are stored *Beboputer* style,

---

[3]Again, you should not actually modify our subroutine, because any programs that use it would become confused. The correct approach would be to make a copy our subroutine, give it a new name, modify the names of all of the labels, and then modify the size of the value returned by the subroutine.

with the most-significant byte "on top" of the least-significant byte. Before considering _SMULT16 itself, let's examine an example of a program that might call this subroutine:

```
# The following program declares two 16-bit unsigned numbers
# called VALUEA and VALUEB. The program sets things up in such a
# way that, when it calls the subroutine, VALUEA is multiplied by
# VALUEB.
           .ORG    $4000         # Start of program is address $4000
VALUEA:    .2BYTE  $0056         # 1st 16-bit number ( 86 in decimal)
VALUEB:    .2BYTE  $0171         # 2nd 16-bit number (369 in decimal)
ANSWER:    .2BYTE                # Save a 16-bit field for the result

                                 # Set everything up so that the
                                 # subroutine will multiply VALUEA
                                 # by VALUEB

           LDA     [VALUEB+1]    # Load ACC with LS byte of VALUEB
           PUSHA                 # and push it onto the stack
           LDA     [VALUEB]      # Load ACC with MS byte of VALUEB
           PUSHA                 # and push it onto the stack
           LDA     [VALUEA+1]    # Load ACC with LS byte of VALUEA
           PUSHA                 # and push it onto the stack
           LDA     [VALUEB]      # Load ACC with MS byte of VALUEA
           PUSHA                 # and push it onto the stack

           JSR     [_SMULT16]    # Jump to the "_SMULT16" subroutine
                                 # to multiply VALUEA by VALUEB
                                 # (the code for the subroutine
                                 # would be somewhere else in the
                                 # program)

           POPA                  # Retrieve the MS byte of the
                                 # result
           STA     [ANSWER]      # from the stack and store it
           POPA                  # Retrieve the LS byte of the result
           STA     [ANSWER+1]    # from the stack and store it
            :         :                      :
```

Before calling the subroutine, we first have to place the two 16-bit numbers that we want to multiply together on the stack ($0056 and $0171 in this example). As usual, the order in which the numbers are put on the stack doesn't particularly matter in the case of a multiplication. After the subroutine has thrashed around, we can retrieve the least-significant 2 bytes of the 4-byte result from the stack and do whatever we wish with them (these least-significant 2 bytes will contain $7BF6 in this example). Alternatively, we could leave this value on the stack and use it as one of the values to be passed into another subroutine, such as the _ADD16 we introduced earlier.

```
#################################################################
# Name:      _SMULT16                                           #
#                                                               #
# Function: Multiplies two 16-bit signed numbers (in the range  #
#           -32767 to +32767) and returns a 16-bit signed result.#
#                                                               #
# Entry:     Top of stack                                       #
#            Most-significant byte of return address            #
#            Least-significant byte of return address           #
#            MS Byte of 1st 16-bit number (multiplicand)        #
#            LS Byte of 1st 16-bit number (multiplicand)        #
#            MS Byte of 2nd 16-bit number (multiplier)          #
#            LS Byte of 2nd 16-bit number (multiplier)          #
#                                                               #
# Exit:      Top of stack                                       #
#            Most-significant byte of result                    #
#            Least-significant byte of result                   #
#                                                               #
# Modifies: Accumulator                                         #
#            Index register                                     #
#                                                               #
# Size:      Program = 201 bytes                                #
#            Data    =   9 bytes                                #
#################################################################
_SMULT16:  BLDX   17             # Load the index register with 17,
                                 # which equals the number of times
                                 # we want to go around the loop +1

           POPA                  # Retrieve MS byte of return
           STA  [_AF_RADD]       # address from stack and store it
           POPA                  # Retrieve LS byte of return
           STA  [_AF_RADD+1]     # address from stack and store it
           POPA                  # Retrieve MS byte of multiplicand
           STA  [_AF_MAND]       # from stack and store it
           POPA                  # Retrieve LS byte of multiplicand
           STA  [_AF_MAND+1]     # from stack and store it

# Note that the result is 4 bytes in size (_AF_RES+0, +1, +2,
# and +3), where _AF_RES+0 is the most-significant byte
           POPA                  # Retrieve MS multiplier from stack
           STA  [_AF_RES+2]      # and store it in byte 2 of result
           POPA                  # Retrieve LS multiplier from stack
           STA  [_AF_RES+3]      # and store it in byte 3 of result
           LDA   0               # Load the accumulator with 0 and
           STA  [_AF_RES]        # store it in byte 0 of result then
           STA  [_AF_RES+1]      # in byte 1 of result
####
#### Invert input values if necessary and load the output flag
####
_AF_TSTA:  LDA  [_AF_MAND]       # Load MS multiplicand and save
           STA  [_AF_FLAG]       # it to the flag
```

```
          JNN   [_AF_TSTB]      # If multiplicand is positive then
                                # jump to '_AF_TSTB', otherwise ..
          LDA   0               # ..load the accumulator with 0
          SUB   [_AF_MAND+1]    # ..subtract LS byte of multiplicand
          STA   [_AF_MAND+1]    # ..(no carry in) store result
          LDA   0               # ..load the accumulator with 0
          SUBC  [_AF_MAND]      # ..subtract MS byte of multiplicand
          STA   [_AF_MAND]      # ..(yes carry in) store result

_AF_TSTB: LDA   [_AF_FLAG]      # Load the flag,
          XOR   [_AF_RES+2]     # XOR it with MS byte of multiplier,
          STA   [_AF_FLAG]      # then store the flag again

          LDA   [_AF_RES+2]     # Load MS multiplier into the ACC
          JNN   [_AF_DUMY]      # If multiplier is positive then
                                # jump to '_AF_DUMY', otherwise ..
          LDA   0               # ..load the accumulator with 0
          SUB   [_AF_RES+3]     # ..subtract LS byte of multiplier
          STA   [_AF_RES+3]     # ..(no carry in) store result
          LDA   0               # ..load the accumulator with 0
          SUBC  [_AF_RES+2]     # ..subtract MS byte of multiplier
          STA   [_AF_RES+2]     # ..(yes carry in) store result

_AF_DUMY: ADD   0               # Add zero to the accumulator (dummy
                                # instruction whose sole purpose is
                                # to set the carry flag to 0)
####
#### Hold tight - this is the start of the main multiplication
#### loop
####
_AF_LOOP: JNC   [_AF_SHFT]      # If carry=0, jump to start shifting
          LDA   [_AF_RES+1]     # otherwise add 16-bit multiplicand
          ADD   [_AF_MAND+1]    # to the 16 MS bits of the result.
          STA   [_AF_RES+1]     # Add LS 8-bits first and store
          LDA   [_AF_RES]       # Now add MS 8-bits (with carry)
          ADDC  [_AF_MAND]      # and store (note we're interested
          STA   [_AF_RES]       # in any carry out)

_AF_SHFT: LDA   [_AF_RES]       # Might not already be loaded
          RORC                  # Rotate the accumulator (MS byte of
                                # result) 1-bit right. This shifts
                                # the carry flag into the MS bit and
                                # also updates the carry flag with
                                # the bit that "falls off the end"
          STA   [_AF_RES]       # Now store the MS byte of result
                                # (doesn't affect the carry flag)
          LDA   [_AF_RES+1]     # Load ACC with next byte of result
                                # (doesn't affect the carry flag)
          RORC                  # Rotate this byte of the result
                                # 1-bit right. This shifts the carry
                                # flag into the MS bit and also
                                # updates the carry flag with the
```

```
                                 # bit that "falls off the end"
          STA   [_AF_RES+1]      # Now store this byte of result
                                 # (doesn't affect the carry flag)

          LDA   [_AF_RES+2]      # Load ACC with next byte of result
                                 # (doesn't affect the carry flag)
          RORC                   # Rotate this byte of the result
                                 # 1-bit right. This shifts the carry
                                 # flag into the MS bit and also
                                 # updates the carry flag with the
                                 # bit that "falls off the end"
          STA   [_AF_RES+2]      # Now store this byte of result
                                 # (doesn't affect the carry flag)

          LDA   [_AF_RES+3]      # Load ACC with LS byte of result
                                 # (doesn't affect the carry flag)
          RORC                   # Rotate the LS byte of the result
                                 # 1-bit right. This shifts the carry
                                 # flag into the MS bit and also
                                 # updates the carry flag with the
                                 # multiplier bit that "falls off the
                                 # end"
          STA   [_AF_RES+3]      # Now store the LS byte of result
                                 # (doesn't affect the carry flag)

          DECX                   # Decrement the index register
                                 # (which doesn't affect the carry
                                 # flag). If the index register
          JNZ   [_AF_LOOP]       # isn't 0 then jump
                                 # back to the beginning of the loop
####
#### Breathe out - this is the end of the main multiplication loop
#### Now check the flag and negate the output result if necessary
####
_AF_TSTC: LDA   [_AF_FLAG]       # Load ACC with the flag
          JNN   [_AF_SAVE]       # If MS bit of flag is 0 then
                                 # jump to '_AF_SAVE', otherwise ..
          LDA   0                # ..load the accumulator with 0
          SUB   [_AF_RES+3]      # ..subtract LS byte of result
          STA   [_AF_RES+3]      # ..(no carry in) store result
          LDA   0                # ..load the accumulator with 0
          SUBC  [_AF_RES+2]      # ..subtract next byte of result
          STA   [_AF_RES+2]      # ..(yes carry in) store result
          LDA   0                # ..load the accumulator with 0
          SUBC  [_AF_RES+1]      # ..subtract next byte of result
          STA   [_AF_RES+1]      # ..(yes carry in) store result
          LDA   0                # ..load the accumulator with 0
          SUBC  [_AF_RES]        # ..subtract MS byte of result
          STA   [_AF_RES]        # ..(yes carry in) store result
####
#### Save the result on the stack and then let's bug out of here
#### Remember we're only returning LS 16 bits of 32-bit result
####
```

```
_AF_SAVE:   LDA   [_AF_RES+3]      # Load ACC with LS byte of result
            PUSHA                  # and stick it on the stack
            LDA   [_AF_RES+2]      # Load ACC with next byte of result
            PUSHA                  # and stick it on the stack

            LDA   [_AF_RADD+1]     # Load ACC with LS byte of return
                                   # address from temp location and
            PUSHA                  # stick it back on the stack
            LDA   [_AF_RADD]       # Load ACC with MS byte of return
                                   # address from temp location and
            PUSHA                  # stick it back on the stack

            RTS                    # That's it, exit the subroutine

_AF_RADD:  .2BYTE                  # Reserve 2-byte temp location for
                                   # the return address
_AF_MAND:  .2BYTE                  # Reserve 2-byte temp location for
                                   # the multiplicand
_AF_RES:   .4BYTE                  # Reserve 4-byte temp location for
                                   # the result
_AF_FLAG:  .BYTE                   # Reserve 1-byte to be used as a
                                   # flag for negating the result (or
                                   # not)
```

☞ If we did decide to return all 4 bytes of the result, all we would have to do would be to add two more pairs of **LDA** and **PUSHA** instructions in the **_AF_SAVE** section of the subroutine (just before we push the return address onto the stack).

16-bit Unsigned Division (_UDIV16)

And so, finally, we turn our attention to division, which is one of the most difficult operations for a computer to do. To understand why this should be so, consider the way in which you would divide 14 into 661 (Figure G.10).

Assuming that you didn't have our calculations in front of you, your thought processes would probably go something like this: You know that you can't divide 14 into 6, so you'd take the next option and try to divide 14 into 66. But how would you set about doing this? The majority of us would probably hunt around in our minds and on our fingers, saying domething like: "3 x 14 = 42, but that's too small; 5 x 14 = 70, but that's too big; 4 x 14 = 56, and that's as close as we can get."

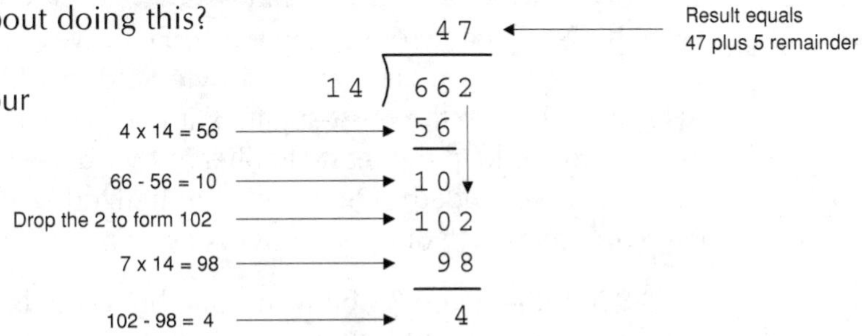

```
                                              47  ←——————  Result equals
                                                           47 plus 5 remainder
                                     14 ) 6 6 2
                    4 x 14 = 56 ————————→   5 6 |
                   66 - 56 = 10 ————————→   1 0 ↓
          Drop the 2 to form 102 ————————→  1 0 2
                    7 x 14 = 98 ————————→      9 8
                                            ———————
                  102 - 98 = 4 ————————→        4
```

Figure G.10: Performing a long division in decimal

So now we know that the first digit of our result is 4 (from the 4 x 14). Next we subtract 56 from 66 leaving 10, drop the 2 down to form 102, and go through the process again, saying: "6 x 14 = 84, but that's too small; 8 x 14 = 112, but that's too big; 7 x 14 = 98, and that's as close as we can get." Thus, we now know that the second digit of our result is 7. Finally we subtract 98 from 102 leaving 4, which is too small to divide by 14 (remember that we're performing an integer division), so we know that our result is 47 with a remainder of 4.

The point is that our CPU has to go through a similar process, which means that it has to iterate on the result by taking a stab in the dark, seeing if it went too far, and backtracking if it did. To confuse the issue even further, we sort of end up doing everything backwards, because we use the same sort of cunning tricks that we employed to make our multiplications easier for the CPU to handle. To cut a long story short, assume that we have two 16-bit numbers called the *dividend* and the *divisor*, and we wish to divide the former by the latter (Figure G.11).

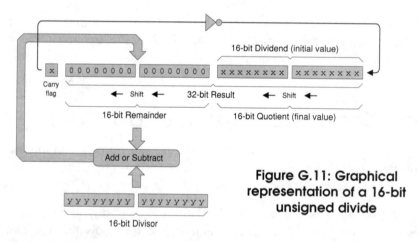

Figure G.11: Graphical representation of a 16-bit unsigned divide

The way in which this works may seem kind of difficult to follow, but everything will come out in the wash. First, we reserve a 2-byte field in which to store our divisor and a 4-byte field in which to store our result. Also, we initialize the most-significant two bytes of the result to contain all zeros, and we load the least-significant two bytes with our dividend (the number to be divided). Once we've initialized everything, we perform the following sequence of operations sixteen times:

a) Shift the entire 32-bit result one bit to the left (shift a zero into the least-significant bit).

b) Subtract the 2-byte divisor from the most-significant 2 bytes of the result and store the answer back into these 2 bytes.

c) If the carry flag is 0 following step (b), then this indicates a positive result, which means that the divisor was smaller than the 2 most-significant bytes if the result. In this case, force the least-significant bit of the result to 1.

Otherwise, if the carry flag is 1, then this indicates a negative result, which means that the divisor was bigger than the 2 most-significant bytes if the result. In this case, leave the least-significant bit of the result as a 0 (from the shift), add the 2-byte divisor back to the most-significant 2 bytes of the result, and store the answer back into these 2 bytes.

Note particularly the case in which the carry flag contains a 1 when we enter step (c). Every time this occurs, it means that the divisor was too big to subtract from the portion of the dividend that we're currently examining. But we've discovered this too late, because we've already performed the subtraction, which means that we have to add the divisor back in. In fact this is known as a *restoring-division* algorithm for just this reason; namely, that we have to keep on restoring things every time we "go too far." There are also *nonrestoring-division* algorithms which are somewhat more efficient, but also a tad more complicated ...... so we'll ignore them in the hope that they'll go away.

Now, unless you've got a size-16 brain (and one of the models equipped with turbo cooling at that), the above has probably left you feeling overheated, confused, lost, and alone. Don't be afraid, because computer divisions can bring the best of us to our knees. The easiest way to understand this (or, at a minimum, to convince ourselves that it actually works as promised) is to examine a much simpler test-case based on 4-bit numbers. For example, consider how we'd divide 1011_2 (11 in decimal) by 0011_2 (3 in decimal). The first step would be to set up our initial conditions (Figure G.12).

Remembering that our thought-experiment is based on 4-bit numbers, this means that the most-significant 4 bits of what will eventually be our 8-bit result are set to zero, while our dividend will be loaded into the least-significant 4 bits of the result. Now consider what happens during the first cycle of the process (Figure G.13).

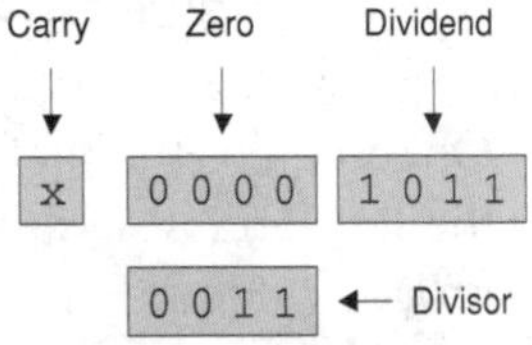

Figure G.12: Initial Conditions

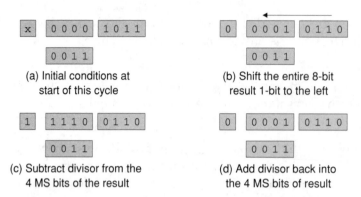

Figure G.13: First cycle of our 4-bit division test case

Commencing with our initial conditions at the start of this cycle (Figure G.13a), the first thing we do is to shift the entire 8-bit result one bit to the left, and also shift a *logic 0* into the least-significant bit during the process (Figure G.13b). Next we subtract the divisor from the 4 most-significant bits of the result (Figure G.13c), but this sets the carry flag to a *logic 1*, which tells us that we've gone too far. Thus, we complete this cycle by adding the divisor back into the 4 most significant bits of the result. As fate would have it, the second cycle offers another helping of the same thing (Figure G.14).

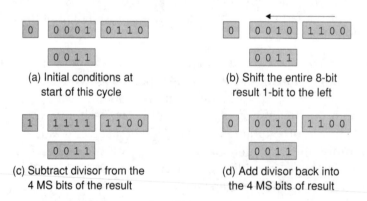

Figure G.14: Second cycle of our 4-bit division test case

Once again, the first thing we do is to shift the entire 8-bit result one bit to the left, and also shift a *logic 0* into the least-significant bit during the process. (Figure G.14b). Next we subtract the divisor from the 4 most-significant bits of the result (Figure G.14c), but this sets the carry flag to a *logic 1*, which tells us that we've gone too far. Thus, we complete this cycle by adding the divisor back into the 4 most significant bits of the result. We can but hope that the third cycle will do something to break the monotony (Figure G.15).

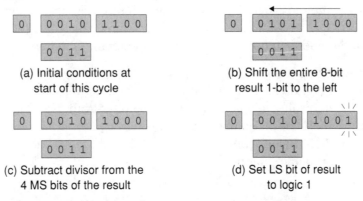

(a) Initial conditions at
start of this cycle

(b) Shift the entire 8-bit
result 1-bit to the left

(c) Subtract divisor from the
4 MS bits of the result

(d) Set LS bit of result
to logic 1

Figure G.15: Third cycle of our 4-bit division test case

As usual we commence this cycle by shifting our 8-bit result one bit to the left (Figure G.15b) and subtracting the divisor from the 4 most-significant bits of the result (Figure G.15c). But in the case of this cycle, the carry flag is left containing a *logic 0*, which means that the only thing we have to do is to force the least-significant bit of the result to a *logic 1* (Figure G.15d). Now the excitement really starts to mount, because we've only got one more cycle to go, but we don't appear to be closing in on a result. Can things possible work out to our satisfaction? (Figure G.16).

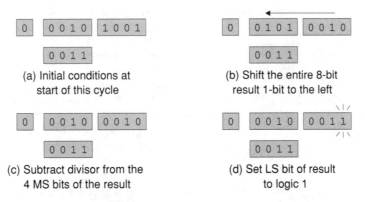

(a) Initial conditions at
start of this cycle

(b) Shift the entire 8-bit
result 1-bit to the left

(c) Subtract divisor from the
4 MS bits of the result

(d) Set LS bit of result
to logic 1

Figure G.16: Fourth and final cycle of our 4-bit division test case

Did you doubt us for a moment? We start off by shifting the 8-bit result one bit to the left (Figure G.16b) and subtracting the divisor from the 4 most-significant bits of the result (Figure G.16c). Once again, the carry flag is left containing a *logic 0*, which means that the only thing we have to do is to force the least-significant bit of the result to a *logic 1* (Figure G.16d).

When we divide 11 by 3, we expect a quotient (result) of 3 and a remainder of 2. Well tickle our toes with a turtle, just look at what's lurking in our 8-bit result. The most-significant 4 bits (which represent the remainder) contain 0010_2 (2 in decimal), while the least-significant 4 bits (which represent the quotient) contain 0011_2 (3 in decimal). Good grief, it works![4]

Now it's time to put our theory into practice, by creating a subroutine called _UDIV16 that will divide one 16-bit unsigned number into another and return a 16-bit result (we'll consider the remainder from the division later), where all of these 16-bit numbers can represent values in the range 0 through +65,535. Before considering _UDIV16 itself, let's first examine an example of a program that might call this subroutine:

```
# The following program declares two 16-bit unsigned numbers
# called VALUEA and VALUEB. The program sets things up in such a
# way that, when it calls the subroutine, the first value to be
# pushed onto the stack is divided by the second value pushed onto
# the stack
            .ORG    $4000       # Start of program is address $4000
VALUEA:     .2BYTE  $0056       # 1st 16-bit number ( 86 in decimal)
VALUEB:     .2BYTE  $7BF6       # 2nd 16-bit number (31734 in
                                # decimal)
ANSWER:     .2BYTE              # Save a 16-bit field for the result

                                # Set everything up so that the
                                # subroutine will divide VALUEB
                                # by VALUEA

            LDA     [VALUEB+1]  # Load ACC with LS byte of VALUEB
            PUSHA               # and push it onto the stack
            LDA     [VALUEB]    # Load ACC with MS byte of VALUEB
            PUSHA               # and push it onto the stack
            LDA     [VALUEA+1]  # Load ACC with LS byte of VALUEA
            PUSHA               # and push it onto the stack
            LDA     [VALUEB]    # Load ACC with MS byte of VALUEA
            PUSHA               # and push it onto the stack

            JSR     [_UDIV16]   # Jump to the "_UDIV16" subroutine
                                # to divide VALUEB by VALUEA (the
                                # code for the subroutine would be
                                # somewhere else in the program)

            POPA                # Retrieve the MS byte of the result
            STA     [ANSWER]    # from the stack and store it
            POPA                # Retrieve the LS byte of the result
            STA     [ANSWER+1]  # from the stack and store it
             :        :                       :
```

---

[4]If you're feeling frisky with your newfound knowledge, try picking on a passerby and attempt to explain just *how* it works!

Before calling the subroutine, we first have to place our 16-bit dividend on the stack followed by our 16-bit divisor ($7BF6 and $0056, respectively in this example). Note that the order in which the numbers are put on the stack *is* important in the case of a division. Once the subroutine has finished its task, we can retrieve the least-significant 2 bytes of the 4-byte result from the stack and do whatever we wish with them (these least-significant 16-bits will contain $0171 in this example). Alternatively, we could leave this value on the stack and use it as one of the values to be passed into another subroutine, such as the _ADD16 we introduced earlier.

```
####################################################################
# Name:     _UDIV16                                                #
#                                                                  #
# Function: Divides two 16-bit unsigned numbers (in the range      #
#           0 to 65,535) and returns a 16-bit unsigned result.     #
#                                                                  #
# Entry:    Top of stack                                           #
#           Most-significant byte of return address                #
#           Least-significant byte of return address               #
#           MS Byte of 1st 16-bit number (divisor)                 #
#           LS Byte of 1st 16-bit number (divisor)                 #
#           MS Byte of 2nd 16-bit number (Dividend)                #
#           LS Byte of 2nd 16-bit number (Dividend)                #
#                                                                  #
# Exit:     Top of stack                                           #
#           Most-significant byte of result                        #
#           Least-significant byte of result                       #
#                                                                  #
# Modifies: Accumulator                                            #
#           Index register                                         #
#                                                                  #
# Size:     Program = 148 bytes                                    #
#           Data    =   8 bytes                                    #
####################################################################
_UDIV16:  BLDX   16            # Load the index register with 16,
                               # which equals the number of times
                               # we want to go around the loop

          POPA                 # Retrieve MS byte of return
          STA    [_AG_RADD]    # address from stack and store it
          POPA                 # Retrieve LS byte of return
          STA    [_AG_RADD+1]  # address from stack and store it

          POPA                 # Retrieve MS byte of the divisor
          STA    [_AG_DIV]     # from the stack and store it
          POPA                 # Retrieve LS byte of the divisor
          STA    [_AG_DIV+1]   # from the stack and store it
# Note that the result is 4 bytes in size (_AG_RES+0, +1, +2,
# and +3), where _AG_RES+0 is the most-significant byte
          POPA                 # Retrieve MS dividend from stack
```

```
                STA   [_AG_RES+2]     # and store it in byte 2 of result
                POPA                  # Retrieve LS dividend from stack
                STA   [_AG_RES+3]     # and store it in byte 3 of result
                LDA   0               # Load the accumulator with 0 and
                STA   [_AG_RES]       # store it in byte 0 of result then
                STA   [_AG_RES+1]     # in byte 1 of result
####
#### Check that we're not trying to divide by zero. If we are then
#### it's an ERROR, so just return zero and bomb out
####
_AG_TSTZ:       LDA   [_AG_DIV]       # Load MS byte of the divisor and OR
                OR    [_AG_DIV+1]     # it with the LS byte of the divisor
                JNZ   [_AG_LOOP]      # If the result isn't zero then
                                      # we've got at least one logic 1, so
                                      # jump to the start of the loop.
                PUSHA                 # Otherwise push the zero in ACC
                                      # onto the stack twice, then
                PUSHA                 # jump to the last chunk of the
                JMP   [_AG_RET]       # return routine
####
#### Hold tight - this is the start of the main division loop
####
_AG_LOOP:       LDA   [_AG_RES+3]     # Load ACC with LS byte of dividend
                SHL                   # and shift left 1 bit
                STA   [_AG_RES+3]     # Store it
                LDA   [_AG_RES+2]     # Load ACC with MS byte of dividend
                ROLC                  # and rotate left 1 bit
                STA   [_AG_RES+2]     # Store it
                LDA   [_AG_RES+1]     # Load ACC with LS byte of remainder
                ROLC                  # and rotate left 1 bit
                STA   [_AG_RES+1]     # Store it
                LDA   [_AG_RES]       # Load ACC with MS byte of remainder
                ROLC                  # and rotate left 1 bit
                STA   [_AG_RES]       # Store it
                # Now we want to subtract the 16-bit divisor from the
                # most-significant two bytes of the result
                LDA   [_AG_RES+1]     # Load ACC with LS byte of remainder
                SUB   [_AG_DIV+1]     # Subtract LS byte of divisor
                STA   [_AG_RES+1]     # Store it in LS byte of remainder
                LDA   [_AG_RES]       # Load ACC with MS byte of remainder
                SUBC  [_AG_DIV]       # Subtract MS byte of divisor
                                      # (w carry)
                STA   [_AG_RES]       # Store it in MS byte of remainder
                # If the carry flag is zero, set the LS bit of the
                # result to logic 1 and jump to the end of the loop.
                # Otherwise undo the harm we've just done by adding the
                # 16-bit divisor back into the MS two bytes of the
                # result
```

```
          JNC   [_AG_ADD]      # If carry flag not zero jump to
          LDA   [_AG_RES+3]    # to _AG_ADD, otherwise load ACC
                               # with LS byte of result,
          OR    $01            # use OR to set LS
          STA   [_AG_RES+3]    # bit to 1, then store it and jump
                               # to AG_TSTL (test at end
          JMP   [_AG_TSTL]     # of the loop)
_AG_ADD:  LDA   [_AG_RES+1]    # Load ACC with LS byte of remainder
          ADD   [_AG_DIV+1]    # Add LS byte of divisor (w/o carry)
          STA   [_AG_RES+1]    # Store it in LS byte of remainder
          LDA   [_AG_RES]      # Load ACC with MS byte of remainder
          ADDC  [_AG_DIV]      # Add MS byte of divisor (with
                               # carry)
          STA   [_AG_RES]      # Store it in MS byte of remainder
_AG_TSTL: DECX                 # Decrement the index register. If
          JNZ   [_AG_LOOP]     # the index register isn't 0 then
                               # jump back to the beginning of the
                               # loop
####
#### Breathe out - this is the end of the main division loop
#### Save result on the stack and bug out of here. Remember that
#### we're only returning the 16-bit quotient portion of the
#### result
####
_AG_SAVE: LDA   [_AG_RES+3]    # Load ACC with LS byte of quotient
          PUSHA                # and stick it on the stack
          LDA   [_AG_RES+2]    # Load ACC with MS byte of quotient
          PUSHA                # and stick it on the stack
_AG_RET:  LDA   [_AG_RADD+1]   # Load ACC with LS byte of return
                               # address from temp location and
          PUSHA                # stick it back on the stack
          LDA   [_AG_RADD]     # Load ACC with MS byte of return
                               # address from temp location and
          PUSHA                # stick it back on the stack
          RTS                  # That's it, exit the subroutine
_AG_RADD: .2BYTE               # Reserve 2-byte temp location for
                               # the return address
_AG_DIV:  .2BYTE               # Reserve 2-byte temp location for
                               # the divisor
_AG_RES:  .4BYTE               # Reserve 4-byte temp location for
                               # the result. The MS two bytes of
                               # which will contain the remainder
                               # and the LS two bytes the quotient
```

☞ Remember that the 2-byte remainder from the division ends up in the most significant two bytes of the result (_AG_RES and _AG_RES+1). Thus, if we decided that we wanted our subroutine to return this remainder, all we would have to do would be to add two more pairs of LDA and PUSHA instructions in the _AG_SAVE section of the subroutine (just before we push the return address onto the stack). However, it's more usual to create a separate subroutine that just returns the remainder. Alternatively, another common technique would be to modify this subroutine to have multiple entry and exit points, depending on whether we wish it to return the remainder or the quotient. Both of these techniques save us from passing the remainder back and forth when we don't wish to use it.

16-bit Signed Division (_SDIV16)

The _SDIV16 subroutine is very similar to the _UDIV16 subroutine we just looked at, except that this one can be used to divide two signed 16-bit numbers together, where said numbers must be in the range -32,767 through +32,767.

Unfortunately, our division algorithm will not perform correctly if faced with negative values, so we have to perform similar tricks to those we used in the case of our signed multiplication subroutines. Thus, we need to check the signs of the numbers first, change any negative values into their positive counterparts using twos complement techniques, perform the division, then correct the sign of the result if necessary (see also the notes at the end of the subroutine).

The main body of a program would call this _SDIV16 subroutine in exactly the same way that we'd call its _UDIV16 cousin, so what say we cut to the chase and leap directly into the body of the subroutine itself?

```
###############################################################
# Name:      _SDIV16                                          #
#                                                             #
# Function:  Divides two 16-bit signed numbers (in the range  #
#            -32,767 to +32,767): returns a 16-bit signed result #
#                                                             #
# Entry:     Top of stack                                     #
#            Most-significant byte of return address          #
#            Least-significant byte of return address         #
#            MS Byte of 1st 16-bit number (divisor)           #
#            LS Byte of 1st 16-bit number (divisor)           #
#            MS Byte of 2nd 16-bit number (Dividend)          #
#            LS Byte of 2nd 16-bit number (Dividend)          #
#                                                             #
# Exit:      Top of stack                                     #
#            Most-significant byte of result                  #
#            Least-significant byte of result                 #
```

```
#                                                                    #
# Modifies: Accumulator                                              #
#           Index register                                           #
#                                                                    #
# Size:     Program = 226 bytes                                      #
#           Data    =   9 bytes                                      #
######################################################################
_SDIV16:   BLDX   16             # Load the index register with 16,
                                 # which equals the number of times
                                 # we want to go around the loop

           POPA                  # Retrieve MS byte of return
           STA    [_AH_RADD]     # address from stack and store it
           POPA                  # Retrieve LS byte of return
           STA    [_AH_RADD+1]   # address from stack and store it

           POPA                  # Retrieve MS byte of the divisor
           STA    [_AH_DIV]      # from the stack and store it
           POPA                  # Retrieve LS byte of the divisor
           STA    [_AH_DIV+1]    # from the stack and store it
# Note that the result is 4 bytes in size (_AH_RES+0, +1, +2,
# and +3), where _AH_RES+0 is the most-significant byte
           POPA                  # Retrieve MS dividend from stack
           STA    [_AH_RES+2]    # and store it in byte 2 of result
           POPA                  # Retrieve LS dividend from stack
           STA    [_AH_RES+3]    # and store it in byte 3 of result
           LDA    0              # Load the accumulator with 0 and
           STA    [_AH_RES]      # store it in byte 0 of result then
           STA    [_AH_RES+1]    # in byte 1 of result
####
#### Check that we're not trying to divide by zero. If we are then
#### it's an ERROR, so just return zero and bomb out
####
_AH_TSTZ:  LDA    [_AH_DIV]      # Load MS byte of the divisor and OR
           OR     [_AH_DIV+1]    # it with the LS byte of the divisor
           JNZ    [_AH_TSTA]     # If the result isn't zero then
                                 # we've got at least one logic 1, so
                                 # jump to the bit to test for -ve
                                 # number.
           PUSHA                 # Otherwise push the zero in ACC
                                 # onto the stack twice,
           PUSHA                 # then jump to the last chunk
           JMP    [_AH_RET]      # of the return routine
####
#### Invert input values if necessary and load the output flag
####
_AH_TSTA:  LDA    [_AH_DIV]      # Load ACC with MS byte of divisor
           TA     [_AH_FLAG]     # and save it to the flag
           JNN    [_AH_TSTB]     # if the divisor is positive then
                                 # jump to '_AH_TSTB', otherwise ..
           LDA    0              # ..load the accumulator with 0
```

```
                SUB   [_AH_DIV+1]   # ..subtract LS byte of divisor
                STA   [_AH_DIV+1]   # ..(no carry in) store result
                LDA   0             # ..load the accumulator with 0
                SUBC  [_AH_DIV]     # ..subtract MS byte of divisor
                STA   [_AH_DIV]     # ..(yes carry in) store result
_AH_TSTB:       LDA   [_AH_FLAG]    # Load the flag,
                XOR   [_AH_RES+2]   # XOR it with MS byte of dividend,
                STA   [_AH_FLAG]    # then store the flag again

                LDA   [_AH_RES+2]   # Load MS dividend into the ACC
                JNN   [_AH_LOOP]    # If dividend is positive then
                                    # jump to '_AH_LOOP, otherwise ..
                LDA   0             # ..load the accumulator with 0
                SUB   [_AH_RES+3]   # ..subtract LS byte of dividend
                STA   [_AH_RES+3]   # ..(no carry in) store result
                LDA   0             # ..load the accumulator with 0
                SUBC  [_AH_RES+2]   # ..subtract MS byte of dividend
                STA   [_AH_RES+2]   # ..(yes carry in) store result
####
#### Hold tight - this is the start of the main division loop
####
_AH_LOOP:       LDA   [_AH_RES+3]   # Load ACC with LS byte of dividend
                SHL                 # and shift left 1 bit
                STA   [_AH_RES+3]   # Store it
                LDA   [_AH_RES+2]   # Load ACC with MS byte of dividend
                ROLC                # and rotate left 1 bit
                STA   [_AH_RES+2]   # Store it
                LDA   [_AH_RES+1]   # Load ACC with LS byte of remainder
                ROLC                # and rotate left 1 bit
                STA   [_AH_RES+1]   # Store it
                LDA   [_AH_RES]     # Load ACC with MS byte of remainder
                ROLC                # and rotate left 1 bit
                STA   [_AH_RES]     # Store it
                # Now we want to subtract the 16-bit divisor from the
                # most-significant two bytes of the result
                LDA   [_AH_RES+1]   # Load ACC with LS byte of remainder
                SUB   [_AH_DIV+1]   # Subtract LS byte of divisor
                STA   [_AH_RES+1]   # Store it in LS byte of remainder
                LDA   [_AH_RES]     # Load ACC with MS byte of remainder
                SUBC  [_AH_DIV]     # Subtract MS byte of divisor
                                    # (w carry)
                STA   [_AH_RES]     # Store it in MS byte of remainder
                # If the carry flag is zero, set the LS bit of the
                # result to logic 1 and jump to the end of the loop.
                # Otherwise undo the harm we've just done by adding the
                # 16-bit ivisor back into the MS two bytes of the
                # result
                JNC   [_AH_ADD]     # If carry flag not zero jump to
                LDA   [_AH_RES+3]   # to _AH_ADD, otherwise load ACC
                                    # with LS byte of result,
```

```
            OR    $01             # use OR to set LS
            STA   [_AH_RES+3]     # bit to 1, then store it and jump
                                  # to AH_TSTL
            JMP   [_AH_TSTL]      # (test at end of the loop)

_AH_ADD:    LDA   [_AH_RES+1]     # Load ACC with LS byte of remainder
            ADD   [_AH_DIV+1]     # Add LS byte of divisor (w/o carry)
            STA   [_AH_RES+1]     # Store it in LS byte of remainder
            LDA   [_AH_RES]       # Load ACC with MS byte of remainder
            ADDC  [_AH_DIV]       # Add MS byte of divisor (with
                                  # carry)
            STA   [_AH_RES]       # Store it in MS byte of remainder
_AH_TSTL:   DECX                  # Decrement the index register. If
            JNZ   [_AH_LOOP]      # the index register isn't 0 then
                                  # jump back to the beginning of the
                                  # loop
####
#### Breathe out - this is the end of the main division loop
#### Now check the flag and negate the quotient portion of the
#### result if necessary (see also the notes following the
#### subroutine)
####
_AH_TSTC:   LDA   [_AH_FLAG]      # Load ACC with the flag
            JNN   [_AH_SAVE]      # If MS bit of flag is 0 then
                                  # jump to '_AH_SAVE', otherwise ..
            LDA   0               # ..load the accumulator with 0
            SUB   [_AH_RES+3]     # ..subtract LS byte of quotient
            STA   [_AH_RES+3]     # ..(no carry in) store result
            LDA   0               # ..load the accumulator with 0
            SUBC  [_AH_RES+2]     # ..subtract MS byte of quotient
            STA   [_AH_RES+2]     # ..(yes carry in) store result
####
#### Save result on the stack and bug out of here. Remember that
#### we're only returning the 16-bit quotient portion of the
#### result
####
_AH_SAVE:   LDA   [_AH_RES+3]     # Load ACC with LS byte of quotient
            PUSHA                 # and stick it on the stack
            LDA   [_AH_RES+2]     # Load ACC with MS byte of quotient
            PUSHA                 # and stick it on the stack
_AH_RET:    LDA   [_AH_RADD+1]    # Load ACC with LS byte of return
                                  # address from temp location and
            PUSHA                 # stick it back on the stack
            LDA   [_AH_RADD]      # Load ACC with MS byte of return
                                  # address from temp location and
            PUSHA                 # stick it back on the stack
            RTS                   # That's it, exit the subroutine
_AH_FLAG:   .BYTE                 # Reserve 1-byte field to be used as
```

```
                              # flag to decide whether or not to
                              # negate the result
_AH_RADD:   .2BYTE            # Reserve 2-byte temp location for
                              # the return address
_AH_DIV:    .2BYTE           # Reserve 2-byte temp location for
                              # the divisor
_AH_RES:    .4BYTE           # Reserve 4-byte temp location for
                              # the result. The MS two bytes of
                              # which will contain the remainder
                              # and the LS two bytesthe quotient
```

☞ As we're not concerned with returning the remainder in this subroutine, we've managed to sidestep a rather convoluted problem. This problem may be summarized as follows: *"If you divide a positive number with a negative number (or a negative number with a positive number), then what sign should the remainder have?"* To put this another way, if we divide +3 into -17, we know that the quotient is going to be -5, but should the remainder be +2 or -2? In fact one can get completely bogged down on this subject (and there are even more esoteric considerations that we aren't even going to touch upon). The bottom line is that if *you* decide that *you* do indeed want to return the remainder from a signed division, then it's up to *you* to stroll down to your local library, read as many books on computer mathematics as you can stomach, and then make *your own* decision as to what you want the sign of the remainder to be.[5]

Tradeoffs involved in using subroutines

There is no doubt that subroutines can be extremely useful and, if you create programs of any size, you'll probably end up using a lot of them. However, there are advantages and disadvantages to everything, and subroutines are no exception.

On the bright side, having a grab-bag of useful subroutines can be extremely convenient when you're writing a program, because they allow you to concentrate on the main body of your program, speed the process of capturing your program, and improve the legibility of your source code. Also, if you craft a subroutine and test it thoroughly, then you have a reasonably high level of confidence that this piece of the code works, thereby allowing you to spend the bulk of your time debugging the main body of the program.

Yet another reason for using subroutines is that they can significantly reduce the total size of your program in terms of both the source code and the

---

[5]Yes, we *are* weaseling out of a tortuously tricky topic.

machine code (although recursive subroutines can still commandeer a lot of memory in the form of the stack when they're running). Having said this, subroutines with small bodies relative to the number of their parameters may actually increase the size of the source code.

The main downside of using subroutines (as opposed to in-line code) is that they usually add an overhead in the form of additional instructions that have to be executed, including passing parameters into the subroutine, retrieving results from the subroutine, and executing the JSR and RET instructions themselves. The effect of these additional instructions is to slow the execution of the resulting program.

At the end of the day, the way to learn what to put into a subroutine and what to leave out is best learned by practicing. Also, the more time you take planning your code up front, the smaller and more efficient will be the resulting programs.[6]

Can you beat our subroutines?

One of the great things about writing programs in assembly language is that there are almost always better ways of doing things. By swapping an instruction here and using a cunning trick there, you can usually squeeze out a few bytes and make the code smaller and more efficient (or sometimes add a few bytes and make it larger and more efficient).

When we wrote the subroutines above, we were mainly concerned with legibility and understandability, so it is almost certainly possible to improve these routines in one way or another. Yes, we're talking to you ..... go on, be brave, improve our subroutines and email us to tell us what you did, why you did it, and how well it worked. Also, if you send us a copy (with documentation), we may well put it up on our web page for others to peruse, use, and admire.

---

[6] *"If I had more time, I would have written you a shorter letter."* – Blaise Pascal

Appendix H

Answers to "Quick Quiz" Questions

Contents of Appendix H

Quick quiz #1

1) What color socks did some Vikings wear?

From scraps of fabric discovered at archeological digs, it appears that more than a few Vikings were partial to woolen socks of the bright red persuasion.

2) When did the term computer originate?

Mathematical tables in the 1800s were created by teams of mathematicians working day and night on primitive mechanical calculators. Due to the fact that these people performed *computations* they were referred to as *computers*.

3) What is a general definition of a computer?

In its broadest sense, a computer is a device that can accept information from the outside world, process that information, make decisions based on the results of its processing, and then return the information to the outside world in its new form.

4) What technologies can be used to implement computers?

Computers can theoretically be implemented in almost any technology, including mechanical, fluidic, and pneumatic variants. However, the overwhelming majority of today's computers are electronic, because electronic components are much smaller and faster than their counterparts in the other technologies.

5) What is the difference between analog and digital information?

Analog information represents a continuously varying quantity, such as the brightness of a lamp controlled by a dimmer, while digital information represents a quantity that can be considered as being in one of a number of discrete states, such as a light switch which is either ON or OFF.

6) Which devices acted as switches in the first true electronic computers?

The first truly electronic computers, such as ENIAC, which was constructed between 1943 and 1946 at the University of Pennsylvania, employed vacuum tubes in the role of switches.

7) What is a semiconductor and what is the most commonly used semiconductor?

A semiconductor is a material that can be persuaded to act as both a conductor and an insulator, which makes it suitable for use in constructing electronic switches in the form of transistors. The most commonly used semiconductor is silicon; transistors formed from other materials, such as gallium arsenide (GaAs), may switch faster and use less power than their silicon counterparts, but these materials are not as robust and they are harder to work with.

8) When was the first point-contact transistor constructed?

Bell Laboratories in the United States began research into semiconductors in 1945, and physicists *William Shockley, Walter Brattain,* and *John Bardeen* succeeded in creating the first point-contact germanium transistor on December 23rd, 1947.

9) In what way can a transistor be considered to act like a switch?

If a mechanical switch is CLOSED, electricity can flow between its terminals, but if the switch is OPEN, the flow of electricity is blocked. Similarly, in the case of the transistor, the presence or absence of an electrical signal at its control terminal causes the transistor to be ON or OFF (corresponding to the mechanical switch being CLOSED or OPEN), thereby facilitating or blocking the flow of electricity between the other two terminals.

10) What is an integrated circuit?

An integrated circuit has transistors and the connections between them formed on the surface layer of a sliver, or chip, of a single piece of semiconductor (usually silicon). Modern integrated circuit manufacturing techniques allow the construction of transistors whose dimensions are measured in fractions of a millionth of a meter, and a single device a few millimeters square can contain millions of these transistors.

Quick quiz #2

1) How many deaths does a coward die?

Cowards only physically die a single time, just like the rest of us. The saying: *"A coward dies a thousand deaths – a brave man only once,"* refers to the fact that cowards spend so much time worrying about the possible outcome of a particular course of action that they suffer defeat in their own minds long before they actually get around to attempting anything.

2) Which number system is used inside digital computers?

Although some experiments have been performed with tertiary (three-state) logic, the vast majority of today's digital computers use the binary number system, which employs two digits: 0 and 1. Also, any number system having a base that is a power of two (2, 4, 8, 16, 32, and so forth) can be easily mapped into its binary equivalent, and vice versa. For this reason, humans often use the *hexadecimal* (base-16) system to represent numbers inside computers.

3) **Which part of the computer makes decisions and performs logical and arithmetic operations?**

The *central processing unit (CPU)* is where all of the number crunching and decision making is performed. In the majority of today's home computers, the entire CPU is implemented as a single integrated circuit. These single-chip CPUs are known as *microprocessors*, and computers based on microprocessors are called *microcomputers*.

4) **What are the data, control, and address busses used for?**

The CPU uses its address bus to point to a location in the memory (or to other components in the system) from which it wishes to read or write data; the data bus is used to convey the data; and the control bus is used to orchestrate operations.

5) **Name four different types of information that might be conveyed by the data bus.**

A pattern of logic 0s and 1s can be used to depict anything that we wish it to represent at any particular time. Thus, values on the data bus may be used to represent instructions, numbers (or portions thereof), alphanumeric characters, simple patterns of 0s and 1s, or anything else we desire.

6) **What are the clock, ~reset, ~read, and ~write signals used for?**

The clock signal is used to synchronize the internal actions of the CPU, and also to synchronize the actions of the CPU with other units in the system. (Asynchronous CPUs that do not use clocks have been created for experimental purposes, but commercial digital computers are almost universally based on synchronous, or clocked techniques). The ~reset signal is used to initialize the CPU and the rest of the system (the reason this signal has a tilde character ("~") as part of its name is to indicate that its active state is a *logic 0*). The CPU generates the ~read and ~write signals, and uses them to inform other components in the system as to whether it wishes to read data from them or write data to them.

7) **What are ROMs and RAMs used for and what are the major differences between them?**

Read-only memories (ROMs) and random-access memories (RAMs) are special types of integrated circuits that can store binary data for use by the computer. The data contained by ROMs is hard-coded into them during their construction, which means that CPU can read (extract) data from these devices, but cannot write (insert) new data into them. By comparison, data can be read out of RAM devices and, if required, new data can be written back into them. When power is first applied to a system, RAM devices initialize containing random *logic 0* or *logic 1* values. Thus, any meaningful data stored inside a RAM must be written into it by the CPU after the system has been powered-up.

8) What does 1 K-Byte actually mean?

Although the suffix K (Kilo) is generally taken to represent one thousand, digital computers are based on the binary (base-2) number system, and the closest power of two to one thousand is 2^{10}, which equals 1,024. Therefore, 1 K-Byte actually refers to 1,024 bytes.

9) What is a memory map used for?

A memory map is a diagram that is commonly used to illustrate the way in which the computer's memory is organized. These maps may be drawn with the most-significant address at the top and address zero at the bottom, but it's more common to see them with address zero at the top, because this tends to reflect the way in which we document our programs.

10) What do input and output ports do and how do they do it?

A CPU uses its input ports to read information from the outside world. Input ports are connected to the data bus using tri-state buffers, which usually serve to isolate the ports from the bus. However, when the CPU reads from an input port, that port's tri-state buffers are enabled, thereby allowing data from the outside world to pass through the port onto the data bus, from whence it can be accessed by the CPU.

Similarly, the CPU uses its output ports to write data to the outside world. There are a variety of different types of output ports, but a common flavor stores whatever value is on the data bus when the CPU writes to the port. In this case, the output port typically continues to present this data to the outside world until the CPU returns to overwrite its contents with some new data.

Quick quiz #3

1) What did computer memory have to do with ladies knitting?

One of the first forms of computer memory that might be considered to be reasonably useful by today's standards was *magnetic core memory* (also known as *core store* or simply *core*), which consisted of tiny ferromagnetic beads threaded onto wires. The early core stores were effectively "knitted" together by teams of ladies with the appropriate skills, but automated techniques soon took over.

2) What was magnetic core store and how did it work?

As was noted in the previous question, magnetic core store was an early form of computer memory which consisted of tiny ferromagnetic beads threaded onto wires. The wires were arranged as a matrix of "rows" and "columns," with a bead at each row-column intersection. If a sufficient amount of current was passed through a pair of row and column wires, the bead at the intersection between them would be magnetized. The polarity of the current determined the direction in which the bead was magnetized, so it was possible to use each bead to represent a *logic 0* or *logic 1* value for later use.

3) What were switch and display panels used for in early computers?

Early computers were not equipped with sophisticated input and output devices such as typewriter-type keyboards and television-style screens. Instead, operators used a bank of switches called a switch panel to instruct the computer as to which operations it was to perform. Similarly, a display panel of flashing lights was one of the main techniques for the operator to see what was actually going on inside the computer.

4) What does a RAM contain when power is first applied to a computer system?

Modern semiconductor RAM devices are *volatile*, which means that any data they contain is lost when power is removed from the system. When power is re-applied to the system, these devices initialize containing random logic 0 and 1 values. Thus, any meaningful data stored inside a RAM must be written into it by the computer after the system has been powered up.

5) What is a hard disk?

A hard disk is a bulk-storage device that can be used to store a large amount of data relatively cheaply. This form of media maintains its data when power is removed from the system, so it is said to be *non-volatile*. The hard disk in a home computer consists of a circular disk a few inches in diameter, which is covered with a magnetic material and which is spun at high speed. The hard disk unit also contains special read/write heads (similar in concept to the record/playback heads in a music cassette recorder). These read/write heads can move across the surface of the disk, record data onto the disk, and recover it later. A home computer can use its hard disk to store hundreds of millions of bytes (megabytes) of information.

6) What are flowcharts and what are they used for?

Flowcharts are a graphical technique for describing a sequence of operations; they do this by charting the flow, or passing of control, from one operation to the next. Flowcharts are extremely useful for documenting the operation of a computer program and they provide an excellent means of communicating the intent of a program, but although they are strong on *"what"* and *"how,"* they are a little weaker on *"when"* and *"why."*

7) What is a program?

The term "program" refers to a sequence of logical, arithmetic, and related operations that are to be performed by a computer in order to solve a computational problem or accomplish some other task. The term may be used to refer to the source code specified in some programming language, and also to the resulting machine code that is executed by the computer.

8) What do you understand by the terms "opcode" and "operand" at this stage in our discussions?

The first byte of each instruction is called the *opcode*, which is an abbreviation of "operation code." The opcode instructs the CPU as to the type of operation it is to perform. Any additional data bytes associated with an opcode are referred to as the *operand*. (Note that this answer assumes a simple computer, such as the *Beboputer*, which is based on an 8-bit data bus and 8-bit instructions).

9) What were the main tasks performed by a monitor routine?

In the context of the discussions in Chapter 3, a monitor routine (or program) would be used to read the state of the switch panel, write values to the lights on the display panel, load data from the switch panel into specified memory locations, and eventually hand control over to another program.

10) Where would you expect to find an accumulator and what does it do?

The accumulator, which is a general-purpose register inside a CPU, is used to gather, or accumulate intermediate results.

Quick quiz #4

1) Who invented the accordion (and why)?

The *accordion* was invented in 1829 by the British physicist and inventor Sir Charles Wheatstone, but we may only speculate as to why he unleashed this monster on an unsuspecting world (unless he was a secret devotee of Polka music).

2) What were the main reasons for the widespread use of paper tapes and punched cards in the 1960s and 1970s?

Computer designers needed some mechanism for storing and transporting programs and data. Paper tapes and punched cards offered a reliable, low-cost solution.

3) Can you spot any interesting features associated with the subset of Morse Code shown in Table 4.1?

If you stare at this table long enough you can spot any number of interesting things, some of which may even be meaningful. But perhaps the most obvious point is that the characters that are used most frequently tend to have the shortest codes. For example, the most commonly used letter in the English language is 'E', whose equivalent Morse Code is a single dot.

4) When was paper tape first used for the preparation, storage, and transmission of data?

In 1857, only twenty years after the American inventor Samuel Finley Breese Morse developed his Morse Telegraph, Sir Charles Wheatstone introduced the first application of paper tapes as a medium for the preparation, storage, and transmission of telegraph data. Sir Charles' paper tape used two rows of holes to represent Morse's dots and dashes. Outgoing messages could be prepared off-line on paper tape and transmitted later.

5) What were the major features of an IBM 1-inch paper tape?

Well it's certainly safe to say that one of the IBM 1-inch paper tape's major features was the fact that it was one inch wide. Data was stored on the tape by punching rows of holes across the width of the tape. The pattern of the holes in each *data row* represented a single data value or character. The individual hole positions forming the data rows were referred to as *channels* or *tracks*, and IBM's 1-inch tapes supported eight channels, with 0.1 inches between the holes.

6) What was the difference between a paper tape generated by a teleprinter and one created by a computer?

The paper tapes generated by teleprinters were formatted in ASCII or some similar code, in which each row of holes represented an alphanumeric character or control code. However, computers could not directly execute a program represented in this form, so a special program was used to read an ASCII paper tape and generate an equivalent tape in binary.

7) In what context were the terms "source" and "object" originally used in regard to paper tapes?

The ASCII and binary paper tapes referenced in the previous question were referred to as the *source* and *object* tapes, respectively. The term "source" was used to indicate the "root" or "beginning," while the term "object" probably indicated that generating this tape was the "object" of the exercise.

8) When and by whom were punched cards first used in a data-processing role?

The practice of punching holes in cards to record data dates back to the early 1800s, when a French silk weaver, Joseph Marie Jacquard, invented a way of automatically controlling the warp and weft threads on a silk loom by recording patterns as holes in a string of thin wooden boards or cards. However, the first practical use of punched cards in a data processing role is credited to the American inventor Herman Hollerith. During the 1880s, Hollerith decided to use Jacquard's punched cards to represent the data gathered for the American census, and then to read and collate this data using an automatic machine.

9) What were the main advantages of punched cards over paper tapes?

The main advantages of punched cards over paper tapes were: (a) It was easy to replace any cards containing errors; and (b) the textual equivalent of the patterns of holes could be printed along the top of the card (one character above each column), which made it easier for the programmer to see what he or she had done.

10) What are the primary differences between main store and bulk storage?

The main store is where the computer keeps any programs and data that are currently active, while bulk storage is used to hold dormant programs and data. We may generalize the main store as being relatively fast, large, expensive, and (typically) volatile, while bulk storage is relatively slow, small, cheap, and (always) non-volatile. Note that referring to bulk storage devices as being "small" and "cheap" has to be taken in the context of the amount of data that they hold. This means that if you compare main store with bulk storage in terms of cubic-inches-per-megabyte and dollars-per-megabyte, then bulk storage is much smaller and cheaper.

Quick quiz #5

1) **What is the average life span of any electronic product in an environment containing small children?**

   Unfortunately, there's no empirical data on this subject, so we have to rely on personal experience, which indicates that the average life-span of any article in an environment containing small children is typically measured in hours if you're lucky.

2) **What are diodes and what do they do?**

   A diode is an electronic component that has two terminals and that only conducts electricity in one direction. The first diodes were created using vacuum tubes, but these were eventually superseded by semiconductor equivalents.

3) **What is the main difference between standard diodes and LEDs?**

   Standard diodes and light-emitting diodes (LEDs) function in a similar manner, in that they both conduct electricity in only one direction. The main difference between these devices is that LEDs emit light when they are conducting. Another difference is that a LED must be packaged in a material that is transparent to the wavelength of light that it emits (otherwise we couldn't see it glow, which would sort of defeat the point of the whole thing).

4) **What are the main differences between incandescent light bulbs and LEDs?**

   Incandescent light bulbs are comparatively large, power-hungry, and tend to have relatively limited life-spans, while LEDs are small, energy-efficient, and exceptionally durable.

5) **Why did early digital calculators and watches use red LEDs as opposed to other colors?**

   Depending on the materials used, it is possible to create LEDs that emit red, green, yellow, orange, and, most recently, blue light. The red ones are the cheapest and the easiest to make, while the blue ones are comparatively rare and expensive. In addition to being cheap and easy to make, red LEDs were the first to become commercially available, which is why all of the original calculators and digital watches used them.

6) In the case of our simple 8-bit displays, why did we use red and green LEDs to represent logic 0 and logic 1 values respectively?

There's no particular reason for us to have used red and green LEDs where we did – we could have swapped them over or even exchanged them for different colors. It's simply that, when we designed our output displays, we took a vote and decided that *logic 0s* and *logic 1s* would be represented by red and green, respectively.

7) Are 7-segment displays always preferable to simple 8-bit displays?

No. Your choice of display depends on the information you're trying to convey to the observer. If you desire to present simple ON/OFF conditions, then 8-bit displays usually have the edge, but 7-segment displays tend to be preferably if your intent is to communicate numerical data.

8) What do the terms "common anode" and "common cathode" mean in the context of diodes?

Diodes have two terminals, which are called the *anode* and the *cathode*. When we're using a group of LEDs to create a device such as a 7-segment display, we might connect all of their anodes to a common power supply and use individual signals to drive their cathodes, in which case this would be referred to as a *common anode* configuration. By comparison, if all of the cathodes terminals are connected to a common supply, the LEDs are said to be in a *common cathode* configuration.

9) The single decoded 7-segment display we used in lab 3 was said to be based on a common cathode configuration; hence the truth table shown in Figure 5.17. Create the corresponding truth table for a single decoded 7-segment display based on a common anode configuration (Figure H.1).

out_data[3:0]	Hex	dec_out_data[6:0]
0 0 0 0	0	1 0 0 0 0 0 0
0 0 0 1	1	1 1 1 1 0 0 1
0 0 1 0	2	0 1 0 0 1 0 0
0 0 1 1	3	0 1 1 0 0 0 0
0 1 0 0	4	0 0 1 1 0 0 1
0 1 0 1	5	0 0 1 0 0 1 0
0 1 1 0	6	0 0 0 0 0 1 0
0 1 1 1	7	1 0 1 1 0 0 0
1 0 0 0	8	0 0 0 0 0 0 0
1 0 0 1	9	0 0 1 1 0 0 0
1 0 1 0	A	0 0 0 1 0 0 0
1 0 1 1	B	0 0 0 0 0 1 1
1 1 0 0	C	1 0 0 0 1 1 0
1 1 0 1	D	0 1 0 0 0 0 1
1 1 1 0	E	0 0 0 0 1 1 0
1 1 1 1	F	0 0 0 1 1 1 0

Figure H.1: Truth table for common-anode 7 segment decoder

10) **What are the relative advantages and disadvantages of undecoded and decoded 7-segment displays?**

An undecoded 7-segment display has the advantage that it can be used to construct $2^7 = 128$ different patterns of lit and unlit segments, while its decoded counterpart can only display $2^4 = 16$ (which are used to represent the hexadecimal digits '0' through '9' and 'A' through 'F'). However, the undecoded display occupies seven bits of an output port (one for each segment), while a decoded display only requires four. Also, a decoded display can directly accept a binary number and immediately display its hexadecimal equivalent, while an undecoded version requires the programmer to perform some kind of conversion.

Quick quiz #6

1) **Why is it preferable to view digital logic in terms of primitive gates as opposed to transistors?**

Complex digital functions, such as microprocessors, can contain a huge number of transistor-based switches, and it would be almost impossible to design or comprehend a system represented at this level of abstraction. The solution is to view things at higher levels of abstraction, the first such level being the primitive logic gates NOT, AND, NAND, OR, NOR, XOR, and XNOR.

2) **What does a NOT gate do and how does it do it?**

A NOT gate, which has a single input and output, is constructed in such a way that a *logic 0* presented to its input will enable or disable the transistors forming the gate so as to cause the output to drive a *logic 1*; similarly, a *logic 1* on the input will cause a *logic 0* on the output.

3) **What does a bobble on the output of the symbol for a primitive gate indicate?**

A small circle (referred to as a *bobble* or *bubble*) on the output of the symbol for a primitive logic gate indicates that this is an inverting function; that is, the output from such a function is the logical negation of that function's non-inverting counterpart.

4) **What is the difference between an AND gate and a NAND gate?**

An AND gate is the logical counterpart of a NAND gate and vice versa. In the case of an AND, the output of the gate only drives a *logic 1* value if all of the inputs are *logic 1*; if any of the inputs are *logic 0*, the output is also *logic 0*. By comparison, if all of the inputs to a NAND are *logic 1*, its output is a *logic 0*; if any of the inputs to the NAND are *logic 0*, it's output drives a *logic 1* (Figure H.2).

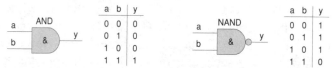

a	b	y
0	0	0
0	1	0
1	0	0
1	1	1

a	b	y
0	0	1
0	1	1
1	0	1
1	1	0

Figure H.2: AND versus NAND gates and truth tables

We can coerce an AND gate to act like a NAND by inverting its output with a NOT. Similarly, a NAND can be caused to act like an AND by inverting *its* output with a NOT. If the gates are implemented using the CMOS technology, a NAND gate will require fewer transistors than an AND; for example, 2-input NAND and AND gates require 4 and 6 transistors, respectively.

5) **Describe the similarities and differences between decoders and multiplexers.**

Both multiplexers and decoders have control inputs, and applying a binary value, or address, to these inputs causes each of the functions to perform a certain action. In the case of a multiplexer, the control inputs select between a number of data inputs, and convey the logical value on the selected input to the function's output. By comparison, a decoder doesn't have any data inputs; instead, the control signals are used to select between a number of outputs, and to assert the selected output by driving it to its active logic value.

6) **Create the symbol and truth table for a 3:8 decoder with active-high outputs (Figure H.3).**

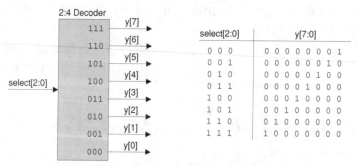

select[2:0]	y[7:0]
0 0 0	0 0 0 0 0 0 0 1
0 0 1	0 0 0 0 0 0 1 0
0 1 0	0 0 0 0 0 1 0 0
0 1 1	0 0 0 0 1 0 0 0
1 0 0	0 0 0 1 0 0 0 0
1 0 1	0 0 1 0 0 0 0 0
1 1 0	0 1 0 0 0 0 0 0
1 1 1	1 0 0 0 0 0 0 0

**Figure H.3: Symbol and truth table for a
3:8 decoder with active-high outputs**

Note that we don't have any "bobbles" on the symbol's outputs, because this particular function has active-high outputs and "bobbles" are used to indicate active-low outputs (similarly, the outputs are now named y[7:0] as opposed to ~y[7:0]).

7) Describe the difference between combinational and sequential functions.

In the case of a combinational (or combinatorial) function, the logic values at that function's outputs are directly related to the current *combination* of values on its inputs. By comparison, the logic values on a sequential function's outputs depend not only on the function's current input values, but also on previous input values; that is, the output values depend on a *sequence* of input values.

8) Create the symbols and truth tables for a D-type latch with an active-high enable and a D-type flip-flop with a negative-edge clock (Figure H.4).

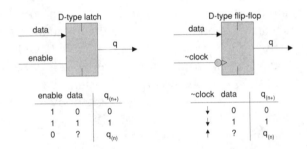

Figure H.4: D-type latch (active-high enable) and
D-type flip-flop (negative-edge clock)

9) What is a tri-state buffer used for and what does a logic Z value represent?

A tri-state buffer is similar to its standard counterpart, except that it has an additional control input. When the buffer is enabled it conveys whatever signal is presented to its data input through to its output, while disabling the gate means that it is effectively disconnected from its own output. The result is that the outputs from multiple tri-state buffers can be used to drive the same wire, so long as only one of the buffers is enabled at any particular time. In the case of a computer system, tri-state buffers act as interfaces between the data bus and the devices that drive it. With regards to the *logic Z*, this isn't a real value at all. Unlike *logic 0s* and *logic 1s*, which are ultimately related to physical voltage levels, a *logic Z* represents a condition known as *high-impedance*, which means that there isn't anything being driven onto the wire.

10) **Create symbols and truth tables for tri-statable OR and NOR gates (Figure H.5).**

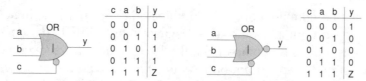

c	a	b	y
0	0	0	0
0	0	1	1
0	1	0	1
0	1	1	1
1	1	1	Z

c	a	b	y
0	0	0	1
0	0	1	0
0	1	0	0
0	1	1	0
1	1	1	Z

Figure H.5: Tri-statable OR and NOR gates (active-low enables)

Quick quiz #7

1) **Why do digital computers use the binary number system?**

Digital computers are constructed from logic gates that can represent only two states; thus, they are obliged to employ the binary number system, which employs only two digits: 0 and 1. Note that there have been experiments with logic gates based on three voltage levels, which therefore employ the tertiary (base-3) number system, but systems based on these techniques have never become commercially viable or available. Also note that the high-impedance Z is typically not considered in the context of this question (see also the answer to Quiz #6, Question 9).

2) **Why are numbers in a computer different from numbers written on a piece of paper?**

Numbers written on paper (in any number system) can be as large as one wishes. By comparison, numbers within a computer have to be mapped onto a physical system of logic gates and wires. Thus the maximum value of an individual numerical quantity inside a computer is dictated by the width of the computer's *data bus*; that is, by the number of bits available to describe that value.

3) **What is the difference between unsigned and signed binary numbers?**

Unsigned binary numbers can only be used to represent positive values, while the signed binary format can be used to represent both positive and negative values.

4) What range of numbers can be represented by a 4-bit field if it (a) represents an unsigned quantity and (b) represents a signed quantity?

If an n-bit field is used to portray an unsigned binary number, it can represent values in the range 0 through $(2^n - 1)$, so a 4-bit field can represent values of 0 through 15. By comparison, if the n-bit field is used to portray signed binary numbers, it can represent values in the range $-2^{(n-1)}$ through $(2^{(n-1)} - 1)$, so a 4-bit field can represent values of -8 through +7.

5) What is the two's complement of 00110101_2?

One way to generate the two's complement of a binary number is to invert all of the bits and to then add 1 to the result. As an alternative, we can commence with the least-significant bit of the value to be complemented, copy each bit each bit up to and including the first 1, and then invert the remaining bits. Using either of these techniques reveals that the two's complement of 00110101_2 is 11001011_2 (Figure H.6).

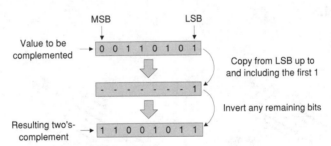

Figure H.6: Using the shortcut technique to generating the two's complement

6) What is the carry flag used for in binary additions?

In the case of binary additions, the carry flag is used to indicate whether or not the result generated by adding two *unsigned* binary numbers will fit in the accumulator (a *logic 0* in the carry flag indicates that the result did fit, while a *logic 1* indicates that it didn't). The contents of the carry flag can then be used by the programmer to detect an error condition, or as part of a subsequent addition using an **ADDC** instruction, thereby facilitating the addition of multi-byte values. Note that the overflow flag performs the equivalent function for *signed* binary numbers.

7) Use two's complement techniques to generate the result of 00110101_2 - 01001010_2 (Figure H.7).

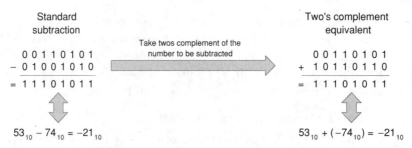

Figure H.7: Performing a binary subtraction using two's complement techniques

8) Show how a 6-bit data bus could be used to represent signed and unsigned binary values (yes, we really mean six bits) (Figure H.8).

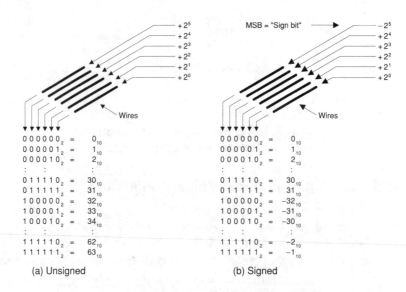

Figure H.8: Using 6 bits to represent unsigned and signed binary numbers

9) **What range of numbers could be represented by a 6-bit bus if we were using a signed-magnitude format, as opposed to standard signed binary numbers?**

In a signed-magnitude format, the most-significant bit is simply used to indicate the sign of the number (0 = positive, 1 = negative), while the remaining bits are used to represent the actual value. In the case of a 6-bit field, the least-significant 5 bits can be used to represent values of 0 through 31, so a 6-bit sign-magnitude number can represent values in the range -31 through +31 (Figure H.9a).

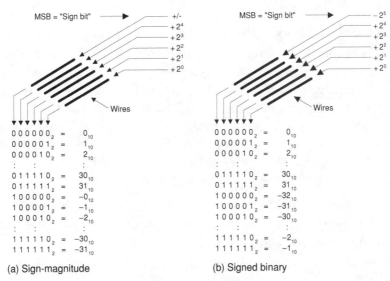

(a) Sign-magnitude   (b) Signed binary

Figure H.9: Sign-magnitude versus signed binary numbers

By comparison, in the case of a signed binary number, the most-significant bit actually represents a negative quantity (-32 in the case of a 6-bit field), so a 6-bit signed binary number can represent values in the range of -32 through +31 (Figure H.9b).

10) **What are the advantages and disadvantages of standard signed binary numbers, as compared to using a signed-magnitude format?**

The sign-magnitude format is conceptually easy for us to understand, because it maps directly onto the way in which we usually visualize numbers in decimal. However, one problem with sign-magnitude numbers is that they support both +0 and -0 values, which introduce complications when a computer is trying to decide whether or not a given value is less than or equal to zero. Another problem is that they make calculations inside a computer overly complicated.

By comparison, the two's complement (signed binary) format is conceptually quite difficult for us to understand when we're first exposed to it. Also, two's complement numbers support an asymmetrical range of values (-128_{10} through $+127_{10}$ for an 8-bit field), which can cause problems, such as the fact that we can't negate the maximum negative value. However, two's complement numbers only give us one value of 0 to worry about, and they are extremely efficient when it comes to performing calculations inside a computer.

Quick Quiz #8

1) **If we were designing a computer that could only support two addressing modes, which ones would we choose?**

We would chose the implied and absolute addressing modes. Actually, we wouldn't have a lot of choice in the case of the implied mode, because this mode is fundamental to the way in which instructions like HALT and INCA work. Although the immediate mode is certainly useful the absolute mode can easily replace it, but the reverse isn't true. Similarly, modes such as indexed and indirect definitely have their advantages, but we can finagle our way around them using the absolute mode.

2) **Is there any particular reason why instructions such as ADD and SUB don't support the indirect, pre-indexed indirect, and indirect post-indexed addressing modes?**

In the case of the *Beboputer*, the main reason these instructions don't support these modes is that its designers (the authors of this book) decided not to bother. To be more precise, the authors decided not to offer these instruction/addressing mode combinations to emphasize the fact that CPU designers can dictate which instructions and modes will be supported and which won't.

3) **Why doesn't the *Beboputer* support NOT, NAND, NOR, and XNOR instructions?**

   a) To keep the *Beboputer's* instruction set as small and concise as possible.

   b) Generally speaking these instructions tend to be used less frequently than their counterparts (such as AND and OR), which *are* included in the *Beboputer's* instruction set.

   c) The functionality of these instructions can be replicated using combinations of other instructions, and doing so is educational in its own right.

4) **In our discussions on the extended ALU, we forced the multiplexer in the negator block to select $FE (-2 in decimal) for a DECA; is there another way in which we could have implemented this instruction?**

Yes. If you refer to Figure 8.34, you'll see that the DECA instruction causes the multiplexer generating the Ciadd signal to feed a *logic 1* value into the adder function's carry-in input. Thus, the resulting operation is equivalent to *accumulator + (-2) + 1*, which boils down to *accumulator -1*.

As an alternative, we could have forced the multiplexer in the negator block to select $FF (-1 in decimal), and caused the multiplexer generating the Ciadd signal to feed a *logic 0* value into the adder function's carry-in input. In this case, the resulting operation would have been equivalent to *accumulator + (-1)*, which once again boils down to *accumulator -1*.

The reason we didn't use this alternative approach was that we found it aesthetically pleasing to gather the ADD and INCA instructions into one group and the SUB and DECA instructions into another (insofar as controlling the multiplexer generating the Ciadd signal). This also gave us the advantage of causing the SUB and DECA instructions to behave in a similar manner, thereby providing consistency to the discussions on these instructions.

5) **Which instructions would be most affected if the *Beboputer's* instruction set also included SETC (*"set carry flag to 1"*) and CLRC (*"clear carry flag to 0"*) instructions?**

The instructions that would be most affected would be ADD and SUB, because we would no longer need them! For example, the main reason we have an ADD is to allow us to implicitly force the carry-in input to the adder function to a *logic 0* when performing an addition, but we could replace the ADD with a CLRC followed by an ADDC. Similarly, the main reason we have an SUB is to allow us to implicitly force the carry-in input (acting in the role of a *borrow* in this case) to the adder function to a *logic 1* when performing a subtraction, but we could replace the SUB with a SETC followed by an SUBC.

6) **Describe two or more ways in which we might augment or enhance the *Beboputer's* CMPA (*"compare accumulator"*) instruction.**

The existing CMPA instruction sets the carry flag to *logic 1* if the value in the accumulator is greater than the value we're comparing it to, and it sets the zero flag to a *logic 1* if the two values are equal. This means that determining whether the value in the accumulator is *less than* the value we're comparing it to requires us to perform two tests: one on the carry flag followed by one on the zero flag (or vice versa). Thus, one way in which we could enhance the CMPA instruction would be to set another flag (say the overflow flag) to a *logic 1* if the value in the accumulator is *less than* the value we're comparing it to.

Also, the existing CMPA instruction assumes that both of the values being compared represent unsigned binary numbers. Thus, we could augment this instruction (or, more precisely, we could augment the *Beboputer's* instruction set) by providing two versions, such as CMPAU ("compare accumulator unsigned") and CMPAS ("compare accumulator signed").

7) **Why do we use certain status flags to represent multiple conditions (for example, the zero flag is also used to indicate equality in the case of the CMPA instruction)?**

Providing individual flags for every type of condition we wish to capture would increase the complexity of the CPU's physical implementation. Also, we would have to add more conditional jump instructions (two for each flag: "*jump if condition is true*" and "*jump if condition is false*"), which would also increase the complexity of the CPU.

8) **Describe a way in which we might enhance the *Beboputer's* SHR ("*shift accumulator right*") instruction.**

One way in which we could enhance the SHR instruction would be to allow ourselves to specify by how many bits the accumulator should be shifted. To illustrate this, consider two techniques by which we could extend our instruction set:

Method #1		Method #2	Comment
SHR1	or	SHR 1	# Shift accumulator 1 bit right
SHR2	or	SHR 2	# Shift accumulator 2 bits right
SHR3	or	SHR 3	# Shift accumulator 3 bits right
SHR4	or	SHR 4	# Shift accumulator 4 bits right
:		:	:

Method #1 would require us to add a whole slew of new mnemonics, while method #2 allows us to append the number of bits to be shifted to our original three-letter mnemonic (this technique would be the preferred approach). Irrespective of the way in which we choose to represent these instructions, and assuming that we want these instructions to continue to use the implied addressing mode, each shift (1 bit, 2 bits, 3 bits, and so forth) would require its own unique opcode.

Alternatively, we might decide to modify the CPU such that the SHR instruction used the immediate addressing mode. In this case, the SHR opcode would now be followed by an operand byte to specify the number of bit-positions to be shifted. Furthermore, if we do decide to allow the SHR instruction to use immediate addressing, then we could also extend it to support other modes, such as absolute and indirect addressing.

9) **What are the advantages and disadvantages of the ROLC and RORC instructions rotating the accumulator through the carry flag?**

The advantage of rotating through the carry flag is that this greatly facilitates multi-byte operations. The main disadvantage is that it makes life awkward if we simply want the accumulator to *"wrap-around"* on itself. In fact many CPUs also support ROL and ROR instructions, which do cause the accumulator to "wrap around" (the bit that "falls off the end" would still be copied into the carry flag). Fortunately, we can achieve the same effect as an ROL or ROR by performing a ROLC or RORC, testing the state of the carry flag, and then using an AND or OR instruction to clear or set the appropriate bit in the accumulator. Although this is somewhat ungraceful, life would be a whole lot worse if the *Beboputer* only supported ROL and ROR instructions, because finagling these to achieve the same ends as their ROLC and RORC counterparts is *really* painful. If you don't believe us, you can easily try it out for yourself. Pretend that you only have ROL and ROR instructions (no ROLC or RORC), and then see how much fun you have trying to implement the _UMULT16 subroutine in Appendix G.

10) **How is it possible for us to use the value in the accumulator to drive the ALU, to perform an operation using the ALU, and to store the result back in the accumulator without messing everything up?**

This is possible because all of the functional blocks forming the CPU have some amount of internal delay. This means that it takes a finite amount of time for the signals to propagate through the ALU and back to the accumulator's inputs. Thus, when we load the result from an operation back into the accumulator, it can store this data before the act of changing its contents ripple through the system and reappear at its inputs.

Quick quiz #9

1) **What are the advantages and disadvantages of the hex keypad compared to the switch and display panels?**

The only advantages of the switch and display panels are that they're conceptually very simple to understand, and they map almost directly onto the way in which the computer processes information internally. In almost every other respect the hex keypad trounces them soundly: it's faster, easier, and more efficient to enter data using a keypad, and its also easier to detect errors, because we find it difficult to relate to binary data in the form employed by the switch and display panels.

2) **How many diodes would be required to encode the hex keypad's buttons (excluding the ON/OFF and Reset buttons) using the mapping described in Chapter 9?**

From Figure 9.3 we know that the mapping for the buttons is as follows:

Button	Binary Value	Button	Binary Value	Button	Binary Value
'0'	00000000	'8'	00001000	Address	00010000
'1'	00000001	'9'	00001001	Data	00100000
'2'	00000010	'A'	00001010	Clear	00110000
'3'	00000011	'B'	00001011	Enter	01000000
'4'	00000100	'C'	00001100	Step	10000000
'5'	00000101	'D'	00001101	Run	11000000
'6'	00000110	'E'	00001110		
'7'	00000111	'F'	00001111		

From Figure 9.4 we can see that we require a diode at every intersection between row and column wires at which we wish to introduce a *logic 0*. Thus, we require a diode for each '0' in the binary values above, which gives us a total of 136 diodes.

3) **What are the advantages of using hierarchical flowcharts?**

Hierarchical flowcharts allow us to represent programs at a high level of abstraction and to partition them into manageable "chunks". Representing a program in this way facilitates its implementation, and also makes it easier to understand and modify in the future.

4) **Why did we choose to load the stack pointer with $4FFF at the beginning of the program?**

This was a purely arbitrary decision. We could have initialized the stack pointer to point to almost anywhere in the RAM portion of the memory map (as long as we ensure that there is no chance of the data we eventually put on the stack overwriting our program). In this particular case, our program commenced at location $4000, so we just decided to initialize the stack pointer to the end of this 4K block of RAM at address $4FFF.

5) **In the "Initializing the Variables" section of the program, we noted that it wasn't strictly necessary to initialize the variable in memory location $4004. Why is this the case?**

Locations $4002, $4003, and $4004 are used to store the number of "hundreds," "tens", and "ones", respectively. The way in which this particular program is written requires us to initialize the "hundreds" location to zero, because the program uses this value as a starting point when it extracts the number of "hundreds" (similarly for the "tens" location). Whatever value remains after we've extracted the "hundreds" and "tens" is loaded directly into the "ones" location, thereby overwriting its existing contents, so the initial value of this location is immaterial.

6) **Describe how a JNC (*"jump if not carry"*) instruction works.**

The JNC instruction tests the value in the carry flag, which may have been cleared to a *logic 0* or set to a *logic 1* during the course of a previous instruction. If the carry flag contains a 0, then the JNC (*"jump if not carry"*) causes the CPU to jump to the address specified in the operand bytes; otherwise the CPU skips the operand bytes and proceeds to the next instruction.

7) **When we were extracting the "hundreds" and the "tens," we compared the value in the accumulator to 99 and 9, respectively. Why didn't we compare the value in the accumulator to 100 and 10, respectively?**

Consider the case of the "hundreds". What we wish to do is determine if the value in the accumulator is greater than or equal to 100. The most appropriate instruction available to us is the CMPA, which compares the value in the accumulator to another value in memory. CMPA loads the carry flag with a *logic 1* if the value in the accumulator is the larger, or it loads zero flag with a *logic 1* if the two values are equal. Thus, if we compared the value in the accumulator to 100, we would potentially have to perform two tests: one on the carry flag to see if the accumulator contained a value greater than 100 and, if this failed, a second test on the zero flag to see if the value in the accumulator was equal to 100. However, if we compare the value in the accumulator to 99, the carry flag will be set to logic 1 if the accumulator's contents are greater than 99, which is another way of saying "greater than or equal to 100" (which is the condition we're really testing for). A similar argument applies to the case of the "tens"; by comparing the value in the accumulator to 9, the carry flag will be loaded with *logic 1* if the accumulator's contents are greater than or equal to 10.

8) What would you expect to happen if you click on "Big Red' while the *Beboputer* is speaking a number?

Whenever you click Big Red it will become active, irrespective of whether the *Beboputer* is speaking a number or not. The fact that Big Red has been activated will be stored in the latch associated with this switch, thereby causing Big Red to light up. However, activating Big Red won't affect the *Beboputer* until the next time the CPU happens to read a value from Big Red's input port.

9) Why is it easier to map from binary to hexadecimal than it is to map from binary to decimal?

The hexadecimal (base-16) number system has a base that is a power of two ($16 = 2^4$). Any number system having a base that is a power of two (2, 4, 8, 16, 32, and so on) can be easily mapped into its binary equivalent, and vice versa. By comparison, mapping between binary and a number system whose base is not a power of two (such as decimal) requires more effort.

10) The programs in Chapter 9 assumed that the 8-bit switches represented unsigned binary numbers in the range 0_{10} through 255_{10}. How would you approach rewriting these programs such that they treated the 8-bit switches as representing signed binary numbers in the range -128_{10} through $+127_{10}$?

The easiest way to do this would be to modify the portion of the program that reads and stores the value on the 8-bit switch input device. When we load the value from the switches into the accumulator, the negative flag will be set if the most significant bit in the accumulator is a logic 1, thereby indicating a negative value (assuming that we're considering the switches to represent signed binary numbers). In this case, we could use a temporary location to store the fact that we have a negative number, and we could then convert the value in the accumulator into its two's complement. Thus, the accumulator always ends up containing a positive value, and the tasks of extracting the "hundreds", "tens", and "ones" would remain unchanged.

The act of displaying the number would also remain unchanged insofar as using the solo display to represent the "hundreds" and the dual display to represent the "tens" and "ones". However, we would also have to employ our undecoded 7-segment device to represent the minus sign for any negative numbers (Figure H.10).

Thus, the only real modification to the display routine would be to check the temporary location in which we store whether our original number was positive or negative; if negative, we write the appropriate value to the undecoded 7-segment display to light its middle segment. Similarly, in the case of speaking a number aloud, we would first check our temporary location to decide whether or not to say the work *"minus"* before speaking the rest of the number.

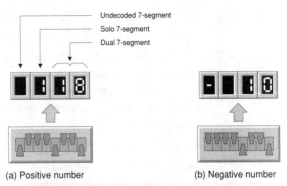

Undecoded 7-segment
Solo 7-segment
Dual 7-segment

(a) Positive number   (b) Negative number

Figure H.10: Modifying the program to handle signed binary values

Quick quiz #10

1) Why was the first commercial typewriter like a sewing machine?

The manufacturer of the first commercial typewriter was E. Remington and Sons, who specialized in guns and sewing machines. The designer they assigned to the typewriter project was William K. Jenne, whose expertise was in the design of sewing machines. Thus, the first commercial typewriter, which was released in 1874, ended up with a foot pedal to advance the paper and sweet little flowers on the sides!

2) Why are the keys on a typical computer keyboard arranged the way they are?

One problem with the first typewriter was that its keys jammed when the operator typed at any real speed, so its inventor, Christopher Latham Sholes, designed the keyboard so as to separate letters that are frequently written or typed one after the other. The jamming problem was later overcome by the use of springs, but existing users didn't want to change and there was no turning back.

3) What are the advantages and disadvantages of a Dvorak compared to a Sholes (QWERTY) keyboard?

The Dvorak keyboard is designed such that that letters which are commonly typed together are physically close to each other, and also such that the (usually) stronger right hand performs the bulk of the work, while the left hand has control of the vowels and the less-used characters. By comparison, the Sholes keyboard separates letters that are commonly typed together and forces the (usually) weaker left hand to perform the bulk of the work.

Using a Dvorak keyboard, the typist's fingers spend 70% of their time on the home row and 80% of this time on their home keys. Thus, as compared to the approximately 120 words that can be constructed from the home row keys of the Sholes keyboard, it is possible to construct more than 3,000 words on Dvorak's home row. Also, Dvorak's scheme reduces the motion of the hands by a factor of three, improves typing accuracy by approximately 50%, and typing speed by up to 20%.

Thus, the only advantage that can really be claimed for the Sholes keyboard is that there are a lot of them about and everyone is used to this layout, which means that it would be expensive and time-consuming to replace all of the existing keyboards and retrain everybody.

4) What does "ASCII" stand for?

ASCII stands for the *American Standard Code for Information Interchange*.

5) Why is ASCII said to be a 7-bit code?

Standard ASCII only defines 128 codes for alphabetic, numeric, punctuation, and special control characters, which means that we only require a 7-bit field to represent these codes.

6) What are the ASCII codes for 'A', 'a', 'Z', and 'z' in hexadecimal, decimal, and binary?

Character	Hexadecimal	Decimal	Binary
'A'	$41	65	01000001
'a'	$61	97	01100001
'Z'	$5A	90	01011010
'z'	$7A	122	01111010

7) What is the difference between even parity and odd parity?

Parity generation and checking is one of the simplest techniques that can be used for error detection. This form of checking requires the presence of an extra bit called the *parity bit* to be associated with the field under consideration. For example, in the case of a 7-bit ASCII code, the most-significant bit in the 8-bit byte can be used to represent the parity bit. In the case of even parity, special logic is used to count the number of *logic 1s* in the field under consideration. If there are an even number of *logic 1s*, the parity bit would be loaded with a *logic 0*, but if there were an odd number of *logic 1s*, the parity bit would be loaded with a *logic 1*. The end result of an even parity check is that there are always an *even* number of *logic 1s* in the final value, which comprises both the original field and the parity bit. (By comparison, an odd parity check ensures that there are always an *odd* number of *logic 1s* in the final value).

8) **What does the term "sticky" mean in the context of a key on a computer keyboard?**

A "sticky" key is one that toggles back and forth between two modes of operation. For example, pressing the CAPS key causes it to become active, and it will remain active until it is pressed again. By comparison, a non-sticky key, such as the SHIFT key, is only active as long as the operator continues to hold it down, and it automatically returns to its inactive state as soon as it is released.

9) **How can we modify our program such that, irrespective of the state of the CAPS and SHIFT keys, whenever an alpha key is pressed the program will always display the uppercase code for that character (for example, if the user clicks on 'a', the code for 'A' will be displayed)?**

As we know, the ASCII code for an 'A' is $41, and the codes increase sequentially up to $5A for 'Z'. Similarly, the ASCII code for 'a' is $61, and the codes increase sequentially up to $7A for 'z'. Thus, whenever we read a code from the keyboard into the accumulator, all we need to do is to test the value in the accumulator to see if it's both greater than or equal to $61 and less than or equal to $7A. If the value is in this range, then we know that we have a lower-case letter. In this case, we can subtract $20 from the value in the accumulator to generate the ASCII code for the upper-case version of the letter, and then write our new code to the dual 7-segment displays.

10) **How could we write a program to cause our virtual keyboard to act like a Dvorak keyboard?**

This is similar to the last question, but it's a little bit trickier. Consider the illustrations of the Sholes and Dvorak keyboards shown in Figures 10.1 and 10.2, respectively. If we press the number '2' on the *Beboputer's* Sholes-style keyboard, it will (not surprisingly) generate the ASCII code for a '2', but we actually want to end up with the ASCII code for a '7', which is the corresponding character on the Dvorak keyboard. Thus, whenever we find the ASCII code for a '2' in our accumulator, we're going to have to replace it with the code for a '7', and similarly for all of the other keys on our keyboard. One way in which we could achieve this is to perform a laboriously sequence of tests as follows (assume that we've just loaded the accumulator with a value from the keyboard, and note that the syntax shown here is more fully discussed in Chapter 12):

```
COMP_2:    CMPA   $32        # Compare ACC to ASCII code for '2'
           JNZ    [COMP_3]   # If not equal jump to 'COMP_3'
                  LDA  $37   # Load ACC with ASCII code for '7'
           JMP    [DISPLAY]  # Jump to display routine

COMP_3:    CMPA   $33        # Compare ACC to ASCII code for '3'
           JNZ    [COMP_4]   # If not equal jump to 'COMP_4'
                  LDA  $35   # Load ACC with ASCII code for '5'
           JMP    [DISPLAY]  # Jump to display routine

COMP_4:    ...... And so it goes for all of the keys
```

As we can see, this is a perfectly reasonable technique, but it's also excruciatingly tedious, because we would have to include 10 tests for the numeric characters, 26 tests for the upper-case alphabetic characters, 26 tests for the lower-case alphabetic characters, and yet more tests for all of the punctuation and special characters ..... Eeeeek!

A much better alternative would be to create a look-up table containing the ASCII codes for the Dvorak key positions, and to then employ the ASCII code received from our Sholes keyboard as an index into the loop-up table (using the indexed addressing mode).

Quick quiz #11

1) Summarize the process of reproducing images using Nipkow disks.

German inventor Paul Gottlieb Nipkow proposed the use of Nipkow disks for capturing, transmitting, and reproducing pictures in 1884. These devices were based on flat circular disks with holes punched in them in a spiral formation. A strong light source was used to project a photographic image onto the surface of a spinning disk. As each hole passed through the image, the light and dark areas in the image modified the intensity of the light passing through the hole. This light was projected onto a light-sensitive phototube, thereby modulating the electrical signal generated by the phototube. At the other end of the process was a brilliant lamp and a second spinning Nipkow Disk. The electrical signal coming out of the phototube was used to modulate the lamp, which was projected onto the second disk. The modulated light passed through the holes in the second disk to build up a line-by-line display on a screen.

2) Summarize the functions of the electron gun, grid, deflection plates, and shadow mask in a video tube.

The electron gun is used to provide a source of free electrons. The positively charged grid, which is mounted a little way in front of the electron gun, focuses the electrons into a beam and accelerates them towards the screen. The deflection plates (or magnetic coils) are used to control the path of the electron beam and dictate its motion across the face of the screen. The shadow mask is a positively charged grid, which is mounted a fraction of an inch from the screen's fluorescent coating. The shadow mask helps to accelerate the electrons forming the electron beam, giving them more energy which results in a brighter picture. More importantly, the shadow mask helps to focus the beam, because any electrons that deviate even slightly from the required path hit the mask and are conducted away, thereby producing a sharper image.

3) **Considering the raster scan technique shown in Figure 11.2, can you suggest an alternative path we could make the spot (electron beam) follow?**

First of all, there are a variety graphical patterns which are of interest due to their recursive nature, a simple example of which are Hilbert curves, which are named after the mathematician D. Hilbert who invented them in 1891 (Figure H.11).

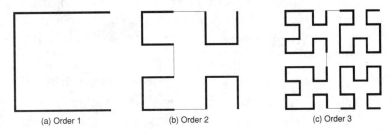

(a) Order 1   (b) Order 2   (c) Order 3

Figure H.11: Hilbert curves of order 1, 2, and 3

With the exception of the first pattern, each curve is formed by taking four "shrunk-down" copies of the preceding pattern, rotating them by various amounts, and linking them with three connecting lines (the first pattern is a special case, but it could be regarded as four "empty" patterns linked by three straight lines).

Why is this of interest? Well we could use a similar recursive pattern to describe the path our electron beam follows as it wends its way across the screen. Also, it has been suggested that similar techniques would provide the means to upgrade our computer and television equipment in the future. For example, suppose that a new television were developed that supports four times the number of pixels as existing sets. This would in turn require television signals to contain four times the information, which will necessitate higher frequencies and so forth. But what about all of the people who had the old television sets, and who therefore don't have enough pixels to display all of this data. The idea is that the new television signals could be based on the next highest order of the recursive pattern, which essentially means that the beam covers four times the pixels in the same area. Existing users would only require a new receiver/decoder module that would perform some simple interpolation algorithm to filter the data so as to be suitable for the lower-resolution screen. (Note that none of the above is commercially available, it's just an idea).

4) Describe the difference between the additive, subtractive, and psychological primary colors.

Primary colors are those which can be combined to form all of the other colors. In the case of light, the primary colors are red, green, and blue. Adding different colored lights together increases the components of the spectrum that reach our eyes, so these are referred to as the *additive primaries*. By comparison, the primary colors for pigments are yellow, magenta, and cyan. Adding different colored pigments together decreases the components of the spectrum that reach our eyes, so these are referred to as the *subtractive primaries*. It is also common to refer to red, yellow, green, blue, white, and black as being the *psychological primaries*, because we subjectively and instinctively believe that these are the basis for all of the other colors.

5) Summarize the main features of a memory-mapped display?

A memory-mapped display regards the screen as consisting of rows and columns of "boxes," where each box can contain a character. The patterns of dots for each character are stored in a special character ROM device, and the display's controller uses ASCII codes stored in the main system's memory to select the particular characters of interest in the character ROM. Memory-mapped displays are extremely efficient in terms of their memory requirements, and are still employed in such applications as bank teller machines. However, this technique find little use in modern computers, which require the ability create sophisticated graphics and to control each pixel on an individual basis.

6) Why did the early memory-mapped displays commonly support 80 columns of characters?

Because one of the main techniques for storing data at that time was by means of IBM punched cards, which supported 80 columns of holes (or 80 characters of information, depending on your point of view). The designers of the first computer terminals certainly didn't want to display fewer characters than were on an IBM punched card, and there didn't seem to be any major advantage to displaying more characters than were on a card.

7) **Assuming that the video card is in its graphics mode and using its default base address for this mode, how would you calculate the video RAM address for the graphic block in the mth column of the nth row?**

a) We know that the default base address of our video RAM in its graphics mode (the address of the block at row 0 column 0) is $E400

b) We know that we have forty-eight rows numbered from 0 through 47, which means that the first row is actually referred to as *row 0*, the second row as *row 1*, the third row as *row 2*, and so on.

c) We know that each row contains sixty-four columns numbered from 0 through 63, which means that the first column is actually referred to as *column 0*, the second column as *column 1*, and so on.

d) So, we can quickly calculate the address of column 0 on any row 'n' using the formula: *address = base address of video RAM + ('n' x $40)*, where $40 is the hexadecimal equivalent of 64 in decimal:

Row ('n')	Formula	Resulting address
0	$E400 + (0 x $40)	= $E400 (row 0 col 0)
1	$E400 + (1 x $40)	= $E440 (row 1 col 0)
2	$E400 + (2 x $40)	= $E480 (row 2 col 0)
3	$E400 + (3 x $40)	= $E4C0 (row 3 col 0)
:	:	:

e) Similarly, for any column 'm', we know that the address of that column is going to be equal to the address of column 0 on that row plus 'm'. Once again, it's easy to see how this works by looking at the following examples for the third row (*row 2*):

Column ('m')	Formula	Resulting address
0	$E480 + 0	= $E480 (row 2 col 0)
1	$E480 + 1	= $E481 (row 2 col 1)
2	$E480 + 2	= $E482 (row 2 col 2)
3	$E480 + 3	= $E483 (row 2 col 3)
4	$E480 + 4	= $E484 (row 2 col 4)
5	$E480 + 5	= $E485 (row 2 col 5)
:	:	:

8) **Create a flowchart that illustrates the major actions performed by the last program in Chapter 11 (the one that randomly places colored blocks on the memory-mapped display) (Figure H.12).**

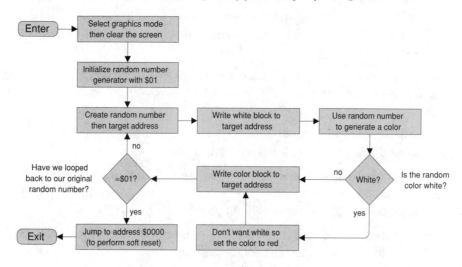

Figure H.12: Flowchart

9) **With regard to the previous question, how could we modify this program such that it never generates a black color?**

In the middle of the body of the existing program we perform a test to see if the randomly generated color is white and, if it is, we set it to red (or any other color we choose) before writing it to the video RAM. Either before or after this test, we could perform a similar test to see if our randomly generated color was black and, if it was, we could set it to another color of our choice.

10 **With regard to the previous question, why would it be such a pain to actually perform these modifications?**

Because we would have to insert extra instructions in the middle of our program, which means that we would have to re-enter the rest of the program after this point. Also, we might have to modify the target address of a jump instruction depending on where we inserted this new test (in a larger program we might have to change the target addresses of many jump instructions). Note that these problems are resolved when we move to use assembly language (or higher-level languages) as discussed in Chapter 12.

Quick quiz #12

1) **Summarize the advantages of writing programs in assembly language as opposed to writing them in machine code.**

   Writing programs in assembly language is substantially faster and less error-prone than creating them in machine code, and assembly language representations are much easier to understand, debug, and modify. With regard to modification, it's easy to insert or delete instructions in assembly language, because the assembler program automatically determines the address operands associated with jump instructions (this can be a major pain when working at the machine code level).

2) **What do the terms *"syntax"* and *"semantics"* mean in the context of computer languages?**

   In the context of computer languages, "syntax" refers to the grammar of the language, such as the ordering of the words and symbols in relation to each other, while "semantics" refers to the underlying meaning of the words and symbols and the relationships between the things they denote.

3) **What are the differences between unary and binary operators?**

   A unary operator only requires a single operand; for example, the unary operator '!' in the expression !$16, which means "invert all of the bits in the $16 operand" (resulting in $E9). By comparison, a binary operator requires two operands; for example, the binary operator '+' in the expression $16 + $25. Also, unary operators have a higher precedence than binary operators, which means that any unary operators are evaluated before their binary counterparts.

4) **Summarize the differences between one-pass and two-pass assemblers.**

   A one-pass assembler translates as much of the assembly code into machine code as it can during its one and only pass through the source code. During this process, the assembler keeps track of any unresolved references and labels, and then retrofits the appropriate values into the machine code at the end of the pass. By comparison, a two-pass assembler uses it's first pass through the source code to construct a table relating any labels to their final addresses; this form of assembler now has access to all of the information required to generate the machine code on its second pass through the source code.

5) What is a nested subroutine?

A nested subroutine is one which has been called from another subroutine, as opposed to one that has been called from the main body of the program. Whether or not a subroutine is nested may be a function of time. For example, if the body of the program calls subroutine A, then this subroutine is not nested at this time. However, if the body of the program calls subroutine B, which in turn calls subroutine A, then subroutine A is nested at this time.

6) If you've just created a computer, is it better to hand-edit your first assembler and use it to assemble your first editor, or is it preferable to hand-assemble your first editor and use it to create your first assembler?

This is a trick question for several reasons. First, there's no right or wrong answer: the authors discussed this point with computer designers who actually went through this process in the past, and each designer had his or her own preference. Second, if one creates a new computer today, one would use an existing computer to generate these tools for the new computer.

7) Summarize the differences between a standard assembler and a cross-assembler.

A standard assembler is one which runs on the same computer for which it generates machine code, while a cross assembler runs on one computer and generates machine code for another.

8) What are the main problems with disassemblers?

A disassembler accepts machine code as input and generates source code as output. One problem with a disassembler is that it has no way of regenerating any useful comments that were contained in the original assembly source code. Another problem is that the source code generated by the disassembler contains arbitrary label names, such as L00001, L00002, L00003, and so forth, because the disassembler has no way of generating truly meaningful label names.

9) How would you go about modifying our "Etch-A-Sketch-like" program to allow you to interactively change the color of the dots?

First, we should note that the existing program already makes use of a byte labeled COLOR, where the contents of this byte reflect the color of the blocks to be drawn on the screen. When the existing program detects that the user has pressed a key, it performs a series of comparisons to determine whether that key was one of the cursor control keys. If we wished, we could decide to associate certain keys with certain colors; for example, 'B' = "blue", 'R' = "red", 'Y' = "yellow", and so forth. In this case we could easily add comparisons for these keys to the end of the existing tests. Whenever we subsequently detected that one of these keys had been pressed, we could load the accumulator with the appropriate value for that color and then save it into the COLOR byte.

10) **Create an assembly language program that can write the phrase** *"Hello World"* **to our memory-mapped display, and that could be easily modified to write a different phrase.**

```
MMSPORT:   .EQU    $F028        # O/P port to mem-mapped screen
CLRCODE:   .EQU    $10          # Code to clear mem-mapped screen
BASEADDR:  .EQU    $EE00        # Base address of text screen

           .ORG    $4000        # Start of program is address
                                # $4000

           BLDX    $0000        # Initialize index reg to zero
           LDA     CLRCODE      # Load ACC with code to clear
                                # screen
           STA     [MMSPORT]    # and write it to the O/P port

LOOP:      LDA     [TEXT,X]     # Load ACC with first/next
                                # character
           JZ      [$0000]      # If ACC = $00, return to monitor
           STA     [BASEADDR,X] # else write character to the
                                # display
           INCX                 # Now increment the index
                                # register
           JMP     [LOOP]       # and loop back to get next
                                # character

## The following statements reserve space for the phrase
## "Hello World" which is stored as a series of ASCII codes, one
## for each character (these codes were described in Chapter 10)

TEXT:      .BYTE   $48, $65, $6C, $6C, $6F,   $20
           #        'H'  'e'  'l'  'l'  'o'   <SPACE>

           .BYTE   $57, $6F, $72, $6C, $64,   $00
           #        'W'  'o'  'r'  'l'  'd'   <NULL>

           .END
```

This is really a very simple program, with only a few points worth noting as follows:

a) We use the index register to point to both the next character in the phrase and the next free location on the memory mapped display.

b) There's no particular reason why we used two .BYTE statements to separate the words onto two separate lines in the source code (except that it looked nicer this way).

c) We have to include $20 codes wherever we want a space to appear.

d) The way this program works requires us to terminate the phrase with the code for a NULL character, $00, which allows us to perform an easy test to determine whether or not we've reached the end of the message.

Quick quiz #13

1) **Summarize the differences between ROMs, PROMs, EPROMs, and EEPROMs.**

The contents of a ROM (that is, the patterns of 0s and 1s contained within the device) are formed when the device is constructed, and they cannot be modified by the user. The contents of a PROM can be modified by the user, but only once. The contents of both EPROMs and EEPROMs can be modified and cleared by the user many times, but the former is cleared using ultraviolet light while the latter is cleared using electrical signals.

2) **To what does the phrase "in-system programmable" refer?**

The phrase "in-system programmable" refers to devices that can be programmed while remaining resident on the circuit board.

3) **What is a JEDEC file?**

There are a variety of standard file formats that might be used to represent the contents of programmable logic devices, and JEDEC is simply one of the more common ones.

4) **What is a Character ROM?**

A Character ROM is the device used to store the patterns of 0s and 1s that are employed to create characters or symbols on a memory-mapped screen.

5) **How does a Character ROM differ from a normal ROM?**

It doesn't. A Character ROM *is* a normal ROM. The only reason it's called a Character ROM is to inform us as to its intended purpose in the scheme of things.

6) **Summarize the process of creating a new Character ROM.**

The first step is to decide on the characters and symbols we wish to represent. Next we use some sort of tool to capture the patterns of 0s and 1s, and to store these patterns in a machine-readable format such as a JEDEC file. Next we use a programming device to load the patterns of 0s and 1s from the JEDEC file into a physical device. Finally, we power-down the system and exchange the old Character ROM for our new device.

7) **Why do we associate our character patterns with ASCII codes when creating a Character ROM ?**

When a system has multiple devices that generate or display characters, these devices require a common way of distinguishing between the characters. There are a number of codes that might be used for this purpose, and ASCII is one such code. In the case of the *Beboputer*, the keys on our QWERTY keyboard generate ASCII codes, so it obviously makes sense for the equivalent characters in the Character ROM to be associated with the same codes.

8) **Summarize the process of creating a new System ROM.**

First we use an assembler (or some other tool) to generate the machine code for one or more programs or useful subroutines; this machine code may be stored in one or more "*.rom" files. Next we use a programming device to load the patterns of 0s and 1s from these "*.rom" files into a physical device. Finally, we power-down the system and exchange the old System ROM for our new device.

9) **Why might you wish to create a new System ROM?**

Suppose that we create a number of useful programs and subroutines. As opposed to having to manually load all of these "tools" from a storage device into the system's RAM, it can make life a lot easier to have them readily available in the System ROM. Also, in the case of a microcontroller (which may be considered to be a microprocessor dedicated to performing control applications), the system may only consist of the microcontroller, along with some RAM and ROM (sometimes all of these units are fabricated on a single device). For example, consider a microcontroller used to control a washing machine; the last thing the designer wants to do is to include a hard disk in such a system, so it makes sense to store any programs required by the microcontroller in its system ROM.

10) **Why do you think that we (the authors) decided the effects of exchanging the default Character and System ROMs would only persist for the duration of the current session?**

This was a tricky one. On the one hand the system would be more true-to-life if the effects of a new Character or System ROM persisted indefinitely (or until you changed them for other devices). However, we decided that this could cause confusion if you returned to an earlier lab, which might behave differently with the new devices. This problem would only be exacerbated in those cases where multiple users have access to one *Beboputer*; for example, at school or college. Thus, we concluded that causing the effects of any new Character or System ROMs to only persist for the duration of the current session was the better option.

Quick quiz #14

1) **Why did we decide to assign the calculator keys '0' through '9' to the codes $00 through $09?**

The fact that we assigned the keys '0' through '9' to the codes $00 through $09 makes it easy for us to process these codes, because they directly map onto the numbers they represent.

2) **Why does the calculator return a value of $FF when no key has been pressed (as opposed to the QWERTY keyboard, which returns $00 in the absence of a key being pressed)?**

Our QWERTY keyboard is based on the ASCII code, in which the value $00 is the code for a NUL character, and the numbers '0' through '9' are represented by the codes $30 through $39. Thus, in the case of the QWERTY keyboard, we can use the NUL code to indicate that no key has been pressed. However, in the case of our calculator, we've already decided to use the $00 value to represent the number '0', so we have to employ some other value to represent the fact that no key has been pressed. The reason we decided on $FF was that it was distinctive, but any unused code would have sufficed. Having said this, it's worth noting that $FF is the only one of our key-codes that has a *logic 1* in its most-significant bit (the sign bit), which therefore allows us to us **JN** and **JNN** instructions to test the sign bit to see if a key has been pressed. Remembering that we're going to be performing this test many times, we see that it's more efficient to determine whether or not a key has been pressed by testing the sign bit as opposed to performing a **CMPA** instruction, which, in this case would have to be followed by a **JZ** or **JNZ** instruction to test for equality.

3) **Why did we decide that your calculator was only required to work with numbers in the range -32,767 through +32,767?**

The *Beboputer* is based on an 8-bit data bus, so whatever size numbers we decide to represent will be a function of how many bytes we use to represent them. The simplest approach would be to use 1-byte values, but this would only allow us to represent signed numbers in the range -128 through +127, which wouldn't be a whole lot of fun. The next step up is to use 2 bytes to store each number, which allows us to represent signed numbers in the range -32,768 through +32,767. We could have decided to use more bytes to represent bigger numbers, but we thought that 2-byte fields would be sufficient to introduce you to performing arithmetic on multi-byte values. Note that although a 2-byte field can represent signed numbers in the range -32,768 through +32,767, we decided to restrict you to numbers in the range -32,767 through +32,767 (see also the next question).

4) **With regard to the previous question, why didn't we allow your calculator to work with numbers in the range -32,768 through +32,767?**

As we've already discussed, a 2-byte field can represent signed numbers in the range -32,768 through +32,767. Unfortunately, this unbalanced range can lead to problems; for example, we can't negate a value of -32,768, because the largest positive value that our 2-byte field can represent is +32,767. Thus, it makes our lives much easier all round if we arbitrarily decide to restrict the range of permitted values to -32,767 through +32,767.

5) **What do we mean when we say that the keys on the calculator are logically and physically distinct from the display area?**

When we say "physically distinct," we mean that clicking a key on the calculator's keypad does not of itself cause anything to happen in the display area. To put this another way, your program has to monitor the keypad, decide what to do when a key is pressed, and then send the appropriate codes to the display area. By comparison, when we say "logically distinct," we mean that there's no inherent reason why the codes associated with the keys on the keypad should be identical to the codes used by the display area. For example, we could associate one code with the clear key, and use another code to clear the display. However, this would be counter-intuitive, so we tend to use identical codes for both portions of the calculator because it makes everything more understandable.

6) How should one approach a programming task such as this calculator?

There are three key points with regards to approaching a programming task such as our calculator. First, it is important to ensure that you have a good understanding as to what you want the program to do. In this case, you might decide to play around with existing calculators (both hardware and software versions) to see how they interact with the user, and make notes as to the things you like and dislike about them. Second, you need to plan your line of attack, including playing "thought games" as to the non-standard things a user might do (such as pressing the '+' key twice in a row), and how you want your program to respond. Third, you need to partition the problem into well-defined sub-tasks, thereby facilitating the creation, debugging, and modification of your solution.

7) What result would you expect if you entered "243 - 382 x 14 = " on your calculator (after you've created the program of course)?

This is not as strange a question as it may at first appear. Some calculators consider the '+' '-', 'x', and '/' operators as having equal precedence, in which case the above calculation will be solved "left-to-right". In this case the calculator will first solve the "243 - 382" portion of the problem, and then multiply the result by 14, thereby returning a result of -1946. By comparison, some calculators treat the 'x' and '/' operators as having a higher precedence than '+' and '-' . In this case the calculator will first solve the "382 x 14" portion of the problem, and then subtract the result from 243, thereby returning a result of -5105. Ultimately, the result you expect on your calculator depends on how you implement your program (see also Appendix I for additional discussions on this sort of thing, but only after you've designed your own solution).

8) How should your calculator respond to the sequence "- 243 =" as opposed to the sequence "0 - 243 =" ?

You are the one who is creating the program, so the way in which your calculator responds is up to you. However, once you've completed your solution, you might want to glance at Appendix I for additional discussions on this sort of thing.

9) Assuming that you've just entered the sequence "0 - 243 = ", what should occur if you now enter the sequence "+ 10 ="?

We refer you to the answer to question 8.

10) **How should your calculator respond to the sequence "10 + + 42 = " ?**

Once again, we refer you to the answer to question 8.

Quick quiz #15

1) **What were *"Napier's Bones"*?**

Napier's Bones, which were invented in the early 1600s by the Scottish Mathematician John Napier, were multiplication tables written out on strips of wood or bone.

2) **Who invented the first mechanical calculator?**

Many references cite the French mathematician, physicist, and theologian, Blaise Pascal as being the inventor of the first mechanical calculator. This device, which Pascal called his *Arithmetic Machine*, was introduced in 1642. However, two of Leonardo da Vinci's notebooks, which were discovered in 1967, contained drawings of a mechanical calculator that Leonardo conceived (although probably never constructed) sometime around the 1500s.

3) **Who invented the first mechanical computer?**

The first mechanical device that might be considered to be a computer in the modern sense of the word was the *Analytical Engine*, which was conceived (although never completed) by the eccentric British mathematician and inventor Charles Babbage around 1830.

4) **Who invented the first light bulb?**

The first experimental light bulb was invented in 1860 by the English physicist and electrician Sir Joseph Wilson Swan. Unfortunately, this prototype didn't work, and it wasn't until 1878 that Swan demonstrated a fully-functional incandescent bulb. Having said this, the American inventor Thomas Alva Edison invented and produced the first *commercially viable* light bulb in 1879.

5) **When was the *Jevons' Logic Machine* invented and why was it so notable?**

The Jevons' Logic Machine was invented by the British logician and economist William Stanley Jevons in 1869. One of the main reasons this device was so notable is because it was the first machine that could solve a logical problem faster than the problem could be solved without the aid of the machine!

6) **What is a "Turing Machine"?**

A "Turing Machine" is an abstract computing device that was invented by the English mathematician Alan Turing around 1936-1937.

7) **What are the basic elements of a stored program computer as described by von Neumann?**

a) *A memory* containing both data and instructions, and the ability for both data and instruction memory locations to be read from, and written to, in any desired order.

b) *A calculating unit* capable of performing both arithmetic and logical operations on the data.

c) *A control unit*, which can interpret an instruction retrieved from the memory and select alternative courses of action based on the results of previous operations.

8) **Who invented the first transistor?**

Many references state that the first transistor was invented by the physicists William Shockley, Walter Brattain, and John Bardeen at Bell Laboratories on the 23rd of December, 1947. However, although this was almost certainly the world's first functional transistor, the question as to whom "invented" the transistor is a little more complex. For example, as far back as 1926, Dr. Julius Edgar Lilienfield from New York filed a patent on what we would now recognize as being an NPN junction transistor.

9) **Who invented the first integrated circuit?**

The idea of fabricating entire circuits on a single piece of semiconductor is credited to the British radar expert G.W.A. Drummer in a paper presented in 1952. However, the first such device was not actually constructed until the summer of 1958 by Jack Kilby at Texas Instruments.

10) **Who invented the first microprocessor and why?**

The first microprocessor, the 4004, was designed by Marcian "Ted" Hoff at Intel in 1970 and constructed in 1971. Hoff was actually given the task of designing a set of twelve chips to implement a calculator for the Japanese company Busicom. However, Hoff realized that rather than design the special-purpose devices requested by Busicom, he could create a single integrated circuit with the attributes of a simple, general-purpose computer.

Appendix
I

Solution for Calculator Sign-Off Project

Contents of Appendix I

Restating the problem

Just to refresh our memories from Chapter 14, the calculator shell is a very simple construct with almost no intelligence of its own. This device features a keypad area containing sixteen buttons, and a display area that can contain up to five decimal digits along with an optional minus sign (Figure I.1).

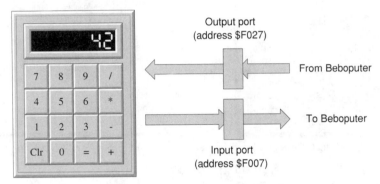

Figure I.1: The calculator shell

The keypad contains an 8-bit latch that's connected to one of the *Beboputer's* input ports (the port at address $F007). By default this latch will contain $FF (or 1111 1111 in binary) to indicate that no buttons have been pressed. When one of the buttons *is* pressed (that is, clicked by the mouse), an associated 8-bit code is loaded into the latch, where it will be stored until the *Beboputer* is ready to read the input port (Figure I.2a). When the *Beboputer* does get around to reading the data from this input port, the latch will be automatically reset to contain $FF.

The buttons on the keypad are logically and physically distinct from the display area. To put this another way, clicking a button on the keypad does not, of itself, affect the display area. The only way to modify the contents of the display area is for the *Beboputer* to write codes to the output port at address $F027 (Figure I.2b). For example, writing a value of $10 to this output port will clear the display.

The display does have a limited amount of hardware-assist to make our lives a little easier. For example, assume that we've cleared the display by writing $10 (the 'Clr' code) to the output port driving the calculator, and that we now wish to display the number "42". If we first write $04 to this port, the number '4' will appear in the right hand column of the display area. If we next write $02 to the port, the number '4' will automatically move one place to the left and the number '2' will appear in the right hand column.

Button	Code (%=Bin, $=Hex)	
0	%0000 0000	$00
1	%0000 0001	$01
2	%0000 0010	$02
3	%0000 0011	$03
4	%0000 0100	$04
5	%0000 0101	$05
6	%0000 0110	$06
7	%0000 0111	$07
8	%0000 1000	$08
9	%0000 1001	$09
Clr	%0001 0000	$10
-	%0010 0000	$20
+	%0011 0000	$30
/	%0100 0000	$40
*	%0101 0000	$50
=	%0110 0000	$60
Nothing	%1111 1111	$FF

(a) Input Port (to *Beboputer*)

Display	Code (%=Bin, $=Hex)	
0	%0000 0000	$00
1	%0000 0001	$01
2	%0000 0010	$02
3	%0000 0011	$03
4	%0000 0100	$04
5	%0000 0101	$05
6	%0000 0110	$06
7	%0000 0111	$07
8	%0000 1000	$08
9	%0000 1001	$09
Clr	%0001 0000	$10
-	%0010 0000	$20
Bell	%0111 0000	$70

(b) Output Port (from *Beboputer*)

Figure I.2: Calculator codes

Our mission is to write a program that uses the calculator keypad to add, subtract, multiply, and divide numbers. For the sake of simplicity, we've decided that this calculator is only required to work with numbers in the range -32,767 through +32,767.

Reading numbers and displaying them at the same time

Whenever we tackle a problem like our calculator sign-off project, it's usually advisable to partition it into smaller, more easily digestible chunks. For example, one of the tasks we're going to have to perform is to read decimal numbers as they're entered on the calculator's keypad, and to display these numbers on the calculator's output display at the same time. For the sake of discussion, assume that the only keys we're interested in at the moment are '0' through '9' and 'Clr', then consider the following flowchart (Figure I.3).

The first thing we do when we enter this routine is to initialize the display by clearing it and writing a number '0' to it. In some respects we'd prefer not to write the '0', so why do we bother? The simple answer is that this is how real calculators typically work — when you power them up or press the clear key they display a '0' — so that's what we decided to do.

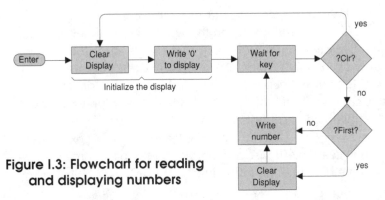

Figure I.3: Flowchart for reading and displaying numbers

Once we've initialized the display, we enter a loop which waits for a key to be pressed on the calculator's keypad. When a key is pressed, the first thing we do is to check whether it is the 'Clr' key and, if it is, we jump back to the start of the program and re-initialize the display (remember we're only interested in the '0' through '9' and 'Clr' keys in this simple test case). Alternatively, if the key represents a decimal digit, we perform a second test to determine whether or not it is the first digit in our new number. If it is the first digit, we clear the display again (to rid ourselves of the '0' that's currently there) and write the digit, otherwise we simply write the digit. To illustrate this process in a slightly different way, consider the sequence of events that we wish to occur if we enter the number 2467, then click the 'Clr' key, then enter the number 42 (Figure I.4).

Figure I.4: Reading and displaying numbers

From our flowchart we know that the first thing we want our program to do is clear the display and write '0' to it, so this will be our initial value. We then want our program to loop around waiting for a digit to be pressed ('2' in this example). As this is the first digit in our number, our program should clear the display (so as to lose the '0') and then writes the '2' to it. The program should continue to loop around reading and writing digits until it sees a 'Clr', at which point we want it to clear the display and write a '0' again. And so we find ourselves back where we started; that is, with an initial value of '0', waiting for a new number to be entered.

Note that our flowchart does not include any tests to determine whether the numbers we're entering are legal (less than or equal to 32,767). Thus, if we were to enter the number 99,999, our program simply wouldn't realize that there was a problem. Similarly, even though we know that our display can only contain five digits and an optional minus sign, our program would happily allow us to enter a number like 653,482,997. In this case the program would merrily keep on reading and writing the digits, which would eventually start to "fall off" the left-hand side of the display. It would certainly be possible to add tests to the program and make the display "beep" if there were a problem, but we'll leave that as an exercise for the reader (you). Instead, we'll just concentrate on the basic program, which could look something like the following:

```
CLR_KEY:     .EQU    $10         # Code associated with 'Clr' key
CLR_CODE:    .EQU    $10         # Code to clear the display

IN_PORT:     .EQU    $F007       # Address of input port from
                                 # keypad
OUT_PORT:    .EQU    $F027       # Address of output port to
                                 # display


             .ORG    $4000       # Start of program is address
                                 # $4000

RESET:       BLDSP   $4FFF       # Initialize the stack pointer
             LDA     CLR_CODE    # Load ACC with clear code
             STA     [OUT_PORT]  # Clear the display

             LDA     0           # Load ACC with code for number '0'
             STA     [OUT_PORT]  # Write it to the display

             JSR     [GET_NUM]   # Jump to the subroutine 'GET_NUM'
             JMP     [RESET]     # The only way to return from
                                 # 'GET_NUM' is if we receive
                                 # a control code, so return
                                 # to 'RESET' and start again

####
#### This is the start of subroutine 'GET_NUM', which keeps on
#### reading keys from the input port and writing them to the
#### display until it sees a control code (anything greater than
#### '9')
GET_NUM:     LDA     1           # Load ACC with '1' and write it
                                 # to a location called 'FLAG',
             STA     [FLAG]      # which will tell us if this
                                 # is the first digit ('0' = NO,
                                 # '1' = YES)
GN_LOOP:     LDA     [IN_PORT]   # Read a value from the input port
             JN      [GN_LOOP]   # If the most significant bit is
                                 # '1',then no key pressed, so jump
                                 # back to 'GN_LOOP' and try again
```

```
GN_COMP:    CMPA    9               # Compare the value in the ACC
                                    # to '9'
            JC      [GN_RET]        # If ACC is greater than '9', then
                                    # we're dealing with a control key
                                    # so return to the calling program
                                    # ...

GN_TEST:    STA     [TEMP8]         # Store ACC to a temporary location
                                    # called 'TEMP8'
            LDA     [FLAG]          # Load ACC with contents of flag
            JZ      [GN_CONT]       # If '0' then jump to
                                    # 'GN_CONT (continue),
            LDA     0               # otherwise load ACC with 0 and
                                    # store it back to the flag,
            STA     [FLAG]          # then load the
            LDA     CLR_CODE        # ACC with the clear code and use
            STA     [OUT_PORT]      # it to clear the display


GN_CONT:    LDA     [TEMP8]         # Retrieve the value from the
                                    # temporary location, write it
            STA     [OUT_PORT]      # to the display,then jump back
            JMP     [GN_LOOP]       # and wait for next key

GN_RET:     RTS                     # Return to the main calling
                                    # program
####
#### This is the end of subroutine 'GET_NUM'
####

FLAG:       .BYTE                   # Reserve location to be used as a
                                    # flag
TEMP8:      .BYTE                   # Reserve a temporary 8-bit
                                    # location

            .END
```

You may wish to compare this code to our flowchart and satisfy yourself that they match up. First we use some .EQU directives to assign values to constant labels that will make our program easier to read. The reset sequence following the .ORG loads the stack pointer with $4FFF (we have to initialize the stack pointer if we want to use a subroutine ...... and we do), clears the calculator's display and writes the number '0' to it, then calls the subroutine GET_NUM.

This subroutine kicks itself off by writing a value of '1' into a 1-byte location called FLAG that we reserve at the end of the program; we're going to use this flag to tell us whether or not we're looking for the first digit of a number. Next we start to loop around at GN_LOOP waiting for the user to press a key. We can save a little effort here, because we don't have to use a CMPA instruction to test for a value of $FF (which indicates that no key has been pressed). Instead, all we have to do is test whether the most-significant bit is a '1' using the JN ("*jump if negative*") instruction, because pressing any of the calculator's keys will set this bit to '0'.

Once a key is pressed, we use a CMPA ("*compare accumulator*") instruction at GN_COMP to check to see whether or not this is a digit in the range '0' to '9' or whether it's a control code (all of the control codes have values greater than '9'). If this was a control key, then its code will be greater than '9' and the carry flag will be set to a *logic 1*, so we can use a JC ("*jump if carry*") instruction to jump to GN_RET, from whence we will exit out of the subroutine.

If the key isn't a control code, then we fall through to GN_TEST, where we store the key's value to the temporary location TEMP8. We do this because we're just about to modify the contents of the accumulator, and we don't want to lose the value of this key. Next we load the accumulator with the contents of FLAG. If these contents are '0' (indicating that this isn't the first digit in a number), then we use the JZ ("*jump if zero*") instruction to jump to GN_CONT, otherwise we store a '0' in FLAG, clear the display, then fall through to GN_CONT. Whichever way we reach GN_CONT, all we do is to retrieve the value of the key from our TEMP8 location, write it to the display, then jump back to GN_LOOP to await the next key to be pressed.

The main "shortcut" we've used in this example occurs when we exit from the GET_NUM, subroutine. For the purposes of this example we've assumed that the user will only press the keys '0' through '9' and 'Clr'. Thus, when we return to the main body of the program, we don't actually bother to test for 'Clr', but instead jump straight back into our initialization sequence at RESET. The advantage of this approach is that we don't run into any problems if the user happens to select one of the other control keys ('+', '−', '*', '/', or '=').

Converting numbers to internal representations

The sample program described in the previous section reads and displays numbers as they're entered on the keypad, but it doesn't store them in a way we can use. We could reserve a set of locations using the .BYTE directive, and then store each digit in a separate byte, but this wouldn't do us a lot of good. In fact, we actually require our program to convert the series of individual digits forming a number into an internal 16-bit representation. Before we look at the code required to achieve this, let's consider an algorithmic representation of what we're trying to do. Assume that we have a 16-bit field called VALUE, and that we wish to enter the number 2467 (Figure I.5).

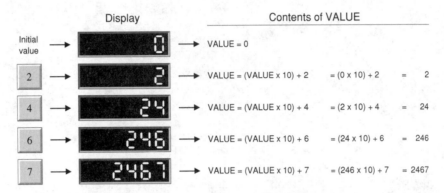

Figure I.5: Converting numbers to internal representations

As we see, the algorithm commences by loading VALUE with zero, then, whenever we receive another digit, we multiply the contents of VALUE by 10 and add the new digit to the result. There are numerous ways in which we could implement this algorithm, but, for reasons that will become apparent, we've decided to employ the stack (the new areas of our program are shown shaded grey):

```
CLR_KEY:   .EQU   $10        # Code associated with 'Clr' key
CLR_CODE:  .EQU   $10        # Code to clear the display

IN_PORT:   .EQU   $F007      # Address of input port from keypad
OUT_PORT:  .EQU   $F027      # Address of output port to display

           .ORG   $4000      # Start of program is address $4000

RESET:     BLDSP  $4FFF      # Initialize the stack pointer
           LDA    CLR_CODE   # Load ACC with clear code
           STA    [OUT_PORT] # Clear the display

           LDA    0          # Load ACC with code for number '0'
           STA    [OUT_PORT] # Write it to the display

           JSR    [GET_NUM]  # Jump to the subroutine 'GET_NUM'
           JMP    [RESET]    # The only way to return from
                            # 'GET_NUM'is if we receive a
```

```
                                    # control code, so return to 'RESET'
                                    # and start again

####
#### This is the start of subroutine 'GET_NUM', which keeps on
#### reading keys from the input port and writing them to the
#### display until it sees a control code (anything greater than
#### '9')
####
GET_NUM:   POPA                     # Retrieve MS byte of return address
           STA    [RET_ADDR]        # and store it
           POPA                     # Retrieve LS byte of return address
           STA    [RET_ADDR+1]      # and store it

           LDA    0                 # Load ACC with zero and push two
           PUSHA                    # copies of this onto the top of
           PUSHA                    # the stack

           LDA    1                 # Load ACC with '1' and write it to
                                    # a location called 'FLAG',
           STA    [FLAG]            # which will tell us if this is the
                                    # first digit ('0' = NO, '1' = YES)
GN_LOOP:   LDA    [IN_PORT]         # Read a value from the input port
           JN     [GN_LOOP]         # If the most significant bit is
                                    # '1',then no key pressed, so jump
                                    # back to 'GN_LOOP' and try again

GN_COMP:   CMPA   9                 # Compare the value in the ACC to
                                    # '9'.
           JC     [GN_RET]          # If ACC is greater than '9', then
                                    # we're dealing with a control key
                                    # so return to the calling program
                                    # ...

GN_TEST:   STA    [TEMP8]           # Store ACC to a temporary location
                                    # called 'TEMP8'
           LDA    [FLAG]            # Load ACC with contents of flag. If
           JZ     [GN_CONT]         # '0' then jump to 'GN_CONT
                                    # (continue),
           LDA    0                 # otherwise load ACC with 0 and
                                    # store it back to the flag,
           STA    [FLAG]            # then load the
           LDA    CLR_CODE          # ACC with the clear code and use it
           STA    [OUT_PORT]        # to clear the display
GN_CONT:   LDA    [TEMP8]           # Retrieve the value from the
                                    # temporary
           STA    [OUT_PORT]        # location, write it to the display,
           JSR    [_UMULT10]        # Multiply the 16-bit number on the
                                    # top of the stack by ten
           LDA    [TEMP8]           # Retrieve the value from the
                                    # temporary location and push it
```

```
        PUSHA                   # on the stack then push a 0 on
        LDA    0                # the stack to form
        PUSHA                   # the MS byte of a 2-byte value
        JSR    [_ADD16]         # Call a 16-bit addition subroutine
        JMP    [GN_LOOP]        # then jump back and wait for next
                                # key

GN_RET: PUSHA                   # Push the control code onto the top
                                # of the stack
        LDA    [RET_ADDR+1]     # Load ACC with LS byte of return
        PUSHA                   # address and push it onto the stack
        LDA    [RET_ADDR]       # Load ACC with MS byte of return
        PUSHA                   # address and push it onto the stack
        RTS                     # Return to the main calling program
####
#### This is the end of subroutine 'GET_NUM'
####
FLAG:      .BYTE                # Reserve location to be used as a
                                # flag
TEMP8:     .BYTE                # Reserve a temporary 8-bit location
RET_ADDR:  .2BYTE               # Reserve a 2-byte location to hold
                                # the return address from our
                                # subroutine

####
#### This is where we'd insert our subroutines _UMULT10 and _ADD16
#### (using the technique discussed in Chapter 12)
####
           .END
```

Neglecting the addition of a new 2-byte temporary location called RET_ADDR ("*return address*") at the end of the program, there are only three areas of modifications. The first occurs at the beginning of our GET_NUM subroutine. When the program commences running, the stack is empty and the stack pointer is pointing at location $4FFF (Figure I.6a). When the body of the program uses the JSR ("*jump to subroutine*") instruction to call GET_NUM, the CPU automatically places the return address on the top of the stack, which is the way things are when we enter GET_NUM (Figure I.6b). Unlike our first example program, this new version of GET_NUM is going to juggle things around on the stack, so the first thing we do upon entering the subroutine is to pop the return address off the top of the stack and store it in our 2-byte temporary location RET_ADDR (Figure I.6c). The last modification in this batch occurs when we load the accumulator with zero and push two copies of this value onto the top of the stack (Figure I.6d).

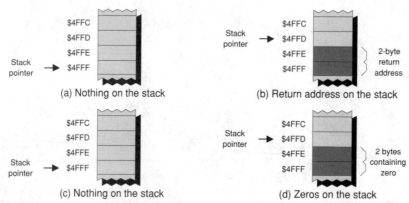

Figure I.6: The condition of the stack as we enter the GET_NUM subroutine

The GET_NUM subroutine then continues to perform the same actions as before, loading **FLAG** with 1 to indicate that it's looking for the first digit, looping around waiting for a key to be pressed, testing to see if it's received a control key, clearing the display and loading **FLAG** with 0 if this was the first digit, and writing our digit our to the display. It is at this point, just after we've executed the first two instructions at **GN_CONT**, that we run into our next batch of modifications.

However, before we proceed further, we need to mention the subroutines _UMULT10 and _ADD16. Hopefully you've already perused Appendix G, which describes the set of general-purpose subroutines that we've provided with your *Beboputer*. Some of these subroutines were used in Chapter 12, which also discussed the mechanism by which you can insert these subroutines into your programs. We will be using certain of these routines to implement our calculator as follows:

> _ADD16   Adds two 16-bit numbers (signed or unsigned)
>
> _SUB16   Subtracts two 16-bit numbers (signed or unsigned)
>
> _SMULT16   Multiplies two signed 16-bit numbers
>
> _SDIV16   Divides two signed 16-bit numbers

In addition to _SMULT16 (for signed 16-bit values), there is also a _UMULT16 subroutine, which can be used to multiply two unsigned 16-bit values together. From our discussions at the beginning of this section, we know that we have to multiply a 16-bit value by a factor of 10, and we could certainly use our general-purpose _UMULT16 subroutine to perform this task. However, we decided that it would be more efficient to take a copy of _UMULT16, rename it as _UMULT10, and then modify this new routine to perform a dedicated "multiply-by-ten."

If you're interested in the internal machinations of _UMULT10, you first need to digest the contents of Appendix G, then use the *Beboputer's* assembler to examine the source code for this routine (which we have also supplied with your *Beboputer*). For the nonce, we need only be aware that _UMULT10 retrieves a 16-bit number from the top of the stack, multiplies it by ten, places the 16-bit result on the top of the stack, and returns control to the program that called it. Similarly, _ADD16 (which is fully described in Appendix G) retrieves two 16-bit numbers from the top of the stack, adds them together, and returns the 16-bit result on the top of the stack.

To put this another way, the first time we reach GN_CONT, we know that the top of the stack contains two bytes containing zero (the ones that we put there during our first set of modifications) (Figure I.7a). As per our earlier discussions, we're assuming that we intend to enter the number 2467, so we know that the first key to be pressed will be a '2'. When we reach GN_CONT and call _UMULT10, it multiplies the 16-bit value on the top of the stack by ten and leaves the 16-bit result on the top of the stack (Figure I.7b). As our original 16-bit value was zero, multiplying it by ten didn't have any affect, but it will the next time we roll around the loop. Next we retrieve the value of our key ('2' in this case), and push it onto the stack, then we push a further zero byte onto the stack to form a 16-bit number (Figure I.7c). Finally we call the _ADD16 subroutine, which retrieves our two 16-bit values from the top of the stack, adds them together, and returns a 16-bit result (Figure I.7d).

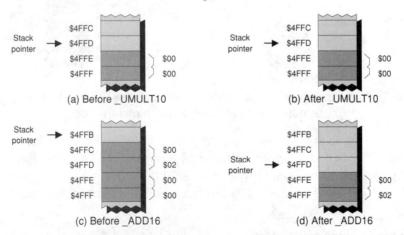

Figure I.7: The condition of the stack as we call the _UMULT10 and _ADD16 subroutines the first time round the loop

Now, this may not appear to be tremendously exciting on our first pass around the loop, but remember that we've only entered the first digit ('2') of our number 2467. Now consider what happens the next pass around the loop as we enter our second digit ('4'). When we reach GN_CONT this time, the top of the stack contains the $0002 that we left there from our last trek through the loop (Figure I.8a), so when we call _UMULT10, it will multiply the $0002 on the top of the stack by 10 and return $0014 (20 in decimal) (Figure I.8b). Next we retrieve the value of our key ('4' in this case), and push it onto the stack, followed by the zero byte required to form a 16-bit number (Figure I.8c). Finally we call our _ADD16 subroutine which retrieves the two 16-bit values from the top of the stack, adds them together, and returns the 16-bit result of $0018 (24 in decimal) (Figure I8.d).

Note that _ADD16 and _UMULT10 both modify the contents of the accumulator and leave it in an undefined state (_UMULT10 also modifies the contents of the index register). Thus, if we desire to use the contents of these registers in the future, we have to take steps to preserve them *before* calling these subroutines, which is one of the reasons we saved the value of the key into TEMP8.

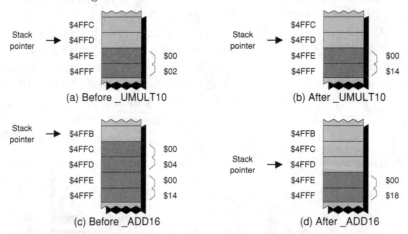

Figure I.8: The condition of the stack as we call the _UMULT10 and _ADD16 subroutines the second time round the loop

And so it goes. Every time we enter an individual digit on the calculator's keypad, GET_NUM incorporates that digit into the 16-bit number that it's constructing. Eventually, after we've entered all four digits of our number 2467, the two bytes on the top of the stack will contain $09A3, which is the equivalent value in hexadecimal.

Try to hang in there with us, because we've almost hammered this section into the ground. After we've entered all of the digits forming our number, we're going to press one of our control keys, at which point our routine will jump to GN_RET where we find our third, and final set of modifications. When we reach GN_RET, we know that the accumulator contains the code for one of the control keys (we know this because this is what caused us to jump to GN_RET in the first place). So the first thing we do is to push this control code onto the top of the stack. Next we retrieve the least- and most-significant bytes of GET_NUM's return address from the temporary location RET_ADDR (which is where we stored it when we entered this subroutine) and place them onto the top of the stack, which means that we're just about ready to return to the main body of the program (Figure I.9a).

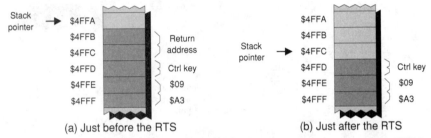

(a) Just before the RTS   (b) Just after the RTS

Figure I.9: The condition of the stack as we return from GET_NUM

The very last instruction in GET_NUM is the RTS (*"return from subroutine"*), which informs the CPU that it's time to exit the subroutine and return to the main body of the program. To do this, the CPU automatically retrieves the return address from the top of the stack and modifies the stack pointer accordingly.[1] Thus, when we come to return to the main body of the program after GET_NUM has performed its role in life, we know that the three bytes on the top of the stack will contain the value of whatever control key was pressed along with our 16-bit number (Figure I.9b). Of course, the current implementation of our program doesn't actually use this data yet, but it will, Oh yes, it will.

Scrunching 16-bit numbers and displaying them

From our discussions above, we now know how to read individual digits from the keypad and convert them into internal 16-bit representations.

---

[1] An enterprising young programmer might spot the fact that, by "tweaking" the value of the return address before executing the RTS instruction, we can fool the CPU into transfering control to wherever we desire. In fact this "trick" is occasionally employed, but it's incredibly dangerous (in programming terms), so one is advised to use it sparingly and with extreme caution.

Eventually it is these 16-bit representations that our calculator will manipulate while performing its wily calculations, but we haven't reached that point yet. After our calculator has performed whatever tasks we require of it, we will have to convert any 16-bit results back into a form we can use to drive the output display. For example, assume that the result of a particular calculation is $F65D (−2467 in decimal), and consider the algorithmic steps we are going to have to perform (Figure I.10).

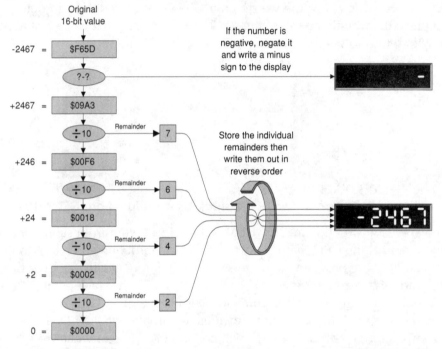

Figure I.10: Algorithm used to scrunch 16-bit numbers and display them

Our first action is to test the number to see if it represents a negative value. Remember that signed numbers are stored internally in a twos complement form, but we wish to display our results using traditional sign-magnitude decimal representations. Thus, if the internal value is negative, we need to negate it (that is, convert it into its positive equivalent) and also write a minus sign out to the display.

Next we repeatedly divide our internal value by ten, storing the remainder from each division operation, until our value has wound down to zero. The reason we need to store the remainders is that we have to write them out to the display in reverse order. As we see, with the exception of a few minor niggles, this process is almost the mirror image of the one used to construct our internal representations in the previous section.

Without further ado, let's examine some code that can implement this algorithm. Note that, for the sake of simplicity, we've chopped out the GET_NUM subroutine and temporarily added a few lines of dummy code to provide us with a number to scrunch up and display. As before, any additions to our program are shown shaded grey:

```
CLR_KEY:    .EQU    $10          # Code associated with 'Clr' key
CLR_CODE:   .EQU    $10          # Code to clear the display
NEG_CODE:   .EQU    $20          # Code for a minus sign

IN_PORT:    .EQU    $F007        # Address of input port from keypad
OUT_PORT:   .EQU    $F027        # Address of output port to display

            .ORG    $4000        # Start of program is address $4000

RESET:      BLDSP   $4FFF        # Initialize the stack pointer
            LDA     CLR_CODE     # Load ACC with clear code
            STA     [OUT_PORT]   # Clear the display

            LDA     0            # Load ACC with code for number '0'
            STA     [OUT_PORT]   # Write it to the display

            #### The next four instructions are simply used to push
            #### a number on the stack for us to play with
            LDA     $5D          # Load ACC with LS byte of 2-byte
            PUSHA                # value and push onto the stack
            LDA     $F6          # followed by the MS byte (the full
            PUSHA                # 2-byte (16-bit) number is $F65D)

            JSR     [DISP_NUM]   # Jump to the subroutine 'DISP_NUM'
            JMP     [$0000]      # to scrunch the number and display
                                 # it. Afterwards jump straight to
                                 # address $0000 to kill the program

####
#### This is the start of subroutine 'DISP_NUM', which grabs a
#### 2-byte (16-bit) value from the top of the stack, scrunches
#### it up, and writes it out to the calculator's output display
####
DISP_NUM:   POPA                 # Retrieve MS byte of return address
            STA     [RET_ADDR]   # and store it
            POPA                 # Retrieve LS byte of return address
            STA     [RET_ADDR+1] # and store it

            POPA                 # Retrieve MS byte of number to be
            STA     [TEMP16]     # scrunched and store it
            POPA                 # Retrieve LS byte of number to be
            STA     [TEMP16+1]   # scrunched and store it, then push
            PUSHA                # it back onto the top of the stack
            LDA     [TEMP16]     # Now reload ACC with stored MS byte
            PUSHA                # of number and push it onto the
                                 # stack

            #### The next four instructions start off by loading
            #### our temporary location 'TEMP8' with 0. We're going
```

```
           #### to use this location to keep a count of the number
           #### of digits to be displayed. Then we clear the
           #### display
           LDA     0              # Load ACC with '0' and write it to
                                  # a location called 'TEMP8'.
           STA     [TEMP8]        # Load ACC with the clear code and
           LDA     CLR_CODE       # write it to the display
           STA     [OUT_PORT]     #

           #### The next section starts off by checking to see if
           #### the MS bit of the MS byte is 0. If it is the
           #### number is positive, so use the JNN instruction
           #### to jump to 'DN_ITPOS'. Otherwise convert the
           #### negative number into its positive equivalent
DN_CKNEG:  LDA     [TEMP16]       # Reload ACC with stored MS byte
           JNN     [DN_ITPOS]     # If MS bit of ACC = 0 then jump to
           LDA     NEG_CODE       # 'DN_ITPOS, otherwise load ACC with
           STA     [OUT_PORT]     # code for minus and write to
                                  # display

           LDA     0              # Load ACC with 0 and push two
           PUSHA                  # copies of this zero byte onto
           PUSHA                  # the top of the stack

           LDA     [TEMP16+1]     # Load ACC with copy of the MS byte
                                  # of the number and push it onto the
           PUSHA                  # stack followed by a copy of the
           LDA     [TEMP16]       # LS byte of the number ....
           PUSHA                  # ....then call subroutine '_SUB16'
           JSR     [_SUB16]       # then jump to 'DN_LOOPA'
           JMP     [DN_LOOPA]

DN_ITPOS:  LDA     [TEMP16+1]     # Load ACC with copy of the MS byte
                                  # of the number and push it onto the
           PUSHA                  # stack followed by a copy of the
           LDA     [TEMP16]       # LS byte of the number
           PUSHA

           #### The next section loops around extracting the
           #### individual remainders which sort of end up on the
           #### stack, but it's a bit tricky to explain here, so
           #### see the notes at the end (sorry about that :-)
DN_LOOPA:  JSR     [_UDIV10]      # Call subroutine '_UDIV10'
           LDA     [TEMP8]        # Retrieve the value we're using as
           INCA                   # a counter, then increment it and
           STA     [TEMP8]        # store it away again.

           POPA                   # Pop the first byte off the top of
           JNZ     [DN_LOOPA]     # the stack. If it's 1 (set by the
                                  # _UDIV10 subroutine) then there's
                                  # more to do, so jump back and loop

           #### The next section is the one that actually writes
           #### our remainders to the display in reverse order
```

```
             #### (once again, see the notes at the end)
DN_DISP:     POPA              # Pop the first two bytes off the
             POPA              # stack and lose them because we
                               # don't need them any more

DN_LOOPB:    POPA              # Pop a remainder off the stack and
             STA    [OUT_PORT] # write it to the display

             LDA    [TEMP8]    # Retrieve the value we're using as
                               # a counter, decrement it and store
             DECA              # it. Also, if it's not zero then
             STA    [TEMP8]    # there are more remainders to
             JNZ    [DN_LOOPB] # display, so jump back and loop

DN_RET:      LDA    [RET_ADDR+1]# Load ACC with LS byte of return
             PUSHA             # address and push it onto the stack
             LDA    [RET_ADDR] # Load ACC with MS byte of return
             PUSHA             # address and push it onto the stack
             RTS               # Return to the main calling program
####
#### This is the end of subroutine 'DISP_NUM'
####

FLAG:        .BYTE             # Reserve location to be used as a
                               # flag
TEMP8:       .BYTE             # Reserve a temporary 8-bit location
TEMP16:      .2BYTE            # Reserve a temporary 16-bit
                               # location
RET_ADDR:    .2BYTE            # Reserve a 2-byte location to hold
                               # the return address from our
                               # subroutine

####
#### This is where we'd insert our subroutines _UDIV10 and _SUB16
#### (using the technique discussed in Chapter 12)
####
             .END
```

Stop quivering your lower lip and wipe those tears away, because this really is a lot simpler than it looks. The only reason this listing appears to be so mean is because it's jam-packed with comments. If we were to strip the comments out, there would be hardly anything left (have we ever lied to you before?).[2]

Before we examine this subroutine in detail, note that we've added a new constant label called **NEG_CODE** into the declarations section at the beginning of the program. Writing this code to the calculator's display will cause a minus sign to appear. Also note that we've reserved a new 2-byte temporary storage location called **TEMP16** at the end of the program.

---

[2]Don't answer that!

Immediately following our old reset sequence at the beginning of the program, we've added a few dummy instructions to push the 16-bit value $F65D (-2467 in decimal) onto the stack. This is the value we're going to attempt to display. Once we've stored this value onto the stack, we immediately call our new DISP_NUM subroutine. As usual, the CPU will automatically place the subroutine's return address onto the top of the stack, so when we actually come to enter the subroutine there will be four bytes on the stack (Figure I.11a).

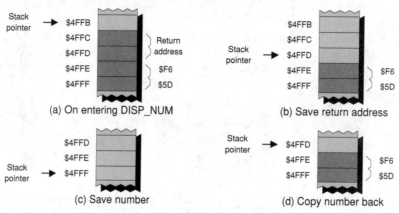

Figure I.11: The condition of the stack as we commence the DISP_NUM subroutine

As soon as we enter DISP_NUM we retrieve the 2-byte return address from the top of the stack and squirrel it away in the temporary location RET_ADDR (Figure I.11b). Next we retrieve our 2-byte number from the new top of the stack and place it in the temporary location TEMP16 (Figure I.11c). However, when we get to the main calculator program in the next section, we're going to want to be able to access this value, so our last action in this preamble is to take a copy of the 2-byte value that we just stored in TEMP16 and stick it back onto the top of the stack (Figure I.11d) (note that this doesn't change the copy in TEMP16).

We're almost ready to begin the interesting part, but first we store a zero into our TEMP8 location, because we're going to use TEMP8 as a counter to keep track of how many digits we have to display. Next we write a CLR_CODE to the output port to clear the display in anticipation of our new number.

It's when we get to the label DN_CHKNEG ("check if the number's negative") that we really start to cook on a hot stove. At this point we've still got the most-significant byte of our 16-bit number in the accumulator, so we can check its most-significant bit to determine whether or not the number is negative (0 = positive, 1 = negative). In this particular case we decided to use a JNN ("*jump if not negative*") instruction: if the number is positive we'll jump down to DN_ITPOS, at which point we'll place a second copy of our 16-bit value onto the top of the stack. However, the number in this example is negative, so we have to play a little jiggery-pokery. First we write a copy of NEG_CODE to the display, which causes it to display a minus sign. Next we load two bytes containing zero onto the top of the stack (Figure I.12a), then we place our 16-bit number on top of these (Figure I.12b), and finally we call the predefined subroutine _SUB16 that we supplied with your *Beboputer* (Figure I.12c).

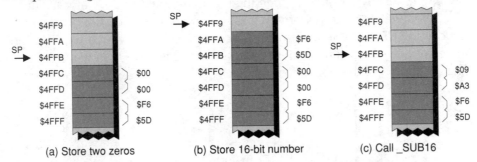

(a) Store two zeros   (b) Store 16-bit number   (c) Call _SUB16

Figure I.12: The condition of the stack as we negate our number

The way in which _SUB16 works is fully described in Appendix G. For the purposes of these discussions, we need only know that it subtracts the 16-bit value it finds on the top of the stack from the 16-bit value below it, and replaces both of these values with a 16-bit result. Thus, in this case, we've subtracted our negative value of $F65D (-2467 in decimal) from $0000, which results in our obtaining the positive equivalent of $09A3 (2467 in decimal).

To recap, if our original number had been positive, we'd have stored it directly onto the top of the stack. As it wasn't, we wrote a minus sign to our output display, negated the number, and left *that* on the top of the stack. In both cases we end up with a positive version of our number on the top of the stack, at which point we find ourselves at the label DN_LOOPA.

From the algorithm we introduced in Figure I.10, we know that we're going to have to repeatedly divide our number by ten. In fact we've provided two general-purpose division subroutines called _UDIV16 and _SDIV16 with your *Beboputer*, which can be used to perform unsigned and signed 16-bit divisions, respectively. However, once again, it proved to be more efficacious for us to take a copy of one of these general-purpose subroutines (_UDIV16 in this case), rename it to _UDIV10 ("*unsigned divide-by-ten*"), and tailor it to our needs. (As usual, we supplied this subroutine with your *Beboputer*, so you can use the assembler to root around to see how it works).

Our first action at **DN_LOOPA** is to call **_UDIV10**, which takes whatever 16-bit number it finds on the top of the stack and divides it by ten. Now this is the clever part, because **_UDIV10** returns four bytes of data on the top of the stack (Figure I.13b). The byte at the bottom of the pile is the remainder from the division; the next two bytes are the quotient from the division (the original value divided by ten); and the last byte (on the top of the stack) is a flag. If this byte is a zero, then there's nothing left to do, but if it's non-zero, then we've got to perform at least one more division. Thus, following the call to **_UDIV10**, we increment our count in **TEMP8** (which we're using to keep track of the number of remainders we've found), then we pop our flag off the top of the stack (Figure I.13c).

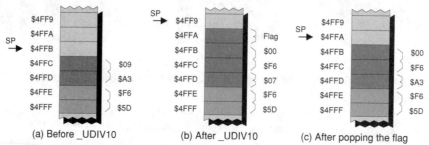

(a) Before _UDIV10   (b) After _UDIV10   (c) After popping the flag

Figure I.13: The condition of the stack on the first pass round DN_LOOPA

As we see, the remainder from this first division is $07, which is sort of what we'd expect if we divide $09A3 (2467 in decimal) by ten. Similarly, the quotient from the division is $00F6 (246 in decimal), which is also what we'd expect. The clever part is that the 16-bit number we now need to divide is just where we want it to be …… on the top of the stack. The end result is that, as we cycle around this loop, we leave a trail of remainders growing up the stack, with whatever number we next wish to divide by ten riding on top of them.

In the case of this particular example, after four passes around the loop we're presented with four remainders on the stack and nothing left to divide, where this *"nothing left to divide"* appears in the form of two bytes containing zero on the top of the stack. Thus, when we arrive at label **DN_DISP**, the first thing we do is to pop these two zero bytes off the top of the stack and throw them away. Next we enter the loop called **DN_LOOPB**, which cycles around popping the remainders off the stack and writing them to our display. The way in which we stored the remainders on the stack means that they arrive at the display in the reverse order to the one in which we generated them, which is just what our algorithm called for.

Note that once we've popped our last remainder off the stack and written it to the display, we're still left with our original number (positive or negative) at the new top of the stack. This means that when we eventually return to the main body of our program, DISP_NUM will leave the stack in exactly the same condition that it found it. Last but not least, we retrieve DISP_NUM's return address from the temporary location RET_ADDR, push it onto the top of the stack, and return to the main body of the program.

The main body of the program

We think that you're just about to receive a nice surprise. With all that's gone before, you're probably anticipating that this final section is going to be incredibly long and torturous. In fact, nothing could be further from the truth. All the hard work is behind us, which means that this section is going to be short, sharp, and to the point.

But, as usual, before we look at the code itself, we first need to perform some up-front work deciding on the usage model that we wish our calculator to follow. Consider a simple task we might wish our calculator to perform; something like:

$$243 - 382 \times 14 = ?$$

How do we want our calculator to behave? Be warned, this is not as obvious as it might at first seem. Some calculators (like the one provided with Windows 95) will consider the '+'. '−', 'x', and '/' operators to have equal precedence, and will therefore perform the operations in the order in which they appear (from left-to-right). Thus, this form of calculator will subtract 382 from 243 and multiply the result by 14. Other calculators take the stance that the 'x' and '/' operators have a higher precedence than '+' and '−', so this form of calculator would multiply 382 by 14 and subtract the result from 243.

As it happens, we've decided to go with the former (equal precedence) model, because this is conceptually simpler and also easier to implement. However, there's more to it than this, because we still have to decide exactly what happens every time we press a key. You might wish to take a few moments to think about this and jot your thoughts down on a piece of paper, then consider the illustration in Figure I.14.

Initial values at the beginning of each sequence before any keys are pushed

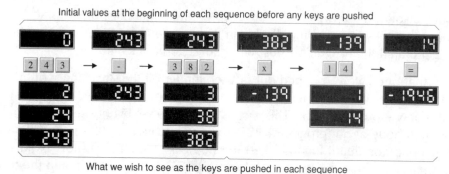

What we wish to see as the keys are pushed in each sequence

Figure I.14: Exactly what should happen every time we press a key

We commence in our reset state with a '0' on the display, then, as we begin to enter the number 243, the '2' replaces the '0' and the '4' and '3' slide in from the right-hand side. Next we enter the '-', but nothing happens until we begin to enter the number 382, at which time the '3' replaces the 243 and the '8' and '2' slide in from the right.

The really interesting thing occurs when we enter the 'x', because this is the point where the previous '−' operation is performed and the intermediate result of -139 appears on the display. This value remains on the display until we begin to enter the next number, 14. The reason we say this is *"the really interesting thing,"* is that it defines the way the calculator works most of the time. That is, when we're in the middle of a sequence of commands, every time we select one of the '+', '-', 'x', and '/' operators, the calculator actually executes the *previous* operation and displays the results.

The only tricky bits occur at the beginning and the end of the sequence. Not surprisingly, these are known as the *end conditions,* and, when you begin to create your own programs, you'll quickly find that it's the end conditions that are the bane of a programmer's life. Consider what happens following the reset condition when we select the '-' operator after entering the number 243. How can we execute the *previous* operation when we haven't entered one yet. Even worse, suppose that when a user commences, she or he decides to use the '0' that's already on the display, so (s)he simply enters the sequence "+ 243". Eeek, now our calculator receives an operator before it's even been presented with a number. Similarly, we have to decide what we wish to happen following an '=' if the user:

a) Commences a new sequence with a number.

b) Kicks off the new sequence with another operator.

c) Decides to click on '=' again just to see what will happen.

In fact point (c) opens up a whole new realm of questions, such as what do we wish to occur if the user clicks the same operator two or more times in a row (for example "123 + + 123"), or what should happen if the user clicks two or more different operators one after the other (for example "123 + x 123").

Fortunately, assuming that you're not working on a mission-critical project in which lives are involved, there is a pretty good way out for the majority of questions like this, which is to say: *"It's not designed to work like that, so the results are undefined in these cases."* This is not a joke. Practice chanting these words like a mantra until you can reel them off without pausing for thought, because they can literally save you hundreds of hours of work. Otherwise, a moment's hesitation can result in your boss uttering the dread words: *"We really ought to tie this sort of thing down."* Once this happens you're lost. You can now look forward to spending days, weeks, months, or the rest of your working life specifying every conceivable way in which an idiot might misuse your product; modifying your program to handle such situations; and then, the final humiliation of all, documenting it in a user manual so that other programmers can laugh at you until the tears roll down their cheeks.

But we've wandered off into the weeds again. If we put our minds into gear, it's usually possible to play a few cunning tricks so as to minimize any problems associated with the end conditions. So let's use everything we've learnt thus far to hammer out one of the many possible solutions to our calculator problem. Once again, any new material is shown shaded grey.

```
CLR_KEY:   .EQU    $10        # Code for 'Clr' key
SUB_KEY:   .EQU    $20        # Code for 'Subtract' key ('-')
ADD_KEY:   .EQU    $30        # Code for 'Add' key ('+')
DIV_KEY:   .EQU    $40        # Code for 'Divide' key ('/')
MULT_KEY:  .EQU    $50        # Code for 'Multiply' key ('*')
EQU_KEY:   .EQU    $60        # Code for 'Equals' key ('=')

CLR_CODE:  .EQU    $10        # Code to clear the display
NEG_CODE:  .EQU    $20        # Code for a minus sign
BEL_CODE:  .EQU    $70        # Code to make a "beep"

IN_PORT:   .EQU    $F007      # Address of input port from keypad
OUT_PORT:  .EQU    $F027      # Address of output port to display

           .ORG    $4000      # Start of program is address $4000

RESET:     BLDSP   $4FFF      # Initialize the stack pointer
           LDA     CLR_CODE   # Load ACC with clear code
           STA     [OUT_PORT] # Clear the display
           LDA     0          # Load ACC with code for number '0'
           STA     [OUT_PORT] # Write it to the display
```

```
                PUSHA                      # Push two zero bytes onto the stack
                PUSHA                      # to give us a dummy 16-bit number
                LDA       ADD_KEY          # Initialize the 'LAST_OP' field
                                           # with the code for the '+' key
                STA       [LAST_OP]
MAINLOOP:       JSR       [GET_NUM]        # Call 'GET_NUM' subroutine to get a
                POPA                       # number and a control key, then pop
                STA       [THIS_OP]        # the control key off the top of the
                                           # stack and store it
TST_CLR:        CMPA      CLR_KEY          # If the clear key HAS been pressed
                JZ        [RESET]          # jump to 'RESET'
TST_EQU:        CMPA      EQU_KEY          # If equals key HASN'T been pressed
                JNZ       [TST_OPS]        # jump to 'TST_OPS' and test the last
                LDA       ADD_KEY          # operation, otherwise play a trick
                STA       [THIS_OP]        # by saying that "this op" was an ADD
TST_OPS:        LDA       [LAST_OP]        # Now load ACC with the last
                                           # operation
TST_ADD:        CMPA      ADD_KEY          # If the add key hasn't been pressed
                JNZ       [TST_SUB]        # jump to 'TST_SUB', else call the
                JSR       [_ADD16]         # '_ADD16' subroutine then jump to
                JMP       [CLEAN_UP]       # label 'CLEAN_UP'
TST_SUB:        CMPA      SUB_KEY          # If the sub key hasn't been pressed
                JNZ       [TST_MULT]       # jump to 'TST_MULT', else call the
                JSR       [_SUB16]         # '_SUB16' subroutine then jump to
                JMP       [CLEAN_UP]       # label 'CLEAN_UP'
TST_MULT:       CMPA      MULT_KEY         # If the mult key hasn't been
                                           # pressed jump to 'IST_DIV',
                JNZ       [ITS_DIV]        # else call the '_SMULT16' subroutine
                JSR       [_SMULT16]       # then jump to label 'CLEAN_UP'
                JMP       [CLEAN_UP]
ITS_DIV:        JSR       [_SDIV16]        # If it's non of the preceding then
                                           # the last op must have been a div
                                           # so call '_SDIV16' subroutine then
                                           # fall through to 'CLEAN_UP'
CLEAN_UP:       LDA       [THIS_OP]        # Retrieve code for this operation
                STA       [LAST_OP]        # and store it in location for last
                                           # op, then display the result using
                JSR       [DISP_NUM]       # the 'DISP_NUM' subroutine,
                JMP       [MAINLOOP]       # then jump back to the beginning
                                           # of the loop
FLAG:           .BYTE                      # Reserve location to be used as a
                                           # flag
TEMP8:          .BYTE                      # Reserve a temporary 8-bit location
TEMP16:         .2BYTE                     # Reserve a temporary 16-bit location
RET_ADDR:       .2BYTE                     # Reserve a 2-byte location to hold
                                           # the return address from our
                                           # subroutine
```

```
LAST_OP:   .BYTE                # Location to store last operation
THIS_OP:   .BYTE                # Location to store current operation
####
#### This is where we'd insert the GET_NUM and DISP_NUM
#### subroutines #### that we created in the previous sections.
####

####
#### This is where we'd insert our general-purpose subroutines
#### (_ADD16, _SUB16, _SMULT16, and _SDIV16) and our special-
#### purpose subroutines (_UMULT10 and _UDIV10) using the
#### technique discussed in Chapter 12)
####
           .END
```

You see, there's nothing to it. We kick off the program by clearing the display and writing a '0' to it just like before. The first real change is that we push two zero bytes onto the stack and load **LAST_OP** with the code for an addition operation. Both of these actions are designed to *"prime the pump,"* in that they will fool our program into believing that it's already received a number and that it knows what the previous operator was. You might have to think about this for a while, but the way in which this works is that the calculator always starts off a new sequence following a 'Clr' by taking the first number you enter and adding it to zero, thereby removing many of the problems associated with the end conditions that we discussed previously.

Thus, when we hit the **MAINLOOP** label for the first time, we already have a 16-bit zero value on the top of the stack (Figure I.15a). Our first action in the main loop is to call our **GET_NUM** subroutine. This returns the latest control key on the top of the stack with our new 16-bit number underneath (Figure I.15b). As soon as we return from **GET_NUM**, we pop the control key off the top of the stack and store it away in **THIS_OP**, which means that we're left with two 16-bit numbers on the top of the stack (Figure I.15c).

As soon as we've popped the control key off the top of the stack we check to see if it was a 'Clr'. If it was a 'Clr', we forget everything we've done thus far and jump back to the reset sequence again; otherwise we check to see if it was an '=', in which case we play a little trick by loading **THIS_OP** with the code for an addition.

Now we retrieve whatever the last operation was from **LAST_OP** and check to see whether it was a '+', '−', 'x', or '/'. Whichever one it was, we call the relevant general-purpose subroutine, **_ADD16**, **_SUB16**, **_SMULT16**, or **_UMULT16**, respectively. Each of these subroutines retrieves two 16-bit numbers off the top of the stack, performs the appropriate mathematical operation, and leaves the 16-bit result on the top of the stack.

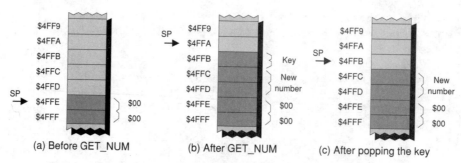

Figure I.15: The condition of the stack at the beginning of MAINLOOP on our first pass round this loop

Finally, we retrieve the key code that we stored in THIS_OP and squirrel it away in LAST_OP, thereby positioning ourselves for the next pass around the loop. Next we use our DISP_NUM subroutine to display the result of the operation, then we jump back to the beginning of the main loop to do the whole thing again. The reason why all of this is so cunning is that whenever we reach the start of the main loop (either from a reset condition or because we've already gone around the loop), we always commence with a single 16-bit value on the top of the stack and some operation stored in LAST_OP. As we said, this goes a long way towards solving the problems of the end conditions.

And there you have it. Note that out solution isn't one hundred percent bullet proof; for example, what *does* happen if we click multiple operators one after the other?[3] As it happens, our program is reasonably robust, in that it won't crash if you do something silly like this, but the results might be *"interesting."* Last but not least, there are many ways in which *you* could improve our program, such as modifying it to *"beep"* (by writing BEL_CODE to the output port) if the user does something inopportune, such as attempting to divide a number by zero.

---

[3] As a wise man once said: *"It's not designed to work like that, so the results are undefined in these cases."*

Appendix J

"The Best Clam Chowder in the World"

Contents of Appendix J

Maintaining your brain at full root-ti-toot-toot power

By the time you've draped your cerebral cortex around the myriad juicy topics in *Bebop Bytes Back*, you'll be in sore need of sustenance to enable your brain to keep barreling along at its full root-ti-toot-toot power. As we all know from our mother's knee, seafood is brain food, so what could be better than wrapping your laughing tackle around a fishy dish? But for what kind of fishy dish could we wish?

When the prequel to this illustrious tome hit the streets,[1] it included the recipe for a *"No-holds-barred Seafood Gumbo"* that promised to *"Swing you sybaritically around the room in a syncopated symphony of delight, and leave you groveling on your knees, gnashing your teeth, and gasping for more."* Well that recipe lived up to its reputation, and more than one reviewer stated: *"This book is well worth the price for the gumbo recipe alone ......"*

Only one man was less than happy! After plowing through the book, a friend of the authors, Chuck Paglicco, stumbled across the seafood gumbo recipe in the wee hours of the morning. Chuck was so disturbed that he was moved to come beating on our doors screaming *"Seafood gumbo? Seafood gumbo? How could you stoop so low when we* [Chuck and his wife Rita] *have the recipe for the best clam chowder in the world?"*

Being a somewhat volatile Bostonian of Italian decent, Chuck isn't a man to be argued with when it comes to matters of haute cuisine, so we prostrated ourselves humbly, apologized profusely, and promised faithfully that our very next book would revel in concoctions of chowder-like nature ...... so here we are.

> Beware ! If you are under 21, male, or a politician, don't attempt to do anything on the culinary front without your mother's permission and supervision, because kitchens contain sharp things, hot things, and a variety of other potentially dangerous things.

---

[1] Bebop to the Boolean Boogie (An Unconventional Guide to Electronics)

Preparing the clams

First of all, start off by cleaning any pots and other debris that happen to be hanging around the kitchen, put everything away in its rightful place, and wipe down all of your work-surfaces. Trust us, this is the only way to cook and you'll enjoy the experience a whole lot more.

- 2 quarts (4 pints) of fresh clams.
- 3 cups of water.
- 2 medium to large-ish cloves of garlic.

a) Thoroughly scrub and rinse your clams (the ocean isn't as clean as it used to be).

b) Finely dice the garlic and add it to 3 cups of water in a saucepan.

c) Bring your water and garlic mixture to the boil, then use it to steam the clams for about eight minutes until their shells are open.

d) Remove the clams and put them to one side.

e) Reserve the liquid used to steam the clams in a jug for later use.

Preparing the stock

Before commencing work on the stock, clean any pots that you used while preparing the clams, put everything away, and wipe down all of your work-surfaces.

- $1/2$ a cup of water.
- $1/2$ a cup of dry Vermouth (substitute water if you're under 21 or a teetotaler).
- 1 cup of the clam liquid that you reserved from preparing the clams.
- 1 stick of celery.
- 1 medium to large-ish carrot.
- 1 medium to large-ish onion.

f) Put 1 cup of the clam liquid that you reserved from the previous section into a saucepan, along with $1/2$ cup of water and $1/2$ cup of dry Vermouth (remember that you can substitute water for the Vermouth if you wish).

g) Wash your stick of celery and peel the carrot and onion. Chop everything into small-ish chunks and add them to the contents of the saucepan.

h) Bring to a boil then simmer for about half an hour.

i) Strain the contents of the saucepan through a coffee filter. The result is your stock (the broth, not the coffee filter or its contents, which you should dispose of in a humane way).

j) Reserve 2 cups of this stock (you can freeze any excess for future use).

Note that, while the stock is simmering, you can fruitfully employ your time by washing everything that you've used thus far and putting it away, followed by shucking the clams and preparing the remaining ingredients as discussed in the next (and final) section.

Making the Chowder

This is where the real fun begins. We're beginning to salivate just writing this, not the least that we've got a pot simmering away on the stove - how else could we vouch for this taste-fest sensation?

- 1 cup of clam liquid (reserved from the first section).
- 2 cups of stock (reserved from the second section).
- 1 cup of milk and 1 cup of single cream (or 2 cups of "half-and-half").
- 2 cloves of garlic.
- 1 1/2 cups halved button mushrooms.
- 1 1/2 cups of finely chopped onion.
- 2 cups cubed potato (1/2 inch cubes).
- 1/2 pound of mild white fish.
- 6 thick slices of bacon.
- 1 teaspoon of salt.
- 1/4 teaspoon of black pepper.
- 1/4 teaspoon of white pepper.
- 2 tablespoons of cornstarch.
- 3 tablespoons of butter.

k) Shuck the clams - your kids can help with this if they're underfoot - and chop them into small-ish pieces (the clams, not the kids).

l) Broil your fish until it's cooked and just a little crisp, then flake it up and set to one side.

m) Finely dice the onion and half the button mushrooms and put them to one side in separate bowls.

n) Chop the potatoes into 1/2 inch cubes and put them into a bowl of water.

o) Chop the bacon into 3/4 inch squares, saute it with the butter in a large pot on a medium heat until its almost crisp, add the onion and saute until it's almost cooked, then throw in the mushrooms and saute until they're golden brown. **Beware!** Watch out for flying grease splatters.

p) Add the potatoes (along with 1 1/2 cups of the water they were soaking in) to the bacon and onions. Also add the salt and pepper (both black and white), then cook uncovered on a medium heat for around fifteen minutes until the potatoes are fork-soft. **Be careful!** Don't overcook the potatoes such that they fall apart.

q) Whisk the cornstarch into 1 cup of the clam liquid (from the first section) and 2 cups of clam stock (from the second section). Add this mixture to the pot and continue cooking on low to medium heat.

r) Once everything has heated through, add the white fish, the clams, the milk, and the cream. Continue heating until it's steaming, and keep it this way until you're convinced the clams are thoroughly cooked (at least 5 minutes).

Serving your taste-fest sensation

Once you've prepared your chowder, there are numerous ways in which you can serve it and guzzle it down, including liberally scattering oyster crackers on top of it and dunking French bread into it. However, our preferred technique is the way in which chowder is served on Fisherman's Wharf in San Francisco as described below.

Take one loaf of sourdough bread for every pair of people who are fortunate enough to be present. Cut the loaves in half and hollow them out, leaving approximately 1/2 inch of bread attached to the crust. Ladle the chowder into the half-loaves, add Tabasco sauce to taste, then guzzle the chowder with a spoon and munch down on the bread.

There's nothing to compare to the experience of standing at the end of Fisherman's Wharf eating steaming hot chowder with a stiff breeze blowing off the bay and the roar of the Sea Lions in your ears. Of course, if you're serving this dish in Alabama in the middle of summer, then the heat and humidity may detract somewhat from the experience (the outside temperature is 105 degrees Fahrenheit as we pen these words).[2] But you can always try replicating the feel of the wharf by turning the air conditioning on full and having a friend douse you with a bucket of iced water every ten minutes or so.[3]

Enjoy!

---

[2]For your edification, zero degrees in the Fahrenheit scale was originally defined as the freezing point of fortified wine.
[3]We strongly advise your closing the drapes first, otherwise the neighbors are sure to talk

Appendix K

Lexicon

Contents of Appendix K

A treasure-trove of words

Our original intention when writing this book was to accommodate younger readers by avoiding over-complex or unfamiliar words, but sadly we failed. The problem is that words are fun, and the fun increases the more you know. Sometimes a particular word is just so ...... it's just so ...... golly gosh, it's just so *efficacious* (there, we said it and we just don't care).

There's a certain satisfaction that comes when one knows the most apposite words for the task and can wield them with confidence and disdain. For example, rather than responding to an unkind jibe with the retort *"Yeah, sez you!,"* imagine the gratification that could be yours if the following were to roll resoundingly off your tongue: *"It is my conjecture that you are a perpilocutionist of no small repute and a trombenik of distinction."*[1]

In a more serious vein (as Count Dracula might say), this book is intended to educate and illuminate on multiple levels. Thus, every now and then we've slipped in the occasional poser of a word to stimulate the old gray matter. However, it's not our intention to make your life more torturous than it already is, so to save you constantly scurrying to the dictionary we've compiled this short lexicon to increase your delectation and delight.

antipodes (antipodean): Anything that is diametrically opposed to
something else; also those regions on the opposite side of the globe
from any given point.
Sounds like: "ann–tip–oh–dees"
Example: *"His statements were at the antipodes of popular opinion."*
Synonyms (noun): antithesis.
Synonyms (adjective): contrary, opposite.
Origin: From the Greek *anti*, meaning "against" or "opposite", and
pous or *podos*, meaning "foot"; thus, the literal meaning of
antipodes is "having the feet opposite". Later Latin speakers
adopted the word to mean "people on the other side of the
world". More recently, the English began to use the word
antipodean to refer to things Australian; for example: *"The
phrase 'Australian Rules Football' is one of the finest examples
of antipodean humor."*

---

[1]A perpilocutionist is someone who doesn't know what he or she is talking about, while a trombenik is a loud and boring person (from the Polish word for a brass horn). (These really are proper words, but they're sort of old, so you rarely find them in modern dictionaries.)

apposite: Something that is appropriate, relevant, or to the point.
Sounds like: "ap–pos–eet"
Example: *"He made an apposite remark."*
Synonyms (adjective): applicable, appropriate, befitting, germane, pertinent, relevant.
Origin: Unknown (to the authors).

arcane: Known or understood by only a few.
Sounds like: "are–cane"
Example: *"The legal documents were arcane to say the least."*
Synonyms (adjective): classified, confidential, esoteric, private, restricted, secret.
Origin: From the Latin adjective *arcanus*, meaning "hidden" or "secret", and the noun *arcanum* (usually used in the plural *arcana*), meaning "mysterious secrets".

behoove: To be necessary, proper, or incumbent upon.
Sounds like: "bee–who–veh"
Example: *"It behooves the authors of this book to act like gentlemen".*
Origin: From the old English word *behofian*, meaning "need", or *behof*, meaning "profit" or "need".

caprice: An impulsive change of mind, freakish idea, or passing fancy.
Sounds like: "cap–reese"
Example: *"It was caprice that made her squeeze the clown's nose."*
Synonyms (noun): fancy, impulse, notion, silly thought, vagary, whim.
Synonyms (adjective): changeable, erratic, mercurial, unstable.
Origin: From the Italian noun *capriccio*, which itself is derived from *capo*, meaning "head", and *riccio*, meaning "hedgehog"; thus, the literal meaning of *capriccio* is "hedgehog head" or "hair standing up like a hedgehog".

conjecture: A guess or shot in the dark.
Sounds like: "con–ject–yur"
Example: *"It is my conjecture that you are a gobemouche".*[2]
Synonyms (noun): guess, hypothesis, speculation, supposition, suspicion.
Synonyms (verbs): guess, hypothesize, speculate, suppose, surmise, suspect.
Origin: From the Latin *conjectura*, meaning an "inference", "conclusion", or "interpretation". This was derived from *conicere*, meaning "throw together", which was, in turn, a compound of the prefix *con-* (a form of *com-*), meaning "together". and *jacere*, meaning "throw".

constituent: Forming part of, being an element in, or helping to compose.
 Sounds like: "con–stit–you–ent"
 Example: "*The main constituent of sand is silicon.*"
 Synonyms (noun): component, element, ingredient, part.
 Synonyms (adjectives): combining, component, constituting, elemental,
  forming.
 Origin: A derivative of "constitute". From the Latin *constitut-(um)*, which was
  derived from *constituere* meaning "fix" or "establish", which was, in
  turn, a compound of the prefix *con-* (a form of *com-*), meaning
  "together," and *statuere*, meaning "set up".

cornucopia: An overflowing supply.
 Sounds like: "corn– you–cope–ee–ya"
 Example: "*This book is a cornucopia of fun and frivolity.*"
 Synonyms (noun): abundance, overflowing supply.
 Origin: From the Latin *cornu copiae*, meaning "horn of plenty", which
  referred to the horn of the goat Amalthaea which suckled Zeus
  without being deplenished.

decimate: To eliminate by violent means a large proportion of a group of
  individuals.
 Sounds like: "dess–ee–mate"
 Example: "*Little old ladies may use virtual reality systems to decimate
  loathsome creatures*".
 Synonyms (verb): butcher, devastate, kill, massacre, murder, slaughter,
  slay, wipe out.
 Origin: From the Latin *decimat-(um)*, which was derived from *decimare*,
  meaning the removal or destruction of one tenth, which was, in turn,
  derived from *decem*, meaning "ten". The word *decimare* referred to
  the Roman practice of punishing a group of soldiers or prisoners for
  some crime by randomly putting one out of every ten to death.
  As this one-in-ten style of punishment is rarely used these days
  (except in high schools), decimate is now taken to mean "to kill or
  destroy most of".

---

[2]A gobemouche (literally a "fly swallower") is someone who will believe anything you tell
them, no matter how ridiculous. For example, did you know that the word *gullible* isn't to be
found in an English dictionary?

delectation: The process of pleasing, pleasure, or delight.
    Sounds like: "del–ekt–ay–ssh–yon"
    Example: *"Wearing a silly hat rarely increases the delectation that comes from guzzling a bowl of clam chowder."*
    Synonyms (noun): delight, ecstasy, enjoyment, happiness, joy, pleasure, rapture.
    Origin: From the Latin *delectation-(em)*, meaning to "charm", "delight", "attract", "entice", or "allure".

digress: To depart from the main theme.
    Sounds like: "die–gr–ess"
    Example: *"I could talk about this subject for hours, but I digress ......"*
    Synonyms (verbs): depart, deviate, diverge, ramble, stray, wander.
    Origin: From the Latin *digress-(um)*, which was, in turn, derived from *digredi*, meaning to "step aside" (a combination of the prefix *di-* and *gradi*, meaning "to step"). Digress may be used to indicate leaving a direct course, turning aside, or straying, but is more usually used as a verbal expression to indicate departing from the main theme or temporarily turning aside to consider a different subject.

ensconce: To cover or hide securely, or to settle securely or snugly.
    Sounds like: "ens–con–ss"
    Example: *"Father was happily ensconced in his favorite armchair, when suddenly ......"*
    Synonyms (verb): establish, install, settle.
    Origin: From the now defunct English word *Sconce*, meaning "a small fort", which in turn came from the Dutch word *schans*, via the High German *schanze*, from the Italian *scanso*, meaning "defense", from the vulgar Latin *excampsare*, meaning "turn around", "sail by", or "hide behind a fortification".

gregarious: Sociable; seeking and enjoying the company of others; belonging to the flock.
    Sounds like: "gre–ger–ree–oss"
    Example: *"She was always a gregarious child."*
    Synonyms (adjective): affable, congenial, convivial, friendly, sociable.
    Origin: Derived from (and acting in opposition to) the word *segregate*, meaning "set apart", which itself comes from the Latin *segregare*, (*se-*, meaning "apart" and *grex* meaning "flock").

hierarchy: Any system of persons or things in a graded order.
> Sounds like: "higher–ark–ee"
> Example: *"He was pathetically low down in the hierarchy of the Organization"*.
> Synonyms (noun): system, society, power structure, pecking order, regime.
> Origin: From the Greek *Hierarkhas*, meaning "Chief Priest", which itself came from *hieros*, meaning "sacred" or "holy," and *arkhos*, meaning "ruling". The word hierarchy was first used in English in the context of the medieval categorization of angels, cherubs, seraphs, powers, and dominions. In the early seventeenth century "hierarchy" was extended to the categorization of the clergy, and it subsequently came to be applicable to any graded system.

inexorable: Unyielding or unalterable; not to be turned from path or purpose.
> Sounds like: "in–x–or–able"
> Example: *"This book was written in an inexorable manner"*.
> Synonyms (adjective): relentless, rigorous, ruthless, stern.
> Origin: From the Latin *inexorabil-(is)*, meaning "not to be persuaded, moved or affected by prayers or entreaties".

jape: A joke or a jest.
> Sounds like: "jay–puh"
> Example: *"Hiding the government inspector's toupee was a jolly jape"*
> Synonyms (noun): jest, joke, quip.
> Synonyms (verb): jest, joke.
> Origin: From the French *japper*, meaning "to bark like a dog".

legerdemain: Sleight of hand, specious argument, or clever unscrupulous action.
> Sounds like: "ledger–duh–main"
> Example: *"Although he appeared to be handcuffed to a camel, it was actually a cunning Legerdemain"*.
> Synonyms (noun): deception, hocus-pocus, trickery.
> Origin: From the French *leger-de-main*, meaning "lightness of hand".

malapropos: Out of place.
>   Sounds like: "mall–a–prop–ose"
>   Example: *"His behavior with the custard pie was completely malapropos."*
>   Synonyms (adjective): inappropriate, inopportune, out of place, untimely.
>   Synonyms (adverbs): inappropriately, unseasonably.
>   Origin: From the French *mal,* meaning "badly", and *apropos,* meaning "to the purpose".

metaphor: Word or phrase used to denote or describe something entirely different.
>   Sounds like: "met–a–for"
>   Example: *"Camels are ships of the desert."*
>   Synonyms (noun): allegory, simile.
>   Origin: From the Latin *metaphore,* meaning "transference".

paradox: Seemingly contradictory statement that may nonetheless be true.
>   Sounds like: "para–dox"
>   Example: *"The professor was an extremely clever fool".*
>   Synonyms (noun): contradiction, incongruity.
>   Origin: From the Latin *para,* meaning "beyond," and *doxa,* meaning "opinion".

penchant: Strong inclination, definite liking (incline or leaning).
>   Sounds like: "pen–shan't"
>   Example: *"He had a penchant for breakfasts featuring kippers".*
>   Synonyms (noun): inclination, taste, partiality, liking.
>   Origin: From the French *pencher,* meaning "incline" or "leaning," which itself came from the Latin adjective *pendulus,* meaning "hanging", and the verb *pendere,* meaning "to hang".

pillage: To rob by force, openly and with violence.
>   Sounds like: "pill–age"
>   Example: *"The Vikings always enjoyed pillaging a village or two on their holiday weekends."*
>   Synonyms (nouns): destruction, devastation, rapine, spoliation.
>   Synonyms (verbs): despoil, loot, plunder, rape, ravage, rob, sack.
>   Origin: Either derived from the French word *piller,* meaning "to rob", or from the Latin *pilare,* meaning to "remove hair" or "fleece".

sequence: Following in order of time or place; occurring as a consequence or result.

Sounds like: "see–kwen–ss"

Example: *"His death was the inevitable sequence of the crime".*

Synonyms (noun): sequent, succeeding.

Origin: From the Latin *sequi*, meaning "to follow".

transmogrify: To change (as if by magic) into a different (especially bizarre) shape or form.

Sounds like: "tran–ss–mog–ree–fie"

Example: *"The magician transmogrified his assistant into a chocolate cookie".*

Synonyms (verb): alter, change, convert, transform, transmute.

Origin: Unknown (to the authors).

Utopia: An ideal place.

Sounds like: "you–tow–pee–a"

Example: *"Everyone dreams of living in Utopia".*

Synonyms (noun): golden age, heaven on earth.

Origin: Coined by Sir Thomas More, from the Greek *ou*, meaning "not", and *topos*, meaning "place". Thus, *Utopia* originally meant "nowhere", but in the seventeenth century it was adapted to its present meaning of a place that was too perfect to really exist.

wanton: Unrestrained, not under control; to frolic without restraint.

Sounds like: "one–ton"

Example: *"His wanton behavior was the talk of the neighborhood".*

Synonyms (adjective): immoral, lewd, promiscuous, unchaste, wayward, wild.

Origin: From the Middle English word *wan-un*, which was itself composed from *wane*, meaning "lacking", and *towen*, from *togen*, which is the past participle of *teon*, meaning "to pull", "to bring up", "to train", or "to discipline". Thus, wanton originally meant "lacking in discipline".

Index

---

bold number = key definition, ‡ = footnote, § = sidebar

bold number = key definition, ‡ = footnote, § = sidebar

bold number = key definition, [‡] = footnote, [§] = sidebar

C

---

bold number = key definition, ‡ = footnote, § = sidebar

bold number = key definition, ‡ = footnote, § = sidebar

---

bold number = key definition,   [‡] = footnote,   [§] = sidebar

bold number = key definition, [‡] = footnote, [§] = sidebar

---

bold number = key definition, [‡] = footnote, [§] = sidebar

bold number = key definition, [‡] = footnote, [§] = sidebar

bold number = key definition, [‡] = footnote, [§] = sidebar

bold number = key definition, ‡ = footnote, § = sidebar

J

---

bold number = key definition, ‡ = footnote, § = sidebar

bold number = key definition,   [‡] = footnote,   [§] = sidebar

bold number = key definition, ‡ = footnote, § = sidebar

bold number = key definition, ‡ = footnote, § = sidebar

bold number = key definition,   ‡ = footnote,   § = sidebar

---

bold number = key definition, [‡] = footnote, [§] = sidebar

bold number = key definition, ‡ = footnote, § = sidebar

bold number = key definition, ‡ = footnote, § = sidebar

bold number = key definition, ‡ = footnote, § = sidebar

bold number = key definition, ‡ = footnote, § = sidebar

---

bold number = key definition, ‡ = footnote, § = sidebar

bold number = key definition,   ‡ = footnote,   § = sidebar

---

bold number = key definition, [‡] = footnote, [§] = sidebar

V

W

bold number = key definition, [‡] = footnote, [§] = sidebar

This page is intentionally left blank

ORDER FORM

Please send _____ copy(s*) of Bebop BYTES Back ($49.^{95} each) at a total cost of $_____

S&H = $7 - Priority Mail ☐   *For ordering more than one book, and for shipping outside of the
or $4.50 - Book Rate ☐   U.S. contact Doone Publications for shipping and handling prices.

If I am not completely satisfied I can return the book for a full refund within 15 days
of delivery.

Name ....
Company ....
Address ....
City ....
State ....
Zip ....
Daytime phone no. ....

☐ check or money order enclosed

charge my
☐ visa   ☐ mastercard

Acc.no. ....
Expiration date ....
Signature ....
• All orders must be prepaid

Discounts are available for orders of 3 or more books: contact the publisher.

Fill and return to:
Doone Publications
7950 Hwy 72W, #G106, Madison, AL 35758, USA
Tel: 1-800-311-3753, Fax: 205-837-0580
e.mail: asmith@doone.com